T0214483

Communications
in Computer and Information Science   1077

Commenced Publication in 2007
Founding and Former Series Editors:
Phoebe Chen, Alfredo Cuzzocrea, Xiaoyong Du, Orhun Kara, Ting Liu,
Krishna M. Sivalingam, Dominik Ślęzak, Takashi Washio, and Xiaokang Yang

Editorial Board Members

More information about this series at http://www.springer.com/series/7899

Marten van Sinderen · Leszek A. Maciaszek (Eds.)

Software Technologies

13th International Conference, ICSOFT 2018
Porto, Portugal, July 26–28, 2018
Revised Selected Papers

 Springer

Editors
Marten van Sinderen
Information Systems Group
University of Twente
Enschede, The Netherlands

Leszek A. Maciaszek
Wrocław University of Economics
Wrocław, Poland

Macquarie University
Sydney, Australia

ISSN 1865-0929 ISSN 1865-0937 (electronic)
Communications in Computer and Information Science
ISBN 978-3-030-29156-3 ISBN 978-3-030-29157-0 (eBook)
https://doi.org/10.1007/978-3-030-29157-0

This Springer imprint is published by the registered company Springer Nature Switzerland AG
The registered company address is: Gewerbestrasse 11, 6330 Cham, Switzerland

Preface

The present book includes extended and revised versions of a set of selected papers from the 13th International Conference on Software Technologies (ICSOFT 2018), held in Porto, Portugal, during 26–28 July, 2018.

ICSOFT 2018 received 130 paper submissions from 28 countries, of which 14% are included in this book. The papers were selected by the event chairs and their selection is based on a number of criteria that include the classifications and comments provided by the Program Committee members, the session chairs' assessment and also the program chairs' global view of all papers included in the technical program. The authors of selected papers were then invited to submit a revised and extended version of their papers having at least 30% new material.

The purpose of the ICSOFT conferences, including its 13th edition in 2018, is to bring together researchers, engineers, and practitioners interested in software technologies. The conference solicits papers and other contributions in themes ranging from software engineering and development via showcasing cutting edge-software systems and applications to addressing foundational innovative technologies for systems and applications of the future. The papers were presented in one of three conference areas: "Software Engineering and Systems Development", "Software Systems and Applications", and "Foundational and Trigger Technologies".

The papers included in this book align with the purpose of ICSOFT conferences, with the following main topics covered: software quality (11, 19), empirical software engineering (7, 10), software testing (8, 12, 17), requirements engineering (13, 18), software development (3, 5, 16), software architecture (2, 4, 6), and model transformation and refinement (9, 14).

We would like to thank all the authors for their contributions and the reviewers for ensuring the quality of this publication.

July 2018

Marten van Sinderen
Leszek Maciaszek

Organization

Conference Chair

Leszek Maciaszek   Wrocław University of Economics, Poland
and Macquarie University, Sydney, Australia

Program Chair

Marten van Sinderen   University of Twente, The Netherlands

Program Committee

Markus Aleksy	ABB Corporate Research Center, Germany
Waleed Alsabhan	KACST, UK
Soumyadip Bandyopadhyay	BITS Pilani K K Birla Goa Campus, India
Wolfgang Bein	University of Nevada, Las Vegas, USA
Fevzi Belli	Izmir Institute of Technology, Turkey
Jorge Bernardino	Polytechnic Institute of Coimbra - ISEC, Portugal
Mario Berón	Universidad Nacional de San Luis, Argentina
Thomas Buchmann	University of Bayreuth, Germany
Andrea Burattin	University of Innsbruck, Austria
Nelio Cacho	Federal University of Rio Grande do Norte, Brazil
Jose Calvo-Manzano	Universidad Politécnica de Madrid, Spain
Gerardo Canfora	University of Sannio, Italy
Ana Cavalli	TELECOM SudParis, France
Rui César das Neves	Directorate-General of Health, Portugal
Marta Cimitile	Unitelma Sapienza, Italy
Rem Collier	University College Dublin, Ireland
Agostino Cortesi	Università Ca' Foscari di Venezia, Italy
Lidia López Cuesta	Universitat Politècnica de Catalunya, Spain
Boguslaw Cyganek	AGH University of Science and Technology, Poland
Sergiu Dascalu	University of Nevada, Reno, USA
Sergio de Cesare	University of Westminster, UK
Cléver Ricardo de Farias	University of São Paulo, Brazil
Jaime Delgado	Universitat Politècnica de Catalunya, Spain
Steven Demurjian	University of Connecticut, USA
Chiara Di Francescomarino	FBK-IRST, Italy
Philippe Dugerdil	Geneva School of Business Administration, University of Applied Sciences of Western Switzerland, Switzerland
Morgan Ericsson	Linnaeus University, Sweden
Jean-Rémy Falleri	Bordeaux INP, France

João Faria	FEUP - Faculty of Engineering of the University of Porto, Portugal
Luis Fernandez Sanz	University of Alcala, Spain
Kehan Gao	Eastern Connecticut State University, USA
Felix Garcia Clemente	University of Murcia, Spain
Mauro Gaspari	University of Bologna, Italy
Hamza Gharsellaoui	Khurmah University College, Taif University, Saudi Arabia
Paola Giannini	University of Piemonte Orientale, Italy
John Gibson	Mines-Telecom - Telecom SudParis, France
Gregor Grambow	Hochschule Aalen, Germany
Christiane Gresse von Wangenheim	UFSC - Federal University of Santa Catarina, Brazil
Hatim Hafiddi	INPT, Morocco
Slimane Hammoudi	ESEO, MODESTE, France
Jean Hauck	Universidade Federal de Santa Catarina, Brazil
Pedro Henriques	University of Minho, Portugal
Jose Herrera	Universidad del Cauca, Colombia
Mercedes Hidalgo-Herrero	Universidad Complutense De Madrid, Spain
Jose R. Hilera	University of Alcala, Spain
Andreas Holzinger	Medical University Graz, Austria
Jang-Eui Hong	Chungbuk National University, South Korea
Shihong Huang	Florida Atlantic University, USA
Ivan Ivanov	SUNY Empire State College, USA
Judit Jasz	University of Szeged, Hungary
Lingxiao Jiang	Singapore Management University, Singapore
Bo Jørgensen	University of Southern Denmark, Denmark
Maria Jose Escalona	University of Seville, Spain
Hermann Kaindl	Vienna University of Technology, Austria
Dimitris Karagiannis	University of Vienna, Austria
Carlos Kavka	ESTECO SpA, Italy
Dean Kelley	Minnesota State University, USA
Chris Kemerer	University of Pittsburgh, USA
Foutse Khomh	École Polytechnique, Canada
Mieczyslaw Kokar	Northeastern University, USA
Jitka Komarkova	University of Pardubice, Czech Republic
Jun Kong	North Dakota State University, USA
Martin Kropp	University of Applied Sciences Northwestern Switzerland, Switzerland
Winfried Kühnhauser	Ilmenau University of Technology, Germany
Rob Kusters	Open Universiteit Nederland, The Netherlands
Wing Kwong	Hofstra University, USA
Giuseppe Lami	Consiglio Nazionale delle Ricerche, Italy
Konstantin Läufer	Loyola University Chicago, USA
David Lorenz	Open University, Israel
Ivan Lukovic	University of Novi Sad, Serbia

Stephane Maag	Telecom SudParis, France
Ivano Malavolta	Vrije Universiteit Amsterdam, The Netherlands
Eda Marchetti	ISTI-CNR, Italy
Katsuhisa Maruyama	Ritsumeikan University, Japan
Manuel Mazzara	Innopolis University, Russia
Tom McBride	University of Technology Sydney, Australia
Francesco Mercaldo	National Research Council of Italy (CNR), Italy
Antoni Mesquida Calafat	Universitat de les Illes Balears (UIB), Spain
Gergely Mezei	Budapest University of Technology and Economics, Hungary
Mattia Monga	Università degli Studi di Milano, Italy
Antao Moura	Federal University of Campina Grande (UFCG), Brazil
Antonio Muñoz	University of Malaga, Spain
Takako Nakatani	The Open University of Japan, Japan
Elena Navarro	University of Castilla-La Mancha, Spain
Joan Navarro	La Salle - Universitat Ramon Llull, Spain
Viorel Negru	West University of Timisoara, Romania
Paolo Nesi	University of Florence, Italy
Jianwei Niu	University of Texas at San Antonio, USA
Rory O'Connor	Dublin City University, Ireland
Claus Pahl	Free University of Bozen-Bolzano, Italy
Marcos Palacios	University of Oviedo, Spain
Vincenzo Pallotta	HEIG-VD (Swiss Applied Science University, Vaud), Switzerland
Luis Pedro	University of Aveiro, Portugal
Jennifer Pérez	Universidad Politécnica de Madrid (UPM), Spain
Dana Petcu	West University of Timisoara, Romania
Giuseppe Polese	Università Degli Studi Di Salerno, Italy
Roman Popp	Vienna University of Technology, Austria
Rosario Pugliese	Universita' di Firenze, Italy
Traian Rebedea	University Politehnica of Bucharest, Romania
Michel Reniers	Eindhoven University of Technology, The Netherlands
Werner Retschitzegger	Johannes Kepler University, Austria
Colette Rolland	Université De Paris1 Panthéon-Sorbonne, France
António Miguel Rosado da Cruz	Instituto Politécnico de Viana do Castelo, Portugal
Gustavo Rossi	Lifia, Argentina
Matteo Rossi	Politecnico di Milano, Italy
Stuart Rubin	University of California San Diego, USA
Chandan Rupakheti	Rose-Hulman Institute of Technology, USA
Gunter Saake	Institute of Technical and Business Information Systems, Germany
Krzysztof Sacha	Warsaw University of Technology, Poland
Maria-Isabel Sanchez-Segura	Carlos III University of Madrid, Spain
Davide Sangiorgi	Università di Bologna, Italy

Elad Schiller	Chalmers University of Technology, Sweden
Lionel Seinturier	University of Lille, France
Istvan Siket	Hungarian Academy of Science, Research Group on Artificial Intelligence, Hungary
Harvey Siy	University of Nebraska at Omaha, USA
Michal Smialek	Warsaw University of Technology, Poland
Yeong-Tae Song	Towson University, USA
Cosmin Spahiu	University of Craiova, Romania
Anongnart Srivihok	Kasetsart University, Thailand
Miroslaw Staron	University of Gothenburg, Sweden
Ketil Stølen	SINTEF, Norway
Hiroki Suguri	Miyagi University, Japan
Bedir Tekinerdogan	Wageningen University, The Netherlands
Claudine Toffolon	Université du Maine, France
Joseph Trienekens	Open University Heerlen, The Netherlands
Michael Vassilakopoulos	University of Thessaly, Greece
Dessislava Vassileva	Sofia University st. Kliment Ohridski, Bulgaria
László Vidács	University of Szeged, Hungary
Sergiy Vilkomir	East Carolina University, USA
Jie Wang	Indiana University Northwest, USA
Dietmar Winkler	Vienna University of Technology, Austria
Andreas Winter	Carl von Ossietzky University Oldenburg, Germany
Jinhui Yao	Xerox Research, USA
Murat Yilmaz	Çankaya University, Turkey
Jingyu Zhang	Macquarie University, Australia

Additional Reviewers

Mohammed Alharbi	Florida Atlantic University, USA
Doina Bein	California State University, Fullerton, USA
Yann Ben Maissa	INPT, Morocco
Dominik Bork	University of Vienna, Austria
Juan Chagüendo Benavides	Universidad Carlos III de Madrid, Spain
Alexandru Cicortas	West University Timisoara, Romania
Estrela Cruz	Instituto Politécnico de Viana do Castelo, Portugal
Teerath Das	Gran Sasso Science Institute, Italy
Victoria Döller	University of Vienna, Austria
German-Lenin Dugarte-Peña	Carlos III University of Madrid, Spain
Gencer Erdogan	SINTEF, Norway
Aritra Ghosh	Florida Atlantic University, USA
Vladimir Ivancevic	University of Novi Sad, Serbia
Vimal Kunnummel	University of Vienna, Austria
Christian Muck	University of Vienna, Austria
Francesco Nocera	Polytechnic University of Bari, Italy
Dara Nyknahad	University of Nevada, Las Vegas, USA

Hui Song   SINTEF, Norway
Michael Walch   University of Vienna, Austria

Invited Speakers

Gian Pietro Picco   University of Trento, Italy
Jan Mendling   Vienna University of Economics and Business, Austria
Tobias Hoellwarth   EuroCloud Europe, Austria
Miguel P. Correia   Universidade de Lisboa, Portugal

Contents

Software Engineering and Systems Development

Using Semantic Metrics to Predict Mutation Equivalence 3
  Amani Ayad, Imen Marsit, Nazih Mohamed Omri, JiMeng Loh,
  and Ali Mili

A Rating Tool for the Automated Selection of Software Refactorings
that Remove Antipatterns to Improve Performance and Stability 28
  Nikolai Moesus, Matthias Scholze, Sebastian Schlesinger,
  and Paula Herber

Model-Based On-the-Fly Testing of Web Applications
and Multilingual Websites 55
  Winfried Dulz

On the Impact of Order Information in API Usage Patterns 79
  Ervina Çergani and Mira Mezini

A Practical Approach for Constraint Solving in Model Transformations 104
  Youness Laghouaouta and Pierre Laforcade

An Integrated Requirements Engineering Framework for Agile Software
Product Lines 124
  Hassan Haidar, Manuel Kolp, and Yves Wautelet

Systematic Refinement of Softgoals Using a Combination of KAOS
Goal Models and Problem Diagrams 150
  Nelufar Ulfat-Bunyadi, Nazila Gol Mohammadi, Roman Wirtz,
  and Maritta Heisel

Simplifying the Classification of App Reviews Using Only
Lexical Features 173
  Faiz Ali Shah, Kairit Sirts, and Dietmar Pfahl

Smart Measurements and Analysis for Software Quality Enhancement 194
  Sarah Dahab, Stephane Maag, Wissam Mallouli, and Ana Cavalli

Modular Programming and Reasoning for Living with Uncertainty 220
  Naoyasu Ubayashi, Yasutaka Kamei, and Ryosuke Sato

Software Systems and Applications

Empowering Continuous Delivery in Software Development:
The DevOps Strategy 247
  Clauirton Siebra, Rosberg Lacerda, Italo Cerqueira,
  Jonysberg P. Quintino, Fabiana Florentin, Fabio B. Q. da Silva,
  and Andre L. M. Santos

Can Commit Change History Reveal Potential Fault Prone Classes?
A Study on GitHub Repositories............................... 266
  Chun Yong Chong and Sai Peck Lee

An Agent-Based Planning Method for Distributed Task Allocation 282
  Dhouha Ben Noureddine, Atef Gharbi, and Samir Ben Ahmed

Automatic Test Data Generation for a Given Set of Applications Using
Recurrent Neural Networks 307
  Ciprian Paduraru, Marius-Constantin Melemciuc,
  and Miruna Paduraru

Guiding the Functional Change Decisions in Agile Project:
An Empirical Evaluation 327
  Asma Sellami, Mariem Haoues, Nour Borchani, and Nadia Bouassida

Wise Objects for IoT (WIoT): Software Framework and Experimentation ... 349
  Ilham Alloui, Eric Benoit, Stéphane Perrin, and Flavien Vernier

A Software Product Line Approach to Design Secure Connectors
in Component-Based Software Architectures...................... 372
  Michael Shin, Hassan Gomaa, and Don Pathirage

Towards an Automatic Verification of BPMN Model Semantic Preservation
During a Refinement Process 397
  Yousra Bendaly Hlaoui, Salma Ayari, and Leila Jemni Ben Ayed

Author Index 421

Software Engineering and Systems Development

Using Semantic Metrics to Predict Mutation Equivalence

Amani Ayad[1], Imen Marsit[2], Nazih Mohamed Omri[2], JiMeng Loh[1], and Ali Mili[1(✉)] (iD)

[1] New Jersey Institute of Technology, Newark, NJ 07102-1982, USA
mili@njit.edu
[2] University of Monastir, 5000 Monastir, Tunisia

Abstract. Equivalent mutants are a major nuisance in mutation testing because they introduce a significant amount of bias. But weeding them out is difficult because it requires a detailed analysis of the source code of the base program and the mutant. In this paper we argue that for most applications, it is not necessary to identify equivalent mutants individually; rather it suffices to estimate their number. Also, we explore how we can estimate their number by a cursory/automatable analysis of the base program and the mutant generation policy.

Keywords: Redundancy · Mutant equivalence · Mutant survival ratio · Software metrics

1 Equivalent Mutants

Mutation is used in software testing to analyze the effectiveness of test data or to simulate faults in programs, and is meaningful only to the extent that the mutants are semantically distinct from the base program [1–4]. But in practice mutants may sometimes be semantically equivalent to the base program while being syntactically distinct from it [5–11]. The issue of equivalent mutants has mobilized the attention of researchers for a long time. Yet, in a recent survey of mutation testing [12], Papadakis et al. cite the problem of mutation equivalence as one of the outstanding/unresolved issues in mutation testing.

Given a base program P and a mutant M, the problem of determining whether M is equivalent to P is known to be undecidable [13]. If we encounter test data for which P and M produce different outcomes, then we can conclude that M is not equivalent to P, and we say that we have *killed* mutant M; but no amount of testing can prove that M is equivalent to P. In the absence of a systematic/algorithmic procedure to determine equivalence, researchers have resorted to heuristic approaches. In [7], Gruen et al. identify four sources of mutant equivalence: the mutation is applied to dead code; the mutation alters the performance of the code but not its function; the mutation alters internal states but not the output; and the mutation cannot be sensitized; we argue that

This paper is an extended version of the paper titled: *Impact of Mutation Operators on Mutant Equivalence*, by I. Marsit, M. N. Omri, J. M. Loh and A. Mili. Proceedings, ICSOFT 2018, Madrid, Spain, July 2018, pages 55–66. This paper extends the original by justifying the definition of the metrics and by showing the details of the regression model.

M. van Sinderen and L. A. Maciaszek (Eds.): ICSOFT 2018, CCIS 1077, pp. 3–27, 2019.
https://doi.org/10.1007/978-3-030-29157-0_1

the metrics we discuss in this paper reflect some of the conditions mentioned in the work of Gruen et al.; but they also reflect other conditions of equivalence. In [14] Offutt and Pan argue that the problem of detecting equivalent mutants is a special case of a more general problem, called the *feasible path problem*; also they use a constraint-based technique to automatically detect equivalent mutants and infeasible paths. Experimentation with their tool shows that they can detect nearly half of the equivalent mutants on a small sample of base programs. Program slicing techniques are proposed in [15] and subsequently used in [16, 17] as a means to assist in identifying equivalent mutants. In [18], Ellims et al. propose to help identify potentially equivalent mutants by analyzing the execution profiles of the mutant and the base program. Howden [19] proposes to detect equivalent mutants by checking that a mutation preserves local states, and Schuler et al. [20] propose to detect equivalent mutants by testing automatically generated invariant assertions produced by Daikon [21]; both the Howden approach and the Daikon approach rely on local conditions to determine equivalence, hence they are prone to generate sufficient but unnecessary conditions of equivalence; a program P and its mutant M may well have different local states but still produce the same overall behavior; the only way to generate necessary and sufficient conditions of equivalence between a base program and a mutant is to analyze the programs in full (vs analyze them locally). In [22], Nica and Wotawa discuss how to detect equivalent mutants by using constraints that specify the conditions under which a test datum can kill the mutant; these constraints are submitted to a constraint solver, and the mutant is considered equivalent whenever the solver fails to find a solution. This approach is as good as the generated constraints, and because the constraints are based on a static analysis of the base program and the mutant, this solution has severe effectiveness and scalability limitations. In [23] Carvalho et al. report on empirical experiments in which they collect information on the average ratio of equivalent mutants generated by mutation operators that focus on preprocessor directives; this experiment involves a diverse set of base programs, and is meant to reflect properties of the selected mutation operators, rather than the programs per se. In [24] Kintis et al. put forth the criterion of *Trivial Compiler Equivalence* (TCE) as a "simple, fast and readily applicable technique" for identifying equivalent mutants and duplicate mutants in C and Java programs. They test their technique against a benchmark ground truth suite (of known equivalent mutants) and find that they detect almost half of all equivalent mutants in Java programs. In [12] Papadakis et al. present a sweeping survey of mutation testing, spanning several decades, and covering all aspects of the practice; they conclude by discussing outstanding research issues, and cite mutant equivalence and mutant redundancy as important venues for future research.

It is fair to argue that despite several years of research, the problem of automatically and efficiently detecting equivalent mutants for programs of arbitrary size and complexity remains an open challenge. In this paper we adopt an orthogonal approach, based on the following premises:

- For most practical applications of mutation testing, it is not necessary to identify equivalent mutants individually; rather it is sufficient to know their number. If we generate 100 mutants and we want to use them to assess the quality of a test data set, then it is sufficient to know how many of them are equivalent: if we know that 20 of them are equivalent, then the test data will be judged by how many of the remaining 80 mutants it kills.

- Even when it is important to identify individually those mutants that are equivalent to the base, knowing their number is helpful: as we kill more and more non-equivalent mutants, the likelihood that the surviving mutants are equivalent rises as we approach the estimated number of equivalent mutants.

- For a given mutant generation policy, it is possible to estimate the ratio (over the total number of generated mutants) of equivalent mutants that a program is prone to produce, by static analysis of the program. We refer to this parameter as the *ratio of equivalent mutants* (*REM*, for short); because mutants that are found to be distinct from the base program are said to be killed, we may also refer to this parameter as the *survival rate* of the program.

This paper represents an extended version of the paper titled *Impact of Mutation Operators on Mutant Equivalence* [25]; in [25] we focus on how the choice of mutation operators affects the REM of a program; whereas in this paper, we focus on the details of how we derive a regression model of the REM for a fixed mutant generation policy. The question of how the choice of mutation operators affects the regression model is addressed, as an extension of the core statistical model.

In Sect. 2, we argue that, for a given mutant generation policy, what determines the REM of a program P is the amount of redundancy of program P; based on this conjecture, we claim that if we can quantify the redundancy of a program, we can find statistical relations between the redundancy metrics of a program and its REM. In Sect. 3, we present a number of entropy-based measures of program redundancy, and put forth analytical arguments to the effect that these are reliable indicators of the preponderance of equivalent mutants in a program. In Sect. 4, we report on an empirical study that bears out our analysis; specifically, we find significant correlations between the redundancy metrics and the REM's of sample benchmark programs, and we derive a regression model that has the REM as dependent variable and the redundancy metrics as independent variables. In Sect. 5 we turn our attention to the other source that may determine the survival rate in a mutation experiment, namely the mutant generation policy. We conclude in Sect. 6 by summarizing our main results and sketching directions for future research.

2 The Key to Immortality

2.1 Equivalence and Redundancy

The agenda of this paper is not to identify and isolate equivalent mutants, but instead to estimate their number. To estimate the number of equivalent mutants, we consider question RQ3 raised by Yao et al. in [5]: What are the causes of mutant equivalence? For a given mutant generation policy, this question can be reformulated more precisely as: what attribute of a program makes it likely to generate more equivalent mutants?

We formulate this question in more precise terms: what attribute makes a program P prone to maintain the same function despite the application of a mutation? Given that mutations are intended to simulate faults, we can reformulate this question as: what attribute makes a program P prone to maintain the same function despite the presence of a fault? A program that maintains the same function despite the presence of a fault is known as a fault-tolerant program. Hence this question can be reformulated as: what attribute makes a program P fault tolerant? We know the answer to this question: redundancy. Hence if only we could find a way to quantify the redundancy of a program, we could conceivably relate it to the rate of equivalent mutants generated from that program. But the ratio of equivalent mutants of a program does not depend exclusively on the program, it also depends on the mutation generation policy; in Sect. 5, we discuss the impact of the mutation generation policy on the REM; in the meantime, we assume that we have a default/fixed mutation generation policy, and we focus on the impact of the program's redundancy metrics.

Because our measures of redundancy use Shannon's entropy function [26], we briefly introduce some definitions, notations and properties related to this function, referring the interested reader to more detailed sources [25]. Given a random variable X that takes its values in a finite set, which for convenience we also designate by X, the *entropy* of X is the function denoted by $H(X)$ and defined by:

$$H(X) = -\sum_{x_i \in X} p(x_i) \log(p(x_i)),$$

where $p(x_i)$ is the probability of the event $X = x_i$. Intuitively, this function measures (in bits) the uncertainty pertaining to the outcome of X, and takes its maximum value $H(X) = log(N)$ when the probability distribution is uniform, where N is the cardinality of X.

We let X and Y be the two random variables; the *conditional entropy* of X *given* Y is denoted by $H(X|Y)$ and defined by:

$$H(X|Y) = H(X, Y) - H(Y),$$

where $H(X, Y)$ is the joint entropy of the aggregate random variable (X, Y). The conditional entropy of X given Y reflects the uncertainty we have about the outcome of X if we know the outcome of Y. If Y is a function of X, then the joint entropy $H(X, Y)$ is equal to $H(X)$, since the outcome of Y is determined by that of X, hence the conditional entropy of X given Y can simply written as:

$$H(X|Y) = H(X) - H(Y).$$

All entropies (absolute and conditional) take non-negative values. Also, regardless of whether Y depends on X or not, the conditional entropy of X given Y is less than or equal to the entropy of X (the uncertainty on X can only decrease if we know Y). Hence for all X and Y, we have the inequality:

$$0 \leq \frac{H(X|Y)}{H(X)} \leq 1.0.$$

3 Analytical Study

In this section, we review a number of entropy-based redundancy metrics of a program, reflecting a number of dimensions of redundancy. For each metric, we discuss, in turn:

- How we define this metric.
- Why we feel that this metric has an impact on the rate of equivalent mutants.
- How we compute this metric in practice (by hand for now).

Because our ultimate goal is to derive a formula for the REM of the program as a function of its redundancy metrics, and because the REM is a fraction that ranges between 0 and 1, we resolve to let all our redundancy metrics be defined in such a way that they range between 0 and 1.

3.1 State Redundancy

What is State Redundancy? State redundancy is the gap between the declared state of the program and its actual state. Indeed, it is very common for programmers to declare much more space to store their data than they actually need, not by any fault of theirs, but due to the limited vocabulary of programming languages. An extreme example of state redundancy is the case where we declare an integer variable (entropy: 32 bits) to store a Boolean variable (entropy: 1 bit). More common and less extreme examples include: we declare an integer variable (entropy: 32 bits) to store the age of a person (ranging realistically from 0 to 128, to be optimistic, entropy: 7 bits); we declare an integer variable to represent a calendar year (ranging realistically from 2018 to 2100, entropy: 6.38 bits).

Definition: State Redundancy. Let P be a program, let S be the random variable that takes values in its declared state space and σ be the random variable that takes values in its actual state space. The *state redundancy* of Program P is defined as:

$$\frac{H(S) - H(\sigma)}{H(S)}$$

Typically, the declared state space of a program remains unchanged through the execution of the program, but the actual state space (i.e. the range of values that program variables may take) grows smaller and smaller as execution proceeds, because the program creates more and more dependencies between its variables with each assignment. Hence we are interested in defining two versions of state redundancy: one pertaining to the initial state, and one pertaining to the final state.

$$SR_I = \frac{H(S) - H(\sigma_I)}{H(S)},$$

$$SR_F = \frac{H(S) - H(\sigma_F)}{H(S)},$$

where σ_I and σ_F are (respectively) the initial state and the final state of the program, and S is its declared state. Since the entropy of the final state is typically smaller than that of the initial state (because the program builds relations between its variables as it proceeds in its execution), the final state redundancy is usually larger than the initial state redundancy.

Why is State Redundancy Correlated to Survival Rate? State redundancy measures the volume of data bits that are accessible to the program (and its mutants) but are not part of the actual state space. Any assignment to/modification of these extra bits of information does not alter the state of the program. The more extra bits there are, the more likely it is for a mutant to affect those and keep relevant bits unaffected, hence producing an equivalent mutant.

How do we Compute State Redundancy? We must compute the entropies of the declared state space ($H(S)$), the entropy of the actual initial state ($H(\sigma_I)$) and the entropy of the actual final state ($H(\sigma_F)$). For the entropy of the declared state, we simply add the entropies of the individual variable declarations, according to the following table (for Java) (Table 1):

Table 1. Entropies of basic variable declarations.

Data type	Entropy (bits)
Boolean	1
Byte	8
Char, short	16
Int, float	32
Long, double	64

For the entropy of the initial state, we consider the state of the program variables once all the relevant data has been received (through read statements, or through parameter passing, etc.) and we look for any information we may have on the incoming data (range of some variables, relations between variables, assert statements specifying the precondition, etc.); the default option being the absence of any condition. When we automate the calculation of redundancy metrics, we will rely exclusively on assert statements that may be included in the program to specify the precondition. Another source of information on the entropy of the initial actual state of the program: any exception handling statement that is invoked if the precondition of the program is not satisfied; right after the exception handling statement, we know with certainty that the negation of the exception's condition holds; this can be used to characterize the entropy of the initial actual state.

For the entropy of the final state, we take into account all the dependencies that the program may create through its execution. When we automate the calculation of redundancy metrics, we may rely on any assert statement that the programmer may have included to specify the program's post-condition; we may also keep track of functional dependencies between program variables by monitoring what variables appear on each side of assignment statements. As an illustration, we consider the following simple example:

```
public void example(int x, int y)
   {assert (1<=x && x<=128 && y>=0);
   long z = reader.nextInt();
   //  initial state
   Z = x+y; //  final state
   }
```

We find:

- $H(S) = 32 + 32 + 64 = 128\ bits$.
  Entropies of x, y, z, respectively.
- $H(\sigma_I) = 10 + 31 + 64 = 105\ bits$
  Entropy of x is 10, because of its range; entropy of y is 31 bits because half the range of int is excluded.
- $H(\sigma_F) = 10 + 31 = 41\ bits$.
  Entropy of z is excluded because z is now determined by x and y.

Hence

$$SR_I = \frac{128 - 105}{128} = 0.18,$$

$$SR_F = \frac{128 - 41}{128} = 0.68.$$

3.2 Non Injectivity

What is Non Injectivity. A major source of program redundancy is the non-injectivity of program functions. An injective function is a function whose value changes whenever its argument does; and a function is all the more non-injective that it maps several distinct arguments into the same image. A sorting routine applied to an array of size N, for example, maps N! different input arrays (corresponding to N! permutations of N distinct elements) onto a single output array (the sorted permutation of the elements). To introduce non-injectivity, we consider the function that the program defines on its state space from initial states to final states. A natural way to define non-injectivity is to let it be the conditional entropy of the initial state given the final state: if we know the final state, how much uncertainty do we have about the initial state? Since we want all our metrics to be fractions between 0 and 1, we normalize this conditional entropy to the entropy of the initial state. Hence we write:

$$NI = \frac{H(\sigma_I | \sigma_F)}{H(\sigma_I)}.$$

Since the final state is a function of the initial state, the numerator can be simplified as $H(\sigma_I) - H(\sigma_F)$. Hence:

> **Definition: Non Injectivity.** Let P be a program, and let σ_I and σ_F be the random variables that represent, respectively its initial state and final state. Then the *non-injectivity* of program P is denoted by NI and defined by:
>
> $$NI = \frac{H(\sigma_I) - H(\sigma_F)}{H(\sigma_I)}.$$

Why is Non-injectivity Correlated to Survival Rate? Of course, non-injectivity is a great contributor to generating equivalent mutants, since it increases the odds that the state produced by the mutation be mapped to the same final state as the state produced by the base program.

How do we Compute Non-injectivity? We have already discussed how to compute the entropies of the initial state and final state of the program; these can be used readily to compute non-injectivity. For illustration, we consider the sample program above, and we find its non-injectivity as:

$$NI = \frac{105 - 41}{105} = 0.61.$$

3.3 Functional Redundancy

What is Functional Redundancy? A program can be modeled as a function from initial states to final states, as we have done in Sects. 3.1 and 3.2 above, but can also be modeled as a function from an input space to an output space. To this effect we let X be the random variable that represents the aggregate of input data that the program receives (through parameter passing, read statements, global variables, etc.), and Y the aggregate of output data that the program delivers (through parameter passing, write statements, return statements, global variables, etc.).

Definition: Functional Redundancy. Let P be a program, and let X be the random variable that ranges over the aggregate of input data received by P and Y the random variable that ranges over the aggregate of output data delivered by P. Then the *functional redundancy* of program P is denoted by FR and defined by:

$$FR = \frac{H(Y)}{H(X)}.$$

Why is Functional Redundancy Related to Survival Rate? Functional redundancy is actually an extension of non-injectivity, in the sense that it reflects not only how initial states are mapped to final states, but also how initial states are affected by input data and how final states are projected onto output data. Consider for example a program that computes the median of an array by first sorting the array, which causes an increase in redundancy due to the drop in entropy, then returning the element stored in the middle of the array, causing a further massive drop in entropy by mapping a whole array onto a single cell. All this drop in entropy creates opportunities for the difference between a base program and a mutant to be erased, leading to mutant equivalence. Consider for example that if the program P sorts the array in increasing order and the mutant M sorts it in decreasing order (and if the array size is odd, or the median is duplicated) then M and P are equivalent.

How do we compute Functional Redundancy? To compute the entropy of X, we survey all the sources of input data into the program, including data that is passed in through parameter passing, global variables, read statements, etc. Unlike the calculation of the entropy of the initial state, the calculation of the entropy of X does not include internal variables, and does not capture initializations. To compute the entropy of Y, we survey all the channels by which the program delivers output data, including data that is returned through parameters, written to output channels, or delivered through return statements. For illustration, we consider the following program:

```
public void example(int u, int v)
    {assert (v>=0);
    int z = 0;
    while (v!=0) {z=z+u; v=v-1;}
    return z;
    }
```

We compute the entropies of the input space and output space:

- $H(X) = 32 + 31 = 63\,bits$.
  Entropy of u, plus entropy of v (which ranges over half of the range of integers).
- $H(Y) = 32\,bits$.

Hence,

$$FR = \frac{32}{63} = 0.51.$$

3.4   Non Determinacy

What is Non Determinacy? In all the mutation research that we have surveyed, mutation equivalence is equated with equivalent behavior between a base program and a mutant; but we have not found a precise definition of what is meant by *behavior*, nor what is meant by *equivalent* behavior. We argue that the concept of *equivalent behavior* is not precisely defined: we consider the following three programs,

```
P1: {int x,y,z; z=x; x=y; y=z;}
P2: {int x,y,z; z=y; y=x; x=z;}
P3: {int x,y,z; x=x+y;y=x-y;x=x-y;}
```

We ask the question: are these programs equivalent? The answer to this question depends on how we interpret the role of variables x, y, and z in these programs. If we interpret these as programs on the space defined by all three variables, then we find that they are distinct, since they assign different values to variable z (x for P1, y for P2, and z for P3). But if we consider that these are actually programs on the space defined by variables x and y, and that z is a mere auxiliary variable, then the three programs may be considered equivalent, since they all perform the same function (swap x and y) on their common space (formed by x, y). Consider a slight variation on these programs:

```
Q1: {int x,y;{int z; z=x; x=y; y=z;}}
Q2: {int x,y;{int z; z=y; y=x; x=z;}}
Q3: {int x,y; x=x+y;y=x-y;x=x-y;}
```

Here it is clear(er) that all three programs are defined on the space formed by variables x and y; and it may be easier to be persuaded that these programs are equivalent.

Rather than making this a discussion about the space of the programs, we wish to turn it into a discussion about the test oracle that we are using to check equivalence between the programs (or in our case, between a base program and its mutants). In the example above, if we let xP, yP, zP be the final values of x, y, z by the base program and xM, yM, zM the final values of x, y, z by the mutant, then oracles we can check include:

```
O1:{return xP==xM && yP==yM && zP==zM;}
O2:{return xP==xM && yP==yM;}
```

Oracle O1 will find that P1, P2 and P3 are not equivalent, whereas oracle O2 will find them equivalent. The difference between O1 and O2 is their degree of non-determinacy; this is the attribute we wish to quantify.

Whereas all the metrics we have studied so far apply to the base program, this metric applies to the oracle that is being used to test equivalence between the base program and a mutant. We want this metric to reflect the degree of latitude that we allow mutants to differ from the base program and still be considered equivalent. To this effect, we let σ^P be the final state produced by the base program for a given input, and we let σ^M be the final state produced by a mutant for the same input. We view the oracle that tests for equivalence between the base program and the mutant as a binary relation between σ^P and σ^M. We can quantify the non-determinacy of this relation by the conditional entropy $H(\sigma^M|\sigma^P)$: Intuitively, this represents the amount of uncertainty (or: the amount of latitude) we have about (or: we allow for) σ^M if we know σ^P. Since we want our metric to be a fraction between 0 and 1, we divide it by the entropy of σ^M. Hence the following definition.

Definition: Non Determinacy. Let O be the oracle that we use to test the equivalence between a base program P and a mutant M, and let σ^P and σ^M be, respectively, the random variables that represent the final states generated by P and M for a given initial state. The *non-determinacy* of oracle O is denoted by ND and defined by:

$$ND = \frac{H(\sigma^M | \sigma^P)}{H(\sigma^M)}.$$

Why is Non Determinacy Correlated with Survival Rate? Of course, the weaker the oracle of equivalence, the more mutants pass the equivalence test, the higher the ratio of equivalent mutants.

How do we Compute Non Determinacy? All equivalence oracles define equivalence relations on the space of the program, and $H(\sigma^M | \sigma^P)$ represents the entropy of the resulting equivalence classes. As for $H(\sigma^M)$, it represents the entropy of the whole space of the program. For illustration, let the space of the program be defined by three integer variables, say x, y, z. Then $H(\sigma^M) = 96\,bits$. As for $H(\sigma^M | \sigma^P)$, it will depend on how the oracle is defined, as it represents the entropy of the resulting equivalence classes. We show a few examples below:

Table 2. Non determinacy of sample oracles.

O#	Oracle	$H(\sigma^M | \sigma^P)$	ND
O1	xP==xM&&yP==yM&&zP==zM	0 bits	0.0
O2	xP==xM&&yP==yM	32 bits	0.33
O3	xP==xM&&zP==zM	32 bits	0.33
O4	yP==yM&&zP==zM	32 bits	0.33
O5	xP==yM	64 bits	0.66
O6	yP==yM	64 bits	0.66
O7	zP==zM	64 bits	0.66
O8	true	96 bits	1.00

Explanation: Oracle O1 is deterministic (assuming the space is made up of x, y, z only), hence its equivalence classes are of size 1; the corresponding conditional entropy is zero, and so is ND. Oracles O2, O3, O4 check for two variables but leave one variable unchecked, leading to a conditional entropy of 32 bits and a non-determinacy of 0.33 (32/96). Oracles O5, O6, O7 check for one variable but leave two variables unchecked, leading to a conditional entropy of 64 bits and a non-determinacy of 0.66 (64/96). Oracle O8 returns true for any σ^M. Hence knowing that a mutant passes this test does not inform us on any of xM, yM, nor zM. Total uncertainty is 96, hence ND = 1.

Imagine now, for the sake of illustration, that we have a single integer variable, say x. Then we can define the following oracles, in the order of decreasing strength, and increasing non-determinacy.

The interpretation of rows O1 and O8 is the same as the table above. For O7, for example, consider that if we know that xM satisfies oracle O7, then we know the rightmost bit of xM, but we do not know anything about the remaining 31 bits; hence the conditional entropy is 31 bits, and the non-determinacy is 0.969, which is 31/32. Oracle O2 informs us about the 12 rightmost bits of xM hence leaves us uncertain about the remaining 20 bits. The non-determinacy of the other oracles can be interpreted likewise.

Table 3. Non determinacy of sample integer oracles.

O#	Oracle	$H(\sigma^M \mid \sigma^P)$	ND
O1	xP==xM	0 bits	0.000
O2	xP % 4096 == xM % 4096	20 bits	0.625
O3	xP % 1024 == xM % 1024	22 bits	0.687
O4	xP % 64 == xM % 64	26 bits	0.812
O5	xP % 16 == xM % 16	28 bits	0.875
O6	xP % 4 == xM % 4	30 bits	0.937
O7	xP % 2 == xM % 2	31 bits	0.969
O8	True	32 bits	1.000

4 Empirical Study

4.1 Experimental Conditions

In order to validate our conjecture, to the effect that the survival rate of mutants generated from a program P depends on the redundancy metrics of the program and the non-determinacy of the oracle that is used to determine equivalence, we consider a number of sample programs, compute their redundancy metrics then record the ratio of equivalent mutants that they produce under controlled experimental conditions, for a fixed mutant generation policy. Our hope is to reveal significant statistical relationships between the metrics (as independent variables) and the ratio of equivalent mutants (as a dependent variable). Because we currently compute the redundancy metrics by hand, we limit ourselves to programs that are relatively small in size.

We consider functions taken from the *Apache Common Mathematics Library* (http://apache.org/); each function comes with a test data file. The test data file includes not only the test data proper, but also a test oracle in the form of assert statements, one for each input datum. Our sample includes 19 programs.

We use PITEST (http://pitest.org/), in conjunction with maven (http://maven.apache.org/) to generate mutants of each program and test them for possible equivalence with the base program. The mutation operators that we have chosen include the following:

- Op1: Increments_mutator.
- Op2: Void_method_call_mutator,
- Op3: Return_vals_mutator,
- Op4: Math_mutator,
- Op5: Negate_conditionals_mutator,
- Op6: Invert_negs_mutator,
- Op7: Conditionals_boundary_mutator.

Of course, we realize that the ratio of equivalent mutants may depend on the choice of mutation operators; but because the focus of this section is to analyze how the ratio of equivalent mutants depends on the base program and the oracle used for determining equivalence, we use a fixed set of mutants for the time being, and postpone the analysis of the impact of mutant operators to Sect. 5.

When we run a mutant M on a test data set T and we find that its behavior is equivalent (per the selected oracle) to that of the base program P, we may not conclude that M is equivalent to P unless we have some assurance that T is sufficiently thorough. In practice, it is impossible to ascertain the thoroughness of T short of letting T be all the input space of the program, which is clearly impractical. As an alternative, we mandate that in all our experiments, line coverage of P and M through their execution on test data T equals or exceeds 90%. This measure also reduces the risk of having mutants that are equivalent to the base program by virtue of the mutation being applied to dead code. In our experiment, most instances had a line coverage of 100%, in fact.

In order to analyze the impact of the non-determinacy of the equivalence oracle on the ratio of equivalent mutants, we revisit the source code of PITEST to control the oracle that it uses. As we discuss above, the test file that comes in the Apache Common Mathematics Library includes an oracle that takes the form of assert statements in Java (one for each test datum). These statements have the form:

```
Assert.assertEqual(yP,M(x))
```

where x is the current test datum, yP is the output delivered by the base program P for input x, and M(x) is the output delivered by mutant M for input x. For this oracle, we record the non-determinacy (ND) as being zero. To test the mutant for other oracles, we replace

```
AssertEqual(yP,M(x))
with
AssertEquivalent(yP,M(x))
```

for various instances of equivalence relations. If the space of the base program includes several variables, we use some of the oracles listed in Table 2, and we take note of their non-determinacy. Also, if yP and $M(x)$ are integer variables, then we use some of the equivalence relations discussed in Table 3, and we take note of their non-determinacy.

4.2   Raw Data

The raw data that results from this experiment is displayed in Table 4. This table also shows (in the last row) the correlations between the redundancy metrics and the ratio of equivalent mutants, as defined in our experiment.

Table 4. Raw data, REM vs Redundancy metrics.

Function	loc	Oracle	SRi	SRf	FR	NI	ND	COV	S/T	REM
gcd	56	Equal	0.89	0.94	0.50	0.49	0	90	16/103	0.155
		Eq%2					0.98		22/103	0.214
		Eq%4					0.95		19/103	0.184
		Eq%16					0.94		16/103	0.155
muland check	42	Equal	0.862	0.931	0.50	0.43	0	95	6/43	0.14
		Eq%2					0.98		6/43	0.14
fraction	68	Equal	0.88	0.961	0.33	0.66	0	96	22/95	0.234
		dEq					0.5		23/95	0.242
		dEq%2					0.84		26/95	0.273
reduced fraction	26	Equal	0.86	0.98	1.00	0.77	0	96	17/46	0.37
		dEq					0.5		19/46	0.413
erfInv	88	Equal	0.62	0.63	1.00	0.03	0	99	9/126	0.071
ebeDiv	20	Equal	0.89	0.90	0.50	0.10	0	97	1/13	0.077
getDist	19	Equal	0.89	0.90	0.50	0.10	0	97	1/17	0.059
ArRealVec	12	Equal	0.90	0.95	0.90	0.48	0	97	2/10	0.020
ToBlocks	42	Equal	0.89	0.90	1.00	0.08	0	95	3/31	0.097
getRowM	27	Equal	0.88	0.95	0.98	0.59	0	95	7/23	0.304
orthogM	87	Equal	0.91	0.93	0.75	0.28	0	100	20/151	0.132
Equals	31	Equal	0.85	0.94	0.20	0.56	0	90	6/21	0.286
Density	18	Equal	0.88	0.96	0.25	0.23	0	95	5/30	0.167
Abs()	20	Equal	0.89	0.93	0.50	0.33	0	96	2/20	0.10
Pow	55	Equal	0.51	0.61	0.67	0.20	0	97	6/52	0.115
setSeed	17	Equal	0.80	0.90	1.00	0.51	0	100	4/16	0.25
Asinh	17	Equal	0.89	0.91	1.00	0.15	0	97	13/82	0.159
Atan	143	Equal	0.90	0.92	0.40	0.08	0	97	14/136	0.103
nextPrime	35	Equal	0.793	0.896	0.40	0.5	0	94	3/58	0.05
		Eq%2					0.96		34/58	0.58
Correlations vs REM			0.055	0.31	0.14	0.65	0.43			

4.3   Statistical Analysis

Table 5 shows a matrix of scatter plots between each pair of the metrics and the REM. For example, in the bottom row of scatter plots, the y-axis is the REM (S/T), and the x-axis are, going from left to right, for metrics SRI, SRF, FR, NI and ND. On inspection of the plots, each of the metrics seems to show some positive correlation with S/T, the strongest being NI. We note that the ND values are confined to 0 or values very close to 1. In our models below, we assume a linear relationship, even though there is no data with moderate values of ND. Finally, we also note that SRI and SRF appear to be highly correlated. Inclusion of both variables in a model can result in unstable estimates. However, it turns out (see below) that both variables are not included in the final model.

Since the response, REM, is a proportion, we use a logistic linear model for the survival rate so that the response will be constrained to be between 0 and 1. More specifically, the logarithm of the odds of equivalence $\left(\frac{REM}{1-REM}\right)$ is a linear function of the predictors:

$$\log\left(\frac{REM}{1-REM}\right) = \alpha + \beta \times X.$$

For any model M consisting of a set of the covariates X, we can obtain a residual deviance D(M) that provides an indication of the degree to which the response is unexplained by the model covariates. Hence, each model can be compared with the null model of no covariates to see if they are statistically different. Furthermore, any pair of nested models can be compared (using a chi-squared test).

We fit the full model with all five covariates, which was found to be statistically significant, and then successively drop a covariate, each time testing the smaller model (one covariate less) with the previous model. We continue until the smaller model was significantly different, i.e. worse than the previous model. Using the procedure described above, we find that the final model contains the metrics FR, NI and ND, with coefficient estimates and standard errors given in the table below:

Metric	Estimate	Standard error	P value
Intercept	−2.765	0.246	≪0.001
FR	0.459	0.268	0.086
NI	2.035	0.350	≪0.001
ND	0.346	0.152	0.023

Hence, the model is

$$\log\left(\frac{REM}{1-REM}\right) = -2.765 + 0.459 \times FR + 2.035 \times NI + 0.346 \times ND.$$

Each of the estimates are positive, hence, the survival rate increases with each of the three metrics. An increase in FR of 0.1 results in an expected increase in the odds by a factor of exp(0.1 × 0.459), or approximately 5%. Similarly increases of 0.1 in NI and ND each yields an expected increase of 22% and 3.5% respectively in the odds of survival.

The sequence of models we tested, including their residual deviances, as well as the results of comparisons between them, are shown in the table below:

No.	Model	Deviance	Degrees of freedom	Test	P value
1	Null model	122.856	26		
2	SRI, SRF, FR, NI, ND	42.888	21	Models 2 and 1	≪0.001
3	SRF, FR, NI, ND	57.447	22	Models 3 and 2	0.0001
4	SRI, FR, NI, ND	57.484	22	Models 4 and 2	0.0001
5	FR, NI, ND	57.74	23	Models 5 and 3	0.588
6	NI, ND	60.667	24	Models 6 and 5	0.087
7	FR, NI	62.955	24	Models 7 and 5	0.022

For the training data, the mean square error of the survival rate is 0.0069 and the mean absolute error is 0.049. We re-checked the analysis by performing take-one-out cross-validation, i.e., we removed each row of data in turn, fit the list of models from our previous analysis on the remaining data, then used the fitted models to predict the data point that was removed. For each model, the error is the difference between the predicted value from that model, and the actual value. The mean squared and absolute errors of 0.0087 and 0.057 respectively for the above final model were the smallest out of the list of models.

The plot below shows the relative errors of the model estimates with respect to the actuals; virtually all the relative errors are within less than 0.1 of the actuals.

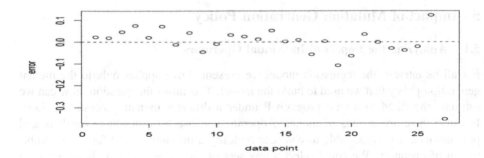

Table 5. Scatter plot, redundancy metrics and ratio of equivalent mutants

5 Impact of Mutation Generation Policy

5.1 Analyzing the Impact of Individual Operators

For all its interest, the regression model we present above applies only to the mutant generation policy that we used to build the model. This raises the question: how can we estimate the REM of a base program P under a different mutant generation policy? Because there are dozens of mutation operators in use by different researchers and practitioners, it is impossible to consider building a different model for each combination of operators. We could select a few sets of operators, that may have been the subject of focused research, or have a documented practical value [2–4, 26] and derive a specific estimation model for each. While this may be interesting from a practical standpoint, it presents limited interest as a research matter, as it does not enhance our understanding of how mutation operators interact with each other. What we are interested to understand is: if we know the REM's of a program P under individual mutation operators $op_1, op_2, \ldots, op_n$, can we estimate the REM of P if all of these operators are applied jointly?

Answering this question will enable us to produce a generic solution to the automated estimation of the REM of a program under an arbitrary mutant generation policy:

- We select a list of mutation operators of interest (e.g. the list suggested by Laurent et al. [27] or by Just et al. [2], or their union).
- Develop a regression model (similar to the model we derived above) based on each individual operator.
- Given a program P and a mutant generation policy defined by a set of operators, say $op_1, op_2, \ldots, op_n$, we apply the regression models of the individual operators to compute the corresponding ratios of equivalent mutants, say $REM_1, REM_2, \ldots, REM_n$.
- Combine the REM's generated for the individual operators to estimate the REM that stems from their simultaneous application.

5.2   Combining Operators

For the sake of simplicity, we first consider the problem above in the context of two operators, say op_1, op_2. Let REM_1, REM_2 be the REM's obtained for program P under operators op_1, op_2. We ponder the question: can we estimate the REM obtained for P when the two operators are applied jointly? To answer this question, we interpret the REM as the probability that a random mutant generated from P is equivalent to P. At first sight, it may be tempting to think of REM as the product of REM_1 and REM_2 on the grounds that in order for mutant M_{12} (obtained from P by applying operators op_1, op_2) to be equivalent with P, it suffices for M_1 to be equivalent to P (probability: REM_1), and for M_{12} to be equivalent to M_1 (probability: REM_2). This hypothesis yields the following formula of REM:

$$REM = REM_1 \times REM_2.$$

But we have strong doubts about this formula, for the following reasons:

- This formula assumes that the equivalence of P to M_1 and the equivalence of M_1 to M_{12} are independent events; but of course they are not. In fact we have shown in Sect. 4 that the probability of equivalence is influenced to a considerable extent by the amount of redundancy in P.
- This formula ignores the possibility that mutation operators may interfere with each other; in particular, the effect of one operator may cancel (all of or some of) the effect of another, or to the contrary may enable it.
- This formula assumes that the ratio of equivalent mutants of a program P decreases with the number of mutation operators; for example, if we have five operators that yield a REM of 0.1 each, then this formula yields a joint REM of 10^{-5}. We do not see why that should be the case; in fact we suspect that the REM of combined operators may be larger than that of individual operators.

- This formula also assumes that if a mutant by itself has an REM of 0, then any set of operators that includes it also has an REM of zero; but that is not consistent with our observations: it is very common for single operators to produce an REM of zero by themselves, but a non-trivial REM once they are combined with another.

For all these reasons, we expect $REM_1 \times REM_2$ to be a loose (remote) lower bound for REM, but not be a good approximation thereof. Elaborating on the third item cited above, we argue that in fact, whenever we deploy a new mutation operator, we are likely to make the mutant more distinct from the original program, hence it is the probability of being distinct that we ought to compose, not the probability of being equivalent. This is captured in the following formula:

$$(1 - REM) = (1 - REM_1)(1 - REM_2),$$

which yields:

$$REM = REM_1 + REM_2 - REM_1 REM_2.$$

In the following sub-section we test our assumption regarding the formula of a combined REM.

5.3   Empirical Validation

In order to evaluate the validity of our proposed formula, we run the following experiment:

- We consider the sample of seventeen Java programs that we used to derive our model of Sect. 4.3.
- We consider the sample of seven mutation operators that are listed in this paper.
- For each operator Op, for each program P, we run the mutant generator Op on program P, and test all the mutants for equivalence to P. By dividing the number of equivalent mutants by the total number of generated mutants, we obtain the REM of program P for mutation operator Op.
- For each mutation operator Op, we obtain a table that records the programs of our sample, and for each program we record the number of mutants and the number of equivalent mutants, whence the corresponding REM.
- For each pair of operators, say (Op1, Op2), we perform the same experiment as above, only activating two mutation operators rather than one. This yields a table where we record the programs, the number of mutants generated for each, and the number of equivalent mutants among these, from which we compute the corresponding REM. Since there are seven operators, we have twenty one pairs of operators, hence twenty one such tables.
- For each pair of operators, we build a table that shows, for each program P, the REM of P under each operator, the REM of P under the joint combination of the two operators, and the residuals that we get for the two tentative formulas:
  F1: $REM = REM_1 REM_2$,
  F2: $REM = REM_1 + REM_2 - REM_1 REM_2$.

At the bottom of each such table, we compute the average and standard deviation of the residuals for formulas F1 and F2.

* We summarize all our results into a single table, which shows the average of residuals and the standard deviation of residuals for formulas F1 and F2 for each (of 21) combination of two operators.

5.4   Analysis

The final result of this analysis is given in Table 6. The first observation we can make from this table is that, as we expected, the expression $F1: REM_1 REM_2$ is indeed a lower bound for REM, since virtually all the average residuals (for all pairs of operators) are positive, with the exception of the pair (Op1, Op2), where the average residual is virtually zero. The second observation is that, as we expected, the expression $F2$: $REM_1 + REM_2 - REM_1 REM_2$ gives a much better approximation of the actual REM than the F1 expression; also, interestingly, the F2 expression hovers around the actual REM, with half of the estimates (11 rows) below the actuals and half above (10 rows). With the exception of one outlier (Op4, Op5), all residuals are less than 0.2 in absolute value, and two thirds (14 out of 21) are less than 0.1 in absolute value. The average (over all pairs of operators) of the absolute value of the average residual (over all programs) for formula F2 is 0.080.

We have conducted similar experiments with three and four operators, and our results appear to confirm the general formula of the combined REM for N operators as:

$$REM = 1 - \prod_{i=1}^{N} (1 - REM_i).$$

Still, this matter is under further investigation.

Table 6. Testing tentative formulas.

Operator pairs	Residuals, F1		Residuals, F2		Abs(Residuals)	
	Average	Std dev	Average	Std dev	F1	F2
Op1, op2	0.1242467	0.1884347	−0.016362	0.0459150	0.1242467	0.0163621
Op1, op3	−0.0008928	0.0936731	0.0241071	0.0740874	0.0008928	0.0241071
Op1, op4	0.3616666	0.4536426	0.1797486	0.5413659	0.3616666	0.1797486
Op1, op5	0.1041666	0.2554951	0.0260416	0.3113869	0.1041666	0.0260416
Op1, op6	0.0777777	0.2587106	0.0777777	0.2587106	0.0777777	0.0777777
Op1, op7	0.0044642	0.0178571	−0.0625	0.25	0.0044642	0.0625
Op2, op3	0.1194726	0.122395	0.0658514	0.1397070	0.1194726	0.0658514
Op2, op4	0.1583097	0.1416790	−0.124639	0.2763612	0.1583097	0.1246387
Op2, op5	0.1630756	0.1588826	0.0535737	0.1469494	0.1630756	0.0535737
Op2, op6	0.2479740	0.4629131	0.0979913	0.332460	0.2479740	0.0979913
OP2, op7	0.1390082	0.1907661	−0.053526	0.2445812	0.1390082	0.0535258
Op3, op4	0.1601363	0.1411115	0.1436880	0.3675601	0.1601363	0.1436880

(continued)

Table 6. (*continued*)

Operator pairs	Residuals, F1		Residuals, F2		Abs(Residuals)	
	Average	Std dev	Average	Std dev	F1	F2
Op3, op5	0.0583333	0.0898558	−0.0447916	0.1019656	0.0583333	0.0447916
Op3, op6	0.0166666	0.1409077	−0.0083333	0.0845893	0.0166666	0.0083333
Op3, op7	0.0152173	0.0504547	−0.0642468	0.2496315	0.0152173	0.0642468
Op4, op5	0.5216666	0.4221049	0.2786375	0.4987458	0.5216666	0.2786375
Op4, op6	0.3166666	0.2855654	0.1347486	0.4101417	0.3166666	0.1347486
OP4, op7	0.3472951	0.3530456	0.125903	0.3530376	0.3472951	0.125903
Op5, op6	0.075	0.1194121	−0.003125	0.1332247	0.075	0.003125
Op5, op7	0.078125	0.1760385	−0.0669642	0.2494466	0.078125	0.0669642
Op6, op7	0.0349264	0.0904917	−0.0320378	0.2735720	0.0349264	0.0320378
Averages	0.1487287		0.0297332		0.1488137	0.0802188

6   Concluding Remarks

6.1   Summary

The presence of equivalent mutants is a constant source of aggravation in mutation testing, because equivalent mutants distort our analysis and introduce biases that prevent us from making assertive claims. This has given rise to much research aiming to identify equivalent mutants by analyzing their source code or their run-time behavior. Analyzing their source code usually provides sufficient but unnecessary conditions of equivalence (as it deals with proving locally equivalent behavior); and analyzing run-time behavior usually provides necessary but insufficient conditions of equivalence (just because two programs have comparable run-time behavior does not mean they are functionally equivalent). Also, static analysis of mutants is generally time-consuming and error-prone, and wholly impractical for large and complex programs, and for large numbers of mutants.

In this paper, we submit four simple premises for the study of equivalent mutants:

- First, for most practical purposes, determining which mutants are equivalent to a base program (and which are not) is not important, provided we can estimate their number.
- Second, even when it is important to single out equivalent mutants, knowing their number can greatly facilitate the task of singling them out; it could in fact be automated.
- Third, what makes a program prone to produce equivalent mutants is the same attribute that makes it fault tolerant, since fault tolerance is by definition the property of maintaining correct behavior in the presence of faults. The attribute that makes programs fault tolerant is well-known: redundancy. Hence we can estimate the ratio of equivalent mutants of a program by analyzing/quantifying its level of redundancy.

- Fourth, it may be possible to estimate the ratio of equivalent mutants of a program for an arbitrary set of mutation operators, assuming we have a regression model for estimating the REM of a program for each individual operator.

6.2 Assessment and Threats to Validity

Even though much of this paper is devoted to the derivation of a regression model that determines the REM of a program from an analysis of its redundancy metrics, we do not consider that the statistical model per se is the main contribution; rather the main contribution of this work is the premise that the REM can be derived from a static analysis of the redundancy metrics of the base program, and a static analysis of the mutant generation operators.

Another interesting contribution of this paper is the formula that it proposes for the REM of a set of mutation operators as a function of the REM's obtained for individual operators. We strongly suspect that this formula is valid not only for individual mutation operators, but for sets of operators. Even though the empirical data of Sect. 5 appears to bear out our formula, and even though other experiments we ran for three and four operators appear to support this formula

$$REM = 1 - \prod_{i=1}^{N} (1 - REM_i),$$

we feel that we need further analytical and empirical evidence to confidently adopt it.

The quantitative approach we advocate to the study of equivalent mutants appears to be useful for a broader quantitative analysis of mutation testing. In addition to providing a basis for the study of mutant equivalence, the REM also enables us to analyze the redundancy of a set of mutants: if we generate 100 mutants and find that the REM is 0.2, then we can infer that 80 mutants are not equivalent to P. What remains to be investigated is whether the remaining 80 mutants are distinct from each other or whether some of them are equivalent to each other. A test data set may kill all 80 mutants, but whether it is a good test data set or not depends on whether the 80 mutants it killed are distinct from each other (in which case this is a good test set), or say they are partitioned into two classes of 40 equivalent mutants each (in which case the test data set is as good as if it killed just two mutants). Using the REM, we can estimate the number of equivalence classes of the set of mutants that are distinct from P.

Threats to the validity of our study include the fact that it fails to take into account mutations that are applied to dead code. This is inherent to our approach, in that it is based on an analysis of the functional properties of the program at hand, whereas dead code is essentially a structural attribute of the program. We address this issue partially by monitoring the line coverage provided by the test data: we exclude from our statistical analysis any execution that does not ensure a line coverage greater than or equal to 90%; but only 100% coverage ensures the absence of dead code.

6.3   Research Prospects

Our future research plan includes the following directions:

- The design of a Java compiler than parses Java code and computes the redundancy metrics.
- The Use of this compiler to build statistical models for the derivation of the REM of a base program, for a predefined catalog of mutant generators.
- Integration of these statistical models into a tool that takes a program and a mutant generator selection as input, and returns the list of mutants generated from the program by the selected generator, along with an estimate of the REM.
- Along with the generated mutants, the tool estimates the number of mutants that are equivalent to the base program.
- Among those mutants that are not equivalent to the base program, the tool estimates the number of equivalent classes (modulo semantic equivalence).
- For a given number of killed mutants by some test data set T, the tool estimates the number of equivalence classes that have been covered (that have at least element that has been killed). This can be used as a more precise measure of mutation score.

On the conceptual side, we envision to further investigate the relation between the RFEM's generated by a set of mutants and those computed for individual mutants deployed in isolation.

Acknowledgement. This research is partially supported by a grant to the last author from the (US) National Science Foundation, number DGE 1565478.

References

1. Jia, Y., Harman, M.: An analysis and survey of the development of mutation testing. IEEE Trans. Softw. Eng. **37**(5), 649–678 (2011)
2. Just, R., Jalali, D., Inozemtseva, L., Ernst, M.D., Holmes, R., Fraser, G.: Are mutants a valid substitute for real faults in software testing. In: Foundations of Software Engineering, Hong Kong, China (2014)
3. Andrews, J.H., Briand, L.C., Labiche, I.: Is mutation an appropriate tool for testing experiments. In: International Conference on Software Testing, St. Louis, MO, USA (2005)
4. Namin, A.S., Kakarla, S.: The Use of mutation in testing experiments and its sensitivity to external threats. In: ISSTA 2011, Toronto, Ontario, Canada (2011)
5. Yao, X., Harman, M., Jia, Y.: A study of equivalent and stubborn mutation operators using human analysis of equivalence. In: Proceedings, International Conference on Software Engineering, Hyderabad, India (2014)
6. Schuler, D., Zeller, A.: Covering and uncovering equivalent mutants. J. Softw. Test. Verification Reliab. **23**(5), 353–374 (2012)
7. Gruen, B.J., Schuler, D., Zeller, A.: The impact of equivalent mutants. In: MUTATION 2009. Denver CO., USA (2009)
8. Just, R., Ernst, M.D., Fraser, G.: Using state infection conditions to detect equivalent mutants and speed up mutation analysis. In: Dagstuhl Seminar 13021: Symbolic Methods in Testing, Wadern, Germany (2013)

9. Just, R., Ernst, M.D., Fraser, G.: Efficient mutation analysis by propagating and partitioning infected execution states. In: ISSTA 2014, San Jose, CA, USA (2014)
10. Wang, B., Xiong, Y., Shi, Y., Zhang, L., Hao, D.: Faster mutation analysis via equivalence modulo states. In: ISSTA 2017, Santa Barbara, CA, USA (2017)
11. Papadakis, M., Delamaro, M., Le Traon, Y.: Mitigating the effects of equivalent mutants with mutant classification strategies. Sci. Comput. Program. **95**(12), 298–319 (2014)
12. Papadakis, M., Kintis, M., Zhang, J., Jia, Y., Le Traon, Y., Harman, M.: Mutation testing advances: an analysis and survey. In: Advances in Computers (2019)
13. Budd, T.A., Angluin, D.: Two notions of correctness and their relation to testing. Acta Informatica **18**(1), 31–45 (1982)
14. Offutt, J.A., Pan, J.: Automatically detecting equivalent mutants and infeasible paths. J. Softw. Test. Verification Reliab. **7**(3), 164–192 (1997)
15. Voas, J., McGraw, G.: Software Fault Injection: Inoculating Programs Against Errors. Wiley, New York (1997)
16. Harman, M., Hierons, R., Danicic, S.: The relationship between program dependence and mutation analysis. In: MUTATION 2000, San Jose, CA, USA (2000)
17. Hierons, R.M., Harman, M., Danicic, S.: Using program slicing to assist in the detection of equivalent mutants. J. Softw. Test. Verification Reliab. **9**(4), 233–262 (1999)
18. Ellims, M., Ince, D.C., Petre, M.: The Csaw C mutation tool: initial results. In: MUTATION 2007, Windsor, UK (2007)
19. Howden, W.E.: Weak mutation testing and completeness of test sets. IEEE Trans. Softw. Eng. **8**(4), 371–379 (1982)
20. Schuler, D., Dallmaier, V., Zeller, A.: Efficient mutation testing by checking invariant violations. In: ISSTA 2009, Chicago, IL, USA (2009)
21. Ernst, M.D., Cockrell, J., Griswold, W.G., Notkin, D.: Dynamically discovering likely program invariants to support program evolution. IEEE Trans. Softw. Eng. **27**(2), 99–123 (2001)
22. Nica, S., Wotawa, F.: Using constraints for equivalent mutant detection. In: Workshop on Formal Methods in the Development of Software (2012)
23. Carvalho, L., Guimaraes, M.A., Fernandes, L., Al Hajjaji, M., Gheyi, R., Thuem, T.: Equivalent mutants in configurable systems: an empirical study. In: VAMOS 2018, Madrid, Spain (2018)
24. Kintis, M., Papadakis, M., Jia, Y., Malevris, N., Le Traon, Y., Harman, M.: Detecting trivial mutant equivalences via compiler optimizations. IEEE Trans. Softw. Eng. **44**(4), 308–333 (2018)
25. Marsit, I., Omri, M.N., Loh, J.M., Mili, A.: Impact of mutation operators on mutant equivalence. In: ICSOFT, Madrid, Spain (2018)
26. Shannon, C.E.: A mathematical theory of communication. Bell Syst. Tech. J. **27**, 379–423 (1948)
27. Laurent, T., Papadakis, M., Kintis, M., Henard, C., Le Traon, Y., Ventresque, A.: Assessing and improving the mutation testing practice of PIT. In: ICST, Vasteras, Sweden (2018)

A Rating Tool for the Automated Selection of Software Refactorings that Remove Antipatterns to Improve Performance and Stability

Nikolai Moesus[1], Matthias Scholze[1], Sebastian Schlesinger[2],
and Paula Herber[3(✉)]

[1] QMETHODS – Business & IT Consulting GmbH, Berlin, Germany
{nikolai.moesus,matthias.scholze}@qmethods.com
[2] Software and Embedded Systems Engineering, Technische Universität Berlin,
Berlin, Germany
sebastian.schlesinger@tu-berlin.de
[3] Embedded Systems Group, University of Münster, Münster, Germany
paula.herber@uni-muenster.de

Abstract. Antipatterns are known to be bad solutions for recurring design problems. To detect and remove antipatterns has proven to be a useful mean to improve the quality of software. While there exist several approaches to detect antipatterns automatically, existing work on antipattern detection often does not solve the detected design problems automatically. Although there exist refactorings that have the potential to significantly increase the quality of a program, it is hard to decide which refactorings effectively yield improvements with respect to performance and stability. In this paper, we present a rating tool that makes use of static antipattern detection together with software profiling for the automated selection of refactorings that remove antipatterns and are promising candidates to improve performance and stability. Our key idea is to extend a previously proposed heuristics that utilizes software properties determined by both static code analyses and dynamic software analyses to compile a list of concrete refactorings sorted by their assessed potential to improve performance with an approach to identify refactorings that may improve stability. We do not impose an order on the refactorings that may improve stability. We demonstrate the practical applicability of our overall approach with experimental results.

Keywords: Software refactoring · Performance ·
Stability antipattern detection

1 Introduction

Performance and stability issues are a common reason why software needs refactoring. However, due to the variety of possible causes for performance and stability issues, finding appropriate refactorings is a complicated task. To tackle this

© Springer Nature Switzerland AG 2019
M. van Sinderen and L. A. Maciaszek (Eds.): ICSOFT 2018, CCIS 1077, pp. 28–54, 2019.
https://doi.org/10.1007/978-3-030-29157-0_2

problem, antipattern detection as well as measurement-based performance engineering have been proposed. Antipattern detection is a static analysis that aims at detecting code flaws and violations against good practice [22]. While antipattern detection often succeeds in detecting critical code sections that cause performance bottlenecks, it tends to yield a great number of proposed refactorings of which only a very small fraction can be considered relevant for performance. To resolve all proposed issues is therefore neither efficient nor feasible. Additionally, a bad performing piece of code that gets only rarely called usually is not the cause of severe performance problems. Measurement-based performance engineering relies on dynamic analysis techniques that are applied when the program under development is running [37]. Those analyses generate huge amounts of heterogeneous data like response times, function call durations, stack traces, memory footprints or hardware counters. To find the important chunks of information that help solving performance issues takes time and also requires skill and experience. Hence, manually searching for an appropriate refactoring is an expensive task.

This paper is an extended version of [25]. There, we have presented a novel approach for the automated selection of refactorings that are promising candidates to improve performance. In this paper, we provide the following extensions compared to [25]: First, we discuss not only performance, but also antipatterns and refactorings that concern the stability of a program. Second, we have added a more extensive discussion of the antipatterns considered in our rating tool, and justified the decision for the antipattern detection tool PMD [6]. Third, we have added a section about the implementation of our rating tool. Fourth and finally, we have added a more detailed discussion of our experimental results. The key idea of our approach is to use both static and dynamic analyses and combine the results to generate a heuristics that determines those refactorings that are most promising with respect to performance. The major contributions are twofold: First, to quantify the expected effect of a refactoring, we present a novel rating function that incorporates the analysis data from both static and dynamic analysis, and thus enables us to heuristically assess the effectiveness of concrete refactorings. The output is a list of proposed refactorings sorted by their potential to yield a strong positive effect on performance, together with a list of refactorings that may improve stability. The reasoning behind our heuristics is to assess which portions of source code get executed frequently, such that a refactoring there pays off more than anywhere else. We combine this with a factor that provides an estimate for the general effectiveness of a given refactoring, independent of its position in the code. Second, we present an evaluation of the general effectiveness of a given set of refactorings that are generally assumed to improve performance, independent of their use in a concrete program. To achieve this, we have implemented micro benchmarks and measured their effectiveness with respect to the execution time and memory consumption. We use the results from our micro benchmarks together with static and dynamic code properties in our ranking function to provide a heuristics that automatically assesses the expected effect of a concrete refactoring in a given program.

To demonstrate the practical applicability of our approach, we present the results from two experiments. In the first experiment, we have intentionally manipulated a given example program such that it contains typical antipatterns and investigate the impact on performance and how high the rule violations are rated by our heuristics. In the second experiment, we apply our rating function to a given program, implement the top rated refactorings and examine the performance improvement.

The rest of this paper is structured as follows: In Sect. 2, we introduce the preliminaries that are necessary to understand the remainder of this paper. In Sect. 3, we discuss related work. In Sect. 4, we present our approach for the automated selection of refactorings. In Sect. 5, we briefly discuss our implementation of the rating tool and micro benchmarks, and we present micro benchmark results as well as our case studies and experimental results. We conclude in Sect. 6.

2 Background

In this section, we introduce the preliminaries that are necessary to understand the remainder of this paper, namely software performance, stability, antipatterns and refactorings.

2.1 Performance

In the field of software, the notion of performance comprises multiple run time aspects [30], all of them classified as non-functional properties. In this paper, we focus on execution time as measure for performance. In a complex software system with multiple components, execution times of single services sum up to the overall execution time.

Performance plays an important role in every software. This is not necessarily apparent as long as the performance is sufficient, e.g. due to modern CPUs, high speed connections or efficient operating systems. From a users perspective, sufficient performance often is taken for granted and is barely noticed, but a lack of performance jeopardizes the success of an application as users become frustrated and search for alternatives. In the case of simulation software, performance sets boundaries to the level of detail or other functional aspects of a simulation because too complex calculations might literally never finish.

To measure the execution time of a software technically no more than a subtraction of two timestamps is necessary. However, a lack of accuracy of the hardware or operating system that takes the timestamps may be a problem. Because it is not possible to increase the time measurement accuracy a common work-around is the utilization of performance benchmarks.

2.2 Stability

The term software stability refers to either absence of failures or consistency of source code over time [10,31]. In this paper, we use the former definition and when speaking of a stable software we think of a program that does not crash or erroneously abort user actions, that does not require restarts due to increasing memory consumption or illegal states, and that can handle any possible input in a reasonable manner. A lack of stability results from bugs or design flaws in any part of the software system.

Stability plays a comparatively important role as performance and is likewise taken for granted by users. A software that frequently crashes and perhaps even looses data is frustrating and can cause great damage. Therefore, an unreliable software should not be used in a production environment.

To measure the stability of software is a difficult task especially in complex programs. Common metrics are the number of failures in a time period and time between failures [24]. The technical measurements is complicated since the most appropriate time unit is CPU time, which is hard to take at an arbitrary moment when a failure occurs. Furthermore, to carry out a measurement, the software under test must be used for a representative time under realistic conditions in order to obtain valid statistics. However, there exist methods that we can make use of to detect potential threats to stability in the source code of a program.

2.3 Software Antipatterns

Software design patterns describe good solutions to recurring problems in an abstract and reusable way. A software antipattern is very similar, only that it describes a bad, unfavored solution [21]. The motivation to write those down is to prevent their use and to provide appropriate refactorings into better designs. An example for an antipattern described in [32] is *The Ramp*, where tasks have an increasing execution time due to a growing list that has to be searched but is never cleaned up.

Listing 1.1. Example Performance Antipattern.

```
1  String [] p = { "These", "are", "separate", "parts" };
2  String str = p[0];
3  for (int i = 1; i < p.length; ++i){
4      str = str + "_" + p[i];
5  }
```

Performance antipatterns are the class of patterns that lead to bad performance. As an example for a performance antipattern in the programming language Java, consider Listing 1.1. In this example, strings are concatenated with the '+' operator. The reason why using the + operator as shown is considered an antipattern is based on the internal implementation in Java. The + operator is natively overloaded for String, although in Java operator overloading in general is not possible. However, this piece of syntactic sugar brings along a disadvantage concerning performance. Because objects of String are immutable, the additional characters cannot simply be appended. Instead, internally a Java StringBuilder object is allocated, concatenates the strings in its char buffer and returns the new immutable string. If such procedure is repeated in a loop as shown in Listing 1.1, each iteration allocates and dismisses a `StringBuilder` and an intermediate string. It is veiled from the programmer that there lies an inefficiency in the simple + syntax. The example demonstrates the low degree of complexity of the antipatterns we deal with. Refactorings for this kind of antipattern are often relatively simple as well. Also, they are mostly predetermined and barely a subject to situational alternation.

2.4   Software Refactorings

A software refactoring is a change in source code that keeps the external behavior of a software unaffected but yet improves the internal design or other non-functional properties [13]. Examples for refactorings are splitting up large classes into multiple units, increasing encapsulation of classes or replacing inefficient operations. Refactoring is a structured process with specified steps and a defined goal. For many situations there is a refactoring that describes a sequence of steps and things to take care of in order to achieve a certain goal, which is better code. Due to the structured procedure, refactorings are an elegant way of improving software, in contrast to uncoordinatedly changing something in the code.

A refactoring may be a large scale operation that affects several units and takes much effort to fully implement. In this paper, we focus on micro refactorings [26], which affect only a few lines of code and are realizable in a short time or even automatically. Concerning performance, micro refactorings can have noticeable benefits, especially in often called functions or inside frequently executed loops. Therefore, micro refactorings have the potential of an excellent cost-benefit ratio.

The proposed performance refactoring for the example in Listing 1.1 is to allocate only one `StringBuilder` outside the loop and use it instead of the + operator, such that no temporary objects accumulate.

3   Related Work

In [33, 34], the authors present approaches to automatically detect software design patterns based on static information extracted from Java bytecode. The model uses a directed graph representation of the class diagram and utilizes matrices to calculate similarities between modeled design patterns and the software. The approach is extended to distinguish between design patterns with a similar structure in [34]. By taking the version history into account the source code before the introduction of the design pattern is inspected for code smells. Depending on the formerly present smells the correct design pattern is determined. However, they focus on the detection of classical design patterns [14] and are not concerned with their effect on performance. It is also possible to detect patterns in source code with formal methods as suggested in [36]. There, the authors examine class relations in a formal concept analysis to detect repeating patterns without the need of prior pattern knowledge. The analysis is expensive, though, and is not feasible for a large code base. Additionally, the impact of the detected patterns on performance is not considered.

According to the survey on design pattern detection presented in [29], the majority of published approaches combines structural and behavioral analyses of the software. Although behavioral analyses are not necessarily implemented as dynamic analyses, for example, the approach introduced in [20] uses static and dynamic analyses similar to how we use them: The static analysis provides a set of design pattern candidates, which is narrowed down in a dynamic analysis. For each design pattern they prepare a set of rules concerning the interaction of classes and discard every candidate that violates any of the rules. Slightly different is the approach of building call graphs during the dynamic analysis as presented in [35]. The authors search both abstract syntax graphs and call graphs for design patterns and rate each candidate. The combination of both ratings helps to determine actual design patterns. Although both approaches combine static and dynamic analyses, they again only detect patterns and are not concerned with their effect on performance.

In [4], the authors detect design patterns in a graph representation according to a meta model specifically designed for this purpose. They develop a domain specific language that allows precise definitions of patterns with inheritance between them to ease the creation of variants. They achieve a high detection precision but again, they are not concerned with the effect on performance.

An approach to detect performance antipatterns and suggest refactorings is proposed in [1,2]. However, they work on software architectural models, and propose refactorings within the model, possibly even before the software is implemented, while we focus on implementations.

In [7], the authors achieve a rating of performance antipatterns based on their so called guiltiness. The algorithm that calculates the guiltiness requires a complete set of antipatterns and the set of performance requirements for the system as input. Each antipattern and requirement is associated to one or more system entities, e.g. a processor. Depending on to what extend a requirement is not fulfilled the associated system entities spread the guilt among all their associated antipatterns while taking into account the antipattern's estimated impact on the respective system entity. Although this approach succeeds in selecting the most effective performance antipatterns, it requires an expensive modeling step to capture the component model, as the software needs to be transformed into a Palladio Component Model (PCM) [3] to carry out the antipattern detection and a performance assessment, which is necessary to estimate an antipattern's impact.

In [8], the authors propose assembly code optimization by means of static antipattern detection and dynamic value profiling. They use a knowledge database for assembly antipatterns that have shown bad performance in micro benchmarks and attempt to find those with a static analyzer. The dynamic analysis benefits from very low instrumentation cost on the assembly level and captures data like cache miss rate. Although this approach is closely related to ours in many ways, e.g. the focus on micro refactorings, it utilizes the dynamic analysis as independent addition instead of combining its yield with the results from static analyses, and it does not target a high-level programming language, which is often preferrable for software evolution and maintenance.

In [23], the authors present a machine learning system that examines execution traces of the software under test and calculates new input values for the next execution that are most promising to uncover a performance bottleneck. Finally, an analysis of the captured execution traces is carried out and a ranked list with presumed performance bottlenecks is compiled. Even though in our approach we utilize very different techniques, the result, namely an ordered list of specific performance issues, is similar. However, they do not automatically propose a solution to the detected performance issue.

In [11], the authors use supervised learning to train a model that finds antipatterns and rates their severity. This relieves them from the necessity to formalize the antipatterns in order to perform the detection. However, they rely on external detection algorithms to support the generation of training data, which is tedious work. Additionally, they do not focus on performance and therefore propose no measure to determine the impact of antipatterns on performance.

To the best of our knowledge, no existing approach enables the automatic selection of refactorings that are most promising to increase performance.

4   Automated Selection of Refactorings

Static code analyses for antipattern detection issue too many alleged defects in a not prioritized fashion, rendering the information hard to work with efficiently. Dynamic software analyses, on the other hand, yield a lot of heterogeneous data which is not easy to interpret and will not directly lead to a refactoring proposition in the source code. Apparently, both techniques have their individual disadvantages.

To overcome these problems, we propose an approach for the automated selection of refactorings that utilizes software properties determined by both static code analyses and dynamic software analyses. By combining the best out of both worlds into one heuristics, we compile a list of concrete refactorings sorted by their assessed potential to improve performance and stability.

Our key idea is that with the help of dynamically retrieved runtime information we rank statically detected antipatterns by their importance regarding the expected impact on performance and stability. By connecting runtime data with specific antipatterns in the code, we derive a precise recommendation which refactorings are most promising to improve the performance and stability.

Figure 1 shows our overall approach. In the top left, a static analysis takes the software source code and a set of antipattern detection rules as input to produce an unordered list of antipatterns, e.g. the undesired use of the '+' operator. In the bottom left, a dynamic analysis examines the software while it is executed in its runtime environment consuming some input data. Various performance measures are the output of this process, e.g. the execution time. In the final step, we introduce a rating function, which uses the dynamic performance measures together with a factor that measures the general effectiveness of a given refactoring to assign a severity value to each statically detected antipattern.

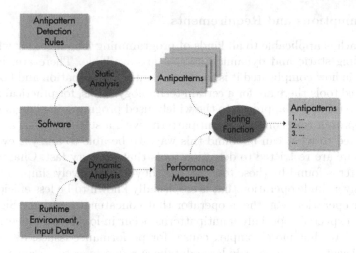

Fig. 1. Automated selection approach [25].

As a result, we get an ordered list where the top entries represent the antipatterns along with their proposed refactorings that have the highest potential of improving performance. Thus, there is no more need to manually handle neither the performance measures nor the huge amount of antipatterns. Instead, it is possible to deal with the most promising refactorings and defer the revision of the others.

Concerning stability antipatterns, making up a meaningful order by means of dynamic analysis results is hardly possible. The certainty that a specific antipattern *may* cause severe stability issues does not necessarily mean that a specific occurrence causes any harm. None of the available measures seems appropriate to make a profound and reliable assessment of severity. Additionally, stability is not measurable like performance. It is much harder to say if an improvement set in after a couple of refactorings, in order to evaluate the quality of an antipattern selection process. Values like downtime of a server application or failure rate cannot easily be measured in a micro benchmark. For these reasons, we separate stability antipatterns from the others and put them into an individual list where no particular order is assumed.

To realize our goal of automatically selecting refactorings, there are multiple challenges to face. The large amount of static detection rules has to be checked for those which may have a positive effect on performance or stability. The many different available runtime parameters have to be evaluated in consultation with an experienced performance engineer in order to find those that point to potential performance leaks. Finally, we aim at defining a parameterized rating function that is capable of melting all information into one value to allow sorting between the statically detected antipatterns.

4.1   Assumptions and Requirements

Our approach is applicable to all kinds of programming languages for which the corresponding static and dynamic analyses are available. There are, however, differences in how complicated it is to obtain runtime information and how many sophisticated tools there are for a certain technology. Thus, for practical reasons, we decide to tailor our approach to the widely used programming language Java.

Our approach relies on finding antipatterns with a static analysis and therefore is limited to what can be found this way. To be able to analyze even large code bases we are restricted to detection tools that are very fast. Characteristic for antipatterns found by those tools is that they are relatively simple and often concern only a single operation that is empirically known to be less efficient than some other operation, e.g. the + operator that concatenates strings. Significant savings are expected especially if antipatterns occur in loops or frequently called functions. Note that more complex causes for performance issues, like memory leaks, inefficient or unnecessarily large database requests or too frequent remote service calls, are hardly detectable by a static analyses in a fail-safe fashion. Expensive techniques, e.g. symbolic execution, would be required, but they still cover only a small part of the considered domain. Additionally, a high rate of false positives must be prevented because the acceptance of a tool and the confidence in its well-functioning would diminish rapidly.

Considering this, we expect our approach to work best for applications where the same source code is executed very often and thus the achievable performance improvement of refactoring antipatterns is high. This decisive criterion is assumed to hold for large business applications, e.g. server software or micro services that get thousands of similar request a second. Nevertheless, our approach works for other software as well, just with smaller performance gains.

Note that for the static antipattern detection, we require access to the source code, while for the dynamic analysis a runtime environment, and realistic input data must be available.

4.2   Rating Criteria

We aim at ordering the detected performance antipatterns according to their severity, i.e., their potential of improving performance. To achieve this, we determine some rating criteria. Those may be either static properties, e.g., the location in the source code where an antipattern is detected together with its loop depth, or properties that can be obtained through dynamic analysis, e.g., the execution time and frequency of the surrounding method.

Static Properties. The core of our static analysis is the static antipattern detection, which provides a list of antipatterns together with their location in the code. As an additional static property we use the loop depth at the corresponding program location as a rating criterion, i.e. within how many layers of loops a specific antipattern is nested. We choose this property because source code within loops has the potential of being executed very often. If an antipattern represents an inefficiency, the many repeated executions give it a higher impact on performance and therefore it is more important to refactor.

Note that we do not use the actual amount of executions of a loop or the nesting depth of a given antipattern. To determine the actual amount of executions of a loop for arbitrary inputs is an undecidable problem, thus we cannot use this information as rating criterion. How deep an antipattern is nested in arbitrary control flow structures, i.e., the nesting depth, is easy to determine. One could argue that source code within, e.g., an if-statement is executed less often. However, we have no evidence that control flow structures other than loops form a reliable correlation that can be used as basis for a rating.

Runtime Properties. An important runtime property is the total execution time of a method. It is defined as the sum of all execution times of a method in a given program run. Therefore, it gives an impression on how much time the program spends in a specific method. The time spent in subroutines is counted towards the respective subroutine but not the calling method. Thereby, we get a correlation between the time spent and a very limited number of code lines. A high total execution time indicates that either some very expensive operations are performed or the number of executions must be high, e.g. due to a loop. In the second case an antipattern in this method has a higher impact on performance.

Another interesting property is the call count, i.e. how often a method is called during runtime. Using the same reasoning as above, we consider antipatterns in frequently called methods to have a higher impact on performance.

The third runtime property is the memory consumption of a method. To capture the memory consumption of a given method in Java, we use the suspension count. As Java is a memory-managed language, the garbage collector suspends the currently executed method from time to time. The suspension count tells how often the garbage collector suspended a certain method to perform a collection. We choose this property as indicator for high memory consumption with the reasoning that if a method suffers suspensions disproportionately often, it probably allocates a lot of memory. The claimed correlation is based on the assumption that a garbage collection takes place whenever all memory is used up, which statistically happens more often in allocation intensive methods. Although different implementations of garbage collectors behave very differently in many ways, the assumption that more suspensions by the garbage collector indicate a higher memory consumption presumably holds. Note that for many other languages there exist profiling tools like Google's gperftools for C or the Memory Profiler for Python, which report the memory consumption of each method in a given program. Our rating function can easily be adapted to include these measures instead of the suspension count.

A runtime property that we leave out is the increase of execution time under increasing load. If a method takes significantly more time just because the system is under load, this indicates that the method contains some operation that impairs the performance. Often, the problem is about waiting time that is spent e.g. for synchronization between multiple threads [16]. We still do not consider this property for two reasons. First, none of our antipatterns causes waiting times. Second, measuring the increase of execution time under increasing load in a completely automated fashion is very complicated, e.g., because a dedicated testing environment for the measured software is required. For the same reasons we do not utilize synchronization and waiting times. Neither do we consider the API breakdown, because the information which component takes the most time is not detailed enough to form a connection with specific antipattern occurrences.

Antipattern Properties. As a further important rating criterion, we use the properties of the antipattern itself. We expect some antipatterns to bring high performance gains through refactoring while others yield only small improvements. To assess the general effectiveness of a given set of refactorings, we have implemented a micro benchmark for each class of antipattern and its refactored counterpart in a before-afterwards fashion (cf. Sect. 5). In doing so, we evaluate the effectiveness of each refactoring and thus can derive meaningful weights for our rating function.

Note that we have the choice to utilize either the relative improvement after the refactoring or the absolute improvement. As we are mostly interested in a positive effect on the performance of the whole software it makes sense to consider the absolute gain. The relative improvement is only of limited meaning because an operation that takes quasi no time has few saving potential even if it can be made faster by a factor of 50. Therefore, we select the absolute effectiveness of refactorings as rating criterion.

4.3 Rating Function

Our final goal is to provide a heuristics for the prioritization and selection of antipatterns regarding their negative impact on performance for a given program. To achieve this, we present a novel rating function that can be used as a heuristics to estimate the severity of a detected antipattern in terms of the expected effect of refactoring the antipattern on performance. Note that our rating function does not rank stability antipatterns, but adds the corresponding refactorings to the recommended refactorings in an unsorted list. Our rating function is based on the various criteria discussed above and forms the heart of innovation in our approach as it actually combines the statically and dynamically obtained data.

We define our rating function, which determines the expected effectiveness of refactoring a given antipattern AP, as follows:

$$severity = exec \cdot (calls + b \cdot loop) \cdot f_{t,AP}$$
$$+ (\beta \cdot susp + 1) \cdot (calls + b \cdot loop) \cdot f_{m,AP}$$

where $exec$ is the total execution time, $susp$ the suspension count, $calls$ the call count, $loop$ the loop depth, $f_{t,AP}$ an antipattern time factor and $f_{m,AP}$ an antipattern memory factor. The antipattern time and memory factors $f_{t,AP}$ and $f_{m,AP}$ capture the general effectiveness of refactoring the antipattern AP.

We have determined these factors using micro benchmarks. The idea behind this is as follows: If the execution time of a single piece of code only consisting of a given antipattern can be reduced by a factor of 10 using the proposed refactoring for this antipattern, we assess the general effectiveness of this refactorings to have a time factor of $f_{t,AP} = 10$. If, for the same experiment, the memory consumption is reduced to 50%, the memory factor of this refactoring is $f_{m,AP} = 2$. We describe our micro benchmarks to determine the time and memory factors for a given set of antipatterns in Sect. 5 and present the resulting factors in Table 3. To fine-tune our rating function, we introduce the weighting factors b and β, where b weights the relative relevance of the loop depth compared to the call count, and β the relative relevance of memory consumption compared to the execution time. The user can use these factors to adjust the rating function to her need, emphasizing the importance of the loop depth compared to the call count by raising b, or putting additional importance on memory consumption compared to the execution time by increasing β.

The ratio behind our rating function is to identify antipatterns that are at locations in the source code that are executed very often. Refactorings at those locations have a larger potential of improving performance than elsewhere and should receive a higher rating. If, e.g., the execution time of a method is high, it is probable that this method is either called very often or contains a loop with many runs. If an antipattern is located in such a method with a high call count, we assume that it is executed often. Consequently, in this case the term $exec \cdot calls$ becomes large and leads to a higher rating. If on the other hand the call count is low but the antipattern lives within a loop, we likewise assume many executions. This time the term $exec \cdot loop$ becomes large and again leads to a higher rating. When merged together under the premise that either of the two cases should result in a higher rating, we get the term $exec \cdot (calls + b \cdot loop)$ in the rating function. The weighting factor b can be used to normalize the loop depth with respect to the call count (the loop depth is typically between 0 and 4, while the call count has much larger numbers), and to express a domain- or application-specific relevance of loop depth and call count. In applications or domains where the loop depth is not expected to significantly influence the performance, b can be reduced, and vice versa. The antipattern time factor $f_{t,AP}$ gives an estimate for the general impact of the antipattern on execution time and is therefore multiplied. Altogether, this yields the first summand of the rating function.

The derivation of the second summand is very similar. For methods that get frequently suspended for garbage collection we assume a higher memory consumption. This leads to the term $susp \cdot (calls + b \cdot loop)$. We again multiply with the antipattern memory factor $f_{m,AP}$ to take the general impact of the antipattern on memory consumption into account. A particularity of the suspension count is that for most methods it simply is zero, since overall garbage collection kicks in relatively seldom. Because we do not want to zero out the whole impact on memory, we add the constant one and get $(susp + 1)$.

Finally, we put together the two terms, each representing an independent indication of a high impact on performance. Since execution times can easily grow large while the suspension count keeps low, the weighting factor β should be used to align the magnitude. In addition, the software developer can increase β to search for refactorings that are promising to reduce the memory consumption, and decrease β to focus on refactorings that are promising to reduce the overall execution time. Note that in $(\beta \cdot susp + 1)$ the constant one is not scaled by β. The reasoning is that in case of zero suspensions the summand should have little influence and only break the tie between otherwise similarly rated antipatterns. If scaled, the second summand could grow significantly large, although the suspension count is zero and there actually is no evidence for a high memory consumption.

4.4 Weight Determination

To normalize the loop depth with respect to the call count and the memory suspensions with respect to the execution time, we determine initial values of the weighting factors b and β. As mentioned above, they can be adjusted to fine-tune the ranking function to certain domains or to a desired performance goal.

The weighting factor b defines the relation between call count and loop depth. To scale the loop depth range of 0 to 4 such that it matches the magnitude of call counts common for the current antipattern selection process, we choose

$$b = \frac{1}{N_m} \sum_{methods} calls$$

with N_m as the number of methods. In other words, we choose b such that it equals the average call count of a method. In our experiments, the call count average is a multiple of the median. Thus, the loop depth has an adequate effect on the antipatterns rating but the extreme call counts still surpass the loop depth in effect. Note that b has to be calculated once in an antipattern selection process.

The weighting factor β defines the relation between execution time and suspension count:

$$\beta = \alpha \cdot \frac{\sum_{methods} exec}{\sum_{methods} susp}$$

In other words, β equals the total execution time divided by the total suspension count. The idea is to calculate the average of how much time corresponds to one suspension and scale the suspension count accordingly. The factor α can be used to reduce the suspension counts influence because it is suspected to be less reliable and accurate than the execution time, as the numbers generally are very low and a proper statistical distribution sets in very late. In our experiments, we use $\alpha = 0.2$. The weighting factor β has to be calculated once per antipattern selection process.

4.5   Selection of Detection Tools and Rules

In this subsection, we justify our decision for the tool we use for the antipattern detection and how we select the detection rules.

As stated above, the common tools for static analysis of Java source code that are available for selection are PMD, Checkstyle and FindBugs [22]. They are freely accessible and come each with a predefined list of detection rules.

An important difference between the tools are their respective lists of predefined rules. To get an overview, we thoroughly inspected the several hundred rules with their descriptions and examples. Finally, we come to the conclusion that PMD is suited best for our purpose. Compared to the others, it has the most rules for performance antipatterns and a fair amount of stability rules.

Checkstyle has a stronger focus on coding style and an overall smaller set of rules. It offers hardly any performance or stability antipattern detection rule that PMD does not offer. Therefore its additional use would not be very beneficial for our cause.

FindBugs does not work with source code but with Java byte code and therefore requires Java class files to operate. Its focus mostly is, like the name suggests, finding bugs and not detecting performance antipatterns. Regardless, it has a rules section dedicated to performance. But still, those rules do not add much new to what we get from PMD. Moreover, the mentioned rules concern only very specific inefficiencies and we estimate the potential to really improve performance to be relatively low.

Based on the inspection of all PMD rules we compose two subsets. One set focuses on performance and the other on stability. This first selection is performed only on the textual documentation of the rules [27]. It is notable that most of the more than 150 rules do not concern performance or stability issues. However, there actually is one category called *Optimization*. But not all performance relevant rules are in there. In particular, the category *String and StringBuffer* also contains some important rules. In Table 1 all selected rules are listed.

5   Evaluation

We have implemented our approach in Java. We perform the static code analysis with PMD [6], which uses detection rules to find patterns in the source code. Compared to other tools like Checkstyle [5] and FindBugs [28], PMD has more rules for performance antipatterns and thus is best suited for our approach. For the recording of runtime properties, we use the monitoring tool Dynatrace AppMon [9]. It is widely used in practice and provides all the dynamic properties we need.

In this section, we first present our micro benchmarks and experimental evaluation of the general effectiveness of a given set of refactorings independent of a concrete program. Then, we demonstrate two experiments we have conducted in order to evaluate our approach for the automated selection of refactorings that

Table 1. Selected PMD detection rules.

Performance rules	
BooleanInstantiation	Avoid to instantiate Boolean objects
AvoidUsingShortType	short requires cast to int before arithmetics
FinalFieldCouldBeStatic	static members save memory
OptimizableToArrayCall	Allocate proper array size in toArray
IntegerInstantiation	Avoid to instantiate Integer objects where possible
ByteInstantiation	Avoid to instantiate Byte objects where possible
ShortInstantiation	Avoid to instantiate Short objects where possible
LongInstantiation	Avoid to instantiate Long objects where possible
AvoidInstantiatingObjectsInLoops	Check if repeated allocation is required
SimplifyStartsWith	Replace str.startsWith("x") with str.charAt(0) == 'x'
UseStringBufferForStringAppends	Avoid using + operator iteratively for strings
UseArraysAsList	Use Arrays.asList wrapper instead of copying all data
AvoidArrayLoops	Prefer System.arraycopy over manual copying
UnnecessaryWrapperObjectCreation	Avoid intermediate instances of Integer etc
AddEmptyString	Do not use + "" to cast to string
RedundantFieldInitializer	Spare initializations to Java default values like int a = 0
ExceptionAsFlowControl	Use exceptions for exceptional situations, not control flow
AvoidThrowingNewInstanceOfSameException	Avoid re-creating exceptions with new
StringInstantiation	Avoid to instantiate String objects with new
InefficientStringBuffering	Avoid using + operator with StringBuilder
UnnecessaryCaseChange	Prefer equalsIgnoreCase over case changing
UseStringBufferLength	Prefer StringBuilder.length over toString
AppendCharacterWithChar	Append single char with append('x')
ConsecutiveAppendsShouldReuse	Put consecutive append in a single instruction
UseIndexOfChar	Search for single char with indexOf('x')
InefficientEmptyStringCheck	Prefer isWhitespace in a loop over trim
InsufficientStringBufferDeclaration	Initialize StringBuilder with appropriate size
UnnecessaryConversionTemporary	Avoid intermediate instances of Integer etc
Stability rules	
ReturnFromFinallyBlock	Avoid return inside a finally block
AvoidThreadGroup	Avoid the not thread-safe class ThreadGroup
CloseResource	Do not forget to close resources after opening them
MissingBreakInSwitch	Do not forget break in switch-statements
SingletonClassReturningNewInstance	Do not make getInstance create new instances
PreserveStackTrace	Do not dump exceptions stack trace
AvoidCatchingThrowable	Do not catch the too general Throwable
AvoidCatchingNPE	Do not hide NullPointerException by catching it
AvoidLosingExceptionInformation	Use return values of functions without side effects
UseEqualsToCompareStrings	Use equals to compare strings contents
UselessOperationOnImmutable	Use return values of functions without side effects

are promising to have a high impact on the performance of a given program. As a case study, we use STATE, a SystemC to Timed Automata Transformation Engine written in Java and developed at TU Berlin [17–19]. Although this is not the class of software our approach is designed for and thus the performance gain is small, the obtained findings demonstrate the practical applicability of our approach. Furthermore, we show some example output and give a first impression of the potential of our approach.

We carried out all experiments on an Intel(R) Core(TM) i7-2620M CPU @ 2.7 GHZ, 2 Core with 8 GB RAM running the Microsoft Windows 10 Pro operating system. We use the Oracle JVM version 8.

5.1 Micro Benchmarks

We have implemented micro benchmarks to determine the general effectiveness of a given set of antipatterns independent of a concrete program. We measure the effectiveness in terms of time and memory factors $f_{t,AP}$ and $f_{m,AP}$, which represent the relative severity of the various antipatterns. Since we are interested in the relative effectiveness of performance refactorings, only the relation between the performance of code containing the antipattern and code containing the refactored version is important and the absolute results do not matter.

Challenges of Java Micro Benchmarks. Micro benchmarks are not easy to design, especially in a language like Java. There are some general pitfalls and some that stem from how Java and its virtual machine work [15].

The first thing to go wrong is that something completely different is measured than what was intended. A naive example is a benchmark to measure some arithmetical operation that writes each result to the console. What impacts the performance in such a setting is mostly the output and not the actual arithmetics. To avoid this, we put only the absolutely necessary operations into the measurement code.

The accuracy of the CPU clock is by far not high enough to capture times in the magnitude of CPU cycles. Thus, we nest the operations we want to measure into a simple, repeating loop. The repetition count must be high enough to reach overall computation times where the accuracy is sufficiently good.

A Java specific pitfall is the just-in-time compiler (JIT compiler), which automatically compiles frequently executed portions of the program while leaving the rest for interpretation as usual. This can corrupt a measurement because half of the executions are interpreted and the other half compiled. We encounter this challenge with a so called warm-up. This means that we run the benchmark code 20000 times before the actual measurement is started. This guarantees that the JIT compiler translates the benchmark code and we measure only the compiled version.

Another general difficulty is the compiler optimization in benchmarks. As the executed code does not fulfill any contentual purpose the compiler may find out and optimize it away, rendering the whole benchmark useless. To solve this problem, we always return a number that in some way contains values involved in the measured code. Like this, we avoid optimization with a negligible overhead.

The garbage collection in Java is another mechanism we take into account with our micro benchmark design. If, for example, a garbage collection is performed during a benchmark the execution time increases significantly. Hence, before each measurement, we demand a garbage collection to happen to achieve similar starting conditions. Actually, the JVM cannot be forced to carry out a garbage collection but according to our experiments it always obeys. Thus, if a garbage collection takes place, it is because so much memory was consumed.

When taking a measurement, the result is subject to deviations. Therefore, we repeat the measurement several times. In a series there probably are outliers, e.g., due to some irregular background process on the machine that executes the benchmarks. For this reason we discard the extreme values and take the average over the remaining as final outcome.

Micro Benchmark Implementation. We have implemented the micro benchmarks as an Apache Tomcat servlet [12]. This allows a user friendly control in the web browser through a simple HTML interface. To cover all PMD performance rules, we have implemented 20 benchmark pairs, each consisting of one benchmark for the antipattern and one for its refactored version. The core of each benchmark is a specific function that executes an antipattern or its refactored counterpart in a loop with a certain repetition count N, in our case $N = 100000$. Around this benchmark function the measurement process is built up. One benchmark measurement consists of two parts of which the first measures memory consumption and the second measures execution time.

For the memory consumption, we take the difference in heap size of the JVM before and after the benchmark function. Because in Java garbage collection can happen at any time, it has to be considered for the measurement, otherwise the alleged memory consumption even may become negative. To solve this problem, we use a callback function, which is triggered by each garbage collection run and which records how much space got cleared. We use this to calculate the memory consumption as follows:

$$memConsumption = (heapAfter + \sum_{GCRuns} collected) - heapBefore$$

We repeated this process 50 times before taking the average, which we consider the true memory consumption. First experiments showed that the callback function does not reliably execute timely before the measurement in which it was triggered is over. Therefore, after every measurement we schedule a wait of (100 ms) to catch late coming garbage collections and assign the numbers to the appropriate measurement.

For the execution time measurement, we take the difference in the system time before and after the benchmark function. To achieve a reliable value we calculate an average over 50 measurements, where we discard the lowest and highest four values beforehand. In order to accomplish an even more reliable result we calculate such an average for ten different cases, where in each case the repetition count is modified according to $repCount = i \cdot N$ with $i = 1, 2, ..., 10$. In doing so, we get a series of supposedly equidistant execution time averages. We calculate the distance between every two successive results, which represents the increase in time for another N runs. Over these distances we take the average and finally consider it the true execution time of N runs of the benchmarked antipattern or its refactored counterpart. The deviation of the minimal distance and the maximal distance from the average indicate the quality of the measurement, with a low deviation confirming the outcome.

Results and Interpretation. The results from our micro benchmarks are shown in Table 3. Note that benchmarks marked with * were executed with $N = 1000$ due to long execution times. The table comprises short, descriptive names for the benchmarks and the corresponding average times and the average memory consumptions as described above. The time factor describes by what factor the execution time changed in the refactored version compared to the antipattern, with a high value indicating that the refactoring is effective. The time saving describes the absolute gain in execution time achieved by the refactoring. Analogously, the values are calculated for memory consumption.

The time factors are in a range of 0.8 to 21497.92, i.e., some refactorings even have a negative impact while others are incredibly effective. The time savings are in a range of -0.16 to 4275.11 ms per 100k repetitions and it is notable that a high factor does not necessarily appear together with a high absolute saving. Regarding memory consumption, the factor range is 0.21 to 10086.67 and the savings range is -0.09 to 198.17 MB per 100k repetitions. For those pairs where the refactored version consumes no memory the factor becomes NaN.

The results fit well with the expectations we had based on the antipattern description. For example, we now have evidence that performing arithmetics with the **short** type takes additional execution time due to the internal type casts but saves memory. In conclusion, we are very confident that our effort to design good benchmarks payed off by providing useful results that we can use in the rating function to distinguish between more or less severe antipatterns.

The measurements taken with the micro benchmarks are not only good for determining the antipattern factors used in the rating function. They have a value in themselves because the effectiveness of refactoring the antipatterns gets quantified in a relative and an absolute way. The results show that there are several refactorings that reduce execution time or memory consumption by large factors. At the same time, we get an overview of how much can be saved through refactoring this kind of antipatterns. While for some the savings are close to zero, for others they are multiple seconds per 100k calls. Those values suggest that in general our approach of refactoring this kind of statically detectable antipatterns has some effect, as long as not every occurrence is considered but only systematically selected ones. The results from our micro benchmarks also provide a valuable insight to the general effectiveness of performance refactorings and can be used by further research on antipatterns and performance refactorings.

5.2   Rating Tool Chain

As preparation for the rating tool, we have configured the data sources, namely PMD and Dynatrace AppMon, to capture the required data. We have explored the output formats of the data sources in order to finally design and implement the rating tool itself.

The rating tool that we have implemented is the core component of the rating tool chain. It comprises routines to read all data required for the rating function from PMD, Dynatrace AppMon and the benchmarks. It uses a data model that we have designed to represent the collected information in a consistent way, finally applies the rating function, sorts the antipatterns according to their severity and writes an output file with the most important information.

Configure and Operate PMD. A XML file is required to configure PMD to use a certain set of detection rules. Therefore, we have composed such a file containing all rules selected according to Sect. 4.5. When executed, PMD analyses the requested source code and writes an output XML file. It contains a `violation` element for each detected antipattern with information about the affected code lines, the violated rule and which class and method it occurred in.

Implement Loop Depth Detection. We use the loop depth in the rating formula. An easy way to reliably identify the loop depth is traversing an abstract syntax tree (AST), especially easier than parsing the pure source code. Fortunately, PMD internally uses an AST and even offers an API to hook into its traversal. The API is originally meant to enable writing custom detection rules but can be misused for our purpose of compiling a list containing all the loops.

Hence, we have implemented a custom PMD rule that detects loop depth. In order to store the information and because the rating tool works with XML anyway, we have enabled the custom PMD rule to write another XML file. We have designed the loop depth file to contain `method` elements which contain `loop` elements that hold all required data. PMD constructs an AST for each compilation unit separately. This brings up the problem of when to finalize the loop depth file, i.e. to close the last XML element, flush the data and close the file handle because we never know if a next unit follows or not. As a work-around we have introduced an empty file with a name such that it gets sorted to the last position by the file system. When coming across, it triggers the loop depth rule to finalize the XML file.

Configure and Operate Dynatrace AppMon. The setup of Dynatrace AppMon involves some configuration in the client which we do not be explained in detail. The placement of the Java agent that collects data in the software under test simply requires including a specific argument in the launch call. The rest is taken care of automatically.

In Dynatrace AppMon there are so called dashboards where the user can arrange various information to be displayed. For those dashboards a REST API is offered through which the information is made accessible. Consequently, we have arranged a dashboard containing all the required data and have prepared a REST request that makes Dynatrace AppMon write that data into another XML file. The generated XML file contains the method call count, the total execution time and the suspension count for all recorded methods.

Usually, Dynatrace AppMon aims for very little overhead but it also can be configured to record many to all method calls for the cost of performance. In our development environment we record every method call to quickly build up an extensive data set, but in a production environment it is important that the monitoring overhead does not grow too large. Hence, in production it is not feasible to record the full method call information but only a small part of it. Still, if the monitoring is carried out for a longer time, sufficiently detailed values emerge.

Implement the Rating Tool. For the core part of our implementation we have chosen Java as programming language because this whole story already takes place in the Java world. We have not bothered to put some shiny little GUI together and rely on the command line. The required invocation arguments are the XML files with the analysis data.

The data model that we use to bring all information together consists of three classes. On highest level there is `SourceFile`, where the file path and the contained methods are stored. In the middle, there is `Method` where call count, execution time and suspension count are stored. Additionally, a list of antipatterns found inside the method is maintained. The third class is `Antipattern` and represents exactly one occurrence of an antipattern. The violated detection rule, the source code line and the loop depth are stored there. After the severity has been calculated, it is kept there as well.

As the input data comes from different sources, the information is not encoded in a uniform manner. For example does the Dynatrace AppMon output not contain the source files where the listed methods are implemented, although it contains most other information considering the methods. Therefore, the corresponding source files are extracted from the PMD output. On the other hand, the loop depth XML only contains the source files and tells from where to where the loops reach.

The largest part of the rating tool takes care of importing the information from XML files and populating the internal data structures. The actual application of the rating function is handled in only 23 lines of code, including the sorting of antipatterns by severity. The results are written as simple text format, where the top most entry represents the top rated antipattern.

Table 2. Experiments with STATE [25].

	Average time	Absolute diff	Relative impact
Original	2232.47 ms	-	-
Injected	2242.03 ms	+9.56 ms	0.428%
Refactored	2218.07 ms	−14.4 ms	0.645%

5.3   Experimental Evaluation

We have evaluated our approach with the software STATE [17,19] in version STATE-2.1. It is licensed as open source under the GNU General Public License version 3 and consists of approx. 30,000 lines of code in 285 classes. We chose one of the shipped examples from STATE to do our measurements, namely b_transport.

Experiment 1: Antipattern Injection. In our first experiment, we have injected some antipatterns in the source code of STATE, measured their impact on performance and evaluated how they get rated by our ranking tool. To achieve this, we have duplicated the STATE source code. Then, in one copy we have manipulated two methods by replacing all occurrences of StringBuilder with the less efficient + operator. In this process, we have altered about 60 lines of code and replaced in total 49 calls to append. The rest of the source code remains unchanged.

Our expectation is that the manipulated copy runs slower, i.e. the measured execution times are increased. We base this expectation on the benchmark results where the string concatenation antipattern showed strong impact on performance. Another expectation is that the introduced antipatterns get ranked high in a follow up analysis of the manipulated copy, because they were injected into a prominent method and have large antipattern factors.

The upper two rows of Table 2 show the execution times of the original STATE version compared to the worsened version where we have injected antipatterns. The average execution time of the original STATE software is 2232.47 ms. The average execution time of the worsened version with antipatterns injected is 2242.03 ms, resulting in an absolute difference of 9.56 ms. Thus, the refactoring of the injected antipatterns, i.e. the restoration of the original state, achieves a performance improvement of 0.428%. The subsequent rating tool analysis reveals that the injected antipatterns are found by our tool. The 24 occurrences appear among the 26 top rated antipatterns.

According to our expectation, the STATE version with antipatterns injected shows worse performance than the original. The execution time difference of about half a percent is small, but we have to keep in mind that STATE has very different characteristics to a large-scale server software or micro service, where our approach is supposed to exploit its full potential. Considering this, half a percent is already a good result, especially in relation to the very low effort it takes to implement some simple, local refactorings.

Table 3. Micro benchmarks for antipatterns [25].

Micro benchmark	Avg time [ms]	Avg mem [kB]	Time factor [1]	Time saving [ms/100k]	Mem factor [1]	Mem saving [MB/100k]
StringBuilder using equals("")	1.30	4133	30.62	1.24	24.52	3.96
StringBuilder using length() == 0	0.04	140				
Concatenate 10 strings with plus operator	74.42	246622	2.09	40.70	5.06	198.17
Concatenate 10 strings with StringBuilder	37.21	48900				
Multiple append in multiple statements	9.22	60202	0.99	−0.05	1.00	−0.09
Multiple append in only one statement	9.28	60215				
Instantiate Boolean object	0.05	140	1.25	0.01	NaN	0.14
Reference pooled Boolean	0.04	0				
Arithmetics with short	0.05	17	1.25	0.01	0.21	−0.07
Arithmetics with integer	0.04	82				
Instantiate object with final member *	23.45	553	1.01	22.95	1.02	0.01
Instantiate object with static final member *	23.18	544				
Call toArray with empty array	0.86	6471	0.84	−0.16	1.00	0.00
Call toArray with correctly sized array	1.02	6471				
Create many small objects	0.44	2740	2.10	0.23	3.42	1.94
Create separate data arrays	0.21	802				
Check first char with startsWith	0.04	0	0.80	−0.01	NaN	0.00
Check first char with charAt(0)	0.05	0				
Copy array iteratively into List *	50.30	40539	10962.82	4275.11	1313.69	37.92
Wrap array with asList	0.39	2623				
Copy array iteratively into array	10.02	15	1.02	0.16	1.07	0.00
Copy array with copyarray	9.86	14				
Convert to string with + ""	4.12	12732	1.15	0.53	2.31	7.22
Convert to string with toString	3.59	5510				
Instantiate with explicitly initialized member *	27.47	570	1.08	182.75	1.01	0.01
Instantiate with implicitly initialized member *	25.32	565				
Throw an exception *	30.35	1068	21497.92	2579.63	10086.67	1.06
Set flag and check if it's set	0.12	9				
Create string with new	0.57	1876	14.25	0.53	NaN	1.88
Create pooled string with quotes	0.04	0				
Check string equality casting both upper case	12.70	20872	2.76	8.10	NaN	20.87
Check string equality ignoring case	4.60	0				
Append character with double quotes	4.17	2366	2.47	2.48	1.45	0.74
Append character with single quotes	1.69	1629				
Search character with double quotes	0.93	0	1.02	0.02	NaN	0.00
Search character with single quotes	0.91	0				
Check if string is empty with trim	1.00	2408	25.00	0.96	NaN	2.41
Check is string is empty with loop	0.04	0				
Initialize StringBuilder too short	4.46	33252	1.17	0.64	1.18	5.09
Initialize StringBuilder sufficiently large	3.82	28163				

```
[3280529] exec=    97.00 | susp= 0 | calls=13595 | loop=0
    Antipattern 'AppendCharacterWithChar' in method 'toString' at
    line 288 in file Location.java
[2592057] exec= 1674.51 | susp= 3 | calls=    5 | loop=1
    Antipattern 'AvoidInstantiatingObjectsInLoops' in method '
    parseParallel' at line 123 in file UppaalXMLManager.java
[1548647] exec= 1504.23 | susp= 0 | calls=    5 | loop=1
    Antipattern 'AppendCharacterWithChar' in method 'embed' at line
    103 in file ParallelUppaalXMLEmbedder.java
[1280611] exec=    58.58 | susp= 0 | calls= 8770 | loop=0
    Antipattern 'AppendCharacterWithChar' in method 'toString' at
    line 221 in file Transition.java
[1280611] exec=    58.58 | susp= 0 | calls= 8770 | loop=0
    Antipattern 'AppendCharacterWithChar' in method 'toString' at
    line 222 in file Transition.java
```

Fig. 2. Extract of rating tool results for STATE [25].

Experiment 2: Performance Refactorings. In our second experiment, we have performed a preliminary analysis of STATE with the rating tool and subsequently refactored the top rated antipatterns. Afterwards, we measured if the performance was improved by the refactorings. With our approach, we get a list of detected antipatterns sorted according to their assigned ratings. Figure 2 shows the first five lines of the output file slightly shortened. The large number in square brackets is the rating assigned to the antipattern. The other information helps to comprehend the rating and to find the antipattern in the source code.

In our experiment, we have implemented the proposed refactorings for 17 of the top rated 19 antipatterns. Two antipatterns remain untreated. One is an unavoidable object instantiation inside a loop and the other would require a **StringBuilder** to prepend text, which it is not intended for. Apart from the 17 refactorings the source code remains unchanged.

Our expectation is that the refactored version runs faster than the original, i.e. the measured execution times are reduced. Although the analyzed software is not in our target domain of large-scale server software, this experiment shows exactly how our approach is meant to be used in practice.

The last row of Table 2 shows the results for our second experiment. The average execution time of the refactored version of STATE is 2218.07 ms. Compared to the original version, this results in a difference of 14.40 ms. Thus, the refactoring of the 17 top rated antipatterns achieves an overall performance improvement of 0.645%.

Overall, we can see our expectation satisfied, since the refactored version effectively executes faster than the original STATE. Again, slightly more than half a percent is a small performance improvement but the same argumentation as above holds and we still consider the result a success. It shows that the rating tool succeeds in proposing refactorings that improve performance and suggests that its application on a server software or micro service can yield great performance gains with a small refactoring effort.

5.4 Added Values of Automated Refactoring Selection

In order to justify a technique that basically combines two well-known techniques, we aim at giving evidence that it is in some way superior to just using the others. In fact, with two experiments we have shown that our approach adds additional value to the static and dynamic analysis.

Using solely PMD detects many antipatterns but the vast majority of them does not need be taken care of. A PMD analysis of the STATE source code that already only considers the performance antipatterns selected in the course of this paper yields 843 issues. Of those, only 339 received a rating greater than zero and promise a positive effect on performance through refactoring at all. But even that number is high and resolving all issues means a significant effort with a questionable cost-benefit ratio. In contrast, refactoring 17 of the highest rated antipatterns is an easy task and very promising at the same time. Hence, by using solely PMD either lots of unimportant refactorings are implemented, which is mostly squandered effort, or they are ignored all together, which wastes a good opportunity to improve performance.

Dynatrace AppMon On the other hand, using solely Dynatrace AppMon to capture runtime properties leaves one with a bunch of information without any concrete instruction on what to do. Experience in the topic may help to follow unwritten heuristics to find spots where improvements can be realized. But additional to the required, extensive know-how the process of investigation takes precious time. Furthermore, it is crucial that after locating a suspicious method the occurrence of an antipattern is recognized and detected with the eye. Hence, by using solely Dynatrace AppMon one is dependent on an experienced performance engineer who has the time and capability to manually search for conspicuous runtime data and antipatterns in the source code.

Dynatrace AppMon certainly is a very sophisticated monitoring and analysis tool which provides many opportunities of using broad data to manually find performance issues. However, many projects do not have access to this commercial software. But even tools with much less functional scope, where manual performance tweaking may be very hard, can provide data appropriate to our approach. Thus, with the automated selection of refactorings we enable projects with no budget for performance engineering to relatively easy achieve a measurable boost.

6   Conclusion

In this paper, we have proposed a novel approach to combine static and dynamic software analyses to automatically select refactorings that improve the performance and stability of a given program. Our major contributions are twofold: First, we have presented a rating function for antipatterns, which assesses their respective potential to improve performance and stability through refactoring based on both static and dynamic properties. Second, we have implemented micro benchmarks that assess the general effectiveness of a given set of performance antipatterns independent of a specific program. Our benchmarks clearly show that the antipatterns actually have an effect on performance, although the effects vary. Due to the mostly small savings, in the majority of cases a refactoring is only reasonable if the antipattern is executed frequently, e.g. in a loop or frequently called method. This illustrates the importance of a feasible approach to select the most effective refactorings in a given program.

We have implemented our approach for the automated selection of refactorings that are most promising to improve the performance and stability of a given program using PMD [6] for static code analyses and Dynatrace AppMon [9] for dynamic software analysis to capture performance measures. The result is a list of recommended refactorings ordered by effectiveness.

We have demonstrated the practical applicability of our approach with a sample software that consists of 30,000 lines of code. Although our approach works best for large scale server software, it still yields some improvement for our much smaller case study from a totally different domain. We therefore assess the potential in a large scale server software as high, especially due to the good cost-benefit ratio.

Our approach enables us to select only the most important antipatterns out of the huge amount of antipatterns that are typically provided by static antipattern detection tools. At the same time, it drastically reduces the cost of interpreting data delivered by dynamic analyses. Due to the automated interpretation and the precisely recommended refactorings, little expertise is required.

In future work, we plan to carry out a field experiment in which we improve the performance of a large scale server software. Furthermore, we plan to investigate more complex refactorings. As this is the intended area of application, an evaluation of the yielded benefits from such a field experiment will greatly show the true potential of the approach and where tweaks still are necessary. The currently included static analysis only detects single operations for which there are more efficient alternatives. This is on a very small scale and therefore requires a great many of repetitions to become effective. A future task is to extend the static analysis with sophisticated techniques already found in the literature, e.g. symbolic execution. This will be very beneficial since more antipatterns become detectable in the static analysis, especially such that have a larger potential for improvement per execution.

References

1. Arcelli, D., Berardinelli, L., Trubiani, C.: Performance antipattern detection through fUML model library. In: Proceedings of the 2015 Workshop on Challenges in Performance Methods for Software Development, pp. 23–28. ACM (2015)
2. Arcelli, D., Cortellessa, V., Trubiani, C.: Antipattern-based model refactoring for software performance improvement. In: Proceedings of the 8th international ACM SIGSOFT conference on Quality of Software Architectures, pp. 33–42. ACM (2012)
3. Becker, S., Koziolek, H., Reussner, R.: The Palladio component model for model-driven performance prediction. J. Syst. Softw. 82(1), 3–22 (2009)

4. Bernardi, M.L., Cimitile, M., Di Lucca, G.A.: A model-driven graph-matching app-roach for design pattern detection. In: 2013 20th Working Conference on Reverse Engineering (WCRE), pp. 172–181. IEEE (2013)
5. Burn, O.: Checkstyle (2017). http://checkstyle.sourceforge.net/index.html
6. Copeland, T., Le Vourch, X.: PMD (2017). https://pmd.github.io/
7. Cortellessa, V., Martens, A., Reussner, R., Trubiani, C.: A process to effectively identify "Guilty" performance antipatterns. In: Rosenblum, D.S., Taentzer, G. (eds.) FASE 2010. LNCS, vol. 6013, pp. 368–382. Springer, Heidelberg (2010). https://doi.org/10.1007/978-3-642-12029-9_26
8. Djoudi, L., Barthou, D., Carribault, P., Lemuet, C., Acquaviva, J.T., Jalby, W.: Exploring application performance: a new tool for a static/dynamic approach. In: Proceedings of the 6th LACSI Symposium. Los Alamos Computer Science Institute (2005)
9. Dynatrace: Dynatrace AppMon (2017). https://www.dynatrace.com/
10. Fayad, M.E., Altman, A.: Thinking objectively: an introduction to software stabil-ity. Commun. ACM **44**(9), 95 (2001)
11. Fontana, F.A., Zanoni, M.: Code smell severity classification using machine learn-ing techniques. Knowl.-Based Syst. **128**, 43–58 (2017)
12. Foundation, A.S.: Apache Tomcat (2017). http://tomcat.apache.org/
13. Fowler, M., Beck, K.: Refactoring: Improving the Design of Existing Code. Addison-Wesley Professional, Massachusetts (1999)
14. Gamma, E., Helm, R., Johnson, R., Vlissides, J.: Design Patterns: Elements of Reusable Object-oriented Software. Addison-Wesley Longman Publishing Co. Inc, Boston (1995)
15. Goetz, B.: Anatomy of a flawed microbenchmark (2005). https://www.ibm.com/developerworks/java/library/j-jtp02225/
16. Grabner, A.: Performance analysis: how to identify synchronization issues under load? (2009). https://www.dynatrace.com/blog/performance-analysis-how-to-identify-synchronization-issues-under-load/
17. Herber, P., Fellmuth, J., Glesner, S.: Model checking SystemC designs using timed automata. In: International Conference on Hardware/Software Codesign and Inte-grated System Synthesis (CODES+ISSS), pp. 131–136. ACM press (2008)
18. Herber, P., Glesner, S.: A HW/SW co-verification framework for SystemC. ACM Trans. Embed. Comput. Syst. **12**, 61 (2013)
19. Herber, P., Pockrandt, M., Glesner, S.: STATE-A SystemC to timed automata transformation engine. In: 2015 IEEE 7th International Symposium on Cyberspace Safety and Security (CSS), 2015 IEEE 12th International Conference on Embed-ded Software and Systems (ICESS), 2015 IEEE 17th International Conference on High Performance Computing and Communications (HPCC), pp. 1074–1077. IEEE (2015)
20. Heuzeroth, D., Holl, T., Hogstrom, G., Lowe, W.: Automatic design pattern detec-tion. In: 2003 11th IEEE International Workshop on Program Comprehension, pp. 94–103. IEEE (2003)
21. Long, J.: Software reuse antipatterns. ACM SIGSOFT Softw. Eng. Notes **26**(4), 68–76 (2001)
22. Louridas, P.: Static code analysis. IEEE Softw. **23**(4), 58–61 (2006)
23. Luo, Q., Nair, A., Grechanik, M., Poshyvanyk, D.: Forepost: finding performance problems automatically with feedback-directed learning software testing. Empir. Softw. Eng. **22**(1), 6–56 (2017)

24. Lyu, M.R.: Software reliability engineering: a roadmap. In: 2007 Future of Software Engineering, pp. 153–170. IEEE Computer Society (2007)
25. Moesus, N., Scholze, M., Schlesinger, S., Herber, P.: Automated selection of software refactorings that improve performance. In: Proceedings of the 13th International Conference on Software Technologies, ICSOFT 2018, Porto, Portugal, 26–28 July 2018, pp. 67–78 (2018)
26. Owen, K.: Improve the smell of your code with microrefactorings (2016). https://www.sitepoint.com/improve-the-smell-of-your-code-with-microrefactorings/
27. PMD: PMD Rulesets index (2017). https://pmd.github.io/pmd-5.8.1/pmd-java/rules/index.html
28. Pugh, B., Hovemeyer, D.: FindBugs (2015). http://findbugs.sourceforge.net/
29. Rasool, G., Streitfdert, D.: A survey on design pattern recovery techniques. IJCSI Int. J. Comput. Sci. Issues $8(2)$, 251–260 (2011)
30. Reitbauer, A., Grabner, A., Kopp, M.: Java Enterprise Performance: [Performance und Skalierbarkeit von Java-Enterprise-Anwendungen verstehen und managen]. Press, Entwickler (2011)
31. Rutter, T.: Stable vs stable: what 'stable' means in software (2010). https://bitdepth.thomasrutter.com/2010/04/02/stable-vs-stable-what-stable-means-in-software/
32. Smith, C.U., Williams, L.G.: New software performance antipatterns: more ways to shoot yourself in the foot. In: International CMG Conference, pp. 667–674 (2002)
33. Tsantalis, N., Chatzigeorgiou, A., Stephanides, G., Halkidis, S.T.: Design pattern detection using similarity scoring. IEEE Trans. Softw. Eng. $32(11)$, 896–909 (2006)
34. Washizaki, H., Fukaya, K., Kubo, A., Fukazawa, Y.: Detecting design patterns using source code of before applying design patterns. In: 2009 Eighth IEEE/ACIS International Conference on Computer and Information Science, ICIS 2009, pp. 933–938. IEEE (2009)
35. Wendehals, L.: Improving design pattern instance recognition by dynamic analysis. In: Proceedings of the ICSE 2003 Workshop on Dynamic Analysis (WODA), Portland, USA, pp. 29–32 (2003)
36. Wierda, A., Dortmans, E., Somers, L.J.: Detecting patterns in object-oriented source code - a case study. In: ICSOFT (SE). pp. 13–24. INSTICC Press (2007)
37. Woodside, M., Franks, G., Petriu, D.C.: The future of software performance engineering. In: 2007 Future of Software Engineering, FOSE 2007, pp. 171–187. IEEE (2007)

Model-Based On-the-Fly Testing of Web Applications and Multilingual Websites

Winfried Dulz[✉]

TestUS Consulting, Nuremberg, Germany
dulz@testus.eu

Abstract. This paper examines techniques for the model-based testing of web applications and multilingual websites. For this purpose, the simple web game application `GuessNumbers` is used to explain the essential steps for a model-based test process that applies statistical usage models to generate appropriate test suites. We also discuss methods for performing on-the-fly testing by means of an executable usage model. Model-based techniques that provide graphical representations of usage models make it easy to set the test focus on specific regions of the system under test that shall be tested. In addition, adapted profiles support the selective generation of test suites. We also show how generic usage models that are adapted to specific environments during the test execution, enable multilingual websites to be tested. Using the TestPlayer tool chain, a model-based testing approach is easily done.

Keywords: Model-based testing · Statistical usage model ·
Test suite generation · On-the-Fly testing · Website testing · Selenium

1 Introduction

Developing complex software and embedded systems usually consists of a series of design, implementation and test phases. Due to the increasing complexity of networked systems, for example for IoT (Internet of things) applications, model-based development approaches are becoming increasingly popular. Each software engineering step is guided by a suitable method and is usually supported by a special tool.

1.1 Model-Based Testing

One method in which the test cases are generated from a model is called *Model-based Testing* [1,2]. The relationship between a model that describes those parts of a given SUT (*system under test*) that need to be tested in order to generate (automatically) test cases derived from the (graphical) model is illustrated in Fig. 1. In general, a distinction is made between

- *system specifications*, which describe functional or non-functional aspects of the SUT and

© Springer Nature Switzerland AG 2019
M. van Sinderen and L. A. Maciaszek (Eds.): ICSOFT 2018, CCIS 1077, pp. 55–78, 2019.
https://doi.org/10.1007/978-3-030-29157-0_3

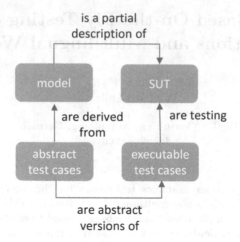

Fig. 1. General approach of model-based testing [20].

- *usage models* that model the usage behavior of the possible users or user classes of the system when they interact with the SUT in different ways.

Test cases, which are generated from a system specification [3] are often used in the so-called component or unit test. Usage models are mostly applied to generate test cases for the system or acceptance test.

Since complete testing of real systems is not feasible in practice, a suitable set of test cases must be selected to achieve a specific test objective. With the help of statistical usage models, also called *Markov chain usage models* (MCUM) [4], [5], individual test cases or complete test suites can (automatically) be derived by traversing the MCUM.

Markov chains are graphical models to define all possible usage steps and scenarios on a given level of abstraction as shown in Fig. 2. MCUM are used to represent

- *usage states* for modeling the user behavior during the interaction with the system, as well as
- *state transitions* to specify the reaction of the system on a user's interaction.

The probability that a particular user interaction triggers an event e_j is called *transition probability* and is given behind a colon, e.g. $e_4 : 0.3$ to change from `Usage State A` into `Usage State B` (Fig. 2). By adjusting the probability values of the usage distribution, i.e. the *operational usage profile* [6], it is easy to specify a varying usage behavior for different *user classes*. In this way, the test engineer can automatically create distinct test cases for different system users.

A *test case* is given by a statistical traversal of the Markov chain beginning in the `Start State` and ending in the final `Stop State`, considering the probabilities of the selected usage profile.

A *test suite* is a set of test cases to achieve a specific test objective, e.g. to cover all usage states or to traverse all transitions at least once during the test

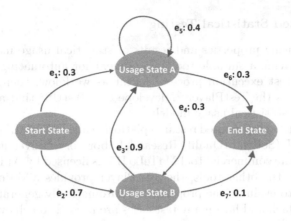

Fig. 2. Statistical Markov chain usage model for modeling the usage behavior of system users [20].

execution. How to derive the usage distribution for a Markov chain usage model in a more systematic way is discussed in [4, 7–10].

The main goals when using a MCUM for statistical test case generation can be summarized in

- automatic *generation* of sufficient many test cases
- calculation of meaningful *metrics* for the test suite
- determine *stopping criteria* for terminating the test execution.

Computations for statistical usage models are the result of years of work by many different people and summarized by Stacy Prowell in [11]. Kirk Sayre's research provided many new and useful analytical results, and provided stopping criteria for statistical testing [12]. Walter Gutjahr demonstrated how a statistical usage model could be modified to bias test generation toward low-use critical function, and how the bias could be removed in the results [13].

In a recent contribution to ICSOFT 2018, Dulz presented a tool environment based on Eclipse and the TestUS[1] tool TestPlayer for performing model-based testing of web applications. The key conclusions of the paper are [20]:

- Model-based techniques that use graphical usage models are helpful for even inexperienced test engineers to prepare and perform their tests.
- Graphical usage models facilitate the setting of the test focus on those areas of the SUT that need to be tested.
- Generic usage models, which can be adapted to different languages during the test execution, allow the testing of multilingual websites.

In this paper, we extend the approach in [20] by applying an executable user model for performing on-the-fly tests. This means that the transitions between usage states create executable test steps that directly test the SUT without first generating an abstract test-suite.

---

[1] https://www.testus.eu/.

1.2   Automated Statistical Testing

Given the promising properties and results of statistical usage models, there is a demand to provide a suitable tool environment for automating the test case generation and test execution process. As far as we know, there are just two other tools besides the TestPlayer©, developed by TestUS[2] that are focused on the testing with statistical usage models.

A more scientifically oriented research platform called JUMBL[3] [14] was developed at the SQRL (Software Quality Research Laboratory, University of Knoxville Tennessee) and the commercial tool MaTeLo [15] is licensed by ALL4TEC[4].

Compared to the other tools, the TestPlayer provides additional graphical representations to evaluate the properties of automatically generated test suites and to decide which and how many test cases are needed to achieve a particular test objective [16].

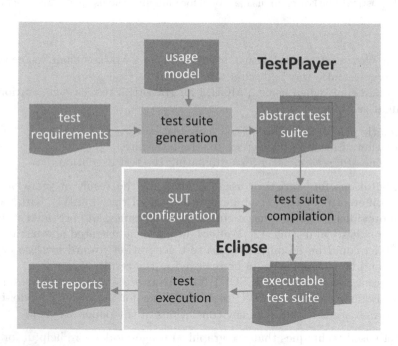

Fig. 3. A versatile tool environment consisting of the TestPlayer and Eclipse [20].

As illustrated in Fig. 3, the Eclipse modeling platform is well suited for compiling an *executable* test suite and for performing the test execution after the TestPlayer has generated an *abstract* test suite from a given usage model and additional test requirements.

In the next sections we take a closer look on the underlying test case generation processes. Using a simple web game application and the corresponding usage

---

model, we demonstrate how typical tasks in modeling, test case generation, analysis and the selection process can be performed. We will also examine some metrics that will enable us to control the selection of the test suite and to decide which test cases are best suited to meet certain test requirements to test game.

2   Automatic Test Suite Generation

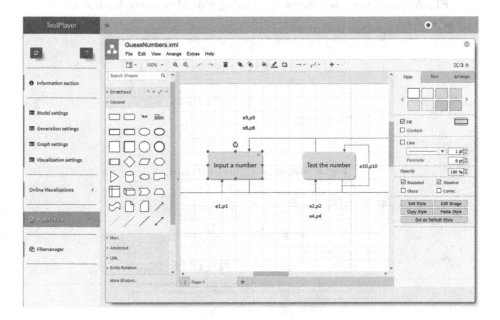

Fig. 4. The graphical TestPlayer model editor.

The TestPlayer can be executed in any modern web browser via a graphical user interface based on RESTful web technologies. Specific elements in the TestPlayer Dashboard allow a comfortable and user-friendly control of all sub-tasks, which must be performed for statistical usage tests.

2.1   Creation of a Usage Model

Usage models can be created in the Model editor section of the TestPlayer dashboard by means of a graphical editor that is based on draw.io[5] (Fig. 4).

In the following, we will briefly present the web game **Guess Numbers**[6] (Fig. 5), which serves as a running example to explain the basic approach. The goal is to find a secret random number between 1 and 100, on the condition that the player has a maximum of 7 attempts. The game widgets consist of an *information field*, a *numerical input field*, an *input button*, a *reset button* and a *result output*.

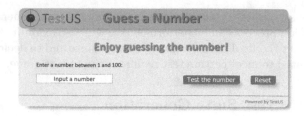

Fig. 5. Web game `GuessNumbers`: Entering a number in the input field.

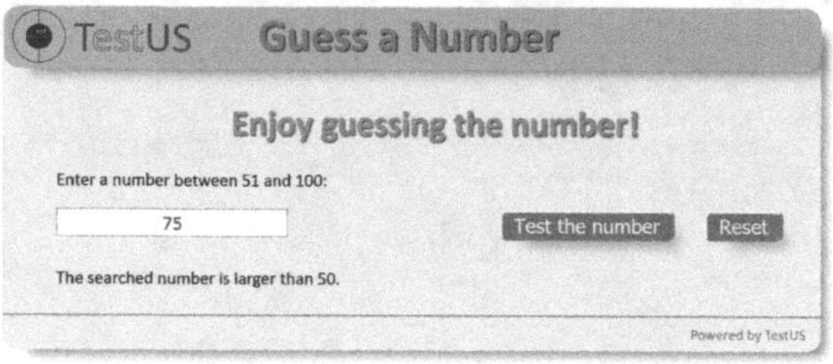

Fig. 6. Result of a guess attempt.

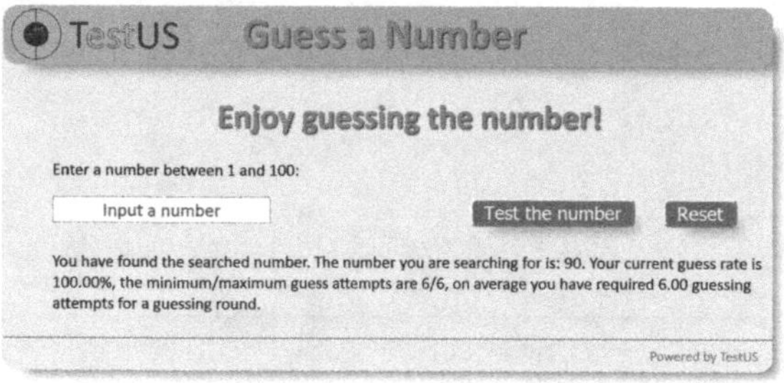

Fig. 7. Successful guess attempt and output of the guess statistics.

The diagrams in Figs. 6 and 7 illustrate how the game `GuessNumbers` behaves when the button `Test the number` is pressed. The numerical input field `Input a number` is used by the player to enter the next number. If the number entered is not equal to the random number searched for, the result output below the input field and the information field above provide information about what the player has to do next. If the hidden number is found, the guess statistics summarizing the guess attempts so far are displayed. Pressing `Reset` will reset the guess statistics to their initial values.

A corresponding statistical usage model, which serves as the basis for the TestPlayer to automatically generate test cases, is shown in Fig. 8.

After starting the game in start state [, usage states `Input a number`, `Test the number` and `Reset` can be selected next, indicated by the state transitions (e_1, p_1), (e_2, p_2) and (e_3, p_3) respectively. When the player makes a new guess

---

[5] https://about.draw.io/.

[6] https://testus.eu/GuessNumbers/.

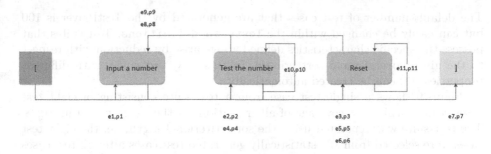

Fig. 8. Statistical usage model for the web game `GuessNumbers`.

attempt usage state `Input a number` follows usage state `Test the number` and transition (e_8, p_8) is selected. It is also possible to return to the same usage state `Test the number` or `Reset`, which is achieved by the transitions (e_{10}, p_{10}) and (e_{11}, p_{11}) respectively. Finally, when the correct number is found the final state `]` is reached from usage state `Test the number` via transition (e_7, p_7).

The *generic* probabilities $p1$ up to $p11$ at the edges behind the input events define the transition probabilities for selecting the respective input event $e1$ up to $e11$. Prior to the generation of the test cases, the TestPlayer replaces the generic values by *concrete* probability values that either originate from a given test profile or are calculated based on a *uniform geometric* distribution.

2.2   Creation of a Usage Model

In the TestPlayer Dashboard section *Model Settings* the essential parameters for the automatic generation of test cases and test suites can be specified. These include

- `Models`: file name of the usage model
- `Model start state`: name of the start state of the usage model
- `Model end state`: name of the final state of the usage model
- `Profile usage`: declaration, whether a statistical usage profile (`yes`) or a uniform distribution (`no`) will be employed for the generation algorithm of the test cases
- `Profiles`: file name of the statistical usage profile.

2.3   Automatic Generation of Test Cases

By applying the given usage model, the TestPlayer Dashboard offers simple user interactions to automatically generate test suites that have specific characteristics, i.e.

- complete coverage of all usage states
- coverage of all possible transitions between the usage states
- coverage of all loop-free paths between the start state `[` and the final state `]`, i.e. no transition is selected twice within the same test case.

The default number of test cases that are generated by the TestPlayer is 100 but can easily be changed within the `Testcase definitions`. Test suites that possess the specific characteristics defined above arise by reduction with respect to the given coverage and sort criteria. In this way, test suites with different properties [17] can be created automatically.

Figure 9 shows a single test case from a test suite consisting of eight test cases, which achieves a coverage of all transitions of the usage model in Fig. 8. The test suite was generated using the sort criterion `length`, i.e. the eight test cases were selected from 100 statistically generated test cases after all test cases were sorted according to their length.

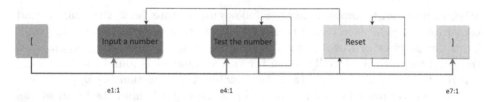

Fig. 9. Test case visualization for the web game `GuessNumbers` (Color figure Online)

Test cases are visualized by highlighting the relevant states and transitions (bold orange coloring) and show the already achieved coverage of usage states or state transitions (represented by a light orange coloring). The number behind the colon of the click events indicates how often the specified state transition is performed during the execution of the test case. In the case of longer loops during the execution of test cases, a single transition can be traversed several times.

In addition to the graphical representations, the TestPlayer provides a textual description of the generated test suite. Textual variants of the test suite are intended for documentation purposes as well as to export test cases for the test execution using a JSON-like notation.

The *JSON-like* test suite description is as follows (see [20]):

- a *test suite* T consists of test cases $TC_1 \cdots TC_m$ notated as $[[TC_1], [TC_2], \cdots [TC_m]]$
- a *test case* T consists of test steps $TS_1 \cdots TS_n$ notated as $[[TS_1], [TS_2], \cdots [TS_n]]$
- a *test step* TS consists of usage states US_{from} and US_{to} and the transition event E notated as $[US_{from}, E, US_{to}]$

A concrete test step example for the test case visualization in Fig. 9 looks as follows:

```
["Input a number", "e4", "Test the number"]
```

The complete test case visualized in Fig. 9 in the JSON-like description is as follows:

```
[
    ["[", "e1", "Input a number"],
    ["Input a number", "e4", "Test the number"],
    ["Test the number", "e7", "]"]
]
```

How to use a test suite in the JSON-like representation for an automated test execution process is discussed in the next section.

2.4 Graphical Representation of the Test Suite Metrics

Once a test-suite has been generated, specific metrics can be used to graphically analyze and evaluate its properties and to assess the quality of the test suite.

Metric *SSP* compares the probability distribution of usage states in statistical equilibrium for the usage model and the relative frequencies of the corresponding usage states in the generated test suite. As can be seen in Fig. 10, the theoretical probability values for the individual usage conditions of the MCUM are well mapped in the test suite.

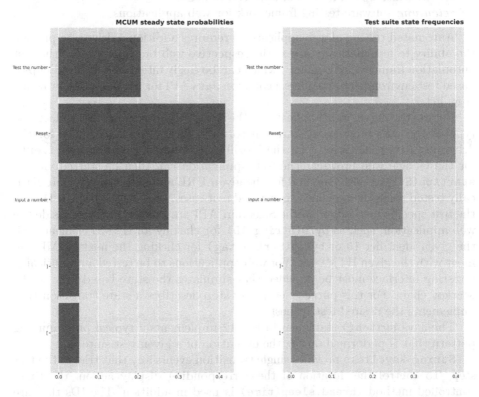

Fig. 10. Steady state probabilities of the MCUM vs. relative frequencies of the test suite.

In addition, the TestPlayer offers further metrics, which are discussed in more detail in [17]:

- *SSV*: comparison of the average number of test cases that are necessary to visit a usage state once in the usage model and during the test execution
- *KL*: visualization of the Kullback/Leibler divergence and the mean weighted deviation [16] between the usage model and the test suite
- *SSP.N*, *SSV.N*, *KL.N*: corresponding metrics for test suites that cover all nodes of the usage model
- *SSV.T*, *KL.T*: corresponding that for test suites that cover all transitions of the usage model.

3   Eclipse for the Automated Test Suite Execution

Eclipse is an open source programming environment for modeling and developing all kinds of (application) software, which fits ideally into the comprehensive test framework. There exist plug-ins for all common programming approaches, e.g.

- *Java*: applications, client/server side programming, Android, $\cdots$
- *PHP*: server side programming
- *JavaScript/CSS/HTML5*: web applications
- *JUnit*: white box unit tests of Java components
- *Selenium*: software-testing framework for web applications

Automated testing of web applications requires additional drivers to provide the ability to automatically access the respective web browser. We use the test automation framework Selenium[7], which can be easily integrated into an Eclipse-based test environment and offers a common Java API for the main web browsers (Fig. 11).

Before testing a web application, the test engineer must first select the type of the web browser to start the correct driver. Concrete values for the driver are `FirefoxDriver()` for the Mozilla web browser and `ChromeDriver()` for the Google web browser. The web application can then be started via the `startApp(String URL)` method for the given URL and subsequently automatically tested using the previously generated test cases, as shown in Fig. 11. During the test specific methods from the Selenium API are used to navigate inside the web application, such as `byID(String ID)` for clicking an HTML element with the given identifier ID or `byTag(String tag)` for clicking the next HTML element with the given HTML tag. For web applications to be tested automatically, a testing interface must be provided that simulates the state-based logic of the Markov chain. For this purpose, each test step describes a state transition that implements the desired test request.

The Java `switch()` statement in Fig. 12 implements a typical programming pattern that is performed during the execution of a given test suite.

`String keyclicks` provides single transition events `key` that trigger the test step. To control the duration of the corresponding display action, the time-controlled method `Thread.sleep(time)` is used in addition. The IDs that are

---

[7] https://www.seleniumhq.org/.

```
// ...
String browser=null;
// select browser type from command line
browser=args[0];
if (browser.equalsIgnoreCase("Firefox")) {
  // browser path
  String pathToGeckoDriver="geckodriver";
  System.setProperty("webdriver.gecko.driver",
                     pathToGeckoDriver);
  driver=new FirefoxDriver();
} else if (browser.equalsIgnoreCase("Chrome")) {
  // browser path
  String pathToChromeDriver="chromedriver";
  System.setProperty("webdriver.chrome.driver",
                     pathToChromeDriver);
  driver=new ChromeDriver();
} else {
  throw new Exception("Browser not defined!");
}
// ...
// start app from URL
public static void startApp(String URL){
  driver.get(URL);
}

// find HTML element by ID
public static void byID(String ID) {
  driver.findElement(By.id(ID)).click();
}

// find HTML element by HTML tag
public static void byTag(String tag) {
  driver.findElement(By.tagName(tag)).click();
}
// ...
```

Fig. 11. Elements of the Selenium web driver Java API for Eclipse [20]

used as input parameters for method byID() are the corresponding HTML id
attributes in the index.html file for the web game, e.g.

```
<button id="ResetButton" class="sbtn"
  type="button" onclick="reset();">Reset
</button>
```

When testing web game GuessNumbers using the test suite shown in Fig. 13,
test results are logged in the Eclipse console window and show which transition
event of the usage model from Fig. 8 has been executed by each test case (Fig. 14).

```
for (String key : keyClicks) {
  switch (key) {
    case "e1":
      byID("Input");
      // actions for transition e1
      Thread.sleep(time);
    break;
    case "e2":
      byID("InputButton");
      // actions for transition e2
      Thread.sleep(time);
    break;
    case "e3":
      byID("ResetButton");
      // actions for transition e3
      Thread.sleep(time);
    break;
    // ...
  }
}
```

Fig. 12. Main Java `switch()` for executing a single test step.

The particular challenge in testing `GuessNumbers` is to guess the hidden random number at the end. Since the used TestPlayer generation strategy `length` tries to create test cases with minimum length in order to satisfy the state coverage criterion, the generated test suite is too short for finding the hidden random number.

A first solution to overcome this problem is using a more complex test suite, i.e. the TestPlayer sorting strategy `add.prob` (additive probability) is applied instead, which produces longer test cases that have a better chance of guessing the secret number. Other sorting strategies that are provided in the TestPlayer `Strategies` section are

- `unsorted`: test cases are generated randomly for a given usage profile
- `frequency`: test case list is sorted by the relative frequency of the test cases
- `length`: test case list is sorted by the length of the test cases
- `multiplicative probabilities`: test case list is sorted by the occurrence probability of the test cases
- `additive probabilities`: test case list is sorted by the additive probabilities of all test steps
- `complexity`: test case list is sorted by the complexity of the test cases

In this way test suites, which have quite different properties are created automatically and are discussed in more detail in [17].

The result is as expected, i.e. the second test case of a test suite consisting of two longer test cases now contains the line `You have found the searched number` (Fig. 15).

```
[
  [
    ["[", "e2", "Test the number"],
    ["Test the number", "e7", "]"]
  ],
  [
    ["[", "e1", "Input a number"],
    ["Input a number", "e4", "Test the number"],
    ["Test the number", "e7", "]"]
  ],
  [
    ["[", "e3", "Reset"],
    ["Reset", "e9", "Input a number"],
    ["Input a number", "e4", "Test the number"],
    ["Test the number", "e7", "]"]
  ],
  {}
]
```

Fig. 13. Test suite that covers all states of the web game `GuessNumbers` in Fig. 8.

4 Model-Based On-the-Fly Testing

Another approach to the problem of not being able to guess the hidden number is to apply an *executable* Markov chain usage model for performing *on-the-fly testing*. That means the transitions between the usage states implement executable test steps that directly test the IuT, i.e. the web game, without first generating an abstract test suite.

The principle techniques for on-the-fly testing can be classified into *specification-based* and *usage-based* approaches. In [18] formal model programs are written in the high level specification language `AsmL`. On-the-fly testing is presented as a method in which test derivation from a model program and test execution are combined into a single algorithm. On the other hand, in [19] use case diagrams containing functional and non-functional requirements are transformed into a statistical usage model. Test cases and the evaluation of test verdicts are interpreted on-the-fly during the execution of a TTCN-3 test suite, providing an executable usage model.

In this paper we applied the second approach and implemented a simple Java pattern (Fig. 16) to provide an executable MCUM consisting of

- an *enumeration* `State` that contains all usage states defined by the identifier set S_i $(i = 1, 2, \cdots)$,...
- an implementation of an *abstract method* `doTransition()` that is executed during state transitions and
  - performs *state dependent* test step operations
  - provides next usage state S_j $(j = 1, 2, \cdots)$ as output.

```
==========================================
TestCase[1]=<e2 e7>
        |R: InputButton
        |R: End of test case
Execution time for TestCase[1]=0.352 s
==========================================
TestCase[2]=<e1 e4 e7>
        |R: Input
        |R: InputButton
        |R: End of test case
Execution time for TestCase[2]=0.682 s
==========================================
TestCase[3]=<e3 e9 e4 e7>
        |R: ResetButton
        |R: Input
        |R: InputButton
        |R: End of test case
Execution time for TestCase[3]=0.788 s
==========================================
Result of Test Case Execution:

Total number of executed test cases: 3
Number of test cases that passed: 3
Number of test cases that failed: 0
==========================================
```

Fig. 14. Test results logged in the Eclipse console window.

Guided by the Java pattern it is easy to provide a solution for on-the-fly testing for the web game GuessNumbers and the corresponding usage model in Fig. 8.

A Java code block that realizes usage state Start by implementing the abstract methods doTransition() is given in Fig. 17. Code blocks for InputState, TestState and Reset are implemented in an analog way. Here, *Start*, $N1$, $N2$, $N3$ and *Stop* are state identifiers representing the usage states [, Input a number, Test the number, Reset and] respectively. The choice, which usage state will be selected next depends on the given usage profile, i.e. the actual values of the generic probabilities $p1, \cdots, p11$. The *implementation pattern* is always the same:

1. Summarize the given probabilities for all outgoing probabilities leaving the usage state, e.g. sum=p1+p2+p3 for usage state [
2. Generate a random number p=Math.random() in the interval [0,1]
3. Compare the values of the probabilities against the random number, e.g. if(p<p1/sum), if(p<(p1+p2)/sum) and do some actions that are related to the selected test step, e.g. MCUM.clickByID("InputButton") that performs an automated click on the selected HTML element given by the attribute id="InputButton".

```
=================================================
TestCase[2]=<e1 e4 e8 e4 e10 e6 e9 e4 e10
             e8 e4 e8 e4 e8 e4 e10 e7>
        |R: Input
        |R: InputButton
        |R: Input
        |R: InputButton
        |R: InputButton
        |R: ResetButton
        |R: Input
        |R: InputButton
        |R: InputButton
        |R: Input
        |R: InputButton
        |R: Input
        |R: InputButton
        |R: Input
        |R: You have found the searched number
        |R: The number you are searching for is: 31
        |R: Your current guess rate is 100.00%
        |R: the minimum/maximum guess attempts are 4/4
        |R: InputButton
        |R: End of test case
Execution time for TestCase[2]=3.473 s
=================================================
```

Fig. 15. Test results indicating a successful guess attempt.

The output statements MCUM.tc.write() also record the test steps for generating test cases on-the-fly. The output format has the same JSON-like syntax as explained in subsection *Automatic Generation of Test Cases*.

The advantage is that a *replay* option is given to test the web game later with the same test cases to reproduce a comparable behavior of the IuT.

The diagram in Fig. 18 shows the main loop for on-the-fly testing of the usage model given in Fig. 8. Each test case starts in State.Start and will end in State.Stop that sets the Boolean MCUM.finish to true. At the end of the test the generated test cases are saved in a text file test_cases.timestamp.txt and can be re-used for a subsequent replay. In addition, a second file, On-the-fly.timestamp.txt, logs the test result and records whether the hidden numbers were guessed.

5   Model-Based Testing of Multilingual Websites

So far, we have shown how simple web applications can be tested by means of model-based testing. Now we are going a step further and focus on testing multilingual websites. For this purpose, a suitable usage model must first be

```
public enum State {
Si {
    // usage state Si
    State doTransition() {
        // test step operations
        // ...
        // go to next usage state Sj
        return Sj;
    }
},
// ...
}
abstract State doTransition();
```

Fig. 16. Java pattern to implement an executable MCUM.

```
Start { // <[>
    State doTransition() {
        double p1 = 1, p2 = 0.1, p3 = 0.05;
        double sum = p1 + p2 + p3;
        double p = Math.random();
        if (p < p1 / sum) {
            // System.out.println("<[> -> <Input a number>, event = e1");
            try {
                MCUM.tc.write( "\n\t[\n\t\t[\"[\", \"e1\", ");
            } catch (IOException e) {}
            MCUM.tcLength++;
            // go to usage state <Input a number>
            return N1;
        } else if (p < (p1 + p2) / sum) {
            // System.out.println("<[> -> <Test the number>, event = e2");
            try {
                MCUM.tc.write( "\n\t[\n\t\t[\"[\", \"e2\", ");
            } catch (IOException e) {}
            MCUM.tcLength++;
            // go to usage state <Test the number>
            return N2;
        } else {
            // System.out.println("<[> -> <Reset>, event = e3");
            try {
                MCUM.tc.write( "\n\t[\n\t\t[\"[\", \"e3\", ");
            } catch (IOException e) {}
            MCUM.tcLength++;
            // go to usage state <Reset>
            return N3;
        }
    }
},
```

Fig. 17. Java code implementing usage state [of the MCUM in Fig. 8.

```
// start a new MCUM
MCUM myMCUM = new MCUM();
MCUM.tcNumber = 0;
for (int j = 0; j < MCUM.rounds; j++) {
    MCUM.finish = false;
    MCUM.tcNumber++;
    System.out.println("Test case " + MCUM.tcNumber);
    MCUM.tcLength = 0;
    MCUM.state = State.Start;
    while (!MCUM.finish) {
        // sleep between state transitions
        sleep(MCUM.time);
        myMCUM.nextState();
    }
}
```

Fig. 18. Main loop for on-the-fly testing of an executable MCUM.

created. In the following, we will explain how the TestUS[8] homepage can be tested (see also [20], where we used a slightly different usage model from a previous version of the website).

5.1 Language-Dependent Usage Models

The corresponding usage model of the website is given in Fig. 19.

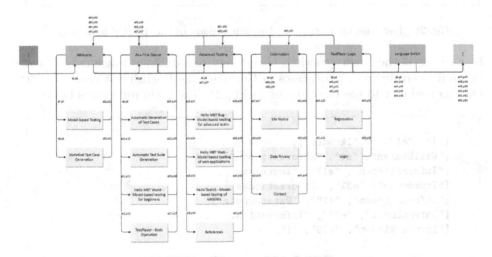

Fig. 19. Usage model of the TestUS home page.

The TestUS homepage always starts in the usage state `Welcome`. From there, you can reach the main usage states `At a First Glance`, `Advanced Testing`, `Information`, `TestPlayer Login` and `Language Switch`. The main usage states

---

[8] https://testus.eu.

correspond to the selection menus in the top menu bar of the TestUS homepage. From the main usage states, you get to the other usage states of the website, e.g. `Welcome` provides access to

- `Model-based Testing` and
- `Statistical Test Case Generation`

  ...

`TestPlayer Login` offers the access to

- `Sign-Up` and
- `Login`

and `Language Switch` switches the representation language of the website between English and German.

A typical test case generated automatically by the TestPlayer looks like the one that is shown Fig. 20. After changing the language from English to German

```
[
  ["[", "e1", "Welcome"],
  ["Welcome", "e4", "Information"],
  ["Information", "e17", "Site Notice"],
  ["Site Notice", "e32", "Information"],
  ["Information", "e18", "Data Privacy"],
  ["Data Privacy", "e33", "Information"],
  ["Information", "e49", "]"]
]
```

Fig. 20. Test case for testing the English version of the TestUS homepage.

by clicking on the language switch of the website a different usage model must be used to create correct test cases in German. The English test case (Fig. 20) has changed now to the German one in Fig. 21. The main differences between

```
[
  ["[", "e1", "Willkommen"],
  ["Willkommen", "e4", "Informationen"],
  ["Informationen", "e17", "Impressum"],
  ["Impressum", "e32", "Informationen"],
  ["Informationen", "e18", "Datenschutz"],
  ["Datenschutz", "e33", "Informationen"],
  ["Informationen", "e49", "]"]
]
```

Fig. 21. Test case for testing the German version of the TestUS homepage.

the two usage models are the different names of the usage states in the selected language. The structure and the generic transition events are not affected by this change.

5.2   Generic Usage Model

For that reason, it makes sense to provide a usage model containing *generic state names* that can be mapped to concrete names of the respective languages during the test execution. This task can be performed by the TestPlayer that can add generic state names Ni ($i = 1, \cdots$) to an incomplete usage model. The result is a generic usage model having 20 generic usage states $N1$ to $N21$ and 62 generic transition events $e1$ to $e62$.

The concrete English test case in Fig. 20 can now be derived from following generic one in Fig. 22.

```
[
  ["[", "e1", "N1"],
  ["N1", "e4", "N4"],
  ["N4", "e17", "N17"],
  ["N17", "e32", "N4"],
  ["N4", "e18", "N18"],
  ["N18", "e33", "N4"],
  ["N4", "e49", "]"]
]
```

Fig. 22. Generic test case for multilingual testing of the TestUS homepage.

To test websites successfully with the presented techniques, individual HTML elements must be labeled with unique identifiers. Therefore, the HTML source code of the English, respectively German TestUS homepage contain HTML markups and identifiers that are composed of the generic state names and a label for the language that is used. During the test execution, the test system must switch to the other language when the language switch is detected inside a test case. The Java code in Fig. 23 shows how Eclipse is performing this task.

For websites to be tested automatically, a testing interface must be provided that simulates the state-based logic of the usage model. In analogy to Fig. 12, we use a Java `switch()` statement consisting of 62+1 entries for the generic transition events and an additional default entry to react when an invalid input occurs.

The Eclipse `Run Configuration` can be set via the parameter s (scroll mode) to indicate whether the individual pages should be scrolled during testing of the website. This feature is used for controlling the run-time of the test execution. In case of a lengthy test suite, e.g. for a desired transition coverage, the scroll mode can be switched off to get a quick overview of the behaviour of the website. When the scroll mode is activated the duration of the display and the scroll action are time-controlled via the class attribute `mainTime` and the sleep method `Thread.sleep()`.

The Java code fragment in Fig. 24 shows the actions that are triggered when selecting the TestUS `Login` page within a test case, which is indicated by the generic

```java
                    // set web site language
                    public static void switch_Language() {
                        if (webSiteLanguage.equals("en")) {
                            // switch to other language
                            webSiteLanguage = "de";
                            N1 = "N1_de";
                            // ...
                            N20 = "N20_de";
                            N21 = "N21_de";
                            //
                            N1_Text = "Willkommen";
                            // ...
                            N20_Text = "Registrierung";
                            N21_Text = "Login";
                        } else if (webSiteLanguage.equals("de")) {
                            // switch to other language
                            webSiteLanguage = "en";
                            N1 = "N1_en";
                            // ...
                            N20 = "N20_en";
                            N21 = "N21_en";
                            //
                            N1_Text = "Welcome";
                            // ...
                            N20_Text = "Registration";
                            N21_Text = "Login";
                        }
                    }
```

Fig. 23. Java code for switching the language during the test.

state name $N21$. When the generic transition event $e21$ appears in a test case the `TestPlayer Login` item is clicked automatically in the selected web driver by performing the method `clickLinkByPartialText(N21_Text)`, which is wrapping the Selenium code `driver.findElement(By.partialLinkText(N21_Text))`. String variable `N21_Text` is set by the actual language condition and contains the Login string either in English or German (see Fig. 23). After a predefined timeout of `mainTime`, which controls the web page display time, the JavaScript engine of the web browser must execute the JavaScript code `window.scrollBy(0,50)` to scroll down by 50 pixels. When the bottom part of the web page is reached, the browser scrolls automatically to the top of the web page by executing the JavaScript code `window.scrollTo(0,0)`.

5.3   Test Focusing by Means of Adapted Usage Profiles

Of special importance for the validation of the `SuT` (System under Test) are customer-specific usage profiles that focus the test execution on selected usage states or sets of usage states. This is achieved by

- avoiding a transition (Si, Sj) that is starting in usage state Si and ending in usage state Sj by setting the corresponding probability value $p(Si, Sj)$ to zero, i.e. $p(Si, Sj) = 0$
- forcing a transition (Si, Sj) by setting the corresponding probability value $p(Si, Sj)$ to one, i.e. $p(Si, Sj) = 1$.

```
case "e21":
    Thread.sleep(100);
    moveMouse(5,0);
    Thread.sleep(100);
    //byID(N21);
    clickLinkByPartialText(N21_Text);
    // scroll part
    if (scrollMode == 1) {
        Thread.sleep(mainTime);
        for (int second = 0;; second++) {
            if (second >= 50) {
                break;
            }
            jsExecutor.executeScript("window.scrollBy(0,50)");
            Thread.sleep(100);
        }
        jsExecutor.executeScript("window.scrollTo(0,0)");
    } else
        Thread.sleep(mainTime);
    break;
```

Fig. 24. Java code for testing the TestUS Login page.

The result is an adapted usage profile that is used to generate the test-suite. In this way, you can easily describe various user classes that visit the website in different ways. A test case, which *must* be performed during the test procedure due to special safety requirements, is often referred to as the *happy path*. The implementation of a happy path can also be easily realized with the concept of adapted usage profiles.

Figure 25 shows an accumulated test case for an adapted test suite that focuses only on those visitors of the TestUS website (Fig. 19) who access the top menu At a First Glance and Fig. 26 contains a test case visualization that is automatically provided by the TestPlayer when generating the test suite.

```
[
    ["[", "e1", "Welcome"],
    ["Welcome", "e2", "At a First Glance"],
    ["At a First Glance", "e10", "Automatic Test Suite Generation"],
    ["Automatic Test Suite Generation", "e25", "At a First Glance"],
    ["At a First Glance", "e51", "]"]
]
```

Fig. 25. Test case for an adapted test suite focusing on usage state At a First Glance of the usage model in Fig. 19.

The corresponding usage profile is as follows:
p1=1, p2=1, p37=0, p38=0, p40=0, p43=0

Visualization of 5 accumulated test cases (state coverage, strategy: sorted by length)
Test case #5

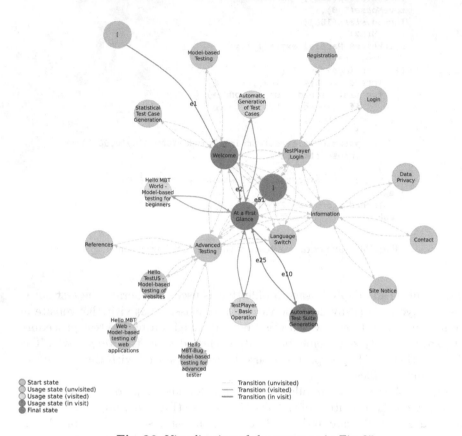

Fig. 26. Visualization of the test case in Fig. 25.

6   Conclusion and Final Remarks

This paper presents various techniques that allow to prepare and perform model-based on-the-fly testing of web applications and multilingual websites by using the TestPlayer tool chain.

For this purpose, the essential steps for a model-based test process which applies statistical usage models for the generation and evaluation of suitable test suites are explained on the basis of the simple web game application GuessNumbers.

Compared to a conventional test project, in which test cases are prepared in a tabular format, for example, a model-based test project requires the development of a test model. This model represents the usage behavior from a test perspective and contains all scenarios, constraints and dependencies that are relevant for testing.

Modeling can involve considerable effort, especially if the input documents do not have the required level of detail and frequent requests are required. On the other hand, this is an excellent way to identify errors and inconsistencies at an early stage before the implementation phase.

Thus, this initial investment helps to avoid serious problems in later phases of the project and to significantly improve the maintainability of the tests.

The key insights from our projects in recent years and this paper can be summarized as follows:

- Due to many successive development cycles, more and more functions must be tested. The increasing testing effort can only be managed by automated testing and model-based testing techniques.
- A model-based tester uses models to control test design and analysis and takes advantage of models for other test activities such as test case generation and test report generation.
- Avoid the reuse of a model that has also been used for code generation. If both the code and the tests are generated from the same model, no deviations will be detected. Instead, try to create a specific model from the test perspective.
- Model-based techniques that use graphical representations of usage models can help even inexperienced test engineers prepare and perform their tests. Graphical usage models facilitate the setting of the test focus on those areas of the SUT that need to be tested.
- Adapted profiles support the selective generation of test suites. Based on adapted profiles different user groups that interact with the SUT can be distinguished by different test suites that are used during the test execution. How to systematically derive an adapted profile is explained in more details in [10].
- The Eclipse modeling framework in combination with the TestPlayer tool chain provides a versatile tool environment for model-based testing of web applications and websites. Nevertheless, the TestPlayer is independent of special application areas and can be used in many different ways.

References

1. El-Far, I.K., Whittaker, J.A.: Model-based software testing. In: Marciniak, J.J. (ed.) Encyclopedia on Software Engineering. Wiley, New York (2001)
2. Legeard, B., Utting, M.: Practical Model-Based Testing. Elsevier, Amsterdam (2007)
3. Rosaria, S., Robinson, H.: Applying models in your testing process. Inf. Softw. Technol. **42**, 815–824 (2000)
4. Whittaker, J.A., Poore, J.H.: Markov analysis of software specifications. ACM Trans. Softw. Eng. Methodol. **2**(1), 93–106 (1993)
5. Walton, G.H., Poore, J.H., Trammell, C.J.: Statistical testing of software based on a usage model. Softw. Pract. Exp. **25**(1), 97–108 (1995)
6. Musa, J.D.: The operational profile. In: Özekici, S. (ed.) Reliability and Maintenance of Complex Systems. NATO ASI Series (Series F: Computer and Systems Sciences), vol. 154, pp. 333–344. Springer, Heidelberg (1996). https://doi.org/10.1007/978-3-662-03274-9_18

7. Walton, G., Poore, J.: Generating transition probabilities to support model-based software testing. Softw. Pract. Exp. **30**(10), 1095–1106 (2000)
8. Poore, J., Walton, G., Whittaker, J.: A constraint-based approach to the representation of software usage models. Inf. Softw. Technol. **42**(12), 825–833 (2000)
9. Takagi, T., Furukawa, Z.: Constructing a usage model for statistical testing with source code generation methods. In: Proceedings of the 11th Asia-Pacific Software Engineering Conference (APSEC 2004) (2004)
10. Dulz, W., Holpp, S., German, R.: A polyhedron approach to calculate probability distributions for Markov chain usage models. Electron. Notes Theor. Comput. Sci. **264**(3), 19–35 (2010)
11. Prowell, S.: Computations for Markov chain usage models. Technical report, Software Engineering Institute, Carnegie-Mellon University, Pittsburgh, USA, 2000. UT-CS-03-505 (2000)
12. Sayre, K., Poore, J.: Stopping criteria for statistical testing. Inf. Softw. Technol. **42**(12), 851–857 (2000)
13. Gutjahr, W.: Importance sampling of test cases in Markovian software usage models. Probab. Eng. Inf. Sci. **11**, 19–36 (1997)
14. Prowell, S.J.: JUMBL: a tool for model-based statistical testing. In: HICSS, pp. 3–37 (2003)
15. Dulz, W., Zhen, F.: MaTeLo - statistical usage testing by annotated sequence diagrams, Markov chains and TTCN-3. In: IEEE International Conference on Quality Software (QSIC 2003), pp. 336–342 (2003)
16. Dulz, W.: A comfortable testplayer for analyzing statistical usage testing strategies. In: ICSE Workshop on Automation of Software Test (AST 2011), Honolulu, Hawaii (2011)
17. Dulz, W.: Model-based strategies for reducing the complexity of statistically generated test suites. In: Winkler, D., Biffl, S., Bergsmann, J. (eds.) SWQD 2013. LNBIP, vol. 133, pp. 89–103. Springer, Heidelberg (2013). https://doi.org/10.1007/978-3-642-35702-2_7
18. Veanes, M., Campbell, C., Schulte, W., Kohli, P.: On-The-fly testing of reactive systems. Technical report, Microsoft Research, Redmond, WA, USA, 2005. MSR-TR-2005-05 (2005)
19. Dulz, W.: On-the-fly testing by using an executable TTCN-3 Markov chain usage model. In: Maciaszek, L.A., González-Pérez, C., Jablonski, S. (eds.) ENASE 2008. CCIS, vol. 69, pp. 17–30. Springer, Heidelberg (2010). https://doi.org/10.1007/978-3-642-14819-4_2
20. Dulz, W.: A versatile tool environment to perform model-based testing of web applications and multilingual websites. In: 13th International Conference on Software Technologies (ICSOFT 2018), pp. 45–56 (2018)

On the Impact of Order Information in API Usage Patterns

Ervina Çergani[(✉)] and Mira Mezini[(✉)]

Software Technology Group, Technische Universität Darmstadt, Darmstadt, Germany
{cergani,mezini}@st.informatik.tu-darmstadt.de,ecergani@gmail.com

Abstract. Many approaches have been proposed for learning Application Programming Interface (API) usage patterns from code repositories. Depending on the underlying technique, the mined patterns may (1) be strictly sequential, (2) consider partial order between method calls, or (3) not consider order information. Understanding the trade-offs between these pattern types with respect to real code is important in many applications (e.g. misuse detection), given that APIs often have usage constraints, such as restrictions on call order. *API misuses*, i.e., violations of these constraints, may lead to software crashes, bugs and vulnerabilities.

In this paper, we present the results of a work that addresses this need. We have constructed a benchmark based on an episode mining algorithm that can be configured to learn three type of patterns: sequential, partial, and no-order patterns. We use the benchmark in two ways. First, we use it to empirically study the different types of the mined API usage patterns based on three well-defined metrics: expressiveness, consistency and generalizability. Second, we evaluate the effect of the different pattern types within the real application context of using them as an input to a misuse detector. We run the benchmark on two existing datasets consisting of: (1) 360 C# code repositories, and (2) four Java projects. We use the C# data set to empirically study the resulting API usage patterns, and the Java data set to evaluate the effect of different pattern types on the application context of misuse detection. For this purpose, we build EMDetect for detecting API misuses in Java projects.

Our results show practical evidence that not only do partial-order patterns represent a generalized super set of sequential-order patterns, partial-order mining also finds additional patterns missed by sequence mining, which are used by a larger number of developers across code repositories. Additionally, our study empirically quantifies the importance of the order information encoded in sequential and partial-order patterns for representing correct co-occurrences of code elements in real code. On the application context of misuse detection, our results show that sequential-order patterns perform better in terms of precision by ranking true positives higher in the top findings, while partial-order patterns perform better in terms of recall by being able to find more misuses in the source code. Last but not least, our benchmark can be used by other researchers to explore additional properties of API patterns, and for building-up other applications based on API usage patterns.

© Springer Nature Switzerland AG 2019
M. van Sinderen and L. A. Maciaszek (Eds.): ICSOFT 2018, CCIS 1077, pp. 79–103, 2019.
https://doi.org/10.1007/978-3-030-29157-0_4

Keywords: API usage pattern types · API misuse detection ·
Events mining · Empirical study · Benchmark

1   Introduction

Application Programming Interfaces (APIs) provide effective means for code
reuse. Client developers of an API must be aware on how to correctly use it
in order to avoid errors. An *API usage pattern* encodes a set of API methods
that are frequently used together, optionally complemented by constraints like
the order in which methods must be called. API patterns are used as the basis
for various applications such as API documentation generation [21], automated
code completion [25], bug or anomaly detection [39], and code search [41].

Many techniques have been proposed to learn three kinds of patterns from
code repositories [34]: (1) *No-order patterns* are unordered sets of frequently
used methods (e.g.,[22,23]) and encode that calls of methods, say a, b, and c,
frequently co-occur in code, but do not include information about the order of
calls. (2) *Sequential-order patterns* (e.g., [29,33]) additionally encode facts such
as that a has to be called before b, and b before c. (3) *partial-order patterns*
(e.g., [25]) are modeled as graphs and can encode e.g., that a must be called
first, but how b or c are called afterwards is irrelevant.

However, so far, we lack systematic studies of the tradeoffs between the different types of patterns in representing source code in practice. A comparison
of different pattern types with regards to some pre-defined metrics is challenging, because each approach in the literature uses a different learning technique
with configurations specific to its data set (e.g., frequency threshold), a different
representation for usage examples and patterns, and might even be specifically
tied to a particular programming language or input form (e.g., source code vs.
bytecode).

In previous work [10], which this paper extends, we address this challenge
and present the first empirical comparison of API pattern types in representing
API usages in the wild. In this work, we go one step further and analyze the
effectiveness of the different pattern types in the context of a particular application of mined usage patterns, that of misuse detection. Incorrect usages of an
API, or *API misuses*, are violations of usage constraints of the API. API misuses
lead often to software crashes, bugs, and vulnerabilities in the source code.

To provide a fair setting, we build a benchmark for performing our empirical
comparisons. The benchmark includes the following components:

1. Two data sets to provide support for two different programming languages,
   (a) the C# data set consisting of 360 open-source Github repositories with
   over $68M$ lines of code [30]. This data set is used in previous work [10] to
   perform the empirical comparison between the different pattern types. (b)
   The Java data set (MUBench [8]) used as the ground-truth to compare the
   different pattern types within the application context of misuse detection.
2. An adaptation of the established mining algorithm, called episode mining [1],
   to the domain of mining code patterns. This algorithm is selected because

it can be customized to mine all three types of patterns, thus enabling a fair and systematic comparison of them. *Episode mining* is a well-known machine learning technique used to discover partially ordered sets of *events* from a stream, called *episodes* (*patterns* in our terminology). In our setting, *events* are method declarations or invocations (cf. Sect. 3.2). We can mine all three pattern types by adjusting certain parameters of the episode mining algorithm.

3. Three metrics: expressiveness, consistency, and generalizability, on which we base our empirical comparison between the different pattern types [10]. We summarize the observations we make in the study and derive implications from our observations, which can help in building better applications of mined API usage patterns.

4. A misuse detector (EMDetect) in order to evaluate the effectiveness of the different pattern types and the validity of the implications we derive from the comparison of pattern types [10] in a real application context. We compare the pattern types in terms of both, precision and recall.

5. We make our experimental infrastructure as a benchmark publicly available[1], so that can be used by other researchers to evaluate additional metrics for API usage pattern types and to building other applications based on API usage patterns.

The rest of this paper is organized as follows: Sect. 2 discusses related work of different API usage patterns learning approaches, other empirical studies that have also studied API usages, and a description of four misuse detectors from the literature that we use to compare our results of EMDetect with. Section 3 describes the episode mining algorithm that we use for learning API usage patterns, how we adapt it for learning patterns from source code, and a description of our misuse detector. Section 4 continues with the experimental setups by describing: the data sets, analyses of the threshold values used by the mining algorithm, the three metrics we base our comparison of the different pattern types, and the experiments performed to evaluate our misuse detector. After that, we present the results of our evaluations of the comparison of the different pattern types in representing source code, the implications that we derive from this comparison and evaluate pattern types performance in the special context of a misuse detector, respectively in Sects. 5, 6 and 7. At the end we discuss threats to validity and conclusions in Sects. 8 and 9 respectively.

2 Related Work

Here, we present existing API usage mining techniques and representations, discuss other studies that have investigated API usages in practice, and present four state of the art API misuse detectors from the literature which we use to compare the performance of EMDetect with.

---

[1] http://www.st.informatik.tu-darmstadt.de/artifacts/patternTypes/

2.1 API Usage Representations

API usage representations can be divided into three types: *no-order*, *sequential-order*, and *partial-order*.

No-order Patterns: The simplest form of learning API usage patterns is to look at frequent co-occurrences of code elements, while ignoring the order they occur in. *Frequent item-set mining* is an example in this category and variations of it have been commonly used [19,22,23].

Sequential-order Patterns: To take code semantics into account, many API usage representations consider order information. For example, calling the constructor of an API type must happen before calling any of its methods. The patterns mined by *sequence mining* encode strict sequential order between code elements in a pattern. Existing approaches are based on, but not limited to, using information from the API's source code [3,39], API documentation [42], program control-flow structure [32], and program execution traces [12,29]. Statistical models have also been used to predict the next code element (e.g. method call), given a current context (e.g., sequences of already seen method calls). Examples include n-gram language models [33] or statistical generative models [28]. Additionally after identifying sequences, some techniques rely on clustering to build pattern abstractions [9,37,41].

Partial-order Patterns: This pattern type allows more flexibility in representing code semantics, e.g., that code elements b and c must occur after code element a, but that their order (b before or after c) is not relevant. *Graph-based* techniques like GraLan [24], GraPacc [25], and JSMiner [26] represent source code in a *graph* to identify frequent sub-graph patterns. *Automata-based* techniques or Finite State Machine (FSM) represent code as a set of states (e.g. method calls) and a transition function between the states. The framework by Acharya et al. [4] extract API usage patterns directly from client code. This framework is based on FSMs for generating execution traces along different program paths. In their terminology, partial-order expresses choices between alternative code elements. In our terminology, a partial-order pattern includes strict and/or unordered pairs of code elements.

2.2 Empirical Studies of API Usages

Researchers have extracted API usages through mining software repositories and studied the characteristics of these usages or used them in various applications. Usage patterns are explored in [15] from the Java Standard API with an early version of the Qualitas Corpus which contains 39 open source Java applications. A study on a larger corpus (5,000 projects) on usages of both core Java and third-party API libraries is performed in [31]. The diversity of API usages in object-oriented software is empirically analyzed in [18]. In their context, diversity is defined as the different statically observable combinations of method calls on the same project. Multiple dimensions of API usages are explored in [11], such as the scope of projects and APIs, the metrics of API usages (e.g., number of project classes extending API classes), the API's metadata, and project versus API-centric views.

The empirical study on API usages presented in [40], focuses on how different types of APIs are used. Our work is mainly concerned with API patterns instead of single usages. Furthermore, most of previous work focuses on comparing one learning technique with other learning techniques that mine the same pattern type. For example, the framework presented in [29] is used to evaluate three mining approaches that learn all sequences of API method calls. Instead, we focus on understanding the trade-offs between different pattern types.

The work in [34] provides a more comprehensive survey on API property inference and discusses over 60 techniques developed for mining frequent API usage patterns. Overall, existing studies focus on different aspects of API usages, but do not analyze the differences between API usage pattern types. Our work fills this gap and investigates the trade-offs between different API usage pattern types in practice with respect to three metrics: expressiveness, consistency, and generalizability, and in the misuse detection application context.

2.3 API Misuse Detectors

Given that we use MUBench as our ground-truth for evaluating the performance of our detector in Sect. 7, we also compare its results with the four state of the art detectors evaluated by Amann et al. [6] using the same framework.

GrouMiner [27]: Tranforms source code into directed acyclic graphs, where method calls, field accesses and control structures are represented by nodes, and control-/data dependencies by directed unlabelled edges.

GrouMiner uses sub-graph smining to learn patterns, and then detects violations of these patterns as potential misuses. GrouMiner detects: missing method calls, misplaced method calls, missing control sequences.

JADET [39]: Encodes call-order relation in each API usage as pairs. It's purpose is to identify missing pairs, but it fails in identifying violation of patterns containing only one pair. TIKANGA [38] is based on the same algorithm, but encodes API usages using temporal properties (CTL). JADET and TIKANGA detect: missing and misplaced method calls.

DMMC [20]: Transforms source code into sets of method calls that are called on the same receiver type. It outputs potential misuses using the ratio of the number of equal usages over the number of usages with exactly one additional method call. DMMC detects only missing method calls, since it does not consider order information.

3 API Pattern Mining and Misuse Detection

We briefly overview the episode mining algorithm and then explain how we use it to mine patterns from open-source C# GitHub repositories and Java projects, in three steps: (a) generate an event stream by transforming source-code into a stream of events, (b) apply episode mining algorithm to mine API usage patterns, and (c) filter the resulting partial-order patterns. After that we explain how we use the learned API usage patterns for detecting potential API misuses in the source code.

3.1 Episode Mining Algorithm

To support the detection of sequential-order, partial-order, and no-order patterns in source code, we use the episode mining algorithm [1] for the following reasons. *First*, it facilitates the comparison of different pattern types, since it provides one configuration parameter for each type. The other option would be to use different learning algorithms, one per pattern type. In this case, ensuring the same baseline for the empirical comparisons will be difficult, since each algorithm might use different configurations and input formats. *Second*, it is a general purpose machine learning algorithm, which has performed well in other applications: text mining [2], positional data [13], multi-neuronal spike data [1]. *Third*, the implementation of the episode mining algorithm [1] is publicly available.

The term *episode* is used to describe a partially ordered set of events. *Frequent episodes* can be found in an event stream through an Apriori-like algorithm [5]. Such an algorithm exploits principles of dynamic programming to combine already frequent episodes into larger ones [16]. The algorithm alternates episode candidates generation and counting phases so that infrequent episodes are discarded due to the downward closure lemma [1]. The counting phase tracks the occurrence of episodes in the event stream using Finite State Automaton (FSA). More specifically, at the k-th iteration, the algorithm generates all possible episodes with k events by self-joining frequent episodes from the previous iteration consisting of $k-1$ events each. The resulting episodes are episode candidates that need to be verified in the subsequent counting phase. A given episode is *frequent* if it occurs often enough in the event stream. A user-defined *frequency threshold* defines the minimum number of occurrences for an episode to be frequent. An *entropy threshold* determines whether there is sufficient evidence that two events occur in either order or not. All frequent episodes that fulfill the minimum *frequency* and *entropy* threshold are outputted by the algorithm in a given iteration k, and all infrequent episodes are simply discarded. The next iteration begins with generating candidate episodes of size $k+1$.

The *entropy threshold* is specific to partial-order patterns. It has a value between 0 and 1, inclusive. A value of 0 means that no order will be mined, resulting in no-order patterns. A value of 1 means a strict ordering of events, resulting in sequential-order patterns. Values between 0 and 1 result in partial-order patterns, with varying levels of strictness. We mine the three pattern types by adjusting the configuration parameter of the episode mining algorithm: *NOC* for

No-Order Configuration, *SOC* for Sequential-Order Configuration, and *POC* for Partial-Order Configuration. More details about the algorithm can be found in the work by Achar et al. [1].

3.2 Mining API Usage Patterns

Event Stream Generation. In our context, an *event* is any method declaration or method invocation. To transform a repository of source code into the stream representation expected by the episode mining algorithm, we iterate over all source files and traverse each Abstract Syntax Tree (AST) depth-first. Whenever we encounter a method declaration or method invocation node in the AST, we emit a corresponding event to a stream. We use a fully-qualified naming scheme for methods to avoid ambiguous references. The following is how we deal with the two types of nodes we are interested in:

- Method invocation is the fundamental information that represents an API usage, for which we want to learn patterns. While a resolved AST might point to a concrete method declaration, we generalize this reference to the method that has originally introduced the signature of the referenced method, i.e., a method that was originally declared in an interface or an abstract base class. The reason is that the original declaration defines the *contract* that all derived classes should adhere to, according to *Liskov's substitution principle* [17]. Assuming that this principle is universally followed, we can reduce noise in the dataset by storing the original reference.
- Method declarations represent the start of an enclosing method context that groups the contained method calls. We emit two different kind of events for the encountered method declaration. *Super Context:* If a method overrides another one, we include a reference to the overridden method, i.e., the encountered method overrides a method in an abstract base class. This serves as context information that might be important for the meaning of a pattern. *First Context:* Following the same reasoning as for super context, we include a reference to the method that was declared in an interface that originally introduced the current method signature, which could be further up the type hierarchy of the current class.

In both cases, method declaration or invocation, the generated events have the following format: `[RT:QT] [T].M([PT] [PT] ...)`, where `RT` is the return type, `M` is the method name, `QT` is the fully qualified name of it's declaring type and `T` is it's simple name. For constructor calls, we use the label of the form `ctor` as method name. We use the declaring type in the event signature to abstract over the different static receiver types. The `PT` label stands for parameter types, in order to distinguish overloaded methods by their parameter entities.

We apply heuristics to optimize the event stream generation. (1) We filter duplicated source code, e.g., projects that include the same source files in multiple solutions or that add their references through nested submodules in the version control system. (2) We ignore auto-generated source code (e.g., UI classes generated from XML templates), since they do not reflect human written code. (3) We ignore references in the data set that point to unresolved types or type elements. These cases indicate transformation errors of the original dataset, that were caused by -for example- an incomplete class path. (4) We do not process empty methods, nor include their method declarations in the event stream.

In addition to the heuristics mentioned above, in previous work [10] we also ignore methods of project-specific APIs (i.e., declared within the same project) to avoid learning project-specific patterns. The reason for this is because in [10], the goal is to learn general patterns that have the potential to be re-used across contexts, while in this work we mine patterns and detect misuses on a per project basis in order to also be able to detect misuses that come from project-specific APIs.

Learning API Usage Patterns. We feed the generated event stream to the episode mining algorithm after fixing the threshold values: frequency and entropy (as evaluated in Sect. 4.2). An *episode*, outputted by the mining algorithm, represents a partially ordered sets of events as a graph with labelled nodes and directed edges. Nodes represent a method declaration or a method invocation, and the directed edges represent the order in which they are called in the source code.

Figure 1 shows episode representations for the different pattern types. A no-order pattern would present the method calls as a set, as shown in Fig. 1(c). Two sequential-order patterns would be needed to present the two valid sequences presented by the partial-order pattern, respectively shown in Figs. 1(a) and (b). Note that methods m2() and m3() can occur in either order as defined by the partial-order pattern.

Filtering Episodes. In order to optimize the episodes outputted by the episode mining algorithm to the special context of misuse detection, we apply two heuristics. *First*, we ignore sub-episodes, e.g., episodes that are part of some other larger episodes. Given that episode mining is an apriori-based algorithm, a sub-episode ($a \rightarrow b$) might be part of another episode ($a \rightarrow b \rightarrow c$), if the later occurs frequently enough according to the frequency and entropy thresholds. The ($a \rightarrow b$) constraint is a redundant constraint already included into the ($a \rightarrow b \rightarrow c$) constraint, that's why we filter it out. *Second,* while SOC and NOC generate episode candidates that are either sequences or sets of events respectively, POC might generate episode candidates from all three types, since it contains the sequential and no-order types as special cases. In case all the episode candidates in POC are considered frequent episodes during the counting phase, then all of them are outputted by the algorithm. This implies that in every iteration (i.e, pattern size), POC might output redundant patterns containing the same set of events but differ in the order information. For illustration, assume that POC generates episode candidates in iteration 3 by combing the following patterns from iteration 2: $a \rightarrow b$ and $a \rightarrow c$. The episode candidates in iteration 3 will be: $a \rightarrow b \rightarrow c$ and $a \rightarrow c \rightarrow b$ as sequences, and $a \rightarrow$ *(b, c)* as partial-order, all possible orderings between the two newly connected

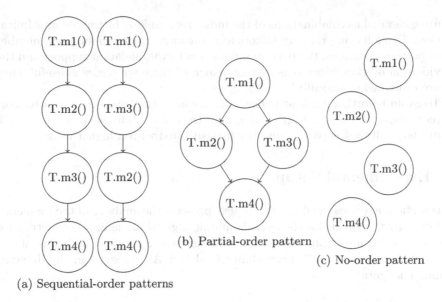

(a) Sequential-order patterns

(b) Partial-order pattern

(c) No-order pattern

Fig. 1. Episode representations for different pattern types.

events b and c. The partial-order episode $a \to (b, c)$ represents both $a \to b \to c$ and $a \to c \to b$. However, if all three episode candidates turn out to be frequent in the subsequent counting phase, the two other sequences will also be carried over to the next iteration. These redundant patterns are meaningless for source code representation though and we filter them out in each iteration.

3.3 Detecting API Misuses

Given the graph representation of the patterns we learn, we use the algorithm presented by Amann et al. [7] for detecting and ranking potential API misuses found in source code. The detection algorithm takes as input the set of learned patterns, the target source code, where we detect potential API misuses, and outputs a ranked list of potential misuses. In a nutshell, the algorithm works as follows. More details about the detection algorithm can be found in the work by Amann et al. [7].

1. The detection algorithm checks and discovers for each pair of a pattern and target source code, full occurrences (instances) and partial occurrences (potential misuses).
2. Potential misuses that are subgraphs of instances of another pattern are filtered out, since they represent alternative correct usages of the same API. Hence they don't represent an API misuse.
3. After identifying all potential misuses in the target source code, the detection algorithm ranks the findings using different ranking strategies. Some of these ranking strategies come from the literature [14,20,27,35,36,38,39], and others

are generated as combinations of the individual ranking factors by multiplication. The following ranking factors are considered: pattern support, number of pattern violations, the pattern uniqueness factor, violation support and the violation overlap. Since it is unclear which of these strategies is useful, they are evaluated empirically.

4. To avoid reporting duplicate misuses (i.e. usages that violate alternative correct usages of the same API), the algorithm filters out misuses involving a method call that is part of another misuse listed with a higher rank.

4 Experimental Setup

This section describes the data sets we use, presents the analyses of the frequency and entropy thresholds for the episode mining algorithm, defines the metrics for the empirical comparison between the different pattern types, and present the setup we use to assess EMDetect ability to detect API misuses in the different mining configurations.

4.1 Data Sets

C# Data Set. We use an established dataset that consists of a curated collection of $2,857$ C# solutions extracted from 360 GitHub repositories [30] with a total of $68M$ lines of source code covering a wide range of applications and project sizes that provide many examples for API usages. The data set uses a specialized AST-like representation of source code with fully-qualified type references and elements. This relieves us from the burden of compiling it to get resolved typing information and makes it easier to transform the source code into the event stream.[2]

We find $138K$ type declarations in the dataset that extend a base class or implement an interface. These type declarations contain $50K$ method declaration (first context plus super context), which override or implement a method declaration introduced in a dependency. The same dependency can be used in other projects, so focusing on these reusable methods provides valuable context information for the API usages. We find $2M$ method invocations across all method bodies of the data set.

Java Data Set. For evaluating EMDetect in terms of both precision and recall, we need an annotated data set of correct and incorrect API usages. To the best of our knowledge, such a data set does not exist for C# code, that's why we need to extend our benchmark [10] to support another programming language for which there exists a ground-truth of known API misuses. We chose to use MUBench [8] as our ground-truth, which contains API method call misuses with examples of correct usages, derived from the fix of the corresponding misuse. The API method call misuses come from real-world Java projects. Furthermore, MUBench comes

---

[2] We use the visitors in the dataset for the transformation.

with MUBenchPipe [6], a public automated benchmarking pipeline built on top of MUBench. MUBenchPipe reveals us from the burden of preparing the target projects and executing the detector, since everything is already integrated into the automated, publicly available pipeline.

4.2 Frequency and Entropy Thresholds

The episode mining algorithm uses two thresholds: *frequency* and *entropy*. The threshold values directly impact the number of patterns learned (higher threshold values means stronger evidence in the source code that a given pattern occurs), and as a consequence also the performance of the misuse detector (according to the patterns learned, the detector may or may not identify misuses in the source code). In this section, we show how we empirically evaluate the effects of the threshold values on the application context of misuse detection. Details about the threshold analyzes for the empirical comparison of the different patterns types can be found in [10].

In the application context of misuse detection, we empirically evaluate the effect of frequency and entropy thresholds on the performance of EMDetect in terms of: (1) The number of misuses detected, based on the ground truth of known method call misuses that we have on the Java projects. (2) The performance of the ranking algorithm (presented in Sect. 3.3) on ranking true positives on top of the list of findings.

Initial Analyzes: Given that we have to analyze the findings of the detector manually, we perform our analyzes for the frequency and entropy thresholds on one Java project from MUBench. For this we chose the one with the highest number of the method call misuses. After fixing the Java project (*initial*) on which we perform our threshold analyzes on, we choose an arbitrary value for the frequency threshold, and analyze the effect of different entropy thresholds on the performance of the detector. After defining the optimal entropy threshold, we repeat our analyzes to study the effect of the different frequency values. Our analyzes reveal an optimal frequency threshold of 20, and entropy threshold of 0.4 for the *initial* project we perform our analyzes on.

Automating for Different Projects. Since different projects have different sizes (number of events), the frequency threshold highly influences the number of patterns learned in each project. For this reason, we decided to automate the calculation of the frequency threshold according to the project sizes. For this we considered the total number of events, the number of unique events, and the average occurrences of events in each of the projects. According to our analyzes, the best function for this calculation resulted the one that compares a *target* project with the *initial* project, on the average occurrence of events. The function used for calculating frequency threshold in every project:

$$frequency = \left(1 + \frac{avg.Target}{avg.Initial}\right) * InitialFreq \tag{1}$$

where *avg. Target* and *avg.Initial* is the average occurrence of events in the target and initial project respectively, and *InitialFreq* is the frequency threshold used in the initial project. The output of this function we round up to the 5th closest integer, for example if the function outputs either 22.2 or 24.8 they are both rounded up to 25.

4.3   Metrics for Pattern Comparison

We define the following metrics to quantify different properties of the mined patterns in our empirical comparison of different pattern types.

Expressiveness. Using a formal language terminology, an API usage pattern can be seen as a *grammar rule* of a language over an *alphabet* of method declaration/invocation (events). The more words the sub-language it defines has, the more expressive a pattern is. A *sequential-order* pattern $(a \to b \to c)$ when seen as a grammar rule defines a language with a single word $\{abc\}$. A *partial-order* pattern $(a \to (b, c))$ defines a language with two words, $\{abc, acb\}$. A *no-oder* pattern (a, b, c) defines a language with six words $\{abc, acb, bac, bca, cab, cba\}$. The expressiveness of a pattern type is determined by the number of patterns (grammar rules) it defines, and how well these patterns abstract over the variety of concrete API usages observed in source code.

To investigate how the three configurations (SOC, POC, and NOC) compare to each other in terms of expressiveness, we calculate three metrics for each configuration pair (c1, c2): (a) `exact(c1,c2)` is the number of patterns that are exactly the same in c1 and c2; (b) `subsumed(c1,c2)` = (x,y) is a pair that represents the number of patterns x learned by c1 that subsume y patterns learned by c2. We say that a pattern $p1$ subsumes a pattern $p2$ iff they relate the same set of events and all words defined by $p2$ are also defined by $p1$, e.g. the grammar rule of a no-order pattern (a, b, c) subsumes both the grammar rules $(a \to (b, c))$ and $(a \to b \to c)$ from the partial and sequential-order patterns respectively; (c) `new(c1,c2)` is the number of patterns learned by c1 that include events for which c2 does not learn any pattern.

Consistency. The three pattern types differ in the extent to which they preserve code structure. While *no-order* patterns cannot represent any structure, *sequential-order* patterns can encode an absolute order of events, and *partial-order* patterns can even represent complex control flow that is imposed by control structures like `if`. We establish the *consistency* metric as a way to quantify how important the order information encoded by sequential-order and partial-order patterns is in practice. The metric takes values in $]0.0, 1.0]$, and is defined as the ratio of number of occurrences of a pattern p and the number of co-occurrences of events in p regardless of their order. A high consistency emphasizes the importance of the encoded order. A low consistency means that in most cases, the respective code elements occur in an order different to the one encoded in the pattern, suggesting that the structural information encoded by the pattern is irrelevant.

Generalizability. Finding instances of a pattern in multiple contexts indicates that the pattern represents an abstraction over a set of similar API usages, e.g., used by multiple developers. On the other hand, a very *local* pattern might suggest that it does not generalize beyond a specific context, e.g., it might only be used by a specific developer. To quantify the *generalizability* of a pattern, we count the number of contexts in which we can observe it at two different levels of granularity that complement each other: (a) The *method declaration* level measures whether instances of a pattern are found within a single method declaration (the latter refers to the highest declaration in the type hierarchy that originally introduced the current method signature) or across method declarations (method-specific versus cross-method pattern). (b) The *code repository* level measures whether instances of a pattern are found in one or in multiple repositories (repository-specific versus cross-repository pattern). Knowledge about the generalizability of patterns is important for judging the versatility of the pattern in later applications.

4.4   EMDetect Experimental Setup

We evaluate EMDetect performance on both precision and recall. For the evaluations, we use an entropy threshold of $e = 0.4$, and varying frequency threshold according to project sizes as presented in Sect. 4.2. We run the experiments using MUBenchPipe [6], a public automated benchmarking pipeline built on top of MUBench [8], containing the ground-truth data set. Since the patterns mined by the episode mining configurations consist of events that correspond to method calls and method declarations only, we run EMDetect on a subset of projects from MUBench that contain API method call misuses. Since we compare the performance of EMDetect with state of the art detectors presented in Sect. 2.3, we apply a second filter on the projects to select the one that are also used by Amann et al. in [6]. This left us with a total of four Java projects. The first author reviewed the detector findings, in order to decide whether the findings correctly identify misuses. We introduce the experiments in more detail in the following paragraphs.

Recall. We run EMDetect on four projects from MUBench (containing API method call misuses and used in [6]), and on the different mining configurations. Following the same evaluation logic as in [6], we detect violations on a per-project basis. Then, we manually review all potential hits. As the ground truth, we use the known API method call misuses from MUBench. We report the number of misuses identified by each of our mining configurations. This gives us the recall of the detector with respect to known misuses and, at the same time, crosscheck which of the mining configurations' findings are also identified by the other configurations and/or by the state of the art detectors.

Precision. We run the detector on the four projects from MUBench, to mine patterns and detect violations on a per-project basis, and on the different mining configurations. Since EMDetect reports several hundreds of violations, reviewing all violations of all mining configurations and on four projects is practically infeasible. Therefore, we review the top-20 findings per configuration on each of the projects, as determined by the ranking algorithm to identify true and false positives. The new true positives found that are not part of the ground-truth, are candidates to be included in MUBench.

5   Empirical Comparison of Pattern Types

This section presents the results of our experiments for the empirical comparison for the different pattern types. In the empirical comparison, all experiments are performed with a frequency threshold of 345. For *POC*, we use an entropy threshold of 0.72 (as evaluated in [10]). First, we show statistics about the learned patterns, and then study them along the dimensions presented in Sect. 4.3.

5.1   Pattern Statistics

Our approach learns patterns with up to 7 events in each configuration in the C# data set, and with up to 8 events in the Java data set. The number of patterns learned decreases for larger pattern sizes with the same ratio in each configuration. Almost all mined patterns (97%) involve 5 events or less. The result matches the intuition that it is less probable that many developers write large code snippets in exactly the same way.

All the patterns learned, 75% in C# and 99% in Java, involve interactions between events from multiple API types (across configurations). In C# data set, only 28% of the patterns with 2–4 events involve interactions between events from a single API type, while all patterns with 5 or more events involve multiple API types. The maximum number of API types involved within a pattern is 5 types in C# and 6 types in Java code. In C# data set patterns involving two API types make the majority (40%), while in Java data set this majority is made by patterns involving 4 and 5 API types with 80%.

5.2   Evaluation Results

This section presents an overview of the empirical comparison for the different pattern types in terms of the three predefined dimensions: expressiveness, consistency and generalizability. The experimental results are presented for the C# data set, and the number of patterns learned by each configuration are: *POC* $1,234$, *SOC* $1,204$ and *NOC* 981. For more details, please refer to [10].

Expressiveness. Quantifies the richness of the language corresponding to a pattern type, whose grammar rules are the mined patterns.

POC vs. SOC. 70% of the patterns learned by the partial order configuration (exact(POC, SOC) = 858), define a strict order between the events. This metric defines the following observation.

> **Observation 5.1**
> Most of the API usage patterns define in the wild strict-order between events (70%), while the other 30% abstract over different API usage variants.

Furthermore, subsumed(POC, SOC) = $(260;346)$. The 260 partial-order patterns encode 572 different sequences, i.e., the 346 sequences mined by SOC plus 226 others. Recall that multiple sequential-order patterns can be represented by a single partial-order pattern. Finally, new(POC, SOC) = 116, meaning that for the events included in 116 partial-order patterns, there are no sequences learned by SOC. From these results, we can conclude that:

> **Observation 5.2**
> The API usage specifications encoded by partial-order patterns fully represent the specifications encoded by sequential-order patterns. Furthermore, they learn 116 additional patterns of events for which sequence mining cannot learn any sequence for.

NOC vs. POC. 20% of the patterns learned by partial-order configuration, define no-order between events: exact(NOC, POC) = 248. Recall that no-order patterns are mined in POC when the involved events occur often enough in either order.

> **Observation 5.3**
> In 20% of the cases, partial-order patterns encode events that occur in either order in the wild.

Furthermore, subsumed(NOC, POC) = $(716; 986)$. Note that one no-order pattern simplifies several partial-order patterns that misses order information. Finally, new(NOC, POC) = 17. These patterns are missed by POC because either: (a) none of the sequences between the events occur frequently enough, recall that sequences are a special case of partial-order patterns, and/or (b) there is not enough evidence in the source code that events occur frequently enough in either order (specified by entropy threshold). From these results we can conclude that no-order patterns represent a superset of partial-order patterns.

NOC vs. SOC. Since NOC learns only set of events and SOC learns only strict-order sequences, there are no overlap between the patterns learned by these two configurations. We find that subsumed(NOC, SOC) = $(853; 1,204)$. Note that multiple sequential-order patterns can be simplified into a single no-order pattern by removing order constraints. Finally, new(NOC, SOC) = 128.

> **Observation 5.4**
> No-order patterns match all sequential-order patterns; furthermore, the no-order configuration learns 128 additional patterns for which sequential-order configuration could not learn any sequence for.

Consistency. Based on the expressiveness dimension results, one may conclude that no-order patterns define a richer language compared to the other two types. The question raises: Why should one use expensive mining approaches (sequence or partial mining), if we can learn a richer language from source code using less computationally expensive mining approaches such as frequent itemset mining? However, this would be a valid conclusion, only if the words in the language mined by NOC are valid, i.e., the order between events in a pattern does not really matter. To analyze this, we investigate the consistency of the mined sequential and partial-order patterns with co-occurrences of events in code.

Our results reveal high consistency in sequential (avg. 0.9) and partial-order patterns (avg. 0.96). This suggests that order information encoded in both sequential and partial-order patterns is crucial for the correct co-occurrences of events in the wild, and simplifying them into no-order patterns will result in losing important order information between events.

Observation 5.5
Partial and sequential-order mining learn important order information regarding co-occurrences of events within a pattern.

Based on this observation, we will perform the empirical evaluation of `EMDetect` in Sect. 7 only on sequential and partial-order patterns, since no-order patterns do not encode any code structure which is crucial for source code representation.

Generalizability. Here, we present the generalizability metric results on two granularity levels as explained in Sect. 4.3: method declaration and code repository.

Method Declaration. Our results empirically show that most of the patterns learned (98%) by each configuration, are used across method declarations. If a pattern occurs across method declarations, it means that it generalizes to different implementation tasks.

Observation 5.6
Most of the patterns learned find applicability to a large variety of implementation tasks.

Next we analyze if the patterns learned are used by multiple developers, or if they represent specific coding styles for a given repository and its developers.

Code Repository. Our results show that the patterns learned by *POC* and *SOC* have almost the same percentage of generalizability (48% vs. 47%), regardless of their size. This means that more than half the patterns mined by each configuration are learned from API usages from the same repository. While such repository-specific patterns are useful to the developers of that particular repository, they may reflect a very specific way of using certain API types, which may not be useful to a general set of developers. On the other hand, *NOC* learns slightly more general patterns (58%). However, recall that these more generalizable patterns come at the cost of missing order information between events.

Observation 5.7

No-order patterns tend to be more generalizable (58%) compared to sequential and partial-order patterns (47% and 48%), which tend to be over-specified due to the order constraints they encode.

We analyzed the patterns learned exclusively by *POC* (new(*POC,SOC*)), and found that 114 out of 116 patterns are general patterns used across repositories. To find out why most of the patterns learned exclusively by *POC* are general patterns, we check if there is any relation between generalizability and pattern-order. We find that strict-order patterns (exact(*POC, SOC*)) are less generalizable (37%) compared to patterns that contain partial-order between events (*subsumed* - 62%, and *new* - 98%). This confirms our hypothesis that there is a relation between generalizability and pattern-order. Furthermore, most of the patterns (90%) learned exclusively by *POC* include method calls only from the standard library, which further explains their generalizability.

Across configurations, the percentage of general patterns learned is higher for smaller patterns, and significantly decreases for bigger patterns. Furthermore, for patterns with 6-events and more, we learn only repository-specific patterns. Specifically, around 70% of general patterns (independent of the configuration) are 2 and 3-event patterns. Most of the patterns with 4-events or more are repository-specific patterns. This makes sense since the probability that multiple developers with different coding styles and different application domains writing a similar and long piece of code is very low.

Observation 5.8

Small code patterns of 2 and 3 events are more generalizable compared to larger code patterns of 4 or more events that mainly encode constraints of API usages from a single repository.

We further analyzed the repository-specific patterns and found that 93% of them are learned from testing code, and they include API types that refer to an old version of a common assembly that is used in no other repository. Filtering out testing code may help mining algorithms learn only general patterns. An empirical validation of this hypothesis, however, needs to be performed in the future.

Remark: For the sake of completeness, we experimented with other threshold values (frequency and entropy), and analyzed the generalizability of the patterns across repositories. The results we received did not show higher generalizability ratios in neither of the pattern types, compared to the ones presented above. This confirms the correctness of the threshold values selected as presented in [10].

6 Implications

Based on the pattern statistics (Sect. 5.1) and results in Sect. 5.2, we derive the following:

Implication 1 (derived from Sect. 5.1). Mining techniques based on frequency occurrence of source code in code bases are unlikely to learn large code patterns (more than 7 method calls using our concrete parameters), since it is less probable that developers write large code snippets exactly in the same way. If the main goal is to learn large code patterns, then other techniques need to be considered.

Implication 2 (derived from Sect. 5.1). Code analyses techniques should consider interactions between objects of different API types, while extracting facts from source code. Even though these analyses are expensive since data-flow dependencies need to be considered, they are important in mining relevant patterns from source code.

Implication 3 (derived from Observations 5.1 and 5.5). While covering a good amount of usages seen in source code, sequential-order mining may lead to false positives in applications such as misuse detection. For example, if the pattern is $a \to (b, c)$, but a strict-order pattern has only learned $a \to b \to c$ and the code written by the developer is $a \to c \to b$. On the other hand, while no-order mining might seem to learn a larger variety of API usages in source code, it might result in false negatives in such applications. Following the same example, the developer might have written $b \to a \to c$, and a no-order pattern cannot detect that b and c should occur strictly after a. We can conclude that, partial-order mining learns better API usage patterns for such applications.

Implication 4 (derived from Observation 5.2). Partial-order mining might be more appropriate for learning API usage patterns in applications such as code recommendation since multiple sequences can be represented by a single partial-order pattern, decreasing the total number of patterns that need to be part of the model. In sequence mining, multiple patterns need to be recommended to the developer for the same set of events and might even risk missing valid sequences if they do not occur frequently enough in the training source code.

Implication 5 (derived from Observation 5.5). Before deciding which mining approach to use in a specific application, developers need to know their trade-offs in terms of order information and computation complexity. Sequential and partial-order mining are computationally expensive approaches but learn important order information about the co-occurrence of events in a pattern, while no-order mining approaches do not require expensive computations but on the other hand do not learn any order information about the co-occurrence of events in a pattern.

Implication 6 (derived from Observation 5.8). If the main goal is to learn large code patterns (4–7 events), then recommenders should focus on a repository-specific mining approach and produce catered recommendations to the repository's developers. However, if the goal is to learn general patterns that can be used by many developers, then researchers should know that they might end up mining small patterns (2 and 3 events).

Table 1. Precision measured in the top-20 findings.

Detector	Precision		Recall	
	True positives	%	True positives	%
$EMDetect_{POC}$	3	3.8%	8	42.1%
$EMDetect_{SOC}$	12	15%	5	26.3%
$DMMC$	2	3.3%	3	15.8%
$JADET$	4	7.7%	8	42.1%
$GROUMiner$	3	3.3%	7	36.8%
$TIKANGA$	2	5%	2	10.5%

7   EMDetect Evaluation Results

In this section, we present the results of our experiments for comparing sequential and partial-order patterns in the application context of API method call
misuse detection. We use our misuse detector (`EMDetect`) to compare the pattern types in terms of both precision and recall. The experiments in this section
are performed on the Java data set, using MUBench [8] as a ground-truth of
correct and in-correct API usages for evaluating the detector performance. For
the sake of completeness, we compare the performance of `EMDetect` also with
the other 4 misuse detectors studied by Amann et al. [6]. For evaluating the
detectors, we consider the same set of projects as used in [6] and select the ones
that contain API method call misuses. This let us with a total of 4 Java projects
to perform our evaluations on: bcel, chensum, jigsaw and testing.

7.1   Precision

The first part of Table 1 summarizes the results of measuring the detectors'
precision in their top-20 findings.

Observation 7.1
$EMDetect_{POC}$ report 80 violations in the top-20 findings in four projects.
Among these violations, we find three true positives, two of which were previously unknown. This results in precision of 3.8%, which exceeds the precision
of 2 of the detectors from the literature.

Observation 7.2
$EMDetect_{SOC}$ report 80 violations in the top-20 findings in four project.
Among these violations, we find 12 true positives, 9 of which were previously
unknown. This results in precision of 15%, which exceeds the precision of all
detectors from the literature.

The two observations above show that $EMDetect_{SOC}$ performs better in terms of precision compared to $EMDetect_{POC}$, by ranking more true positives in the top-20 findings. This comes due to: (1) higher number of patterns learned by POC compared to SOC as we found in Observation 5.2, and (2) missing of the order information between some of the events in partial-order patterns. The higher number of patterns means that more false positives are ranked in the top-20 findings, while the missing of the order information impacts the matching algorithm, which is based on nodes (method calls) and edges (order information).

7.2 Recall

For measuring the detectors's recall, we use 19 publicly available method call misuses from the four filtered projects from MUBench. The last part of Table 1 summarizes the results.

Observation 7.3
$EMDetect_{POC}$ identifies 8 out of the 19 known misuses, which results in recall of 42.1%. This result exceeds the recall of three out of four detectors from the literature, except for JADET, which performs the same.

Observation 7.4
$EMDetect_{SOC}$ identifies 5 out of the 19 known misuses, which results in recall of 26.3%. This result exceeds the recall of two out of four detectors from the literature.

The two observations above show that $EMDetect_{POC}$ performs better in terms of recall compared to $EMDetect_{SOC}$, by finding more known misuses from our ground-truth data set. This comes due to the fact that POC abstracts over several usages in the source code, which increases the patterns support. On the other hand SOC learns only sequences of method calls and, when a given sequence does not occur often enough, it is missed by the learning algorithm.

$EMDetect_{POC}$ correctly identifies three misuses that $EMDetect_{SOC}$ does not identify, and one misuse that none of the detectors from the literature nor $EMDetect_{SOC}$ identifies. $EMDetect_{POC}$ misses 8 misuses that one of the detectors from the literature finds. Three of these misuses are missed, because the projects contain few usage examples compared to the frequency threshold used by MUDetect for the pattern mining algorithm. Four of these misuses are missed because they contain a missing call in case an exception occurs. Since MUDetect does not handle exception conditions (it only identifies if a method is missing or not in the target code), it fails in identifying such cases. One of these misuses is missed due to the matching algorithm.

7.3 Discussion

Our evaluation results in the application context of misuse detection show that $EMDetect_{SOC}$ performs better in term of precision by ranking true positives higher in the top-20 findings, while $EMDetect_{POC}$ outperforms $EMDetect_{SOC}$ in terms of recall, since it is able to abstract over several API usages with low occurrence making SOC fail in learning such patterns.

Compared to the other four detectors from the literature, we can conclude that $EMDetect_{SOC}$ outperforms all of them in terms of precision by at least 2 times, and $EMDetect_{POC}$ performs better (DMMC, GrouMiner and Tikanga) or the same (JADET) in terms of recall. Depending on whether we give higher priority to either precision or recall, we can decide on the mining approach to use, either POC or SOC. Our results also show that it is possible to outperform other detectors in the literature with a general purpose machine learning approach (EMDetect) that does not require much domain-specific tuning.

8 Threats to Validity

Internal Validity. We generate the event stream based on static analyses, not on dynamic execution traces. Even though this may not represent valid execution traces, it does represent how the code is written by developers. In this paper, we focus on learning code patterns to represent source code as it is written in code editors. Also, our event stream considers only intra-procedural analysis since we are interested to learn patterns that occur within methods.

The episode mining algorithm learns only *injective* episodes, where all events are distinct, i.e., the algorithm does not handle multiple occurrences of the same event in a pattern. For example, method invocations: `IEnumerator.MoveNext()` or `StringBuilder.Append()` are usually called multiple times in the code. The patterns we learn contain a single instance of such events. While this is a limitation, it is also an advantage in terms of pattern generalizability. Specifically, the mined pattern would not have a strict number of occurrences that would lead to mismatches because of the difference in the number of occurrences.

The algorithm relies on user-defined parameters: frequency-threshold, entropy-threshold. While the configuration parameter depends on the type of patterns one is interested in, deciding on adequate frequency and entropy thresholds is not an easy task, which affect the results. We mitigate this threat by empirically evaluating the thresholds and choosing the best combination of frequency and entropy thresholds for the given data set (cf. Sect. 4.2).

The episode mining algorithm is available only in a sequential (non-parallelized) implementation, hence is inefficient. However, this paper does not advocate using episode mining per se, but rather uses it as a baseline for comparing different configurations. This limitation can be improved by parallelizing the algorithm's implementation.

External Validity. We learn code patterns only for *method declarations* and *invocations*, excluding all other code structures such as *loops, conditions, exceptions* etc. This is because the focus of this paper is on comparing different code pattern types (sequential, partial, and no-order), instead of specifically learning complex patterns that include all code structures. Since learning code patterns while considering other code structures is important for supporting certain development tasks, we plan to enrich the code patterns that we learn with additional code structures. This requires modifying our event stream generation, which is an engineering task rather than a conceptual limitation.

Finally, we analyze the trade-offs between different pattern types based on two data sets. We also use a single learning algorithm that we configure to produce different pattern types. However, we cannot generalize our results beyond our current datasets and learning algorithm.

9   Conclusions

In this paper, we extend the benchmark presented in [10] for analyzing the trade-offs between different pattern types (sequential, partial and no-order) with respect to real code. The extended benchmark consist of the following components: (1) Two data sets providing support for two different programming languages, C# and Java. (2) An adaptation of an event mining algorithm to the special context of pattern mining for software engineering. (3) Three well defined metrics, on which we base the empirical comparison between the different pattern types. (4) EMDetect to evaluate the effectiveness of the different pattern types within the application context of misuse detection.

Our empirical investigation shows that there are different types of patterns learned in code repositories. While there are tradeoffs between pattern types in terms of *expressiveness, consistency* and *generalizability*, they are comparable in terms of the patterns size and number of API types. Our results empirically show that the *sweet spot* in representing source code are *partial-order* patterns, which are a superset of *sequential-order* patterns, without losing valuable information like *no-order* patterns. Partial-order mining learns additional patterns compared to sequence mining, which generalize across repositories. In the application context of misuses detection, this results in better performance of partial-order patterns ($EMDetect_{POC}$) in terms of recall, but very low precision compared to sequential-order patterns ($EMDetect_{SOC}$). Compared to other detectors from the literature, ($EMDetect_{SOC}$) outperforms all of them in terms of precision, and ($EMDetect_{POC}$) performs the same (compared to Jadet) or better (compared to three others) in terms of recall in the typical per-project setting.

Our findings are useful indications for researchers who work with code patterns in applications of code recommendation and misuse detection.

References

1. Achar, A., Laxman, S., Viswanathan, R., Sastry, P.: Discovering injective episodes with general partial orders. Data Min. Knowl. Disc. **25**, 67–108 (2012)
2. Achar, A., Sastry, P.: Statistical significance of episodes with general partial orders. Inf. Sci. **296**, 175–200 (2015)

3. Acharya, M., Xie, T.: Mining API error-handling specifications from source code. In: Chechik, M., Wirsing, M. (eds.) FASE 2009. LNCS, vol. 5503, pp. 370–384. Springer, Heidelberg (2009). https://doi.org/10.1007/978-3-642-00593-0_25
4. Acharya, M., Xie, T., Pei, J., Xu, J.: Mining API patterns as partial orders from source code: from usage scenarios to specifications. In: European Software Engineering Conference and the ACM SIGSOFT Symposium on the Foundations of Software Engineering, pp. 25–34 (2007)
5. Agrawal, R., Imieliński, T., Swami, A.: Mining association rules between sets of items in large databases. In: ACM SIGMOD, pp. 207–216 (1993)
6. Amann, S., Nguyen, H.A., Nadi, S., Nguyen, T.N., Mezini, M.: A systematic evaluation of static API-misuse detectors. IEEE Trans. Softw. Eng. 1–1 (2018). abs/1712.00242
7. Amann, S.: A systematic approach to benchmark and improve automated static detection of Java-API misuses. Ph.D. thesis, Darmstadt University of Technology, Germany (2018)
8. Amann, S., Nadi, S., Nguyen, H.A., Nguyen, T.N., Mezini, M.: Mubench: a benchmark for API-misuse detectors. In: International Conference on Mining Software Repositories, pp. 464–467 (2016)
9. Buse, R.P., Weimer, W.: Synthesizing API usage examples. In: Proceedings of the 34th International Conference on Software Engineering, pp. 782–792. IEEE Press (2012)
10. Çergani, E., Proksch, S., Nadi, S., Mezini, M.: Investigating order information in API-usage patterns: a benchmark and empirical study. In: International Conference on Software Technologies, ICSOFT 2018, Porto, Portugal, 26–28 July 2018, pp. 91–102 (2018)
11. De Roover, C., Lammel, R., Pek, E.: Multi-dimensional exploration of API usage. In: 2013 IEEE 21st International Conference on Program Comprehension (ICPC), pp. 152–161. IEEE (2013)
12. Gabel, M., Su, Z.: Javert: fully automatic mining of general temporal properties from dynamic traces. In: ACM SIGSOFT International Symposium on Foundations of Software Engineering, pp. 339–349 (2008)
13. Haase, J., Brefeld, U.: Mining positional data streams. In: Appice, A., Ceci, M., Loglisci, C., Manco, G., Masciari, E., Ras, Z.W. (eds.) NFMCP 2014. LNCS (LNAI), vol. 8983, pp. 102–116. Springer, Cham (2015). https://doi.org/10.1007/978-3-319-17876-9_7
14. Li, Z., Zhou, Y.: PR-Miner: automatically extracting implicit programming rules and detecting violations in large software code. In: ACM SIGSOFT Software Engineering Notes, pp. 306–315 (2005)
15. Ma, H., Amor, R., Tempero, E.: Usage patterns of the java standard API. In: Software Engineering Conference 2006, pp. 342–352 (2006)
16. Mannila, H., Toivonen, H., Inkeri Verkamo, A.: Discovery of frequent episodes in event sequences. Data Min. Knowl. Discov. 1, 259–289 (1997)
17. Martin, R.C.: Agile Software Development: Principles, Patterns, and Practices. Prentice Hall PTR, Upper Saddle River (2003)
18. Mendez, D., Baudry, B., Monperrus, M.: Empirical evidence of large-scale diversity in API usage of object-oriented software. In: Source Code Analysis and Manipulation, pp. 43–52 (2013)
19. Michail, A.: Data mining library reuse patterns using generalized association rules. In: International Conference on Software Engineering, pp. 167–176 (2000)
20. Monperrus, M., Mezini, M.: Detecting missing method calls as violations of the majority rule. ACM Trans. Softw. Eng. Methodol. (TOSEM) 22(1), 7 (2013)

21. Montandon, J.E., Borges, H., Felix, D., Valente, M.T.: Documenting APIs with examples: lessons learned with the APIMiner platform. In: WCRE, pp. 401–408 (2013)
22. Negara, S., Codoban, M., Dig, D., Johnson, R.E.: Mining fine-grained code changes to detect unknown change patterns. In: International Conference on Software Engineering, pp. 803–813 (2014)
23. Nguyen, A.T., et al.: API code recommendation using statistical learning from fine-grained changes. In: ACM SIGSOFT International Symposium on Foundations of Software Engineering, pp. 511–522 (2016)
24. Nguyen, A.T., Nguyen, T.N.: Graph-based statistical language model for code. In: International Conference on Software Engineering, pp. 858–868 (2015)
25. Nguyen, A.T., et al.: Graph-based pattern-oriented, context-sensitive source code completion. In: International Conference on Software Engineering, pp. 69–79 (2012)
26. Nguyen, H.V., Nguyen, H.A., Nguyen, A.T., Nguyen, T.N.: Mining interprocedural, data-oriented usage patterns in javascript web applications. In: International Conference on Software Engineering, pp. 791–802 (2014)
27. Nguyen, T.T., Nguyen, H.A., Pham, N.H., Al-Kofahi, J.M., Nguyen, T.N.: Graph-based mining of multiple object usage patterns. In: Proceedings of the the 7th Joint Meeting of the European Software Engineering Conference and the ACM SIGSOFT Symposium on the Foundations of Software Engineering, pp. 383–392. ACM (2009)
28. Pham, H.V., Vu, P.M., Nguyen, T.T., et al.: Learning API usages from bytecode: a statistical approach. In: International Conference on Software Engineering, pp. 416–427 (2016)
29. Pradel, M., Bichsel, P., Gross, T.R.: A framework for the evaluation of specification miners based on finite state machines. In: IEEE International Conference on Software Maintenance, pp. 1–10 (2010)
30. Proksch, S., Amann, S., Nadi, S., Mezini, M.: A dataset of simplified syntax trees for c#. In: International Conference on Mining Software Repositories, pp. 476–479 (2016)
31. Qiu, D., Li, B., Leung, H.: Understanding the API usage in java. Inf. Softw. Technol. **73**, 81–100 (2016)
32. Ramanathan, M.K., Grama, A., Jagannathan, S.: Path-sensitive inference of function precedence protocols. In: International Conference on Software Engineering, pp. 240–250 (2007)
33. Raychev, V., Vechev, M., Yahav, E.: Code completion with statistical language models. In: ACM SIGPLAN Notices, pp. 419–428 (2014)
34. Robillard, M.P., Bodden, E., Kawrykow, D., Mezini, M., Ratchford, T.: Automated API property inference techniques. IEEE Trans. Softw. Eng. **39**, 613–637 (2013)
35. Thummalapenta, S., Xie, T.: Alattin: Mining alternative patterns for detecting neglected conditions. In: International Conference on Automated Software Engineering, pp. 283–294 (2009)
36. Thummalapenta, S., Xie, T.: Mining exception-handling rules as sequence association rules. In: Proceedings of the 31st International Conference on Software Engineering, pp. 496–506. IEEE Computer Society (2009)
37. Wang, J., Dang, Y., Zhang, H., Chen, K., Xie, T., Zhang, D.: Mining succinct and high-coverage API usage patterns from source code. In: Proceedings of the 10th Working Conference on Mining Software Repositories, pp. 319–328. IEEE Press (2013)
38. Wasylkowski, A., Zeller, A.: Mining temporal specifications from object usage. Autom. Softw. Eng. **18**(3), 263–292 (2011)

39. Wasylkowski, A., Zeller, A., Lindig, C.: Detecting object usage anomalies. In: European Software Engineering Conference and the ACM SIGSOFT Symposium on The Foundations of Software Engineering, pp. 35–44 (2007)
40. Zhong, H., Mei, H.: An empirical study on API usages. IEEE Trans. Softw. Eng. **45**, 319–334 (2018)
41. Zhong, H., Xie, T., Zhang, L., Pei, J., Mei, H.: MAPO: mining and recommending API usage patterns. In: Drossopoulou, S. (ed.) ECOOP 2009. LNCS, vol. 5653, pp. 318–343. Springer, Heidelberg (2009). https://doi.org/10.1007/978-3-642-03013-0_15
42. Zhong, H., Zhang, L., Xie, T., Mei, H.: Inferring resource specifications from natural language API documentation. In: International Conference on Automated Software Engineering, pp. 307–318 (2009)

A Practical Approach for Constraint Solving in Model Transformations

Youness Laghouaouta[(✉)] and Pierre Laforcade

Computer Science Laboratory of Le Mans University, Le Mans, France
{youness.laghouaouta,pierre.laforcade}@univ-lemans.fr

Abstract. In model transformation scenarios, expressing a Constraint Satisfaction Problem (CSP) is a complex and error prone activity. Indeed, transformation techniques do not provide fully integrated supports for solving constraints, and external solvers are not well adapted. This chapter presents a practical approach for constraint solving in model transformations. The base principle is to consider a pattern matching problem as a high level specification of a CSP. Besides, a transformation infrastructure that underpins the conceptual proposal can be generated in a semi-automatic manner. This infrastructure provides support for pattern specification, match model search, and transformation into valid target models. An application case extracted from the *Escape It!* serious game has been selected to illustrate our contribution.

Keywords: Model driven engineering · Model transformation ·
Pattern matching · Constraint satisfaction problem

1 Introduction

In Model Driven Engineering (MDE), the primary focus is on models rather than computing concepts. Models represent all artifacts handled by a software development process and can be used as first class entities in dedicated model management operations (e.g. model transformation, model composition, model validation...).

The model transformation operation is a pillar of MDE. It underpins the automatic generation of target models from source ones (i.e. generally higher level models). The managed models conform to the metamodels that define the structure and well-formedness rules. Besides, a transformation specification/definition includes descriptions of how constructs of source metamodels can be transformed into constructs of target metamodels [15]. Several related techniques have been proposed to provide developers with supports to implement transformation scenarios (e.g. [6,11,16]).

The obtained target models have to conform to the structuring defined by the implied metamodel and satisfy all the related constraints. In practice, constraints cannot be expressed by means of metamodel constructs and require the use of additional formalisms (e.g. OCL [17]). Likewise, model transformation

© Springer Nature Switzerland AG 2019
M. van Sinderen and L. A. Maciaszek (Eds.): ICSOFT 2018, CCIS 1077, pp. 104–123, 2019.
https://doi.org/10.1007/978-3-030-29157-0_5

techniques are not well supported for enforcing all constraints. Indeed, developers are constrained to use external constraint solvers or libraries.

However, expressing a Constraint Satisfaction Problem (CSP) is a complex and error prone activity. This is due to the fact that constraint solvers support numeric values while model transformations are expressed by means of model elements. Hence, developers are faced with the two domains divergence and have to establish and manage non evident mappings between these domains.

Our contribution is then a practical constraint solving approach for model transformations. The objective is to allow enforcing constraints on target models while simplifying the expression of the constraint based problem. To this aim, a CSP is considered as a pattern matching problem specified by means of model elements. Besides, the pattern matching is included in a global process that allows producing the expected target models of a given transformation scenario. In [13], we have presented the base principles of the proposed approach and provided the primary results. The current chapter extends this work and focuses on parametric patterns.

The remainder of this chapter is structured as follows. In Sect. 2, we present the context of this research work and motivate the need for a practical constraint solving approach for model transformations. Section 3 gives a global overview of the proposed approach, while Sect. 4 focuses on implementation details. In Sect. 5, we demonstrate the soundness of our approach using an illustrative transformation scenario. Section 5 lists related work. Finally, Sect. 6 summarizes this chapter and presents future work.

2   Motivation

This research work is conducted in the context of the *Escape it!* project. The objective is to develop a serious game to train visual skills of children with ASD (Autistic Syndrome Disorder). Given the specific needs of autistic children, it was crucial to involve ASD experts in the first development stage. The aim is to guarantee that the proposed game fits to ASD characteristics while being individually adaptive to each child.

MDE provides principles and techniques that allow domain experts to take part of the design activity and guide the development of the game. Indeed, the domain elements (i.e. children profiles, game components and game scenarios) can be expressed in a high level of abstraction so that the implication of domain experts does not require a technical background. Also, model transformations make it possible to deal with the scenarization process (i.e. the other alternative would be to design and implement all possible configurations of scenarios). Indeed, the profile model and game component model can be transformed to automatically produce adapted scenarios. These latter are used to validate the domain elements and rules that are relevant for the generation of scenarios and will subsequently form a basis for real exploitation within the game.

In [12], we have proposed a metamodel for structuring all the dimensions related to the game. As for the generation of scenarios adapted to children profiles, it is implemented as a model transformation written in Java/EMF [20].

Certainly, the proposed implementation allows optimizing the validation task so that game scenarios are generated in demand and without additional effort. However, the problem arises when domain experts suggest alterations of the domain rules that drive the generation.

The identification of transformation fragments impacted by an expressed change is a complex task. Indeed, the way the transformation is specified does not reveal mappings between each experts direction/requirement (i.e. considered here as a constraint) and the transformation fragments that allow building target models. In addition, the experts directions/requirements are not easy to implement even when the transformation is specified from scratch. Several constraints are expressed in order of priority and they are global constraints that are attached to a set of model elements and not to separated ones. In fact, the proposed model transformation uses an external constraints solving library to tackle some very specific generation steps.

As a feedback from the co-design sessions conducted with ASD experts, we realize that MDE provides support for adaptive generation of scenarios and allows varying situations proposed to domain experts without significant effort. However, the proposed implementation of the production of learning scenarios is problematic (i.e. especially when changes are expressed). Hence, we have exploited other model transformations languages/supports (i.e. ETL language [11] and the meta-language *Melange* [3]) to express the generation of scenarios.

Although ETL allows specifying the transformation in a much more structured way compared to Java/EMF (e.g. rules, operations, pre and post blocks), the lack of a CSP support raises a significant issue. As for *Melange* (i.e. a language workbench that allows expressing operational semantics by augmenting meta-classes with behaviors), the generation concern is specified in a modular manner which helps to identify the components (e.g. metaclasses, operations) related to an expressed change. Also, it is possible to reuse existing Java libraries for CSP solving. However, like the Java/EMF transformation, it is not easy to express the directions/requirements of ASD experts by means of a CSP. This is due to the divergence between domains of values supported by the CSP solver (essentially integer and real values) and the concerned model elements.

The next section details our proposal for a model transformation approach that facilitates the expression of the implied CSP. Our goal is to deal with the objectives below:

1. the generation of target models by transforming source ones.
2. the specification of constraints applied to target models in a simple manner and constraint solving.
3. the modification or reconfiguration of the transformation in case of constraint changes.

We have to notice that details concerning the last objective are out of the chapter scope.

3   Global Overview

This section explains how a model transformation implying constraint solving can be considered as a pattern matching problem. We give the base principles of our approach and present an illustrative example. Thereafter, we detail the structuring of patterns.

3.1   Base Principles

Basically, a CSP is defined as a set of variables, variable domains (i.e. possible values for each variable) and a set of constraints. A solution is an assignment of values to each variable that satisfies every constraint. As for graph pattern matching, it is based on *(sub)graph isomorphism* and requires finding an image (i.e. match) of a given graph (i.e. pattern graph) in another graph (i.e. source graph) [14].

In the literature, several works address the joint use of CSP and pattern matching [14,19,21]. Essentially, the graph pattern matching is expressed and resolved as a CSP. The aim is to improve matching performance by exploiting the rich and advanced research work done in the CSP field. In order to obtain the CSP equivalent of a pattern matching problem, some mappings have been established between concepts of the two domains [19]:

- CSP variables correspond to the objects of the pattern graph.
- variable domains correspond to the source graph objects to be matched into.
- constraints correspond to the restrictions that apply to a graph morphism.

Our approach is based on a reverse use of these matches. The base principle is to consider a pattern matching problem as a high level specification of a CSP. Hence, a CSP problem over a model can be directly expressed by means of model elements rather than establishing non evident matches to basic variable domains supported by CSP solvers (e.g. integers, reals).

Figure 1 gives a global overview of our approach. A model transformation that implies constraint solving is decomposed into two steps: a pattern matching step and a transformation step. The idea is to express all constraints to enforce on target models through a relevant pattern. A found match is then transformed into valid target models. Therefore, the expression of the pattern has to consider the following requirements:

- although the pattern is expressed by means of source model elements, it has to ensure the satisfaction of all constraints related to target models.
- a match model has to be sufficient enough to ensure a complete generation of target models.

Furthermore, the expression of a pattern is decomposed into two parts. The structure part refers to the elements to be matched into source models, while the constraint part refers to the different constraints that force the identification of a match model. This decoupling makes it possible to associate multiple constraints (i.e. classed by order of priority) to the same pattern. Also, variation of a constraint does not affect the transformation because this latter is specified using the pattern structure.

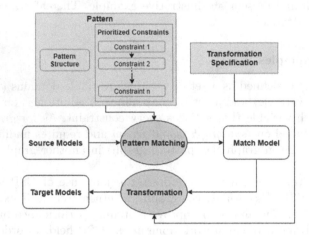

Fig. 1. Global overview of the transformation process [13].

3.2   Illustrative Example

The transformation scenario we have chosen to illustrate the base principles of our proposal consists in producing a piling up of triangles. These triangles are matched from those belonging to the source model (see Fig. 2). This latter contains a set of squares with a colored background with numbered triangles of different areas. Each produced triangle must preserve the same area of its source equivalent and have the background color of the container square. Besides, the produced model must include as many triangles as source squares.

As for constraints to be satisfied by the target model, they are listed by order of priority:

1. the piling up must be coherent (i.e. the area of the contained triangle must be less than the container one) and the target triangles must have different color.
2. the piling up must be coherent (if constraint 1 could not be satisfied).

For this transformation scenario, the pattern structure consists of an ordered set of three triangles (i.e. because the source model contains three squares). Each one can match one of the source triangles. As for the constraints part, it specifies that the piling up must be coherent and triangles must have different colors. The less prioritized constraint allows producing a coherent piling up of triangles regardless their colors. We have to notice that the two constraints have to be satisfied by target models, but they cannot be directly applied on the pattern structure elements. In fact, other source constraints are derived from the expressed ones to specify the validation logic of a model matched using the pattern structure. The relevant mappings are given below:

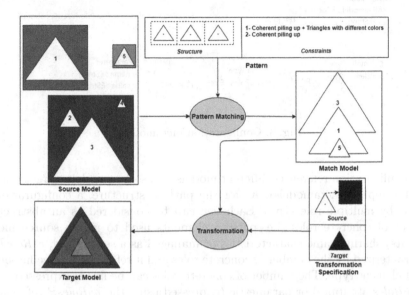

Fig. 2. Simple application example.

- the piling up must be coherent: the matched triangles are in descending order of area.
- target triangles must have different color: the matched triangles must belong to different squares.

The matching process uses the source constraints to search for a valid model. If no match is found (e.g. considering that triangles 1 and 5 have the same area), models matched using the pattern structure are validated against the less prioritized constraint. Once a valid match occurs, the transformation is applied on each matched triangle for copying it and assigning the background color of its container. We have to notice that squares are not matched by the pattern. They are derived from matched triangles.

3.3 Configuration Metamodel

As discussed before, the pattern specification (i.e. structure and constraints parts) underpins the proposed transformation approach. The relevant information is considered as a configuration for generating the transformation infrastructure. It is stored in a model that conforms to the metamodel depicted in Fig. 3.

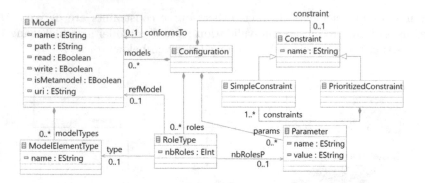

Fig. 3. Configuration metamodel.

A configuration references different models (i.e. source models, target models and the implied metamodels). As for the pattern structure, a configuration is defined by multiple role types. Each one can be considered as an abstraction of a set of concrete roles (i.e. pattern elements used to match source model elements) sharing same characteristics or managed as a set. Indeed, a *RoleType* is characterized by the number of concrete roles and it references a specific source model element type. The number of concrete roles can be fixed (expressed using the *nbRoles* attribute) or parametric (expressed using the *nbRolesP* reference).

For example, the pattern depicted in Fig. 2 can be expressed by one *Role-Type* instance. This latter references the model element type corresponding to triangles, while the number of concrete roles is parametric and corresponds to the number of source squares. Therefore, the declared role type is an abstraction of three concrete roles and each of them is used to match a unique triangle of the source model.

As for to the pattern constraints part, a configuration expresses if a match model is validated against one constraint level (*SimpleConstraint*) or multiple and prioritized constraints (*PrioritizedConstraint*). A constraint is characterized by a name that gives an idea of the validation logic. One can note that the complete constraints specification (i.e. by means of conditions for example) is not covered by the proposed metamodel. Indeed, the configuration model does not ensure the generation of the entire transformation infrastructure. This latter includes resources that have to be manually completed by developers. The next section details these aspects by presenting the infrastructure generation process.

4   Transformation Infrastructure

In this section, we detail the generation process of the infrastructure supporting our approach for CSP solving in model transformations (see Fig. 4).

4.1   Generate Configuration

The first step to produce the transformation infrastructure is the generation of the configuration. For that, we provide developers with a GUI allowing them to specify all paths of the managed models and metamodels to which they conform. A configuration model can then be automatically generated. It includes the input information as well as other automatically derived data (e.g. metamodels URIs, model elements types).

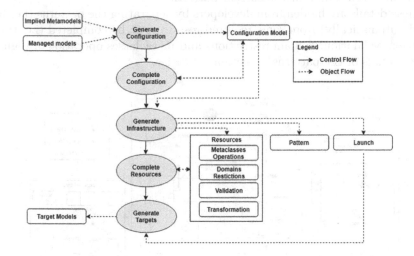

Fig. 4. Process for generating the transformation infrastructure [13].

4.2   Complete Configuration

Recaling from Sect. 3.3, the configuration model has to be completed with the pattern structure and the constraints type (i.e. simple or prioritized). To make this task easier for developers, we have associated a textual concrete syntax to the configuration metamodel and implemented a dedicated XText editor [1].

4.3   Generate Infrastructure

Once the configuration is completed, developers can ask for the automatic generation of the transformation infrastructure. This is concretely done by associating a specific EPL pattern [9] to each constraint level (i.e. in case of prioritized constraints).

EPL is a language that provides support for the specification and detection of structural patterns in models that conform to diverse metamodels [9]. Essentially, an EPL pattern consists of a set of typed roles used to capture adequate combinations from source models and a match condition to evaluate the validity of a combination. In our case, typed roles are derived from *Role Type* instances (i.e. with respect to *nbRoles*, *nbRolesP*, *type* and *refModel* values) while the match condition is viewed as a boolean operation that references a considered constraint.

Besides, the sequencing of the patterns execution is described as an ANT-based Epsilon workflow [8]. For each EPL pattern, a dedicated target and task pair is generated. Besides, *depends* properties of each generated target are specified in order to prohibits the execution of a successor pattern (i.e. with respect to constraints priority which is derived from the order of declaration) if a match has already been found for the current pattern.

These details are hidden from developers by separating the patterns (i.e. generated automatically) from some required resources to be completed (i.e. transformation, validation, domain restrictions and metaclasses operations). Figure 5 depicts details of the patterns execution activities.

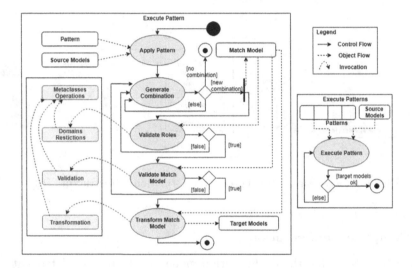

Fig. 5. Patterns execution.

4.4   Complete Resources

Since the generated EPL patterns have the same structure (i.e. derived from the configuration model), a developer needs to provide only one specification for transforming match models. The transformation is specified by means of EOL operations [10] that are applied to match model elements in order to produce valid target models.

Regarding constraints, they are expressed in the validation resource. Indeed, for each constraint, a specific EOL operation is generated and it allows accessing the match model elements. The generated operations must be implemented by the developer in order to express the validation logic (i.e. when a model captured by pattern roles is considered to be a valid match).

Domain restriction resources make it possible to refine the constraints specification. Unlike the validation which applies on an entire match model, the restriction concerns only one single role (e.g. do not capture a triangle if its area exceeds a threshold). Finally, the remaining resource allows the developer to assign operations to metaclasses. These operations can be called from other resources.

4.5 Generate Targets

In order to encapsulate the patterns execution details, the transformation infrastructure includes a launch configuration that allows automatically calling the ANT workflow and therefore producing the target models. Nevertheless, changing the source models implies the synchronization of the transformation infrastructure. Indeed, the ANT workflow and the launch file have to be regenerated in order to reference the new models paths. In addition, the patterns have to be adapted with respect to the resolved values of parametric numbers of concrete roles. The different resources remain unchanged because they are independent from the managed models and the number of concrete roles.

The way in which the transformation infrastructure is structured brings further benefits. When a constraint changes, the transformation resource is not impacted. Besides, the operations associated to the implied metaclasses can be reused when changing the pattern structure or the transformation scenario as long as the same metamodels are involved.

5 Application

This section is dedicated to the application of the proposed approach. First, we briefly present the serious game that motivates the overall proposal and we describe the selected application case. Then, we illustrate each step of the process of generating the transformation infrastructure.

5.1 Application Case

The application context is the *Escape it!* project which aims to develop a mobile learning game (i.e. a serious game with learning purposes) dedicated to children with ASD (Autistic Syndrome Disorder). The game intends to support the learning of visual skills and it will be used both to reinforce and generalize the learning skills. These skills will be initiated by "classic" working sessions with tangible objects. The proposed serious game is based on a minimalist "escape-room" gameplay. The child (player) has to drag objects, sometimes hidden, to their correct locations in order to unlock the room's door and get to the next level.

The global domain elements required for the generation of game sessions are structured into three related parts: game description elements, profile-related elements, and scenario elements. The required constructs have been defined by a dedicated metamodel [12].

The game description model describes all the real game elements (e.g. skills, resources or exercisers, in-game objects...). As for the profile model, it represents a player's (child's) profile. These models are transformed into a game scenario. This latter is built after three steps.

- objective scenario: it is related to the selection of the visual performance skills in accordance with the current child profile.
- structural scenario: it refers to the selection of learning game exercises (i.e. scenes where game levels will take place). This scenario extends the previous one. It is generated from knowledge domain rules stating the relations between scenes and the targeted skills they can deal with.
- features scenario: it expresses the additional inner-resources/fine-grained elements to be associated to each selected scene (e.g. objects appearing in a scene, their positions...). The features scenario includes components of previous scenarios. It specifies the overall information required by a game engine to drive the set-up of a learning game session.

In [13], we have selected the generation of objective scenarios as an illustrative application case (top part of Fig. 6). This chapter extends the application scope by presenting the way structural scenarios can be generated using the proposed constraint solving approach. The selected transformation scenario (bottom part of Fig. 6) takes as input the objective scenario presented in [13] as well as an extended version of the game description model that includes the structural dimension (i.e exercises). The managed models conform to the metamodel depicted in Fig. 7. It is worth noting that the presented metamodel is an excerpt of the global one that defines all the game constructs [12].

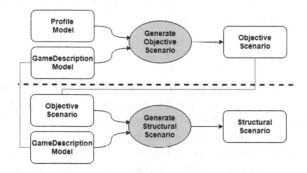

Fig. 6. Selected transformation scenario.

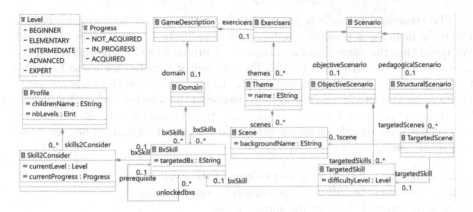

Fig. 7. Excerpt of the "Escape It!" metamodel.

The expression of the game description model is based on ASD experts requirements. It expresses four visual performance skills B3-B4-B8-B25 (respectively matching object to object, matching object to image, sorting categories of objects, making a seriation) and their dependency relations. The game description model expresses also the different supported scenes organized into themes. Figure 8 shows an excerpt of this model that focuses on exercisers. Relations between scenes and the targeted skills are depicted with dashed lines.

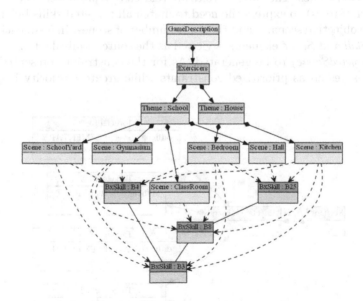

Fig. 8. Game description model.

The structural scenario is generated from the objective scenario depicted in Fig. 9. It includes a possible combination of skills to be trained by the child. We recall that the corresponding fictive child profile as well as details about the generation process are given in [13]. The number of targeted scenes to be added to the structural scenario has to be equal to the number of the targeted skills. Besides, each selected scene corresponds to one of the selected targeted skills (i.e. based on the *targets* reference). In addition, the domain experts have expressed some constraints to enforce on the generated structural scenario. They are listed by priority order:

1. all scenes must be different and belong to the same theme.
2. all scenes must be different (no constraints on themes).
3. all scenes must belong to the same theme.

5.2   Infrastructure Generation

In order to perform the described transformation scenario, we start by generating the relevant configuration. This latter can be completed by defining the pattern structure and identifying constraints through a dedicated Xtext editor (Fig. 10).

For the presented application case, the pattern comprises three role types. The first one allows matching an *ObjectiveScenario*, the second role type corresponds to the *targetedSkill* instances to be matched, and the last one corresponds to the selected scenes. The two last roles are related to a parameter (i.e. parametric number of roles) to express the need to match all targeted skills belonging to the source objective scenario and the same number of scenes. Indeed, each pair of *TargetedSkill* and *Scene* elements is viewed as the source equivalent of a targeted scene (*TargetedScene*) to be generated. As for the constraints presented above, they are expressed as prioritized constraints while greatest priority is given to

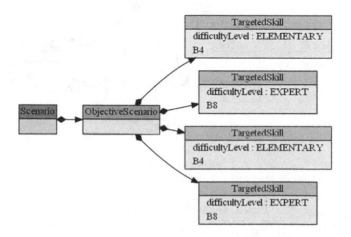

Fig. 9. Objective scenario [13].

the first declared one. Aside from the pattern structure and constraints parts, all other elements are automatically generated.

```
Configuration{
    Models:
        metamodel "mmcs" "C:/Eclipse/workspace/IcsoftExt/models/GameDescription.xmi"
            uri: "http://mmcs/1.0/"
            Types:
                "Domain"
                "BxSkill"
                "GameDescription"
                "Exercisers"
                "Scene"
                "Profile"
                "Skill2Consider"
                "Scenario"
                "ObjectiveScenario"
                "StructuralScenario"
                "TargetedSkill"
                "TargetedScene"
                "Theme"
        model "m1" "C:/Eclipse/workspace/IcsoftExt/models/Scenario.xmi" read write mmcs
        model "m2" "C:/Eclipse/workspace/IcsoftExt/models/GameDescription.xmi" read mmcs
    Pattern:
        roleType m1!mmcs.ObjectiveScenario[1]
        roleType m1!mmcs.TargetedSkill [$p]
        roleType m2!mmcs.Scene [$p]
    Parameters:
        "p": "m1.Scenario.conceptualscenario.targetedskill"
    Constraint:
    ComplexConstraint "scenesConstraint":
        SimpleConstraint "dSuT"
        SimpleConstraint "dS"
        SimpleConstraint "uT"
}
```

Fig. 10. Configuration model.

Once the configuration model is completed, the transformation infrastructure can be generated (see Fig. 11). Recalling from Sect. 4.3, an EPL pattern is automatically generated for each constraint level and the related details are hidden from developers by separating patterns and the required resources. For the application example, three EPL patterns are generated respectively for the aforementioned constraints (cf. Sect. 5.1). Listing 1 illustrates an excerpt of the pattern generated for constraint 2 (i.e. all scenes must be different). For convenience, the excerpt focuses on the pattern structure and the resources invocation. Some code fragments (e.g variables declaration, stop searching, randomness...) have been removed to simplify the pattern's interpretation.

As for the domain restriction resource, it is possible to specify guard conditions in order to restrict the possible elements to be caught by a role. Given that the restriction mechanism is not applicable for the selected application case, the generated operations remains unchanged and they allow capturing all possible elements (cf. Listing 2).

Listing 3 depicts an excerpt of the validation resource. Three operations are automatically generated with respect to the constraints names. We complete these operations with action blocks that express the specific validation logic for models matched by the pattern (the added code is underlined). For example, the second operation implements the validation logic for constraint 2 (i.e. all scenes must be different). The first statement verify if the matched targeted skills are all different (i.e. because EPL allows matching the same element multiple times) while the second one is applied on the matched scenes. Also, the *For* statement verify if each matched scene is compatible with one of the targeted skills. the *targets*() operation implements this behavior and it is expressed in the context of the *Scene* metaclass (i.e. metaclass operations resources).

As for *allDifferent*(), it is a predefined operation. Indeed, we defined a list of operations (e.g. *followingNotMatch*(), *sort*(), *randSequence*()...) which are automatically added to the operations resource.

```
pattern  Pattern
     r0  :  m1!ObjectiveScenario
          guard  :  r0.ObjectiveScenarioDomainRestriction(),
     r1  :  m1!TargetedSkill
          guard  :  r1.TargetedSkillDomainRestriction(),
     r2  :  m1!TargetedSkill
          guard  :  r2.TargetedSkillDomainRestriction(),
     r3  :  m1!TargetedSkill
          guard  :  r3.TargetedSkillDomainRestriction(),
     r4  :  m1!TargetedSkill
          guard  :  r4.TargetedSkillDomainRestriction(),
     r5  :  m2!Scene
          guard  :  r5.SceneDomainRestriction(),
     r6  :  m2!Scene
          guard  :  r6.SceneDomainRestriction(),
     r7  :  m2!Scene
          guard  :  r7.SceneDomainRestriction(),
     r8  :  m2!Scene
          guard  :  r8.SceneDomainRestriction(),
{
match:  continue and
     validatePatterndS(r0,Sequence{r1,r2,r3,r4},Sequence{r5,r6,r7,r8})
onmatch
     {
     //code fragment depends on the matching mechanism (all possible match, first
          match, random match)
     //the continue boolean is used to stop searching for possible combinations.
     }
     do{
     //code fragment depends on the matching mechanism
     transformPattern(r0,Sequence{r1,r2,r3,r4},Sequence{r5,r6,r7,r8});
     }
}
```

Listing 1. Excerpt of the EPL pattern generated for constraint 2.

```
operation m1!ObjectiveScenario ObjectiveScenarioDomainRestriction(): Boolean{
return true;
}
operation m1!TargetedSkill TargetedSkillDomainRestriction(): Boolean{
return true;
}
operation m2!Scene SceneDomainRestriction(): Boolean{
return true;
}
```

Listing 2. Domain restriction resource.

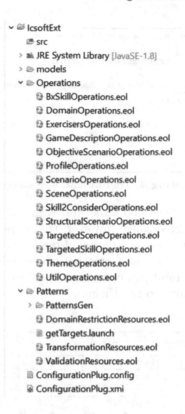

Fig. 11. Transformation infrastructure.

```
operation validatePatterndSuT(r0 : m1!ObjectiveScenario,r1 : Sequence ,r5 :
    Sequence ) :Boolean{
    //code fragment implementing the constraint 1
}
operation validatePatterndS(r0 : m1!ObjectiveScenario,r1 : Sequence ,r5 :
    Sequence ) :Boolean{
    if(not allDifferent(r1)) return false;
    if(not allDifferent(r5)) return false;
    for(i in Sequence{0..r1.size()-1}){
        if(not r5.get(i).targets(r1.get(i))){
            return false;
        }
    }
    return true;
}
operation validatePatternuT(r0 : m1!ObjectiveScenario,r1 : Sequence ,r5 :
    Sequence ) :Boolean{
    //code fragment implementing the constraint 3
}
```

Listing 3. Validation resource.

As for the transformation resource (see Listing 4), we completed it with actions to be applied on the match model in order to produce a valid structural scenario. Basically, a new *StructuralScenario* element is created as a target equivalent of the matched objective scenario. In addition, for each targeted skill, the compatible scene is selected (with respect to the sequencing order), and both elements are used to create a new *TargetedScene* element.

```
operation transformPattern(r0 : m1!ObjectiveScenario,r1 : Sequence ,r5 : Sequence ){
    var ss=createStructuralScenario(r0);
    for(i in Sequence{0..r1.size()-1}){
        ss.targetedscene.add(createTargetedScene(r1.get(i),r5.get(i)));
    }
}
operation createStructuralScenario(p0 : m1!ObjectiveScenario) : m1!StructuralScenario {
    var ss= new m1!StructuralScenario;
    p0.eContainer().pedagogicalscenario=ss;
    return ss;
}
operation createTargetedScene(p0 : m1!TargetedSkill,p1 : m3!Scene) : m1!TargetedScene {
    var ts= new m1!TargetedScene;
    ts.targetedskill=p0;
    ts.scene=p1;
    return ts;
}
```

Listing 4. Transformation resource.

Figure 12 depicts the generated structural scenario. The selected scenes are compatible with the targeted skills. However, the proposed skills do not belong to the same theme. In fact, no combination of possible skills allows enforcing the first constraint. For that, the transformation generates a scenario with respect to a less prioritized constraint (i.e. constraint 2). Indeed, the selected scenes are all different but they belong to two themes.

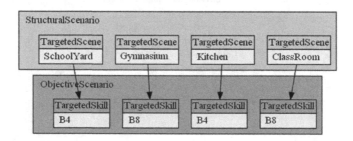

Fig. 12. The generated structural scenario.

6 Related Work

Our approach for constraint solving is based on expressing constraints to enforce on target models by means of source model elements. This proposal is inspired from graph transformations techniques where constraints on the involved graphs can be expressed through application conditions [4]. Besides, the proposed transformation process (i.e. including the match and transformation steps) is similar to the application of graph transformations. For these latter, the source graph fragments concerned with the application of a transformation are first determined with respect to the LHS (Left Hand Side) graph. Then, the matched fragments are replaced with the structure of the RHS (Right Hand Side) graph.

The main difference is the way the pattern is defined. In fact, the pattern structure is separated from constraints. This allows expressing different and prioritized constraints for the same pattern. Besides, it is much easier to express complex constraints within our approach (e.g. textual syntax, feature navigation, predefined operations...). In contrast, for graph transformations the pattern is defined as one block (i.e. the LHS graph) and constraints are expressed like sub-graphs.

Several proposals have addressed the problem of directly enforcing constraints on target models. Petter et al. [18] have proposed an implementation to extend the QVT-Relations language [16] with constraint solving capabilities. However, the proposal focuses on constraints related to attribute values and disregards global constraints.

Other related works address the automatic generation of models. In this case, models are not considered as targets of applying model transformations but are viewed as valid instances of constrained metamodels [7]. Cabot et al. [2] have proposed an approach where metamodels and OCL constraints are translated into a CSP and a dedicated solver allows producing a valid instance. Based on similar principles, Ferdjoukh et al. [5] have proposed an approach for model generation while dealing with performance.

In the limited scope of the presented application case, we have experimented the use of model generation techniques to perform the transformation scenario. The idea was to express the source models information, the way to construct the target model and the expert requirements, as OCL constraints. Hence, a model generation support (we chose Grimm [5]) can be used to deal with the generation of the expected scenario. However, the tool failed because it does not support some essential OCL operations.

7 Conclusion

This chapter presents a practical approach for constraint solving in model transformations. The base principle is to consider a pattern matching problem as a high level specification of a CSP. Besides, a transformation infrastructure that underpins the conceptual proposal can be generated in a semi-automatic manner. Indeed, this infrastructure provides support for pattern specification, match model search, and transformation into valid target models. An application case extracted from the *Escape It!* serious game has been selected to illustrate these tasks.

The way the pattern definition is carried out offers some benefits. By decoupling the pattern structure from the validation constraints, it is possible to associate multiple constraints to a same pattern and therefore allows specifying shared transformation rules for all validation constraints. In addition, the proposal supports parametric patterns. Hence, the same pattern definition can be used in various transformation scenarios even if involving slightly different match models.

The integration of our proposal in the co-design framework for the presented serious game opens up many perspectives. The future work deal with two main issues: (i) the cognitive effort to be implicated by the domain expert in order to specify/interpret the pattern and (ii) the change impact analysis of domain rules.

To address the first issue, we are exploring a new approach to express the constraint satisfaction problem by means of target model elements. The corresponding source pattern can be automatically generated by exploiting some relevant information (i.e. source-target mappings, one time or multiple match...). As for the change of domain rules, the regeneration of the transformation infrastructure must consider the extent of the variation expressed by the expert (e.g. adding a constraint must imply changing the validation resource without impacting the transformation and operations resources).

References

1. Bettini, L.: Implementing domain-specific languages with Xtext and Xtend. Packt Publishing Ltd., Birmingham (2016)
2. Cabot, J., Claris, R., Riera, D., et al.: Verification of UML/OCL class diagrams using constraint programming. In: First International Conference on Software Testing Verification and Validation, ICST 2008, pp. 73–80. IEEE (2008)
3. Degueule, T., Combemale, B., Blouin, A., Barais, O., Jézéquel, J.M.: Melange: a meta-language for modular and reusable development of dsls. In: Proceedings of the 2015 ACM SIGPLAN International Conference on Software Language Engineering, pp. 25–36. ACM (2015)
4. Ehrig, H., Ehrig, K., Habel, A., Pennemann, K.-H.: Constraints and application conditions: from graphs to high-level structures. In: Ehrig, H., Engels, G., Parisi-Presicce, F., Rozenberg, G. (eds.) ICGT 2004. LNCS, vol. 3256, pp. 287–303. Springer, Heidelberg (2004). https://doi.org/10.1007/978-3-540-30203-2_21
5. Ferdjoukh, A., Baert, A.E., Chateau, A., Coletta, R., Nebut, C.: A CSP approach for metamodel instantiation. In: 2013 IEEE 25th International Conference on Tools with Artificial Intelligence, pp. 1044–1051. IEEE (2013)
6. Jouault, F., Kurtev, I.: Transforming models with ATL. In: Bruel, J.-M. (ed.) MODELS 2005. LNCS, vol. 3844, pp. 128–138. Springer, Heidelberg (2006). https://doi.org/10.1007/11663430_14
7. Kleiner, M., Del Fabro, M.D., Albert, P.: Model search: formalizing and automating constraint solving in MDE platforms. In: Kühne, T., Selic, B., Gervais, M.-P., Terrier, F. (eds.) ECMFA 2010. LNCS, vol. 6138, pp. 173–188. Springer, Heidelberg (2010). https://doi.org/10.1007/978-3-642-13595-8_15
8. Kolovos, D., Rose, L., Garcia-Dominguez, A., Paige, R.: The epsilon book (2017)
9. Kolovos, D.S., Paige, R.F.: The epsilon pattern language. In: 9th IEEE/ACM International Workshop on Modelling in Software Engineering, MiSE@ICSE 2017, pp. 54–60. IEEE (2017)
10. Kolovos, D.S., Paige, R.F., Polack, F.A.C.: The epsilon object language (EOL). In: Rensink, A., Warmer, J. (eds.) ECMDA-FA 2006. LNCS, vol. 4066, pp. 128–142. Springer, Heidelberg (2006). https://doi.org/10.1007/11787044_11
11. Kolovos, D.S., Paige, R.F., Polack, F.A.C.: The epsilon transformation language. In: Vallecillo, A., Gray, J., Pierantonio, A. (eds.) ICMT 2008. LNCS, vol. 5063, pp. 46–60. Springer, Heidelberg (2008). https://doi.org/10.1007/978-3-540-69927-9_4
12. Laforcade, P., Laghouaouta, Y.: Supporting the Adaptive Generation of Learning Game Scenarios with a Model-Driven Engineering Framework. In: Pammer-Schindler, V., Pérez-Sanagustín, M., Drachsler, H., Elferink, R., Scheffel, M. (eds.) EC-TEL 2018. LNCS, vol. 11082, pp. 151–165. Springer, Cham (2018). https://doi.org/10.1007/978-3-319-98572-5_12

13. Laghouaouta, Y., Laforcade, P., Loiseau, E.: A pattern-matching based approach for problem solving in model transformations. In: Proceedings of the 13th International Conference on Software Technologies, ICSOFT 2018, Portugal, pp. 113–123. SciTePress, Setúbal (2018). https://doi.org/10.5220/0006847901130123
14. Larrosa, J., Valiente, G.: Constraint satisfaction algorithms for graph pattern matching. Math. Struct. Comput. Sci. **12**(4), 403–422 (2002)
15. Mens, T., Gorp, P.V.: A taxonomy of model transformation. Electron. Notes Theor. Comput. Sci. **152**, 125–142 (2006)
16. OMG: Meta object facility (mof) 2.0 query/view/transformation specification (2008)
17. OMG: Object constraint language 2.4 specification (2014)
18. Petter, A., Behring, A., Mühlhäuser, M.: Solving constraints in model transformations. In: Paige, R.F. (ed.) ICMT 2009. LNCS, vol. 5563, pp. 132–147. Springer, Heidelberg (2009). https://doi.org/10.1007/978-3-642-02408-5_10
19. Rudolf, M.: Utilizing constraint satisfaction techniques for efficient graph pattern matching. In: Ehrig, H., Engels, G., Kreowski, H.-J., Rozenberg, G. (eds.) TAGT 1998. LNCS, vol. 1764, pp. 238–251. Springer, Heidelberg (2000). https://doi.org/10.1007/978-3-540-46464-8_17
20. Steinberg, D., Budinsky, F., Paternostro, M., Merks, E.: EMF: Eclipse Modeling Framework 2.0, 2nd edn. Addison-Wesley Professional, Boston (2009)
21. Taentzer, G., Ermel, C., Rudolf, M.: The AGG approach: language and tool environment. In: Handbook of graph grammars and computing by graph transformation, vol. 2, 551–603 (1999)

An Integrated Requirements Engineering Framework for Agile Software Product Lines

Hassan Haidar[1]([⊠]), Manuel Kolp[1], and Yves Wautelet[2]

[1] UCLouvain, LouRIM/CEMIS, Louvain-la-Neuve, Belgium
{hassan.haidar,manuel.kolp}@uclouvain.be
[2] KULeuven, FEB, Leuven, Belgium
yves.wautelet@kuleuven.be

Abstract. Requirements engineering (RE) techniques play a determinant role within Agile Product Lines development methods; these notably allow to establish the relevance to adopt or not the product line approach for software-intensive systems production. This paper proposes an integrated goal and feature-based meta-model for agile software product lines development. The main objective is to permit the sepecification of the requirements that precisely capture stakeholder's needs and intentions as well as the management of product line variabilities. Adopting practices from requirements engineering, especially goal and feature models, helps designing the domain and application engineering tiers of an agile product line. Such an approach allows a holistic perspective integrating human, organizational and agile aspects to better understand product lines dynamic business environments. It helps bridging the gap between product lines structures and requirements models, and proposes an integrated framework to all actors involved in the product line architecture. In this paper we show how our proposed metamodel can be applied to the requirements engineering stage of an agile product line development mainly for feature-oriented agile product lines such as our own methodology called AgiFPL.

Keywords: Agile product line engineering · Requirements · Engineering goal model · Feature · Feature model · AgiFPL

1 Introduction

"Agile Product Lines Engineering" has been proposed as an approach that deals with the growing complexity of information systems and the handling of competitive and changing needs of the IT production industry [1]. This approach offers better support for reusable and evolving software artefacts and helps managing changes in requirements, promoting product quality, decreasing development costs and reducing time to market. Thus, the main goal of this approach is to ensure better systematic development of a family of software systems by identifying and managing their similarities and variations [2]. Successful adoption of an agile product line methodology requires a deep organizational mind shift since, in fact, all software engineering processes are affected from requirements to maintenance and evolution activities.

© Springer Nature Switzerland AG 2019
M. van Sinderen and L. A. Maciaszek (Eds.): ICSOFT 2018, CCIS 1077, pp. 124–149, 2019.
https://doi.org/10.1007/978-3-030-29157-0_6

Agile Product Lines Engineering has emerged as the result of merging both the "Agile techniques" and "Product Lines Engineering (PLE)" approaches [3]. By using the term "Agile Product Lines", we refer to Product Lines development methodologies compliant with agile principles. These have organized agile software development activities and practices in ways that prescribe the workflows that should be performed and explain how the products should be produced and handled, along these flows. The flow of activities respects agile principles. In our research works and related projects, we consider that the agility attribute of Agile Product Lines methodologies concern the software development process (and not the developed product).

According to [4], software development methodologies consist of two integral parts. The first one is a modeling language and the second one is a process. Thus, it is clear that any proposed methodology uses to handle, on the one hand, a requirements engineering perspective (including modeling and other related tasks) and, on the other hand, the dynamic perspectives such as development, implementation, or maintenance, etc. Since one of our major goals is to propose a complete methodology, we therefore take into account these two parts.

Requirements engineering (RE) – more precisely here, Goal-Oriented Requirements Engineering (GORE) – and Feature Modeling including elicitation, analysis, specification, verification, and management [5], plays a determinant role when defining a new Agile Product Lines methodology and making the decision to adopt (one of) them to meet the business goals of an organization. Compared with RE for a single custom-built system, RE for a software-intensive systems family focuses more on systematic reuse, not only from the technical perspective, but from the organizational, and process perspectives as well [6]. Therefore, many crucial decisions have to be made during the requirements engineering stages that influence the structure, development, and implementation of an agile product line.

Managing product line requirements is non-trivial since they reflect stakeholders' diverse perspectives, have complex configuration dependencies (e.g., requires, uses, excludes, extends, ...), and are expressed in various forms (e.g., textual, goals) and at different granularity levels (e.g., features, qualities) [7]. We have recently proposed an integrated goal and feature-based metamodel for managing requirements phases of Agile Product Line in [8]. The aim was to allow analysts and developers to produce specifications that precisely capture the stakeholder's needs and intentions as well as to manage product line variabilities. In addition, our motivation was to understand and build an efficient structure of the requirements engineering of a feature-oriented product line in an agile context with the research question of building a RE approach for an agile product line to efficiently represent stakeholders' intentions and goals, as well as product line variabilities and communalities.

In [8], we have defined and formalized a specific metamodel for describing product lines using the Z specification language [9]. The present paper extends the contributions of [8] by defining how the metamodel can be applied to requirements engineering stages of an agile product line methodology called AgiFPL that has been introduced in [10]. The metamodel application process starts (1) by specifying the concerned requirements processes of the methodology; (2) detailing the integration of the metamodel with these processes; (3) validating on a real-world case study; and (4) comparing our proposal to existing approaches. This paper focuses on the first two points, the other ones are left for future work.

Our method, called AgiFPL (Agile Framework for managing evolving Product Lines) is a feature-oriented approach involving two classical tiers of product line engineering: *Domain Engineering* and *Application Engineering*.

The domain engineering deals with all the aspects of managing reusable assets (artifacts), while the application engineering aims at developing a specific product for a particular stakeholder. Therefore, requirements engineering approaches have to cope with the different organizational levels and architectural complexity. Specifically, for product lines, requirements engineering, captures both commonality and variability among product line members [11]. Our proposed metamodel follows a holistic approach that allows the modeling of the organizational and operational context of a product line within a flexible and rapidly evolving environment. It offers thus a better understanding of the representation of product lines requirements and their stakeholders' requirements.

The remainder of the paper is structured as follows. Section 2, briefly reviews the literature about RE for agile product lines and some related work. Section 3 presents our research method and describes the main concepts of our metamodel. Section 4 presents the integration of our proposed metamodel to our AgiFPL methodology. Section 5 highlights an example of application of our proposal. Section 6 concludes the paper.

2 Related Work

Research works such as [12–15] have demonstrated the difficulty of integrating agile methods with product line engineering due to the plan-driven and sequential nature of product line approaches versus the iterative and flexible nature of agile frameworks. However, they have highlighted that adding agility to product line engineering is not only possible but can also be highly beneficial [14]. This paper focuses on the requirements engineering part of this particular integration issue; we hereafter present how the requirements engineering stage has been considered in the existent agile product line approaches.

Generally speaking, both agile methods and software product line approaches recognize that changes to the requirements during the product development are going to occur inevitably. However, they handle different strategies to deal with the requirements and the occurred changes.

Table 1 compares how agile methods and product line approaches take in charge "Requirements", "Architecture", and "Reuse". Change management strategies for Agile methods deal with occurred changes to requirements by focusing on incremental development and close interactions with stakeholders mainly through the product owner role [16]. These agile methods consider organizations as complex adaptive systems in which requirements are emergent rather than pre-specifiable, therefore, project teams rarely perform comprehensive requirements' elicitation, specification, analysis, validation, or even management activities [17]. On the contrary, the strategies to deal with requirements in product line approaches focus on finding solutions to meet stakeholders' needs by customizing the core assets [2, 5, 18] and concerned teams give importance to the process of formal and written specification and documentation.

In fact, they try to predict changes in the beginning of the process and maintain the variability models (such as Feature Models) as core assets. Therefore, requirements engineering in product line approaches is done by defining the product line scope [19]. In order to define the domain scope, first, the right products for the domain have to be targeted, and second, factors used to know similar systems (i.e. communalities) and future market demands must be determined. Too large or small scope will deteriorate the capabilities of product line approaches to achieve variabilities and desired economies. Requirements and their changes in product line approaches are carried out through analysis, careful predications and smart selections [5]. If a customer's desired product is out of the product line scope, then, the cost associated with amending and revising the core assets to meet their needs will be higher than the cost of products in the scope. Thus, the clients have to whether accept the high cost or modify their initial requirements in order to gain benefits such as better maintainability and faster delivery [12]. In addition, stakeholders' collaboration is managed through "customer interface management practice". A number of customer representatives (e.g. domain experts, product managers, etc.) have explicitly assigned roles and responsibilities and act as a bridge that connect stakeholders and development teams [20, 21].

Table 1. Agile methods versus product line approaches.

	Agile methods	Product line approaches
Requirements	Emphasis on quick response to requirements' changes with short iterations and small increments for the application. Direct stakeholders collaboration; stakeholders (i.e. owner, etc.) have to participate in the whole software project lifecycle	Domain requirements and application requirements are both engineered. Indirect stakeholders' collaboration using *well-trained* customer (and user) representatives
Architecture	Minimal emphasis on the application architecture features beyond the immediate iteration	Domain and Application architecture are both engineered
Reuse	Optimistic use of COTS; Applies streamlined domain engineering activity without emphasis on development of reusable artifacts	Special emphasis on maturity and reliability of COTS Foundation of the method is "re-using core assets (i.e. artifacts) defined in domain engineering tier"

On their side, agile methods emphasize on simplicity. They call for removing or not taking into account architectural features that are not of immediate interest for the current iteration [24]. However, product line approaches consider the "mass production" principal which requires the definition and maintenance of a product line architecture in order to satisfy the general requirements of the product line and the individual requirements of products by explicitly recognizing a set of variation points required to support the family of products within the scope of the targeted domain [25].

Agile methods can make opportunistic reuse of existent artifacts and pre-developed software components in an application development. In fact, agile methods apply streamlined domain engineering activity without emphasis on development of reusable core assets [26]. However, as said, the software product line engineering paradigm separates two main processes: Domain Engineering and Application Engineering.

The domain engineering process is fundamentally dedicated for establishing the reusable artifacts and thus defining the commonality and the variability of the product line. The application engineering process is essentially dedicated for developing a single product from reusable artifacts created within the domain engineering process [5].

After reviewing some foundations of agile methods and product line approaches, it appears that classical product line approaches have to deal with the increasing rapid pace of changing requirements to satisfy market needs as well as to be within the framework of existing and changing norms and standards which lead to an increasing need for rapid development and adaptability [27].

Due to their actual benefits, agile methods could help product line teams and companies to deal with the highlighted issue and thus being agile. In fact, if the known requirements, on the basis of which the product line development teams perform the project scoping are not sufficiently detailed for a thorough analysis, agile methods can be applied. Indeed, further these allow to elicit requirements and/or manage changes in the already identified ones. Agile methods may also help these teams (in both domain engineering and application engineering tiers) to produce prototypes swiftly and modify them quickly according to any occurred change in requirements. In addition, applying agile methods may clarify gradually the targeted scope [14, 28]. Therefore, integrating requirements engineering practices as well as development practices from agile methods could enhance product line approaches.

Several concrete methods and models that integrate agile methods and product line approaches are available. Each proposed method combines product line engineering with selected agile approaches and techniques [28]. Since the main target of this paper is to propose a requirements engineering framework for agile product lines, hereafter, we identify the requirements engineering techniques by surveying some relevant agile product line approaches.

Babar et al. [29] have promoted the integration of agile software development and product line engineering as means of reducing time-to-market, increasing productivity, and improving quality. They establish a phase called "Exploration before agile product development" as requirements engineering process. This process uses the "Product Roadmaps" in order to perform a "Feature Analysis" and thus define the "Product Backlog" that contains "Feature Description". Based on the "Product Backlog", the "Sprint Backlog" for the implementation is structured.

Ghanam et al. [30] have introduced an agile product line method (i.e. Test Driven Development (TDD)) that emphasizes on writing tests before writing code as a means of ensuring the satisfaction of customer requirements, and reinforcing good design habits. To satisfy the customer requirements, they have proposed "Acceptance Tests" in order to identify what features are to be delivered by the implemented product lines. Acceptance tests are considered as "executable specifications" and they are usually written in a format accessible to both technical and non-technical audiences; they can always be a reference of what was requested by the customer, what has been done so far and what is to be done next.

O'Leary et al. [31] have proposed an agile process model for deriving products in software product line engineering. The model was developed through industry-based case study research. The requirements engineering activities are done during the phase "Preparing for Derivation". In this phase the requirements are determined, prioritized, and assigned to development iterations. The purpose of this phase is to achieve agreement among all the stakeholders on the product requirements.

Díaz et al. [32] have introduced an agile product line approach called "Agile Product-Line Architecting (APLA)" that integrates a set of mechanisms in order to support agile architecting of the Product lines. The APLA process has been deployed in Scrum [33] by the smooth integration of its mechanisms in this agile method. According to the APLA process, the first task consists of capturing the requirements of the "Software Product Line Owner" from the product vision (i.e. features). These features can be decomposed into a list of "user stories (US)" and "tasks" known as "Software Product-Line Backlog". In addition, Santos Jr. and Lucena Jr. [34] have presented the ScrumPL approach that supports iterative domain and application engineering based on Scrum.

Table 2. RE Tools/approach and activities, identified in studied agile product line approaches.

RE approach/tools	RE activities
- Structured text	- Plan and elicit
- Use cases	- Model and analyze
- Features	- Communicate and agree
- Orthogonal variability models	- Realize and evolve
- User stories	

Table 2 summarizes the requirements engineering approaches/tools and activities used within the identified publications that propose agile product lines models or approaches. These works underline the need for a performant requirements engineering framework that ensure the agile transformation while preserving existing software product lines. To answer that, we try here to propose a convenient framework that can be applied to requirements engineering stage of feature-oriented agile product lines.

3 A Metamodel for Agile Product Lines

A framework for managing the requirements stage of Agile Product Lines should serve the analysis of software product lines processes, the definition of a (conceptual) process language, and the implementation of software processes using tools [35]. In this section, before detailing our metamodel itself; we first present how it was crafted. However, the implication on Agile-Product-Lines' processes analysis, design and implementation will be discussed in future work.

According to [36], the procedure for constructing metamodels that support Life Cycle Management adopts the following steps:

- Define domain and disciplines;
- Produce domain model of software engineering concepts;
- Select notations;
- Define artifacts types;
- Define the software engineering process models;
- Select tools, techniques and utilities.

Based on the approach presented in [36] and to target the research question mentioned above, the proposed metamodel is based on the comprehensive analysis of common data types, representation schemes and relationships that exist in Agile Product Lines approaches and then represented through a Unified Modeling Language (UML) class diagram [37]. Three major steps are taken (iteratively):

- *Step 1*: identification of the basic RE concepts of Agile Product Lines methodologies;
- *Step 2*: Analysis of the relationships between concepts. Four types of relationships
- are used, namely *generalization*, *composition*, *aggregation* and *association*. The existence of relationships between concepts needs to be identified and their types distinguished;
- *Step 3*: Formal expression of the metamodel according to the basic concepts and relationships gathered in the first steps, including UML class diagram graphical representation.

As stated above, our motivation is to understand and build an efficient structure of the requirements engineering of a feature-oriented product line in an agile context. This leads us to define a goal and feature-oriented specification to provide modeling constructs that permit:

- Representations of stakeholder's intentions and goals;
- Variability, commonality and technical elements of the agile product line;
- Requirements artifacts and their relationships used by agile teams.

The proposed metamodel defines two main perspectives. The first one is the product line engineering perspective itself, in which goal (i.e. Family goal model) and feature models provide different variability perspectives and the rationale of the variability. The second one is the agile development perspective, in which the agile requirements artifacts and goal models provide an exhaustive structure for the implementation of product line's features and products derivation.

Standard goal model frameworks like i* [38, 39] can represent intentional variability, but lack mechanisms for representing differences between intentional spaces of various systems (i.e., product line variability in the intentional space). Therefore, Asadi et al. [40] have introduced the notion of family goal model to extend standard goal modeling techniques, which we apply in this paper to iStar 2.0 [41], the second version of i*.

Our metamodel connects family goal models and features models through mappings. They provide bidirectional relationships and traceability links between high-level stakeholders' business objectives, which are described by goal models and implementation units enclosed within features in feature models. In addition, we seek to support the stakeholders of a product line, especially in the application engineering tier, through iStar 2.0 models, which provide a graphical and comprehensive vision of the stories and their relationships. Our proposed model connects Backlog items (i.e., user stories,...), and family goal models by mappings performed through heuristics rules proposed in [42] and [18].

Figure 1 introduces the main entities and relationships of our metamodel. We subdivide it into four sub-models:

- The *Organizational sub-model*, describing the members (i.e. actors, teams, ...) of the product line, their organizational roles, responsibilities, capabilities and relationships;
- The *Goal-oriented sub-model*, describing the intentions of the product line stakeholders and generating a stakeholder's view of feature models;
- The *Feature-oriented sub-model*, illustrating the product line variability;
- The *Agile requirements artifacts sub-model* defining the requirements artifacts used by agile teams, as well as the relationships among these artifacts.

The primitives of our framework are also of different types. We classify them as:

- Meta-concepts: Goal, Feature, Actor, User Story ...
- Meta-relationships: Qualifies, Refines, Composition, Aggregation, Generalization ...
- Meta-attributes: Power, Motivation ...
- Meta-constraints: implications between features located in different parts of the feature hierarchy.

All meta-concepts, meta-relationships and meta-constraints have the following mandatory meta-attributes: *Name* and *Description*. *Name* allows unambiguous reference to the instance of the meta-concept and *Description* provides a precise and unambiguous description of the corresponding instance of the meta-concept. The description should contain sufficient information for a formal specification to be derived for use in requirements specifications for a future product or application of the product line.

Figure 1 insists on meta-concepts and meta-relationships. Meta-attributes and meta-constraints are formalized with the Z state-based specification language [9]. We use Z since it provides sufficient modularity, abstraction and expressiveness to describe the requirements engineering aspects of agile product line and the wider context in which they are used in a consistent and structured way. In addition, Z offers a pragmatic approach to specifications by allowing a clear transition between specification and implementation of product lines' applications. Moreover, it is widely adopted in the software development industry and academia.

This paper details next the organizational, goal-oriented, feature-oriented sub-models and their integration, and the user story concept. It also discusses their relevance for agile product lines requirements engineering.

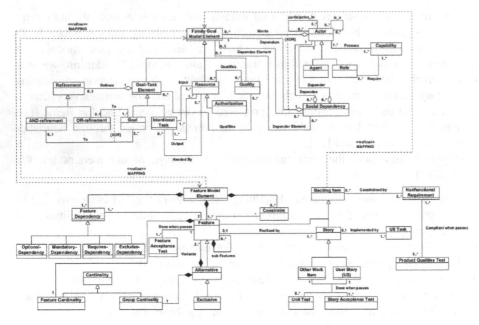

Fig. 1. Requirements-oriented meta-model for agile product lines [8].

3.1 Organizational Sub-model

The main entities and relationships of the organizational sub-model defined in our metamodel are presented on the right corner of the bottom of Fig. 1. The Organizational sub-model, describes the members (i.e. actors, teams, …) of the product line, their organizational roles, responsibilities, capabilities and relation-ships. In fact, this sub-model identifies the relevant **Actors** of the product line, the **Roles** they occupy, the **Capabilities** they possess, and the **Dependum** for which Actors depend on one another.

Actor

Most of stakeholders are represented as actors. Actors can be human, organizations, technical systems (i.e. hardware, software), or any combination thereof. Actors are active, autonomous entities that aim at achieving their goals by exercising their know-how in collaboration with other actors. According to the iStar 2.0 language, two types of actors can be distinguished [41, 46]:

- **Role:** *an abstract characterization of the behavior of a social actor within some specialized context or domain of endeavour.*
- **Agent:** *an actor with concrete, physical manifestations, such as a human individual, an organization, or a department.*

Actor's intentionality is made explicit through the actor boundary, which is a graphical container for their intentional elements.

[Name]
[Informal_Defintion]
[Actor_Type] := Role | Agent
[Goal]

_____**Actor**_____

name : *Name*
description : *Informal_Definition*
is_a : *Actor_Type*
want : *set Goal*
own : *set Resource*
possess : *set Capability*

_____

(want ≠ ø) ∧ (possess ≠ ø)   **(c1)**
(∀ act : *Actor*) act.is_a = Agent ⇒ act.own ≠ ø   **(c2)**

The **Actor** schema above shows the Z formal specification of the Actor concept. The first part of the specification represents the definition of types. The Actor specification first defines the type Name (which represents the **Name** attribute) by writing [Name]. This declaration introduces the set of all names, without making assumptions about the type (i.e. whether the name is a string of characters and numbers, or only characters,…). The type [Actor_Type] is defined as being either a *Role* or an *Agent* or even just an *Actor*.

More complex and structured types are defined with specific schemata. For instance, the **Actor** schema is partitioned horizontally into two sections:

- The *declaration section* introduces a set of named, typed variable declarations;
- The *predicate section* provides predicates that constrain values of the variables. We use identifiers e.g. "(c1)" to refer to predicate, i.e. constraint (c1) of the schema.

In essence an *Actor* of an agile product line *wants* to fulfil the product line *Goals* as well his/her own *Goals*. In fact, an Actor possesses his/her specific *Capabilities* and owns a set of *Resources*. Each Actor applies plans that are part of his/her *Capabilities* and uses *Resources* in order to achieve the *Goal* that he/she *wants*. As the *Actor* is present in a rapid and flexible environment, he/she takes into account the changing *Intentional Elements* related to the product line as well as the ones related to specific customers' needs, in order to adapt its behavior to environmental circumstances. Considering these changes is crucial when eliciting product line requirements as well as stakeholders (i.e. product owner, etc.) requirements. Since an *Actor* can be also a *Role* or an *Agent*, two different types of actor links exist:

- *is-a*: represents the concept of generalization or specification. Only *Roles* can be specialized into *Roles*, or general *Actors* into general *Actors*. However, *Agents* cannot be specialized via is-a, as they are concrete instantiations;
- *participates-in*: represents any kind of association, other than generalization or specialization, between two *Actors*. No restriction exists on the type of actors linked by this association. Note that every *Actor* can *participates-in* multiple other *Actors*.

Thus, a *is-a* relationship applies only between pairs of *Roles* or pairs of *Actors*. There should be no *is-a* cycles. In addition, there should be no *participate-in* cycles. A pair of *Actors* can be linked by at most one actor link. It is not possible to connect two actors via both *is-a* and *participates-in*. An *Actor* can (sometimes, has to) cooperate with another *Actor* to fulfil common *Goals* to the *Roles* that each of these *Actors* occupies.

Role

As stated above, an organizational *Role* of the product line is an abstract characterization of expected behavior of an *Actor* within some specified context of the product line. An *Actor* can occupy multiple *Roles* and multiple *Actors* can occupy a *Role*.

The following **Role** schema shows the Z formal specification of Role concept within a product line. Each Role requires a set of Capabilities to fulfil or contribute to Goals for which it is responsible. An Actor can occupy the Role only if it possesses the required Capabilities (**c4**). Moreover, to entering Roles, Actors should be able to leave Roles at runtime (**c5**).

Roles are responsible for *Goals* (**c6**) and can control their fulfilment. This control procedure requires that a single *Actor* can never occupy distinct *Roles* that are responsible of and control the fulfilment of the *Goal* (**c7**). In addition, *Roles* can have different levels of authority. Consequently, a Role can have authority on other Roles. The authority on relationship specifies the hierarchical structure of the product line.

[Goal_control_Status]

Role_____

name : *Name*
description : *Informal_Definition*
require : *set Capability*
responsible : *set Goal*
control : *set (Goal, Goal_control_status)*
authoroty_on : *set Role*

(require ≠ ø) ∧ (responsible ≠ ø)	(**c3**)
(∀ act : *Actor* ; r : *Role*)	(**c4**)
r ∈ act.occupy ⟹ r.require ⊂ act.possess	
(∀ act : *Actor* ; r : *Role*)	(**c5**)
act.leave ⟹ r ∉ act.occupy	
(∀ r : *Role* ; g : *Goal*)	(**c6**)
g ∈ r.responsible ⟹ g.sec_is_a = Goal	
(∀ r_1 , r_2 : *Role* ; g : *Goal* ; a_1 , a_2 : *Actor*)	(**c7**)
(g.sec_is_a = Goal ∧ g ∈ r_1.responsible ∧ g ∈ r_2.control ∧ r_1 ≠ r_2 ∧ r_1 ∈ act.occupy ∧ r_2 ∈ act.occupy) ⟹ a_1 ≠ a_2	

Dependum

In social models such as iStar 2.0, dependencies represent social relationships. A dependency is defined as a relationship with five arguments:

- *Depender* is the actor that depends for something (the dependum) to be provided;
- *DependerElmt* is the intentional element within the depender's actor boundary where the dependency starts from, which explains why the dependency exists;

- *Dependum* is an intentional element that is the object of the dependency;
- *Dependee* is the actor that should provide the dependum;
- *DependeeElmt* is the intentional element that explains how the dependee intends to provide the dependum.

Dependencies link the *dependerElmt* within the *depender* actor to the dependum, outside actor boundaries, to the *dependeeElmt* within the *dependee* actor.

The type of the dependum specializes the semantics of the relationship:

- *Goal*: the dependee is expected to achieve the goal, and is free to choose how;
- *Quality:* the dependee is expected to sufficiently satisfy the quality, and is free to choose how;
- *Task:* the dependee is expected to execute the task in a prescribed way;
- *Resource:* the dependee is expected to make the resource available to the depender.

[Dependum_Type] := Goal | Quality | Task | Resource

_Dependum______

name : *Name*
description : *Informal_Definition*
type : *Dependum_Type*
depender : set *Role*
dependee : set *Role*

(type $\neq$ ø) $\wedge$ (depender $\neq$ ø) $\wedge$ (dependee $\neq$ ø)   (c8)
($\forall$ d : *Dependency* ; dpd : *Dependum* ; r_1, r_2 : *Role*)   (c9)
$r_1 \neq r_2 \wedge$ (d $\equiv r_1$ x dpd x r_2) $\Rightarrow$ (depender = $r_2 \wedge$ dependee = r_1)
($\forall$ d : *Dependency* ; dpd : *Dependum* ; r_1, r_2 : *Role*)   (c10)
$r_1 \neq r_2$ (d $\equiv r_1$ x dpd x r_2) $\wedge$ (dpd.type = authorization)
$\Rightarrow r_1 \in r_2$.authoroty_on
($\forall$ res : *Resource* ; a_1, a_2 : *Actor* ; cap_1, cap_2 : *Capability* ;
t_1, t_2 : *Task* ; r_1, r_2 : *Role*)   (c11)
($a_1 \neq a_2 \wedge cap_1 \neq cap_2 \wedge t_1 \neq t_2 \wedge$ ($t_1 \in cap_1$.composed_of $\wedge$
$cap_1 \in a_1$.possess) $\wedge$ ($t_2 \in cap_2$.composed_of $\wedge cap_2 \in a_2$.possess) $\wedge$ res $\in t_1$.postcondition $\wedge$
res $\in t_2$.input $\wedge r_1 \in a_1$.occupy $\wedge r_2 \in a_2$.occupy $\wedge$ { r_1, r_2} $\notin$ { a_1.occupy $\cap a_2$.occupy})
$\Leftrightarrow$ ($\exists$ dm: Dependum $\wedge$ dm.type = Resource $\wedge$ dm.name = res.name $\wedge$ dm.depender = $r_2 \wedge$
dm.dependee = r_1)

The **Dependum** schema above shows the formal specification of the *Dependum*. *Resource* dependency allows us to represent any specialization of the *Resource* concept as a *Dependum*. For example, a *Role (r₁)* might depend on another *Role (r₂)* for an *Authorization*. This has implication on the authority on relationship, as this dependency means that r_2 must have authority on r_1 (i.e. **c11**). In addition, the constraint (**c11**) demonstrates that the existence of a *Resource Dependum* among *Roles* has implications on the *Input* and *Postcondition* of *Tasks* accomplished by *Actors* that occupy these *Roles*.

3.2   Goal Sub-model

Intentional elements are the actors' needs. As such, they model different kinds of requirements and are central to our proposal. The following elements are considered as *Intentional Elements (Family Goal Model Elements)* in this work:

- *Goal:* a state of affairs that the actor wants to achieve and that has clearly cut criteria of achievement;
- *Quality:* an attribute for which an actor desires some level of achievement;
- *Task:* an action that an actor wants to be executed, usually with the purpose of achieving some goal;
- *Resource:* a physical or informational entity that the actor requires in order to perform a task.

The **Family Goal Model** schema below highlights the formal specification of the *Family Goal Model* adopted in our proposal. Constraint **(c12)** states that Goals and Tasks must have a non-empty status. In addition, if there is a set of Tasks *(tset)*, such that the *Goal* is a subset of *tset*, then the *Goal is fulfilled* **(c13)**. Moreover, a Goal is a *Requirement* if there is some *Agent Actor act* which occupies a *Role* which in turn is responsible for the Goal **(c14)**. A Goal is an *Expectation*, if there is some specific *Role* that is responsible for the *Goal* **(c15)**.

[Family_Goal_Element] := Goal | Quality | Task | Resource
[Goal_Type] := Requirement | Expectation
[Goal_Pattern] := Achieve | Cease | Maintain | Avoid
[Status] := Fulfilled | Unfulfilled
[Refinement_Alternative]

Family Goal Model_____
name : *Name*
description : *Informal_Definition*
intentional_elmt_is_a : *Family_Goal_Element*
goal_is_a : *Goal_Type*
pattern : *Goal_Pattern*
status : *Status*
refined_by : set *Refinement_Alternative*

($\forall$ g: *Goal* ; t: *Task*) g.intentional_elmt_is_a = Goal $\land$
t.intentional_elmt_is_a = *Task* $\Rightarrow$ (g.status $\neq$ $\emptyset$) $\land$ (t.status $\neq$ $\emptyset$)   **(c12)**
($\forall$ g: *Goal*) g.intentional_elmt_is_a = *Goal*
$\land$ $\exists$ tset = {t_1 , ... , t_2} $\Rightarrow$ g.status = Fulfilled   **(c13)**
($\forall$ g : *Goal* ; r : *Role* ; act : *Actor*)   **(c14)**
(g.intentional_elmt_is_a = *Goal* $\land$ r $\in$ act.occupy $\land$ g $\in$ r.responsible $\land$ act.isa = *Agent*) $\Rightarrow$
g.goal_is_a = *Requirement*
($\forall$ g : *Goal* ; r : *Role* ; ac t: *Actor*)   **(c15)**
(g.intentional_elmt_is_a = Goal $\land$ r $\in$ act.occupy $\land$ g $\in$ r.responsible $\land$ act.isa = Role) $\Rightarrow$
g.goal_is_a = Expectation

Several types of link exist in order to connect intentional elements. These links are: *refinement, needed-by, contribution* and *qualification*.

Refinement is an n-ary relationship relating one parent to one or more children. An intentional element can be the parent in at most one refinement relationship. There are two types of refinement – applied to any kind of parent (i.e. Goal or Task) – that define the logical operator relating the parent with the children:

- *AND-refinement*: the fulfillment of all the n children (n $\geq$ 2) makes the parent fulfilled;
- *Inclusive OR*: the fulfillment of at least one child makes the parent fulfilled.

The *Needed-By* relationship links a task with a resource and indicates that the actor needs the resource in order to execute the task. The *Contribution* links represent the effects of intentional elements on qualities, and are essential to assist analysts in the decision-making process among alternative goals or tasks. Contribution links lead to the accumulation of evidence for qualities. The *Qualification* relationship relates a quality to its subject (i.e. a task, goal, or resource).

In our proposal the goal model called Family Goal Model, represents the intentional space of a domain for which the product line is developed. The adopted goal-oriented approach helps to build artifacts that represent stakeholders' objectives and strategies.

3.3 Feature Sub-model

As stated above, our proposal offers feature-oriented design and implementation for which feature models are a standard visual representation. Feature models support a natural description of a wide range of variability schemata.

Several definitions to what domain experts call "feature" exist in the literature (see [43]). Due to the lack of space, we will not list them here and adopt the following definition of the term feature based on [43]: *A feature is a characteristic or end-user-visible behavior of a software system. Features are used in product line engineering to specify and communicate commonalities and differences of the products between stakeholders, and to guide structure, reuse, and variation across all phases of the software life cycle* [19].

A feature model is a tree of which nodes are labelled with feature names. It also proposes various parent-child relationships between features and their constraints. In fact, if a feature *f* is a child of another feature *p*, *f* can be selected only when *p* is also selected. Typically, a feature model includes mutual relations between features. In addition, *Mandatory* and *Optional* features are distinguished within the feature model. Note that in our proposal we focus on *Boolean features* identified by a name. In principle, *non-Boolean features* or *attributes of features* may also be of interest in distinguishing applications of the product line. In this paper, we cover essentially Boolean features; non-Boolean features will be studied in future work.

[Feature_Type] := Parent | Child | Abstract | Concrete
[Feature_Availability] := Available | Unavailable
[Feature_Constraint_Type] := Mandatory | Optional | Alternative | Or

Feature Model_____
name : Name
description : Informal_Definition
is_a : Feature_Type
availability : Feature_Availability
constraint_type : Feature_Constraint_Type
_____
root (f) ≡ f   (c16)
mandatory (p, f) ≡ f ⇔ p   (c17)
optional (p, f) ≡ f ⇒ p   (c18)

alternative (p, {f$_1$, ... , f$_n$}) ≡ ((f$_1$ ∨ ... ∨ f$_n$) ⇔ p) ∧ ($\bigwedge_{i<j}$ ¬ (f$_i$ ∧ f$_j$))   (c19)
Or (p, {f$_1$, ... , f$_n$}) ≡ (f$_1$ ∨ ... ∨ f$_n$) ⇔ p   (c20)

The **Feature Model** schema above formalizes the *Feature Model* concepts. All feature names from the set F of feature names are interpreted as propositional variables, p, f and f_i represents members of F. Each edge in the tree is defined by exactly one feature constraint, that is, by a declaration of one of the feature constraint types *mandatory*, *optional*, *alternative*, or *"or"*. A *mandatory* feature definition between a parent feature and a child feature corresponds to a logical equivalence. That is, whenever the parent feature is selected, so must the child and vice-versa (**c17**). An *optional* feature corresponds to implication. The implication states that the parent feature may be chosen independently from the child feature, but the child feature can only be chosen if the parent feature is selected (**c18**). The *alternative* constraint defines a one-out-of-many choice. The definition of the constraint (**c19**) has the parent feature as first parameter and a non-empty set of child features as second parameter. This constraint is a disjunction in which, at least, one child feature is selected when the parent is chosen. In addition, we ensure for each pair of child features that no two child features are selected together. An unrestricted *choice* or *"or"* defines a some-out-of-many choice. Again, the constraint (**c20**) has a non-empty set of child features as second parameter. The selection of parent feature is equivalent to a disjunction of the child features. Additionally, a set of cross-tree constraints may be defined in the feature model. The corresponding propositional formula of the feature constraints and the cross-tree constraints are conjoined resulting in one logic formula that represents the semantics of the whole feature model.

4 User Story Concept

Our proposed metamodel focuses on agile perspectives. Relevant agile requirements artifacts thus play, a core role within the proposal. This section details the user story concept, which the proposed metamodel integrates. User stories are considered here due to their wide use and to take profit from their effectiveness. Leffingwell [44] and Chon [22], consider them as an increasingly popular textual notation to capture requirements in agile software development. User stories are statements that use a simple template such as *"As a ⟨role⟩, I want ⟨goal⟩, [so that ⟨benefit⟩]"*.

The **User Story** schema above formalizes the *User Story* (μ_i) concept. Let $U = \{\mu_1, \mu_2, \ldots\}$ a set of user stories in a project. A user story μ is a 4-tuple $\mu_i = \langle r_i, m_i, E_i, f_i \rangle$ where r is the role, m is the means, $E = \{e_1, e_2, \ldots\}$ is a set of ends, and f is the format. In addition, a means m is a 5-tuple $m = \langle s, av, do, io, adj \rangle$ where s is a *"subject"*, av is an *"action verb"*, do is a *"direct object"*, io is an *"indirect object"*, and adj is an *"adjective"* (io and adj may be null).

A user story μ_1 is an exact duplicate of another user story μ_2 when they are identical (**c21**). The constraint (**c22**) indicates that a user story μ_1 duplicates the request of μ_2, while using a different text (i.e. Semantic Duplicate). (**c23**) denotes two or more user stories that have the same end, but achieve this using different means. (**c24**) represents the case in which two or more user stories use the same means to reach different ends. For the case where two or more user stories with different roles, but same means and/or ends we formalize the constraint (**c25**). When there is a strong semantic relationship between two user stories, it is important to add *explicit dependencies* to the user stories, although this breaks the *independent* criterion (**c26**). Uniformity in the context of user stories means that a user story format is consistent with the one of the majority of user stories in the same set. Therefore, the format f_1 of an individual user story μ_1 is syntactically compared to the most common format f_{std} to determine whether it adheres to the uniformity criterion (**c27**).

[User_Story_Element] := Format | Role | Means | Ends
[Mean] := Subject | Action_Verb | Direct_Object | Indirect_Object | Adjective
[End] := Clarification | Dependency | Quality
[Status] := To_Do | In_Progress | Testing | Done

User Story

identifier : *Identifier*
user_story_elmt_is_a : *User_Story_Element*
mean_is_a : *Mean*
end_is_a : *End*
status : *Status*

($\forall$ μ_1 , μ_2 : User_Story)   **(c21)**
is_Full_Duplicate (μ_1, μ_2) $\leftrightarrow$ μ_1 $=_{syn}$ μ_2
($\forall$ μ_1 , μ_2 : *User_Story*)   **(c22)**
is_Sem_Duplicate (μ_1 , μ_2) $\leftrightarrow$ μ_1 = μ_2 $\wedge$ μ_1 $\neq_{syn}$ μ_2
($\forall$ μ_1 , μ_2 : *User_Story* ; m_1, m_2 : *Means* ; E_1, E_2 : *Ends*)   **(c23)**
diff_Means_same_Ends (μ_1 , μ_2) $\leftrightarrow$ m_1 $\neq$ m_2
$\wedge$ E_1 $\cap$ E_2 $\neq$ $\emptyset$
($\forall$ μ_1 , μ_2 : *User_Story* ; m_1, m_2 : *Means* ; E_1, E_2 : *Ends*)   **(c24)**
same_Means_diff_Ends (μ_1 , μ_2) $\leftrightarrow$ m_1 = m_2 $\wedge$ (E_1 \ E_2 $\neq$ $\emptyset$ $\vee$ E_2 \ E_1 $\neq$ $\emptyset$)
($\forall$ μ_1 , μ_2 : *User_Story* ; m_1, m_2 : *Means* ; E_1, E_2 : *Ends* ; r_1, r_2 : *Role*)   **(c25)**
same_Role_diff_Story (μ_1 , μ_2) $\leftrightarrow$ r_1 $\neq$ r_2 $\wedge$ (m_1 = m_2 $\vee$ E_1 $\cap$ E_2 $\neq$ $\emptyset$)
($\forall$ μ_1 , μ_2 : *User_Story* ; m_1, m_2 : *Means* ; E_1, E_2 : *Ends*)   **(c26)**
purpose_is_Means (μ_1 , μ_2) $\leftrightarrow$ E_1 = \{m_2\}
($\forall$ μ_1 : *User_Story* ; f_1, f_{std} : *Format*)   **(c27)**
is_not_Uniform (μ_1, f_{std}) $\leftrightarrow$ f_1 $\neq_{syn}$ f_{std}
($\forall$ μ_1 : *User_Story* ; av_1, av_2 : *Action_Verb* ; do_1, do_2 : *Direct_Object*)   **(c28)**
has_Dep (μ_1 , μ_2) $\leftrightarrow$ depends (av_1, av_2) $\wedge$ do_1 = do_2
($\forall$ μ_1 , μ_2 $\in$ U : *User_Story* ; do_1, do_2 : *Direct_Object*)   **(c29)**
has_is_a_Dep (μ_1 , μ_2) $\leftrightarrow$ $\exists$ μ_2 $\in$ U . is_a (do_1, do_2)
($\forall$ μ_1 , μ_2 $\in$ U : *User_Story* ; av_1, av_2 : *Action_Verb* ; do_1, do_2 : *Direct_Object*)   **(c30)**
void_Dep (μ_1) $\leftrightarrow$ depends (av_1, av_2) $\wedge$ $\nexists$ μ_2 $\in$ U . do_1 = do_2

In some cases, it is necessary that one user story μ_1 be completed before the developer can start on another story μ_2. Formally, the predicate *has-Dep(μ_1, μ_2)* holds when μ_1 causally depends on μ_2 **(c28)**. Moreover, an object of one user story μ_1 can refer to multiple other objects of stories in *U*, indicating that the object of μ_1 is a parent or superclass of the other objects. Formally, predicate *has-is-a-Dep(μ_1, μ_2)* is true when μ_1 has a direct object superclass dependency based on the sub-class do_2 o do_1 **(c29)**.

Implementing a set of user stories *U* should lead to a feature-complete application. While user stories should not thrive to cover 100% of the application's functionality preemptively, crucial user stories should not be missed, for this may cause a show stopping feature-gap. The predicate *void-Dep(μ_1)* holds when no story μ_2 satisfies a dependency for μ_1's direct object **(c30)**.

In a nutshell, our proposed metamodel offers a better understanding of the representation of product lines requirements and their stakeholders' requirements. In addition, it takes inspiration from research in GORE frameworks such as iStar 2.0 [41], and from feature-oriented modeling [19], related to agile requirements practices like user stories [22, 23, 44, 45].

5 The AgiFPL Methodology

This section illustrates how our proposed metamodel can be adopted for the requirements engineering stage of agile product lines, when using methodology called AgiFPL [10]. Like classical agile product lines methodologies, AgiFPL is a feature-oriented approach involving two classical tiers of product line engineering: Domain Engineering and Application Engineering.

AgiFPL also considers two spaces: the Problem and Solution ones. The problem space calls attention to the perspective of stakeholders and their problems, requirements, and views of the entire domain and individual products. The solution space represents the developers' and vendors' perspectives [19]. The Solution Space is not targeted in this work since our proposed metamodel is designed essentially for the requirements engineering concerned by the Problem Space.

Integrating our proposed metamodel to AgiFPL allows modelling and managing intentions, goals, variabilities and commonalities of the product lines. For example, the "Family Goal Models" of our proposed metamodel will guide the development of variability of the product line in the domain engineering, while they are used for the configuration of products in the application engineering. Note that in this paper we will not present all processes of AgiFPL. However, we will detail the processes that concern the requirements engineering in both tiers of the methodology (i.e. Domain requirements engineering process and Application requirements engineering process).

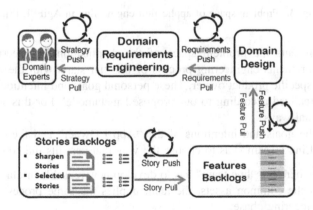

Fig. 2. Problem space of domain engineering in AgiFPL [8].

Figure 2 illustrates the problem space of the Domain Engineering tier. The figure depicts the main steps of the RE process followed in the domain engineering. Based on the strategy of a software vendor who decides to adopt AgiFPL, *Domain Experts* and *concerned teams* apply our proposed metamodel as follows:

1. Execute a sub-process for modeling the family goal models. (i.e. goal-oriented requirements engineering);
2. Apply the stated practices and rules of our proposal in order to generate the correspondent feature models (specifies and design the desired domain – i.e. Domain Design & Feature Backlog);
3. Prioritize the identified features of the designed domain and then document the required user stories (apply the correspondent agile requirements practices – i.e. Stories Backlog, tests, …).

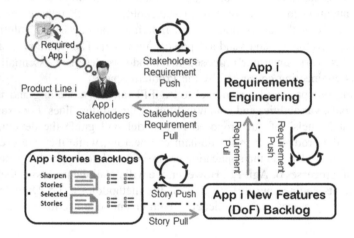

Fig. 3. Problem space of application engineering in AgiFPL [8].

Figure 3 presents the problem space of the Application Engineering tier. The concerned requirements engineering process of this tier starts with the goals and the intentions of a specific product owner. These personal goals and intentions are studied, modelled and realized according to our proposed metamodel. For this stage, we propose two optional ways.

Based on the goals and intentions of the "App i Owner" and the context of the "Line i", the "Line i Team" has to choose the way that best fits the context:

1. In the case where the "line team" has to develop new reusable artefacts that do not exist within the common assets, the team applies the same process used for the domain-engineering phase;
2. In the case where some stakeholders' goals do not affect the product line, have not equivalent features in the common assets and concern a specific product, the "Line Team" produces directly the User Stories and their Backlogs.

Making the relevant decisions for each tier allows analysts and developers of an agile product line to efficiently represent stakeholders' intentions and goals on the one hand and product line variabilities and communalities on the other hand. AgiFPL is thus an agile methodology designed to improve the agility within the software product lines and effectively meet any new emerged business expectations. Its main goal is to move teams from the classical approach to a more evolved APLE framework.

6 Applying the Proposed Metamodel

A simple and short example related to an e-commerce product line is outlined below to describe and show the applicability of our proposed metamodel. The e-commerce case study is available in the SPLOT repository (Software Product Lines Online Tools – http://www.splot-research.org/).

We first design the family goal model related to the case study and then follow the practices of our proposed metamodel to generate the correspondent feature model. Due to the lack of space, we only present the application of Goals and Features sub-models, the mapping from the goal model to its correspondent feature model and an example of user story.

Figure 4 shows a concrete "Family Goal Model" of the "Order Process" related to the e-commerce case study (modeled using iStar 2.0). It represents the intentional elements and relations. For example, the goal <Item_Available> can be achieved by <Prepare_and_Package_Item>, by <Obtain_From_Stock>, and by <Aquire_From_Supplier>. In addition, satisfactions of the tasks <Obtain_From_Stock>, and <Aquire_From_Supplier> lead to satisfaction and dissatisfaction of the quality <Avoid_Unsold_Stock>. In fact, if the "sales department" adopts a "Make to Stock" strategy, it could lead to unsold items. However, adopting "Make to Order" strategy will help to avoid a stock of unsold items.

According to our proposed framework, to represent a mapping we should develop a mapping relation (Φ) for each mapped task. For example, the *Approve Order (AO)* task is mapped to the *Automatic Approval*, and *Manual Approval* features. Therefore, the mapping relation created is the following:

$$\Phi AO\ (Approve\ Order, \{Automatic\ Approval, Manual\ Approval\}).$$

Moreover, the *Receive e-Payment (REP)* task is mapped to *Debit Card Payment*, *Credit Card Payment*, and *Payment Gateway*. Thus, the mapping relation created is the following:

$$\Phi REP\ (Receive\ e\text{-}Payment, \{Debit\ Card\ Payment, Credit\ Card\ Payment, Payment\ Gateway\}).$$

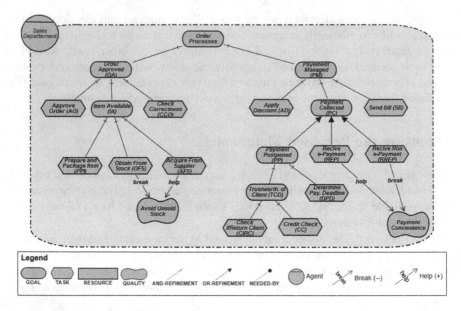

Fig. 4. A FGM for "Order Processes" modeled from the e-commerce case study [8].

Once the "explicit mapping" between tasks in the family goal model and features in feature model is executed, we can start an "implicit mapping" between intermediate tasks, goals, and features. The implicit mapping is performed between "intentional relations" in family goal models and "feature relations" in feature models. For example, following our proposed metamodel, we can infer that the goal *Payment Managed (PM)* in the family goal model (see Fig. 4) is implicitly mapped to the feature *Payment Management (PMa)* (see Fig. 5).

Note that, if a feature is mapped to more than one goal or/and task, then the corresponding feature appears in the mapping relations of all those goals or/and tasks.

Figure 5 shows the corresponding feature model of the family goal model presented in Fig. 4. The obtained feature model is represented using a tree graphical notation that could be translated into propositional logic. In addition, the feature model is generated according to the rules and practices of our proposed metamodel.

Based on the illustrated example, it was shown that the modeled family goal model of "Order Processes" (i.e. Figure 4) captures the intentional variability and describes the intentions behind existing features in the product line of e-commerce. Hereafter, we present some mappings as follows:

Order Processes (G-OP) = Order Management
Order Approved (G-OA) = Order Preparation
Payment Managed (G-PM) = Payment Management
Item Available (G-IA) = Item Preparation
Check Correctness of Order (T-CCO) = Order Confirmation (FC ∨ MC ∨ EC)
Obtain From Stock (T-OFS) = TFW
Acquire From Supplier (T-AFS) = BI
Apply Discount (T-AS) = (CoP ∨ PD)

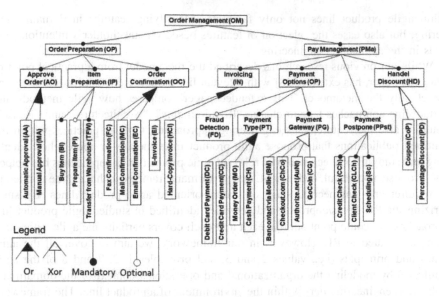

Fig. 5. Correspondent feature model [8].

Finally, as an illustration of user stories generated according to our proposed metamodel from the correspondent features, **<Invoicing>** could be realized by several user stories, such as: *As ⟨Accountant⟩, I want to ⟨Generate and Send Invoices⟩, so that ⟨the Invoice can be paid⟩*.

7   Conclusion

Approaches that combine agility attribute with software product lines have been proposed to practitioners and researchers. Being agile while preserving a software product-line structure implies the adopted Agile Product Line approach conforms to agile values and principles. Requirements engineering issues are main elements to consider when integrating agility to software product lines. Collaborating with customers and responding quickly to changes are principals that have to be supported by any proposed (agile) process. Thus, any Agile Product Line approach should assign a high priority to satisfy customers through early and continuous delivery of valuable software from the start, in addition to accommodate any changing requirements, even coming late in the process.

Following these guidelines, our previous research has proposed an integrated and consistent metamodel for software analysts and developers who adopt agile product line approaches. The main contribution presented in [8] allows capturing intentional variability and describing goals behind existing features in the agile product line. Therefore, by using family goal models we can ensure that existing features and variability relations in feature models are aligned with intentional variability in the family goal models. In addition, we can trace back differences in products from differences in the intentions of stakeholders. Moreover, applying intentional elements within agile product lines not only facilitates identifying features in domain engineering, but also eases the selection of features based on stakeholder's intentions and needs in the application engineering.

While our previous research has described the metamodel from a practical point of view, this paper, has extended [8] with relevant literature review that lead us to define theoretically the metamodel. This extended paper compares how agile methods and product-line approaches take in charge "Requirements", "Architecture", and "Reuse". It studies also the requirements engineering approaches, tools or practices within the identified publications that propose agile product lines models or approaches. Identifying and studying RE techniques of relevant agile product lines approaches has helped us to propose a powerful, convenient, and performant framework that can be applied to the requirements engineering stage of feature-oriented agile product lines. By summarizing the RE Tools/approach and activities identified in studied agile product line approaches, we could point out that each approach covers partially the agile values and principles related to RE. However, in our framework, we aim to cover all the agile values and principles (i.e., values 2 and 3, and principles 1, 2, 7 and 8 of the agile manifesto) by modeling the organizational and operational context of the domain and application engineering tiers within the environment of a product line. The framework allows capturing intentional variability and describing the intentions behind existing features in the agile product line.

Our future priorities aim to develop a procedure to discover inconsistencies in mapping results (i.e., generated goal models and/or generated feature models). We will aim at extending the validation technique to cover other properties such as for example safe composition (i.e., for all goal models modeled within the application engineering tier, they have at least one correspondent feature model and vice versa).

References

1. da Silva, I.F., da Mota Silveira Neto, P.A., O'Leary, P., de Almeida, E.S., de Lemos Meira, S.R.: Agile software product lines: a systematic mapping study. Softw.: Pract. Exp. **41**(8), 899–920 (2011)
2. Clements, P.C., Northrop, L.: Software Product Lines: Practices and Patterns. Addison-Wesley, Boston (2001)
3. Díaz, J., Pérez, J., Alarcón, P.P., Garbajosa, J.: Agile product line engineering - a systematic literature review. Softw.: Pract. Exp. **41**(8), 921–941 (2011)
4. Asadi, M., Ramsin, R.: MDA-based methodologies: an analytical survey. In: Schieferdecker, I., Hartman, A. (eds.) ECMDA-FA 2008. LNCS, vol. 5095, pp. 419–431. Springer, Heidelberg (2008). https://doi.org/10.1007/978-3-540-69100-6_30
5. Pohl, K., Böckle, G., van der Linden, F.J.: Software Product Line Engineering: Foundations, Principles, and Techniques. Springer, Berlin (2005)
6. Coplien, J., Hoffman, D., Weiss, D.: Commonality and variability in software engineering. IEEE Softw. **15**(6), 37–45 (1998)

7. Alves, V., Niu, N., Alves, C.F., Valença, G.: Requirements engineering for software product lines: a systematic literature review. Inf. Softw. Technol. **52**(8), 806–820 (2010)
8. Haidar, H., Kolp, M., Wautelet, Y.: Formalizing agile software product lines with a RE metamodel. In: 13th International Conference on Software Technologies, ICSOFT 2018, pp. 90–101. SciTePress, Porto (2018)
9. O'Regan, G.: Z formal specification language. In: O'Regan, G. (ed.) Mathematics in Computing: An Accessible Guide to Historical, Foundational and Application Contexts, pp. 109–122. Springer, London (2013). https://doi.org/10.1007/978-1-4471-4534-9_6
10. Haidar, H., Kolp, M., Wautelet, Y.: Agile product line engineering: the AgiFPL method. In: 12th International Conference on Software Technologies, ICSOFT 2017, pp. 275–285. SciTePress, Madrid (2017)
11. Borba, C., Silva, C.: A comparison of goal-oriented approaches to model software product lines variability. In: Heuser, C.A., Pernul, G. (eds.) ER 2009. LNCS, vol. 5833, pp. 244–253. Springer, Heidelberg (2009). https://doi.org/10.1007/978-3-642-04947-7_30
12. Tian, K., Cooper, K.: Agile and software product line methods: are they so different. In: 1st International Workshop on Agile Product Line Engineering (2006)
13. Carbon, R., Lindvall, M., Muthig, D., Costa, P.: Integrating product line engineering and agile methods: flexible design up-front vs. incremental design. In: 1st International Workshop on Agile Product Line Engineering (2006)
14. Boehm, B.W.: Get ready for agile methods, with care. IEEE Comput. **35**(1), 64–69 (2002)
15. Navarrete, F., Botella, P., Franch, X.: How agile COTS selection methods are (and can be). In: Proceedings of the 31st EUROMICRO Conference on Software Engineering and Advanced Applications, Porto, Portugal, pp. 160–167. IEEE Computer Society (2005)
16. Noor, M.A., Rabiser, R., Grünbacher, P.: Agile product line planning: a collaborative approach and a case study. J. Syst. Softw. **81**(6), 868–882 (2008)
17. Schön, E.-M., Thomaschewski, J., Escalona, M.J.: Agile requirements engineering: a systematic literature review. Comput. Stand. Interfaces **49**, 79–91 (2017)
18. Highsmith, J., Cockburn, A.: Agile software development: the business of innovation. Computer **34**(9), 120–122 (2001)
19. Apel, S., Batory, D., Kästner, C., Saake, G.: Feature-Oriented Software Product Lines: Concepts and Implementation. Springer, Heidelberg (2013). https://doi.org/10.1007/978-3-642-37521-7
20. Northrop, L., Clement, P.C.: A framework for software product line practice, version 5.0. https://resources.sei.cmu.edu/library/asset-view.cfm?assetID=495357. Accessed 23 Nov 2018
21. Irshad, M., Petersen, K., Poulding, S.: A systematic literature review of software requirements reuse approaches. Inf. Softw. Technol. **93**(C), 223–245 (2018)
22. Cohn, M.: User Stories Applied: For Agile Software Development. Addison Wesley Longman Publishing Co., Boston (2004)
23. Wautelet, Y., Heng, S., Hintea, D., Kolp, M., Poelmans, S.: Bridging user story sets with the use case model. In: Link, S., Trujillo, Juan C. (eds.) ER 2016. LNCS, vol. 9975, pp. 127–138. Springer, Cham (2016). https://doi.org/10.1007/978-3-319-47717-6_11
24. van der Linden, F.J., Schmid, K., Rommes, E.: Software Product Lines in Action: The Best Industrial Practice in Product Line Engineering. Springer, Heidelberg (2007). https://doi.org/10.1007/978-3-540-71437-8
25. Rubin, K.S.: Essential Scrum: A Practical Guide to the Most Popular Agile Process. Addison-Wesley Professional (2012)

26. Wautelet, Y., Heng, S., Kolp, M., Mirbel, I.: Unifying and extending user story models. In: Jarke, M., Mylopoulos, J., Quix, C., Rolland, C., Manolopoulos, Y., Mouratidis, H., Horkoff, J. (eds.) CAiSE 2014. LNCS, vol. 8484, pp. 211–225. Springer, Cham (2014). https://doi.org/10.1007/978-3-319-07881-6_15

27. Broy, M.: Domain modeling and domain engineering: key tasks in requirements engineering. In: Münch, J., Schmid, K. (eds.) Perspectives on the Future of Software Engineering. Springer, Heidelberg (2013). https://doi.org/10.1007/978-3-642-37395-4_2

28. Klünder, J., Hohl, P., Schneider, K.: Becoming agile while preserving software product lines: an agile transformation model for large companies. In: Proceedings of the 2018 International Conference on Software and System Process, Gothenburg, Sweden, pp. 1–10. ACM (2018)

29. Babar, M.A., Ihme, T., Pikkarainen, M.: An industrial case of exploiting product line architectures in agile software development. In: Proceedings of the 13th International Software Product Line Conference, San Francisco, California, USA, pp. 171–179. Carnegie Mellon University (2009)

30. Ghanam, Y., Park, S., Maurer, F.: A test-driven approach to establishing & managing agile product lines. In: Proceedings of the 5th Software Product Line Testing Workshop (SPLiT 2008) in Conjunction with SPLC 2008, Limerick, Ireland (2008)

31. O'Leary, P., McCaffery, F., Thiel, S., Richardson, I.: An agile process model for product derivation in software product line engineering. J. Softw. Maint. Res. Pract. 24(5), 561–571 (2012)

32. Díaz, J., Pérez, J., Garbajosa, J.: Agile product-line architecting in practice: a case study in smart grids. Inf. Softw. Technol. 56(7), 727–748 (2014)

33. Schwaber, K., Beedle, M.: Agile Software Development with Scrum. Prentice Hall PTR, Upper Saddle River (2002)

34. dos Santos Jr., A.F., Lucena Jr., V.F.: SCRUMPL - software product line engineering with scrum. In: Proceedings of ENASE 2010 - Conference on Evaluation of Novel Approaches to Software Engineering, Setubal, Portugal, pp. 239–244. SciTePress (2010)

35. Kuhrmann, M., Tiessler, M.: Crafting a Method Engineering Metamodel – Approach, Methods, Results. TU München, Garching (2014)

36. Engels, G., Sauer, S.: A meta-method for defining software engineering methods. In: Engels, G., Lewerentz, C., Schäfer, W., Schürr, A., Westfechtel, B. (eds.) Graph Transformations and Model-Driven Engineering. Lecture Notes in Computer Science, vol. 5765, pp. 411–440. Springer, Berlin, Heidelberg (2010). https://doi.org/10.1007/978-3-642-17322-6_18

37. OMG: Unified Modeling Language (OMG UML) - version 2.5.1. Technical report (2017)

38. Yu, E., Giorgini, P., Maiden, N., Mylopoulos, J. (eds.): Social Modeling for Requirements Engineering. MIT, Cambridge (2011)

39. Mouratidis, H., Kolp, M., Faulkner, S., Giorgini, P.: A secure architectural description language for agent systems. In: Proceedings of the 4th International Joint Conference on Autonomous Agents and Multiagent Systems, pp. 578–585. ACM, The Netherlands (2005)

40. Asadi, M., Gröner, G., Mohabbati, B., Gasevic, D.: Goal-oriented modeling and verification of feature-oriented product lines. Softw. Syst. Model. 15(1), 257–279 (2014)

41. Dalpiaz, F., Franch, X., Horkoff, J.J.C.: iStar 2.0 Language Guide (v3) 2016. https://arxiv.org/pdf/1605.07767v3.pdf. Accessed 14 Oct 2018

42. Jaqueira, A., Lucena, M., Alencar, F.M.R., Castro, J., Aranha, E.: Using i* models to enrich user stories. In: Proceedings of the 6th International i* Workshop 2013, Valencia, Spain, pp. 55–60. CEUR-WS.org (2013)

43. Haidar, H., Kolp, M., Wautelet, Y.: Goal-oriented requirement engineering for agile software product lines: an overview. LouRIM Working Paper Series, February 2017. http://hdl.handle.net/2078.1/185846

44. Leffingwell, D.: Agile Software Requirements: Lean Requirements Practices for Teams, Programs, and the Enterprise. Addison-Wesley Professional, Boston (2011)

45. Wautelet, Y., Heng, S., Kiv, S., Kolp, M.: User-story driven development of multi-agent systems: a process fragment for agile methods. Comput. Lang. Syst. Struct. **50**, 159–176 (2017)

46. Kolp, M., Do, T., Faulkner, S.: Introspecting agent-oriented design patterns. In: Chang, S.K. (ed.) Handbook of Software Engineering and Knowledge Engineering: Recent Advances: Recent Advances, vol. 3, pp. 151–177. World Scientific Publishing (2005)

Systematic Refinement of Softgoals Using a Combination of KAOS Goal Models and Problem Diagrams

Nelufar Ulfat-Bunyadi[✉], Nazila Gol Mohammadi, Roman Wirtz,
and Maritta Heisel

University of Duisburg-Essen, Duisburg, Germany
{nelufar.ulfat-bunyadi,nazila.golmohammadi,roman.wirtz,maritta.heisel}@uni-due.d

Abstract. Softgoals are goals that do not have a clear-cut criterion for their satisfaction (in contrast to so-called hardgoals). They are considered to be satisfied when there is sufficient positive and little negative evidence for this claim. Thus, they are expected to be satisfied within acceptable limits rather than absolutely. Examples of such softgoals are quality attributes such as safety, security, and trustworthiness. In a previous paper, we showed how the systematic refinement of goals can be supported by combining KAOS goal models and problem diagrams that are created based on the Six-Variable Model. Therein, we mainly focussed on hardgoals. In this paper, we show how the systematic refinement of softgoals can be supported. We mainly focus on security as a softgoal and show how it can be refined in a systematic way. However, our method can be used in the same way to systematically decompose other softgoals as well. The benefit of our method is that it results not only in detailed security requirements but helps also in making expectations to be satisfied e.g. by sensors, actuators, other systems, and users explicit.

Keywords: Softgoal · Goal refinement ·
KAOS goal model · Problem diagram · Security goal ·
Security concern · Security requirement · Assumption · Expectation

1 Introduction

In goal modelling, two types of goals are frequently distinguished: softgoals and hardgoals [1]. In contrast to hardgoals, softgoals are goals that do not have a clear-cut criterion for their satisfaction. A softgoal is considered to be satisfied (or, more precisely, 'satisficed') when there is sufficient positive and little negative evidence for this claim [2]. Quality attributes such as safety, security, and trustworthiness are typical softgoals.

KAOS is a goal-oriented requirements engineering methodology that was developed by van Lamsweerde [3]. In a KAOS goal model, multi-agent goals are refined until they can be assigned to single agents, i.e. either to the software-to-be or to agents in the software's environment (e.g. sensors, actuators, devices,

© Springer Nature Switzerland AG 2019
M. van Sinderen and L. A. Maciaszek (Eds.): ICSOFT 2018, CCIS 1077, pp. 150–172, 2019.
https://doi.org/10.1007/978-3-030-29157-0_7

users). As regards the refinement of goals in KAOS goal models, van Lamsweerde [3] suggests some heuristics to support this task. One heuristic consists in *asking HOW questions* (e.g. How can a goal G be satisfied? Is this subgoal sufficient or is there any other subgoal needed for satisfying G?). Another heuristic is called *Split responsibilities*. According to this heuristic, a goal is refined into subgoals by requiring the subgoals to involve fewer potential agents in their satisfaction than the parent goal. However, these are only heuristics. A systematic approach for achieving such a refinement and arriving at such subgoals is not provided.

In a previous paper [4], we presented a method that fills this gap and supports the systematic refinement of goals in KAOS goal models using an extension (the so-called Six-Variable Model [5]) that was originally made to problem diagrams [6] but is also useful for goal modelling. However, therein, we mainly focussed on hardgoals. In this paper, we therefore want to show how the systematic refinement of softgoals in KAOS goal models can be supported. Decomposing softgoals is more difficult than decomposing hardgoals, because softgoals do not have a have a clear-cut criterion for their satisfaction. For softgoals such as safety, security, and trustworthiness, the decomposition is not straightforward. Security, for example, is frequently decomposed into the three subgoals confidentiality, integrity, availability. However, simply stating that the confidentiality, integrity, and availability of an asset must be protected (e.g. "The user data should be confidential.") is not useful, since such requirements are not verifiable. They are too high-level and imprecise. Therefore, we suggest following a different approach in this paper. We identify security concerns of different stakeholders regarding the assets shown in problem diagrams. These concerns refer to confidentiality, integrity, and availability, but on a much more detailed level. Then, we define security requirements that address these concerns. All the security requirements contribute to satisfying the security softgoal. Thus, our method can be considered rather as a bottom-up approach than a top-down approach. We will mainly focus on security as a softgoal and show how it can be refined in a systematic way. However, our method can be used in the same way for other softgoals as well.

The paper is structured as follows. In Sect. 2, we first introduce the fundamentals of our work. In Sect. 3, we present our method. In Sect. 4, we illustrate its application using an example from the insurance domain. In Sect. 5, we discuss related work. Finally, in Sect. 6, we provide a conclusion and an outlook on future work.

2   Fundamentals

KAOS goal models and problem diagrams are both based on the well-known satisfaction argument developed by Zave and Jackson [7]. This commonality facilitates combining them and transferring or using concepts like the Six-Variable Model (defined for problem diagrams) for goal models as well to overcome shortcomings like the lack of support for a systematic refinement of goals. In this section, we first introduce briefly the satisfaction argument, KAOS goal models, problem diagrams, and the Six-Variable Model. Then, we describe how these were used in our previous method [4].

The Satisfaction Argument. According to Zave and Jackson [7], a *system* consists of the so-called *machine* (i.e. the software-to-be) and its *environment* (i.e. a part of the real world). The current behaviour of the environment is unsatisfactory. The objective of software development is to develop a software that will be inserted into this environment to achieve that the behaviour is satisfactory then. There are three types of statements about the machine, the environment, and the system: the specification S, the domain knowledge D, and the requirements R. Based on these statements, the satisfaction argument is defined as follows: $S, D \vdash R$. The argument says that, if a software is developed which satisfies S and is integrated into an environment as described by D, and S and D are consistent with each other, then R is satisfied.

KAOS Goal Models. Van Lamsweerde [3] calls S *software requirements* and R *system requirements*. As regards the domain knowledge D, he distinguishes between: *domain properties* (facts about the environment) and *assumptions* (about the environment). Assumptions are in turn divided into *domain hypotheses* (to be satisfied by the entire environment) and *expectations* (to be satisfied by single agents in the environment).

A KAOS goal model is an AND/OR graph. An example is shown in Fig. 10. As nodes of the graph, goals (hardgoals and softgoals), domain properties, and domain hypotheses can be modelled. Goals that are further refined are so-called multi-agent goals (i.e. several agents are responsible for satisfying them). Goals that are not further refined (i.e. leaves of the graph) are single-agent goals. This means they are assigned to single agents who are responsible for satisfying them. Single-agent goals assigned to the software-to-be represent *software requirements*. Single-agent goals assigned to the environment represent *expectations*. The AND/OR-refinement relationships between the nodes in the graph show which subgoals need to be satisfied and which domain properties and domain hypotheses need to be valid to satisfy a parent goal. Thus, the goal refinement structure in KAOS goal models reflects Zave and Jackson's satisfaction argument.

Problem Diagrams. Problem diagrams have been introduced by Jackson as part of the problem frames methodology [6]. According to this methodology, first, a context diagram is created showing the machine in its environment. Then, the overall software development problem is decomposed into sub-problems, and each sub-problem is documented in a problem diagram.

The problem diagram notation is shown in Fig. 1. The software-to-be is modelled as the so-called *machine domain*. The environment is represented in terms of so-called *problem domains* which are material or immaterial objects in the environment that are relevant for the machine for satisfying the requirements. Between problem domains, machine domain, and requirements, three types of relationships can be modelled. *Interfaces* exist between machine domain and problem domains or among problem domains. At the interfaces, phenomena (e.g. events, states, values) are shared. Sharing means that one domain controls a phenomenon, while the other observes it. At interfaces, not only the phenomena are annotated but also an abbreviation of the domain controlling them followed by an exclamation mark (e.g. CM!). A requirement is connected to problem domains by means of a *requirement reference* or a *constraining reference*. A requirement reference expresses that the requirement *refers* to phenomena of the domain, while a constraining reference expresses that the requirement *constrains* (i.e. influences) them. An example of a problem diagram is shown in Fig. 6.

While problem diagrams show *what* the software development problem is, the context diagram shows *where* the software development problem is located. The context diagram shows the environment of the machine in terms of problem domains and how the machine domain is related to them. Thus, it does not contain any requirement. It serves as a foundation for decomposing the overall software development problem into sub-problems and creating problem diagrams for each sub-problem. An example of a context diagram is shown in Fig. 5.

The Six-Variable Model. The Six-Variable Model extends the well-known Four-Variable Model [8] which defines the content of software documentation (e.g. of documentations to be created during requirements engineering). A control system typically consists of some control software that uses sensors and actuators for monitoring and controlling certain quantities (variables) in the environment. During requirements engineering, four types of variables and the relationships between them should be documented: monitored variables m (environmental quantities that the software monitors through input devices like sensors), controlled variables c (environmental quantities that the software controls through output devices like actuators), input variables i (data items that the software needs as input), and output variables o (quantities that the software produces as output).

However, it is not always possible to monitor/control exactly those variables one is interested in. Then, sensors and actuators are selected which monitor/control a different set of variables which are related to the ones of real interest. The Six-Variable Model demands that the variables of real interest are documented as well beside the classical four variables m, c, i, and o (see Fig. 1). The two newly introduced variables are the so-called *referenced* and *desired* variables r and d. Referenced variables are environmental quantities that should originally be observed in the environment, i.e. before deciding which sensors/actuators to use for monitoring/controlling. Desired variables are environmental quantities that should originally be influenced in the environment.

Sometimes there is not only one sensor or one actuator between the environmental domain and the machine domain but a chain of sensors or a chain of actuators. Then, there are not only $4 + 2$ variables to be documented but even $4 + n$ variables. Jackson [6] calls problem domains like the sensors/actuators *connection domains* and allows for omitting them from a problem diagram when they are considered to be reliable. However, if they are unreliable, they should be modelled explicitly in the diagrams.

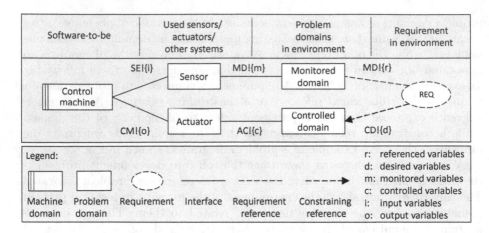

Fig. 1. The Six-Variable Model (taken from [5]).

For problem diagrams created based on the Six-Variable model, the domain hypotheses (*DH*), expectations (*Exp*), and software requirements (*SOF*) can be made explicit as shown in Fig. 2. *DH-MD* is a hypothesis about the monitored domain, which needs to be true. *Exp-SE* is an expectation to be satisfied by the sensors, *Exp-AC* is an expectation to be satisfied by the actuators, and *Exp-CD* is an expectation to be satisfied by the controlled domain. *SOF* represents the software requirements which are to be satisfied by the control machine. The requirements *REQ* can only be satisfied, if *DH-MD* is valid and *Exp-SE, SOF, Exp-AC*, and *Exp-CD* are satisfied. This is expressed by the following satisfaction argument: $DH\text{-}MD, Exp\text{-}SE, SOF, Exp\text{-}AC, Exp\text{-}CD \vdash REQ$.

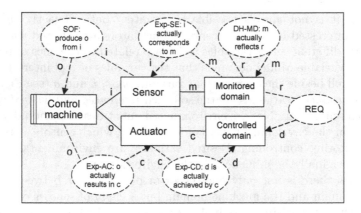

Fig. 2. Assumptions in the Six-Variable Model (taken from [5]).

Systematic Goal Refinement in KAOS using the Six-Variable Model. As described above, KAOS goal models and problem diagrams have in common that they are both based on the satisfaction argument. As shown in Fig. 3, we exploit this commonality for refining goals in KAOS goal models in a systematic way. For each high-level goal in a KAOS goal model, we suggest creating a problem diagram based on the Six-Variable Model. The benefit of problem diagrams which are created based on the Six-Variable Model is that the six variables are made explicit therein. This information is missing in KAOS goal models. Based on the six variables, the expectations, domain hypotheses, and domain properties can be made explicit more easily because they are actually statements describing the relation between two or more variables. For example, the relation between r and m is usually a domain hypothesis, if r and m are different (e.g. if a variable m is monitored which is only an estimation of r). The problem diagram thus results in a decomposition of the high-level goal (G2.2 in Fig. 3) into software requirements, expectations, and domain hypotheses. This decomposition can then also be modelled in the KAOS goal graph.

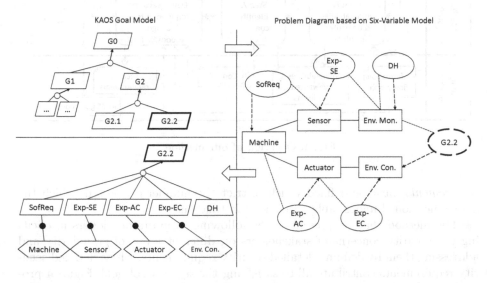

Fig. 3. Combination of KAOS goal models and problem diagrams (taken from [4]).

3   Our Method

Security requirements arise because stakeholders assert that some objects (tangible or intangible) have direct or indirect value. Objects valued in this way are called *assets* (cf. [9]) and the stakeholders want to protect them from harm, for example, from being destroyed, stolen, revealed, or modified. Thus, they have *security concerns* regarding these assets. To address these concerns, *security*

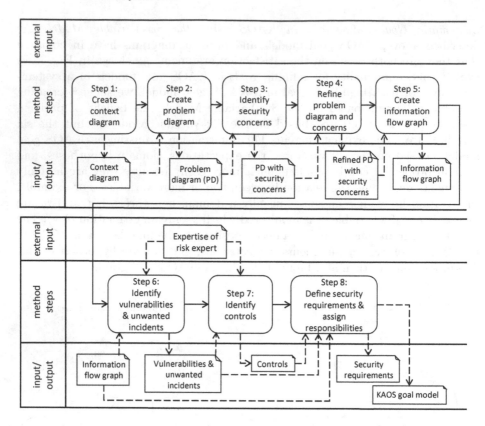

Fig. 4. Overview of our method.

requirements must be defined which restrict the number of cases in which the above-mentioned undesirable outcomes can take place.

The method that we present in the following supports developers in eliciting the security concerns of stakeholders on different levels of granularity and addressing them by defining detailed security requirements. These detailed security requirements contribute all to satisfying the security softgoal. Figure 4 provides an overview of our method showing the steps to be performed as well as input and output of these steps. In the following, we describe each step in detail.

Step 1: Create Context Diagram. As a first step, the requirements engineer creates a context diagram. Note that according to Jackson's problem frames method [6], a context diagram shows the machine domain and the problem domains in its environment. However, we allow also for creating context diagrams that show only the environment, i.e. without the machine domain. Such context diagrams help nevertheless to understand the context (i.e. the environment and the problem that shall be solved) first, before delving into details of the solution (the software).

Step 2: Create Problem Diagram. Based on the context diagram, the requirements engineer creates a problem diagram which contains the machine domain as well as the overall functional requirement to be satisfied by the system (i.e. the machine and its environment). This problem diagram either contains the same problem domains as the ones shown in the context diagram, or it may contain more detailed problem domains as well as more detailed phenomena.

Step 3: Identify Security Concerns. The requirements engineer presents the problem diagram from Step 2 to the stakeholders (e.g. the client, system users) to show them which phenomena (data, events, values) are exchanged between the machine domain and problem domains. Based on this high level problem diagram, the requirements engineer elicits a first set of security concerns that are either related to phenomena or to problem domains in the diagram. These concerns can be documented in the problem diagram as simple comments. To express whose concern they are, an abbreviation indicating the corresponding stakeholder can be added to the ID (identification number) of the concern.

Step 4: Refine Problem Diagram and Security Concerns. During this step, the requirements engineer decomposes the software development problem shown in the problem diagram from Step 2 and creates problem diagrams for each sub-problem based on the Six-Variable Model. This means that he/she first answers the question which problem domains are relevant in the real world because properties of them need to be observed or changed. This results in the real world problem domains that need to be modelled and the r and d variables. Then, the requirements engineer reflects on the way these domains are connected to the machine and tries to make all connection domains explicit. The connection domains are added to the model together with their interfaces. As mentioned before, there may be chains of sensors or chains of actuators that connect the machine to the real world domains. In this way, the Six-Variable Model forces developers (i) to model the referenced and desired variables in the environment which are otherwise often neglected in documentation and (ii) to make connection domains and phenomena at their interfaces explicit, since they may also represent assets and may thus be attacked. Together with the stakeholders, the requirements engineer then refines the security concerns in the refined problem diagrams and adds newly identified concerns, if necessary. It may be the case that the same security concern occurs in several problem diagrams but relates to different phenomena or problem domains in these problem diagrams.

Step 5: Create Information Flow Graph. During this step, the requirements engineer uses the problem diagrams from Step 4 (that show the six variables) to create a so-called information flow graph which shows how phenomena are processed in the problem diagrams and how they are related to each other (i.e. how certain phenomena result in other phenomena after being processed). We introduced the information flow graph in previous work [10]. To create the information flow graph, the requirements engineer must start with the problem domains whose phenomena are referenced by the requirement in a problem diagram and must follow the flow of phenomena from there until arriving at the problem domain(s) which is/are constrained by the requirement. The problem domains are modelled as rectangles (representing the nodes of the graph) and phenomena are annotated at arrows (edges) between them. This step is performed for all problem diagrams and results in one overall information flow graph.

Step 6: Identify Vulnerabilities and Unwanted Incidents. For each security concern shown in the problem diagrams from Step 4, the requirements engineer analyses how the concern could become true, i.e. he/she looks at the information flows in the information flow graph created in Step 5 to identify unwanted incidents in which this concern would actually become true. Each node and edge of the information flow graph is analysed by the requirements engineer to identify unwanted incidents and the vulnerabilities of the system that are exploited therein. For this step, the participation of a risk or domain expert is necessary. Identified vulnerabilities and unwanted incidents (possibly including their consequences) can simply be documented as a table or, for example, using so-called threat diagrams as suggested by Lund et al. [11].

Step 7: Identify Controls. To address the unwanted incidents from Step 6, the requirements engineer identifies controls during this step. Controls may refer to hardware or software. One control may address several unwanted incidents. Again, knowledge from a risk or domain expert is necessary for performing this step. The controls and the unwanted incidents they address can again be documented simply as a table or, for example, using so-called treatment diagrams as suggested by Lund et al. [11]. If the requirements engineer needs more support in performing Steps 6 and 7, any risk assessment method (such as CORAS [11]) can be applied as well.

Step 8: Define Security Requirements and Assign Responsibilities. Based on the identified unwanted incidents, vulnerabilities, and controls for addressing the unwanted incidents, security requirements are defined by the requirements engineer using the following pattern (which is based on the patterns provided by Wirtz et al. [10]):

> Ensure that the risk for [*unwanted incident*] caused by exploitation of [*vulnerability*] is reduced to an acceptable level by applying [*control*].

However, other patterns for documenting security requirements might be used as well as long as they document the identified controls. Then, the responsibilities for realising the controls must be assigned. Sometimes it is the responsibility of the software-to-be, sometimes of other parts of the system to realise them. Therefore, we assign the responsibilities for realising the controls to the corresponding parts of the system during this step. This results in software requirements (when the software-to-be is responsible) and in expectations (when other parts of the system are responsible). We suggest documenting these assignments in a KAOS goal model in the following way. The controls from Step 7 are modelled as goals refining the security softgoal. The software requirements and expectations, which need to be satisfied for each control, are modelled as responsibility assignments for corresponding agents in the goal model.

Benefit of the Method. The benefit of our method is that it (i) helps in identifying the security concerns of different stakeholders, (ii) supports the identification of vulnerabilities, unwanted incidents, and controls which result in a set of detailed security requirements and (iii) facilitates the assignment of responsibilities for satisfying these security requirements. In this way, the security softgoal is decomposed in a systematic way. If all agents (i.e. the software/machine and all other parts of the system) satisfy the goals assigned to them, the security softgoal can be considered to be satisfied.

4   Application Example

To illustrate our method, we use a system that supports the usage-based automobile insurance. This example stems from EU project RestAssured[1] and is described in [12]. The system is called PAYD, which stands for "Pay As You Drive". This means that the policy premium is determined based on the way the driver drives. To this end, telemetric data is collected during the ride (e.g. distance travelled, date, time, speed, direction, and location). The following stakeholders are involved in this scenario:

- A *driver* desires an insurance product and wishes to directly engage with and provide information to an *insurance service provider.*
- The *insurance service provider* engages a *telematics service provider* to manage the delivery of driver data streams to the insurance service provider.
- The *telematics service provider* is the provider of streamed telematic data from the driver's connected car to the insurance service provider. A connected car is a car that is connected to the Internet e.g. by a 3G or 4G mobile gateway and thus provides for interconnectivity to other devices and sensors via technologies such as WiFi and Bluetooth (cf. [12]).
- Both, the *insurance service provider* and the *telematics service provider* individually engage cloud infrastructure and cloud platform providers as part of their infrastructure that support the insurance service provided by the insurance service provider to the driver.
- The *Infrastructure as a Service (IaaS) Providers* provide untrusted cloud infrastructures to the insurance service provider and to the telematic service provider.
- The *Platform as a Service (PaaS) Providers* provide untrusted cloud platforms to the insurance service provider and to the telematic service provider.

---

[1] https://restassuredh2020.eu.

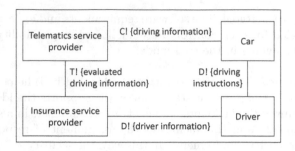

Fig. 5. Context diagram for PAYD.

Step 1: Create Context Diagram. Figure 5 shows the environment without the machine. Important problem domains in the environment are the car driver and the car, as well as the insurance service provider and the telematics service provider. The driver provides driving instructions to the car. Driving information of the ride (e.g. distance travelled, date, time, speed, direction, and location, etc.) is sent to the telematics service provider who evaluates this information and sends only evaluated information (i.e. not the raw data) to the insurance service provider. The insurance service provider also receives driver information of the driver (e.g. name, age, address, payment information, etc.).

Step 2: Create Problem Diagram. The problem diagram created based on the context diagram from Step 1 is shown in Fig. 6. Note that the problem diagram contains some details which are different to the context diagram since it is more concrete. This diagram includes the PAYD machine domain, details about its environment, and the overall functional requirement G0: "Provide PAYD insurance". We use the abbreviation G0 since it is a high level requirement and therefore represents a goal. Instead of the car domain, the domain "gateway in car" is shown, instead of the telematics service provider, a telematics component is shown, and instead of the insurance service provider, an insurance component is shown. The PAYD machine transfers the data it receives from the telematics component to the insurance component. The telematics component receives the driver information and detailed driving information (i.e. measured speed, distance travelled, etc.) from the car's gateway. The telematics provider evaluates this raw data and provides evaluated information (e.g. a score) to the PAYD machine. The PAYD machine transfers this data to the insurance component of the insurance service provider. The insurance component provides then an insurance which corresponds to the evaluated driving information received from the PAYD machine. Note that the telematics component and the insurance component represent other systems that we use, since they are services.

Step 3: Identify Security Concerns. Figure 7 shows the first set of security concerns that have been identified for the high level problem diagram. As part of the ID of a security concern, we indicate the stakeholder whose concern it is by means of an abbreviation (e.g. D stands for driver, TSP for telematics service

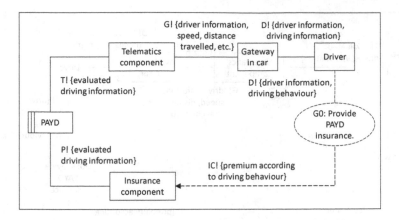

Fig. 6. Problem diagram for G0.

provider, and ISP for insurance service provider). Most of these concerns are security concerns of the driver (SC1-D to SC5-D); some are the concerns of the telematics service provider and of the insurance service provider (SC6-TSP and SC7-ISP). The driver is concerned whether his/her driving behaviour will be monitored correctly, i.e. he/she is concerned that incorrect monitoring data is delivered (SC1-D). The driver is concerned about insecure transmission of data from the car's gateway to the telematics component which may cause that someone else sees his/her data (SC2-D). He/she is also concerned that there is some non-authorised access to the his/her data in the telematics component (SC3-D), about the insecure storage and processing of data in the telematics and insurance components (SC4-D), and about the possibility that incorrect data is sent from the telematics service provider to the insurance service provider (SC5-D). The telematics service provider and the insurance service provider are both concerned about the security compliance with local regulations (e.g. GDPR) and ISO 27000 (SC6-TSP and SC7-ISP).

Step 4: Refine Problem Diagram and Security Concerns. We decompose the overall software development problem "Provide PAYD insurance" (shown as G0 in Fig. 7) into the following three subproblems: G1: "Store data", G2: "Calculate premium", and G3: "Display stored information to driver". In the following, we focus on G1. Figure 8 shows the detailed problem diagram for G1 which was created based on the Six-Variable Model. The two real world domains are the driver and the car. Phenomena of the driver are referred by the requirement. Further connection domains, not considered so far, are the card reader and the car sensors. The driver puts his/her insurance card into the card reader which transfers the driver's profile to the gateway. Similarly, sensors in the car monitor speed, distance travelled, etc. and provide the measured values to the gateway. The gateway transfers all this data to the telematics component. Regarding the telematics component, we made the database used by the component explicit since it is a cloud-based database and there is a high risk of attacks. The same

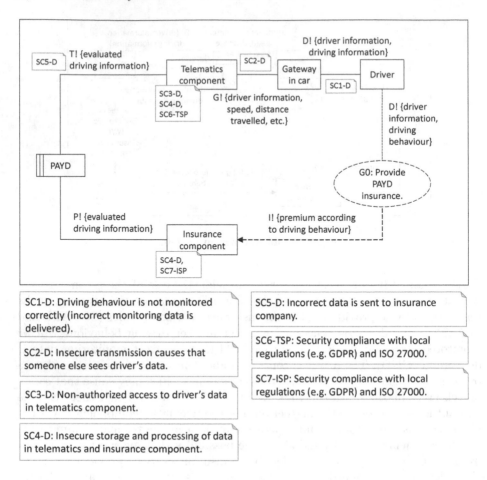

Fig. 7. Problem diagram and security concerns.

holds for the cloud-based database used by the insurance component. Further-more, we added the telematics analyst to the diagram since he/she has access to the telematics component for the purpose of analysis. As shown in Fig. 8, the identified security concerns can now be better assigned to the phenomena they refer to due to the more detailed information resulting from the application of the Six-Variable Model. Some concerns have been decomposed or refined, while others are newly identified concerns. For example, SC1-D from Fig. 7 was refined and resulted in SC1-D (incorrect monitoring) and SC2-D (incorrect transmission of monitored data) in Fig. 8. Similarly, SC4-D from Fig. 7) was decomposed into SC5-D (insecure data storage) and SC6-D (insecure data processing) in Fig. 8. SC8-D in Fig. 8 is completely new, since the diagram shows now that the driver enters his/her driver information by inserting his/her insurance card into a card reader. This new information in the diagram raised a new concern

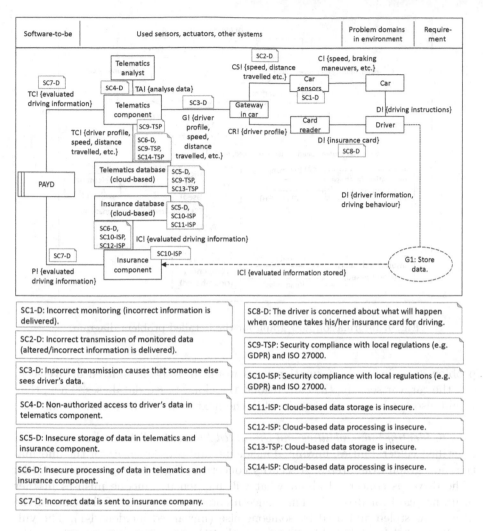

Software-to-be	Used sensors, actuators, other systems	Problem domains in environment	Require-ment

SC1-D: Incorrect monitoring (incorrect information is delivered).

SC2-D: Incorrect transmission of monitored data (altered/incorrect information is delivered).

SC3-D: Insecure transmission causes that someone else sees driver's data.

SC4-D: Non-authorized access to driver's data in telematics component.

SC5-D: Insecure storage of data in telematics and insurance component.

SC6-D: Insecure processing of data in telematics and insurance component.

SC7-D: Incorrect data is sent to insurance company.

SC8-D: The driver is concerned about what will happen when someone takes his/her insurance card for driving.

SC9-TSP: Security compliance with local regulations (e.g. GDPR) and ISO 27000.

SC10-ISP: Security compliance with local regulations (e.g. GDPR) and ISO 27000.

SC11-ISP: Cloud-based data storage is insecure.

SC12-ISP: Cloud-based data processing is insecure.

SC13-TSP: Cloud-based data storage is insecure.

SC14-ISP: Cloud-based data processing is insecure.

Fig. 8. Detailed problem diagram and further security concerns.

of the driver (SC8-D). SC11-ISP, SC12-ISP, SC13-TSP, SC14-TSP are also new concerns which are modelled because the diagram shows that both, the telematics provider and the insurance provider, engage cloud infrastructures for the services they provide. They are both concerned that cloud-based data storage and processing could be insecure.

Step 5: Create Information Flow Graph. Figure 9 shows the information flow graph created for the detailed problem diagram for G1 from Step 4. It shows how the information flows from problem domain to problem domain. Note that the information flow graph contains the information that has been made explicit in Step 4 using the Six-Variable Model. Without this information, important

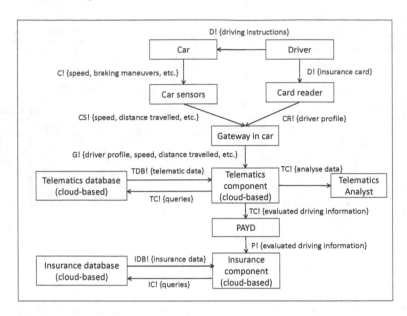

Fig. 9. Information flow graph for the detailed problem diagram.

problem domains and information flows would have been omitted or overseen, e.g. the car, car sensors, the card reader, the cloud-based databases. Then, they would also not have been considered in the next steps of the security analysis.

Step 6: Identify Vulnerabilities and Unwanted Incidents. Table 1 shows the list of identified vulnerabilities, unwanted incidents, and consequences for the information flow graph from Step 5. A security concern in Fig. 8 is, for example, SC8-D: "The driver is concerned about what will happen if someone misuses his/her insurance card for driving". This concern could become true if the card of the driver was stolen and used by someone else (unwanted incident I-1). The vulnerability that is exploited in this case is that the users' insurance cards are the only means for identifying users. No other stronger credentials are used like, for example, fingerprints or PIN numbers. Another security concern is, for example, SC3-D. The driver is concerned that the transmission of his/her data from the gateway to the telematics component is insecure and someone else sees his/her data. This concern could become true in two cases (two unwanted incidents): (i) the card reader could be manipulated by someone to retrieve the card data (I-2) and (ii) the data could be manipulated in the car's gateway (I-3). V-2 and V-3 are the vulnerabilities that are exploited in these cases.

Step 7: Identify Controls. Table 2 contains the controls identified for the unwanted incidents from Step 6. I-1 can, for example, be addressed by using additional credentials like a PIN or fingerprints. I-2 can be addressed by using better hardware (card readers) to avoid skimming attacks.

Table 1. Identified vulnerabilities and unwanted incidents (result of Step 6).

Unwanted incident	Vulnerabilities
I-1: The insurance card of the driver is stolen and another driver misuses his/her card	V-1: Cards are the only means for using the service; no other stronger credentials like fingerprints, PIN numbers, etc. are used
I-2: Card reader is manipulated by someone to retrieve the card data	V-2: Insufficient hardware security
I-3: The software in the car is manipulated and thus monitored data is incorrect	V-3: Software updates can be performed by any garage
I-4: Driver profile and driving information (i.e. speed, distance travelled, etc.) are manipulated in the car's gateway	V-4: Insufficient hardware and software security
I-5: Data sent from the car's gateway is manipulated or is read by an unauthorized party	V-5: Insecure transmission channel
I-6: Telematics component is accessed and the telematics data of the driver is accessed and processed by an unauthorized party	V-6: Telematics component is deployed to insecure cloud infrastructure and has weak access control mechanisms
I-7: Telematics database, i.e. cloud database used by telematics service provider, is compromised	V-7: Telematics data is deployed in an insecure cloud database
I-8: Insurance component receives incorrect data from the telematics component	V-8: Telematics component can be compromised either through cloud component issues or through the telematics analyst or other unauthorized accesses that are possible
I-9: Insurance component is accessed and the driver insurance information is accessed and processed by an unauthorized party (e.g. IaaS provider, PaaS provider as black hat actors)	V-9: Insurance component is deployed to insecure cloud infrastructure and has weak access control mechanisms
I-10: Insurance database, i.e. cloud database used by insurance service provider, is compromised (e.g. IaaS provider, PaaS provider as black hat actors)	V-10: Insurance data of the driver and of the insurance company are deployed in an insecure cloud database

Table 2. Controls and addressed unwanted incidents (result of Step 7).

Identified controls	Unwanted incidents
C-1: Use additional credentials for card	I-1
C-2: Improve hardware security to avoid skimming attacks	I-2
C-3: Allow only car manufacturers to update the software in cars	I-3
C-4: Implement secure checksums and black chain mechanisms	I-4
C-5: Implement strong encryption mechanism (e.g. homomorphic/ polymorphic encryptions)	I-5, I-7, I-10
C-6: Implement appropriate access controls (e.g. sticky policies, etc.)	I-6
C-7: Implement enclaves and database encryption mechanisms. Secure enclaves give a secure processing possibility (e.g. using SGX secure enclaves for insurance and telematics components and databases)	I-6, I-7, I-8, I-9, I-10
C-8: Improve access rights management for telematics analyst (i.e. restrict access rights)	I-8

Step 8: Define Security Requirements. Based on the security requirement pattern, we are able to define more detailed security requirements of the following type:

Ensure that the risk for *I-1* ("The insurance card of the driver is stolen and another driver misuses his/her card.") caused by exploitation of *V-1* ("Cards are the only means for using the service; no other stronger credentials like fingerprints, PIN numbers, etc. are used.") is reduced to an acceptable level by applying *C-1* ("Use additional credentials for card.").

Based on the information flow graph in Fig. 9, we are able to assign the responsibilities for realising the controls identified in Step 7 to different parts of the system. Table 3 documents whether a control results in requirements for the PAYD machine or in expectations for other parts of the system and who is responsible for satisfying the expectations and requirements. Based on this table, we create the KAOS goal model depicted in Fig. 10 which shows the controls as subgoals of the security softgoal in an AND-refinement and responsibility assignments for the controls. Some agents are shown several times, because they have several responsibilities.

5 Related Work

With regard to our method, there are mainly three areas of related work that we discuss in the following.

First, several existing approaches show that it is beneficial to combine (KAOS) goal models and problem diagrams (cf. [13–16]). We exploit the same benefits in our method. However, none of these methods focuses on softgoals as we do.

Second, there are several goal-oriented approaches that support the refinement of the security goal and the derivation of security requirements from these subgoals. Elahi and Yu [17], for example, extend i* goal models to allow for modelling trust relationships among actors and malicious behaviour. They suggest replacing the trusted parties (actors) in the goal model with a corresponding malicious counterpart and analysing how the capabilities and permissions granted to this party can be abused by him/her for malicious purposes. Mouratidis and Giorgini [18] extend the Tropos methodology to enable modelling security constraints on dependencies between actors. Similar to the Tropos methodology, first, the environment is analysed in terms of actors and their dependencies on each other. Then, the software-to-be is considered as a further actor and some of the goals of the other actors are delegated to it. In SecureTropos [18], security constraints on the dependencies between actors are also modelled. They are then assigned to the goals of the actor they restrict and are further analysed/refined. Finally, tasks for the software-to-be are identified to guarantee the security constraints. Meland et al. [19] integrate threat modelling into the socio-technical security modelling language STS-ml. Using these modelling elements, threats and their impact on the goal model can be made explicit. Meland et al. provide also tool support for analysing the impact of a threatening event on the rest of the goal model.

All these approaches identify and analyse vulnerabilities only based on the goal model and the relationships between actors that are documented therein. In contrast to that, we use detailed problem diagrams for identifying security concerns of stakeholders and the information flow graph for identifying vulnerabilities which contain both far more (and more detailed) information about the data exchanged between the software and its environment than goal models. Thus, our analysis yields a more detailed and complete vulnerability analysis which results in a more complete set of identified unwanted incidents and corresponding security requirements to address them. Furthermore, our method is more stakeholder-centric, since we focus on the security concerns of different stakeholders and derive from them security requirements and expectations.

Third, there are several problem-based approaches that support the elicitation of detailed security requirements. However, they do not focus on the security concerns of different stakeholders and thus do not provide support in making them explicit in problem diagrams and in deriving security requirements from them. Furthermore, they do not make responsibility assignments explicit as we do. Nevertheless, we elaborate on them in the following.

Table 3. Controls and Assigned Responsibilities (result of Step 8).

Controls	Expectation on/Requirement for	Responsible for Satisfaction
C-1: Use additional credentials for card	- Expectation on insurance card	Insurance service provider
C-2: Improve hardware security to avoid skimming attacks	- Expectation on card reader	Insurance service provider
C-3: Allow only car manufacturers to update the software in cars	- Expectation on car	Car manufacturer
C-4: Implement secure checksums and black chain mechanisms	- Expectation on gateway	Car manufacturer
C-5: Implement strong encryption mechanism (e.g. homomorphic/ polymorphic encryptions)	- Expectation on gateway - Expectation on telematics component and telematics database	Car manufacturer Telematics service provider
	- Requirement for PAYD	We (as developers of PAYD)
	- Expectation on insurance component and insurance database	Insurance service provider
C-6: Implement appropriate access controls (e.g. sticky policies, etc.)	- Expectation on telematics component	Telematics service provider
C-7: Implement enclaves and database encryption mechanisms. Secure enclaves give a secure processing possibility (e.g. using SGX secure enclaves for insurance and telematics components and databases)	- Expectation on telematics component and telematics database	Telematics service provider
	- Requirement for PAYD - Expectation on insurance component and insurance database	We (as developers of PAYD) Insurance service provider
C-8: Improve access rights management for telematics analyst (i.e. restrict access rights)	- Expectation on telematics component	Telematics service provider

Faßbender et al. [20] describe a method for deriving security requirements from functional requirements which are documented in problem diagrams. Based on these problem diagrams, assets (i.e. problem domains which are considered to be assets) as well as possible attackers and their abilities are identified. For each asset, a so-called access graph is created which shows the access flows from and to this asset. For example, if problem domain A is referred by the requirement RQ1 and problem domain B is constrained by RQ1 in a problem diagram, then a direct access flow (i.e. an edge) is modelled between the problem domains A and B and this edge is annotated with RQ1. Then, another type of graph is created for each

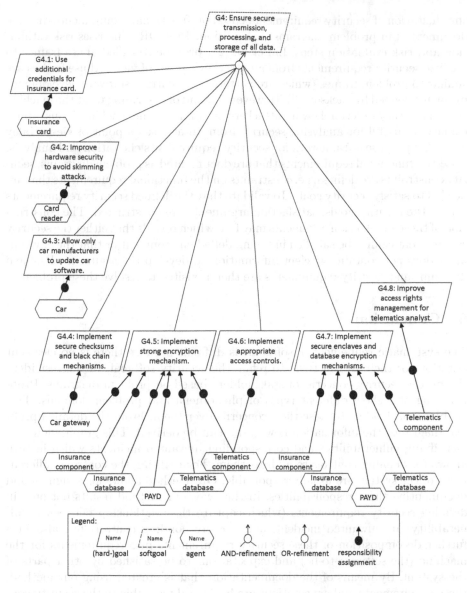

Fig. 10. KAOS goal model showing the refinement of the security softgoal (result of Step 8).

asset that visualizes the information flows from attackers to this asset and vice versa. Since these graphs contain the information where an asset might be threatened by an attacker, the requirements engineer and a security expert can check based on these graphs whether the original functional requirements related to this asset must be augmented with security requirements or not. ProCOR [10] is a risk management process. Similar to the method of Faßbender et al. [20], it supports the elicitation of security requirements based on functional requirements that are documented in problem diagrams. In addition, ProCOR comprises risk estimation and risk evaluation steps. Lin et al. [21] propose so-called abuse frames to analyze security requirements from an attacker's point of view. Abuse frames are similar to problem frames (which are patterns of recurring software development problems defined by Jackson [6]). However, instead of describing what the machine should do, they describe how an attacker could misuse the machine. Thus, abuse frames are useful for analysing security from an attacker's point of view. Haley et al. [22] propose a framework for security requirements elicitation and analysis. Based on functional requirements that are documented as problem diagrams, security constraints are defined, i.e. constraints on the functional requirements that are needed to satisfy security goals. To validate that the defined security requirements satisfy the security goals, satisfaction arguments are constructed. The construction of these satisfaction arguments may fail, which reveals that either the security requirement cannot be satisfied in the modelled environment or that the environment does not contain sufficient information to develop the argument. Problem diagrams and security requirements are then revisited to resolve these problems.

6   Conclusion

The systematic refinement of softgoals is difficult because there is no clear-cut criterion for their satisfaction. To refine the security softgoal, we suggest identifying the security concerns of stakeholders based on problem diagrams. Problem diagrams show different types of phenomena and problem domains. This enables stakeholders to raise their concerns over them. From the detailed problem diagrams, the information flow graph can be derived. This graph allows for identifying vulnerabilities and corresponding unwanted incidents which in turn allows for defining controls to address them. For realising the controls, different parts of the system are usually responsible. Our method allows for assigning and documenting these responsibilities. In this way, our method results not only in detailed security requirements (which capture the relationship between a vulnerability, an unwanted incident, and a corresponding control) but also in a further decomposition of these security requirements into requirements for the machine (the software-to-be) and expectations to be satisfied by other parts of the system. By means of the documentation that is created using our method, these requirements and expectations are backward traceable to the security concerns from which they originate. This information is helpful when changes occur, for example, when it turns out that an expectation cannot be satisfied. Then, it is backward traceable which security concerns are affected and can possibly not be addressed or must be addressed in a different way. Without using the problem diagrams (for eliciting security concerns and deriving finally security requirements), a decomposition of the security softgoal in the KAOS goal model would have been difficult due to the lack of guidance regarding the systematic refinement of softgoals. The method that we presented in this paper can be used in the same way for other quality attributes (softgoals) as well. We used KAOS goal models in our method. Yet, it is possible to use other goal models (e.g. i* goal models) instead. It might then be necessary to extend these goal models, for example, in order to be able to model expectations.

In future work, we want to extend our method with an approach for the detailed quantitative risk analysis and evaluation that needs to be performed as a next step after having applied our method. Furthermore, we plan to perform a comparative evaluation with student groups to compare our method with the KAOS methodology.

Acknowledgment. Research leading to these results received funding from the European Union's Horizon 2020 research and innovation programme under grant agreement number 731678 (RestAssured).

References

1. van Lamsweerde, A.: Goal-oriented requirements engineering: a guided tour. In: Proceedings of RE 2001, pp. 249–263. IEEE Computer Society (2001)
2. Mylopoulos, J., Chung, L., Yu, E.: From object-oriented to goal-oriented requirements analysis. Commun. ACM **42**(1), 31–37 (1999)
3. Van Lamsweerde, A.: Requirements Engineering - From System Goals to UML Models to Software Specifications. Wiley, Hoboken (2009)
4. Ulfat-Bunyadi, N., Gol Mohammadi, N., Heisel, M.: Supporting the systematic goal refinement in KAOS using the Six-Variable Model. In: Proceedings of ICSOFT 2018, pp. 136–145 (2018)
5. Ulfat-Bunyadi, N., Meis, R., Heisel, M.: The six-variable model - context modelling enabling systematic reuse of control software. In: Proceedings of ICSOFT 2016, pp. 15–26 (2016)
6. Jackson, M.: Problem Frames - Analysing and Structuring Software Development Problems. Addison-Wesley, Boston (2001)
7. Zave, P., Jackson, M.: Four dark corners of requirements engineering. ACM Trans. Softw. Eng. Methodol. **6**(1), 1–30 (1997)
8. Parnas, D., Madey, J.: Functional documents for computer systems. Sci. Comput. Program. **25**(1), 41–61 (1995)
9. Haley, C.B., Laney, R.C., Moffett, J.D., Nuseibeh, B.: The effect of trust assumptions on the elaboration of security requirements. In: Proceedings of RE 2004, pp. 102–111 (2004)
10. Wirtz, R., Heisel, M., Meis, R., Omerovic, A., Stølen, K.: Problem-based elicitation of security requirements - the ProCOR method. In: Proceedings of ENASE 2018, pp. 26–38. SciTePress (2018)
11. Lund, M., Solhaug, B., Stolen, K.: Model-Driven Risk Analysis – The CORAS Approach. Springer, Heidelberg (2011). https://doi.org/10.1007/978-3-642-12323-8
12. RestAssured Consortium: Deliverable D8.1: First Validation Plan (2017). https://restassuredh2020.eu/wp-content/uploads/2018/07/D8.1.pdf
13. Bleistein, S., Cox, K., Verner, J.: Requirements engineering for e-business systems: integrating Jackson problem diagrams with goal modelling and BPM. In: Proceedings of APSEC 2004, pp. 410–417. IEEE Computer Society (2004)

14. Mohammadi, N.G., Alebrahim, A., Weyer, T., Heisel, M., Pohl, K.: A framework for combining problem frames and goal models to support context analysis during requirements engineering. In: Cuzzocrea, A., Kittl, C., Simos, D.E., Weippl, E., Xu, L. (eds.) CD-ARES 2013. LNCS, vol. 8127, pp. 272–288. Springer, Heidelberg (2013). https://doi.org/10.1007/978-3-642-40511-2_19

15. Dao, T., Lee, H., Kang, K.: Problem frames-based approach to achieving quality attributes in software product line engineering. In: Proceedings of SPLC 2011, pp. 175–180. IEEE Computer Society (2011)

16. Han, D., Xing, J., Yang, Q., Li, J., Zhang, X., Chen, Y.: Integrating goal models and problem frames for requirements analysis of self-adaptive CPS. In: Proceedings of COMPSAC 2017, pp. 529–535. IEEE Computer Society (2017)

17. Elahi, G., Yu, E.: Trust trade-off analysis for security requirements engineering. In: Proceedings of RE 2009, pp. 243–248 (2009)

18. Giorgini, P., Mouratidis, H.: Secure tropos: a security-oriented extension of the tropos methodology. Int. J. Softw. Eng. Knowl. Eng. 17(2), 285–309 (2007)

19. Meland, P., Paja, E., Gjære, E., Paul, S., Dalpiaz, F., Giorgini, P.: Threat analysis in goal-oriented security requirements modelling. Int. J. Secur. Softw. Eng. 5(2), 1–19 (2014)

20. Faßbender, S., Heisel, M., Meis, R.: Functional requirements under security Pres-SuRE. In: Proceedings of ICSOFT-PT 2014, pp. 5–16 (2014)

21. Lin, L., Nuseibeh, B., Ince, D.C., Jackson, M., Moffett, J.D.: Analysing security threats and vulnerabilities using abuse frames. Technical Report No. 2003/10, October 2003, The Open University, United Kingdom (2003)

22. Haley, C., Laney, R., Moffett, J., Nuseibeh, B.: Security requirements engineering: a framework for representation and analysis. IEEE Trans. Softw. Eng. 34(1), 133–153 (2008)

Simplifying the Classification of App Reviews Using Only Lexical Features

Faiz Ali Shah(✉), Kairit Sirts, and Dietmar Pfahl

Institute of Computer Science, University of Tartu, Tartu, Estonia
{shah,kairit.sirts,dietmar.pfahl}@ut.ee

Abstract. User reviews submitted to app marketplaces contain information that falls into different categories, e.g., feature evaluation, feature request, and bug report. This information is valuable for developers to improve the quality of mobile applications. However, due to the large volume of reviews received every day, manual classification of user reviews into these categories is not feasible. Therefore, developing automatic classification methods using machine learning approaches is desirable. In this study, we address the problem of automatic classification of app review sentences (as opposed to full reviews) into different categories. We compare the simplest textual machine learning classifier using only lexical features – the so-called Bag-of-Words (BoW) approach – with more complex models used in previous work adopting rich linguistic features. We find that the performance of the simple BoW model is very competitive and has the advantage of not requiring any external linguistic tools to extract the features. Moreover, we experiment with deep learning based Convolutional Neural Network (CNN) models that have recently achieved state-of-the-art results in many classification tasks. We find that, on average, the CNN models do not perform significantly better than the simple BoW model. Finally, the manual analysis of misclassification errors and data annotations suggests that classifying review sentences in isolation does not always contain enough information to make a correct prediction. Thus, we suggest that adopting neural models to incorporate additional contextual knowledge might improve the classification performance.

Keywords: App review classifsication · Bag-of-Words · CNN

1 Introduction

App marketplaces such as PlayStore and AppStore offer apps to its users supporting virtually all kinds of services and businesses [1]. These marketplaces provide users a central place to download apps and submit their feedback on them in the form of ratings and reviews. The app market is highly competitive. Therefore, app developers constantly look for information that helps them improve the quality of their apps [22]. User reviews contain information such as

© Springer Nature Switzerland AG 2019
M. van Sinderen and L. A. Maciaszek (Eds.): ICSOFT 2018, CCIS 1077, pp. 173–193, 2019.
https://doi.org/10.1007/978-3-030-29157-0_8

feature requests, bug reports, and feature evaluations, making them an extremely valuable source for app developers to improve the quality of their apps [13].

Developers receive a large number of reviews every day making manual classification of reviews an arduous task. In past research, supervised machine learning methods have been used for automatic classification of app reviews into different categories [7,13]. The study of Maalej et al. [13] performed automatic classification at review level. However, multiple types of information can be mentioned in a single review or a review can contain information that is not informative for app developers. Therefore, other studies have performed automatic classification of reviews at sentence-level [7].

The study by [7] used natural language processing (NLP) tools, such as taggers and parsers, to extract features for classifying review sentences. However, the review-level classification results of [13] suggest that extracting such complex features might not be necessary and comparable classification results could be obtained by using only simple lexical Bag-of-Words (BoW) features. The BoW model, if its performance is on par with more complex feature sets, is an attractive approach for a non-expert because it does not require using any dedicated natural language processing tools. This perspective motivates us to find an answer to the following research question:

RQ1: When classifying app review sentences, how does a model with simple BoW features compare with a model using more complex linguistic features extracted via external NLP tools?

To answer RQ1, we use the dataset of Gu and Kim [7] and train a Maximum Entropy (MaxEnt) model using both feature sets: BoW features and the set of linguistic features proposed by [7]. Our results show that the simple BoW is very competitive, both in terms of feature extraction and computational complexity, for review sentence classification.

Recently, deep learning based models have gained popularity among researchers as they have an ability to learn useful feature representations automatically from a large corpus of labeled data without manual feature engineering effort. Specifically, a deep learning model known as *Convolutional Neural Network* (CNN) has recently achieved encouraging results for various text classification tasks [10]. A recent study of [4] suggests researchers to always compare computationally expensive models with their simple and efficient counterparts. Following this suggestion, we were interested in comparing the powerful deep learning CNN model with the simple BoW model. We formulate the second research question (RQ2) as follows:

RQ2: How does the deep learning based CNN classifier compare with the simple BoW model for app review sentence classification?

To answer RQ2, we experiment with CNN-based models for review sentence classification, adopting the model proposed by Kim [10]. A comparison of the CNN model performance with that of the MaxEnt model with BoW features shows that on average, the CNN-based model performs slightly worse than the BoW model. However, for the review sentence types *feature request* and *bug report*, which are the most informative sentence types to software developers, CNN-based models obtain the highest precision.

In this study, we first extend our previous work [19] with an analysis of the misclassification errors made by the BoW model and the annotated data. We observe that the largest proportion of confusions between the model predictions and the annotations occur between the three most meaningful sentence types (FEATURE EVALUATION, FEATURE REQUEST and BUG REPORT) and the sentence type OTHER, which is a residual category containing sentences that did not fit to any other category. By analyzing the annotated data in the light of these errors, we observe that in some cases individual sentences alone do not contain enough information to make the correct categorization decision. Thus, we suggest that for better app review sentence classification the context in terms of other sentences in the review should be taken into account.

Secondly, we performed more rigorous experiments with our lexical models as follows:

- We performed an additional analysis using MaxEnt models with 1 to 3 word n-gram features.
- For CNN models, we adopted early stopping to avoid overfitting and we re-evaluated the CNN results in this new setting.
- We now report standard deviations for all results observed in model performance over ten independent runs.

Finally, the related work section has been revised and updated to include the most recent work.

The rest of the paper is structured as follows. Section 2 summarizes the related work. In Sect. 3, we describe the dataset used for this study. In Sect. 4, we provide the description of the features and models used in this study. Section 5 details the experimental setting. Section 6 presents the results followed by a discussion in Sect. 7. In Sect. 8, threats to validity are examined. Conclusions are presented in Sect. 9.

2 Related Work

Maalej and Nabil [13] experimented with different classification models to classify reviews into *feature requests*, *bug reports*, *ratings*, and *user experiences*. They experimented with various features, including BoW. Similarly to us, they trained their models on the whole dataset of different apps. However, they evaluated their models on review-level, which fails to properly handle those reviews that simultaneously belong to several different categories.

McIlroy et al. [15] addressed this problem by performing multilabel classification of reviews, so that each review could be assigned several labels. However, their approach does not indicate, which sentence in the review is related to which label.

Other research has operated on sentence level. The most relevant for our work is SUR-Miner, a system proposed by Gu and Kim [7] that classifies review sentences into *feature evaluation*, *bug report*, *feature request*, *praise*, and *other*. They used a MaxEnt model for the classification task with a rich set of lexical and linguistic features extracted with NLP tools. We adopt their dataset and compare their linguistic feature set to the simpler BoW model. Whereas they trained a separate model for each app, we train a single model incorporating sentences of all apps, thus building a more general model with a larger training set, which has an additional advantage that it is not dependent on the existence of the labeled sentences of the apps that the model is applied to.

Chen et al. [1] proposed the system AR-Miner to help developers filter out informative reviews. Their system classifies review sentences into two classes: *informative* and *non-informative*. The study of Panichella et al. [18] first used AR-Miner to filter out non-informative review sentences and then categorized informative review sentences based on user intentions, i.e., *information seeking*, *information giving*, *feature request*, *problem discovery*, and *others*, and trained a learner, which relies on a large number of heuristic linguistic patterns, to automatically classify review sentences into those categories. In the same direction, the study of Sorbo et al. [21] proposed a tool, SURF, which uses a two-level classification approach. At the first level, similar to [18], review sentences are classified based on the user intentions and then on the second level the sentences are grouped into different review topics such as resources, security, pricing, GUI, download, model, company, updates/versions, feature/functionality, contents or app. In a recent study by Gao et al. [5], the review topics extracted using the SURF tool were further analyzed to get an insight about salient topics (i.e., review topics with significantly lower ratings (i.e. salient topic), abnormal topics (review topics having a swift increase in volume during a time period), correlation between two topics, and casual factors to rating or review quantity changes.

The study by Lu et al. [12] focuses on non-functional features. They automatically classified app reviews at sentence-level into four types of quality attributes: *reliability*, *usability*, *portability*, *performance*, and two additional classes *functional requirements*, and *others*. Iacob and Harrison [8] developed a system called MARA that used predefined linguistic patterns for finding feature requests from app reviews, later the system was extended to also find bug reports [9].

For general overviews about app store analysis for software engineering and opinion mining from app user reviews see [6,14].

3   Dataset and Preprocessing

In our study, we used the app review dataset contributed by Gu and Kim [7]. The dataset contains labeled review sentences of 17 apps belonging to different app categories, such as games, communication, books, and music. Each review sentence is assigned a label from a set of mutually exclusive types, which are: (a) FEATURE EVALUATION (E), (b) FEATURE REQUEST (R), (c) BUG REPORT (B), (d) PRAISE (P), and (e) OTHER (O). Table 1 presents the definition and a sample of review sentences for each type.

Table 1. Definition of five review sentence types used by Gu and Kim [7].

Sentence type	Definition	Examples
Praise (P)	Expressing emotions with specific reasons	Excellent!
		I love it!
		Amazing!
Feature Evaluation (E)	Expressing opinions about specific features	The UI is convenient
		I like the prediction text
Bug Report (B)	Reporting bugs, glitches or problems	It always force closes when I click the ".com" button
Feature Request (R)	Suggestion or new feature requests	It's a pity it doesn't support Chinese
Other (O)	Other categories defined in [17]	I've been playing it for three years

Table 2 shows the distribution of sentence types in each app category. It is apparent that the distribution of sentence types is highly skewed. The highest number of sentences belongs to the category OTHER followed by the category PRAISE. The numbers of other three sentence types—FEATURE EVALUATION, FEATURE REQUEST and BUG REPORT—are significantly smaller. However, these are the sentence types we are most interested in because they more likely contain useful information that help developers to improve their app.

The user review texts contain many typos and contractions that can make automatic classification of app review sentences a difficult task. To address this issue, we used a collection of 60 types and contractions[1] identified by Gu and Kim [7] to correct the words in the dataset. During this cleaning process, we replaced the common typos and contractions, e.g. "U" is replaced with "you" and "Plz" is replaced with "Please" etc.

4   Classification Models

This section describes the models designed to answer our research questions RQ1 and RQ2. We describe in detail the textual features we use to train MaxEnt models for review sentence classification. Then, we explain the CNN architecture that combines automatic feature extraction and classifier to classify the same set of review sentences.

4.1   Word N-Grams (BoW)

Word n-grams, also called Bag-of-Words (BoW), is a very simple feature extraction method without much manual effort. For instance, 1 to 2 word n-grams of

---

[1] https://guxd.github.io/srminer/appendix.html.

Table 2. App-wise distribution of sentence types in the dataset of Gu and Kim [7].

App name	App category	Review types					
		E	R	B	P	O	Total
chase mobile	finance	372	152	120	304	1051	**1999**
duolingo	education	370	20	121	614	874	**1999**
swiftkey	productivity	385	98	177	463	876	**1999**
google playbook	books	254	152	198	413	982	**1999**
yelp	food	435	44	54	348	1118	**1999**
google map	map	354	273	141	312	919	**1999**
text plus	social	354	138	75	537	1013	**2117**
wechat	social network	231	132	71	612	953	**1999**
google calender	productivity	466	119	463	109	842	**1999**
spotify calender	music	231	87	90	714	877	**1999**
yahoo weather	weather	493	71	85	508	842	**1999**
temple run 2	game	234	48	17	877	877	**2053**
medscape	medical	464	82	83	522	848	**1999**
espn	sports	472	287	128	161	951	**1999**
camera360	photography	178	67	24	928	928	**2125**
imdb	entertainment	361	115	194	363	966	**1999**
kakotalk	communication	220	69	77	768	865	**1999**
Total		**5874**	**1954**	**2118**	**8553**	**15782**	**34281**

a sentence 'plz fix it' are: *'plz'*, *'fix'*, *'it'*, *'plz fix'*, *'fix it'*. In this approach, first, a dictionary is created from a sequence of words called n-grams occurring in the training corpus. Then, a feature vector for each review sentence is created that stores the frequency of each n-gram in that sentence.

Lexical features are important in characterizing review sentence types. For instance, the words "awesome" and "great" are mostly used to praise the app. Similarly, the words "bug", "crash", and "plz fix" represent bug reports.

While Maalej and Nabil [13] used BoW features to classify app user reviews, we applied the same features on the sentence level. Although user reviews are longer and thus contain more information, we believe that review sentences are more specific and most of them contain enough lexical information to classify them correctly.

4.2   Character N-Grams (BoC)

Character n-grams, also called Bag-of-Characters (BoC), are simple lexical features, analogous to word n-grams. Character n-gram features of a sentence are all n-consecutive letter sequences (without spaces) in the tokens of the given sentence. For example, the 3-grams for the sentence "The UI is Ok" are *The*, *heU*, *eUI*, *UIi*, *Iis*, *isO*, and *sOk*. They have been used successfully in many applications such as malicious code detection and duplicate bug report detection [7].

4.3 Linguistic Features

We extracted the same set of linguistic features as proposed by Gu and Kim [7]. In addition to these linguistic features, Gu and Kim's feature set also includes the BoC features explained in the previous section.

Linguistic features can be useful because review sentences in each category often follow a distinct structural pattern. For instance, for aspect evaluation, the sentence structure tends to have a pattern like "The search (noun) works pretty nice (adjective)" or "It's perfect (adjective) for storing notes (noun)". While for feature request, sentence structure often follows the patterns such as "please add look up feature" or "it could be improved by adding more themes".

Part of Speech (POS): POS tags indicate the type of each word in a sentence. For example, POS tags for the sentence "The user interface is elegant." are "Determiner Noun Noun Verb Adjective". We extracted the PTB POS tags[2] with NLTK[3] and used the concatenation of POS tags of all the words in a sentence as a feature.

Constituency Parse Tree: Constituency parse tree represents the grammatical structure of a sentence. Figure 1 shows the constituency parse tree for a sample review sentence generated using Stanford CoreNLP library.[4] The parse tree shows that the sentence (S) consists of a noun phrase (NP) and a verb phrase (VP). The VP is further decomposed into an adjective phrase (ADJP). The parse tree of a sentence is traversed in breadth first order and the first five nodes are stored. The concatenation of non-terminal labels of these five nodes is then used as a feature.

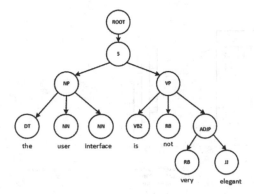

Fig. 1. Constituency parse tree for a review sentence "the user interface is not very elegant". The feature extracted from this tree is "ROOT-S-NP-VP-DT-NN" [19].

---

[2] https://www.ling.upenn.edu/courses/Fall_2003/ling001/penn_treebank_pos.html.
[3] http://www.nltk.org/.
[4] https://stanfordnlp.github.io/CoreNLP/.

Semantic Dependency Graph (SDG): SDG is a directed graph that shows the dependency relations between words in a sentence. Nodes in the graph represent words labeled with POS tags and edges represent dependency relations between words. Figure 2 shows the dependency graph of a sample sentence generated using spaCy[5] library. The word *is* is the ROOT node of the sentence as it does not have any incoming edges. The root has three dependents with the following relationships: a noun subject (nsubj) *interface*, a negation modifier (neg) *not*, and adjectival complement (acomp) *elegant*. The child node *interface* has two children: a determiner (det) *the* and a noun compound modifier (nn) *user*. To extract the feature, the SDG is traversed in a breadth first order and the dependency relations labeling the edges and the POS tags of the words in the nodes are concatenated. Leaf nodes that are not directly connected to the ROOT node are ignored. For example, the textual feature extracted from SDG of a sentence shown in Fig. 2 is "VBZ-nsubj-NN-neg-ADV-acomp-JJ".

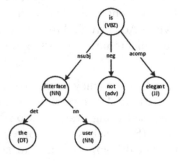

Fig. 2. Semantic Dependence Graph of a sample review sentence "the user interface is not elegant". The feature extracted from this SGD is "VBZ-nsubj-NN-neg-ADV-acomp-JJ" [19].

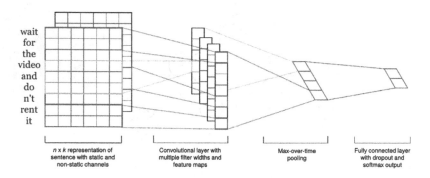

Fig. 3. CNN model architecture for sentence classification (Figure taken from [10]).

---

[5] https://spacy.io/.

Trunk Words. The trunk word feature is simply the root word of a SDG. For instance, the trunk word of the sentence "The user interface is not elegant" is *is*.

4.4 Convolutional Neural Networks (CNNs)

CNN-based classification models have shown encouraging results on various textual classification tasks [2,10]. We adopt the CNN architecture proposed by Kim [10] to classify review sentences.

The architecture of the model is illustrated in Fig. 3. The first layer of the network embeds words into low dimensional vectors. The second layer performs convolutions over the embedded word vectors using multiple filter sizes. The output of these convolutions are max pooled into a long feature vector in the third layer. The fourth layer is a dense layer with dropout applied. Finally, the results are classified using a softmax layer. For more details see [10].

Because neural network models have a large number of trainable parameters, they typically require large training sets to learn properly. However, when the available training sets are not very large, as is the case in this study, initializing CNN-based model with pre-trained word embedding vectors, obtained from a unsupervised neural language model might help to improve model performance [10,20].

Therefore, we train CNN-models both with and without pre-trained word embeddings to assess the effect of using the externally trained word vectors for classifying app review sentences. We use the 300-dimensional Word2Vec embeddings [16] trained on 100 billion words from Google News.[6]

The words that are absent in the vocabulary of pre-trained embeddings are initialized randomly. In particular, we experiment with two different models:

- **CNN (static):** The CNN model is initialized with the pre-trained word vectors but all words including the ones that are randomly initialized are kept static and are not updated during training.
- **CNN (non-static):** Same as CNN (static) but the pre-trained vectors are fine-tuned during model training for our classification task.

In our previous paper [19], we also reported results for the CNN model that did not use pretrained embeddings and where all embeddings were initialized randomly. Because adopting early stopping to avoid overfitting improved the results for both static and non-static CNN while the results with the randomly initialized CNN remained the same, we omitted experiments with the randomly initialized CNN in this paper, but the interested reader can find them in [19].

5   Experimental Setup

We trained and tested all models on the dataset described in Sect. 3. We compared all classification models on the test set by computing precision, recall, and f1-score for each review sentence type.

---

[6] https://code.google.com/archive/p/word2vec/.

For all experiments, labeled review sentences of all apps were merged into one dataset (see Table 2). We trained 10 instances of each model to ensure that the impact on accuracy due to variation in the data has been taken into account.

For each training instance, 80% of the data was randomly sampled as training set and 20% as test set without fixing the seed value. During each run, a model was trained on the training set and evaluated on the test set. The prediction accuracy of the ten evaluations were averaged and reported as the final performance.

We trained three MaxEnt models by extracting the different feature sets from review sentences. Two of the models are the same that we presented previously in [19]. The other two models are variations of the BoW model, one of them using higher order word n-grams and the other using only the character n-grams used in [7].

1. The unigram Bow model - BoW(1) [19];
2. The BoW model with word unigrams, bigrams and trigrams - BoW(3). This model is essentially as simple as the unigram BoW model and the training takes only slightly longer;
3. All features used in the study of Gu and Kim [7], which includes character n-grams of 2 to 4 characters and linguistic features - BoC+L [19];

We used the scikit-learn python library[7] to train, tune and evaluate the MaxEnt models. The regularization hyper-parameter C was fine-tuned separately for each model by performing 5-fold cross-validation on 80% of the randomly sampled data. For the BoW(1) model, the regularization weight was fixed to 0.856 and for the models with character n-grams and Gu's features: BoC and BoC+L, C was fixed to 0.09 and 1.0, respectively. For the model with BoW(3) features, C was fixed to 0.4 and the parameter "class-weight" was set to "balanced" to adjust the weight of each class so that would be inversely proportional to their class frequencies. All the experiments were run on a CPU cluster (2 x Intel(R) Xeon(R) CPU E5-2660 v2 @ 2.20 GHz) with resources of one compute node and 16 GB RAM.

For the CNN model, we used a freely available implementation of [10][8] based on TensorFlow[9] library in Python. For each CNN model, the 80% training sample is further split into 70% training and 10% validation set. The model is evaluation on the validation set after every 100 updates. We stopped the training when the average f1-score of the relevant classes (i.e., E, B, and R) on development set had not improved further during the next 1000 steps, compared to its last best performance. The best performing model was used for the evaluation on the test set. The hyperparameters used in the CNN model are: rectified linear units (ReLU), filter windows of sizes 2, 3 and 4 with 128 feature maps for each filter. The dropout rate of 0.6 and L2 regularization parameter of 0.1 was chosen by performing 5-fold cross-validation on a training set. We used a batch size of 256 and trained the models for 50 epochs. The model was trained with Adam optimizer.

---

[7] http://scikit-learn.org/stable/.
[8] https://github.com/dennybritz/cnn-text-classification-tf.
[9] https://www.tensorflow.org/.

Table 3. The classification performance of all models on all sentence types. In each row, the best result for MaxEnt and CNN models is in bold.

Sentence type	MaxEnt			CNN	
	BoW(1)	BoW(3)	BoC+L	Static	Non-static
Feature Evaluation (E)					
Precision	**77.4 ± 1.4**	75.4 ± 1.2	77.0 ± 1.0	**78.2 ± 2.1**	76.2 ± 3.2
Recall	63.6 ± 1.5	68.1 ± 1.7	**68.5 ± 1.1**	65.0 ± 2.1	**71.0 ± 2.2**
F1-score	69.8 ± 1.3	71.6 ± 1.3	**72.5 ± 0.8**	69.9 ± 0.8	**73.5 ± 1.1**
Feature Request (R)					
Precision	71.2 ± 3.8	63.4 ± 1.7	**73.9 ± 3.1**	**74.9 ± 5.3**	73.8 ± 3.0
Recall	57.8 ± 2.1	**71.0 ± 2.4**	59.1 ± 2.5	60.7 ± 2.9	**63.6 ± 4.1**
F1-score	63.8 ± 2.3	**67.0 ± 1.5**	65.6 ± 2.0	66.9 ± 2.2	**68.2 ± 1.6**
Bug Report (B)					
Precision	73.0 ± 2.8	67.1 ± 2.5	**76.1 ± 2.3**	**74.3 ± 3.3**	72.4 ± 3.3
Recall	57.4 ± 1.6	**68.9 ± 2.2**	60.7 ± 2.6	**64.5 ± 4.2**	62.7 ± 5.9
F1-score	64.2 ± 1.6	**67.9 ± 1.6**	67.5 ± 1.8	**68.9 ± 2.5**	67.0 ± 3.2
Average (E+R+B)					
Precision	73.9 ± 1.7	68.7 ± 1.0	**75.7 ± 1.6**	**75.8 ± 2.0**	74.2 ± 2.4
Recall	59.6 ± 1.1	**69.3 ± 1.1**	62.7 ± 1.0	64.9 ± 1.8	**65.8 ± 2.8**
F1-score	65.9 ± 1.3	**68.8 ± 0.8**	68.5 ± 1.0	**69.8 ± 1.4**	69.5 ± 1.4
Praise (P)					
Precision	83.1 ± 1.0	81.9 ± 0.7	**85.8 ± 0.7**	80.1 ± 1.6	**80.9 ± 0.9**
Recall	85.7 ± 1.3	**88.0 ± 1.2**	87.1 ± 0.7	**85.9 ± 1.5**	84.0 ± 2.3
F1-score	84.4 ± 0.6	84.8 ± 0.7	**86.5 ± 0.5**	**82.9 ± 0.7**	82.4 ± 0.7
Others (O)					
Precision	78.2 ± 0.7	**82.7 ± 0.6**	80.0 ± 0.8	**84.8 ± 1.4**	84.0 ± 1.9
Recall	85.9 ± 0.9	80.7 ± 0.5	**86.9 ± 0.5**	86.4 ± 2.1	**87.0 ± 1.7**
F1-score	81.9 ± 0.6	81.6 ± 0.4	**83.3 ± 0.5**	**85.6 ± 0.7**	85.4 ± 0.6
Overall average (E+R+B+P+O)					
Precision	76.6 ± 1.2	74.1 ± 0.7	**78.6 ± 0.9**	**78.5 ± 1.3**	77.5 ± 1.5
Recall	70.1 ± 0.7	**75.3 ± 0.7**	72.5 ± 0.6	73.4 ± 1.2	**73.7 ± 1.4**
F1-score	72.8 ± 0.9	74.6 ± 0.7	**75.1 ± 0.6**	**75.6 ± 1.0**	75.3 ± 1.0

6 Results

In this section, we present the results for research questions RQ1 and RQ2. The classification accuracies of all models for all sentence types are shown in Table 3. The average performance (i.e., precision, recall and f1-score) for sentence types FEATURE EVALUATION (E), FEATURE REQUEST (R) and BUG REPORT (B) is separately shown as these categories are expected to give the most interesting information for app improvement. The first three columns present the results of the MaxEnt models. The last two columns give the results of the static and non-static CNN models. In each row, the best results for the MaxEnt and CNN models, respectively, are printed in bold font. The results averaged over all sentence types are shown in the last row of Table 3.

In the following, we answer the research questions. RQ1 is concerned with the performance comparison of the three MaxEnt models (the first four columns in Table 3). The first two models only use simple BoW (i.e., word n-grams) features, while the last model uses both character n-grams and, in addition, linguistic features (see Sect. 4.3). On average over all sentence types on MaxEnt models, the model with linguistic features (BoC+L) obtained the best precision and f1-score while the model with only BoW features (i.e. 1 to 3 word n-gram features) achieves the best recall. However, the difference in f1-scores between the BoC+L and BoW(3) models is less than one standard deviation and thus not statistically significant.

Regarding the model performances for the relevant sentence types E, R and B, the average recall of the model with BoW(3) features is better than the recall of the BoC+L model with linguistic features by 6.6 % points. However, the model with linguistic features has the best precision compared to the other models. In terms of f1-score, the BoW(3) model is the best with 68.8, but the difference to BoC+L with linguistic features is non-significant.

In relation to RQ1, we conclude that the simple MaxEnt model with 1 to 3 word n-gram features is computationally the fastest (see Table 4) and as competitive as the MaxEnt model with complex linguistic features.

Table 4. Runtime of different classification models [19].

Model	Average runtime for one run
MaxEnt BoW(1)	9 mins
MaxEnt BoW(3)	12 mins
MaxEnt BoC+L	22 mins
CNN (non-static)	142 mins
CNN (static)	554 mins

RQ2 studies the performance of deep learning based CNN model in comparison with the MaxEnt model with BoW features. Although the static CNN seems to obtain better precision and the non-static models obtains higher recall, the performance of the individual model runs varies a lot and thus, the differences are not statistically significant. Thus, in terms of overall averages, the performance of both the static and the non-static CNN models are on the same level.

On average, for the informative sentence types (i.e. E, R and B), the CNN (static) model is slightly better than both BoW(1) and BoW(3) in terms of f1-score, but these differences are again not statistically significant. When comparing the CNN (static) model to the BoW(3) model, the CNN (static) model obtains higher precision whereas the BoW(3) model has a better recall.

Hence, we conclude with regards to RQ2 that the CNN models (static and non-static) achieve competitive performance in comparison to the MaxEnt models (BoW(1) and BoW(3)) but the superiority of one or the other approach is not clear. However, it is possible that with a larger training set, the CNN models would gain a clearer advantage over the simple MaxEnt models with BoW features.

7 Discussion

The results presented in Sect. 6 indicate that the model performance for automatic classification of review sentences might have potential for improvement, especially with regards to sentence types that contain useful information for developers (i.e. FEATURE REQUEST (R), FEATURE EVALUATION (E) and BUG REPORT (B)). To investigate issues affecting model performance, we first performed an error analysis of the BoW(3) model predictions. Then, we analyzed a random sample of annotated reviews from Gu's dataset to better comprehend the overall procedure that was used to annotate reviews.

Since our first objective is to understand the reasons behind the prediction errors made by the model, we started our analysis by looking at the confusion matrix (shown in Table 5) of the reviews used for evaluation in one of the experimental runs. Each column of the confusion matrix in Table 5 represents the instances of a predicted sentence type while each row represents the instances of a true (annotated) sentence type. All correct predictions are located in the diagonal of the confusion matrix. The confusion matrix clearly shows that the classification model is seriously confused about the prediction of a large number of review sentences labeled as OTHER (O). For instance, 26% (107 out of 411) of the sentences with the true label OTHER are wrongly predicted as BUG REPORT while 22.5% (86 out of 382) of sentences with the true label BUG REPORT have been missed as they have been falsely predicted as type OTHER. Similar percentages of misclassifications also occur for the FEATURE REQUEST sentence type.

Table 5. The confusion matrix of model predictions on reviews in the evaluation-set.

			Predicted label				
		E	R	B	P	O	Total
	E	845	29	22	86	209	1191
	R	24	295	14	10	76	419
True label	B	16	11	265	4	86	382
	P	45	5	3	1537	139	1729
	O	202	117	107	205	2445	3076
	Total	1132	457	411	1842	2995	6979

The classification performance presented in the form of the confusion matrix indicates that a significant number of sentences annotated as OTHER overlaps with sentences annotated as with other classes FEATURE EVALUATION, FEATURE REQUEST, BUG REPORT and PRAISE. A manual analysis of misclassified review sentences in each sentence type can help to investigate the reasons for these misclassifications. Therefore, we manually analyzed the false positives (FPs) and false negatives (FNs) of the sentences annotated as BUG REPORT because this class has the largest proportion of misclassifications regarding sentence type OTHER (the number of instances analyzed are highlighted in Table 5).

It seems reasonable to assume that review sentences labeled as FEATURE EVALUATION, BUG REPORT or FEATURE REQUEST should mention a functional or non-functional aspect of an app. Based on the definitions of the sentence types given in Table 1, this assumption should hold for review sentences labeled as FEATURE EVALUATION and FEATURE REQUEST in Gu's dataset. With sentence type BUG REPORT the definition given in Table 1 is not so clear as it also includes glitches and problems which might be general and not specific to a particular aspect of an app. Indeed, the examples of some FNs (Sentence#1 to Sentence#5) presented in Table 6 show that there are sentences annotated as BUG REPORTS that describe general problems or glitches that the model predicts as belonging to the class OTHER. Similarly, the examples of FPs given in Table 6 (Sentence#6 to Sentence#10) show that there are very similar sentences that have been annotated as OTHERS but that the model has predicted as belonging to the class BUG REPORT. These examples demonstrate that differences between sentences belonging to classes BUG REPORT and OTHER are not always clear and this also confuses the model.

Another possibility is that the sentences annotated as BUG REPORTS in fact contained more specific complaints about the app compared to sentences labeled as OTHERS, which would become evident if the rest of the app review from where the sentence was taken from would be considered. Consider any of the sentences #1 to #5 in Table 6. It is possible that a previous review sentence or sentences might describe more specifically what problem has been referred to. However, by considering these sentences in isolation from the rest of the review it is impossible to tell whether they are part of more specific complaints or not. We suggest that for many of these sentences, the correct type of these sentences remains ambiguous when treated in isolation without the context of the rest of the review.

In order to better understand how widespread the problem of ambiguity is for the given dataset, we selected a stratified random sample of 200 review sentences from Gu's dataset for manual re-annotation analysis. We started with the basic intuition that in order for the review sentences of type FEATURE REQUEST, FEATURE EVALUATION and BUG REPORT to be useful they must contain an app feature. Thus, we first counted the number of review sentences in each sentence type in which a functional or a non-functional aspect has been mentioned. The summary of this analysis is shown in Table 7, showing that on average 24% of review sentences belonging to these three types do not contain any aspect information (although there were none of such sentences of type FEATURE REQUEST in this random sample). In our opinion, the review sentences that belong to type BUG REPORT but not mentioning any aspect term should be labeled as type OTHER

Table 6. Examples of false negatives (FNs) and false positives (FPs) from sentence type 'B'.

Sent#	Review sentence	True label	Pred label
False negatives (FNs)			
1	*Unfortunately stop*	B	O
2	*CAN YOU FIX THAT PROBLEMS?*	B	O
3	*I'd love to give this a 5 star again but not until that's fixed*	B	O
4	*I uninstalled it because of this same glitch before*	B	O
5	*blank screen*	B	O
False positives (FPs)			
6	*It won't work offline anymore*	O	B
7	*Can't remove it*	O	B
8	*The keyboard stals open on my lock screen*	O	B
9	*I can only bookmark the pages*	O	B
10	*fix it*	O	B

Table 7. Analysis of randomly selected 200 review sentences mentioning functional aspect, non-functional aspect, or no aspect.

Sentence type	#Functional aspect	#Non-functional aspect	#No aspect	Total
E	11	14	9	34
R	12	0	0	12
B	2	5	5	12
Subtotal	25	19	14	58
P	1	0	49	50
O	16	9	67	92
Total	42	28	130	200

while the review sentences belonging to type FEATURE EVALUATION that do not mention any aspect information should be either labeled as type OTHER (in the case of negative or neutral sentiment) or type PRAISE (in the case of positive sentiment).

Next, in order to quantify our disagreement with Gu's annotations, the first author of this paper manually re-annotated the same 200 randomly selected review sentences according to the principles describe above, and in the following we refer to these as Shah's annotation. The number of disagreements between Gu's annotation and Shah's annotation are presented in the form of a confusion matrix in

Table 8. Comparison of Shah's annotation against Gu's annotation.

		Shah's label					
		E	R	B	P	O	Total
	E	24	0	1	8	1	34
	R	0	12	0	0	0	12
Gu's label	B	0	0	7	0	5	12
	P	1	0	0	46	3	50
	O	9	5	7	12	59	92
	Total	34	17	15	66	68	200

Table 8. We show the examples of a few disagreements (Sentence#1 to Sentence#5 in Table 9) to demonstrate the annotation differences that stem from our strict criteria about the presence of an aspect term in sentences of types BUG REPORT and FEATURE EVALUATION.[10] Moreover, in Gu's annotations, the review sentences in which user praises the whole app with words: "helpful", "useful" and "effective" are labeled as FEATURE EVALUATION, however, in Shah's annotation we labeled them as type PRAISE (look at sentence#3 and sentence#5 in Table 9). Overall, 35% of review sentence annotated by Gu as type OTHER were relabeled as one of the other four types (FEATURE EVALUATION, FEATURE REQUEST, BUG REPORT or PRAISE) in Shah's annotation, some examples are shown in Table 9 (sentence#6 to sentence#10). Regardless of these disagreements, we cannot rule out the possibility that annotators who labeled the reviews in Gu's dataset might have taken into account the context information when they annotated these review sentences. Since the dataset we received from the authors only contains the review sentences without the context information, we did not have access to this context information during our manual annotation.

The next logical step in the light of this knowledge would be to re-annotate the whole dataset using the principles described. The sentence types FEATURE EVALUATION, FEATURE REQUEST and BUG REPORT must contain a functional or nonfunctional aspect term. Those sentences that do not contain an aspect term should be annotated as PRAISE when the sentiment of the sentence is positive towards the app and the category OTHER should contain all the remaining sentences. However, as the dataset is quite large we were not able to carry out the full re-annotation at this point and thus, we can only hypothesize what effect such re-annotation could have on the machine learning classifiers. We hypothesize that after such re-annotation there boundaries between the three classes containing aspect terms and the OTHER class are more clear and that would improve the performance of the machine learning classifiers.

Our previous analysis (see examples in Tables 6 and 9) suggested that context information might be important for classification of reviews at sentence-level. To illustrate this idea, we present two sample reviews in Table 10. In the table, the first sentence of Review#1 has a negative sentiment word "issue" that, when looking at

---

[10] There are no examples from the sentence type FEATURE REQUEST because all sentences in our sample annotated with that type contained an aspect term.

Table 9. Example of annotations on which Gu and Shah have disagreements.

Sent#	Sentence text	Gu's label	Shah's label
1	*Keeps crashing*	B	O
2	*I've tried more than five times it got stuck at 2% 58% 75% what shall i do?*	B	O
3	*It is very helpful!*	E	P
4	*it works great!*	E	P
5	*Effective!*	E	P
6	*Can't make a deposit after last update*	O	B
7	*It is so prone to mistakes and if we do not double check the dates, we would end up missing the events*	O	B
8	*WoW!*	O	P
9	*Is it possible to ad emojis and a name 'taging' functionality (similar to facebook/instagram) within the ap's yelp talk forum?*	O	R
10	*My husband and I frequently sync calendars which is fuss free*	O	E

the sentence in isolation, hints that the sentence belongs to type BUG REPORT but the word and sentence level information is in fact FEATURE REQUEST. Similarly, in the second review example, the second sentence without wider context would be too vague to consider as BUG REPORT as it does not contain an aspect term. However, the first sentence helps to resolve the coreference and disambiguate the correct sentence type as BUG REPORT.

All examples in Table 9 could be annotated and classified on the review level. However, in this paper we addressed the review classification problem on sentences level because some reviews can address several aspect types. According to [15] between 22% and 30% of app reviews raise multiple issues in the same review. Although these numbers cannot be directly generalized to our setting because [15] quantified the amount of multi-labeled reviews using an annotation set consisting of 14 different labels as opposed to only 5 labels in our dataset, they suggest that the issue of multiple labels per review cannot be overlooked. On the other hand, as we have shown in our discussion, strictly sentence level analysis does not solve the problem either because the meaning of a sentence and to which category it belong might be dependent on the contextual sentences in the review. Thus, we propose that further studies should explore *categorizing review sentences in the context of the rest of the review.*

One option to utilize the context information would be to adopt neural models. Over the past few years, researchers have successfully utilized the context information in neural models using the attention mechanisms [3, 11] in which the model is allowed to focus to contextual information (i.e., previous and next sentences) of the source sentence before generating a prediction. For instance, [23] improved the performance for automatic classification of reviews (i.e., Yelp, IMDB and Amazon) with neural networks by utilizing the word level and sentence level context information. In conclusion, we suggest that future research in app review classification should adopt datasets *annotated on the sentence level within the context of the whole review* and experiment with incorporating this context information into CNN models or other neural text classification models.

Table 10. Context information is useful in predicting the correct type of a review sentence.

Review#	Review text
1	*The main issue I have with this app is that there isn't a 'keep me logged in' feature. Please add and I will reward you greatly (with 5 stars)*
2	*I cannot view my XLS files on iPad.* *Please fix this ASAP.* *Thanks*

8   Threats to Validity

The review dataset used in this study has been collected from PlayStore and was manually labeled by [7]. We do not know the extent to which the results of our study are sensitive to the annotators and annotation guidelines used to label this data. Moreover, the nature or language characteristics of the reviews in other app marketplaces may be different to that of PlayStore. Therefore, we do not claim the generalizability of our results to reviews from other platforms like, e.g., AppStore.

The CNN-based model has a large number of hyperparameters that can be tuned to potentially improve the performance. This set of hyperparameters includes the size of the embeddings, number and sizes of filters, the choice of the optimizer with its parameters, various options for regularization, etc. Tuning all these hypermarameters is unfeasible in practice. Thus, we tuned the drop-out rate and the strength of the L2-regularization. Still, tuning other hyperparameters as well might improve the model performance.

Previous studies have shown that tuning the word vectors to the particular classification task (non-static CNN) improves model performance [10] but in our experiments the performance difference between static and non-static CNN is not significant. One possible reason for this can be that the textual domain of Google News is too different from the texts of app reviews and thus embeddings trained on Google News has not given a good enough starting point for our model. It is possible that word embeddings pre-trained on a large amount of app reviews would perform better in our case.

The number of examples for each sentence type in the dataset are imbalanced. To tackle this imbalance, we experimented with random oversampling and random undersampling techniques in MaxEnt models but did not observe any improvements in F1-score. Many other techniques exist to handle class imbalance and thus it is possible that using one of those would have made a difference. Also, we did not apply the class balancing techniques to neural models where they potentially could have improved the results.

The manual analysis presented in Sect. 7 was performed by only one person and thus might be biased. We tried to address this problem by having the re-labeling decisions reviewed by the other two co-authors. There were only two cases where the decisions were needed to be changed. This happened in agreement among all three authors.

9 Conclusion

We explored the power of simple lexical features in classifying app review sentences. For that, we compared the simple Bag-of-Words feature representation with a more complex feature set proposed in previous work extracted using various NLP tools. We found that, on average, the simple BoW model performs as well as the model with complex linguistic features. Considering that software developers and software engineering researchers are typically not experts in NLP tools, this is a desirable result. We also experimented with deep learning based CNN models which have become very popular due to their ability to learn complex feature representations from simple lexical inputs as well as their good performance in many tasks. In our study, we did not observe any significant advantage of using computationally more expensive CNNs over its simpler BoW counterpart. However, from the manual analysis of annotated reviews and classification errors, we gather that context knowledge could be useful for the classification of review sentences. Therefore, including context information, for instance using attention mechanisms in neural models, might help in improving the classification performance.

Acknowledgments. We are grateful to Xiaodong Gu for sharing the review dataset for this study. This research was supported by the institutional research grant IUT20-55 of the Estonian Research Council and the Estonian Center of Excellence in ICT research (EXCITE).

References

1. Chen, N., Lin, J., Hoi, S.C.H., Xiao, X., Zhang, B.: AR-miner: mining informative reviews for developers from mobile app marketplace. In: Proceedings of the ICSE 2014, pp. 767–778. ACM Press (2014)
2. Collobert, R., Weston, J., Bottou, L., Karlen, M., Kavukcuoglu, K., Kuksa, P.: Natural language processing (almost) from scratch. J. Mach. Learn. Res. **12**(Aug), 2493–2537 (2011)
3. Du, J., Gui, L., Xu, R., He, Y.: A convolutional attention model for text classification. In: Huang, X., Jiang, J., Zhao, D., Feng, Y., Hong, Y. (eds.) NLPCC 2017. LNCS (LNAI), vol. 10619, pp. 183–195. Springer, Cham (2018). https://doi.org/10.1007/978-3-319-73618-1_16

4. Fu, W., Menzies, T.: Easy over hard: a case study on deep learning. In: Proceedings of the 2017 11th Joint Meeting on Foundations of Software Engineering, ESEC/FSE 2017, pp. 49–60. ACM, New York (2017). https://doi.org/10.1145/3106237.3106256, http://doi.acm.org/10.1145/3106237.3106256

5. Gao, C., Zeng, J., Lo, D., Lin, C.Y., Lyu, M.R., King, I.: Infar: insight extraction from app reviews. In: Proceedings of the 2018 26th ACM Joint Meeting on European Software Engineering Conference and Symposium on the Foundations of Software Engineering, ESEC/FSE 2018, pp. 904–907. ACM, New York (2018). https://doi.org/10.1145/3236024.3264595, http://doi.acm.org/10.1145/3236024.3264595

6. Genc-Nayebi, N., Abran, A.: A systematic literature review: opinion mining studies from mobile app store user reviews. J. Syst. Softw. **125**, 207–219 (2017)

7. Gu, X., Kim, S.: What parts of your apps are loved by users? In: 2015 30th IEEE/ACM International Conference on Automated Software Engineering (ASE), pp. 760–770, November 2015. https://doi.org/10.1109/ASE.2015.57

8. Iacob, C., Harrison, R.: Retrieving and analyzing mobile apps feature requests from online reviews. In: Proceedings of the 10th Working Conference on Mining Software Repositories, pp. 41–44. IEEE Press (2013)

9. Iacob, C., Harrison, R., Faily, S.: Online reviews as first class artifacts in mobile app development. In: Memmi, G., Blanke, U. (eds.) MobiCASE 2013. LNICST, vol. 130, pp. 47–53. Springer, Cham (2014). https://doi.org/10.1007/978-3-319-05452-0_4

10. Kim, Y.: Convolutional neural networks for sentence classification. In: Proceedings of the EMNLP 2014, pp. 1746–1751. ACL (2014)

11. Liu, T., Yu, S., Xu, B., Yin, H.: Recurrent networks with attention and convolutional networks for sentence representation and classification. Appl. Intell. **48**(10), 3797–3806 (2018)

12. Lu, M., Liang, P.: Automatic classification of non-functional requirements from augmented app user reviews. In: Proceedings of the 21st International Conference on Evaluation and Assessment in Software Engineering, EASE 2017, pp. 344–353. ACM, New York (2017). https://doi.org/10.1145/3084226.3084241, http://doi.acm.org/10.1145/3084226.3084241

13. Maalej, W., Nabil, H.: Bug report, feature request, or simply praise? On automatically classifying app reviews. In: Proceedings of RE 2015, pp. 116–125. IEEE, August 2015

14. Martin, W., Sarro, F., Jia, Y., Zhang, Y., Harman, M.: A survey of app store analysis for software engineering. IEEE Trans. Softw. Eng. **43**(9), 817–847 (2017)

15. McIlroy, S., Ali, N., Khalid, H., Hassan, A.E.: Analyzing and automatically labelling the types of user issues that are raised in mobile app reviews. Empir. Softw. Eng. **21**(3), 1067–1106 (2016)

16. Mikolov, T., Chen, K., Corrado, G., Dean, J.: Efficient estimation of word representations in vector space. arXiv preprint arXiv:1301.3781 (2013)

17. Pagano, D., Maalej, W.: User feedback in the appstore: an empirical study. In: Proceedings of RE 2013, pp. 125–134 (2013)

18. Panichella, S., Di Sorbo, A., Guzman, E., Visaggio, C.A., Canfora, G., Gall, H.C.: How can i improve my app? Classifying user reviews for software maintenance and evolution. In: Proceedings of the 2015 IEEE International Conference on Software Maintenance and Evolution (ICSME), ICSME 2015, pp. 281–290. IEEE Computer Society, Washington, D.C. (2015). https://doi.org/10.1109/ICSM.2015.7332474, http://dx.doi.org/10.1109/ICSM.2015.7332474

19. Shah, F.A., Sirts, K., Pfahl, D.: Simple app review classification with only lexical features. In: Proceedings of the 13th International Conference on Software Technologies, ICSOFT, vol. 1, pp. 112–119. INSTICC, SciTePress (2018). https://doi.org/10.5220/0006855901460153
20. Socher, R., Lin, C.C.Y., Ng, A.Y., Manning, C.D.: Parsing natural scenes and natural language with recursive neural networks. In: Proceedings of the 28th International Conference on International Conference on Machine Learning, ICML 2011, pp. 129–136. Omnipress, Madison (2011). http://dl.acm.org/citation.cfm?id=3104482.3104499
21. Sorbo, A.D., Panichella, S., Alexandru, C.V., Visaggio, C.A., Canfora, G.: Surf: summarizer of user reviews feedback. In: 2017 IEEE/ACM 39th International Conference on Software Engineering Companion (ICSE-C), pp. 55–58, May 2017. https://doi.org/10.1109/ICSE-C.2017.5
22. Villarroel, L., Bavota, G., Russo, B., Oliveto, R., Di Penta, M.: Release planning of mobile apps based on user reviews. In: Proceedings of the ICSE 2016, pp. 14–24. ACM (2016)
23. Yang, Z., Yang, D., Dyer, C., He, X., Smola, A., Hovy, E.: Hierarchical attention networks for document classification. In: Proceedings of the 2016 Conference of the North American Chapter of the Association for Computational Linguistics: Human Language Technologies, pp. 1480–1489 (2016)

Smart Measurements and Analysis for Software Quality Enhancement

Sarah Dahab[1] , Stephane Maag[1] , Wissam Mallouli[2(✉)] ,
and Ana Cavalli[1]

[1] SAMOVAR, Telecom SudParis, Université Paris-Saclay, Saint-Aubin, France
{sarah.dahab,stephane.maag}@telecom-sudparis.eu
[2] Montimage Research and Development, Paris, France
{wissam.mallouli,ana.cavalli}@montimage.com

Abstract. Requests to improve the quality of software are increasing due to the competition in software industry and the complexity of software development integrating multiple technology domains (e.g., IoT, Big Data, Cloud, Artificial Intelligence, Security Technologies). Measurements collection and analysis is key activity to assess software quality during its development live-cycle. To optimize this activity, our main idea is to periodically select relevant measures to be executed (among a set of possible measures) and automatize their analysis by using a dedicated tool. The proposed solution is integrated in a whole PaaS platform called MEASURE. The tools supporting this activity are Software Metric Suggester tool that recommends metrics of interest according several software development constraints and based on artificial intelligence and MINT tool that correlates collected measurements and provides near real-time recommendations to software development stakeholders (i.e. DevOps team, project manager, human resources manager etc.) to improve the quality of the development process. To illustrate the efficiency of both tools, we created different scenarios on which both approaches are applied. Results show that both tools are complementary and can be used to improve the software development process and thus the final software quality.

Keywords: Software engineering · DevOps team ·
Metrics combination · Metrics reuse · Metrics suggestion ·
Metrics correlation · Software quality

1 Introduction

Metrics play a crucial role to improve software quality development process that is becoming more and more complex [1]. To select the right metrics is also of

Supported by the ongoing European project ITEA3-MEASURE started in Dec. 1st, 2015, and the EU HubLinked project started in Jan. 1st, 2017.

M. van Sinderen and L. A. Maciaszek (Eds.): ICSOFT 2018, CCIS 1077, pp. 194–219, 2019.
https://doi.org/10.1007/978-3-030-29157-0_9

prime importance for a successful software development. They have a strong impact on developers actions and decisions [16].

In order to improve the software quality, we need to introduce new metrics with the required detail and automation. Due to the modern development practices, new tools and methods are also necessary being the traditional metrics and evaluation methods not sufficient anymore. Even more, there is a large body of research related to software metrics that aims to help industry while measuring the effectiveness and efficiency of used software engineering processes, tools and techniques to help management in decision-making [4].

To achieve software quality, it is required to integrate new metrics based on constraints combining safety (the system always behaves as it is supposed to) and security (authentication, data protection, confidentiality, ...) and quality of service. Green metrics also become relevant as they contribute to the reduction of energy consumption.

This paper focuses on the combination, reuse, suggestion and correlation of metrics. We have developed two complementary approaches, one based on metrics reuse, combination and suggestion and the other on metrics correlation. They have been implemented in two tools, Metrics Suggester and Metrics Intelligence Tool (MINT). Both approaches contribute to improve software quality development proposing new techniques for metrics application and evaluation.

Regarding the Metrics Suggester approach, it is based on the optimization of the current measurement process which are manual and static and thus very costly. Metrics Suggester proposes an automated analysis and suggestion approach, by using the learning technique Support Vector Machine[1] (SVM), based on AI algorithms. In summary, it consists of suggesting relevant and efficient measurement plans at runtime using a machine learning algorithm.

Regarding the MINT approach, the idea is to identify and design correlations between metrics that contribute to the improvement of the development process and help developers to take decisions about it. The proposed correlations cover all aspects of the system like functional behavior, security, green computing and timing. For instance, we have defined correlations covering different phases of development. Techniques to correlate metrics are provided and recommendations are given as an outcome to the developer and project manager or any other software stakeholder. Recommendations will affect their actions and decisions.

Both techniques are original and introduce innovation with respect to classical methods. Moreover, the application to the combination of metrics regarding software development, security and green computing is a novelty with respect to them.

Both approaches and tools are part of the European ITEA project MEASURE and they have been integrated in the project PaaS platform[2]. Furthermore, in order to reach that result, a close link has been defined between academia and industry for several years strengthened by the EU HubLinked

---

[1] http://www.statsoft.com/Textbook/Support-Vector-Machines.
[2] https://itea3.org/project/measure.html.

project[3] fostering the U-I relationships (Universities-Industry). In summary, the main contributions of this paper are:

- the design of new complementary approaches to improve software quality development process by introduction of new correlation and suggestion techniques, these lasts based on AI algorithms;
- the development of techniques and tools, Metrics Suggester and MINT, for metrics correlation, reuse, suggestion, and recommendation.
- first functional experimentation of both tools.

This paper is organized as it follows: Sect. 2 presents the related works. Section 3 gives a view of the MEASURE global platform and presents the two approaches and the tools, Metrics Suggester and MINT. Section 4 is devoted to presenting the experiences that are illustrated by experiments and Sect. 5 gives the conclusion and perspectives of our work.

2   Related Works

Many efforts have been done to define metrics for software quality [4,10,21,25]. These works can be associated with standardized quality models such as ISO 9126 quantifying properties with software metrics [5]. Learning techniques are currently arising to effectively refine, detail and improve the used metrics and to target more relevant measurement data. Current works such as [22], [27] and [23] raise that issue by proposing diverse kinds of machine learning approaches for software defect prediction through software metrics. These studies have shown the importance of gathering information on the software engineering process in particular to ensure its quality through metrics and measurements analysis [10]. Thanks to that, standardization institutes worked in that way to propose two well-known norms, ISO/IEC25010 [21] and OMG SMM [4] to guide the measurement plan specification. These two standards have been reviewed by the research and industrial community, and are adapted and applied in many domains [2].

However, even if these techniques have introduced considerable progress to improve the software quality, they have still some limitations. The measurement plan is, in general, manually fixed by the project manager, the implementation of the measures is dependent on the developer and reduce the scalability, maintainability and the interoperability of the measurement process.

For software metrics correlation, there are many works focused on the relations between internal and external software metrics. In [28], the impact of software metrics on software quality is presented and the internal and external attributes of a software product are studied because the relationship between them directly affects its behaviour. The metrics are combination of these attributes. As the number of metrics used in a software project increases, the management and controlling of the project also increases. In [24], the authors

---

[3] http://www.hublinked.eu/.

investigated the relationship between different internal and external software metrics by analyzing a large collection of C/C++ programs submitted to a programming competition, the Online Judge. In [19], they analyze the links between software reliability and software complexity for evaluating the effectiveness of testing strategies.

These works have been applied mainly to establish correlations between internal and external metrics, and to specific ones. They have been very useful for our work published in [7] and extended in this paper. Even though our approaches are generic and can be applied to any metric, we plan to apply our approaches to evaluate the relation between specific and well selected metrics. Besides, the tools we propose are part of a PaaS open source platform called MEASURE[4] dedicated to host several measuring and analysis tools to enhance software engineering process quality.

3   Measurement Approaches and Tools

3.1   The MEASURE PaaS Platform

The MEASURE platform provides services to (1) host, configure and collect measures, (2) store measurements, present and visualize them and (3) analyze them

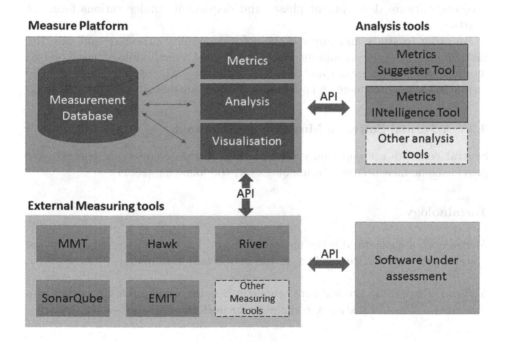

Fig. 1. The MEASURE PaaS platform.

---

[4] https://github.com/ITEA3-Measure/.

and provide recommendations. These measures are first defined in SMM (Structured Metrics Meta-model) standard[5] using the extension of Modelio modelling tool[6] dedicated to SMM modelling. The MEASURE platform is able to collect measurements (data resulting of the execution of an instantiated measure) thanks to external measuring tools (e.g., Hawk [11] for design and modelling related measurements, SonarQube [12] for testing related measurements, MMT[7] for operation related measurements, EMIT [3] for energy consumption related measurements, etc.) (Fig. 1).

Direct measures collect data in physical world while the derived (complex or composed) measures are calculated using previously collected measurements as input. Collected measurements are stored on a NoSQL database designed to be able to process a very large amount of data. To collect measurements, the direct measures can delegate the gathering work to existing measuring tools integrated with the MEASURE PaaS platform.

The measurements can also be processed by analysis tools to present consolidated results. The analysis platform is composed of a set of tools that allow combining and correlating measurements in a meaningful way in order to provide suggestions and recommendations for the software developers and managers.

Finally, stored measurements and recommendations are presented directly to the end user following a business structured way by the Decision-making platform, with a web front-end that allows organizing measures based on projects/software development phases and displays its under various forms of charts.

In order to study and improve the software quality processes and ease the tasks of project engineers and managers, we defined a methodology based on two modules: Metrics Suggester and Metrics Intelligence. The used terminology, the formal modelling language and our two techniques are described in the following.

3.2   A Formal Software Measurement Context

Several concepts are commonly used in the software engineering context. We provide some measurement terminologies in the following [15, 17].

Terminology

Measurand: a measurand is the measured object. In this context, it is a software system, such as software product, in use or software resource.

Software Properties: the software properties are the measurable properties of a software such as, for instance, complexity or performance.

---

[5] https://www.omg.org/spec/SMM/About-SMM/.
[6] https://www.modelio.org/.
[7] http://www.montimage.com/products.html.

Measurement: a measurement is defined as a direct quantification of a measured property [9]. This is the value of an evaluation result in a single time. This is information on the measured property, such as the percentage of the memory used.

Measure: a measure is the definition of a concrete calculation to evaluate a property, such as the calculation of the number of lines of code.

Metric: a metric is a measure space, in other words, the specification of a measurement. This is the formal definition of a measurement of a property of a computer object by specifying the measurand, the measure(s) and the software property to be measured.

Measurement Plan: a measurement plan is an ordered set of metrics (simple or complex). They are all expected to be executed at a specific time t or during a well-defined duration and according to an ordered metrics sequence. They can be run sequentially or in parallel.

The OMG Structured Metrics Meta-model. Our methodology is based on the OMG SMM (Structured Metrics Meta-model) standard to formally model our metrics in terms of measure, scope (subset of measured properties) and measurement but also in order to easily generate the corresponding Java code [6]. Our main purpose is to have a standard documentation on the measurement architecture with the SMM model, which will also optimize the design phase of the implementation of a software measurement. Indeed, this process will enable measurement code generation from a measurement architecture model based on SMM. This will reduce the developer's burden of manual implementation.

SMM is a standard specification that defines a meta-model to specify a software measurement architecture, in other words to specify a *Measure Space* applied to a computer system. It defines the meta-models to express all necessary concepts to specify a measurement context. A wide range of diversified types of measures is proposed to define the dependency type between dependent measures (as the ratio, binary or grade measure). The language allows to define direct/indirect measures and complex metrics:

- Direct Measure: is the measure independent of other measures, thus it refers to the simple evaluation function.
- Indirect Measure: is a measure dependent on other measures.
- Complex metric: a complex metric is a metric composed of indirect measure(s).

As an example, the Fig. 2 represents the model of the computational energy cost metric in SMM with the Modelio tool. This complex metric (represented by 3 stack levels) depends on three other metrics, two of them are direct metrics (represented by a microscope): the memory access count and I/O usage metrics, and the third one is also a complex metric denoted CPU energy model. It returns

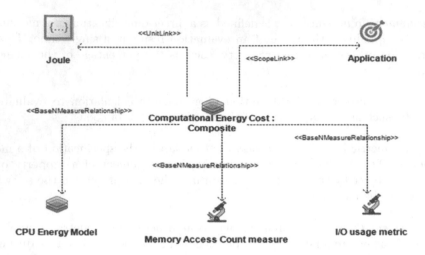

Fig. 2. The computational energy cost metric model in SMM. (Color figure online)

a numerical value in Joule. A low energy cost means a better software. Thus, it is. Then, the unit of measure of the computational energy cost is a Joule and represented in the figure by the yellow symbol "{...}". Finally, this metric is applied on an application, which is represented by the blue target in the model. Each component is modeled as a UML class allowing the code generation from a SMM metric model.

We describe in the following the two approaches and tools composing our methodology.

3.3 The Software Metrics Suggester

As previously mentioned, one of our approaches consists on suggesting relevant and efficient software measurement plans at runtime using a machine learning algorithm. In order to detail our methodology, we first introduce some concepts in the following.

Basics. In our previous paper [7], we developed a supervised learning technique based on SVM with training datasets. These datasets contain vectors labeled by experts. In an industrial context, the labeling process can be complex, time and resource consuming [13]. In this paper, our main objective is to automatically generate our measurement plans from totally unlabeled data. Our goal being to define an unsupervised learning methodology. To do so, we propose an algorithm (Algorithm 1) based on a clustering technique. This latter allows to identify in an automatic way the software classes of interests from unlabeled data that are themselves automatically labeled with dummy classes.

Finally, each obtained cluster will be classified and vectors of measurements automatically labeled to be fed as inputs to our SVM approach. In the following, we formally describe the detailed procedures along with a generalized classifier for the suggestion of measurements plan.

X-means Clustering. First, while measuring a system, we have a continuous stream S of n measurements. These measurements can be considered as events. The concept of event is interesting since it defines a formal link between the two methods proposed in our approach, Metric Suggester and MINT. Each event can be represented as a data point in a space x_i and can be expressed as:

$$\{(x_i)\},\ x_i \in \mathbb{R}^d, i \in \{1, 2, ..., n\} \tag{1}$$

where d is the dimension number of the input space or attributes (a_i), and n is the number of samples.

Generally, we can associated low-level events with high-level or complex events $y_i \in \mathbb{R}$ by a prediction function $f(x_i)$ (Eq. (4)). However, because no labeled event data is assumed, we decided to apply a clustering technique that could categorize the data into classes of metrics. One famous technique commonly applied is the K-means algorithm [18]. Though it is very efficient in many areas, it requires to know the value of K. In our paper, we herein suppose that we do not know its value, that depends on the software metrics in use and the collected data. Therefore, the X-means clustering algorithm is proposed [26]. X-means will allow us to split the input data (1) into K clusters without the need to define the expected number of them at the first stage. The best K subsets are chosen such that all points in a given subset "belong" to some center c_j, $j \in (1, 2, ..., k)$ with a low inter-cluster similarity. Basically, the algorithm aims at minimizing the following distance objective function:

$$J = \sum_{j=1}^{k} \sum_{i=1}^{n} |D_{MH}(x_i^j, c_j)|, \tag{2}$$

where $|D_{MH}(x_i^j, c_j)|$ is the Mahalanobis distance measure between a event data point and a cluster center [8]. Later, we also use this distance measure to define the boundaries of each rule attribute. By using the Eq. (2), we can assign the events data points x_i to the cluster whose distance from the cluster center c_j is lower of all the cluster centers and which satisfies the Bayesian information criterion (BIC). After that, each cluster center is updated by taking the weighted average value of event points in that cluster (3) for better clustering results.

$$C_{j_u pdate} = \frac{1}{|c_j|} \sum_{i=1}^{c_j} x_i \tag{3}$$

Finally, class labels y_i can be assigned for each event cluster automatically by our system. Then, once this assignation is performed, the vectors are labelled and the SVM process can be executed at runtime for beginning the measurement plans suggestion.

Algorithm 1. Event Clustering.

  Input: Unlabeled event data-set $\{x_i\}_{i=1}^n \in \mathbb{R}^d$
  Output: Labeled event data-set $\{(x_i, y_i)\}_{i=1}^n \in \mathbb{R}^d$,
      Clusters centers $C_i^j \in y_i$

1 Initialize an empty stack $\varphi \leftarrow 0$
2 Define initial number of clusters $K_0 \leftarrow 2$
3 Divide unlabeled event data-set into $C_1, C_2, ..., C_{k_0}$ clusters using k-means with
  setting $k \leftarrow k_0$.
4 **repeat**
5 $\quad$ Divide each cluster C_i into $C_i^{k_0}$ sub-clusters using k-means with $k \leftarrow k_0$.
6 $\quad$ Calculate $BIC(C_i)$
7 $\quad$ Calculate $BIC, MNDL(C_i^{k_0})$
8 $\quad$ **if** $BIC(C_i) > BIC'(MNDL(C_i^{k_0}) > MNDL'(C_i^{k_0}))$ **then**
9 $\quad\quad$ The two-divided model is preferred, and the division is continued with
  $\quad\quad C_i \leftarrow C_i^1$.
  $\quad\quad$ // push event data into the stack
10 $\quad\quad x_i \rightarrow \varphi$
11 $\quad\quad C_i^{k_0} \rightarrow \varphi$
12 $\quad\quad BIC(C_i) \rightarrow \varphi$
13 $\quad\quad$ **return** step 5
14 $\quad$ **end**
15 $\quad$ **if** $BIC(C_i) < BIC'(MNDL(C_i^{k_0}) < MNDL'(C_i^{k_0}))$ **then**
16 $\quad\quad$ Clusters C_i are no longer divided and set $C_i \leftarrow C_i^{k_0}$.
17 $\quad\quad$ **if** $\varphi \rightarrow 0$ **then**
18 $\quad\quad\quad$ **goto** step 26
19 $\quad\quad$ **else**
  $\quad\quad\quad$ // Extract all the stacked data
20 $\quad\quad\quad \varphi \rightarrow x_i$
21 $\quad\quad\quad \varphi \rightarrow C_i^{k_0}$
22 $\quad\quad\quad \varphi \rightarrow BIC(C_i)$
23 $\quad\quad\quad$ **return** step 5
24 $\quad\quad$ **end**
25 $\quad$ **end**
  $\quad$ // C_i cluster identification becomes unique.
26 $\quad C_i \leftarrow C_i^*$
  $\quad$ // Initial k_0 divided clusters become unique.
27 $\quad C_j \leftarrow C_j^*$
28 **until** $i \leq k_0$;

Support Vector Machine. A support vector machine (SVM) [29] is a linear classifier defined by a separating hyperplane that determines the decision surface for the classification. Given a training set (supervised learning), the SVM algorithm finds a hyperplane to classify new data. Consider a binary classification problem, with a training dataset composed of pairs $(x_1, y_1), \ldots, (x_l, y_l)$, where each vector $x_i \in R^n$ and $y_i \in \{-1, +1\}$. The SVM classifier model is a hyperplane that separates the training data in two sets corresponding to the desired classes. Equation (4) defines a separating hyperplane (Source [7]):

$$f(\boldsymbol{x}) = \boldsymbol{w}^T \boldsymbol{x} + b = 0 \tag{4}$$

where $\boldsymbol{w} \in R^n$ and $b \in R$ are parameters that control the function. Function f gives the signed distance between a point $\boldsymbol{x}$ and the separating hyperplane. A point $\boldsymbol{x}$ is assigned to the positive class if $f(\boldsymbol{x}) \geq 0$, and otherwise to the negative class. The SVM algorithm computes a hyperplane that maximizes the distance between the data points on either side, this distance is called *margin*. SVMs can be modeled as the solution of the optimization problem given by (5), this problem maximizes the margin between training points (Source: [7]).

$$\min_{\boldsymbol{w}, b} \; \frac{1}{2} \| \boldsymbol{w} \|^2$$
$$\text{subject to:} \quad y_i(\boldsymbol{w}^T \boldsymbol{x}_i + b) \geq 1, i = 1, \ldots, l \tag{5}$$

All training examples labeled -1 are on one side of the hyperplane and all training examples label 1 are on the other side. Not all the samples of the training data are used to the determine the hyperplane, only a subset of the training samples contribute to the definition of the classifier. The data points used in the algorithm to maximize the margin are called *support vectors*.

Features and Classes. The set of measurements that is classified using SVM is defined as a *vector* of *features*. Each feature is a field of a vector and a measurement of one specific measure. Each field is unique. So a feature is a measurement composing a vector for our classification. Further, the vectors are classified into *classes* according to the feature values. Each class refers to a measured software property, such as the maintainability or reliability. The features composing a vector are the measurements which give information on the classes. Some of them can give information on several classes or only one. The features are chosen according to the metrics defined in the starting measurement plan.

The Mapping System. In order to suggest relevant and effective measurement plans, a mapping system is defined between classes and metrics, and between metrics and features. It aims at allowing an automate suggestion procedure. This mapping is performed by the experts of the measured system. According to the type of interest (in terms of numbers of vector contained) of the classes highlighted by the SVM classification, some metrics will be added or removed from the measurement plan. Thus, new features will be gathered and others will no longer be.

Classes-Metrics. A relationship between a class and some metrics is needed to measure specific targeted software properties. The classes are used for the classification of the vectors according to their features values. As above mentioned, our classification method is to classify a vector in the class corresponding to the property whose the values of the vector show a type of interest.

Features-Metrics. The features values inform about the properties (classes) of interest. There are features which give information on only one property and others which can give information on several different properties (complex metrics). Some of the measures can be used by different metrics. Thus, the features associated with a metric are the features corresponding to the measures which composed the metric. In order to ensure the sustainability of measurement cycles by having at each cycle an information on all measured properties, a set of metrics should always be gathered. This set is called mandatory features. To select the mandatory features, we use the RFE technique, explained below, based on SVM.

The Feature Selection. The goal of the Feature Selection (FS) process is to select the relevant features of the raised classes. Its objective is to determine a subset of features that collectively have good predictive power. With FS, we aim at highlighting the features that are important for classification process. The feature selection method is Recursive Feature Elimination (RFE) [20]. RFE performs backward elimination that consists of starting with all the features and test the elimination of each variable until no more features can be eliminated. RFE begins with a classifier that was trained with all the features that are weighted. Then, the feature with the absolute smallest weight is eliminated from the feature set. This process is done recursively until the desired number of features is achieved. The number of features is determined by using RFE and cross validation together. In this process each subset of features is evaluated with trained classifier to obtain the best number of features. The result of the process is a classifier trained with a subset of features that achieve the best score in the cross validation. The classifier used during the RFE process is the classifier used during the classification process.

Measurement Plan Suggestion. Based on the classification, matching and FS, two sets of classes are notified: the one with the most vectors called *Biggest* and the other set constituted of all the other classes called *Others*. The Biggest means that the corresponding property is the most interested element while the Others means that the corresponding properties are not the elements of interest. Thereby, our *Suggestion* procedure is applied for the property corresponding to the Biggest. Indeed, the Biggest property needs a further measurement, while the Others one no longer need it. Basically, based on the procedures *Analysis* and *Selection*, we raise unnecessary features for the classification that should be removed from the measurement plan. Through this method, the measurement load is increased only on needs and decreasing due to less interested properties. This suggestion approach allows to reach a lighter, complete and relevant measurement plan at each cycle of the software project management.

3.4   MINT- Metrics Intelligence Tool

As mentioned in our paper [7], MINT is a software solution designed to correlate metrics from different software development life cycle in order to provide

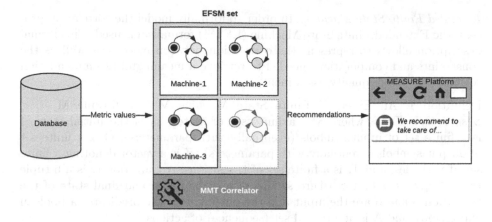

Fig. 3. MINT approach overview.

valuable recommendations to different actors impacting the software development process. MINT considers the different measurements collected by the MEASURE platform as events occurring at runtime. The correlation is designed as extended finite state machines (EFSMs) allowing to perform Complex Event Processing (CEP) in order to determine the possible actions that can be taken to improve the diverse stages of the software life cycle and thus the global software quality and cost (Fig. 3).

Background

Metrics Correlation. The correlation can be defined as a mutual relationship or association between metrics (or the values of its application). Metrics correlation can be the basis for the reuse of metrics; it can help to predict one value from another; it can indicate a causal relation between metrics and can establish relations between different metrics and increase the ability to measure. Examples of correlation are: to correlate two metrics from the same development phase; to correlate the same metric at different times; to correlate a metric (a set of metrics) from phase X regarding metrics of phase Y. As an outcome, recommendations and a selection of metrics will be proposed to the developer to improve the software development. MINT is based on correlation techniques.

Complex Events Processing. Complex event processing (CEP) [14] technology addresses exactly the need of matching continuously incoming events against a pattern. Input events from data streams are processed immediately and if an event sequence is matching a pattern, the result is emitted straight away. CEP works very efficiently and in real-time, as there are no overheads for data storing. CEP is used in many areas that include for instance manufacturing processes, ICT security, etc. and is adapted in this paper for software quality assessment process.

Extended Finite State Machine. In order to formally model the correlation process, the Extended Finite State Machine (EFSM) formalism is used. This formal description allows to represent the correlation between metrics as well as the constraints and computations needed to retrieve a meaningful recommendation related to software quality assessment.

Definition 1. An Extended Finite State Machine M is a 6-tuple M $= < S, s_0, I, O, \vec{x}, Tr >$ where S is a finite set of states, s_0 is the initial state, I is a finite set of input symbols (eventually with parameters), O is a finite set of output symbols (eventually with parameters), $\vec{x}$ is a vector denoting a finite set of variables, and Tr is a finite set of transitions. A transition tr is a 6-tuple tr $= < s_i, s_f, i, o, P, A >$ where s_i and s_f are the initial and final state of the transition, i and o are the input and the output, P is the predicate (a boolean expression), and A is an ordered set (sequence) of actions.

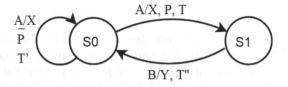

Fig. 4. Example of a simple EFSM with two states (Source [7]).

We illustrate the notion of EFSM through a simple example described in Fig. 4. The ESFM is composed of two states S_0, S_1 and three transitions that are labeled with two inputs A and B, two outputs X and Y, one predicate P and three tasks T, T', and T''. The EFSM operates as follows: starting from state S_0, when the input A occurs, the predicate P is tested. If the condition holds, the machine performs the task T, triggers the output X and passes to state S_1. If P is not satisfied, the same output X is triggered but the action T' is performed and the state loops on itself. Once the machine is in state S_1, it can come back to state S_0 if receiving input B. If so, task T'' is performed and output Y is triggered.

Writing Correlation Processes

Correlation Process Inputs and Outputs. The basic idea behind MINT approach is to specify a set of correlation rules based on the knowledge of an expert of the software development process. These rules can rely on one or different sets of metrics (seen as inputs) and allow different recommendations to be provided (seen as outputs) to different kinds of actors:

- Actors from the DevOps team: Analysts, designers, modellers, architects, developers, tester, operators, security experts, etc.
- Actors from the management plan: product manager, project manager, responsible of human resources, responsible of financial issues etc.

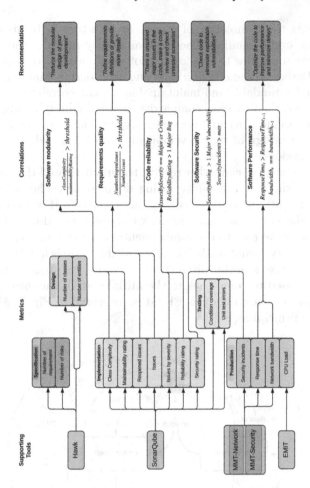

Fig. 5. Example of correlation processes (Source [7]).

The automatic generation of such rules or their continuous refinement based on some artificial intelligence techniques is an ongoing work and out of the paper scope.

Example of Correlation Processes. The correlation processes rely on different measurements that are computed and collected by external tools. Some examples of correlations are presented in the Fig. 5.

Software Modularity. The assessment of the software modularity relies on two metrics provided by the SonarQube tool that are the class complexity and the maintainability rating. The class complexity measure (also called cognitive complexity) computes the cognitive weight of a Java Architecture. The cognitive weight represents the complexity of a code architecture in terms of maintainability and code understanding. The maintainability rating is the ratio of time (according to the total time to develop the software) needed to update or modify the software. Based on these definitions, and considering that a modular code can be more understandable and maintainable, we can correlate the two metrics and compute the ratio $R = class$ complexity/maintainability rating. If this ratio is more than a specific threshold set by an expert, the recommendation "Reinforce the modular design of your development" will be provided to the software architect and developers.

In the initial state, we can either receive the input related the class complexity denote cc or the maintainability rating denoted mr. The process accesses respectively to the states "cc received" or "mr received". If we receive the same measurement related to the same metric, we update its value and loop on the state. Otherwise, if we receive the complementary metric, we compute the ratio $R = class$ complexity/maintainability rating. If this ratio is less than the defined threshold, we come back to the initial state otherwise, we raise the recommendation. Timers are used to come back to the initial state if the measurements are too old. For sake of place, only this EFSM is presented in Fig. 7. All the others follow the same principles (Fig. 6).

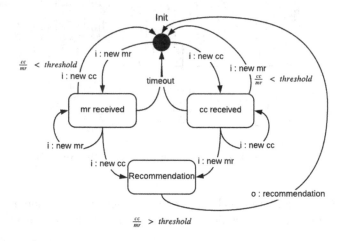

Fig. 6. Software modularity correlation processes (Source [7]).

Requirements Quality. The assessment of the requirements quality can rely on two metrics provided by the SonarQube tool that are the total number of issues and the total number of reopened issues. These numbers are collected during the implementation phase and we can consider that the fact that we reopen an issue many times during the development process can be related to an ambiguous definition of the requirement that needs to be implemented. If we have a ratio R = number of reopened issues/number of issues that is more than a specific threshold, we can consider that the requirements are not well defined and that the development needs more refinement about them. The recommendation "Refine requirement definitions or provide more details" will be provided to the requirements analyst.

Code Reliability. The assessment of the code reliability relies on two metrics provided by the SonarQube tool that are the number of issues categorized by severity and the reliability rating. The issues in SonarQube are presented with severity being blocker, critical, major, minor or info and the reliability rating are from A to E: A is to say that the software is 100% reliable and E is to say that there is at least a blocker bug that needs to be fixed. Based on these definitions and considering that a reliable code should be at last free of major or critical issues, we can check that there is no major, critical nor blocker issues and the reliability rating is < C corresponding to 1 major bug. If this condition is not satisfied, the recommendation "There is unsolved major issues in the code, make a code review and check untested scenarios" will be provided to the software developers and testers.

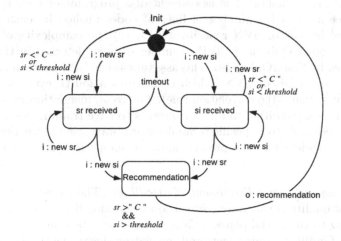

Fig. 7. Software security correlation processes.

Software Security. The assessment of the software security relies on two metrics, one provided by the SonarQube tool that is the security rating (denoted sr in Fig. 7) and the other is provided by MMT that is the number of security incidents (denoted si in Fig. 7). The security rating in SonarQube provide an insight of the detected vulnerabilities in the code and are presented with severity being blocker, critical, major, minor or no vulnerability. The number of the security incidents provided by MMT reports on successful attacks during operation. The evaluation of security demonstrates that if an attack is successful this means that the vulnerability in the code was at least major because an attacker was able to exploit it to perform its malicious activity. Based on these definitions, and considering that a reliable code should be at last free of major vulnerabilities, we can check if there is a major vulnerability and that the number of attacks at runtime are more than a threshold. If this condition is satisfied, the recommendation "Check code to eliminate exploitable vulnerabilities" will be provided to the software developers ans security experts.

Software Performance. The assessment of the software performance relies on two metrics provided by the MMT tool that are the response time and the bandwidth usage. The response time denotes the delay that can be caused by the software, hardware or networking part that is computed during operation. This delay is in general the same for a constant bandwidth (an equivalent number of users and concurrent sessions). Based on this finding, we can correlate the two metrics and compute that the response time is not increasing for during time for the same bandwidth usage. If this response time is increasing, the recommendation "Optimize the code to improve performance and minimize delays" will be provided.

Programmer Code Quality. The assessment of a programmer code quality can rely on three metrics (1) number of lines of codes pushed by each developer and provided by Git or SVN repository API, (2) the complexity of the code computed by SonarQube and (3) the number of bugs detected in this specific code provided by SonarQube also. This assessment can be done each time a new code is pushed on Git or SVN (which constitutes a fourth event in the FSM machine that specifies the correlation rule). The recommendation for developers pushing bad code (resulting to a lot of bugs) is to have training regarding good practices in coding or to a specific technology or library used in the development or/and can provide a hint the project manager about the quality of developers skills.

Project Management and Fulfillment of Deadlines. The assessment of project management quality is generally performed by checking if the project is advancing according to the initial plans. This assessment can be done by checking the percentage of fulfilled requirements and correlating this to the timing plan. If the project is late a recommendation can be to add more developers in the project or to change priorities in the development strategy, if the project is advancing more than expected, reallocation of human resources on other projects can be an option.

4   Experiments

Fifteen software metrics have been selected by experts of the MEASURE platform[8] (mainly its administrator, the project manager and tools engineers). The list of metrics is depicted in the Table 1.

---

[8] http://194.2.241.244/measure/.

Table 1. Each metric and its assigned index during the experiments (Source [7]).

Index	Metric
1	Cognitive Complexity
2	Maintainability Index
3	Code Size
4	Number of issues
5	Response Time
6	Running Time
7	Usability
8	Computational Cost
9	Infrastructure Cost
10	Communication Cost
11	Tasks
12	I/O Errors
13	Precision
14	Stability Response Time
15	Illegal Operations

Then measurements corresponding to these metrics are collected. Our approach is based on the classification of the collected vectors into well-defined classes. However, one of the novelties in that new paper compared to [7] is that the training data set is automatically obtained using our X-means clustering algorithm. It means that our classes are obtained from the results of the algorithm. This is what we depict in the first subsection below. After that, we apply our two techniques and tools on the data collected through the MEASURE platform and detail the results.

4.1   The Training Data Set and the Classification Process

In order to obtain our clusters and then provide our classes, we have run our X-means algorithm on a collection of 1000 vectors containing, each of them, the measurements for the 15 metrics. As this can be noted, we here considered metrics defined from one single metric. Due to the management of the MEASURE project and the dates allowing to collect some data, the schedule when these data have been collected and the data for suggesting the measurement plans had to be tuned. Indeed, the data corresponding to the training data set and the ones collected for the plans suggestion were not matching exactly; and the results when using SVM was not efficient. For these reasons, most of the data used within the procedure of training data set has been manually changed to fit with the platform in use during the learning approach, that is the measurement plans suggestion process.

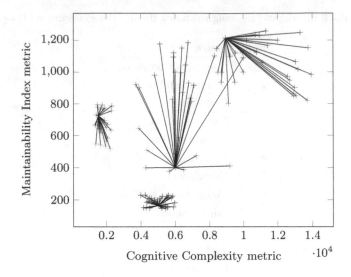

Fig. 8. A visualization of our X-means clustering results.

Based on that data, our X-means approach has been successfully applied. For that purpose, the pyclustering library has been used and configured for our methodology[9]. Therefore, the tool provided four main clusters defined by four centers. We illustrate these results in the Fig. 8. In this figure, we made the choice to consider the two first features, i.e., 'Cognitive Complexity' and 'Maintainability Index' as the two axis. For a sake of visualization clarity, the other axis are not illustrated.

As previously mentioned, our objective is the categorize these clusters in terms of set of metrics. Then the above mentioned experts have analyzed the results of our approach to finally extract the four following classes that basically correspond to software class properties:

– **Maintainability (Class 1):** Cognitive Complexity, Maintainability Index, Code Size, Number of issues.
– **System Performance (Class 2):** Computational Cost, Infrastructure Cost, Communication Cost and Tasks.
– **Performance (Class 3):** Response Time, Running Time and I/O Errors.
– **Functionality (Class 4):** Usability, Precision, Stability Response Time and Illegal Operations.

These classes and the obtained training data set is therefore used for our learning based suggestion approach as described in the following.

---

[9] https://github.com/annoviko/pyclustering.

4.2 Suggester Experiments

The suggestion process is evaluated by analyzing the new measurement plans (MP) based on the results of the classification process. These results are used in the feature selection process in order to identify the class of interest. The objective is to highlight the effects of using the proposed measurement plans and its impact on the classification of new data and on the amount of data collected by this plan.

The used and analyzed measurement data are the measurement results provided by our industrial MEASURE platform. Data are collected at runtime from selected features/metrics.

Setup. We herein considered the following measurement plan determined by our experts. An initial MP can be defined by 15 features, 15 metrics and 4 software quality properties. As previously said, each metric is composed of only one feature and the mapping between metrics and classes has been provided by the previous step with the clustering approach.

Using the previously described plan, we considered the class with the most predicted instances during each cycle. A huge set of 16,000,000 unclassified vectors (unlabelled) were collected and processed (representing a collection of diverse data during a long period of time). This data set was divided into 32

Table 2. Measurement plans used during the suggestion process and the cycles where they were used. Metrics of the plans are represented by the indexes described in Table 1 (Source [7]).

	Metrics	Cycles
MP1	2, 5, 6, 7, 8	1
MP2	4, 5, 6, 12	2, 4, 17, 22, 23, 24
MP3	1, 2, 3, 4, 5, 6, 7, 8, 9, 10, 11, 13, 14, 15	3, 5, 18
MP4	8, 9, 10, 11	6, 30
MP5	7, 8, 9, 10, 11	7, 8, 9
MP6	1, 2, 3, 4, 5, 6, 7, 8, 9, 10, 13, 14, 15	10
MP7	1, 2, 3, 4, 5, 6, 7, 8, 9, 10, 11, 12, 13, 14, 15	11, 19, 20
MP8	2, 3, 4, 5, 6, 7, 8, 9, 10, 11, 12, 13, 14, 15	12, 21
MP9	1, 2, 3, 4, 5, 6, 7, 8, 9, 10, 11, 12, 13, 14	13, 14, 15, 16
MP10	3, 4, 5, 6, 8, 9, 10, 11, 12	25
MP11	1, 2, 3, 4, 5, 6, 7, 8, 9, 10, 11	26, 32
MP12	1, 2, 3, 4, 5, 6, 8, 9, 10, 11	27
MP13	1, 3, 4, 5, 6, 8, 9, 10, 11, 12	28
MP14	1, 2, 3, 4, 5, 6, 7, 8, 9, 10, 11, 12	29
MP15	1, 2, 3, 4, 5, 6, 7, 8, 9, 10	31

subsets each containing 500,000 vectors. For each period of the suggestion process, only one subset was used as input.

The initial measurement plan used during the experiment consisted of the following 5 metrics: Maintainability Index, Response Time, Running Time, Usability, Computational Cost. These metrics where selected by the experts as an example of a measurement plan with a small number of metrics that have links to all software quality properties. During the suggestion process a number was assigned to each metric as depicted in Table 1.

Results. During the suggestion process, 15 metrics (Table 1) were available to suggest new MP. Figure 9 shows how the classification of the vectors was distributed during the cycles and the percentage of the vectors assigned to each class. From these metrics, 15 unique measurement plans were used in the suggestion process. Table 2 lists the plans and in which cycle they were used.

MP1 was only used at the beginning of the process, this was the plan suggested by the expert. We note that MP2 was the most used plan during the process (6 times). This plan is composed by the metrics linked to the Performance property and was suggested when the classification of vector to class 3 overwhelmed the other classes. This tells us that if we focus on the Performance property then the metrics in MP2 are sufficient.

MP3 was suggested when the four classes were present in the classification results and class 4 was the class of interest. The tool suggests to take into consideration more than the linked metrics to the class, it seems that these features help to the classification of class 4.

MP4 was suggested when the input vectors were only classified to class 2, this MP2 consists of the metrics linked to that class. This happens when the input vectors are classified to only one class, the same can be observed in cycle

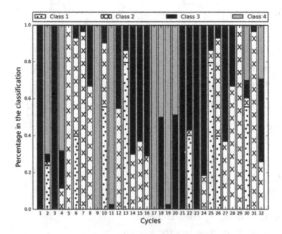

Fig. 9. Classification results of each cycle. The results show the percentage in the predictions of each cycles for the 4 classes (Source [7]).

1 but with class 3. MP5 has only one more metric than MP4, Usability. It is also a MP focused on System Performance property. MP11 was also suggested when class 2 overwhelmed the number of classifications during the classification phase.

MP7, MP8 and MP9 are very similar measurement plans. These plans have the highest number of metrics, MP7 15 metrics and MP8&9 14 metrics. These plans are suggested when the classification results usually have more than 2 classes. This is because the classes do not share any metric between them. A measurement plan with the majority of the metrics is expected to classify well the majority of the classes. MP10, MP12, MP13, MP14 and MP15 where suggested in the same case as the previously mentioned plans but these plans where only suggested one time during the process.

4.3   MINT Experiments

To test the efficiency of the MINT tool, we created 30 scripts enabling to generate different values for the fifteen metrics that are relevant for the correlation processes defined in the Fig. 5. For each correlation, we created 2 scripts: one that meets the condition that satisfies the recommendation and another that does not satisfy it. The 10/30 scripts are summarized in Table 3.

Table 3. Experiments scripts (Source [7]).

Correlation	Script	Metrics constraint
Code modularity	1	Class complexity/maintainability rating > threshold
Code modularity	2	Class complexity/maintainability rating < threshold
Specification quality	3	Number of reopened issues/number of issues > threshold
Specification	4	Number of reopened issues/number of issues < threshold
Management quality	5	Issues by severity = Major or Critical Reliability rating > 1 Major bug
Management	6	Issues by severity $\neq$ Major and $\neq$ Critical or Reliability rating < 1 Major bug
Security	7	Security vulnerability > Major vulnerability Security incident > threshold
Security	8	Security vulnerability < Major vulnerability or Security incident < threshold
Performance	9	Response time$_t$ > response time$_{t-1}$ bandwidth$_t$ = bandwidth$_{t-1}$
Performance	10	Response time$_t$ <= response time$_{t-1}$ or bandwidth$_t$ > bandwidth$_{t-1}$

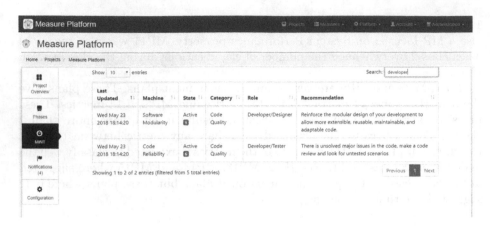

Fig. 10. Recommendation triggered by script 1.

Each script pushes the metric values into an event bus that feeds the 5 correlation processes defined in Sect. 3.4. The results correspond to the desired recommendations and the Fig. 10 displays an example of recommendation provided by the MINT tool for a software developer.

This experiment showed the efficiency of the tool. More work is planned to apply this tool to real datasets provided by real users in the context of the software development process.

5 Conclusion and Perspectives

This paper present an innovative approach to enhance software quality based on the analysis of a large amount of measurements generated during the software development process. The analysis is performed at different phases from the design to the operation and using different measuring tools (e.g., Hawk, SonarQube and MMT). The approach is implemented using two tools: Metric Suggester and MINT tools.

The Metrics Suggester tool is very valuable to reduce the energy and cost in gathering the metrics from different software life cycle phases and allows to reduce the number of the collected metrics according to the needs defined as profiles or clusters. It uses the support vector machine (SVM) that allows to build different classifications and provide the relevant measuring profile, the MP. The algorithm used in the tool as well some experiments demonstrate the efficiency of the tool to focus on relevant metrics depending the engineering process needs.

MINT is a rule based engine that relies on the ESFM formalism. It acts as a complex event processor that corrects the occurrence of measurements on time and provides a near real-time recommendation for the software developers and managers. The tool already integrates a set of default correlation rules that are able to provide valuable recommendations during the software development and operation. The tool has been experimented using different scenarios and demonstrates an interesting added value

The data analysis platform of the MEASURE solution integrates the two tools and implements analytic algorithms (SVM and CEP) to correlate the different phases of software development and perform the tracking of metrics and their value. Correlations cover all aspects of the system like modularity, maintainability, security, timing, etc. and evaluate the global quality of the software development process and define actions (suggestions and recommendations) for improvements. The paper present the innovation of these tools and extended experiment according to the research paper published in [7]. More experiments are planned in the context of MEASURE ITEA-3 project with real use cases provided by industrial partner. We believe that these experimentation will allow to facilitate the exploitation of the tools in industrial contexts.

Acknowledgment. This work is partially funded by the ongoing European project ITEA3-MEASURE started in Dec. 1st, 2015, and the EU HubLinked project started in Jan. 1st, 2017.

References

1. Akbar, M.A., et al.: Improving the quality of software development process by introducing a new methodology-AZ-model. IEEE Access **6**, 4811–4823 (2018). https://doi.org/10.1109/ACCESS.2017.2787981
2. Alshayeb, M., Shaaban, Y., AlGhamdi, J.: SPMDL: software product metrics definition language. J. Data Inf. Qual. **9**(4), 20:1–20:30 (2018). https://doi.org/10.1145/3185049
3. Bagnato, A., da Silva, M.A.A., Abherve, A., Rocheteau, J., Pihery, C., Mabit, P.: Measuring green software engineering in the MEASURE ITEA 3 project. In: Condori-Fernández, N., Procaccianti, G., Calero, C., Bagnato, A. (eds.) Proceedings of the 3rd International Workshop on Measurement and Metrics for Green and Sustainable Software Systems, MeGSuS 2016, Co-Located with 10th International Symposium on Empirical Software Engineering and Measurement (ESEM 2016), Ciudad Real, Spain, 7 September 2016. CEUR Workshop Proceedings, vol. 1708, pp. 33–42. CEUR-WS.org (2016). http://ceur-ws.org/Vol-1708/paper-06.pdf
4. Bouwers, E., van Deursen, A., Visser, J.: Evaluating usefulness of software metrics: an industrial experience report. In: Notkin, D., Cheng, B.H.C., Pohl, K. (eds.) 35th International Conference on Software Engineering, ICSE 2013, San Francisco, CA, USA, 18–26 May 2013, pp. 921–930. IEEE Computer Society (2013). https://doi.org/10.1109/ICSE.2013.6606641
5. Carvallo, J.P., Franch, X.: Extending the ISO/IEC 9126-1 quality model with non-technical factors for cots components selection. In: Proceedings of the 2006 International Workshop on Software Quality, WoSQ 2006, pp. 9–14. ACM, New York (2006). https://doi.org/10.1145/1137702.1137706. http://doi.acm.org/10.1145/1137702.1137706
6. Dahab, S.A., Maag, S., Hernandez Porras, J.J.: A novel formal approach to automatically suggest metrics in software measurement plans. In: 2018 13th International Conference on Evaluation of Novel Approaches to Software Engineering (ENASE). IEEE (2018)

7. Dahab, S.A., Silva, E., Maag, S., Cavalli, A.R., Mallouli, W.: Enhancing software development process quality based on metrics correlation and suggestion. In: Proceedings of the 13th International Conference on Software Technologies, ICSOFT 2018, Porto, Portugal, 26–28 July 2018, pp. 154–165 (2018)

8. De Maesschalck, R., Jouan-Rimbaud, D., Massart, D.L.: The Mahalanobis distance. Chemometr. Intell. Lab. Syst. **50**(1), 1–18 (2000)

9. Fenton, N., Bieman, J.: Software Metrics: A Rigorous and Practical Approach. CRC Press, Boca Raton (2014)

10. Fenton, N.E., Pfleeger, S.L.: Software Metrics - A Practical and Rigorous Approach, 2nd edn. International Thomson, Boston (1996)

11. García-Domínguez, A., Barmpis, K., Kolovos, D.S., da Silva, M.A.A., Abherve, A., Bagnato, A.: Integration of a graph-based model indexer in commercial modelling tools. In: Baudry, B., Combemale, B. (eds.) Proceedings of the ACM/IEEE 19th International Conference on Model Driven Engineering Languages and Systems, Saint-Malo, France, 2–7 October 2016, pp. 340–350. ACM (2016). https://doi.org/10.1145/2976767. http://dl.acm.org/citation.cfm?id=2976809

12. García-Munoz, J., García-Valls, M., Escribano-Barreno, J.: Improved metrics handling in SonarQube for software quality monitoring. In: Omatu, S., et al. (eds.) Distributed Computing and Artificial Intelligence, 13th International Conference. AISC, vol. 474, pp. 463–470. Springer, Cham (2016). https://doi.org/10.1007/978-3-319-40162-1_50

13. Ge, Z., Song, Z., Ding, S.X., Huang, B.: Data mining and analytics in the process industry: the role of machine learning. IEEE Access **5**, 20590–20616 (2017)

14. Grez, A., Riveros, C., Ugarte, M.: Foundations of complex event processing. CoRR abs/1709.05369 (2017). http://arxiv.org/abs/1709.05369

15. Group, O.M.: Structured Metrics Metamodel (SMM) (October), pp. 1–110 (2012)

16. Hauser, J., Katz, G.: Metrics: you are what you measure!. Eur. Manag. J. **16**, 517–528 (1998)

17. ISO/IEC: ISO/IEC 25010 - systems and software engineering - systems and software quality requirements and evaluation (square) - system and software quality models. Technical report (2010)

18. Jain, A.K.: Data clustering: 50 years beyond k-means. Pattern Recogn. Lett. **31**(8), 651–666 (2010)

19. Kevrekidis, K., et al.: Software complexity and testing effectiveness: an empirical study. In: 2009 Annual Reliability and Maintainability Symposium, RAMS 2009. IEEE (2009)

20. Khalid, S., Khalil, T., Nasreen, S.: A survey of feature selection and feature extraction techniques in machine learning. In: Science and Information Conference (SAI), pp. 372–378. IEEE (2014)

21. Kitchenham, B.A.: What's up with software metrics? - A preliminary mapping study. J. Syst. Softw. **83**(1), 37–51 (2010). https://doi.org/10.1016/j.jss.2009.06.041

22. Laradji, I.H., Alshayeb, M., Ghouti, L.: Software defect prediction using ensemble learning on selected features. Inf. Softw. Technol. **58**, 388–402 (2015). https://doi.org/10.1016/j.infsof.2014.07.005

23. Malhotra, R.: A systematic review of machine learning techniques for software fault prediction. Appl. Soft Comput. **27**(C), 504–518 (2015). https://doi.org/10.1016/j.asoc.2014.11.023

24. van der Meulen, M., Revilla, M.A.: Correlations between internal software metrics and software dependability in a large population of small C/C++ programs. In: ISSRE 2007, The 18th IEEE International Symposium on Software Reliability, Trollhättan, Sweden, 5–9 November 2007, pp. 203–208 (2007)
25. Papadopoulos, L., Marantos, C., Digkas, G., Ampatzoglou, A., Chatzigeorgiou, A., Soudris, D.: Interrelations between software quality metrics, performance and energy consumption in embedded applications. In: Stuijk, S. (ed.) Proceedings of the 21st International Workshop on Software and Compilers for Embedded Systems, SCOPES 2018, Sankt Goar, Germany, 28–30 May 2018, pp. 62–65. ACM (2018). https://doi.org/10.1145/3207719.3207736
26. Pelleg, D., Moore, A.W., et al.: X-means: extending k-means with efficient estimation of the number of clusters. In: ICML, vol. 1, pp. 727–734 (2000)
27. Shepperd, M.J., Bowes, D., Hall, T.: Researcher bias: the use of machine learning in software defect prediction. IEEE Trans. Software Eng. **40**(6), 603–616 (2014). https://doi.org/10.1109/TSE.2014.2322358
28. Shweta, S.S., Singh, R.: Analysis of correlation between software complexity metrics. IJISET Int. J. Innovative Sci. Eng. Technol. **2**(8), 902–905 (2015)
29. Vapnik, V.N., Vapnik, V.: Statistical Learning Theory, vol. 1. Wiley, New York (1998)

Modular Programming and Reasoning for Living with Uncertainty

Naoyasu Ubayashi[✉], Yasutaka Kamei, and Ryosuke Sato

Kyushu University, Fukuoka, Japan
{ubayashi,kamei,sato}@ait.kyushu-u.ac.jp

Abstract. Embracing uncertainty in software development is one of the crucial research topics in software engineering. In most projects, we have to deal with uncertain concerns by using informal ways such as documents, mailing lists, or issue tracking systems. This task is tedious and error-prone. Especially, uncertainty in programming is one of the challenging issues to be tackled, because it is difficult to verify the correctness of a program when there are uncertain user requirements, unfixed design choices, and alternative algorithms. If uncertainty can be dealt with modularly, we can add or delete uncertain concerns to/from code whenever they arise or are fixed to certain concerns. This paper proposes a new programming and reasoning style based on *Modularity for Uncertainty*. The *iArch-U* IDE (Integrated Development Environment) is developed to support uncertainty-aware software development. The combined usage of a type checker and a model checker in *iArch-U* plays an important role in verifying whether or not some important properties are guaranteed even if uncertainty remains in a program. Our model checker is based on LTSA (Labelled Transition System Analyzer) and is implemented as an Eclipse plug-in. Agile methods embrace *change* to accept changeable user requirements. On the other hand, our approach embraces *uncertainty* to support exploratory software development.

Keywords: Uncertainty · Known Unknowns · Partial model · Modular uncertainty representation · Modular reasoning · Type checking · Model checking · State explosion problem

1 Introduction

Embracing uncertainty in software development is one of the crucial research topics in software engineering [35,40,42,45,56]. Garlan, D. discusses the future of software engineering from the viewpoint of uncertainty [22]. He claims that *software engineering is founded on a computational myth that no longer fully serves its purpose: that the computational environment is predictable and in principle fully specifiable, and that the systems that compute in those environments can in principle be engineered so that they are trouble-free.* He argues that we must embrace uncertainty within the engineering discipline of software engineering.

© Springer Nature Switzerland AG 2019
M. van Sinderen and L. A. Maciaszek (Eds.): ICSOFT 2018, CCIS 1077, pp. 220–244, 2019.
https://doi.org/10.1007/978-3-030-29157-0_10

Uncertainty is an unavoidable problem in actual software development projects. Most developers suffer from many kinds of uncertainties: it is uncertain when user requirements change; functional specifications cannot be finalized at the initial requirements elicitation phase; and there are multiple design choices due to non-functional requirements such as performance. From our experience, we consider that many developers encounter the situations in which design alternatives cannot be determined or should be delayed to the later development phases. However, many developers tend to believe that uncertainty is not a problem of software technologies but a problem of software processes or operations. This may be a kind of myth in software development. Indeed, most developers consider that uncertainty is the target of risk management and cannot be dealt with without handling by non-technical activities using spread sheets, informal documents, mailing lists, or issue tracking systems. These tasks for dealing with uncertainty are tedious and error-prone. Is uncertainty really non-technical management issues? Can uncertainty really not be dealt with as programming language theories such as modularity, compilation, or formal verification? This paper is motivated by our experience in software development.

This paper, an extended version of our early works [49][1], shows that uncertainty is the target of compilation and verification by introducing the notion of modularity into the world of uncertainty. Modularity is one of the important principles in software engineering [38]. Unfortunately, the state-of-the-art module mechanisms do not regard an uncertain concern as a first-class software module. *Modularity for Uncertainty* is one of the challenges to be tackled by the software engineering research community. If uncertainty can be dealt with modularly, we can add or delete uncertain concerns to/from code whenever these concerns arise or are fixed to certain concerns. Agile methods embrace *change* to accept changeable user requirements. Our approach embraces *uncertainty* to support exploratory software development. Our approach consists of three key ideas: (1) modular programming for uncertainty; (2) modular reasoning for uncertainty; and (3) automated tool support for managing when and why uncertain concerns arise or are resolved. By introducing (1), we can add or delete uncertainty as a module whenever an uncertain concern appears or disappears. By introducing (2), we can check whether some important properties such as functionality and deadlock freedom are guaranteed even if uncertainty exists. We can postpone the decision for dealing with uncertainty to the later software development phase if selection of uncertain alternatives does not affect the correctness of the properties. By introducing (3), a part of traditional risk management tasks can be replaced to automated tool support by integrating version control systems with (1) and (2).

---

[1] We focused on the design and implementation of an uncertainty-aware model checker in our previous work [49]. In this paper, we discuss on not only uncertainty-aware reasoning including the model checker but also uncertainty-aware programming by extending our preliminary work [20,21,52]. We show the world of uncertainty-aware software development and demonstrate the effectiveness of our approach using a concrete usage scenario.

This paper is structured as follows. We survey the definition of uncertainty and related work in Sect. 2. We clarify what kind of problems exist in traditional approaches in Sect. 3. Three key ideas consisting of *Modularity for Uncertainty* are provided in Sects. 4, 5, and 6. The overview of *iArch-U*, an IDE (Integrated Development Environment) supporting our approach, is illustrated in Sect. 6. We discuss on the originality and the applicability of our approach in Sect. 7. Concluding remarks are provided in Sect. 8.

2   Related Work

We classify the definition of uncertainty. After that, we show the state-of-the-art research on uncertainty.

2.1   Taxonomic Classification

Uncertainty is an abstract concept. Many people might feel that *definition of uncertainty is uncertain*. Although it is not easy to define uncertainty explicitly, there is a consensus of its definition in the research community. We show the representative definitions in this section.

There are three types of phenomena affecting software development: *Known Knowns*, *Known Unknowns*, and *Unknown Unknowns* [10]. The *Known Knowns*-type corresponds to the development in which uncertainty does not exist. Many studies on this type have been conducted in traditional software engineering research. In the *Known Unknowns*-type, there are uncertain issues in the process of software development. However, these issues are known and shared among the stakeholders including developers and customers. For example, there are alternative requirements although it is uncertain which alternative should be selected. On the other hand, in the *Unknown Unknowns*-type, it is uncertain what is uncertain. This type is difficult to be dealt with, because it is unpredictable what kind of issues will appear in the future. Due to this reason, current state-of-the-art research mainly focuses on *Known Unknowns*-type uncertainty. Our motivation is to introduce the modularity into *Known Unknowns*.

Perez-Palacin and Mirandola [39] provide a systematic review on uncertainty and summarize as follows: *The most used definitions of uncertainty simply distinguish between natural variability of physical processes (i.e., aleatory or stochastic uncertainty) and the uncertainties in knowledge of these processes (i.e., epistemic or state-of-knowledge uncertainty).* They propose the three-dimension classification consisting of *Location*, *Level*, and *Nature* by referring [51]. Location is categorized into *Context*, *Structural*, and *Input parameters*. Context uncertainty is an identification of the boundaries of a model (or design). Structural uncertainty is contained in a system model itself. The last uncertainty is caused by the vague input parameter values from the real world. Level is categorized into four orders. In the first order of uncertainty, the subject lacks knowledge about something but a developer is aware of such lack (i.e., *Known Unknowns*). The second order indicates lack of knowledge and lack of awareness (i.e., *Unknown Unknowns*). The third order indicates lack of process to find out the lack of awareness. The fourth order indicates uncertainty about orders of uncertainty. Nature is categorized into *Aleatory* and *Epistemic*. In [39], *Source of Uncertainty* is categorized into the followings: (1) *Simplifying assumptions*; (2) *Model drift*; (3) *Noise in sensing*; (4) *Future parameter value*; (5) *Human in the loop*; (6) *Objectives*; (7) *Decentralization*; (8) *Execution context/Mobility*; (9) *Cyber-physical system*; (10) *Automatic learning*; (11) *Rapid evolution*; (12) *Granularity of models*; and (13) *Different sources of information*. For example, *Human in the loop* is classified as *Context* (Location), *1st/2nd/3rd/4th (Level)*, and *Aleatory/Epistemic* (Nature) by using the three-dimension classification in [39]. Uncertain requirements from a stakeholder are labeled as *Human in the loop* in which the location is *Context* (uncertain whether the requirements should be included in a system), the level is the 1st order (*Known-Unknowns*), and the nature is epistemic (the future decisions of the stakeholder are unknown). Although the main target of the three-dimension classification is self-adaptive systems, it is well-formed and applicable to other application domains.

2.2   State-of-the-Art Research on Uncertainty

Recently, uncertainty has attracted a growing interest among researchers. Most of the state-of-the-art studies focus on *Known Unknowns*. As a representative work, a method for expressing *Known Unknowns* using a partial model is proposed in [16,18]. A partial model is a single model containing all possible alternative designs of a system and is encoded in propositional logic. We can check whether or not a model including uncertainty satisfies some interesting properties. The idea of partial model fits the needs in industry, because alternatives can be represented as a single model. For this reason, our approach is based on the partial model as shown in Sect. 4.

Research themes spread over uncertainty of requirements modeling [43,50], software architecture [2,13,15,31], model transformations [11,17], programming [20], testing [10], verification [23,33], and performance engineering [8,25,36,46]. In [43], a partial model is applied to uncertainty in requirements to address the problem of specifying uncertainty within a requirements model, refining a model as uncertainty reduces, providing meaning to traceability relations between models containing uncertainty, and propagating uncertainty-reducing changes between related models. In [2,13,15,31], uncertainty is explored in terms of software architecture. Letier, E et al. present a support method for evaluating uncertainty, its impact on risk, and the value of reducing uncertainty in requirements and architecture [32]. In [44], a method for change propagation in the context of model uncertainty is proposed. Most of these studies focus on epistemic uncertainty. Uncertain< T >, a simple probabilistic programming language for letting programmers without statistics expertise easily and correctly compute with estimates [4]. Uncertain< T > deals with aleatory uncertainty. Elbaum, S. and Rosenblum, D. S. explore how uncertainty affects software testing [10]. Uncertainty in self-adaptive systems is explored in [5,12,14,39,53,54]. Performance and reliability analysis under uncertainty is explored in [8,25,36,46]. Uncertainty has been well studied in the field of formal methods. PRISM [26], a probabilistic symbol model checker, can deal with aleatory uncertainty. Three-valued logic consisting of True, False, and Undefined can represent epistemic uncertainty as in VDM (Vienna Development Method) [19].

Although there are many studies for dealing with uncertainty, none of the state-of-the-art studies regard an uncertain concern as a first-class software module. However, the research on uncertainty-aware module mechanism is important to relax the problems pointed out in Sect. 1.

Lesson Learned

State-of-the-art studies focus on *Known Unknowns* and the idea of partial model representing alternatives fits our needs. It is valuable to provide an uncertainty-aware module mechanism based on the partial model in order to support *Known Unknowns*.

---

3   Towards Conquering Uncertainty

It is important to deal with *Known Unknowns* efficiently in software development as shown in Sects. 1 and 2. Unfortunately, awkward approaches tend to be used in actual development from our experience. In this section, we explore the traditional approaches for conquering uncertainty and show what kind of problems they contain. After that, we show a way for us to go. Below, we use the term *uncertainty* as *Known Unknowns*.

3.1   Pitfalls in Traditional Approaches

When we have to manage unknown API usages, unknown code snippets, unknown return values, and unsure program implementation, we tend to temporally avoid uncertain concerns only using simple language constructs such as comments or conditional statements because current programming languages do not provide a mechanism for describing an uncertain concern as a first-class software module. That is, we temporally comment out the target statements to skip an uncertain concern or insert a superfluous *if* statement to be able to select an alternative uncertain choice. After that, we have to test the program. These comments and conditional statements make difficult to understand the program code, because they impede the separation of concerns in terms of modularity. We explain in details why these traditional approaches are insufficient to deal with uncertainty.

Usage of Comments. This approach is easy to use and most developers prefer it. However, it becomes difficult to maintain the program after a long period of time because the reason of code modification may be forgotten. Meaningless defects may be injected when another developer returns this modification back to the original code.

Usage of Conditional Statements. This approach is often used to deal with uncertainty in terms of behavioral aspects. It is determined by a runtime option which code is executed. If uncertainty is fixed to be certain, complex code modification such as removal of *if-else* statements is needed. This kind of code modification is not only troublesome but also error-prone.

Usage of Preprocessor. C preprocessor is convenient to deal with conditional compilation, although it is not always supported in other programming languages such as Java. This approach is not only easy to modify but also understandable. In the field of SPL (Software Product Lines) [7], conditional compilation is often used to configure a product from a feature model [28]. However, the statements of conditional compilation invade the separation of concerns. It tends to be extremely difficult to understand the combination of uncertain concerns if the number of the conditions increases. Modification places scatter over source code. It is not easy to manage uncertainty using this approach.

Usage of AOP. Using AOP (Aspect-Oriented Programming) [29,30], crosscutting concerns can be separated from the primary concerns. The former and the latter correspond to uncertain code and the original code, respectively. However, we have to write multiple aspects corresponding to each alternative and weave the aspect respectively in order to test all of uncertain alternatives. It is not easy to manage these alternatives.

Usage of Version Control Systems. Currently, usage of version control systems such as Git is one of the standard practices of software engineering. A common practice when dealing with uncertainty is to use multiple branches. When a developer is uncertain about the right way to implement a feature, he or she can branch from the master and develop the own code. When the uncertainty is resolved, the developer merges the new branch with the master. Someone claims that program modifications using comments are needless and we can go back to the original code anytime from the current code. However, there is a pitfall in this scenario. It is difficult to manage which branch deals with uncertainty without some kind of supporting facilities. It is necessary to write the understandable comments when the developer commits the code. If there are no useful commit comments, it difficult to manage uncertainty.

3.2 Way for Us to Go

The exploratory modification process shown above may be repeated again and again until all uncertain concerns are fixed. If an uncertain concern crosscuts over multiple places in a program, the number of comments or conditional statements increases and the version control of the modified code becomes tremendously complex. Moreover, we may have to return all of the modified portions to the original code or one of the final decided code if the uncertain concern is fixed to be certain. This task is error-prone. It may become a cause of a meaningless defect. Many developers have an experience of encountering this kind of problems. Although the approaches above might not cover all patterns for conquering uncertainty, the methods can be considered representative approaches in real software development.

As pointed out in this section, programming under uncertainty is not yet appropriately supported. It would be preferable to be able to modularize uncertain concerns and check whether the important properties concerning to the requirements and designs are satisfied even if there are uncertain concerns. We can continue the development if the properties hold, because the decision can be deferred. To relax the problems pointed out in this section, we propose *Modularity for Uncertainty*. As repeatedly stated, we focus on *Known Unknowns*.

Our Contributions
Modularity for Uncertainty can conquer *Known Unknowns*. Our approach consists of three key ideas: 1) modular programming for *Known Unknowns*; 2) modular reasoning for *Known Unknowns*; and 3) tool support for managing when and why *Known Unknowns* arise or are resolved.

---

4 Modular Programming for Uncertainty

In this section, we introduce an interface-based module mechanism for describing uncertainty. The interface called *Archface-U* [20,21], an architectural interface for uncertainty, plays an important role not only in uncertainty descriptions but also modular reasoning and uncertainty management. Although we use Java as the target programming language in this paper, the proposed concept itself can be applied to other languages.

4.1 Why Interface?

It is a difficult question whether an uncertain concern should be described as an interface or a group of code fragments such as function, class, method, or aspect. Many people might regard only the latter as a module. However, this paper adopts the former approach as a module mechanism. The former does not include an instance of uncertain descriptions but only declares an annotation indicating uncertainty. As mentioned in Sect. 3, many developers use comments or conditional statements to temporarily remove or change uncertain concerns. In this case, uncertain concerns still remain in the original code. Someone may consider that uncertainty can be represented with an abstract method which is implemented if needed or undefined otherwise. It is possible to represent an uncertain concern by using an abstract method if the code location of the concern is already known before programming. However, we have to modify the structure of existing programs to introduce an abstract method if the concern unexpectedly arises during programming. Moreover, we have to remove the abstract method after the uncertain concern is fixed to be certain.

Our approach does not invade the existing programs but introduce an interface annotating uncertain concerns. We only have to add or remove an interface when uncertainty appears or disappears. By only looking at the interface and the corresponding code region, we can understand which portion of code is uncertain. The conformance between the interface and the code is checked by our compiler (to be exact, type checker). Moreover, important properties such as deadlock freedom can be verified only referring the information described in the interface by using our model checker. Nevertheless, these properties are guaranteed in the code if the conformance check is passed by our type checker. Below, we explain in details how to realize this module and verification mechanism.

4.2 Archface-U in a Nutshell

We introduce *Archface-U*, an interface mechanism for dealing with uncertainty. *Archface-U* is an extension of *Archface* [47,48] to support uncertainty. *Archface-U*, which supports *component-and-connector* architecture [1], consists of two kinds of interface: *component* and *connector*. The former declares a class structure (basically same to a Java interface) and the latter defines how to coordinate components.

Syntax. For reader's understandability, we use a simple example to explain the language syntax of *Archface-U* as shown in Fig. 1. This example is a printer-scanner system, a well-known parallel system that falls into a deadlock [34]. Two processes P and Q acquire the lock from each of the shared resources, the printer and the scanner, and then releases the locks.

In *Archface-U*, the symbols {} and [] represent *alternative* and *optional*, respectively. These symbols are introduced to represent *Known Unknowns—Known* which kind of alternatives exists, but *Unknown* which should be selected. *Optional* is syntactical sugar, because *optional* can be expressed using *alternative* (e.g, {A, }). A component is basically the same with ordinary Java interface. A return value or arguments in a method signature can be also specified as *alternative*. For example, the following declaration is available. In this case, it is uncertain whether the argument `setting` is needed.

```
{public void utility();, public void utility(int setting);}
```

A connector, which is specified using the notation similar to FSP (Finite State Processes) [34], defines the message interactions among components. FSP is based on process algebra [37] and generates finite LTS (Labelled Transition Systems). An arrow in FSP indicates a sequence of actions. For example, GET (List 1, line 19) shows that the action `scanner.get` is executed after the action `printer.get` is executed.

Our notation has an expressive power equal to a partial model that compactly yet precisely encodes the entire set of possible models [16]. The GET (List 2, line 14–15) represents the following four behavioral models.

```
[List 1]
01: interface component cPrinter {
02:    public void get();
03:    public void put();
04:    public void print();
05: }
06:
07: interface component cScanner {
08:    public void get();
09:    public void put();
10:    public void scan();
11: }
12:
13: interface component cCopyMachine {
14:    public void copy();
15: }
16: interface connector cSystem (
17:    cCopyMachine P, cCopyMachine Q, cPrinter printer, cScanner scanner) {
18:
19:    GET  = (printer.get -> scanner.get);
20:    PUT  = (printer.put -> scanner.put);
21:    COPY = (scanner.scan -> printer.print);
22:
23:    P.copy = (GET -> COPY -> PUT -> P.copy);
24:    Q.copy = (GET -> COPY -> PUT -> Q.copy);
25: }
```

```
[List 2]
01: interface component uPrinter
02:    extends cPrinter {
03:    [public void utility();]        // optional implementation
04: }
05:
06: interface component uScanner {
07:    extends cScanner {
08:    [public void utility();]        // optional implementation
09: }
10:
11: interface connector uSystem
12:    extends cSystem (uPrinter printer, uScanner scanner) {
13:
14:    GET = ({printer.get -> scanner.get,        // alternative
15:            scanner.get -> printer.get});       // action sequence
16:    COPY = ([snanner.utility] -> scanner.scan ->  // optional
17:            [printer.utility] -> printer.print);  // action sequence
18: }
```

Fig. 1. Archface-U description (Printer-scanner system).

1) P:printer.get -> scanner.get   2) P:scanner.get -> printer.get
   Q:printer.get -> scanner.get   Q:scanner.get -> printer.get
3) P:printer.get -> scanner.get   4) P:scanner.get -> printer.get
   Q:scanner.get -> printer.get   Q:printer.get -> scanner.get

In case of List 2, the combination is more complex because of the two optional methods utility (line 03, 08, 16–17). The partial model consists of 16 behavioral models (16 = 4 * 2 * 2). A developer has to take into account huge number of variabilities even if a small program as in List 1 and 2. Introducing the notation of *Archface-U*, we can represent variabilities compactly.

Pluggable Interface. In *Archface-U*, uncertain concerns are defined as a sub interface as shown in List 2. By extending the existing interface, we can introduce uncertainty modularly. In List 2, it is uncertain how to acquire printer and scanner resources in two processes, P and Q. Additionally, it is uncertain whether

```
[List 3] (*Before* uncertainty appears)
01: public class Printer implements cPrinter {
02:    public void get()  { ... };
03:    public void put()  { ... };
04:    public void print() { ... };
05: }
06:
07: public class Scanner implements cScanner {
08:    public void get()  { ... };
09:    public void put()  { ... };
10:    public void scan()  { ... };
11: }
12:
13: public class CopyMachine implements cCopyMachine {
14:    public void copy() {
15:       // printer and scanner are instantiated elsewhere.
16:       // details for mutual execution are omitted.
17:       printer.get();     scanner.get();
18:       scanner.scan();    printer.print();
19:
20:       // call a method not declared in Archface-U.
21:       methodX();
22:       printer.put();     scanner.put();
23:    }
24: }
```

```
[List 4] (*After* uncertainty appears)
*01: public class Printer implements uPrinter {        // changed to uPrinter
 02:    public void get()     { ... };
 03:    public void put()     { ... };
 04:    public void print()   { ... };
 05: }
 06:
*07: public class Scanner implements uScanner {         // changed to uScanner
 08:    public void get()     { ... };
 09:    public void put()     { ... };
 10:    public void scan()    { ... };
#11:    public void utility() { ... };                  // added if needed
 12: }
 13:
*14: public class CopyMachine implements uCopyMachine { // changed to uCopyMachine
 15:    public void copy() {
 16:       printer.get();     scanner.get();
#17:       scanner.utility();                           // added if needed
 18:       scanner.scan();    printer.print();
 19:       methodX();
 20:       printer.put();     scanner.put();
 21:    }
 22: }
```

Fig. 2. Pseudo Java code before/after uncertainty appears

or not optional utility functions of a scanner and a printer (e.g., setting of the image gray level) are available in this system. We only have to define a sub interface or delete it when we want to add or remove uncertainty.

4.3   Usage Scenario

We show a typical usage scenario using *Archface-U* in order to demonstrate the merits of introducing our approach.

Situation. Alice, a developer, is writing a Java program as shown in List 3 (Fig. 2). List 3 is the pseudo code that omits the details. Assume that Alice becomes aware of the existence of two uncertain concerns: (1) *"I cannot have* *confidence in the order of the* get *operations between two processes P and Q—It is uncertain which algorithm must be selected"*; and (2) *I am uncertain whether exceptional side effects occur if the* utility *method is appended to the* Printer *class or the* Scanner *class in order to support user's new requirements.* The situation of (1) happens when we design an algorithm. On the other hand, (2) happens when we adopt an agile software process. What should Alice do to deal with these uncertainties without using awkward approaches such as comments or superfluous *if* statements?

Annotating Uncertainty. Alice only has to modify *Archface-U* as shown in List 2 and change the implementing interfaces as shown in List 4. The line marked with '*' indicates the code that must be modified. On the other hand, the line marked with '#' indicates the code that may be added to List 3 if Alice wants to add the code fragments implementing the optional method utility. Minimum code modifications are 3 lines (List 4, line 01, 07, and 14). By only specifying *optional* or *alternative* to the *Archface-U* definition (List 2), the utility code region (List 4, line 11) and the message interaction for get and copy operations (List 4, line 17) are annotated as uncertain concerns. The link from *Archface-U* to this code region is guaranteed by type checking explained in details in Sect. 5. Be careful that line 11 and 17 in List 4 must be consistent: utility has to be called if utility is defined in the Scanner class implementing uScanner. Otherwise, utility must not be called. This verification is also performed by the *Archface-U* type checker.

Checking Properties. Using the uncertainty-aware model checker given in Sect. 5, important behavioral properties can be checked. In case of (1), Alice is notified that a deadlock may happen and she understands that this uncertainty has to be fixed immediately. Alice has to delete line 14 and 15 in List 2. The order of get in two processes P and Q must be the same. On the other hand, in case of (2), no counterexamples are generated from the model checker. Alice can postpone the implementation of the utility methods to the later software development phase. In List 4, Alice does not have to implement the utility method in the Printer class. Be careful that this model checking is performed at not the code level (List 4) but the *Archface-U* description level (List 2). Nevertheless, we can guarantee that the code (List 4) satisfies the above properties, because the type checker verifies whether the code simulates one of the possible behavioral models specified in FSP. For this reason, the implementation of the utility methods can be optional in List 4. Currently, only the behavioral properties represented by LTL (Linear Temporal Logic) are available in our verification mechanisms. Counterexamples help both debugging and a better understanding of the impact of uncertain features.

Managing Uncertainty. By checking the code difference between *Archface-U* modifications, Alice can manage what kind of uncertainty arises and how to resolve it as shown in Sect. 6. For example, if line 08 in List 2 is removed and this *Archface-U* is committed into Git at some point, not only Alice but also Bob, a maintenance programmer, can trace that uncertainty about the `utility` method was resolved at that time even if time passes. This trace can be automatically performed if Alice only writes *Archface-U* definitions.

Cost for Writing Archface-U. Alice in this scenario can get valuable help by writing *Archface-U*. Someone might consider that the cost of writing *Archface-U* is an obstacle to software development productivity. However, all programmers write a Java interface when they make a Java program. Our approach adds only *alternative/optional* syntax and FSP descriptions to the ordinary Java interface. Additional cost is considered relative low.

Modular Programming for Uncertainty
Our approach does not invade the existing programs but introduce an interface called *Archface-U* annotating uncertain concerns. We only have to modify *Archface-U* descriptions when uncertainty appears or disappears. By only looking at the *Archface-U* and the corresponding code region, we can understand which portion of code is uncertain.

---

5   Modular Reasoning

Without modular reasoning about uncertainty, a developer has to rely on global reasoning to check whether some properties are satisfied. In this section, we show the *Archface-U*-based verification in details.

5.1   Uncertainty-Aware Verification

We can use the verification power provided by partial model. The behavioral correctness of a program is guaranteed modularly using our compiler (type checker) and model checker. Figure 3 illustrates the verification process. The type checker based on the refinement calculus focusing on simulation checks the conformance between *Archface-U* and its code. The model checker verifies the behavioral properties such as a deadlock by only using the information described in *Archface-U*. Integrating type checker and model checker, we can verify behavioral properties at the code level. Φ_M and Φ_p in Table 1 [16] correspond to logical formula expressing a partial model generated from *Archface-U* and the properties to be checked.

In this paper, we provide two types of true-false decisions for a property p: (1) verified by type checking; and (2) verified by model checking. Φ_p corresponds to the consistency among code or user-defined properties. When a property p is `True`, we can continue to develop even if uncertainty exists. When a property p is `Maybe`, we have to take care of the corresponding properties as a development risk. In other cases, we have to reconsider the code.

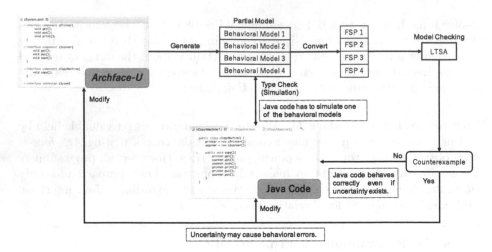

Fig. 3. Modular reasoning for Known Unknowns [49].

Table 1. Checking property on partial model [16].

$\Phi_M \wedge \Phi_p$	$\Phi_M \wedge \neg\Phi_p$	Property p
SAT	SAT	Maybe
SAT	UNSAT	True
UNSAT	SAT	False
UNSAT	UNSAT	(error)

5.2 Type Check

Basic Idea. Uncertainty is a target of compilation. Our type checker verifies (1) whether a partial model Φ_M generated from *Archface-U* satisfies a property Φ_p such as consistency; and (2) whether code is a subset of the partial model Φ_M (or whether code simulates one of the behavioral models contained in the partial model). It is important that (1) is performed by only *Archface-U* definitions. If code conforms to *Archface-U* in terms of (2), Φ_p is also satisfied in the code. That is, the verification of Φ_p results in modular interface checking. All of the code files are needed for property checking without an interface mechanism provided by *Archface-U*. Fixing the inter-model/code inconsistency is an important problem [9]. Our approach can verify inconsistency among code files by type checking even if uncertainty exists. For example, our compiler generates an error message if a method is defined in a component interface and its call is not appeared in the connector interface.

Archface-U and Partial Model. In our compiler, *Archface-U* is translated into a partial model as shown in Fig. 3. The followings is the translation algorithm for *Archface-U* containing *Alternative* uncertainty.

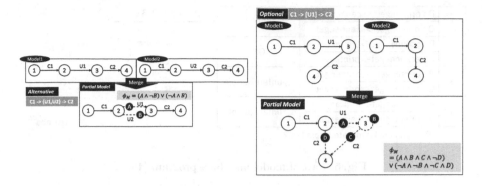

Fig. 4. Partial model generation (Left: Alternative, Right: Optional) [49].

STEP 1. Divide a connector interface including *Alternative* to a set of connector interfaces represented by original *Archface-U* that does not contain uncertainty. Each *Archface-U* description represented by LTS is translated into a state transition model. The upper part of Fig. 4 (left) shows the result of transformation in case of $C1 \rightarrow \{U1, U2\} \rightarrow C2$. The number in Fig. 4 (left) indicates a state.

STEP 2. State transition models generated in STEP 1 are merged into a state transition machine as shown in the lower part of Fig. 4 (left). This state transition model is a partial model. Mandatory edges and nodes appeared in all state transition models are represented by solid lines. Other non-common edges and nodes are represented by dashed lines. After generating a partial model, it can be translated into logical formula.

The algorithm in case of *Optional* uncertainty is basically the same to the above algorithm as illustrated in Fig. 4 (right side). In case of $C1 \rightarrow [U1] \rightarrow C2$, this *Optional* uncertainty is translated into two state transition models as shown in the upper part of Fig. 4 (right side). This procedure corresponds to STEP 1 in *Alternative* uncertainty. After that, these two models are merged into a state transition machine as shown in the lower part of Fig. 4 (right side). This procedure corresponds to STEP 2 in *Alternative* uncertainty. $C2$ is represented by two dashed lines, because the source of transition C (state number 3) is different from that of transition D (state number 2).

Features of Our Type Checker. Our type checker consists of a partial model generator, a refinement verifier, and a consistency verifier. The partial model generator creates a partial model, a set of possible behavior models from FSPs containing *alternative* and *optional* descriptions extended by *Archface-U*. The refinement verifier checks whether the code simulates one model included in the generated partial model. In List 3, a sequence *printer.get* → *scanner.get* → *scanner.scan* → *printer.print* → *methodX* → *printer.put* → *scanner.put* simulates the sequence 1 (Fig. 5) generated from the *Archface-U* definitions (List 1

1	P : printer.get->scanner.get	OK	
	Q : printer.get->scanner.get		
2	P : scanner.get->printer.get	OK	
	Q : scanner.get->printer.get		
3	P : printer.get->scanner.get	Counterexample	
	Q : scanner.get->printer.get		
4	P : scanner.get->printer.get	Counterexample	
	Q : printer.get->scanner.get		

Partial Model generated from List2

Simulate 1, 2, 3 or 4

```
cCopyMachine1.java
public class cCopyMachine1 {
    printer = new cPrinter();
    scanner = new cScanner();

    public void copy(){
        printer.get();
        scanner.get();
        scanner.scan();
        printer.print();
        printer.put();
        scanner.put();
    }
}
```

```
cCopyMachine2.java
public class cCopyMachine2 {
    printer = new cPrinter();
    scanner = new cScanner();

    public void copy(){
        printer.get();
        scanner.get();
        scanner.scan();
        printer.print();
        printer.put();
        scanner.put();
    }
}
```

Java Code

Fig. 5. Partial model and Java program [49].

and 2). The call of `methodX` does not violates an LTS defined by FSP in Lists 1 and 2. As a result, properties satisfied by the LTS are also held in the code that passes compile check. The consistency verifier checks the inconsistency not only among *Archface-U* definitions but also among code files. An error is generated if a method is defined in a component interface and its call does not appear in the connector interface. Our approach can verify the inconsistency even if uncertainty exists.

Our compiler adds only type checking embracing uncertainty to the original Java compiler. Compiled code is executable, because *Archface-U* is just a constraint to the code. Program behavior is also guaranteed, because the code simulates just one of the possible models described in *Archface-U*.

5.3 Model Checking Embracing Uncertainty

Behavioral properties represented by LTL can be automatically verified using existing model checkers. In our uncertainty-aware model checker, LTSA (LTS Analyzer)[2] is used as a model checking engine because *Archface-U* is based on FSP supported by LTSA. *Optional* and *Alternative* are translated into ordinary FSP descriptions as shown in Fig. 6.

If a property is verified by LTSA and the type check is successfully passed, the program satisfies the property too. Although we used LTSA, our approach takes a standard approach and can be implemented with other popular off-the-shelf checkers such as FDR (Failures Divergences Refinement)[3], a refinement checker for the process algebra CSP (Communicating Sequential Processes) [27].

5.4 Usage Scenario

We explain our verification process using a printer-scanner system as an example. There are four possible resource acquisition sequences as shown in Fig. 5. These cases are generated from a partial model described as *Archface-U* (List 2).

---

[2] http://www.doc.ic.ac.uk/ltsa/, Last accessed 18 November 2018.
[3] https://www.cs.ox.ac.uk/projects/fdr/, Last accessed 18 November 2018.

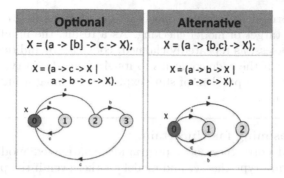

Fig. 6. Expansion of uncertain FSP [49].

Type Checking. Type check is passed if the code simulates one of the four possible resource acquisition sequences in Fig. 5. The Java code (List 3) simulates the sequence 1 and the type check is passed.

Model Checking and Counterexample Generation. As shown in Fig. 3, each behavioral model of a partial model is converted into the corresponding FSP description. Behavioral properties represented by LTL can be automatically verified using our model checker. If counterexamples are not generated by our model checker, Alice can select any sequence (either of 1, 2, 3, or 4 is OK). Alice can proceed development even if uncertain concerns exist, because the code simulating any sequence is correct. Of course, List 3 simulating the sequence 1 is correct. Unfortunately, counterexamples are generated in case of the sequences 3 or 4 and these counterexamples show that the acquisition order must be the same. Alice is notified that uncertainty specified in *Archface-U* (List 2) may cause a deadlock although the code (List 3) is correct. Alice cannot embrace uncertainty in this scenario.

Archface-U Modification for Resolving Uncertainty. Alice should not modify List 3 but change List 2 to remove the alternatives of **get** operation orders. After that, Alice has to run the model checker again and confirm that no counterexamples are generated. As explained here, Alice can resolve uncertain concerns and can make a correct program before debugging and testing.

5.5   State Explosion Problem

State explosion is a crucial problem when applying model checking to a real project. Especially, it is difficult to apply model checking to source code even if several tools such as CBMC (Bounded Model Checker for C and C++)[4] and Java Pathfinder[5] are already provided. On the other hand, in our approach, model

---

[4] http://www.cprover.org/cbmc/, Last accessed 18 November 2018.
[5] https://github.com/javapathfinder/, Last accessed 18 November 2018.

checking is performed in terms of only FSP descriptions in *Archface-U*. Code is not the direct target of model checking. As a result, the number of states is reduced. Nevertheless, as repeatedly claimed, code can be indirectly verified by the model checker if the code conforms to its *Archface-U* via type checker. Our approach mitigates the problem of state explosion by integrating type checking with model checking.

Modular Reasoning for Uncertainty

The behavioral correctness of a program is guaranteed modularly using uncertainty-aware type checker and model checker even if the program contains uncertainty. Our verification mechanism is based on partial model. Integrating type checker and model checker, we can not only verify behavioral properties at the code level but also avoid the state explosion problem.

---

6 Tool Support

The *iArch-U* IDE [52] is an Eclipse-based tool chain supporting *Modularity for Uncertainty*. In this section, we illustrate the tool overview of the *iArch-U* IDE.

The *iArch-U* IDE is open source software and can be downloaded from GitHub[6]. Referring the tutorials and technical documents provided in our GitHub repository, *iArch-U* tool features can be understood in details.

6.1 Overview

The overview of *iArch-U* is illustrated in Fig. 7. The *iArch-U* IDE consists of the tool components below. In this paper, we focused on the design and implementation of *iArch-U/Compiler* and *iArch-U/MC*.

iArch-U/MEditor (Model Editor). This is a UML model editor that can specify uncertain concerns. Using this model editor, a developer can specify *optional/alternative* in class diagrams and sequence diagrams. That is, an optional method or an alternative method call sequence can be modeled. Type checking is also available for these diagrams. Both type checking for a model and code are passed, they are consistent and traceable. *Archface-U* can be automatically generated from these diagrams.

iArch-U/CEditor (Code Editor). This is a code editor for Java programs. Basically, this editor provides the same functionality with the standard Eclipse Java editor.

iArch-U/IEditor (Interface Editor). This is an editor for writing *Archface-U* descriptions.

---

[6] http://posl.github.io/iArch/, Last accessed 18 November 2018.

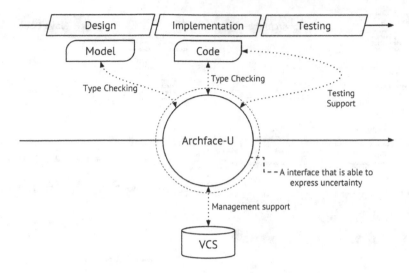

Fig. 7. *iArch-U* overview   (cited from http://posl.github.io/iArch/).

iArch-U/Compiler: This is an *Archface-U* compiler that adds only type checking embracing uncertainty to the original Java compiler. Compiled code is executable. The design and implementation of the type checker is shown in Sect. 5.

iArch-U/MC (Model Checker). This is an uncertainty-aware model checker based on LTSA. The design and implementation of the model checker is shown in Sect. 5.

iArch-U/UT (Unit Test): This is a JUnit-based unit testing tool. Using this unit testing support integrated with JUnit[7] and AspectJ[8], we can execute runtime testing when we want to check properties that cannot be checked statically. Test case drivers are automatically generated as aspects from the *Archface-U optional/alternative* descriptions. By weaving an aspect, we can test each alternative.

iArch-U/UM (Uncertainty Management). This is a Git-based uncertainty management support. We can trace when and why uncertain concerns arise or are resolved by analyzing git commits history.

6.2   Eclipse-Based User Interface

Figure 8 shows a snapshot of the *iArch-U* IDE. In Fig. 8, the user interface of *iArch-U/MC* is shown as an example. Using *iArch-U/MC*, we can explore which

---

[7] https://junit.org/, Last accessed 18 November 2018.
[8] https://www.eclipse.org/aspectj/, Last accessed 18 November 2018.

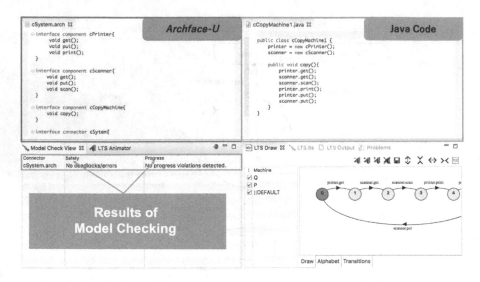

Fig. 8. *iArch-U/MC*: Uncertainty-aware model checker [49].

uncertainty can be permitted by interactively modifying not program code itself but *Archface-U* descriptions and checking the behavioral correctness.

6.3   Implementation

The *iArch-U* IDE is implemented as an Eclipse plug-in. *Archface-U* is defined as a DSL (Domain-Specific Language) by using Xtext[9]. Type checker is implemented by using APIs for analyzing AST (Abstract Syntax Tree) provided in JDT (Java Development Tools). Model editor is implemented by using EMF (Eclipse Modeling Framework)[10] and Graphiti (Graphical Tooling Infrastructure)[11].

---

iArch-U: An IDE for Uncertainty-aware Software Development
The *iArch-U* IDE supporting *Modularity for Uncertainty* consists of UML model editor, Java program editor, *Archface-U* compiler (type checker), LTSA-based model checker, JUnit-based testing support, and Git-based uncertainty management support. This Eclipse-based IDE is open source software and can be downloaded from GitHub.

---

7   Discussion

In this section, we discuss on the originality and the applicability of our idea from several viewpoints.

---

[9] https://eclipse.org/Xtext/, Last accessed 18 November 2018.
[10] https://www.eclipse.org/modeling/emf/, Last accessed 18 November 2018.
[11] https://www.eclipse.org/graphiti/, Last accessed 18 November 2018.

First of all, we have to discuss on the generality of our approach. Uncertainty is an abstract concept. It arises in many different domains/applications/contexts. We cannot provide a generic approach that can deal with uncertainty in every shape and form and in every context. Many people might consider that uncertainty has to be studied in a specific problem context since there is no generic solution that can handle uncertainty at an abstract level and be applicable to every problem context. Although uncertainty has many aspects as shown in Sect. 2, some kinds of *Known-Unknowns* represented by *optional* and *alternative* can be dealt with generally as demonstrated in this paper.

In our approach, uncertainty is encapsulated into an interface description. There might be many opinions about this policy. As shown in Sect. 4, we consider that temporary code patching is crucial in handling the uncertainty. It is not preferable to define an uncertain concern as a solid module (e.g., function, method, etc.) because such a module should be defined in terms of software architecture. The purpose of tradition encapsulation [38] is completely different from that of our approach. The former deals with uncertainty forecasted at the beginning of a design. The latter deals with uncertainty fluently appearing in the process of programming due to several reasons. We feel that uncertainness is often vague in most cases. In our approach, uncertainty is introduced as a pluggable interface. We consider that the notion of *fluent modularization* is needed. Our usage of the word *"modularity"* is slightly different from a tradition definition: a module should have a substantial instance such as classes, functions, and aspects. However, we consider it is valuable to introduce the notion of *fluency* in the world of modularity in some contexts such as uncertainty. As explained in Sect. 3, uncertainty can be represented using AOP. However, we have to write multiple aspects corresponding to each alternative and weave the aspect respectively in order to test all of uncertain alternatives. We introduced *Archface-U* to manage these alternatives easily.

Someone might consider that *Archface-U* is similar to variability modeling in SPL [3]. How different is our approach from SPL? If there is no difference, we can deal with uncertainty by only using SPL technologies. Indeed, uncertainty in structural aspects (a component interface in *Archface-U*) can be represented by defining uncertain features in a feature model. Although it is difficult to represent behavioral aspects of uncertainty (a connector interface in *Archface-U*) in a feature model, there are studies on behavioral variability [6,24,55]. Our most important contribution is to introduce the *interface-based variability* to the world of SPL. As claimed in this paper, this interface enables the valuable integration of code-conformance check via type checker, model checking taking into account abstraction, and uncertainty-aware code localization (traceable to an uncertain code region). Only using current SPL technologies, it is not easy to integrate important facilities mentioned above. Moreover, our idea can be basically applied to SPL by not limiting to variability in uncertain concerns. Similarity to SPL comes from the characteristics of *Known Unknowns* in which uncertainty is a subset of variability. Although the interface mechanism of *Archface-U* can be applied to SPL, the process of SPL is different from that of uncertainty-aware software development. The former focuses on generating a product from a set of features represented by *optional* and *alternatives*. Product structure does not basically change through a software development, although product regeneration may occur several times to deal with small changes. On the other hand, our approach focuses on the management of uncertainty frequently appearing or disappearing in a software development. Product generation is out of scope. The main concern is to verify whether some important properties are guaranteed even if uncertainty exists and to decide whether resolution of uncertainty can be postponed. For this reason, modular reasoning realized by type checking and model checking is important.

Lastly, we discuss on the extension to probabilistic descriptions. As explained in Sect. 2, there are two types of uncertainty: *aleatory* and *epistemic*. The former is supported by probabilistic programming or model checking such as Uncertain $< T >$ or PRISM. Our approach supporting the latter case provides a module mechanism for expressing state-of-knowledge uncertainty. Our approach can be applied to probabilistic programming and model checking by adding probability to connector's arrows. As the next step, we plan to integrate our model checker with LTSA-PCA (Probabilistic Component Automata) [41] to support aleatory uncertainty.

8   Conclusions—Can We Live with Uncertainty?

Garlan, D. claims that embracing uncertainty within the discipline of software engineering causes a shift in perspective along important dimensions: (1) From correctness to utility; (2) From open-loop to closed-loop; and (3) From precise to approximate [22]. This paper focused on only the static aspect of uncertainty— *Archface-U* is statically applied to the code. However, in principle, *Archface-U* can be applied to the existing programs dynamically although further research is needed—e.g., prototype-based *Archface-U*. The aspect of *utility* or *approximation* can be introduced to an application at run-time by dynamically adding or deleting uncertain constraints represented by *Archface-U*.

Acknowledgments. We thank Syunya Nakamura, Keisuke Watanabe, and Takuya Fukamachi for their great contributions. They were students of Naoyasu Ubayashi. This work was supported by JSPS KAKENHI Grant Numbers JP26240007.

References

1. Allen, R., Garlan, D.: Formalizing architectural connection. In: Proceedings of the 16th International Conference on Software Engineering (ICSE 1994), pp. 71–80 (1994)
2. Autili, M., Cortellessa, V., Di Ruscio, D., Inverardi, P., Pelliccione, P., Tivoli, M.: Integration architecture synthesis for taming uncertainty in the digital space. In: Calinescu, R., Garlan, D. (eds.) Monterey Workshop 2012. LNCS, vol. 7539, pp. 118–131. Springer, Heidelberg (2012). https://doi.org/10.1007/978-3-642-34059-8_6

3. Bąk, K., Diskin, Z., Antkiewicz, M., Czarnecki, K., Wąsowski, A.: Clafer: unifying class and feature modeling. Softw. Syst. Model. **15**(3), 811–845 (2016)
4. Bornholt, J., Mytkowicz, T., McKinley, K.S.: Uncertain< T >: a first-order type for uncertain data. In: Proceedings of the 19th International Conference on Architectural Support for Programming Languages and Operating Systems (ASPLOS 2014), pp. 51–66 (2014)
5. Cheng, S.-W., Garlan, D.: Handling uncertainty in autonomic systems. In: Proceedings of the International Workshop on Living with Uncertainties (IWLU 2007) (2007)
6. Classen, A., Cordy, M., Heymans, P., Legay, A., Schobbens, P.Y.: Model checking software product lines with SNIP. Int. J. Softw. Tools Technol. Transfer **14**(5), 589–612 (2012)
7. Clements, P., Northrop, L.: Software Product Lines. Addision-Wesley, Boston (2001)
8. Devaraj, A., Mishra, K., Trivedi, K.S.: Uncertainty propagation in analytic availability models. In: Proceedings of the Symposium on Reliable Distributed Systems (SRDS 2010), pp. 121–130 (2010)
9. Egyed, A., Letter, E., Finkelstein, A.: Generating and evaluating choices for fixing inconsistencies in UML design models. In: Proceedings of the 23rd International Conference on Automated Software Engineering (ASE 2008), pp. 99–108 (2008)
10. Elbaum, S., Rosenblum, D.S.: Known Unknowns: testing in the presence of uncertainty. In: Proceedings of the 22nd ACM SIGSOFT International Symposium on Foundations of Software Engineering (FSE 2014), pp. 833–836 (2014)
11. Eramo, R., Pierantonio, A., Rosa, G.: Uncertainty in bidirectional transformations. In: Proceedings of the 6th International Workshop on Modeling in Software Engineering (MiSE 2014), pp. 37–42 (2014)
12. Esfahani, N., Kouroshfar, E., Malek, S.: Taming uncertainty in self-adaptive software. In: Proceedings of the 8th Joint Meeting of the European Software Engineering Conference and the ACM SIGSOFT Symposium on the Foundations of Software Engineering (ESEC/FSE 2011), pp. 234–244 (2011)
13. Esfahani, N., Razavi, K., Malek, S.: Dealing with uncertainty in early software architecture. In: Proceedings of the 20th International Symposium on the Foundations of Software Engineering (FSE 2012), pp. 21:1–21:4 (2012)
14. Esfahani, N., Malek, S.: Uncertainty in self-adaptive software systems. In: de Lemos, R., Giese, H., Müller, H.A., Shaw, M. (eds.) Software Engineering for Self-Adaptive Systems II. LNCS, vol. 7475, pp. 214–238. Springer, Heidelberg (2013). https://doi.org/10.1007/978-3-642-35813-5_9
15. Esfahani, N., Malek, S., Razavi, K.: GuideArch: guiding the exploration of architectural solution space under uncertainty. In: Proceedings of the 35th International Conference on Software Engineering (ICSE 2013), pp. 43–52 (2013)
16. Famelis, M., Salay, R., Chechik, M.: Partial models: towards modeling and reasoning with uncertainty. In: Proceedings of the 34th International Conference on Software Engineering (ICSE 2012), pp. 573–583 (2012)
17. Famelis, M., Salay, R., Di Sandro, A., Chechik, M.: Transformation of models containing uncertainty. In: Moreira, A., Schätz, B., Gray, J., Vallecillo, A., Clarke, P. (eds.) MODELS 2013. LNCS, vol. 8107, pp. 673–689. Springer, Heidelberg (2013). https://doi.org/10.1007/978-3-642-41533-3_41
18. Famelis, M., Ben-David, N., Sandro, A.D., Salay, R., Chechik, M.: MU-MMINT: an IDE for model uncertainty. In: Proceedings of the 37th International Conference on Software Engineering (ICSE 2015), Demonstrations Track, pp. 697–700 (2015)

19. Fitzgerald, J., Larsen, G.P.: Modeling Systems, Practical Tools and Techniques in Software Development. Cambridge University Press, Cambridge (1998)

20. Fukamachi, T., Ubayashi, N., Hosoai, S., Kamei, Y.: Conquering uncertainty in Java programming. In: Proceedings of the 37th International Conference on Software Engineering (ICSE 2015), Poster Track, pp. 823–824 (2015)

21. Fukamachi, T., Ubayashi, N., Hosoai, S., Kamei, Y.: Modularity for uncertainty. In: Proceedings of the 7th International Workshop on Modelling in Software Engineering (MiSE 2015), pp. 7–12 (2015)

22. Garlan, D.: Software engineering in an uncertain world. In: Proceedings of FSE/SDP Workshop on Future of Software Engineering Research (FoSER 2010), pp. 125–128 (2010)

23. Ghezzi, C., Sharifloo, A.M.: Quantitative verification of non-functional requirements with uncertainty. In: Zamojski, W., Kacprzyk, J., Mazurkiewicz, J., Sugier, J., Walkowiak, T. (eds.) Dependable Computer Systems. AINSC, vol. 97, pp. 47–62. Springer, Heidelberg (2011). https://doi.org/10.1007/978-3-642-21393-9_4

24. Ghezzi, C., Sharifloo, A.M.: Verifying non-functional properties of software product lines: towards an efficient approach using parametric model checking. In: Proceedings of the 15th Software Product Line Conference (SPLC 2011), pp. 170–174 (2011)

25. Goseva-Popstojanova, K., Kamavaram, S.: Assessing uncertainty in reliability of component-based software systems. In: Proceedings of the 14th International Symposium on Software Reliability Engineering (ISSRE 2003), pp. 307–320 (2003)

26. Hinton, A., Kwiatkowska, M., Norman, G., Parker, D.: PRISM: a tool for automatic verification of probabilistic systems. In: Hermanns, H., Palsberg, J. (eds.) TACAS 2006. LNCS, vol. 3920, pp. 441–444. Springer, Heidelberg (2006). https://doi.org/10.1007/11691372_29

27. Hoare, C.A.R.: Communicating Sequential Processes. Prentice Hall, Upper Saddle River (1985)

28. Kang, K.C., Lee, J., Donohoe, P.: Feature-oriented product line engineering. IEEE Softw. 9(4), 58–65 (2002)

29. Kiczales, G., et al.: Aspect-oriented programming. In: Akşit, M., Matsuoka, S. (eds.) ECOOP 1997. LNCS, vol. 1241, pp. 220–242. Springer, Heidelberg (1997). https://doi.org/10.1007/BFb0053381

30. Kiczales, G., Hilsdale, E., Hugunin, J., Kersten, M., Palm, J., Griswold, W.G.: An overview of AspectJ. In: Knudsen, J.L. (ed.) ECOOP 2001. LNCS, vol. 2072, pp. 327–354. Springer, Heidelberg (2001). https://doi.org/10.1007/3-540-45337-7_18

31. Lago, P., Vliet, H.: Explicit assumptions enrich architectural models. In: Proceedings of the 27th International Conference on Software Engineering (ICSE 2005), pp. 206–214 (2005)

32. Letier, E., Stefan, D., Barr, E.T.: Uncertainty, risk, and information value in software requirements and architecture. In: Proceedings of the 36th International Conference on Software Engineering (ICSE 2014), pp. 883–894 (2014)

33. Llerena, Y.R.S.: Dealing with uncertainty in verification of nondeterministic systems. In: Proceedings of the 22nd ACM SIGSOFT International Symposium on Foundations of Software Engineering (FSE 2014), pp. 787–790 (2014)

34. Magee, J., Kramer, J.: Concurrency: State Models & Java Programs, 2nd edn. Wiley, Hoboken (2006)

35. Massey, A., Rutledge, R., Antón, A., Swire, P.: Identifying and classifying ambiguity for regulatory requirements. In: Proceedings of the 22nd International Requirements Engineering Conference (RE 2014), pp. 83–92 (2014)

36. Meedeniya, I., Moser, I., Aleti, A., Grunske, L.: Architecture-based reliability evaluation under uncertainty. In: Proceedings of the 7th International ACM Sigsoft Conference on the Quality of Software Architectures (QoSA 2011), pp. 85–94 (2011)
37. Milner, R.: Communication and Concurrency. Prentice Hall, Upper Saddle River (1989)
38. Parnas, D.L.: On the criteria to be used in decomposing systems into modules. Commun. ACM 15(12), 1053–1058 (1972)
39. Perez-Palacin, D., Mirandola, R.: Uncertainties in the modeling of self-adaptive systems: a axonomy and an example of availability evaluation. In: Proceedings of the 5th ACM/SPEC International Conference on Performance Engineering (ICPE 2014), pp. 3–14 (2014)
40. Raccoon, Dog: Unknownness. ACM SIGSOFT Softw. Eng. Notes 38(5), 8–17 (2013)
41. Rodrigues, P., Lupu, E., Kramer, J.: LTSA-PCA: tool support for compositional reliability analysis. In: ICSE Companion 2014 Companion Proceedings of the 36th International Conference on Software Engineering (ICSE 2014), pp. 548–551 (2014)
42. Rosenblum, D.: Probability and uncertainty in software engineering. In: Keynote Talk at the 2013 National Software Application Conference (NASAC 2013) (2013). http://www.slideshare.net/dsrosenblum/nasac-2013
43. Salay, R., Chechik, M., Horkoff, J., Sandro, A.D.: Managing requirements uncertainty with partial models. Requirements Eng. 18(2), 107–128 (2013)
44. Salay, R., Gorzny, J., Chechik, M.: Change propagation due to uncertainty change. In: Cortellessa, V., Varró, D. (eds.) FASE 2013. LNCS, vol. 7793, pp. 21–36. Springer, Heidelberg (2013). https://doi.org/10.1007/978-3-642-37057-1_3
45. Sommerville, I.: Integrated requirements engineering: a tutorial. IEEE Softw. 22(1), 16–23 (2005)
46. Trubiani, C., Meedeniya, I., Cortellessa, V., Aleti, A., Grunske, L.: Model-based performance analysis of software architectures under uncertainty. In: Proceedings of the 9th International ACM SIGSOFT Conference on the Quality of Software Architectures (QoSA 2013), pp. 69–78 (2013)
47. Ubayashi, N., Nomura, J., Tamai, T.: Archface: a contract place where architectural design and code meet together. In: Proceedings of the 32nd International Conference on Software Engineering (ICSE 2010), pp. 75–84 (2010)
48. Ubayashi, N., Ai, D., Li, P., Li, Y., Hosoai, S., Kamei, Y.: Abstraction-aware verifying compiler for yet another MDD. In: Proceedings of the 29th International Conference on Automated Software Engineering (ASE 2014), pp. 557–562 (2014)
49. Ubayashi, N., Kamei, Y., Sato, R.: iArch-U/MC: an uncertainty-aware model checker for embracing known unknowns. In: Proceedings of the 13th International Conference on Software Technologies (ICSOFT 2018), pp. 176–184 (2018)
50. Uchitel, S., Kramer, J., Magee, J.: Modelling undefined behaviour in scenario synthesis. In: Proceedings of the 2nd International Workshop on Scenarios and State Machines: Models, Algorithms, and Tools at ICSE 2003 (2003)
51. Walker, W.E., et al.: Defining uncertainty. A conceptual basis for uncertainty management in model-based decision support. Integr. Assess. 4(1), 5–17 (2003)
52. Watanabe, K., Ubayashi, N., Fukamachi, T., Nakamura, S., Muraoka, H., Kamei, Y.: iArch-U: interface-centric integrated uncertainty-aware development environment. In: Proceedings of the 9th International Workshop on Modelling in Software Engineering (MiSE 2017) (Workshop at ICSE 2017), pp. 40–46 (2017)
53. Whittle, J., Sawyer, P., Bencomo, N., Cheng, B.H.C., Bruel, J.-M.: Relax: a language to address uncertainty in self-adaptive systems requirement. Requirements Eng. 15(2), 177–196 (2010)

54. Yang, W., Xu, C., Liu, Y., Cao, C., Ma, X., Lu, J.: Verifying self-adaptive applications suffering uncertainty. In: Proceedings of the 29th International Conference on Automated Software Engineering (ASE 2014), pp. 199–210 (2014)
55. Ziadi, T., Hélouët, L., Jézéquel, J.-M.: Towards a UML profile for software product lines. In: van der Linden, F.J. (ed.) PFE 2003. LNCS, vol. 3014, pp. 129–139. Springer, Heidelberg (2004). https://doi.org/10.1007/978-3-540-24667-1_10
56. Ziv, H., Richardson, D.J., Klösch, R.: The uncertainty principle in software engineering (1996). http://citeseerx.ist.psu.edu/viewdoc/summary?doi=10.1.1.39.8700

Software Systems and Applications

Empowering Continuous Delivery in Software Development: The DevOps Strategy

Clauirton Siebra[1,2(✉)], Rosberg Lacerda[2], Italo Cerqueira[2],
Jonysberg P. Quintino[2], Fabiana Florentin[3], Fabio B. Q. da Silva[4],
and Andre L. M. Santos[4]

[1] Informatics Center, Federal University of Paraiba, Joao Pessoa PB, Brazil
clauirton@ci.ufpb.br
[2] CIn/Samsung Laboratory of Research and Development,
UFPE, Recife PE, Brazil
{rll,iac2,jpq}@cin.ufpe.br
[3] SIDI/Samsung, Campinas, SP, Brazil
f.florentin@samsung.com
[4] Centro de Informática, Universidade Federal de Pernambuco, Recife PE, Brazil
{fabio,alms}@cin.ufpe.br

Abstract. Continuous Delivery refers to a software development practice where members of a team frequently integrate their work, so that the process of delivery can be easily conducted. However, this continuous integration and delivery requires a reliable collaboration between development and IT operation teams. The DevOps practices support this collaboration since they enable that the operation staff making use of the same infrastructure as developers for their systems work. Our study aims at presenting a practical DevOps implementation and analyzing how the process of software delivery and infrastructure changes was automated. Our approach follows the principles of infrastructure as code, where a configuration platform – PowerShell DSC – was used to automatically define reliable environments for continuous software delivery. In this context, we defined the concept of "stage for dev", also using the Docker technology, which involves all the elements that enable members of a team to have the same production environment, locally configured in their personal machines and thus empowering the continuous integration and delivery of system releases.

Keywords: Continuous delivery · DevOps · Software deployment

1 Introduction

The lifecycle of an application involves teams that usually work in distinct areas and have incompatible goals. For example, while the development team wants agility; the operation team is more focused on stability issues. In such domains, applications are manually handed over between these teams with minimal communication. Such separation between entities, which are in fact dependent, translates into an increased time to market and negatively impacts the software quality, decreasing the actual value of the product [1].

© Springer Nature Switzerland AG 2019
M. van Sinderen and L. A. Maciaszek (Eds.): ICSOFT 2018, CCIS 1077, pp. 247–265, 2019.
https://doi.org/10.1007/978-3-030-29157-0_11

The fundamental conflict in the software process environment is between developers, which have to produce changes at a rapid pace; and IT Operators, which have to maintain infrastructure configuration and availability along these changes. The term DevOps, which is a blend of the Developers and Operations words, is a concept that assists to facilitate these changes [2]. It builds a living bridge between development and operations and gives them an opportunity to work and collaborate effectively and seamlessly. According to Loukides [3], *DevOps is a culture, movement or practice that emphasizes the collaboration and communication of both software developers and other information technology (IT) professionals while automating the process of software delivery and infrastructure changes. It aims at establishing a culture and environment where building, testing, and releasing software, can happen rapidly, frequently, and more reliably.*

Previous works on DevOps [4, 5] are mainly focused on propose conceptual frameworks, which intend to create a consensus to the own DevOps definition and their features. Some elements such as the culture of collaboration, automation and monitoring; emerged from these works and seem to be the basis for the implementation of DevOps environments. However, while DevOps is becoming very popular between software practitioners; there is still a lack in discussions on frameworks that support its implementation and reports of real experiences that could assist development teams in adopting the DevOps principles [6, 7].

The first focus of this work was on the automation dimension, where the definition of practices related to infrastructure as code creates the basis for an automated process of continuous integration and delivery [8]. Handling infrastructure as code, the following benefits can be obtained [9]:

- A code can be thoroughly tested to reproduce infrastructure consistently at scale;
- Developers could be provided with a simulated production environment, which increases testability and reliability;
- Infrastructure code can be versioned;
- Infrastructure can be provisioned and configured on demand;
- Proactive recovering from failures can be carried out by continuous monitoring of the environment for violations, which can trigger automatic execution of scripts for rollback or recovery.

Our approach followed the principles of infrastructure as code, where a configuration platform, *PowerShell DSC* (Desired State Configuration) was used to automatically define reliable environments for continuous software delivery. This initial environment was designed to work on virtual machines. Differently, our current study shows this approach running together with Docker [10]. Docker is a tool designed to easily create, deploy, and run applications by using containers, which allow developers to package up an application with all of the parts it needs, such as libraries and other dependencies, and ship it all out as one package. In this way, our main aim was to define an environment model, which we call *"stage for dev"*, which involves all the elements that enable members of a team to have the same production environment, locally configured in their personal machines and thus empowering the continuous integration and delivery of system releases. Furthermore, we also present the current discussions regarding the integration of Docker with PowerShell DSC, which is being conducted in the Windows platform.

The remainder of this paper is structured as follows: Sect. 2 summarizes the studies on the automation dimension of DevOps, where the focus is on the infrastructure as code aspects and their implementations. Section 3 presents how DevOps concepts were implemented in our organization and the lessons learned from this experience. Section 4 extends this idea, considering the use of the Docker technology. Section 5 summarizes the current discussions about infrastructure as code, which focus on the integration of Docker and PowerShell DSC. Finally, Sect. 6 concludes this work, stressing the challenges of DevOps implementation and future works that we intend to carry out.

2   Structure as Code

The creation of a DevOps environment is based on principles such as culture of collaboration [11–15], measurement of development efforts [16–18] and monitoring of system health [11, 17, 18]. However, according to Ebert et al. [19], the most important shift over the adoption of DevOps is to treat infrastructure as code, since infrastructure can be shared, tested, and version controlled. Furthermore, development and production could share a homogenous infrastructure, reducing problems and bugs due to different infrastructure configurations. This section discusses the main ideas of this approach and resources that support it.

2.1   Basic Concepts

Infrastructure as Code (IaC) is a DevOps principle used to address problems regarding the manual process of configuration management by means of automatic provision and configuration of infrastructural resources. In this way, the IaC concept is used to describe the idea that almost all actions performed to the infrastructure can be automated. Like any code, developers could create automation logic for different tasks such as to deploy, configure and upgrade computational systems and infrastructures. Patterns to use the infrastructure as code were proposed in [20] and they can be summarized as:

- Automate Provisioning: automate the process of configuring environments to include networks, external services, and infrastructure;
- Behavior-Driven Monitoring: automate tests to verify the behavior of the infrastructure;
- Immune System: deploy software one instance at a time while conducting behavior-driven monitoring. If an error is detected during the incremental deployment, a Rollback Release must be initiated to revert changes;
- Lockdown Environments: lock down shared environments from unauthorized external and internal usage, including operations staff. All changes must be versioned and applied through automation;
- Production-Like Environments: development and production environments must be as similar as possible.

These patterns show that DevOps pushes automation from the development to the infrastructure. Compared with manual infrastructure provisioning, for example, configuration management tools can reduce production provisioning and configuration maintenance complexity while enabling recreation of the production system on the development machines. As discussed in [19], tools are a major DevOps enabler and they are mandatory in automating these and other patterns and tasks. In fact, DevOps considers deliveries with short cycle time. This feature comes from one of the Lean/Agile principles, which stands for "Build incrementally with fast integrated learning cycles". Thus, such a strategy requires a high degree of automation, so that it is fundamental the appropriate choice of tools. See a list of tools in [19].

2.2   Tools for Configuration Management

Configuration management tools are the main resources to implement IaC strategies. Such tools aim at replacing error-prone shell scripts, which are employed to manage the state of machines or environments where development codes are going to execute. Shell scripts are potentially complex to maintain and evolve, since they are neither modular nor reusable. Thus, the aim of approaches for configuration management was to provide languages to specify configuration properties without the limitations (low modularity and reusability) of shell scripts. Three examples of these languages, which follow different implementation strategies, are:

- Puppet: domain specific language implemented in a common programming language (originally Ruby, but with newer versions in C++ and Clojure);
- Chef: uses an existing language (Ruby) for writing system configuration "recipes";
- CFEngine: domain specific language also implemented in a common programming language (C).

These languages are often declarative. This means, they describe the desired state of the system rather than a way to achieve it. There are other languages such as Nix, which is a purely functional programming language with specific properties for configuration; and IBM Tivoli System Automation for Multiplatforms. These languages have similar features but may present particular purposes. The IBM approach, for example, facilitates the automatic switching of users, applications and data from one database system to another in a cluster.

Puppet, Chef and CFEngine are the most popular configuration management alternatives. Therefore, it is important to understand some slight differences among them [21]. Chef and Puppet are very similar since they are based on Ruby. However, Chef seems to present fewer security vulnerabilities than Puppet. Both languages are more "Ops-friendly" due to its model-driven approach. They also present a relatively small learning curve. Differently, CFEngine is more "Dev-friendly" and its learning curve is steep. However, as an advantage, CFEngine has a dramatically smaller memory footprint, runs faster and has far fewer dependencies since it was developed with C. For configuration information, CFEngine uses its own declarative language to create "promises," or policy statements. Puppet, on the other hand, uses a Ruby Domain-Specific Language (DSL) to create its manifests. So those with some Ruby experience may find themselves in more familiar territory with Puppet.

A comparison among these and several other open-source configuration management approaches can be seen in [22].

2.3 Frameworks

As applications need to be developed and tested in production like environments, some organizations are using strategies such as virtualization and more recently containerization [23] to make such environments portable. However, these approaches are also hard to use when they are manually maintained. This scenario motivated the creation of frameworks for setup of more complex development environments.

Two popular examples of frameworks are Vagrant and Docker. Vagrant [24] is a management and support framework to virtualization of development environments. Instead of running all projects locally on a unique computer, having to rearrange the different requirements and dependencies of each project, this framework allows running each project in its own dedicated virtual environment. Docker [10] is a container-based approach that provides virtualization at the operating system level and uses the host kernel to run multiple virtual environments.

A difference between these approaches is associated with their performances. As discussed in the previous paragraph, Docker relies on containerization, while Vagrant utilizes virtualization. In this latter approach, each virtual machine runs its own entire operating system inside a simulated hardware environment provided by special programs. Thus, each virtual machine needs a dedicated amount of static resources (CPU, RAM, storage), generating an overhead of such resources. Approaches based on containerization present a higher performance since containers simply use whatever resources it needs. This means, there is no overhead of resources. Based on this discussion, Docker is lighter than Vagrant. A deeper study in such approaches shows that both have advantages and disadvantages, so that the final decision must be based on the particular features of each project.

There is another important difference between these approaches. Vagrant cannot create virtual machines or containers without virtualization platforms [21] such as VirtualBox, VMware or Docker. Differently, Docker can work without Vagrant. In order, the main advantage of vagrant is that it provides an easy mechanism to reproduce environments. These frameworks can also be used together with configuration management tools/languages to implement more powerful IaC environments. Some examples are given in the next section.

2.4 Tools in Practice

The previous section showed that there are several options regarding frameworks and configuration management tools to support the implementation of the infrastructure as code principles. However, the literature presents few contributions regarding their practical use and the focus of this literature is on the specification of extensions that could improve the limitations of current tools rather than descriptions of real case studies. The work of Hüttermann [25], for example, integrates Vagrant and Puppet and uses them to create a topology for IaC consisting of Vagrant and Puppet artefacts that are continuously built and stored in a version control system. While Vagrant allows the building of lightweight and portable virtual environments, based on a simple textual description; Puppet uses a declarative syntax to describe the desired state of a target environment and allows this description to be executed to create that state on a target machine. Hummer and colleagues [26] propose and evaluate a model-based testing framework for IaC, where an abstracted system model is used to derive state transition graphs. The resulting graph is then used to derive test cases. Their prototype extends the Chef IaC tool. However the authors comment that their approach is general and could be applied to other tools, such as Puppet. The work of Artac *et al.* [27] discusses several technologies involved in supporting IaC. Its main focus is on the OASIS TOSCA, which is an industrial practice language for automated deployment of technology independent and multi-cloud compliant applications.

In order, the majority of examples regarding IaC are focused on Cloud environment and they are related to specific features of such domain. For example, Zhu *et al.* [28] report results from experiments on reliability issues of cloud infrastructure and trade-offs between using heavily-baked and lightly-baked images. Their experiments were based on Amazon Web Service (AWS) OpsWorks APIs (Application Programming Interfaces) and they also used the Chef configuration management tool. Several other works regarding IaC in the Cloud domain are discussed in the literature, such as in [18, 29].

The work of Spinellis [30] is another example of a study that discusses popular tools in the DevOps domain, which include CFEngine, Puppet and Chef. This work stresses the main function of such tools, which is to automate a system's configuration so that users write rules expressing how an IT system is to be configured and the tool will set up the system accordingly. Wettinger *et al.* [13] also show that the DevOps community focuses on providing pragmatic solutions for the automation of application deployment. Then, the communities affiliated with some of the DevOps tools, such as Chef or Puppet, to provide artefacts to build deployment plans for certain application tasks. Thus, these two previous works [13, 30] confirm the trend to some specific tools (Chef and Puppet) and their relation to aspects of automation. Unfortunately, the scientific literature does not discuss the use and evaluation of such tools in a DevOps context, including the Docker technology, considering real development cases. This is the major contribution of our work, as detailed in the next sections.

3   DevOps Implementation: Case Study 1

This section is divided into four parts. We first describe the object of this case study, which is a real application that we call *Xsolution* (pseudo name due to commercial issues). Next we describe the original strategy to deploy this application and the metrics that characterize the problems of such a strategy. Then, we present the implementation of our infrastructure as code approach, which is based on the *PowerShell DCS*, and how this new strategy significantly improved our deployment process. Finally, we stress the advantages of this approach when it is compared to other ways to implement infrastructure as code solutions, such as Chef and Puppet.

3.1   Tools in Practice

Xsolution is a client-server solution that requires the deployment of a server and mobile modules to execute. The abstract architecture of this application is illustrated in Fig. 1.

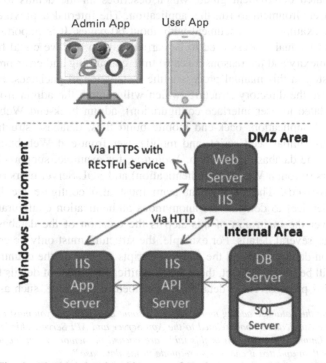

Fig. 1. The high-level architecture of *Xsolution* (adapted from [8]).

Each of the components in this figure (Smartphone, Web server, Internet Information Service – IIS, App Server, API Server, DB Server and SQL Server) requires a specific configuration before the deployment of the application. This configuration used to be manually carried out by the IT team by means of an internal home-made deployment guide that describes all the process (step-by-step), as better detailed in Sect. 3.2.

In order, to prepare the required resources that will support *Xsolution*, or any other application with this architecture (Fig. 1), the next actions must be carried out: (1) Installation of packages; (2) Database installation; (3) Installation of Web application requirements; (4) Installation of Web application; (5) Configuration of the Admin Web Applications; (6) Configuration of the log of errors; and (7) Mobile Web site configuration. Each of these actions has multiple steps and the traditional approach to carry out this process is to follow guides that describe these steps. This approach is described in the next section.

3.2 Manual Deployment Process

The manual deployment of *Xsolution* and other applications of our company, used to be manually carried out by a group of IT collaborators. In this strategy, each application had an associated deployment guide, which describes all the details to prepare the resources and environment to run this application. The internal deployment guide of *Xsolution*, for example, is a document with about 60 pages. It is important to understand how this manual process used to be carried out, so that we could have an idea about its complexity and the reasons it is a so time-consuming and error-prone activity.

The first step in this manual process is the installation of packages. Basically the idea is to create the directory structure, which will contain the admin front-end Web build files (related to user interface configuration), admin back-end Web build files, mobile android application, back-end mobile build files, database structure creation scripts, database initial seed script, and mobile user front-end Web build files. The second step is the database installation. *Xsolution*, for example, supports both Active Directory users (through Windows authentication) and SQL Server users (with custom login and password). The deployment team must also configure the IIS (Internet Information Service) to delegate the anonymous authentication configuration to *Xsolution*. However the main aim of this step is the creation of the database structure, which involves several details. For example, the structure must only be created in the first application deployment and the database scripts depend on the country where the application will be hosted. In fact, there are a significant number of details that must be observed in this process. These details are described in the guide, such as:

> "*if you update the database adding more values for some Enumeration, you must perform the Recycle of the Application Pools related to the App Server and API Server. This is necessary because the Enumerations present in this table are cached in memory when the application starts, rather than updated if changes were made in the database.*"

This type of conditional actions increases the complexity of the configuration and they are usually a common source of errors since they are not part of the normal configuration flow. The use of further support tools, such as the SQL Server management studio to support the database backup procedures, is also described in the guide. In addition, there are also issues when databases are updated. For example:

> "*If you are upgrading the version of the database, you must sequentially run all scripts of the current version to the version you want. If just a script is ignored, the next scripts after that may not run correctly.*"

The third step is the installation of the Web application requirements. This step generally involves the installation of several third-party resources, which act as the Front-end Admin Web, Back-end Admin Web and Mobile User Web. For example, the *Xsolution* requires the installation of the next components: (1) NET Framework 4.5; (2) Internet Information Services 7.5 or 10; (3) ASP.NET; (4) Windows Management Framework 3.0; and (5) IIS URL Rewrite 2.0 module. Each of these components also has their own installation details, which must be observed by the deployment team. For example, the IIS module has its own manual (24 pages) with instructions about the reverse proxy configuration using an IIS server. One of the functions of the IIS is to capture the application log. This task is customized and also presents a set of configurations to properly work according to the features of each Web application.

The version of components is another point to observe. *Xsolution*, for example, allows the use of Windows Server 2008 R2 Service Pack 1 or Windows Server 2016. Depending on the choice, particular details must be observed along the configuration process. The configuration process also has an influence from local laws. For example, due to the new national legislation for Internet (Law No. 12,965 - Internet Civil Landmark) [31], information about the user access to the application needs to be stored for a period of six months. The information required is the IP, the username, the date and time of login. Thus, the components must be configured to maintain such information.

The fourth step is the installation of the own Web application, which involves the creation of the application pool, the choice of Website locations and the assignment of each site to a specific application pool. In order, application pools are processing groups based on specific administrative preferences that isolate Website processes from other website processes on the server, offering strong performance and security benefits. Again, there are several details in this configuration. For example, the Admin Front-end Web and Admin Back-end Web applications could be in the same application pool, but it is strongly recommended that the Back-end Mobile application stays in a separate application pool. Thus, the configuration of two Web servers is required.

The fifth step is the configuration of the Admin Web application. There are several technical details in this step, which are related to authentication options, the configuration of mobile responses and database access permissions. In fact, there are a significant number of parameters (about 50) that must be set and the deployment team must understand these parameters and know the best way to set them.

Finally, the sixth and seventh steps are respectively related to the configuration of the error log and mobile Website. Similarly to the other steps, the guide brings several details and customization options.

This description illustrates just part of the tasks and details regarding the manual deployment process. We can easily observe that this process is prone to errors since it is long and has several details. Furthermore, it is hard to identify which configuration was not properly performed when an error occurs.

To demonstrate these problems and characterize this process in terms of software engineering metrics, we carried out a simple quantitative analysis of this process using *Xsolution* as our object of study. According to the schedule and documents from the *Xsolution* project, the deployment stage of each *Xsolution* release took about 16 h in the best case. This means when the process was performed without errors. Then, if we had 3 sprints per month, a collaborator should be allocated to this task over 6 days (8 h/day) to each new version.

At each new sprint, all the guide items were executed, starting from the first step; while the own guide was also reviewed or updated along with each sprint. This ensures a current and future process free of failures. If any error was identified, all the process was again started from the initial configuration. Thus, the final deployment could spend much more than 16 h.

3.3 Infrastructure as Code Implementation

The infrastructure as code to support the deployment was implemented in our organization as a form to avoid the limitations of the previous manual approach (Sect. 3.2). Furthermore, this approach allows that solutions can be deployed in any environment without the expertise required by the manual approach.

Our strategy is based on the PowerShell DSC (Desired State Configuration), which is a script language that enables the definition of a set of deployment actions. Our experiments showed that several of the previous deployment actions could be automated with this language, such as: (1) install or remove server roles and features; (2) manage registry settings; (3) manage files and directories; (4) start, stop, and manage processes and services; (5) manage local groups and user accounts; (6) install and manage packages such as .msi and .exe; (7) manage environment variables; (8) fix a configuration that has drifted away from the desired state; and (8) discover the actual configuration state on a given node. Furthermore, DSC is a platform build into Windows, so that it is a natural choice for development projects in such platform.

The use of PowerShell DSC involved three phases in our experiments. In the first phase (authoring phase), the DSC configuration was created by means of the PowerShell Integrated Scripting Environment (ISE), which is an authoring tool for DSC configurations. These configurations are translated to one or more MOF files, which contain the necessary information for the configuration of the nodes. MOF (Managed Object Format) is a schema description language used for specifying the interface of managed resources, such as storage, networking, etc.). Thus, they are basically made up of a series of class and instance declarations. A MOF file used in the *Xsolution* deployment, for example, accounts for the configuration of roles and service roles during the installation of the Web application requirements (step 3 discussed in Sect. 3.2). A server role is a set of software programs that, when installed and properly configured, allows a computer to perform a specific function for multiple users or other computers within a network.

Role services are software programs that provide the functionality of a role. In a manual way, the deployment team must access several configuration pages and check a set of options indicated by the manual. Differently, the use of MOF scripts is simple and powerful at the same time since we do not need to indicate any path for the system variables. The own DSC framework already identifies such variables and set them. This process is completely transparent to human operators. However, this configuration was simple because the DSC framework has the "WindowsFeature" as one of its 12 built-in configuration resources. In order, a DSC resource is a Windows PowerShell module, which contains both the schema (the definition of the configurable properties) and the implementation (the code that does the actual work specified by a configuration) for the resource. A DSC resource schema can be defined in a MOF file, and the implementation is performed by a script module. Other examples of built-in resources that were used in our study are:

- DSC File Resource: provides a mechanism to manage files and folders on the target node;
- DSC Package Resource: provides a mechanism to install or uninstall packages, such as Windows Installer and setup.exe packages, on a target node;
- DSC Service Resource: provides a mechanism to manage services on the target node.

The use of the infrastructure as code had a huge impact in our deployment efficiency. The deployment time for each release was decreased to 30 min. Thus, if we had 3 sprints per month, just 90 min will be spent in this process for each new version. Furthermore, all the process is automatic, so that it can be quickly executed from the beginning and the deployment team abandoned both the use of the guide (Sect. 3.2) and its update. Modifications are now carried out in the own scripts and maintained by version control programs.

3.4 Lessons Learned

Some lessons were learned along this first case study with DSC and some of them support previous finds from the literature. DSC enables IT teams in deploying several times their configuration without risks of breaking the infrastructure. Thus, DSC supports the DevOps principle of continuous deployment. We observed two important DSC features that optimize this process of continuous deployment:

- Only settings that do not match will be modified when the configuration is applied. The remainder configurations are skipped so that we obtain a faster deployment time;
- The definition of the configuration data and configuration logic are separated and well-defined. This strategy supports the reuse of configuration data for different resources, nodes and configurations.

A useful DSC strategy is to record errors and events in logs that can be viewed in the Event Viewer application. This function was important mainly at initial phases of the development since the composition of configuration scripts was challenging for members of our team. Thus, the use of logs has facilitated the identification and solving of issues.

DSC provides a declarative syntax to express configurations for infrastructure and information systems. This DSC feature accounts for creating a transparent process, where the IT team do not necessarily have to know how DSC will provide a specific feature or software installation because the declarative syntax is similar to an INI type expression, specifying what should be present on the node, as discussed in [22].

DSC has two modes of operation: push and pull. The pull mode has its scalability as the primary advantage and it seems to be the most used DSC mode. In fact, a single pull server can provide DSC configurations to many connected nodes with the additional benefit of specifying how often the LCM (Local Configuration Manager) on each node should check back with the pull server enforcing a configuration. However, as our task is focused on deployment, whose configuration is applied once for a long period, the push mode was chosen since we do not need periodic configuration checks. Furthermore, the push mode is more appropriate when environments have high security restrictions.

Finally, we used the ability of DSC to create new resources for configurations that are not provided as a built-in resource. This process was straightforward and the resultant resources could be reused in several parts of the deployment script. Thus, this feature was very useful to a complete automation of our deployment process and we also contributed to the open source DSC official repository, which is maintained by Microsoft.

4   The Docker Extension: Case Study 2

4.1   Initial Setup

The previous case study was based on an infrastructure that uses virtualization. However, the aspects of a containerization technology, such as Docker, must be considered as an additional way to facilitate continuous delivery. Containers provide a mechanism for logical packaging in which applications could be abstracted from the environment in which they actually run.

The principal motivation to use containerization in our environment was to enable applications to be easily and consistently deployed, regardless of the type of host (e.g. physical machines, virtual machines, private or public clouds). These hosts become in fact predictable environments, which maintain a default configuration pattern, which we call *stage for dev*. Using containers together with our strategy to Infrastructure as Code, we could go beyond the process of software delivery. In order, rather than delivering the software together with a script to configure the infrastructure, we can instantiate a container, configure the infrastructure in this instance and then delivering a container with the software and its infrastructure ready in terms of configuration. In this way, we could save resources, facilitate the delivery management, provide scalability and portability. In brief, the next definitions of Docker are used in our work:

- Images: a template, sometimes also called recipe, which is used to create containers. An important part of these images is composed of a set of steps that account for installing and running a particular software;
- Containers: they are created from the instructions defined within the source image. Containers act like a compact virtual machine regarding their applications and they share the operating system;
- Client: a client is the interface of the Docker API, which is used to access the Docker daemon. The implementation of a daemon only makes sense if it is going to run in a different machine than the client;
- Host: this component is represented by a physical or virtual machine, where the daemon is running, and contains cached images as well as runnable containers created from images.

Docker follows a client-server architecture, which uses a remote API to create containers based on Docker images. Containers and images have a similar relationship than objects and classes of the object-oriented programming. Thus, we defined our templates (images) to be later instantiated in several containers. The images of our project are used to create four containers:

- Gateway container: contains the gateway module, which is based on a functionality called *Reverse proxy*;
- Web container: contains the web, web_backend, site and helper modules;
- MobileBackend container: contains the mobile_backend module;
- SQL container: contains the database module.

While these containers support the main idea of portability, its integration in our DSC based approach enables that their configuration can also evolve together with the needs of the applications in development. Next section describes the workflow of a traditional Docker application and how/where our approach works in this workflow.

4.2 Workflow

The typical Docker workflow allows creating images, pulling images, publishing images, and running containers. The next schema (Fig. 2) illustrates these actions.

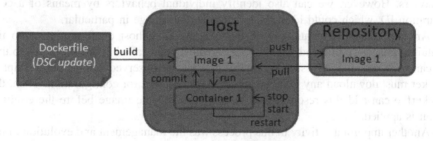

Fig. 2. Schema of the Docker workflow.

This schema shows that images are built from Dockerfiles, which in our approach will be evolved by means of DSC updates. These files have the instructions regarding the configuration of containers. Furthermore, Dockerfiles may also contain instructions on how to pull an image from Docker repositories. After the creation of an image in the host environment, we can run such image to create the containers, which are in fact an isolated runtime environment with applications and other configurations that are specified in the image. In our case, we have three images: Dockerfile_Iis (Xsolu-tionWeb and XsolutionBackend containers), Dockerfile_IisHttps (XsolutionGatway container) and Dockerfile_Database (XsolutionSQL). These containers can be started and stopped and restarted similarly to virtual machines. A container can be committed to making a new image that can be later used to create containers from it. This must be indicated in its configuration. In our case, for example, after the start of a general container, the DSC PowerShell script is executed in each container and these four images can be generated. New images can also be pulled from repositories, while our images can also be pushed to such repositories. This is a possible strategy to share and reuse images already specified by the own team, or other teams around the world when these repositories are global.

4.3   The Docker and PowerShell DSC Integration

As illustrated in the previous schema (Fig. 2), the Dockerfile represents the main form to build Docker images by means of commands for installing and configuring the environment. Together with such files, other files located in the same directory could be incorporated as part of this build process. Our project extension was focused on how DSC scripts could be used to automate the evolution of containers that are created from Dockerfiles. In this scenario, the scripts could be evolved by the own development team, together with the application code and its needs.

The next execution sequence is used in our project to promote this extension. First, the Dockerfile is edited, acting as a template to define a Docker image. Then, this image is instantiated to create one or more containers. Each container has a LCM, which is the DSC engine that runs on every host and accounts for parsing and enacting configurations that are sent to such host. In other words, the LCM executes DSC scripts. The configurable feature of LCM, by means of a meta-configuration, is fundamental in this process. We observed that several options for configuration are related to global behaviors. However, we can also identify individual behaviors by means of a configuration ID, which could identify, for example, an image in particular.

An important investigation is on the integration of host configurations into the container image. To that end, the *Dsc-Service* must be installed in the Windows so that we can work with the DSC strategy. In this process, we observed that the build script of Docker must download any DSC resource that is required for configuration. Then, the Dockerfile can add this resource and its directories to the image before the configuration is applied.

Another important activity in this process was the management and evolution of the meta-configuration. A possible approach to this management is to divide the meta-configuration into two parts. The first part accounts for building the image. The second part is more related to the instantiation of this image, or the creation of containers. To that end, the Dockerfile must contain the reference to a script that applies the static configuration to the LCM. After that, other commands can be used to instantiate the containers based on an image.

4.4   Discussion

Using Docker containers together with our DSC-based approach for configuration, we have tested with success our infrastructure on different types of hosts such as Windows Server 2012 and Windows Server 2016. This means, even with different hosts features, the containers were able to create a unique *stage for dev* that was used by all individuals involved in the development/deployment of the applications.

Along the process, our developers needed to integrate their codes in a branch to try their execution, which usually raised several problems related to the versions of APIs of service and outdated databases. Furthermore, the entire environment needed to be replicated to avoid problems with services or application instances that were offered to other developers.

The team also had problems, before the *stage for dev*, regarding the identification of the right moment to delegate the maintenance of the code related to the infrastructure (infra-code) to the development team. This problem appeared when the DevOps team had an infrastructure script almost concluded, but the evolution of the *Xsolution* was still generating new modifications in this script configuration. In order, when the dev team was evolving the *Xsolution* code in a specific sprint, this used to generate a demand for the infrastructure evolution, which was carried out by the operation team. However, this infrastructure evolution should finish before the next development sprint, so that they could use a complete and functional infra-code. After the conclusion of the *stage of dev*, which integrated the Docker containers with DSC, the concept of Infrastructure as Code was included in the process of development and this team could evolve both the application code and the infrastructure together.

The main restrictions of our experiment were related to aspects of security. These restrictions had a significant impact on the development of our solution. The main examples were:

- No application server could have access to the Internet;
- The communication between the machines should be carried out via just one port (port 80) and no further ports could be liberated;
- No network shared directory could be created;
- We should consider that all machines only had the operating system installed. From this scenario, any required modification should be exclusively carried out by the deployment scripts.

Due to these restrictions, libraries (e.g. non-native PowerShell resources) or embedded tools (e.g. Java Runtime Environment or the URL module for IIS) needed to be sent together with the deployment package. Furthermore, we also concluded that the push mode to deployment is more appropriate to very restrictive environments. In fact, the pull model requires the use of a server that is responsible for providing the configurations (MOF files), or the creation of a shared network directory to maintain these files. Thus, due to our restrictions regarding security, we could not implement any of these approaches.

An important lesson learned was to realize that the bakery model [32] was the correct choice to manage the containers. According to [32], "*A bakery is a form of infrastructure entity that embodies the process of acquiring, building and releasing machine images to allow repeatable deployments of working code. The output of a bakery is a baked image that is used to spin off instances of machines (VMs or containers) in any compatible infrastructure. The compatible infrastructure represents the required environment in the form of hypervisors or container engines that support the deployment of these baked images*". Thus, the bakery output, which is represented by baked images, is compatible with several types of infrastructures. This feature reduces the need for seamlessly tailored images built for each type of infrastructure.

In our project, we used the bakery strategy to deliver the "ingredients and the recipe" rather than delivering the image already ready to use. This means, we deliver a Dockerfile, which comes from the official Microsoft image (microsoft/iis), and then we execute the DSC script. The main reason to use this strategy is the size of the final image, which is around 11 GB.

5   The Current State of PowerShell DSC and Docker

The Windows Server 2016 was the first version in this platform to natively offer support to Docker. However, PowerShell DSC and Docker use to be discussed in the opposite site when the Infrastructure as Code is considered. According to Stoneman [33], DSC works with scripts which declaratively specify the final state of a host. This specification is modular and contains different types of components in different packages, which can be obtained from the Microsoft and related community. Thus, using PowerShell DSC we can write a single script to define the state of a particular type of machine. According to its use, DSC is employed for one-time configuration or configurations that periodically verify if hosts are still correctly set up. Thus, when virtual machines have their correct state modified, scripts can automatically return this state to the correct one.

The idea of Docker is to maintain the host as light as possible. To that end, the main strategy is to install the base OS and Docker tools so that they support the operationalization of applications inside Docker containers on the host. Initially, Docker was developed to use Linux features that provide ways to isolate processes running on its core. Thus, containers could share the same kernel with other Linux processes, avoiding complex strategies (e.g. hypervisor) to separate the containers applications from the host's computer resources.

To follow this Linux strategy, Windows Server 2016 introduced containers as a new layer of virtualization, whose aim was to create a compatible management layer based on Docker. Two initial ideas of containers are *Windows* and *Hyper-V* Containers, whose primary interface managements were implemented in PowerShell. However, according to Dille [34], although this interface module was implemented in the PowerShell way, it did not relate to the management concepts of Docker. New releases of this approach show that the trend is to have Docker as the primary management tool while the PowerShell module for containers should be redesigned and adapted to this situation. This is still an ongoing process, but as described in the experiences of Dille [34], *"After investing a few hours of testing and playing around with Dockerfiles as well as the build and push commands, I am amazed by the current state of the implementation of containers on Windows. Microsoft has managed to bring the management experience of Docker on Linux to Windows Server. This will make containers on Windows Server part of a huge community"*.

6 Conclusion

This work provides an initial analysis on the use and advantages of applying an infrastructure as code strategy for deployment, based on the PowerShell DSC and its integration with Docker. In fact, specialized forums and the software engineering community comment on this lack. We could find comments such as *"I've never seen anyone with a robust production environment using DSC exclusively yet, however there are plenty of examples of Puppet/Chef environments"*. Furthermore, PowerShell DSC and Docker are technologies that are separately discussed. While PowerShell DSC is presented as great for automating the setup of complex components; Docker is showed as great for building small, lean components. Thus, this paper is an initial academic contribution to show in practice as these two technologies could work together since most of the information presented on this subject is from different blogs and sites of the Internet.

Our analysis with PowerShell DSC and Docker was based on a case study, which used a real market application as an object. The quantitative analysis of the efficiency of the approaches shows that the use of these technologies offers the appropriate resources to the automation of the deployment process. Our future researches intend to carry out a better quantitative analysis (e.g. development time) since the infrastructure as code is in fact being implemented in our organization. Thus, several quantitative and qualitative data is going to be generated regarding the real advantages of this deployment approach.

References

1. Humble, J., Farley, D.: Continuous delivery: reliable software releases through build, test, and deployment automation. Addison-Wesley Professional, Boston (2010)
2. Claps, G.G., Svensson, R.B., Aurum, A.: On the journey to continuous deployment: technical and social challenges along the way. Inf. Softw. Technol. 57(1), 21–31 (2015)
3. Loukides, M.: What is DevOps? Infrastructure as Code. O'Reilly Media, Sebastopol (2012)
4. Lwakatare, L.E., Kuvaja, P., Oivo, M.: Dimensions of DevOps. In: Lassenius, C., Dingsøyr, T., Paasivaara, M. (eds.) XP 2015. LNBIP, vol. 212, pp. 212–217. Springer, Cham (2015). https://doi.org/10.1007/978-3-319-18612-2_19
5. Hosono, S.: A DevOps framework to shorten delivery time for cloud applications. Int. J. Comput. Sci. Eng. 7(4), 329–344 (2012)
6. Erich, F., Amrit, C., Daneva, M.: Report: Devops literature review. University of Twente, Technical report (2014)
7. Dyck, A., Penners, R., Lichter, H.: Towards definitions for release engineering and DevOps. In: Proceedings of the IEEE/ACM 3rd International Workshop on Release Engineering (2015)
8. Siebra, C. et al.: From theory to practice: the challenges of a DevOps infrastructure as code implementation. In: Proceedings of the 13th International Conference on Software Technologies (ICSOFT) (2018)

9. Punjabi, R., Bajaj, R.: User stories to user reality: a DevOps approach for the cloud. In: IEEE International Conference on Recent Trends in Electronics, Information & Communication Technology (RTEICT), Bangalore, pp. 658–662 (2016)
10. Miell, I., Sayers, A.H.: Docker in Practice. Manning Publications Co., New York (2016)
11. Bang, S.K., Chung, S., Choh, Y., Dupuis, M.: A grounded theory analysis of modern Web applications: knowledge, skills, and abilities for DevOps. In: Proceedings of the 2nd Annual Conference on Research in Information Technology (RIIT 2013), pp. 61–62. ACM, New York (2013)
12. DeGrandis, D.: Devops: so you say you want a revolution? Cutter Bus. Technol. J. **24**(8), 34–39 (2011)
13. Wettinger, J., Breitenbücher, U., Leymann, F.: Devopslang – bridging the gap between development and operations. In: Villari, M., Zimmermann, W., Lau, K.-K. (eds.) ESOCC 2014. LNCS, vol. 8745, pp. 108–122. Springer, Heidelberg (2014). https://doi.org/10.1007/978-3-662-44879-3_8
14. Tessem, B., Iden, J.: Cooperation between developers and operations in software engineering projects. In: Proceedings of the 2008 International Workshop on Cooperative and Human Aspects of Software Engineering, pp. 105–108 (2008)
15. Walls, M.: Building a DevOps Culture. O'Reilly Media, Sebastopol (2013)
16. Liu, Y., Li, C., Liu, W.: Integrated solution for timely delivery of customer change requests: a case study of using devops approach. Int. J. U- E-Serv. Sci. Technol. **7**, 41–50 (2014)
17. Shang, W.: Bridging the divide between software developers and operators using logs. In: Proceedings of the 34th International Conference on Software Engineering, pp. 1583–1586. IEEE Press, New York (2012)
18. Bruneo, D., et al.: Cloudwave: where adaptive cloud management meets DevOps. In: Proceedings of the IEEE Symposium on Computers and Communications, pp. 1–6. IEEE Press, New York (2014)
19. Ebert, C., Gallardo, G., Hernantes, J., Serrano, N.: DevOps. IEEE Softw. **33**(3), 94–100 (2016)
20. Duvall, M.P.: Continuous Delivery Patterns and AntiPatterns in the Software LifeCycle (2011)
21. Younge, A.J., et al.: Analysis of virtualization technologies for high performance computing environments. In: IEEE International Conference on Cloud Computing, pp. 9–16 (2011)
22. O'Connor, R., Elger, P., Clarke, P.: Continuous software engineering – a microservices architecture perspective. J. Softw. Evol. Process **29**(11), e1866 (2017)
23. Scheepers, M.J.: Virtualization and containerization of application infrastructure: a comparison. In: Proceedings of the 21st Twente Student Conference on IT, pp. 1–7 (2014)
24. Peacock, M.: Creating Development Environments with Vagrant. Packt Publishing Ltd., Birmingham (2015)
25. Hüttermann, M.: Infrastructure as Code. In: DevOps for Developers. Apress, Berkeley (2012)
26. Hummer, W., Rosenberg, F., Oliveira, F., Eilam, T.: Testing idempotence for infrastructure as code. In: Eyers, D., Schwan, K. (eds.) Middleware 2013. LNCS, vol. 8275, pp. 368–388. Springer, Heidelberg (2013). https://doi.org/10.1007/978-3-642-45065-5_19
27. Artac, M., Borovssak, T., Di Nitto, E., Guerriero, M., Tamburri, D.: Devops: introducing infrastructure-as-code. In: Proceedings of the 39th IEEE International Conference on Software Engineering Companion, pp. 497–498 (2017)

28. Zhu, L., Xu, D., Xu, X., Tran, A.B., Weber, I., Bass, L.: Challenges in practicing high frequency releases in cloud environments. In: Proceedings of the 2nd International Workshop on Release Engineering, Mountain View, USA, pp. 21–24 (2014)
29. Scheuner, J., Leitner, P., Cito, J., Gall, H.: Cloud work bench–infrastructure-as-code based cloud benchmarking. In: Proceedings of the IEEE 6th International Conference on Cloud Computing Technology and Science (CloudCom), pp. 246–253 (2014)
30. Spinellis, D.: Don't install software by hand. IEEE Softw. **29**(4), 86–87 (2012)
31. Tomasevicius Filho, E.: Marco Civil da Internet: uma lei sem conteúdo normativo. Estudos Avançados **30**(86), 269–285 (2016). (in Portuguese)
32. Juneja, V.: The Bakery Model for Building Container Images and Microservices. TheNewStack   (2016).   https://thenewstack.io/bakery-foundation-container-images-microservices. Accessed 20 Oct 2018
33. Eagles, H.: DevOps Technology in a Windows World (2016). https://blogs.technet.microsoft.com/uktechnet/2016/05/24/devops-technology-in-a-windows-world/. Accessed 28 Sept 2018
34. Dille, N.: Build, Ship, Run Containers on Windows Server 2016 TP5 with Docker. Automation, DevOps and Containerization (2016). https://dille.name/blog/2016/06/08/build-ship-run-containers-with-windows-server-2016-tp5/. Accessed 22 Oct 2018

Can Commit Change History Reveal Potential Fault Prone Classes? A Study on GitHub Repositories

Chun Yong Chong[1](✉) [ID] and Sai Peck Lee[2] [ID]

[1] School of Information Technology, Monash University Malaysia,
Jalan Lagoon Selatan, 47500 Bandar Sunway, Malaysia
chong.chunyong@monash.edu
[2] Department of Software Engineering,
Faculty of Computer Science and Information Technology,
University of Malaya, 50603 Kuala Lumpur, Malaysia

Abstract. Various studies had successfully utilized graph theory analysis as a way to gain a high-level abstraction view of the software systems, such as constructing the call graph to visualize the dependencies among software components. The level of granularity and information shown by the graph usually depends on the input such as variable, method, class, package, or combination of multiple levels. However, there are very limited studies that investigated how software evolution and change history can be used as a basis to model software-based complex network. It is a common understanding that stable and well-designed source code will have less update throughout a software development lifecycle. It is only those code that were badly design tend to get updated due to broken dependencies, high coupling, or dependencies with other classes. This paper put forward an approach to model a commit change-based weighted complex network based on historical software change and evolution data captured from GitHub repositories with the aim to identify potential fault prone classes. Four well-established graph centrality metrics were used as a proxy metric to discover fault prone classes. Experiments on ten open-source projects discovered that when all centrality metrics are used together, it can yield reasonably good precision when compared against the ground truth.

Keywords: Software fault identification · Software change coupling ·
Commit change data · Mining software repositories · Complex network

1 Introduction

In recent years, research in software engineering in the aspect of representing software systems using complex networks has started to emerge with the aim to gain a high-level abstraction view of the analysed software systems [1, 2]. Representing software systems using complex networks allows software maintainers to gain more insights on the studied software by discovering unique or recurring structural patterns, detecting abnormalities and outliers, or even predicting future evolution trends [3]. For instance, the work by Zimmermann and Nagappan [4] has shown that it is possible to predict

© Springer Nature Switzerland AG 2019
M. van Sinderen and L. A. Maciaszek (Eds.): ICSOFT 2018, CCIS 1077, pp. 266–281, 2019.
https://doi.org/10.1007/978-3-030-29157-0_12

software defects using graph theory metrics to reveal some extra-deterministic information of the software that are otherwise hidden from software maintainers, such as fault prone software components.

However, the ways to represent software-based complex networks are generally not standardized across multiple studies due to the fact that different studies might be addressing some specific issues at different levels of granularity, i.e. package level [5], class level [6, 7], or code level [8]. While most of the existing studies focus on utilizing source code as the main source of information to form a software-based complex network, there is a lack of studies that attempt to harness the data and metadata that are available on source code management systems (SCMS).

Software engineering and big data researchers have been drawn into using SCMS such as GitHub due to its integrated social features and the metadata that can be accessed through its API [9]. Much research including qualitative and quantitative studies have been conducted on GitHub. In qualitative studies, the research focus on analyzing software developers' behavior, in an attempt to identify the traits and characteristics of software developers in successful software development [10]. On the other hand, quantitative studies focus on using commit change data to understand the evolution of a software, and to construct software bug predictors to facilitate its maintenance in the GitHub environment [11]. Due to the vast amount of data available for projects hosted on GitHub, it is easy to retrieve commit change related information of a particular software. Various studies have found the frequency of software change, especially pre or post-release, is positively correlated to its fault proneness [12]. Hence, by studying the commit change requests in GitHub, researchers are able to discover and study recurring patterns of fault prone software components.

However, based on our knowledge through literature review, there is no study that attempts to fully exploit the commit change data mined from SCMS by creating a commit change-based complex network to reveal the co-change behavior of software components from a graph theory point-of-view. We argue that a complex network modelled based on the commit change data of software systems can aid in the identification of bug prone components by applying relevant graph theory metrics. Graph theory metrics such as degree centrality, closeness centrality, and clustering coefficient had been proven to be correlated to the quality of software systems [6]. Hence, applying this set of well-established graph theory metrics on the proposed commit change-based complex network can reveal bug or fault prone classes and other inter-dependent classes that are strongly related to the faulty class, i.e. when ClassA is changed, there is a high probability that ClassB will need to be changed as well.

This paper is an extension of our previous work [13]. In our previous work, we only focus on using community detection techniques to reveal potential fault prone classes, and use another proxy metric, namely change burst metric proposed by [12] as a benchmark. In this extended work, we propose a new way to utilize historical software change and evolution data as an input to model a commit change-based weighted complex network. Through the application of well-established graph centrality metrics, potential fault prone classes are identified. We then construct our own ground truth by parsing the issue tracker report of each test subjects to see if the identified classes are indeed being recognized as faulty by the users or developers of the project. In this way, it creates a more reliable benchmark to evaluate the accuracy of our proposed approach on ten open source projects hosted on GitHub. Experiments show that there is no single graph theory metric that perform consistency better than others. Instead, when all metrics are used together, the proposed method achieve reasonably good precision. This paper is organized as follows: Sect. 2 discusses the background and related works in utilizing complex network analysis to study the structure of software, as well as works on change coupling metrics to identify potential fault prone software components. Section 3 presents the proposed approach to model a commit change-based weighted complex network. Section 4 presents the experimental design, along with the execution of the experiment. Section 5 gives an overall discussion based on the results obtained in the previous section, followed by concluding remarks and potential future work.

2 Related Works

There are several features in graph theory that can be used to analyze the structure and behavior of software systems. Recent studies of representing objected-oriented software systems as complex networks revealed that many of them share some global and fundamental topological properties such as scale free and small world [14–18]. The scale free characteristic in software systems can be interpreted as the level of reuse of important classes, or the number of dependencies between classes, while software-based networks that exhibit small world property signify that the cohesion strength among software components are strong from a graph theory's point of view. Thus, complex networks and graph theory analysis are excellent in evaluating the impact of a particular class with respect to the whole system.

Before applying graph theory metrics onto a software system to be analyzed, one must construct its complex network in advance. An object-oriented software is typically composed of multiple classes. At the source code level, classes in object-oriented software may contain data structures, objects, methods, and variables. Two classes can be considered related if there are actions such as passing of messages. Due to multiple ways of representing nodes and edges, there is a need to perform an in-depth review on existing works that model software systems using complex networks.

2.1 Modelling Software-Based Complex Network

The work by Myers [8] proposed a method to model software systems using complex network by analyzing the interdependencies of source code. A software collaboration graph based on the calling of methods by one another is used to analyze the structure and complexity of software systems. The work by Myers is later extended in the work by LaBelle et al. [19] and Hyland-Wood et al. [5] to include the usage of classes and packages.

On the other hand, the work by Oyetoyan et al. [20] proposed an approach to investigate the relationship between cyclic dependencies and software maintainability. Cyclic dependency graphs are used in this work, where classes are represented as nodes and relationships between classes are represented as edges. The authors examined the change frequency of software components in multiple releases and identified if the classes involved in circular dependencies are more prone to changes. Based on their finding, the authors discovered that circular dependencies are positively correlated to change frequency, and it will adversely affect the maintainability of software systems.

The work by Valverde and Solé [21] discussed the usage of two graphs, namely Class Graph and Class-Method Graph, to analyze the global structure of software systems. Class Graph is derived based on UML class diagrams, where classes are represented as nodes, while relationships among classes, such as dependency and association, are depicted as edges between nodes. Class-Method Graph is modeled based on source code using the similar concept. For both types of graphs, the complexity of nodes and edges is ignored mainly because the authors assumed that internal complexities do not change the global structure of a software.

On the other hand, the work by Zhang et al. [22] proposed to construct a software-based network to analyze the modularity of the examined software. The authors use dynamic execution traces of software to construct a dynamic software network model and attempt to identify the most important node by evaluating the community structure of the software-based network. The experiment results show that the proposed method is reliable and competent enough to software developers to identify refactoring opportunities.

Based on these studies, it is obvious that there are various ways to represent software-based complex network mainly because different studies are addressing different issues at varying levels of granularity. Since the focus of this paper is to identify bug or fault prone software components, information related to the evolution of software components such as change history can be useful to model a software-based complex network. It is widely acknowledged that software components constantly undergoing changes are more likely to be fault prone due to their unstable structure. Hence, by studying the commit change in SCMSs such as GitHub, one can attempt to discover and learn recurring patterns of bug or fault prone software components.

2.2 Change Metric to Identify Bug or Fault Prone Software Components

Studies have found that apart from using popular source code metrics in software bug prediction, change metrics are equally good, if not better, in identifying bug or fault prone software components when compared to code metrics [12, 23, 24]. Change coupling, which is one of the most widely used change metrics, was defined in [25] as the situation associated with recurrent co-changes of software components found in the software evolution or change history. In other words, change coupling between any two classes is measured by observing their co-change or co-evolve patterns over a period of development history [26, 27]. According to the work by Zimmermann et al. [28], the authors treat change coupling as association rules. The association rule defines that if given a situation where when class A is changed, class B is also changed in response to that action, that will result in the association rule of $A \Rightarrow B$.

Various research studies were conducted to analyze the relationships between all the software components, evolution patterns, and relevant information mined from SCMSs such as GitHub and Subversion [29, 30] in order to capture the co-changing behavior. Experimental results had shown that by studying co-change patterns among software components, developers can actually identify hidden dependencies that are not revealed by traditional static code metrics and it can be used to form the basis of bug prediction model [28, 31, 32].

Meanwhile, Nagappan et al. [12] proposed a new code change metric, called the change burst metric, which is capable of accurately predicting fault prone software components in software projects with high frequency of changes. The authors define change burst as a sequence of consecutive changes in a fixed interval of time, i.e. pre-release or post-release of a major software version. If the amount of change burst is relatively high on a piece of code, it could indicate that the code is not tested or designed properly, causing developers to issue emergency post-release patch to fix the issue. With precision and recall exceeding 90% when tested on Windows Vista, the authors have shown that code change metrics can outperform conventional source code metrics for predicting defects in large-scale commercial software.

The work by Guerrouj et al. [33] investigate how lexical smells are correlated to change proneness and fault proneness of three open-source software projects. Lexical smells is defined as recurring poor practices in the naming, documentation, and choice of identifiers during the implementation of software artifacts [34]. The authors attempt to validate their finding by cross-checking if the artifacts with lexical smells were also mentioned in the change logs in the BugZilla or JIRA issue tracking systems of the inspected software. Experiments show that classes with high design and lexical smells tend to change more frequently and is strongly correlated to fault proneness.

Based on the discussed literature, utilizing data mined from software repositories can be a promising way to study the inherent complexity and co-change behavior of software systems. In this paper, an approach to model a commit change-based weighted complex network is proposed. The proposed commit change-based network is capable of revealing extra-deterministic information about the fault proneness of software components with the aid of graph theory metrics such as degree centrality and betweenness centrality. After applying relevant graph metrics, one can identify the important nodes in the network, or in this context, classes that change frequently (due to the fact that the network is modelled based on commit change data of software components) throughout a fixed period of software development lifecycle. The information derived from graph theory analysis can be used to supplement the raw commit change data mined from SCMS to aid in identifying bug-prone software components. The contribution of this paper can be summarized as follows:

1. A novel way to model a commit change-based weighted complex network
2. A way to identify classes that change frequently in order to reveal potential bug prone classes, based on the modelled commit change-based weighted complex network.
3. Evaluation of the proposed approach using ten open-source projects archived in GitHub repositories.

3   Proposed Approach

A complex network, $G = (V, E)$, is made up of a set of nodes V, and a set of edges $E \subseteq V \times V$ that connect pairs of nodes. In general, a complex network can either directed or undirected. In both directed and undirected networks, edges may be associated with weights to denote the similarity of a pair of nodes connected by an edge or the cost of traveling through that particular edge. In a directed network

$G = (V, E)$, $(i, j) \in E$ signifies that there is an edge in E that is linking node i to node j where i is the origin and j is the terminus. On the other hand, in an undirected network $G_u = (V, E)$, if $(i, j) \in E$, then edge $(j, i) \in E$ as well because the origin and terminus are not specified in an undirected network.

Both directed and undirected networks can be represented by their own adjacency matrix A. The matrix A is a $|V| \times |V|$ matrix where the rows and columns represent the nodes of the network. In an undirected network, the entry $A_{ij} = 1$, if $(i, j) \in E$; $\forall i, j \in 1, \cdots, |V|$. Value 0 indicates that there is no relationship in between nodes i and j. Meanwhile for a directed network, the value A_{ij} represents the weight associated with edge (i, j). The value of adjacency matrix A is symmetric for an undirected network such that $A_{ij} = A_{ji}$. In a directed network, however, the relation A_{ij} is asymmetrical.

In OO software systems, objects and classes are normally related through different kinds of binary relationships, such as inheritance, composition and dependency. Thus, the notion of associating graph theory to represent large OO software systems and to analyze their properties, be it structural complexity or maintainability, is feasible.

In this paper, an approach to model a commit change-based weighted complex network is proposed. Table 1 illustrates an example where there exist four commit changes over a period of time. For each commit, all the affected files or classes (including add a new line of codes, modify existing code, or removal of code) are listed in the table. For example, in Commit #1120, three classes, namely A.java, B.java, and G.java were affected. Based on the information provided in Table 1, a way to model the associated weighted complex network is proposed. Figure 1 illustrates an example of the proposed approach to create a commit change-based weighted complex network.

Table 1. Example of four commit changes and classes affected by each commit change. Source [13].

	Commit #1120	Commit #1121	Commit #1122	Commit #1123
Affected classes	A.java	A.java	A.java	C.java
	B.java	G.java	H.java	F.java
	G.java	F.java	H.java	

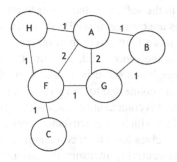

Fig. 1. Example of commit change-based weighted complex network. Source [13].

The proposed approach takes into consideration any kind of changes, including adding one or many lines of code, modifying one or many lines of code, and removing one or many lines of code. Based on the commit change information shown in Table 1, a weighted complex network that resembles the interaction of commit changes among all classes is created. Classes that are affected by the same commit change are linked together with edges, while the frequency of co-changes is used as a basis to calculate the weights of edges. For example, Commit #1120 affects three classes, namely A.java, B.java, and G.java. Hence, edges are created to connect all these three classes affected by the same commit change #1120. As for the frequency of co-changes, Class A.java and G.java were both affected in Commit #1120 and Commit #1121. Hence, a value of 2 is assigned to the edge connecting node A and G.

Once the target software is modelled into its respective weighted complex network, we can then analyze it using graph theory metrics that are correlated to fault proneness of software systems. Before choosing the appropriate metrics, we need to define the characteristics of complex network that are capable of revealing fault proneness of software components.

3.1   Centrality Measures Correlated to Fault Proneness of Software

The work by Zimmermann and Nagappan [4] had shown that graph centrality metrics can be a reliable tool to identify fault prone classes. In general, centrality metrics are used to identify important nodes that exert a certain level of influence on the studied graph. From a commit change-based graph, centrality can help in identifying the pieces of code that are target of numerous co-change dependencies. There are several commonly used centrality metrics.

Degree centrality measure the frequency of co-change between two or more classes. Two classes with high degree centrality indicates that there exist many dependencies in between themselves and they are more fault prone than others [4].

Closeness centrality on the other hand, is calculated as the inverse of the sum of length of the shortest path between the inspected node and all the other nodes in the network. From a commit change graph point-of-view, measuring the closeness centrality of a class can help identify the co-change frequency of all other classes in the software against the inspected class. A class with high closeness centrality indicates that it is central (important) to the software, and closer to all other nodes (high tendency to change when other classes are change as well). Similarly, a class with high closeness centrality indicate that it is more fault prone than others.

Eigenvector centrality on the other hand, measure the influence of a class in the commit change graph. A weightage score is assigned to all the classes based on the assumption that classes that are connected to "important classes" will contribute more to the score. Important classes in this context are classes with high co-change behavior (high degree centrality score). A class with high eigenvector score means that it is connected to many other classes who themselves have high co-change tendencies as well.

Finally, the betweenness centrality measure the amount of shortest path between other classes that pass through the inspected class. Zimmermann and Nagappan had shown that classes with high betweenness centrality are more likely to be faulty due to the higher probability of fault propagation.

Hence, in this work, we had chosen the four centrality metrics, namely degree, closeness, eigenvector, and betweenness as the proxy measure to identify fault prone classes due to evidence from prior research.

We utilize the NetworkX to build the commit change-based complex network and use NetworkX's built-in functions to calculate the centrality score of each node in the network. For all unique classes mined from the commit history, a table is created to show the corresponding centrality score for each classes. Each of these centrality metric sheds light on how important that class is in the repository. All the scores are normalized between the range of zero and one. Using the package matplotlib, each of these metrics are then represented in the form of heat map for each repository. This help in providing a visual aid to spot classes with high centrality score and their commit change-based relationships with other classes. Figure 2 shows an example of visualization for all four centrality score for a python-based open source project, called flask.

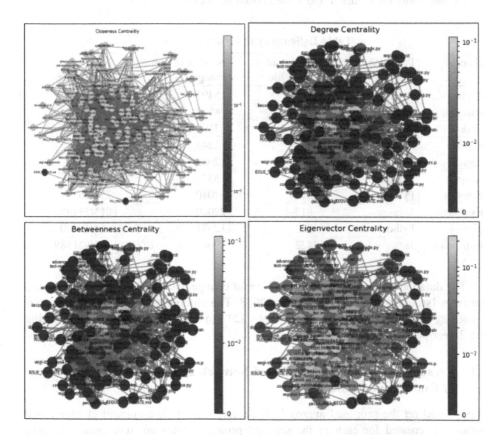

Fig. 2. Heat map for the closeness, degree, betweenness and eigenvector centrality score of project "flask".

4   Experiment Setup

In order to facilitate reproducibility and follow up research, the tool that we used to extract relevant commit change information from GitHub repository is made available to the public [35]. The shell script provides users a way to extract co-change behaviour from any GitHub repository and return the query in a csv format which contains three columns, which are "weight", "source", and "target" respectively. Users can specify the target repository by changing the "repository name" variable. The code also provides a way to specify the range of dates for inspection by modifying the "SINCE" and "UNTIL" variable. The output can be easily exported to NetworkX for further analysis.

Ten open-source software systems written in Java and Python are chosen in this study. The sizes of the software systems vary from 34 to 2422 files to reflect some representative distribution on the population of open-source software systems. Table 2 shows additional information about the chosen projects.

Table 2. Summary of chosen projects.

Name	Programming language	Number of source file	Number of commit changes	Number of nodes/edges
Zappa	Python	34	15491	29/16024
requests	Python	35	4584	30/3378
flask	Python	155	3107	155/1615
tornado	Python	115	2243	110/3791
keras	Python	184	12083	180/8711
scrappy	Python	291	5328	248/2241
ZeroNet	Python	311	7010	234/2059
ExoPlayer	Java	813	22040	813/232358
pipenv	Python	823	12371	464/49440
fastjson	Java	2422	9663	1560/21589

The duration where we captured the commit change data from the selected projects are from 1st January 2016 to 1st January 2018. The number of commit changes varies according to different project, ranging from 2243 to 22040 changes identified during the 2-year period.

4.1   Creation of Commit Change-Based Network and Identification of Fault Prone Classes

Next, based on the proposed approach discussed in Sect. 3, a commit change-based network is created for each of the selected project. Nodes are represented as .java source file (for Java projects) or .py source file (for Python projects), while edges between the nodes are the commit change relationship among those source files. In order to simplify the notion of source file type (.py for Python, .java for Java), we use the term "classes" to refer as the source file for both languages. The commit change-based network is created using NetworkX.

Referring to Table 2, the last column shows the total number of nodes and edges formed in the commit change-based weighted complex network using the proposed approach. The number of commit change for a project does not correlate directly to the number of edges. For instance, it can be observed that during the 2-year inspection period, there were 7010 commit changes on ZeroNet project, but the commit change-based network only contains 2059 edges. This is because there are plenty of commit change that modified the same sets of classes, and there are plenty of commit change that only modified one class. Hence, the number of edges is lesser than the total number of commit changes. On the other hand, there are also cases where the number of edges is more than the number of commit changes, such as the one observed from the ExoPlayer project. From the two-year inspection period, a total of 22040 commit change request were made on ExoPlayer but the total number of edges of the commit change network is recorded as 232358. Upon further inspection, we found that on average at least 8 classes were modified for each commit change request. Hence, the number of edges formed for the commit change-based network is much larger than the total number of commit change requests.

Once the network is created, we utilized the built-in plugin from NetworkX to compute the centrality score for each of the nodes. In order to identify classes that has the highest probability to be fault or error prone, we examine the nodes which have the highest centrality score for each category under degree centrality, betweenness centrality, eigenvector centrality, and closeness centrality. We attempt to experiment using 3 different cut-off points at the 85th percentile, 90th percentile, and 95th percentile. As such, nodes with the highest centrality score at different percentile will be flagged as fault or error prone.

4.2   Identification of Ground Truth

Next, in order to evaluate the accuracy of the proposed approach, we will need to identify the ground truth, i.e. files that are indeed recognized as faulty by the developers or users of the selected projects.

We follow the approach used by Guerrouj et al. [33] to identify the ground truth. First, issue reports from each of the examined projects which are hosted on Github were extracted. Both open and closed issues were extracted. Next, a simple text parser was used to identify the frequency of source file name or classes that were being mentioned in all the published issue reports. For instance, the file flask-handler.py was mentioned in the issue report #2700 in the flask project. Source file or classes that are frequently mentioned in the issue reports are assumed to be faulty and are used as the ground truth in this paper.

We then cross-check to see if source file or classes with high centrality scores (degree, closeness, betweenness, and eigenvector) were also mentioned in the issue report of the inspected software (ground truth). This will allow us to check if the calculated centrality score can be a good proxy measure to identify fault or bug prone classes. The following is the summary of the steps taken to conduct the experiment in this work.

For each project,

1. Download the commit change log from 1st Jan 2016–1st Jan 2018
2. Identify the list of classes modified under each commit change request.
3. Based on the approach proposed in Sect. 3, construct a commit change-based network.
4. Use NetworkX to visualize and calculate the degree, closeness, betweenness, and eigenvector centrality score of each node in the network.
5. Identify the nodes with highest centrality score and flagged them as fault prone classes.
6. Run the text parser to identify files or classes that are frequently mentioned in the issue report and use them as ground truth.
7. Crosscheck the list of identified classes in Step 5 with the ground truth in Step 6 and calculate the precision and recall of the proposed method.

4.3   Experiment Results

As mentioned in Sect. 4.1, in order to capture the list of classes with the highest centrality score, we attempt to experiment using 3 different cut-off points at the 85th percentile, 90th percentile, and 95th percentile.

However, we are unsure if there is one single centrality metrics that can accurately predict fault or bug prone classes. Hence, for each project, we ran the experiments 5 times:

1. Using degree centrality alone to predict fault prone classes
2. Using closeness centrality alone to predict fault prone classes
3. Using betweenness centrality alone to predict fault prone classes
4. Using eigenvector centrality alone to predict fault prone classes
5. Combine four centrality metrics to predict fault prone classes

It is important to note that for each of the five settings mentioned above, we had to run it for 3 times using 3 different cut-off points at 85th, 90th, and 95th percentile. Table 3 shows the experiment results.

To recall, there are a total of 5 different experiment setting for each of the selected project - using four centrality metrics on its own individually, and a mixture of all the metrics. For all 5 different settings, we ran the experiment for 3 times using three percentile cutoff points at 85th percentile, 90th percentile, and 95th percentile. For each cut-off point, the collection of classes or files that falls into the kth percentile will be flagged as fault or bug prone. In order to find out the best performing centrality metric, we do a simple cross-check between the flagged classes against the ground truth (discussed in Sect. 4.2) and calculate the precision and recall.

Precision and recall that score more than 70% are highlighted in Table 3. Looking at each individual repository, the precision of the proposed method varies accordingly to the size of the project. For small project such as Zappa, the precision of the method is relatively high in all 5 different settings. Whereas, other smaller project such as flask and requests also demonstrate similar behavior but the precision of all combined centrality metrics performed at a consistently high level. In general, when the condition to label the classes as faulty or not becomes more stringent, i.e. higher percentile cut-off point, the precision of the proposed approach improve as well. This is an expected behavior at the cost of lower recall value.

For other medium-sized projects (number of files in the range of 100–300), there doesn't seem to have any centrality metrics that stands out in term of precision, except for the combined one: (tornado, 75), (Zero-Net, 75), (scrappy, 80). It is interesting to see that for keras (184 files), there is no single setting that achieve precision of 70% of above. Upon further investigation, we found that keras project has significantly more commit change requests (12083 times) throughout the two-year inspection period when compared to other medium-sized project. With the high commit change request, it also resulted in a commit change-based network that consist of relatively high edge count (8711). It could mean that with large volume of commit change request, the probability of noises (preventive maintenance update) is higher as well, causing the proposed approach to mis-label those files as faulty.

For large-sized projects such as pipenv, ExoPlayer, and fastjson, the accuracy of the proposed approach is even lower. Only pipenv with degree centrality and the combined centrality metrics achieve 75% precision. Once again, we observed that the combined centrality metric recorded higher precision score when compared to each centrality metric on its own.

Table 3. Summary of experiment results.

Project (# of files)		Degree		Closeness		Betweenness		Eigenvector		Combined	
flask (71)	Percentile	Precision	Recall	Precision	Recall	Precision	Recall	Precision	Recall	Precision	Recall
	80th	0.577	0.294	0.56	0.274	0.667	0.314	0.577	0.294	**0.833**	0.196
	90th	0.611	0.216	**0.701**	0.235	0.625	0.196	0.625	0.196	**0.833**	0.098
	95th	**0.875**	0.137	0.667	0.118	**0.75**	0.118	0.625	0.098	1	0.02
requests (35)	Percentile	Precision	Recall	Precision	Recall	Precision	Recall	Precision	Recall	Precision	Recall
	80th	0.231	0.313	0.565	0.271	0.455	0.208	0.8	0.167	**0.75**	0.063
	90th	**0.706**	0.25	**0.733**	0.229	0.6	0.187	0.187	0.187	**0.75**	0.063
	95th	0.667	0.125	0.667	0.125	**0.75**	0.125	**0.875**	0.146	1	0.063
scrappy (291)	Percentile	Precision	Recall	Precision	Recall	Precision	Recall	Precision	Recall	Precision	Recall
	80th	0.318	0.246	0.302	0.228	0.289	0.193	0.342	0.228	0.471	0.140
	90th	0.48	0.211	0.44	0.193	0.36	0.158	0.343	0.211	0.5	0.105
	95th	0.462	0.105	0.385	0.088	0.461	0.105	0.538	0.123	**0.8**	0.070
tornado (115)	Percentile	Precision	Recall	Precision	Recall	Precision	Recall	Precision	Recall	Precision	Recall
	80th	0.591	0.342	0.591	0.342	0.524	0.289	0.619	0.342	**0.75**	0.237
	90th	**0.75**	0.316	0.667	0.316	0.5	0.184	**0.714**	0.263	0.667	0.105
	95th	**0.875**	0.184	**0.857**	0.158	**0.714**	0.132	**0.857**	0.158	0.667	0.053
pipenv (823)	Percentile	Precision	Recall	Precision	Recall	Precision	Recall	Precision	Recall	Precision	Recall
	80th	0.192	0.111	0.2	0.118	0.268	0.192	0.19	0.111	0.192	0.111
	90th	**0.75**	0.044	0.18	0.101	0.268	0.192	0.188	0.198	0.192	0.106
	95th	0.192	0.111	0.23	0.121	0.667	0.118	0.176	0.102	**0.75**	0.044
Zero-Net (311)	Percentile	Precision	Recall	Precision	Recall	Precision	Recall	Precision	Recall	Precision	Recall
	80th	0.364	0.355	0.314	0.244	0.371	0.289	0.343	0.267	0.5	0.111
	90th	0.524	0.244	0.385	0.222	0.417	0.222	0.333	0.2	**0.75**	0.067
	95th	0.583	0.155	0.417	0.111	0.5	0.133	0.333	0.2	0.667	0.044

(*continued*)

Table 3. (*continued*)

Project (# of files)		Degree		Closeness		Betweenness		Eigenvector		Combined	
Zappa (34)	Percentile	Precision	Recall	Precision	Recall	Precision	Recall	Precision	Recall	Precision	Recall
	80th	**0.996**	0.317	**0.996**	0.317	**0.978**	0.172	**0.998**	0.317	**0.993**	0.085
	90th	**0.996**	0.317	**0.987**	0.085	**0.973**	0.101	**0.998**	0.317	**0.993**	0.085
	95th	1	0.075	**0.993**	0.075	**0.973**	0.098	1	0.075	1	0.075
ExoPlayer (813)	Percentile	Precision	Recall	Precision	Recall	Precision	Recall	Precision	Recall	Precision	Recall
	80th	0.133	0.218	0.13	0.218	0.213	0.336	0.126	0.2	0.231	0.136
	90th	0.146	0.154	0.146	0.154	0.25	0.264	0.112	0.118	0.305	0.1
	95th	0.147	0.082	0.172	0.09	0.327	0.173	0.172	0.091	0.533	0.073
keras (184)	Percentile	Precision	Recall	Precision	Recall	Precision	Recall	Precision	Recall	Precision	Recall
	80th	0.297	0.25	0.316	0.273	0.278	0.227	0.278	0.227	0.35	0.159
	90th	0.375	0.204	0.375	0.205	0.25	0.136	0.417	0.227	0.308	0.091
	95th	0.5	0.136	0.462	0.136	0.333	0.091	0.5	0.136	0.5	0.091
fastjson (2422)	Percentile	Precision	Recall	Precision	Recall	Precision	Recall	Precision	Recall	Precision	Recall
	80th	0.106	0.61	0.107	0.61	0.116	0.658	0.106	0.61	0.233	0.585
	90th	0.115	0.488	0.157	0.61	0.147	0.561	0.160	0.61	0.265	0.537
	95th	0.218	0.415	0.269	0.512	0.218	0.415	0.21	0.415	0.424	0.341
Average	Percentile	Precision	Recall	Precision	Recall	Precision	Recall	Precision	Recall	Precision	Recall
	80th	0.381	0.306	0.408	0.289	0.416	0.288	0.438	0.276	0.530	0.182
	90th	0.545	0.244	0.477	0.235	0.439	0.220	0.408	0.253	0.556	0.136
	95th	0.552	0.152	0.512	0.153	0.569	0.151	0.529	0.154	0.734	0.087

We also discovered that the recall rate of the proposed method is very low across all projects and experiment setting. In general, in works related to fault detection, precision of the proposed method is more important than recall because we will always like to strive for less False Positives (mistakenly identify a class as being buggy but in fact they are not) rather than having more False Negatives (missed identifying a class as being not buggy but in fact they are bug or error prone).

To put it in the context of software development and maintenance, getting a False Positive is very costly because if a class is being flagged as being faulty, developers or maintainers will need to diagnose and re-test the flagged component rigorously in order to pinpoint the issue. If it is in fact a false alarm, it will be extremely costly in term of time and monetary value. On the other hand, a False Negative can be less costly if there are already some basic quality assurance in place such as testing, issue tracking, and manual inspection.

We position the proposed approach as an alternative way to help developers to uncover bug prone classes that are otherwise hidden from the developers. Hence, precision is more important in this context. Classes that are obviously bug or error prone will be able to pick up easily by experienced software developers and testers. Hence, we argue that having a low recall is acceptable in this context when compared to having a low precision score.

5 Conclusion and Future Work

While a lot of research were conducted in both software-based network analysis and software change coupling metrics, we found that there is a lack of studies that attempted to combine both approaches to identify potential fault prone software components. In this paper, we have proposed a novel way to model commit change-based weighted complex network based on historical data mined from GitHub. Ten open-source projects were chosen to evaluate our proposed approach. In order to identify potential fault prone classes, we decided to use three well-established graph theory metrics that have been proven to correlate with the structural stability of software components such as the degree centrality, closeness centrality, betweenness centrality, and eigenvector centrality. To validate the accuracy of our proposed approach, create our ground truth (classes that are indeed recognized as faulty by users or developers) by using a simple text parser to capture the name of classes that were mentioned in the published issue report on GitHub. When the chosen centrality metrics were used on its own to identify fault prone classes, the proposed approach achieved mediocre precision and recall. It is when all the chosen metrics were combined and the condition to identify fault prone classes is more stringent (95th percentile), the precision and recall of the proposed approach improved significantly. Although we had achieved reasonably good precision score when combining all centrality metrics, recall is mediocre across all experiment setting. The calculation of precision and recall relies heavily on the issue log (used as ground truth) found in each repository. If the project community is not active in reporting bugs or errors, it might affect the precision of the proposed method.

As part of the future work, we plan to expand the proposed approach by utilizing more graph theory metrics such in order to improve the richness of the graph theory analysis results. With the aid of more graph metrics, we can then experiment the proposed approach on larger-scale open-source or commercial software systems. Besides that, it is also worth investigating if there are any specific centrality metric that is more well-suited to be used to identify fault prone classes on a specific domain of software project.

Acknowledgement. This work was carried out within the framework of the research project FP001-2016 under the Fundamental Research Grant Scheme provided by Ministry of Higher Education, Malaysia.

References

1. Ma, Y.T., He, K.Q., Li, B., Liu, J., Zhou, X.Y.: A hybrid set of complexity metrics for large-scale object-oriented software systems. J. Comput. Sci. Technol. **25**, 1184–1201 (2010)
2. Concas, G., Marchesi, M., Murgia, A., Tonelli, R., Turnu, I.: On the Distribution of Bugs in the Eclipse System. IEEE T Softw. Eng. **37**, 872–877 (2011)
3. Turnu, I., Concas, G., Marchesi, M., Tonelli, R.: The fractal dimension of software networks as a global quality metric. Inform. Sci. **245**, 290–303 (2013)

4. Zimmermann, T., Nagappan, N.: Predicting defects using network analysis on dependency graphs. In: Proceedings of the 30th International Conference on Software Engineering, pp. 531–540. ACM (2008)
5. Hyland-Wood, D., Carrington, D., Kaplan, S.: Scale-free nature of java software package, class and method collaboration graphs. In: Proceedings of the 5th International Symposium on Empirical Software Engineering, Rio de Janeiro, Brasil (2006)
6. Chong, C.Y., Lee, S.P.: Analyzing maintainability and reliability of object-oriented software using weighted complex network. J. Syst. Softw. **110**, 28–53 (2015)
7. Chong, C.Y., Lee, S.P.: Automatic clustering constraints derivation from object-oriented software using weighted complex network with graph theory analysis. J. Syst. Softw. **133**, 28–53 (2017)
8. Myers, C.R.: Software systems as complex networks: structure, function, and evolvability of software collaboration graphs. Phys. Rev. E **68**, 046116 (2003)
9. Kalliamvakou, E., Gousios, G., Blincoe, K., Singer, L., German, D.M., Damian, D.: An in-depth study of the promises and perils of mining GitHub. Empirical Softw. Eng. **21**(5), 2035–2071 (2016)
10. Begel, A., Bosch, J., Storey, M.A.: Social networking meets software development: perspectives from GitHub, MSDN, stack exchange, and TopCoder. Softw. IEEE **30**, 52–66 (2013)
11. Gousios, G., Pinzger, M., Deursen, A.V.: An exploratory study of the pull-based software development model. In: Proceedings of the 36th International Conference on Software Engineering, pp. 345–355. ACM, Hyderabad (2014)
12. Nagappan, N., Zeller, A., Zimmermann, T., Herzig, K., Murphy, B.: Change bursts as defect predictors. In: 2010 IEEE 21st International Symposium on Software Reliability Engineering (ISSRE), pp. 309–318. IEEE (2010)
13. Chong, C.Y., Lee, S.P.: A commit change-based weighted complex network approach to identify potential fault prone classes. In: 13th International Conference on Software Technologies, pp. 471–482 (2018)
14. Potanin, A., Noble, J., Frean, M., Biddle, R.: Scale-free geometry in OO programs. Commun. ACM **48**, 99–103 (2005)
15. Concas, G., Marchesi, M., Pinna, S., Serra, N.: Power-laws in a large object-oriented software system. IEEE Trans. Softw. Eng. **33**, 687–708 (2007)
16. Louridas, P., Spinellis, D., Vlachos, V.: Power laws in software. ACM Trans. Softw. Eng. Methodol. **18**, 1–26 (2008)
17. Pang, T.Y., Maslov, S.: Universal distribution of component frequencies in biological and technological systems. Proc. Nat. Acad. Sci. **110**(15), 6235–6239 (2013)
18. Baxter, G., et al.: Understanding the shape of Java software. In: Sigplan Notices, vol. 41, pp. 397–412 (2006)
19. LaBelle, N., Wallingford, E.: Inter-package dependency networks in open-source software. arXiv preprint arXiv:cs/0411096 (2004)
20. Oyetoyan, T.D., Falleri, J.R., Dietrich, J., Jezek, K.: Circular dependencies and change-proneness: an empirical study. In: 2015 IEEE 22nd International Conference on Software Analysis, Evolution and Reengineering (SANER), pp. 241–250 (2015)
21. Valverde, S., Solé, R.V.: Hierarchical small worlds in software architecture. arXiv preprint arXiv:cond-mat/0307278 (2003)
22. Zhang, B., Huang, G., Zheng, Z., Ren, J., Hu, C.: Approach to mine the modularity of software network based on the most vital nodes. IEEE Access (2018)
23. Muthukumaran, K., Choudhary, A., Murthy, N.L.B.: Mining GitHub for novel change metrics to predict buggy files in software systems. In: 2015 International Conference on Computational Intelligence and Networks, pp. 15–20 (2015)

24. Hassan, A.E.: Predicting faults using the complexity of code changes. In: Proceedings of the 31st International Conference on Software Engineering, pp. 78–88. IEEE Computer Society (2009)
25. Wiese, I.S., Kuroda, R.T., Re, R., Oliva, G.A., Gerosa, M.A.: An empirical study of the relation between strong change coupling and defects using history and social metrics in the apache aries project. In: Damiani, E., Frati, F., Riehle, D., Wasserman, Anthony I. (eds.) OSS 2015. IAICT, vol. 451, pp. 3–12. Springer, Cham (2015). https://doi.org/10.1007/978-3-319-17837-0_1
26. Ambros, M.D., Lanza, M., Robbes, R.: On the relationship between change coupling and software defects. In: 2009 16th Working Conference on Reverse Engineering, pp. 135–144 (2009)
27. Ajienka, N., Capiluppi, A.: Understanding the interplay between the logical and structural coupling of software classes. J. Syst. Softw. **134**, 120–137 (2017)
28. Zimmermann, T., Weisgerber, P., Diehl, S., Zeller, A.: Mining version histories to guide software changes. In: Proceedings of the 26th International Conference on Software Engineering, pp. 563–572. IEEE Computer Society (2004)
29. Kagdi, H., Gethers, M., Poshyvanyk, D.: Integrating conceptual and logical couplings for change impact analysis in software. Empirical Softw. Eng. **18**, 933–969 (2013)
30. Yang, X., Lo, D., Xia, X., Sun, J.: TLEL: a two-layer ensemble learning approach for just-in-time defect prediction. Inf. Softw. Technol. **87**, 206–220 (2017)
31. Xia, X., Lo, D., Pan, S.J., Nagappan, N., Wang, X.: HYDRA: massively compositional model for cross-project defect prediction. IEEE T. Softw. Eng. **42**, 977–998 (2016)
32. Huang, Q., Xia, X., Lo, D.: Supervised vs unsupervised models: a holistic look at effort-aware just-in-time defect prediction. In: 2017 IEEE International Conference on Software Maintenance and Evolution (ICSME), pp. 159–170 (2017)
33. Guerrouj, L., et al.: Investigating the relation between lexical smells and change-and fault-proneness: an empirical study. Softw. Qual. J. **25**, 641–670 (2017)
34. Arnaoudova, V., Di Penta, M., Antoniol, G.: Linguistic antipatterns: what they are and how developers perceive them. Empirical Softw. Eng. **21**, 104–158 (2016)
35. Chong, C.Y.: 01 January 2019. https://github.com/chongchunyong/Commit-Change-based-WCN

An Agent-Based Planning Method for Distributed Task Allocation

Dhouha Ben Noureddine[1,2]($\boxtimes$), Atef Gharbi[1], and Samir Ben Ahmed[2]

[1] LISI, National Institute of Applied Science and Technology, INSAT,
University of Carthage, Tunis, Tunisia
`dhouha.bennoureddine@gmail.com`, `atef.elgharbi@gmail.com`
[2] FST, University of El Manar, Tunis, Tunisia
`samir.benahmed@fst.utm.tn`

Abstract. In multi-agent systems, agents should socially cooperate with their neighboring agents in order to solve task allocation problem in open and dynamic network environments. This paper proposes an agent-based architecture to handle different tasks; in particular, we focus on planning and distributed task allocation. In the proposed approach, each agent uses the fuzzy logic technique to select the alternative plans. We also propose an efficient task allocation algorithm that takes into consideration agent architectures and allows neighboring agents to help to perform a task as well as the indirectly related agents in the system. We illustrate our line of thought with a Benchmark Production System used as a running example in order to explain better our contribution. A set of experiments was conducted to demonstrate the efficiency of our planning approach and the performance of our distributed task allocation method.

Keywords: Multi-agent system · Software architecture ·
Distributed task allocation · Planning · Fuzzy logic

1 Introduction

Nowadays, task allocation in Multi-Agent System (MAS) is a noteworthy research issue. Task allocation problem can be defined as that when an agent has a task which it cannot attain independently, the agent then tries to find other agents which contain the proper resources, and assigns the task or part of the task, to those agents. That's why, they need to be cooperative with their neighboring agents to process tasks and accomplish their objectives. The social cooperation is a crucial challenge in the software engineering fields, especially in the distributed artificial intelligence and MAS [5]. This challenge developed with the progress of the applications, e.g. in wireless ad-hoc networks [6], service-oriented MAS [7], multi-robot system in healthcare facilities [8], file sharing in P2P systems [9], social networks [10], etc. So, cooperation can provide appreciable convenience for these applications by promoting joint goals.

© Springer Nature Switzerland AG 2019
M. van Sinderen and L. A. Maciaszek (Eds.): ICSOFT 2018, CCIS 1077, pp. 282–306, 2019.
https://doi.org/10.1007/978-3-030-29157-0_13

More and more attention has been paid to distributed task allocation approaches. Early researches used centralized approaches (such in [17]) to generate a plan for cooperating all the agents by using a central server able to gather the whole system information. This type of approaches can be a proficient solution in a small network because the central planner has a global view of the whole system and it affects the appropriate tasks to the agents. In such case, communication overhead could be decreased during allocation processes. On the flip side, it also has important disadvantages. First, in some systems, it is hard to have such a central controller. Second, when the central planner is out of order or cracked by some attackers task allocation will endure a major inconvenience in this system.

Other researches pointed out the distributed task allocation approaches (e.g. [15]) as a solution to avoid the risks of deficiencies of the centralized approaches. The distributed task allocation approaches are widely used for interactive MAS, semantic web and grid technologies. However, the decentralized approaches are more scalable and robust but the communication overhead rises.

In this paper, we propose an agent-based architecture to manage tasks and control embedded systems at run-time. We firstly, introduce multi-agent planning in which each agent uses the fuzzy logic technique to select plans. The originality in this approach is that our agents evaluate plans based on their goal achievement satisfaction, which is represented as degrees of membership for each individual agent, their aggregate then represents the satisfaction of the overall goal. Proving that our approach performs better than the central planning processes in other systems. We then propose the distributed task allocation solution which is allowing agents to request help from neighbors, this would be done by allocating tasks to different agents who may be able each, to perform different subsets of those tasks. We use to highlight the performance of our solution using the provision of a benchmarking scenario.

The remainder of this paper is organized as follows. Section 2 provides some current related research in this field. Section 3 introduces the benchmark production system used in our approach. After that, in Sect. 4 a software architecture of MAS will be depicted in detail. Section 5 defines our planning method and demonstrates the simulation and analysis about the quality and performance of our method. Then, a distributed task allocation approach is illustrated as well as its related experiments in Sect. 6. Finally, we discuss and conclude our work in Sect. 7.

2   Related Work

In the literature, the proposed architectures solving the task allocation can be classified into centralized or decentralized. [17] proposed a centralized approach, therefore, they supposed that there is a central planner to allocate tasks to agents. Their main goal was to find a solution with a small team cost and each objective to be allocated to the correct number of various agents. Despite the centralized approaches have the main advantage of computing a global plan dependent on all accessible data, their main drawback, however, is the fact that being a single point of failure.

The decentralized architecture dodges this issue, there is no centralized controller and rather the task allocation process was contributed by all agents. The distributed task allocation approach additionally has the benefit of scalability and robustness. In the multi-agent network, the task allocation remains a complex problem. Many parameters have to be taken into accounts, such as communication protocols, resource sharing, synchronization or the evolution of the priorities assigned to each task, etc. These different parameters are positioned as strong constraints when we consider that they evolve as and when the missions unfold. This raises the question of the effectiveness of a planning or the relevance of a dynamic allocation solution without prior planning. We will send the interested reader back to [15] and [16] for a categorization around different axes such as self-organization, the formalization of coordination and the composition of teams of agents.

Some researchers [18–20] proposed other task allocation approaches in multi-agent network environments including the negotiation-based approaches. [20] introduced a method with uncertain negotiation deadlines. Thereafter, [22] proposed an approach based on negotiation for task allocation by taking into account the uncertain factors such as the deadline and the reserve price. Nevertheless, the negotiation for task allocation in most open, dynamic and distributed environments, practically, takes into consideration more than two uncertain factors. In [23], the authors expanded more uncertainty factors, like resource competition, deadline, reserve price and cost under the assumption of a global view of each resource consumer.

In [21], the authors developed a market-based approach for allocation tasks in the environment that is in reality an approach based on multi-resource negotiation. In their method, the consumer gets the required resources through negotiating with providers for each of the needed resources independently. Against our approach, the separate negotiations always result in a large number of Manager being selected to finish a task, and this may result in communication overload among the chosen managers.

[14] proposed a Greedy Distributed Task allocation Protocol (GDAP) in social networks. There are a few angles at which GDAP is like our approach, e.g., there is no central controller in GDAP, which implies every agent just has local view and agents are connected as a social network which is similar to the one proposed in our approach. However, this protocol just enables neighboring agents to help with a task which may result in a high probability of abandon of tasks when neighbors can't provide sufficient and adequate resources. In this paper, our approach [4] is proposed which allows agents to allocate tasks not only to their neighbors yet, in addition, to submit incomplete tasks to their neighbors for reallocation. Along these lines, the agents can have more opportunities to accomplish a solution to their tasks. Given the characteristics of existing multi-agent task allocation approaches, there remains an important opportunity to develop cost-effective and communication economical decentralized methods to

task allocation in the multi-agent systems. Although additional assumptions like partial observability, and heterogeneity, can additional make difficult this problem. In this paper, we propose a decentralized planning algorithm [4] to the following hypothesis: (i) there are no environmental uncertainties, and (ii) each agent has a full observation of all tasks and the state of other agents.

A combinatorial auction-based algorithm CBBA [24] proposed to solve task allocation problem. This algorithm used combinatorial auctions, where groups of tasks are produced. CBBA has displayed better execution than single-item auctions and has created good results against optimal centralized approaches [25]. A second combinatorial auction-based algorithm was developed by [27] similar to CBBA. However, the baseline of this algorithm performs, empirically, better than the baseline CBBA algorithm [26], with the approach of [27] showing a greatly improved achievement rate with different numbers of tasks and agents, and different network topologies. However, the papers mentioned do not examine handling of uncertainty of the method of [27], as well as CBBA's.

3   Benchmark Production System

We explain our approach using a simple current example called RARM [11] which is implemented in our previous work [1, 2, 4]. The RARM presented in Fig. 1 is composed of two inputs and one output conveyors, a servicing robotic agent and a processing-assembling center. Workpieces to be treated come irregularly one by one. The workpieces of type A are delivered via conveyor $C1$ and workpieces of type B via conveyor $C2$. Only one workpiece can be on the input conveyor. A robotic agent R transfers workpieces one after the other to the processing center. The next workpiece can be put on the input conveyor when it has been emptied by the robotic agent. The technology of production requires that firstly an A-workpiece is inserted into the center M and treated, then a B-workpiece is added to the center, and finally the two workpieces are assembled. Afterwards, the assembled product is taken by the robot and put above the $C3$ conveyor of output. The assembled product can be transferred on $C3$ only when the output conveyor is empty and ready to receive the next produced one.

3.1   Sensing Input

Formally, the statement of benchmark production system is defined like this: $RARM = \{position, A\text{-}workpiece, B\text{-}workpiece, AB\text{-}workpiece, conveyor, states, processing center, robotic agent\}$ where each variable is defined by his values as follows:

- A set of positions $\{p_1, p_2, \dots\}$: the variable **position** is used to localize the workpiece A, B or AB and $p_1, p_2, ..., p_i$ present the values of the variable **position**;
- A set of robotic agents $\{r_1, r_2, \dots\}$: the variable **robotic agent** transfers a workpiece one after one to be processed and $r_1, r_2, ... r_i$ present the values of the variable **robotic agent**;

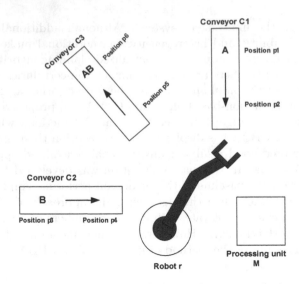

Fig. 1. The benchmark production system RARM.

- A set of workpieces of type A $\{a_1, a_2, \dots\}$: $a_1, a_2, \dots, a_i$ present the values of the variable **A-workpiece**;
- A set of workpieces of type B $\{b_1, b_2, \dots\}$: $b_1, b_2, \dots, b_i$ present the values of the variable **B-workpiece**;
- A set of workpieces of type AB $\{ab_1, ab_2, \dots\}$: $ab_1, ab_2, \dots, ab_i$ present the values of the variable **AB-workpiece**;
- A set of conveyors $\{C_{1i}, C_{2i}, C_{3i}\}$: the variable **conveyor** and his values C_{1i} (resp. C_{2i}, C_{3i}) is responsible for transferring set of workpieces of type A (resp B, AB);
- A set of processing center M $\{M_1, M_2, \dots\}$: first one A-workpiece is inserted into the variable **processing center** M and processed, then one B-workpiece is added into the center M, and last both workpieces are assembled.

The set of the variable **states** is $\{s_0, s_1, s_2, s_3, s_4, s_5, s_6, s_7, s_8, s_9, s_{10}, s_{11}, s_{12}, s_{13}, s_{14}, s_{15}, s_{16}\}$ where:

- s_0 (resp. s_6, s_{15}) is meaning a workpiece of type A (resp. B, AB) is at position $p1$ (resp. $p3$, $p5$);
- s_1 (resp. s_7, s_{16}) is meaning a workpiece of type A (resp. B, AB) is at position $p2$ (resp. $p4$, $p6$);
- s_2 (resp. s_8, s_{14}) is meaning a workpiece of type A (resp. B, AB) is taken by the robotic agent r near to the position $p2$ (resp. $p4$, $p5$) of the conveyor $C1$ (resp. $C2$, $C3$);
- s_3 (resp. s_9, s_{13}) is meaning a workpiece of type A (resp. B, AB) is taken by the robotic agent r near to the processing unit;
- s_4 (resp. s_{10}, s_{12}) is meaning a workpiece of type A (resp. B, AB) is put in the processing unit M.

The robot-like agent connects directly to the environment via sensors. So, these sensing inputs present the observations of RARM in our approach. It is defined as follows:

1. Is there an A-workpiece at the extreme end of the position $p1$? (sens1)
2. Is $C1$ in its extreme left position? (sens2)
3. Is $C1$ in its extreme right position? (sens3)
4. Is there an A-workpiece at the unit M? (sens4)
5. Is $C2$ in its extreme left position? (sens5)
6. Is $C2$ in its extreme right position? (sens6)
7. Is there a B-workpiece at the extreme end of the position $p3$? (sens7)
8. Is there a B-workpiece at the unit M? (sens8)
9. Is $C3$ in its extreme left position? (sens9)
10. Is $C3$ in its extreme right position? (sens10)
11. Is there a AB-workpiece at the unit M? (sens11)
12. Is the robotic agent arm in its lower position? (sens12)
13. Is the robotic agent arm in its higher position? (sens13)

3.2   Action Output

The system can be controlled using the following actuators:

1. move the conveyor $C1$ (act1);
2. move the conveyor $C2$ (act2);
3. move the conveyor $C3$ (act3);
4. rotate robotic agent (act4);
5. move elevating the robotic agent arm vertically (act5);
6. pick up and drop a piece with the robotic agent arm (act6);
7. treat the workpiece (act7);
8. assembly two pieces (act8).

The set of actions is $\{C1\_left,\ C1\_right,\ R1\_left,\ R1\_right,\ C2\_left,$ $C2\_right,\ R2\_left,\ R2\_right,\ C3\_left,\ C3\_right,\ R3\_left,\ R3\_right,\ take_1,$ $take_2,\ take_3,\ load_1,\ load_2,\ load_3,\ put_1,\ put_2,\ put_3,\ process_1,\ process_2\}$ where:

- $C1\_left$ (resp. $C1\_right$) is meaning a workpiece of type A is moving to the left of conveyor $C1$ from position p_1 (resp. p_2) to position p_2 (resp. p_1);
- $C2\_left$ (resp. $C2\_right$) is meaning a workpiece of type B is moving to the left of conveyor $C2$ from position p_3 (resp. p_4) to position p_4 (resp. p_3);
- $C3\_left$ (resp. $C3\_right$) is meaning a workpiece of type AB is moving to the left of conveyor $C3$ from position p_5 (resp. p_6) to position p_6 (resp. p_5);
- $R1\_left$ (resp. $R1\_right$) is meaning the robotic agent taking a workpiece of type A is moving to the left (resp. to the right) from the position p_2 of conveyor $C1$ (resp. the processing unit M) to the processing unit M (resp. the position p_2 of conveyor $C1$);

- $R2\_left$ (resp. $R2\_right$) is meaning the robotic agent taking a workpiece of type B is moving to the left (resp. to the right) from the position p_4 of conveyor $C2$ (resp. the processing unit M) to the processing unit M (resp. the position p_4 of conveyor $C2$);
- $R3\_left$ (resp. $R3\_right$) is meaning the robotic agent taking a workpiece of type AB is moving to the left (resp. to the right) from the the processing unit M (resp. position p_2 of conveyor $C3$) to the position p_2 of conveyor $C3$ (resp. the processing unit M);
- $take_1$ (resp. $take_2$, $take_3$) is meaning the operation of taking a workpiece of type A (resp. B, AB);
- $load_1$ (resp. $load_2$, $load_3$) is meaning the fact of loading a workpiece of type A (resp. B, AB);
- put_1 (resp. put_2, put_3) is meaning the operation of putting a workpiece of type A (resp. B, AB);
- $process_1$ (resp. $process_2$) is meaning the fact of processing a workpiece of type A (resp. B).

4 Agent Architecture

We propose an agent architecture to control embedded systems at runtime. The agent checks the evolution of the environment and reacts when new events occur.

4.1 Formal Specification

We use the state machine to define the dynamic behavior of an intelligent agent controlling the planning. In the state machine, states, inputs and outputs are enumerated. The state machine can be defined as a graph of states and transitions. It treats many events that may execute by detecting them and responding to each one appropriately. We describe a state machine SM_i as follows:

$$SM_i = (S_i, S_{i0}, I_i, O_i, Precond_i, Postcond_i, t_i)$$

- $S_i = \{s_{i1}, .., s_{ip}\}$: the set of states;
- S_{i0} the initial state;
- $I_i = \{I_{i1}, .., I_{im}\}$: the input events;
- $O_i = \{O_{i1}, .., O_{ik}\}$: the output events;
- $Precond_i$: the set of conditions to be verified before the activation of a state;
- $Postcond_i$: the set of conditions to be verified once a state is activated;
- $t_i : S_i \times I_i \rightarrow S_i$: the transition function.

Figure 2 shows a conceptual model for a state machine where we define the classes *State machine*, *State*, *Transition*, *Event* and *Condition*. The class *State Machine* composed by the classes *State* and *Transition*. The class *Transition* is doubly associated linked to the class *State* as long as the transition is considered as an association between two states. Each transition has an event that is considered as a trigger to fire it and a set of conditions to be verified. This association between the class *Transition* and the two classes *Event* and *Condition* exists and it's modeled by the aggregation relation.

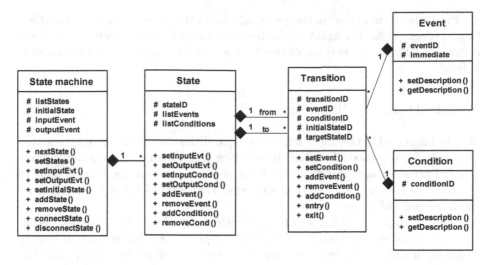

Fig. 2. The state machine model.

4.2 Conceptual Architecture for MAS

A conceptual architecture was proposed for MAS. It consists of four parts: *(i)* the Event Queue which saves different input events that may happen in the system, *(ii)* the Software Agent which reads an input from the event queue and reacts accordingly, *(iii)* the set of state machines, and *(iv)* each state represents a specific information about the system.

The agent using state machine determines the new state of the system to perform depending on the event inputs and the conditions to be satisfied. This approach provides coming characteristics: *(i)* The design of the agent is general enough to adapt to different sorts of embedded-software based application. Consequently, the agent is uncoupled from the application and from its components. *(ii)* The agent is independent of the state machine: it grants to change the structure of the state machine without changing the implementation of the agent. This guarantees the agent keeps on working accurately even if there should arise an occurrence of the modification of state machines.

In the following algorithm, the symbol Q is an event queue which holds incoming event instances, ev refers to an event input, S_i represents a State Machine, and $s_{i,j}$ a state related to a State Machine S_i. The internal behavior of the agent is defined as follow:

1. the agent reads the first event ev from the queue Q;
2. searches from the top to the bottom in the different state machines;
3. within the state machine SM_i, the agent verifies if ev is considered as an event input to the current state $s_{i,j}$ (i.e. $ev \in I$ related to $s_{i,j}$). In this case, the agent searches the states considered as successor for the state $s_{i,j}$ (states in the same state machine SM_i or in another state machine SM_l);
4. the agent executes the operations related to the different states;
5. repeats the same steps (1–4) until no more event exists in the queue to be treated.

First, the agent evaluates the pre-condition of the state $s_{i,j}$. If it is false, then the agent exits, else the agent determines the list of tasks to be executed. Then, it evaluates the post-condition of the state $s_{i,j}$ and generates errors whenever it is false.

5   Multi-agent Planning

We are interested in the use of reflection capabilities and multi-agent interaction protocols for the task allocation. If we place ourselves in an open and loosely coupled framework, it is difficult for a set of agents to combine their actions to reach a goal that it be explicitly described at the system level or implicitly from the local goals of agents.

We will propose an approach to deal with this problem. It suggests a decentralized algorithm for task allocation in complex MAS based on multi-agent planning in which each agent uses the fuzzy logic technique to select plans. The originality in this approach is that our agents evaluate plans based on their goal achievement satisfaction, which is represented as membership degrees for each individual agent, their aggregate then represents the satisfaction of the overall aim. This approach successes to make the collaboration and communication between agents superb and it performs better than the central planning processes in other systems. As it's known the task allocation problem in teams is one of optimally assigning tasks in a team plan to agents to maximize overall team utility.

In this approach, our agents use their introspection and intercession abilities to indicate in runtime what they can do, what they cannot do and why? And change their actions so that they are adaptable.

5.1   Policy

The most approaches concerning planning use a single-agent procedure, in which one agent executes the entire search process, developing the complete action plan to do the task at hand. We are inspired by these approaches to propose our contribution, in which every agent belonging to our system can make a decision by following a simple policy. This policy aids the agent to select a suitable plan of actions to carry out, which led us to solve many issues regarding the openness of the MASs and more precisely the task allocation problems.

We use conjunction operators for *fuzzy relationship* in [2, 4], to make the agent expresses more objectively the decision about the evaluation of a plan (list of events). It is very feasible to apply a membership function in fuzzy mathematics to calculate and assess the *satisfaction degree* of the plan. So, we consider G the problem goal, it is the union of individual goals of all agents denoted by g_i, which are flexible propositions.

$$G = \cup_{i=1..n} g_i \tag{1}$$

These goals can be accomplished with a satisfaction degree. The form of a flexible proposition is $(\rho \; \phi_1, \; \phi_2, ..., \phi_j \; \kappa_i)$, where $\phi_i \in \phi$ and κ_i are elements of totally ordered set, K, which presents the truth degree of the proposition. K is composed of a finite number of membership degrees, $k_\uparrow, k_1, ..., k_\downarrow$, where $k_\uparrow \in K$ and $k_\downarrow \in K$, representing respectively total falsehood and total truth. When dealing with a flexible proposition with a truth value of $k_\uparrow$ or $k_\downarrow$, the boolean style $\neg \; (\rho \; \phi_1, \; \phi_2, ..., \phi_j)$ or $(\rho \; \phi_1, \; \phi_2, ..., \phi_j)$ is adopted. The flexible proposition [12] is described by a *fuzzy relation*, R, which is defined as a membership function $\mu_R(.)$: $\Phi_1{}^*\Phi_2{}^*...{}^*\Phi_j \rightarrow K$, where $\Phi_1{}^*\Phi_2{}^*...{}^*\Phi_j$ is the Cartesian product of the subsets of Φ in the current proposition state. Especially, if each agent accomplishes its individual objectives with a specific satisfaction degree, the public goals of the problem are achieved. The satisfaction degree of a multi-agent flexible planning problem is characterized as the conjunction of the satisfaction degrees of each action and goal.

$$\mu_G = \wedge_{i=1..n}\mu_R(i) \tag{2}$$

The function μ_G [4] signifies how well a given plan is satisfying and can be considered as a value between 0 and 1, 1 represents totally satisfied and 0 represents not satisfied by any means. In our approach, each plan alternative is related to a satisfaction degree. That implies each value is the metric that gives the way to choose a plan among various alternatives. Having the improved mean values calculated, the alternative plan alongside these values are sent to the current state machine. The alternative plan, the need, the objective, and the corresponding values reach the decision-making mechanism first. These values are used by the decision-making mechanism to compare the satisfaction degrees for each alternative plan to find the most satisfactory and acceptable one. The one with the highest satisfaction degree is considered as the most satisfactory plan alternative.

Running Example

Giving $(S, \; A, \; G_s)$ where $S = \{s_i | i = 1 ... \text{n}\}$ is a set of states, $A = \{Ci\_left, Ci\_right, Ri\_left, Ri\_right, take_i, load_i, put_i, process_i | i = 1 ... \text{n}\}$ is a set of actions, and G_s is the problem goal. *if s_0 and $g - \{workpiece \; in \; the \; processing \; unit\}$. Let:*

- π_0: $(C2\_left, take_2, load_2, process_2)$
- π_1: $(load_1, put_1, process_1, C1\_right)$
- π_2: $(C1\_left, take_1, load_1, put_1, process_1, C1\_right)$

We solve multi-agent planning problems by distributed flexible constraint satisfaction problem (CSP) technique [13] and make a trade-off between plan length and the compromise decisions made. The quality of a plan is measured by its satisfaction degree and its length, where the shorter of two plans is better under the same satisfaction degrees. In this example, the definitions of K and L are: $K = \{k_\uparrow, k_1, k_2, k_\downarrow\}$, $L = \{l_\uparrow, l_1, l_2, l_\downarrow\}$.

The multi-agent planning problem is helpful to robot-like agents like in this example. If any actions $\in \{Ci\_left, Ci\_right, Ri\_left, Ri\_right, take_i, load_i,$

put_i, $process_i | i = 2 \ldots n$} will damage the plan, leading to a satisfaction degree l_2, any plan not beginning with $C1\_left$ will result in a satisfaction degree l_2 because it is not applicable to s_0, and when any action is applicable to s_0 and the resulting state is a goal state then the result will be a satisfaction l_1. We obtain π_0 which is a plan of 4 steps with satisfaction l_2 as follows:

- $C2\_left$ has a satisfaction degree l_2
- $take_2$ has a satisfaction degree l_2
- $load_2$ has a satisfaction degree l_2
- $process_2$ has a satisfaction degree l_2

In addition, we obtain π_2 which is a plan of 6 steps with satisfaction $l_\uparrow$ as follows:

- $C1\_left$ has a satisfaction degree $l_\uparrow$
- $take_1$ has a satisfaction degree $l_\uparrow$
- $load_1$ has a satisfaction degree $l_\uparrow$
- put_1 has a satisfaction degree $l_\uparrow$
- $process_1$ has a satisfaction degree $l_\uparrow$
- $C1\_right$ has a satisfaction degree $l_\uparrow$

Then π_0 is not a solution because although it is applicable to s_0, the resulting state is not a goal state; π_1 is not a solution because it's not applicable to s_0; π_2 is the most appropriate solution.

5.2   Experimental Evaluation

We have evaluated our approach to prove, on the one hand, how our software agent having distinctive capacities such as it can perform, simulate the behavior of the agent. On the other hand, to prove how the performance of the robotic agents was impacted by varying their satisfaction degree and the plan length. In order to show the feasibility of our approach, we have presented experimental results on preliminary tests focusing on the analysis of the planning performance using the satisfaction degree by simulating RARM.

The results obtained when running our architecture were shown in Fig. 3. Therefore, we have compared their performance on a set of plans for the RARM state-transitions. Since the second plan of 2 steps with maximum satisfaction degree l_2, the fifth plan of 15 steps with satisfaction $l_\uparrow$. So, it is often possible to find short, satisfactory plans quickly during the decision-making mechanism. The quality of a plan is its satisfaction degree combined with its length, where the shorter of two plans with equivalent satisfaction degrees is better.

These results are demonstrative of the capacity to dynamically treat working conditions among various conveyors, a service robot and a treating-assembling center after some time, assumes a basic role in the determination of actions during the planning. Additionally, the choice of process flexibility was affected by the making decisions. The breakdown of an individual robotic agent impacts in

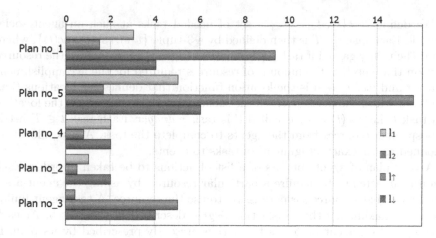

Fig. 3. The experimental results collected the length of the plan and his satisfaction degree [4].

the whole team as a result of the satisfaction degree of the plan which selects the most satisfactory alternative plan depending on the software agent architecture. At the point when the architecture is tested on the multi-robot system RARM, there are a few critical functions that have been performed. The related issues are planning and intelligent decision making.

6   Distributed Task Allocation Approach

To solve the task allocation problem, many researchers have proposed various methods of single-agent planning. Recently other researchers are interested in multi-agent planning (including our approach), they hence focus on a set of heterogeneous agents that work together to develop a course of action that satisfies the purpose of the team. Therefore, multi-agent planning defines a social approach to planning by which multiple intelligent entities work together to solve planning tasks that they are not able to solve by themselves, or to at least accomplish them better by cooperating [28].

6.1   Problem Definition

The social task allocation problem that will be depicted in this section, it can be defined as an agent not satisfactory to complete a task by itself and it needs the collaboration from other agents to achieve an action or service. We denote $A = \{a_1, ..., a_m\}$ a set of agents, that require resources to achieve tasks; and $R = \{r_1, ..., r_k\}$ a set of resources types available to A. Each agent $a \in A$ controls a fixed amount of resources for every resource type in R, which is defined by a resource function: $rsc: A \times R \rightarrow N$. Moreover, we suppose agents are connected by a *social network* as discussed before in [3,4].

We define $T = \{t_1, t_2, ..., t_n\}$ a set of needed tasks at such an agent social network. Each task $t \in T$ is then defined by a 3-tuple $\{u(t), rsc(t), loc(t)\}$, where $u(t)$ is the utility gained if task t is accomplished, $rsc: T \times R \rightarrow N$ is the resource function that specifies the amount of resources required for the accomplishment of task t and $loc: T \rightarrow A$ is the location function that defines the locations (i.e., agents) at which the tasks arrive in the social network. An agent a is the location of a task t, i.e. $loc(t) = a$, is called this task *manager*. Each task $t \in T$ needs some specific resources from the agents to complete the task. A task allocation is defined as the exact assignment of tasks to agents.

A task plan of agent consists of a list of actions to be taken in order. Each action is an attempt to acquire a particular resource, by asking the agent associated with that resource for permission to use the resource. A task agent builds a plan by maximizing the satisfaction degree described in the Sect. 5. At each timestep, a task agent performs the action presently prescribed by its plan. It does this by contacting the agent associated with the targeted resource, and asking it whether it may take the resource.

Now we formally define the important components of the problem:

– Social network: an agent social network $SN = (A, AE)$ is an undirected graph, where A is a set of agents and AE is a set of edges connecting two agents a_i and a_j significant that it exists a social connection between these two agents.
– Each agent $a \in A$ is composed of 4-tuple $\{AgentID(a), Neig(a), Resource(a), State(a)\}$, where $AgentID(a)$ is the identity of agent a, $Neig(a)$ is a set indicating the neighbors of agent a, $Resource(a)$ is the resource which agent a contains, and $State(a)$ demonstrates the state of agent.
– Multi-agent planning problem: we denote π a plan which is described by a 5-tuple $\{T, P(t), E(t), G, \mu_t\}$, where T is a set of tasks, $P(t)$ is the set of action (task) preconditions, $E(t)$ is the set of task effects, G is the problem goal and μ_t the satisfaction degree of a multi-agent flexible planning problem introduced in Sect. 5.
– Task allocation: we consider a set of tasks $T = \{t_1, t_2, ..., t_n\}$, a set of agents $A = \{a_1, ..., a_m\}$, a set of plans $\pi = \{\pi_1, ..., \pi_m\}$, and a set of resources $R = \{r_1, ..., r_k\}$ in a social network SN, a task allocation is a mapping ϕ: $T \times A \times R \times \pi \rightarrow SN$.
– Three types of agents to control system in our software agent architecture $= \{Manager, Participant, Mediator\}$. *Manager* is the agent which requests help for its task, *Participant* is the agent which accepts and performs the announced task and *Mediator* is the agent which receives another commitment of the agent for help to discover participants.
– Three states $= \{Busy, Committed, Idle\}$. In a complex system, an agent can be only in one of the three states at any timestep. When an agent is a Manager or Participant, the state of that agent is *Busy*. When an agent is a Mediator, the agent is in *Committed* state. An agent in *Idle* state is available and not assigned or committed to any task.
– *Resource Announce Message*: it is a message sent from agent a_i to agent a_j for building up neighborhood is 3-tuple described formally as $\{AgentID(a_i),$

$TaskID(t_{a_i})$, $Resource(t_{a_i})$}, where $AgentID(a_i)$ represents the ID of the agent a_i, $TaskID(t_{a_i})$ is the ID of the task of the agent a_i and $Resource(t_{a_i})$ represents the resource required for the task t_{a_i}.

- *Propose Message*: it is sent from agent a_j to agent a_i for proposing a task to be achieving is 4-tuple described formally as {$AgentID(a_j)$, $Resource(a_j)$, $Execute(a_j)$, $Utility(a_j)$}, where $AgentID(a_j)$ represents the identity of the agent which proposes the resource type it contains which is defined as $Resource(a_j)$, $Execute(a_j)$ represents the execution time, and $Utility(a_j)$ represents the utility.

- *Contract*: it is sent from agent a_i to the chosen agent a_j after satisfying with resource proposal of the neighbors a_j, the contract is defined as 4-tuple {$AgentID(a_i)$, $AgentID(a_j)$, $TaskID(t_{a_i})$, $Resource(a_i)$}, where $AgentID(a_i)$ represents the identity of the agent which sends the contract to the agent with the identity $AgentID(a_j)$, $TaskID(t_i)$ represents the ID of the appropriate task to do to $Resource(a_i)$.

- *Commitment*: it is sent from agent a_i to the agent a_j after selection a partial fulfilled task a_j, the commitment is defined as 4-tuple {$AgentID(a_i)$, $AgentID(a_j)$, $TaskID(t_{a_i})$, $rsc(t_{a_i})^1$}, where $rsc(t_{a_i})^1$ is a subset of $rsc(t_{a_i})$, which contains the unfulfilled required resources, $AgentID(a_i)$ represents the identity of the agent which sends the commitment to the agent with the identity $AgentID(a_j)$, $TaskID(t_i)$ represents the ID of the partial fulfilled task to do.

6.2   The Principle of Distributed Task Allocation

As we indicated before, we propose a software agent architecture to manage the openness and to guarantee a coherent behavior of the MAS, in our case the multi-robot system. Accordingly, we propose a distributed task allocation approach, which is allowing agents to request help from neighbors, this would be done by allocating tasks to different agents who may be able each, to perform different subsets of tasks. Moreover, each neighbor selects the most appropriate tasks due to the single-agent planning described in the Sect. 5.

So, we illustrate the following idea: *we suppose that $Neig(a_i)$ stores only directly linked neighboring agents of agent a_i where at each timestep, these task neighboring agents perform the action presently prescribed by their most satisfying tasks. The task neighboring agents do this by contacting the agent associated with the targeted resource, and asking it whether it may take the resource.*

To make our task allocation approach efficient, it is supposed that only an *Idle* agent can be assigned to a new task as a *Manager* or a partial fulfilled task as a *Participant*, or *Committed* to a partial fulfilled task as a *Mediator*. A partial fulfilled task is a task, for which a full group is in formation procedure and has not yet formed. We present our approach which describes an interactive model between agents detailed as follows:

- When a *Manager* denoted by a_{Mn} ought to apply distributed task allocation, it then sends resource announce message to all its neighbors
  $ResAnnounceMess = <\text{AgentID}(a_{Mn}), \text{TaskID}(t_{Mn}), \text{Resource}(t_{Mn})>$;

– These neighboring agents receiving the *ResAnnounceMess* sent by a_{Mn},
  - **If** (*state(neighboring agent)* = *Idle*) **Then** the neighboring agent a_j applies the single-agent planning to select the most appropriate tasks and then sends a propose message
  ProposeMess = <AgentID(a_j), Resource(a_j), Execute(a_j), Utility(a_j)>.
  - **Else** (*state(neighboring agent)* = *Busy*) the neighboring agent a_j refuses and sends the following message *RefuseMess* = <AgentID(a_j)>.
– After answering the resource announce message sent by a_{Mn}
  - **If** (a_{Mn} is satisfied with many resource proposals of the neighbor) **Then** a_{Mn} will pick the agent having the highest utility, denoted by a_j, and the state of a_j will be changed to *Busy*. In case the a_{Mn} finds many agents having the highest utility then it chooses the agent a_j proposing the least execution time with a most appropriate task.
  - **Else** the a_{Mn} is satisfied with only one resource of the neighbor, then the a_{Mn} will choose this agent without any utility consideration.

  Manager a_{Mn} sends a contract to the chosen agent a_j composed of 4-tuple, *Contract* = <AgentID(a_{Mn}), AgentID(a_j), TaskID(t_{Mn}), Resource(a_{Mn})>.
– After obtaining the answer from its different cooperative neighbors, a_{Mn} then compares the available resources from its neighbors, i.e. Resoneig(a_{Mn}), with the resources required for its task t_{Mn}, namely rsc(t_{Mn})
  (Here, Resoneig(a_{Mn}) = $\bigcup_{a_j \in Neig(a_{Mn})} Resource(a_j)$). This comparison would result in one of the following two cases:
  1. **If** (rsc(t_{Mn}) $\subseteq$ Resoneig(a)) **Then** a_{Mn} can form a full group for task t_{Mn} directly with its neighboring agents which they apply the policy of single-agent planning.
  2. **Else** (Resoneig(a) $\subset$ rsc(t_{Mn})), in this condition, a_{Mn} can only form a partial group for task t_{Mn}. It then commits the task t_{Mn} to one of its neighbors. The commitment selection is based on the number of neighbors each neighbor of a_{Mn} maintaining. The more neighbors an agent has, the higher probability that agent could be selected as a *Mediator* agent to commit the task t_{Mn}.
– After selection, a_{Mn} commits its partial fulfilled task t_{Mn} to the *Mediator* agent, denoted as a_{Md}. A commitment consists of 4-tuple,
  Commitment = <AgentID(a_{Mn}), AgentID(a_{Md}), TaskID(t_{Mn}), rsc(t_{Mn})^1 >, where rsc(t_{Mn})^1 contains the unfulfilled required resources. Afterwards, a_{Md} subtracts 1 from N_{max} and attempts to discover the agents with available resources from its neighbors. If any agents satisfy resource requirement, a_{Md} will send a response message, *RespMess*, back to a_{Mn}. The agent a_{Mn} then directly makes contract with the agents which satisfy the resource requirement and have an appropriate plan of tasks. If the neighboring agents of a_{Md} cannot satisfy the resource requirement either, a_{Md} will commit the partial fulfilled task t_{Mn} to one of its neighbors again.
– This process will continue until all of the resource requirements of task t_{Mn} are satisfied, or the N_{max} reaches 0, or there is no more *Idle* agent among the neighbors. Both of the last two conditions, i.e. $N_{max} = 0$ and no more *Idle*

agent, demonstrates the failure of task allocation. In these two conditions, a_{Mn} disables the assigned contracts with the *Participant* s, and the states of these *Participant* are reset to *Idle*.
– When finishing an allocation for one task, the system is restored to its original status and each agent's state is reset to *Idle*.

Figure 4 illustrates briefly a simple example of interaction scenario between a *Manager, Mediator* and *Participants*.

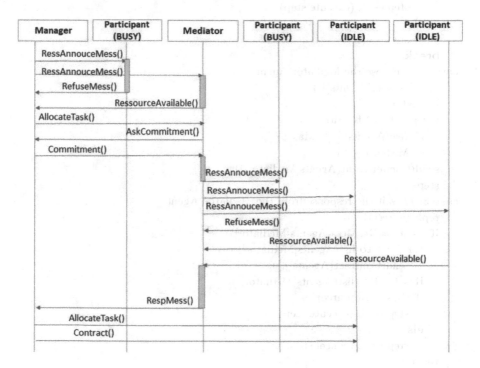

Fig. 4. The interaction process between Manager, Mediator and 4 Participants.

The following algorithm gives the pseudocode of the distributed task allocation algorithm employed by each Manager, Mediator and Participant.

```
Algorithm Communicate()
begin
switch (role)
case Manager:
   switch (step)
   case 0: // send a request to all neighbors Agents
      for j = 1 to NbA do
         send(ResAnnounceMes(Agents[j]));
      step++;
```

```
        break;
    case 1: // Receive accept/refusal from neighbors Agents      reply ← receive();
        if (reply = ProposeMess(Agents[j]))
            send(Contract(Agents[j]));
            Res=Res+Res(Agents[j]);
        Nb++;
        if (Nb = NbA )
            if (Res = Resource)
                step ← 4; (execute step)
            else
                step ++;
        break;
    case 2: // choose the Mediator Agent
        Max ← Neig(Agents[1])
        Mediator ← 1
        for j = 2 to NbA do
            if Neig(Agents[j]) > Max ;
                Mediator ← j
        send(Commitment(Agents[Mediator]));
        step++;
    case 3: // wait the response from the Mediator Agent
        reply ← receive();
        if (reply = ResMess(Agents[Mediator]))
            for j = 1 to list(Agents[Mediator]) do
                send(Contract(Agents[j]));
            Res += Res(list(Agents[Mediator]))
            if (Res = Resource)
                step ← 4; (execute step)
            else
                step ← 5; (cancel step)
        break;
    case 4:
    for j = 1 to length(list(Agents)) do
        send(Execute(list(Agents[j])));
    step ← 0;
    role ← participant;
    break;
    case 5:
    step ← 0;
    role ← participant;
    break;
    End switch
case Mediator:
    switch (step)
    case 0: // wait a message from the Manager Agent
```

```
    reply ← receive();
    if (reply = Commitment)
       step++;
    break;
  case 1: // send a request to all neighbors Agents
     for j = 1 to NbA do
        send(ResAnnounceMes(Agents[j]));
     step++;
     break;
  case 2: // Receive accept/refusal from neighbors Agents     reply ← receive();
    if (reply = ProposeMess(Agents[j]))
       Res=Res+Res(Agents[j]);
  Nb++;
  if (Nb = NbA )
     step ← 3; (inform the manager)
  break;
  case 3: // inform the manager Agent
  send(ResMess(Manager));
     break;
  End switch
case Participant:
   switch (step)
   case 0: // wait a message from the Manager Agent
   reply ← receive();
   if (reply = ResAnnounceMes(Manager))
      if (state = IDLE )
         send(ProposeMess(Manager));
         step++;
      else
         step ← 0;
   break;
   case 1: // wait a CONTRACT from the Manager Agent
   reply ← receive();
   if (reply = CONTRACT(Manager))
      state = BUSY
      step++;
   break;
   case 2: // Receive accept/refusal from neighbors Agents     reply ← receive();
   if (reply = Execute(Manager))
      ExcuteTask();
   state = IDLE
   step← 0;
   break;
   End switch
end
```

6.3   Experiments

We have simulated our distributed task allocation algorithm in different networks. To test the efficiency of our algorithm, we compare it with the Greedy Distributed Allocation Protocol (GDAP) [14]. In this subsection, we briefly define GDAP. Then, we introduce the experiment environment' settings. And we depict in the last sub-subsection the results and the relevant analysis.

GDAP is selected to manage task allocation problem in agent social networks. It's described briefly in [14] as follows: All *Manager* agents $a \in A$ try to find neighboring contractors (the same as *Participant* in this paper) to help them do their tasks $T_a = \{t_i \in T | loc(t_i) = a\}$. They start offering the most efficient task. Among all tasks offered, contractors select the one having the highest efficiency and send a bid to the related manager. A bid consists of all the resources the agent is able to supply for this task. If sufficient resources have been offered, the manager selects the required resources and informs all contractors of its choice. When a task is allocated, or when a manager has received offers from all neighbors but still cannot satisfy its task, the task is removed from its task list. And this is the main disadvantage of GDAP that it only relies on neighbors which may cause several unallocated tasks due to limited resources, that is exactly what our approach tries to solve.

Experimental Settings. We have been implementing our distributed task allocation algorithm and (GDAP) in JAVA and we have been testing them. There are two different settings used in our experiment. The first setup has been done in the *Small-world networks* in which most neighbors of an agent are also connected to each other. The second setup has been done in the *Scale free networks*.

Setting 1: is shown in Table 1. We assume that tasks are distributed uniformly on each *Idle* agent and resources are normally allocated to agents. The only changing variable in this setting is the average number of neighbors. This setting intends to represent the influence of neighbors' number on the performance of both our algorithm and GDAP.

Table 1. The details of Setting 1.

Setting	Quantity
Number of agents	40
Number of tasks	20
Number of different resource's types	5
Average number of resources required by each task	30

Setting 2: is shown in Table 2. We fix the average number of neighbors at 10, the ratio between the number of agents and tasks at 5/3 and the resource ratio at 1.2. The tasks are uniformly distributed. This setting is defined to show the

Table 2. The details of Setting 2.

Setting	Quantity
Number of agents	varies from 100 to 2000
Number of different resource types	20
Average number of resources required by each task	100

scalability of both our proposed algorithm and GDAP in a large scale networks with a fixed average number of neighbors.

The algorithms have been evaluated according to two criteria in this experiment; the *Utility Ratio* and the *Execution Time*, where:

$$UtilityRatio = \frac{\sum Successful - completed - tasks}{Total - of - tasks} \tag{3}$$

The unit of Execution Time is millisecond. For simplicity, we suppose that once a task has been allocated to a Participant, the Participant would successfully finish this task without failure.

Experiment Results and Analysis from Setting 1: We would like to test in this experiment the influence of different average number of neighbors on both algorithms. We notice in Fig. 5 that the Utility Ratio of our algorithm in different networks is more reliable than the GDAP algorithm. For the reason that the distribution of tasks in GDAP is only depending on the Manager neighbors, contrary to ours, in the case of need, other agents are allocated (i.e. not only the neighbors).

We can mention another factor to compare both approaches which is the network type. The results of GDAP in a small world network is higher than in a scale free network, and this could be explained by the fact that the most agents have a very few neighbors in the small network. Opposingly to that, in the scale free network when the average number of neighbors increases, the GDAP performance decreases. Which leads to say that this factor does not affect the performance of our algorithm as we take into consideration enough neighbors to obtain satisfactory resources for processing its tasks without reallocating tasks further.

Figure 6 presents the Execution Time of two algorithms in different networks depending on the average number of neighbors. The Execution Time of our algorithm is higher than that of GDAP since during execution, the agents in our algorithm reallocate tasks when resources from neighbors are unsatisfying. Furthermore, we note that the results of GDAP in a small world network is higher than in a scale free network, but compared to our algorithm are still lower and this is because it considers only neighbors which could decrease the time and communication cost during task allocation process.

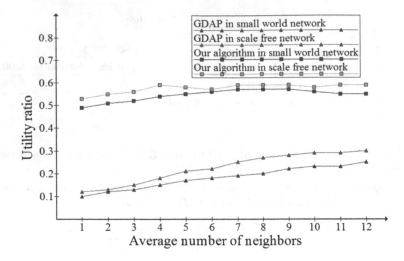

Fig. 5. The Utility ratio of the GDAP and our algorithm depending on the average number of neighbors in different type of networks [4].

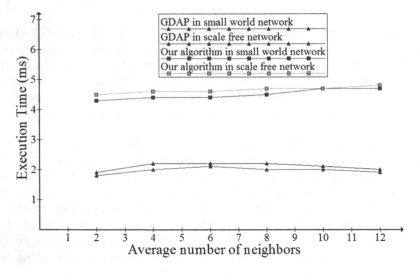

Fig. 6. The Execution time in millisecond of the GDAP and our algorithm depending on the average number of neighbors in different type of networks [4].

Experiment Results and Analysis from Setting 2: We would like to test the scalability of both GDAP and our algorithm in different large network scales like applications running on the internet. The Fig. 7 presents the Utility Ratio of GDAP which is constantly descending while that of our algorithm can save the stability and it is higher than GDAP with the increase of number of agents and simultaneously the number of tasks in a large network scale. In fact, we

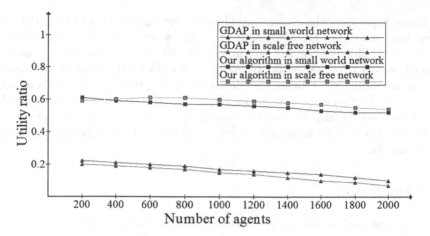

Fig. 7. The Utility ratio of the GDAP and our algorithm depending on the number of agents in different type of networks [4].

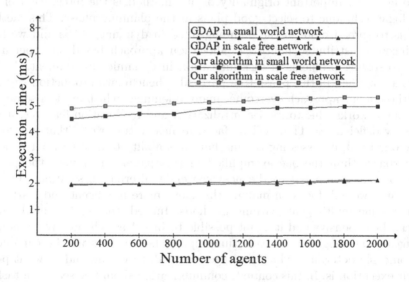

Fig. 8. The Execution time in millisecond of the GDAP and our algorithm depending on the number of agents in different type of networks [4].

can explain this by the proportional rise of the network scale, the tasks and the resource types.

Moreover the condition in small world network is better than that in scale free network. And this is justified by the same reason described above, that in scale free network, several agents only have a few neighbors which is not good for GDAP. Compared with GDAP, our algorithm is more competitive and it is favoured from task reallocation.

Figure 8 presents the Execution Time of our algorithm and GDAP in different network types. GDAP spends less time when there are more agents in the network. This is because there are more tasks despite the average number of neighbors is fixed. Accordingly, more reallocation steps cannot be avoided towards allocating these tasks, that leads to soaring in time and overhead communication. Furthermore, the graphs show that the GDAP and our algorithm almost behaves linearly and the time consumption of GDAP keeps a lower level than ours. This can be supposedly interpreted that GDAP only relies on neighboring agents.

7   Conclusion

We have proposed a software agent architecture to manage services and control embedded systems at run-time to perform self-adaptation. These architecture served us to propose a single-agent planning method that aids agent to make a convenient decision and compose better his services during the communication with others. An important originality of our method is the integration of the fuzzy logic technique to select good plans in the planning phase. This method leads us to spread more in the planning filled in dynamic MASs and we have introduced a distributed multi-task allocation approach based on a pertinent policy to solving problems of task allocation in dynamic environment. All the results are applied in this phase to a particular benchmark production system.

Although our approach overcomes many dilemmas, which exist in some current related works, due to its decentralization and reallocation features, it still has many deficiencies. They will be faced in near future work, that will focus, on the one hand, on assessing the mechanism's ability to deal with larger state action spaces than the one exemplified in this paper and review the performance benefits compared to the heavier-weight alternative solutions. On the other hand, we will focus on making the agent more intelligent and learner by utilizing some multi-agent learning methods. Indeed, the sending of the message can be expensive and it is not possible to broadcast all resource announce messages to all neighbors at each timestep. In fact, agents will be capable to autonomously determine which messages to send, to whom, and at what point in their execution is. In this context, communication should be seen as a task to do in the own decision of the agent that it will deal with both the actions and the possible interactions. We also plan, in the future, to enhance our approach by considering that each agent in the system has multiple resources instead of only one.

References

1. Gharbi, A., Ben Noureddine, D., Ben Halima, N.: Building multi-robot system based on five capabilities model. In: 12th International Conference on Evaluation of Novel Approaches to Software Engineering, Barcelona, Spain, pp. 270–275 (2015)

2. Ben Noureddine, D., Gharbi, A., Ben Ahmed, S.: An approach for multi-robot system based on agent layered architecture. Int. J. Manag. Appl. Sci. (IJMAS) **2**(12), 135–143 (2016)
3. Ben Noureddine, D., Gharbi, A., Ben Ahmed. S.: Multi-agent deep reinforcement learning for task allocation in dynamic environment. In: 12th International Conference on Software Technologies, Madrid, Spain, pp. 17–26 (2017)
4. Ben Noureddine, D., Gharbi, A., Ben Ahmed, S.: A social multi-agent cooperation system based on planning and distributed task allocation: real case study. In: 13th International Conference on Software Technologies, Porto, Portugal, pp. 483–493 (2018)
5. Jennings, N.R., Sycara, K., Wooldridgse, M.: A roadmap of agent research and development. Auton. Agents Multi-agent Syst. **1**, 7–38 (1998)
6. Mejia, M., Peña, N., Muñoz, J.L., Esparza, O., Alzate, M.: DECADE: distributed emergent cooperation through adaptive evolution in mobile ad hoc networks. Ad Hoc Netw. **10**, 1379–1398 (2012)
7. Del Val, E., Rebollo, M., Botti, V.: Promoting cooperation in service-oriented MAS through social plasticity and incentives. J. Syst. Softw. **86**, 520–537 (2013)
8. Das, G.P., McGinnity, T.M., Coleman, S.A., Behera, L.: A distributed task allocation algorithm for a multi-robot system in healthcare facilities. J. Intell. Robot. Syst. **84**, 1–26 (2014)
9. Sun, Q., Garcia-Molina, H.: SLIC: a selfish link based incentive mechanism for unstructured peer-to-peer networks. In: 24th International Conference in Distributed Computing Systems, Tokyo, Japan, pp. 506–515 (2004)
10. Wei, G., Zhu, P., Vasilakos, A.V., Mao, Y., Luo, J., Ling, Y.: Cooperation dynamics on collaborative social networks of heterogeneous population. IEEE J. Sel. Areas Commun. **31**, 1135–1146 (2013)
11. Hruz, B., Zhou, M.: Modeling and Control of Discrete-event Dynamic Systems with Petri Nets and Other Tools. Springer, London (2007). https://doi.org/10.1007/978-1-84628-877-7
12. Miguel, I., Jarvis, P., Shen, Q.: Flexible graphplan. In: 14th European Conference on Artificial Intelligence, Berlin, Germany, pp. 4506–4514 (2000)
13. Miguel, I., Giret, A.: Feasible distributed CSP models for scheduling problems. Eng. Appl. Artif. Intell. **21**(5), 723–732 (2008)
14. Weerdt, M.D., Zhang, Y., Klos, T.: Distributed task allocation in social networks. In: 6th International Conference on Autonomous Agents and Multi-agent Systems Distributed Computing Systems, Honolulu, Hawaii, USA, pp. 500–507 (2007)
15. Farinelli, A., Farinelli, R., Iocchi, L., Nardi, N.: Multi-robot systems: a classification focused on coordination. IEEE Trans. Syst. Man Cybern. Part B (Cybern.) **34**(5), 2015–2028 (2004)
16. Dudek, G., Jenkin, M., Milios, E.: A taxonomy of multirobot systems. In: Robot Teams: From Diversity to Polymorphism, pp. 3–22 (2002)
17. Zheng, X., Koenig, S.: Reaction functions for task allocation to cooperative agents. In: 7th International Conference on Autonomous Agents and Multiagent Systems, Estoril, Portugal, pp. 559–566 (2008)
18. Jennings, N.R., Faratin, P., Lomuscio, A.R., Parsons, S., Wooldridge, M.J., Sierra, C.: Automated negotiation: prospects, methods and challenges. Group Decis. Negot. **10**(2), 199–215 (2001)
19. Fatima, S.S., Wooldridge, M.: Adaptive task and resource allocation in multi-agent systems. In: 5th International Conference on Autonomous Agents, Montreal, QC, Canada, pp. 537–544 (2001)

20. Gatti, N., Giunta, D., Marino, S.: Alternating-offers bargaining with one-sided uncertain deadlines. An efficient algorithm. Artif. Intell. **172**(8), 1119–1157 (2008)
21. An, B., Lesser, V., Sim, K.M.: Strategic agents for multi-resource negotiation. Auton. Agent Multi Agent Syst. **23**(1), 114–153 (2011)
22. An, B., Gatti, N., Lesser, V.: Bilateral bargaining with one-sided two-type uncertainty. In: The International Joint Conference on Web Intelligence and Intelligent Agent Technology, DC, USA, pp. 403–410 (2009)
23. An, B., Lesser, V., Irwin, D., Zink, M.: Automated negotiation with decommitment for dynamic resource allocation in cloud computing. In: 9th International Conference on Autonomous Agents and Multiagent Systems, Toronto, ON, Canada, pp. 981–988 (2010)
24. Choi, H.-L., Brunet, J., How, J.P.: Consensus-based decentralization auctions for robust task allocation. IEEE Trans. Robot. **25**(4), 912–926 (2009)
25. Cramton, P., Shoham, Y., Steinberg, R.: An overview of combinatorial auction. ACM SIGecom Exch. **7**(1), 3–14 (2007)
26. Whitbrook, A., Meng, Q., Chung, P.W.H.: A novel distributed scheduling algorithm for time-critical, multi-agent systems. In: IEEE/RSJ International Conference on Intelligent Robots and Systems, Hamburg, Germany, pp. 6451–6458 (2015)
27. Zhao, W., Meng, Q., Chung, P.W.H.: A heuristic distributed task allocation method for multivehicle multitask problems and its application to search and rescue scenario. IEEE Trans. Cybern. **46**(4), 902–915 (2016)
28. Weerdt, M.D., Clement, B.: Introduction to planning in multiagent systems. Multiagent Grid Syst. **5**(4), 345–355 (2009)

Automatic Test Data Generation for a Given Set of Applications Using Recurrent Neural Networks

Ciprian Paduraru[1]([⊠]), Marius-Constantin Melemciuc[2]([⊠]), and Miruna Paduraru[2]

[1] The Research Institute of the University of Bucharest (ICUB), University of Bucharest, Bd. M. Kogalniceanu 36-46, 050107 Bucharest, Romania
ciprian.paduraru@fmi.unibuc.ro
[2] Department of Computing Science, University of Bucharest, Bucharest, Romania
marius-constantin.melemciuc@my.fmi.unibuc.ro, miruna-gabriela.paduraru@ubisoft.com

Abstract. To address the problem of automatic software testing against vulnerabilities, our work focuses on creating a tool capable in assisting users to generate automatic test sets for multiple programs under test at the same time. Starting with an initial set of inputs in a corpus folder, the tool works by clustering the inputs depending on their application target type, then produces a generative model for each of these clusters. The architecture of the models is falling in the recurrent neural network architecture class, and for training and inferencing the models we used the Tensorflow framework. Online-learning is supported by the tool, thus models can get better as long as new inputs for each application cluster are added to the corpus folder. Users can interact with the tool similar to the interface used in expert systems: customize various parameters exposed per cluster, or override various function hooks for learning and inferencing the model, with the purpose of getting finer control over the tool's backend. As the evaluation section shows, the tool can be useful for creating important sets of new inputs, with good code coverage quality and less resources consumed.

Keywords: Fuzz testing · Recurrent neural networks · LSTM Tensorflow · Pipeline · Taint analysis

1 Introduction

The importance of security in software systems has increased year over year recently, because of the wide interconnectivity between different software pieces. Important resources are invested nowadays in detecting security bugs in these systems before being released on the market. Machine generated test data is desirable for automatizing the process of testing and ensuring a better coverage.

© Springer Nature Switzerland AG 2019
M. van Sinderen and L. A. Maciaszek (Eds.): ICSOFT 2018, CCIS 1077, pp. 307–326, 2019.
https://doi.org/10.1007/978-3-030-29157-0_14

Ideally, the purpose of an automatic test data generation system for programs evaluation should be to generate test data that covers as many branches as possible from a program's code, with the least computational effort possible. The most common technique is *Fuzz testing* [12], which is a program analysis technique that looks for inputs causing errors such as buffer overflows, memory access violations, null pointer dereferences, etc, which in general have a high rate of being exploitable. Using this technique, testing data is generated using random inputs and the program under test is executing them for the purpose of detecting issues like the above mentioned ones. One of the main limitations of fuzz testing is that it takes a significant effort to produce inputs that covers almost all branches of a program's source code. This comes from the fact that using randomness, it results in a high chance of producing inputs that are not correct and rejected in the early outs of a program's execution. If we filter and consider only the inputs that are correct and accepted by the program, there still is a huge area of possible inputs remaining and from these usually only a few are a subset of the corner cases that could trigger unexpected and problematic behaviour. This challenge sits at the core of developing tools to increase the coverage of the branches in the program execution that could point the development team to handle cases omitted in the previous development steps. A constant cycle of releasing program patches having one of the purposes of covering those cases are still desired to be introduced as early as possible in the development process. Considering the randomness aspect, any guidance specifics or additional insights taken from the evaluation of early stages inputs are ideally to be taken into consideration for reducing the computational power and time needed to expose the program issues. The initial seed quality as well as unbalanced seed selection are good aspects to be considered when generating the inputs.

Alternative methods that augment the classic random fuzz testing with different methods were created. Such ideas involved the use of genetic algorithms for better guiding the test data generation towards uncovered areas [24], or by using recurrent neural networks and predicting the probability distribution of the next character knowing a previously generated context [15, 26].

This paper discusses an open-source tool (from the authors' knowledge, the first one at the moment of writing this paper) that given a corpus of different existing test file formats, it performs cluster analysis, then learns a generative model for each cluster, which can be used later to quickly generate new tests with a high rate of being correct (i.e., touching more branches of a program instead of taking the early outs due to incorrect inputs). More specifically, the contributions of this paper in the field of using machine learning for automating software testing are:

- An open-source tool that is capable of storing a database of generative models for sampling new test data for multiple programs at once. These models are learned from a corpus of test data, which can be updated online with newly added content. No manual clusterization of inputs is needed.

- Description of a parallelized implementation for learning the models and sampling from them using Tensorflow [2]. The models also permit checkpoints and online learning.
- Present a technique for assigning begin/end markers in the pre-processed training data that works for all kinds of files, not just the well-known ones. The previous work in the field that uses the same core system as our tool (i.e. recurrent neural networks) is focused only on PDF files.
- Allows users to leverage expert system in oversizing the work and perform custom optimizations and logs for learning or sampling certain categories of file types.
- Describes how to use the recurrent neural networks generative models for applications with binary input context too.

The paper is structured as follows. Next section presents some existing work in the field that inspired the work presented in this paper. Section 3 makes a quick introduction in one of the ways machine learning can be used to generate new texts based on an existing corpus of texts. Section 4 presents our methods for automating the process of test data generation. Evaluation of our tool and methods are discussed in Sect. 5. Finally, conclusions and future work are given in the last section.

2 Related Work

One of the main differences between fuzz testing and symbolic testing is that the former has the potential of getting better code coverage in shorter time and with less resources used, while the latter can exploit all possible branches of a process with less resources consumed overall. It all depends on how complex is the program under test, computational resources available and how many test requests are in a given unit of time. In large companies, or online source-code repositories, which usually need a quick testing of newly committed source code, it is important to have variety that can get code coverage with minimal resource consumption in very short time after each code commit. Thus, fuzz testing can be an efficient method for covering such use cases.

In the field of fuzzing techniques, there are three main categories currently: blackbox random fuzzing [30], whitebox random fuzzing [14], and grammar based fuzzing [25,30]. The first two are automatic methods proving efficiency in finding vulnerabilities in binary-format file parsers. These methods are also augmented with others for better results. For example, in [24] authors present a distributed framework using genetic algorithms that generates new tests by looking at the probability of each branch encountered during the execution. Their fitness function scores a newly generated input test by the probability of the branches encountered in the program's execution trace. This way, the genetic algorithm tries to create input data that drives the program's execution towards rare (low probability) branches inside the program's control flow. They use Apache Spark for parallelization and dynamic tainting to know the paths taken during the execution. Their method obtains better scores than classical random fuzzers and it is one of the solutions that we compare against, including the same two examples: an HTTP and an XML parser.

On the other side, the grammar based fuzzing is not fully automatic: it requires a grammar specifying the input format of the application under test. Typically, this grammar is written by hand and the process becomes time consuming and error prone. It can be viewed as a model-based testing [32], and the work on it started with [16,25]. Having the input grammar, test generation from it can be done either (usually) random [10,27] or exhaustive [19]. Methods that combine whitebox fuzzing with grammar-based fuzzing were discussed in [13,20]. Recent work concentrates also on learning grammars automatically. For instance, [5] presents an algorithm to synthesize a context-free grammar from a given set of inputs. The method uses repetition and alternation constructs for regular expressions, then merging non-terminals for the grammar construction. This can capture hierarchical properties from the input formats but, as mentioned in [15] the method is not well suited for formats such as PDF objects for instance, which include a large diverse set of content types and key-value pair.

Autogram, mentioned in [17] learns context-free grammars given a set of inputs by using dynamic tainting, i.e. dynamically observing how inputs are processed inside a program. Syntactic entities in the generated grammar are constructed hierarchically by observing what parts of the given input is processed by the program. Each such input part becomes an entity in the grammar. The same idea of processing input formats from examples and producing grammars, but this time associating data structures with addresses in the application's address space is presented in [11].

Both approaches described above for learning grammars automatically require access to the program for adding instrumentation. Thus, their applicability and precision for complex formats under proprietary applications such as XML, PNG or ZIP file parsers is unclear. There are two main differences between our method and Autogram:

1. Our method can work on all kind of programming languages while Autogram works only with Java source code. They use Java Virtual Machine to understand variables content by analysing the execution stack. Our method is more generic since the trace tool (Sect. 3) uses in the analysis side the assembly language generated from the source code.
2. We generate grammars and do inference only for the parts of the input stream that affect the execution flow of the program, while Autogram generates and perform inference for all variables that have a connection with the input stream. This should intuitively make our method faster to train and inference.

The method presented in [15] uses neural-network models to learn statistical generative models for such formats. Starting from a base suite of input PDF files (not binaries) they concatenate all and use recurrent neural networks (RNN, and more specifically a sequence - to - sequence network) to learn a generative model for other PDF files. Their work is focused on generative models for non-binary objects.

Dynamic tainting has numerous applications such as finding and analyzing security threats [3,22], software test generation using in combination with concolic execution [6], or in combination with fuzz testing and genetic algorithms [4,21]. One of the most appreciated tools for practical fuzzing today, *AFL* (american fuzzy lop) [1], is based on genetic algorithms and various heuristics to find faster vulnerabilities and achieve good code coverage. We compared it against our solution to find out what is the difference between them. On short, AFL tends to be better sometimes for short time tests done over text-based inputs, while ours can get better results over longer execution times. An improved fuzzing tool, with reported results above AFL is *Angora* [7]. It uses runtime taint analysis and keeps stack context on branch transitions to achieve improved code coverage and bugs finding. However, it is dependent on LLVM and needs access to the source code. Instead, our tool works at binary level (i.e. doesn't need access to the source code), and this is the reason we don't compare our methods against Angora.

This paper is an update of [23] with some improvements over original content: added our new work regarding RNNs usage for binary inputs too, new experiments and comparison with one of the state of the art tools - AFL, another type of application benchmark - a JSON parser, and several text improvements and clarifications.

3   Using Machine Learning to Learn Generative Models for Testing

A statistical learning approach for learning generative models for PDF files was introduced in [15]. Their main idea is to learn the model based on a large corpus of PDF objects using recurrent neural networks, and more specifically a sequence-to-sequence network model [8,29]. This model has been used for machine translation [29] and speech recognition [9], producing state of the art results in these fields. The model can be trained in an unsupervised manner to learn a generative model from the corpus folder, then used to produce new sequences of test data. Recurrent neural networks are a good candidate for this case because these algorithms have an internal memory, compared to other machine learning algorithms, as in they have access to previous states, information cycling through a loop. This detail is important in exploring the problem that we are facing and it gives an important advantage when considering the following iterations, keeping a track of the previous ones in memory. Being able to remember aspects about the input they received, it enables them to be more precise in predicting what's coming next and how to consider the rest of the iterations. This is the main reason why they are preferred algorithm for sequential data.

3.1   Sequence-to-Sequence Neural Network Model

Recurrent neural networks (RNN) are neural network models that operate on a variable input sequence $< x_1, x_2, ..., x_T >$ and have a hidden layer of states h, and an output y. At each time step (t) one element from the input sequence is consumed, modifying the internal hidden state and the output of the network as follows:

$$h_t = f(h_{t-1}, x_t) \tag{1}$$

$$y_t = \sigma(h_t), \tag{2}$$

where σ is a function such as softmax (used typically in learning classifiers) that computes the output probability distribution over a given vocabulary by taking into account the current hidden state, while f is a non-linear activation function used to make the transition between hidden states (e.g. of functions: sigmoid, tanh, ReLU, etc). Thus, the RNN can learn the probability distribution of the next character (x_t) in the vocabulary, given a character sequence as input $< x_1, x_2, ..., x_{t-1} >$, i.e. it can learn the conditional distribution $p(x_t| < x_1, x_2, ..., x_{t-1} >)$.

Sequence-to-sequence model (seq2seq) was introduced in [8]. It consists of two connected recurrent neural networks: one that acts as an encoder, processing a variable input sequence and producing a fixed dimensional representation, and another one that acts as a decoder by taking the fixed dimensional input sequence representation and generating a variable dimensional output sequence. The decoder network uses the output character at time step t as an input character for time step $t+1$. Thus, it learns a conditional distribution over a sequence of next outputs, i.e. $p(< y_1, ..., y_{T1} > | < x_1, ..., x_{T2} >)$. Figure 2 shows the architecture of the model (Fig. 1).

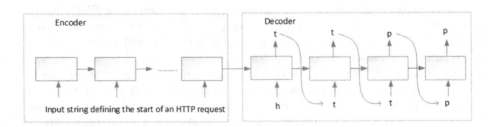

Fig. 1. A sequence-to-sequence graphical representation. In this example, the encoder part takes as input the internal string marker representing the beginning of an HTTP request, while the decoder produces the beginning text of such a request. Source: [23].

The test data of generative models presented in this paper uses the seq2seq models. The corpus of input files are treated as a sequence of characters, so the model itself contains the distribution of the next character in the vocabulary based on a previously generated context. An *epoch* is defined in the machine learning terminology as a full iteration of the learning algorithm over the entire training database (i.e. input files in the corpus). In the evaluation section, we use different epochs (10, 20, 30, 40 and 50) to correlate the time needed to train versus the quality of the trained model.

3.2   Using the Model to Generate New Inputs

After the seq2seq model is trained, it can be used to generate new inputs based on the probability distribution of next characters and the previously generated context. The work in [15] always starts with "obj" string and continuously generates characters using different policies to draw the next characters from the model, until the output produced is the string "endobj". These markers are the ones used to represent the beginning and ending of PDF objects. While our tool is capable of dynamically adapting to new/unknown file types or without any expert knowledge, we use a different strategy for defining the beginning/end markers (see the next section for details).

There are four documented policies that can be used when deciding which character a model should output next:

- No sampling: just use the model as it is without randomness; this will produce deterministic results from any starting point, i.e. the highest probability character will be chosen always.
- Sample: random sampling at each next character according to the probability distribution encapsulated in the model. This strategy produces a diverse set of new inputs combining the patterns learned from data but also mixing with random fuzzing.
- SampleSpace: random sampling only at white spaces. According to the evaluation section, this produces better well-formed new inputs that are not deterministic but that are not as diverse as the Sample model.
- SampleFuzz: A parameter defines the threshold probability for deciding how to choose the next character from the learned model. Then, a random value is drawn at each time step and if it is higher than the threshold, the next character chosen is the one with the highest probability from the learned model. Otherwise, the character with the lowest probability is selected in an attempt to trick the PDF parser. The idea was analysed in [15]. However, in our analysis this shows worse results than Sample and SampleSpace methods.

4   Pipeline for Generating New Tests Based on Existing Corpus

The tool presented in this paper is open-source and currently available at: https://github.com/AGAPIA/river-trace-analysis-and-fuzz. It receives as input a corpus of different input file types, with no previous classification made manually by the user. The content of the folder can be updated online in both directions: either adding new files of existing types, or adding new file types. This is an important requirement since the main requirements from software security companies (such as the one we collaborated with, Bitdefender) are: (1) to be able to learn and produce new inputs of different kinds for many different programs with the purpose of security evaluation, and (2) to automatically and dynamically collect data from users, i.e. new input tests are added online and used to improve the trained model).

4.1   The Training Pipeline

Given the path to an existing corpus folder (*data*), the training pipeline writes its output in two folders:

1. *data_preprocesses*
2. *data_models*

Folder (1) stores the clusterized and preprocessed corpus data. Since the types of the files in there is unknown, our first target is to cluster them by identifying the type of each file in the corpus then put them in a different sub-folder corresponding to each file type. As an example, if the corpus folder (*data*) contains four different input file types such as XML, PDF, JSON and HTTP requests, then the first step will create (if not already existing) four clusters (folders) and add each input file to the corresponding one. Currently, the classification of files to clusters is done using the $file - l$ command in Unix, and getting the output string of the command (we plan to improve this classification in the future work by using unsupervised learning and perform clusterization based on common identified features). Since at each training epoch the entire sequence of character in each file must be processed, and considering that seek operations on disk can be expensive, the strategy used by our training pipeline is to concatenate together all files in each cluster (folder) in a single file to make the training process faster. Thus, each of the four folders in the concrete example above will contain a single file with the aggregated context from the initial ones. The neural-network model of each cluster is trained by splitting the aggregated file content ($C_{Content}$) in multiple training sequences of a fixed size L, which can be customized by user. Thus, the ith training sequence contains $t_i = C_{Content}[i * L : (i + 1) * L]$ (where F[a : b] denotes the subsequence of characters in F between indices a and b). For each of these training sequences, the expected output that the network is trained against is the input one shifted by 1 position to the right, i.e, $o_i = C_{Content}[i * L + 1 : (i+1) * L + 1]$. The model is then trained with all these input/output sequences from a cluster's content and using backpropagation to correct the weights, it learns the probability map of next characters having a given context (prior sequence). This previous context is modeled with the hidden state layer.

However, we need a generic way to mark the beginning and ending of an individual file content, such that the sampling method knows how to start and when to stop. At this moment, the beginning marker is a string *BEGIN#CLUSTERID*, while the end marker is a string *END#CLUSTERID*, where *CLUSTERID* is an integer built using a string to integer mapping heuristic. The input string used for mapping is the full classification output string given by the $file - l$ command when the file was classified in a cluster. A supervisor map checks if all hashcodes are unique and tries different methods until for each cluster there is a unique identifier. The equation below (Source: [23]) shows the content of a cluster's aggregated file, where the $\sum$ and + operators acts as concatenation of strings, and C is a given cluster type.

$$Identifier(C) = GetUniqueClusterIdentifier(C)$$

$$Cluster(C) = \sum_{each file F \in C} (\text{``}BEGIN\text{''} + Identifier(C)$$

$$+ FileContent(F) + \text{``}END\text{''} + Identifier(C))$$

The tool uses Tensorflow [2] for implementing both learning and sampling processes. Each cluster will have its own generative model, saved in *data_models* folder. In the example given above, four models will be created, one for each XML, PDF, JSON, and HTTP input types. A mapping from $CLUSTERID$ to the corresponding model will be created (and stored on disk) to let the sampling process know where to get data from. In the network built using Tensorflow implementation we use LSTM cells for avoiding the problems with exploding or vanishing gradients [33]. By default, the network built has two hidden layers each with 128 hidden states. However, the user can modify this network using expert knowledge per cluster granularity as stated in Sect. 4.4 (the starting point of the process described in this section is defined in *generateModel.py* script, which has a documented set of parameters as help). Tensorflow is also able to parallelize automatically the training/sampling in a given cluster. On a high-level view, the framework allows users to customize a network and its internal compiler/executer decides where to run tasks with the scope of optimizing performance (e.g. minimize communication time, GPU-CPU memory transfer, etc).

Our tool takes advantage of the checkpointing feature available in the Tensorflow framework, i.e. at any time the learned model up to a point can be saved to disk. This helps users by letting them update the generative models if new files were added dynamically to the clusters after the initial learning step. This way, the learned weights in the neural network are reused and if the new files are not completely different in terms of features from the initial ones, the training time scales proportionally to the size of the new content added. At the implementation level, an indexing service keeps the track of the new content in each cluster and informs a service periodically to start the generative models updating for each of the modified clusters. Another advantage of the checkpoint feature is that it allows users to take advantage of the intermediate trained models. Although not optimal, these can be used in parallel with the training process (until convergence) to generate new test data.

4.2 New Inputs Generation

The pseudocode in the listing below shows the method used to generate a new input test. The function receives as input a cluster type (considering that there exists a trained generative model for the given cluster), and a policy functor pointing to one of the four policies defined in the previous section. The first step is to get the custom parameters and the begin/end marker strings for the given cluster. The next step is to feed the entire begin marker string (starting with a zero set hidden layer) and get the resulted hidden state. This will capture

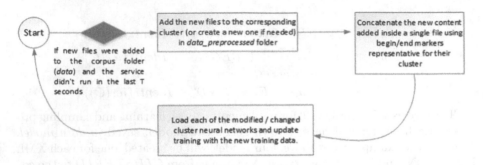

Fig. 2. The process of updating the generative models. Source: [23].

the context learned from the training data at the beginning of the files in that cluster. Then, the code loops producing output characters one by one using the probability distribution map (P) returned by the $FeedForward$ function in the current state (h_state). At each iteration, as seen in Fig. 2, the last produced output character and state are given as parameters to find the probability distribution map over vocabulary. The loop ends when the last part of the output (suffix) is exactly the end marker string (or until a certain maximum size was produced to avoid blocking if the training was not good enough to get to the end marker). The starting point of the concrete implementation can be found in the script file named $sampleModel.py$.

```
SampleNewTest(Cluster, PolicyType):

  Params = GetParams(Cluster)
  BeginMarker, EndMarker = GetMarkers(Params)

  foreach c in BeginMarker:
    h_state, P = FeedForward(h0, internalRNN, c)
    lastChar = c

  output = ""

  while the suffix of output != EndMarker :
    lastChar = Policy(PolicyType, P, lastChar)
    output += lastChar
    h_state, P = FeedForward(h_state,
                     internalRNN, lastChar)
return output
```

Source: [23]

A pseudocode defining sampling policies is presented in the listing below. Roulette-wheel based random selection is used with the Sample policy, and with the SampleSpace one when the previous character generated was a whitespace. If SampleSpace is used but still inside a word, or if SampleFuzz sampling method is used and the random value drawn is higher than the fuzz threshold, then the character with the highest probability from the vocabulary is chosen. Instead, if the random value is smaller than fuzz threshold, the character with the lowest probability is chosen in an attempt to trick the program under test.

```
Policy(PolicyType, P, C):
  switch Type:
    case NoSample:
        return argmax(P)
    case SampleSpace:
        if C == " " return roulettewheel(P)
        else return argmax(P)
    case Sample:
        return roulettewheel(P)
    case SampleFuzz:
        if rand < FuzzThreshold:
            return argmin(P)
        else
            return argmax(P)
    default:
        assert "no such policy"
```

Source: [23]

4.3   Producing Generative Models for Applications with Binary Inputs

Considering N samples of test examples for a specific application Fig. 3, and by using using our *RIVER* tool (https://github.com/bitdefender/, [28]), we can find out which parts of the inputs can affect the branching decision of a program through taint analysis [31]. The intuition is that to achieve efficient result, we should concentrate fuzzing more on those specific areas rather than the whole input. Considering this, our approach is to create generative models for each of the sample and contiguous green region. At inference time, we choose one of the sample, duplicate it in a memory region, call each green area model, and fuzz the rest of the input a little bit. The process is depicted in the listing below.

```
GetNewBinaryInput(AppType A)
  NewInput = GetRandomInputSampleByAppType( A )
  for each model M in NewInput
    PartialInput = SampleNewTest(M)
    Replace the bytes covered by M (green areas) in NewInput with PartialInput

  Random fuzzing 5% of uncovered areas in NewInput
  return NewInput
```

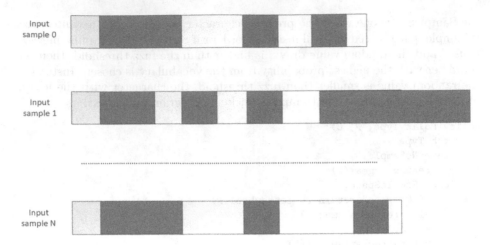

Fig. 3. Different length test samples for a given application from the training set. Marked with green are regions of the input that can affect branching conditions, i.e. the application flow. (Color figure online)

4.4   Expert Knowledge

Different clusters might need different parameters for optimal results. For example, training PDF objects might require more time to get to the same loss result than the threshold set for learning HTTP requests. The optimal parameters can differ starting from simple thresholds to the configuration of the neural network structure, i.e. the number of hidden layers or states. The tool allows users to inject their own parameters for both learning and sampling new results, by using a map data structure that looks more like an expert system. If custom data is available in that map (e.g. [*"HTTP request cluster"*, *num hidden layers*] = 1) for a particular cluster and parameters, then those are used instead of the default ones. Another example is the customization of the beginning/end markers used to know when a certain input data starts and ends. For well-known types, the user can override our default method for assigning the markers with the correct ones (e.g. PDF objects start with "obj" and end with "endobj"). Also, since Tensorflow can provide graphical statistics added by users (Tensorboard) during both training and sampling, the tool allows users to insert customized logs and graphics per cluster type using the function hooks provided.

5   Evaluation

As the previous work in the field [15] already evaluated the training efficiency of the core method, i.e. learning a generative model with RNNs and do inference over it to find new inputs, using PDF file types, we evaluate our tool using three more parser applications: XML parser[1], JSON parser[2], and HTTP parser[3]. However, we use our own mark system for beginning/ending of a file, which works for generic (any kind of) file types as mentioned in Sect. 4. The two new mentioned test applications were used to compare the results directly against the work in [24], which uses random fuzz testing driven by a genetic algorithm to get better coverage over time, and the same two programs for evaluation.

5.1 Experiment Setup and Methodology

The experiments described below involved a cluster of 8 PCs, each one with 12 physical CPU cores, totaling 96 physical cores of approximately the same performance (Intel Core i7-5930K 3.50 GHz). Each of the PC had one GPU device, an Nvidia GTX 1070. The user should note that adding more GPUs into the system could improve performance with our tool since the benchmarks show that the GPU device was in average about 15 times faster than the CPU both for learning models and generating new tests.

In our tests, we ultimately care about the coverage metric of a database of input tests: how many branches of a program are evaluated using all the available tests, and how much time did we spend to get to that coverage? Our implementation uses a tool called Tracer that can run a program P against the input test data and produce a trace, i.e., an ordered list of branch instructions $B_0, \ldots, B_n$ that a program encountered while executing with the given input test: $Tracer(P, test) = B_0 B_1 ... B_n$. Because a program can make calls to other libraries or system executables, each branch is a pair of the module name and offset where the branch instruction occurred: $B_i = (module, offset)$. Note that we divide our program in basic blocks, which are sequences of x86 instructions that contain exactly one branch instruction at its end. We used a tracer tool developed by Bitdefender company, which helped us in the evaluation process, but there are also open-source tracer tools such as Bintrace[4]. Having a set of input test files, we name coverage the set of different instructions (pairs of $(module, offset)$) encountered by Tracer when executing all those tests. We are interested in maximizing the size of this set usually, and/or minimizing the time needed to obtain good coverage.

Specifically, when training generative models, another point of interest is how efficient is the trained model with different setups, i.e. how many newly generated tests are correctly compiled by the HTTP and XML parsers (*Pass Rate* metric)? This could help us make a correlation between the Pass Rate and coverage metrics.

---

[1] http://xmlsoft.org.
[2] https://github.com/nlohmann/json.
[3] https://github.com/nodejs/http-parser.
[4] https://bitbucket.org/mihaila/bintrace.

5.2   Training Data and Generation of New Tests

The training set consisted of XML, JSON, and PDF files that were taken using web-crawling different websites. A total of 12.000 files were randomly selected and stored for each of these three categories. For HTTP requests, we used an internal logger to collect 100.000 of such request. The folder grouping all these inputs is named in our terminology *corpus test set*. A metric to understand how well does the trained model learn is named *Pass Rate*. This estimates (using the output from *grep* tool) the percent of tests (from the generated suite) that are well formatted for the parser under test. As Fig. 4 shows, and as expected, the quality of trained model grows with the number of epochs used for training (i.e. the number of full passes over the entire training data set). Randomizing only on spaces (i.e. using SampleSpace) gives better results for Pass Rate metric since more data is used as indicated as being optimal by the trained model. Tensorflow was used for both training and inference, and the hardware system considered was the one described at the beginning of this section.

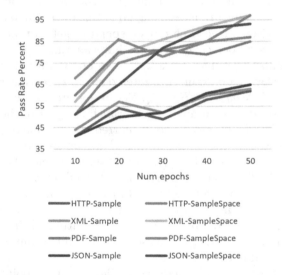

Fig. 4. Pass Rate metric evaluation for different number of epochs and models used to generate new tests.

Table 1 shows the time needed to perform model learning over the entire corpus folder of 12.000 PDF, JSON and XML files, and 100.000 HTTP requests using a different number of epochs. Other parameters are also important, the user should also take a look at the description of those inside the tool's repository and try to parametrize with expert knowledge for more optimizations when dealing with new file types. Table 2 shows the timings for producing 10.000 new inputs for PDF, JSON and XML files, and 50.000 of HTTP requests. As expected, since there is only inference through a learned model, the timings are almost equal between all models (we do not even show the difference between Sample and SampleSpace since the difference is negligible). Actually, from profiling the data tests generation it takes more time to write the output data (i.e. input tests) on disk rather than spending cycles on inference.

Table 1. Time in hours to train models on different number of epochs and using 12.000 files for PDF, JSON, and XML, and 100.000 HTTP requests as training dataset.

Num epochs	HTTP	XML	PDF	JSON
50	8h:25	7h:19	9h:11	8h:01
40	6h:59	5h:56	8h:04	6h:09
30	5h:35	4h:20	6h:15	4h:53
20	3h:48	3h:42	4h:17	3h:24
10	2h:10	1h:12	3h:02	1h:35

Table 2. The average time needed to produce 10.000 new inputs for PDF, JSON, and XML files, and 50.000 new HTTP requests.

File type	Time in minutes
XML	49
HTTP	25
PDF	51
JSON	53

Main Takeaway. The time needed to train the model is fixed, depending on the number of epochs and a few other parameters. After the training phase, the tool can create huge databases of new inputs (valid ones) quickly, which in the end can provide better code coverage than existing fuzzing methods. Those do not need the training phase, but the new tests generated are often rejected from early tests inside the program because of their incorrect format.

5.3 Coverage Evaluation

For the coverage evaluation tables below, we considered only the model trained with 30 epochs, which was the winner in terms of performance versus training cost. Using 40 or 50 epochs increased just with a few new lines the coverage over time, but the training time is significantly higher. Of course, the user should experiment and find the optimal number of epochs depending on training data size for example, and their budget time limit allocated for training.

Tables 3, 5 and 4 show the coverage for XML, JSON and HTTP file types by using three different evaluation methods. The first one, with suffix -fuzz+genetic, considers the fuzzing method driven by genetic algorithms as explained in [24].

Table 3. The number of branch instructions touched in comparison between random fuzzing driven by genetic algorithms, Sample and SampleSpace models for XML files.

Model	9h	15h	24h	72h
XML-fuzz+genetic	1271	1279	1285	1286
XML-Sample	1290	1364	1455	1549
XML-SampleSpace	1291	1375	1407	1553
XML-AFL	1294	1351	1360	1395

Table 4. The number of branch instructions touched in comparison between random fuzzing driven by genetic algorithms, Sample and SampleSpace models for HTTP requests.

Model	9h	15h	24h	72h
HTTP-fuzz+genetic	229	230	230	232
HTTP-Sample	238	249	257	271
HTTP-SampleSpace	241	245	269	279
HTTP-AFL	243	248	251	263

Table 5. The number of branch instructions touched in comparison between random fuzzing driven by genetic algorithms, Sample and SampleSpace models for JSON requests.

Model	9h	15h	24h	72h
JSON-fuzz+genetic	151	174	263	269
JSON-Sample	290	364	455	449
JSON-SampleSpace	298	370	407	453
JSON-AFL	321	335	355	385

The Sample and SampleSpace are the two models used for sampling defined above in this paper which uses our tool. The entries with suffix -AFL are tests performed against AFL tool [1]. The main observation is that with simple fuzzing (i.e. no use of generative models), the coverage value converges quickly to a value, without necessarily growing by having more time allocated. This happens mainly because the random fuzzing methods produce many times inputs that are not correct, being rejected by early outs, or difficult to deviate from a few common branches inside a program even when adopting different policies to guide fuzzing [15,24]. However, fuzzing without learning the input context techniques have their own advantage: they are simple to implement and require no training time. For instance, if smoke tests [18] are needed after changing the user application's source code and input grammar, quick random fuzzing methods are very efficient since they do not require any training time. Learning a generative model is not feasible in this situation due to the limited time needed to respond to the new code change. Actually, techniques can be combined: classic fuzzing can be used for smoke tests, while fuzzing with generative models such as the one presented in this paper can be used to perform longer and more performant tests.

In 72 h using the system described in the setup, the system was able to get approximately 10 to 20% more coverage than the best fuzzing models available on the XML, JSON, and HTTP cases. Also, please note again that the models evaluated were chosen to compare against other documented results. Our tool is able to produce generative models and training tests after training on any kind of user inputs formats (e.g. HTML, DOC, XLS, source code for different programming languages, etc). An interesting aspect is that the Sample method has better results than SampleSpace one, although the Pass Rate metric shows inverse results. Remember that by sampling each character according to the probability distribution in the generative model, it has a higher rate of making inputs incorrect (Fig. 4). One possible explanation for this is that having a high rate of correct inputs can make the program avoid some instructions that were verifying the code's correctness in more detail. Thus, those instructions might be encountered by Tracer only when the inputs given are a mix between correct and (slightly) invalid. In [15] there is also a discussion about performing random fuzzing over the inputs learned using RNN methods, but similar to our evaluation, the results are not better than the Sample method. The other technique presented in [17] that learns the grammar of the input through dynamic tainting and applicable currently only to Java programs, could not be evaluated since the tool is not (yet) open-source and could not be retrieved in any other way.

6   Conclusions and Future Work

This paper presented an open-source tool that addresses the problem of generating automatic test inputs for multiple programs under test at the same time. Starting with a basic set of input in the corpus folder for learning some starting models for each application type under test, the tool allows online-learning to improve the initial set of the generative models quality over time. The support is available for both binary and text input types. Other important features offered by the tool presented in this work are the capability to operate efficiently in distributed computing environments, and the checkpointing support implemented to pause and continue improving the existing models. The evaluation section shows the efficiency of using the recurrent neural network architectures for learning generative models that are able to produce new tests, from two main perspectives: improved instruction coverage over random fuzzing and the percent of correct input files produced from the learned model.

On our future work plans, we are interested in analyzing the effectiveness of using Generative adversarial networks (GANs) in improving tests coverage and compare them against the RNNs. Also, we plan improvements over the user control of the tool, like adding a visual interface for controlling parameters and injecting expert knowledge in learning and generation processes in an easier way.

Acknowledgments. This work was supported by a grant of Romanian Ministry of Research and Innovation CCCDI-UEFISCDI. project no. 17PCCDI/2018 We would like to thank our colleagues Teodor Stoenescu and Alexandra Sandulescu from Bitdefender, and to Alin Stefanescu from University of Bucharest for fruitful discussions and collaboration.

References

1. Afl. (2018). http://lcamtuf.coredump.cx/afl/
2. Abadi, M., et al.: Tensorflow: large-scale machine learning on heterogeneous distributed systems. CoRR abs/1603.04467 (2016). http://arxiv.org/abs/1603.04467
3. Arzt, S., et al.: Flowdroid: precise context, flow, field, object-sensitive and lifecycle-aware taint analysis for android apps. In: PLDI (2014)
4. Avancini, A., Ceccato, M.: Towards security testing with taint analysis and genetic algorithms. In: Proceedings of the 2010 ICSE Workshop on Software Engineering for Secure Systems, SESS 2010, pp. 65–71. ACM, New York (2010). https://doi.org/10.1145/1809100.1809110. http://doi.acm.org/10.1145/1809100.1809110
5. Bastani, O., Sharma, R., Aiken, A., Liang, P.: Synthesizing program input grammars. SIGPLAN Not. **52**(6), 95–110 (2017). https://doi.org/10.1145/3140587.3062349. http://doi.acm.org/10.1145/3140587.3062349
6. Bekrar, S., Groz, R., Mounier, L., Bekrar, C.: Finding software vulnerabilities by smart fuzzing. In: 2011 Fourth IEEE International Conference on Software Testing, Verification and Validation (ICST), pp. 427–430, March 2011. https://doi.org/10.1109/ICST.2011.48. http://doi.ieeecomputersociety.org/10.1109/ICST.2011.48
7. Chen, P., Chen, H.: Angora: efficient fuzzing by principled search. CoRR abs/1803.01307 (2018)
8. Cho, K., van Merrienboer, B., Gülçehre, Ç., Bougares, F., Schwenk, H., Bengio, Y.: Learning phrase representations using RNN encoder-decoder for statistical machine translation. CoRR abs/1406.1078 (2014). http://arxiv.org/abs/1406.1078
9. Chorowski, J., Bahdanau, D., Serdyuk, D., Cho, K., Bengio, Y.: Attention-based models for speech recognition. CoRR abs/1506.07503 (2015). http://arxiv.org/abs/1506.07503
10. Coppit, D., Lian, J.: Yagg: an easy-to-use generator for structured test inputs. In: Proceedings of the 20th IEEE/ACM International Conference on Automated Software Engineering, ASE 2005, pp. 356–359. ACM, New York (2005). https://doi.org/10.1145/1101908.1101969. http://doi.acm.org/10.1145/1101908.1101969
11. Cui, W., Peinado, M., Chen, K., Wang, H.J., Irun-Briz, L.: Tupni: automatic reverse engineering of input formats. In: Proceedings of the 15th ACM Conference on Computer and Communications Security, CCS 2008, pp. 391–402. ACM, New York (2008). https://doi.org/10.1145/1455770.1455820. http://doi.acm.org/10.1145/1455770.1455820
12. Godefroid, P.: Random testing for security: blackbox vs. whitebox fuzzing. In: RT 2007 (2007)
13. Godefroid, P., Kiezun, A., Levin, M.Y.: Grammar-based whitebox fuzzing. In: Proceedings of the 29th ACM SIGPLAN Conference on Programming Language Design and Implementation, PLDI 2008, pp. 206–215. ACM, New York (2008). https://doi.org/10.1145/1375581.1375607. http://doi.acm.org/10.1145/1375581.1375607

14. Godefroid, P., Levin, M.Y., Molnar, D.: Sage: whitebox fuzzing for security testing. Queue **10**(1), 20:20–20:27 (2012). https://doi.org/10.1145/2090147.2094081. http://doi.acm.org/10.1145/2090147.2094081

15. Godefroid, P., Peleg, H., Singh, R.: Learn&fuzz: machine learning for input fuzzing. In: Rosu, G., Penta, M.D., Nguyen, T.N. (eds.) Proceedings of the 32nd IEEE/ACM International Conference on Automated Software Engineering, ASE 2017, Urbana, IL, USA, 30 October–3 November 2017, pp. 50–59. IEEE Computer Society (2017). https://doi.org/10.1109/ASE.2017.8115618

16. Hanford, K.V.: Automatic generation of test cases. IBM Syst. J. **9**(4), 242–257 (1970). https://doi.org/10.1147/sj.94.0242

17. Höschele, M., Zeller, A.: Mining input grammars from dynamic taints. In: Proceedings of the 31st IEEE/ACM International Conference on Automated Software Engineering, ASE 2016, pp. 720–725. ACM, New York (2016). https://doi.org/10.1145/2970276.2970321. http://doi.acm.org/10.1145/2970276.2970321

18. Kaner, C., Bach, J., Pettichord, B.: Lessons Learned in Software Testing. Wiley, New York (2001)

19. Lämmel, R., Schulte, W.: Controllable combinatorial coverage in grammar-based testing. In: Uyar, M.Ü., Duale, A.Y., Fecko, M.A. (eds.) TestCom 2006. LNCS, vol. 3964, pp. 19–38. Springer, Heidelberg (2006). https://doi.org/10.1007/11754008_2

20. Majumdar, R., Xu, R.G.: Directed test generation using symbolic grammars. In: Proceedings of the Twenty-Second IEEE/ACM International Conference on Automated Software Engineering, ASE 2007, pp. 134–143. ACM, New York (2007). https://doi.org/10.1145/1321631.1321653. http://doi.acm.org/10.1145/1321631.1321653

21. Mathis, B.: Dynamic tainting for automatic test case generation. In: Proceedings of the 26th ACM SIGSOFT International Symposium on Software Testing and Analysis, ISSTA 2017, pp. 436–439. ACM, New York (2017). https://doi.org/10.1145/3092703.3098233. http://doi.acm.org/10.1145/3092703.3098233

22. Newsome, J.: Dynamic taint analysis for automatic detection, analysis, and signature generation of exploits on commodity software (2005)

23. Paduraru, C., Melemciuc, M.: An automatic test data generation tool using machine learning. In: Maciaszek, L.A., van Sinderen, M. (eds.) Proceedings of the 13th International Conference on Software Technologies, ICSOFT 2018, Porto, Portugal, 26–28 July 2018, pp. 506–515. SciTePress (2018). https://doi.org/10.5220/0006836605060515

24. Paduraru, C., Melemciuc, M., Stefanescu, A.: A distributed implementation using apache spark of a genetic algorithm applied to test data generation. In: Bosman, P.A.N. (ed.) Genetic and Evolutionary Computation Conference, Berlin, Germany, 15–19 July 2017, Companion Material Proceedings, pp. 1857–1863. ACM (2017). https://doi.org/10.1145/3067695.3084219. http://doi.acm.org/10.1145/3067695.3084219

25. Purdom, P.: A sentence generator for testing parsers. BIT Numer. Math. **12**(3), 366–375 (1972). https://doi.org/10.1007/BF01932308

26. Rajpal, M., Blum, W., Singh, R.: Not all bytes are equal: Neural byte sieve for fuzzing. CoRR abs/1711.04596 (2017). http://arxiv.org/abs/1711.04596

27. Sirer, E.G., Bershad, B.N.: Using production grammars in software testing. SIGPLAN Not. **35**(1), 1–13 (1999). https://doi.org/10.1145/331963.331965. http://doi.acm.org/10.1145/331963.331965

28. Stoenescu, T., Stefanescu, A., Predut, S., Ipate, F.: Binary analysis based on symbolic execution and reversible x86 instructions. Fundam. Inform. **153**(1–2), 105–124 (2017). https://doi.org/10.3233/FI-2017-1533

29. Sutskever, I., Vinyals, O., Le, Q.V.: Sequence to sequence learning with neural networks. CoRR abs/1409.3215 (2014). http://arxiv.org/abs/1409.3215
30. Sutton, M., Greene, A., Amini, P.: Fuzzing: Brute Force Vulnerability Discovery. Addison-Wesley Professional, Reading (2007)
31. Tripp, O., Pistoia, M., Fink, S.J., Sridharan, M., Weisman, O.: Taj: effective taint analysis of web applications. SIGPLAN Not. **44**(6), 87–97 (2009). https://doi.org/10.1145/1543135.1542486. http://doi.acm.org/10.1145/1543135.1542486
32. Utting, M., Pretschner, A., Legeard, B.: A taxonomy of model-based testing approaches. Softw. Test. Verif. Reliab. **22**(5), 297–312 (2012). https://doi.org/10.1002/stvr.456
33. Zaremba, W., Sutskever, I., Vinyals, O.: Recurrent neural network regularization. CoRR abs/1409.2329 (2014). http://arxiv.org/abs/1409.2329

Guiding the Functional Change Decisions in Agile Project: An Empirical Evaluation

Asma Sellami[1(✉)], Mariem Haoues[2(✉)], Nour Borchani[1(✉)],
and Nadia Bouassida[1(✉)]

[1] Mir@cl Laboratory, ISIMS, University of Sfax, BP 242, 3021 Sfax, Tunisia
{asma.sellami,nadia.bouassida}@isims.usf.tn, borchani.nour@gmail.com
[2] Mir@cl Laboratory, FSEGS, University of Sfax, BP 1088, 3018 Sfax, Tunisia
mariem.haoues@isims.usf.tn

Abstract. Agile methods are becoming increasingly used in software industry as a response to the challenges of managing the frequent changes during the software life-cycle. However, an important number of agile projects yield unsatisfactory results and end up with failure. This is due mainly to a lack of structured change control process. A well-defined change control process gives software industry a significant competitive advantage. This paper describes an evaluation of functional changes affecting either an ongoing sprint or an implemented sprint. This evaluation can greatly assist the development teams in making appropriate decisions. We quantitatively and qualitatively evaluate 15 software development projects using agile (scrum) method. We also investigate the use of COSMIC Functional Size Measurement method for a rapid quantification and evaluation of a change request.

Keywords: Functional change · Software requirements ·
Functional size measurement · User story description ·
COSMIC-ISO 19761 · Scrum · User stories · Agile

1 Introduction

Software projects are incredibly hard to manage when compared to other kinds of projects. This is due mainly to invisibility, complexity, conformity and changeability of the software products in comparison to other products [15]. Hence, software managers need an effective change control process to ensure the trade-offs between the particular project constraints (budget, duration and scope), while ultimately satisfying the customers' needs.

At the beginning of the Software Life-Cycle (SLC), requirements are often unclear, ambiguous, and incomplete. Hence, they may change frequently during the software development. In addition, other reasons may cause the requirements change (*e.g.,* missing functionality, defects corrections, etc.) [7]. However, the cost of a requirements change at an early phase of the SLC is relatively low compared to the cost of changing requirements at a later phase [15]. For this reason, researchers

© Springer Nature Switzerland AG 2019
M. van Sinderen and L. A. Maciaszek (Eds.): ICSOFT 2018, CCIS 1077, pp. 327–348, 2019.
https://doi.org/10.1007/978-3-030-29157-0_15

adapted two strategies to reduce the cost of software requirements change: (i) anticipating changes, and (ii) use flexible models more adapted to embrace change such as Agile methods.

Currently, agile methods (*e.g.,* extreme programming, scrum, crystal, etc.) are increasingly being adopted in software organizations. eXtreme Programming and Scrum methods are the most popular [13]. They are flexible and more adapted to the software evolution. In addition, agile methods encourage an active collaboration between development teams and the customer/user (*i.e.,* product owner), who is present during each phase of the SLC.

Although scrum is gaining popularity in comparison with other agile methods, Gilb considers that 61% of agile projects end up with failure [17]. This is due mainly to the lack of comprehensive documentations in scrum [16], the inappropriate application of scrum concepts, the limited use of standardized measures, and the poorly change control. For a successful project development, Gilb reported that it is important to use standardized measurement on reviewing development progress, re-evaluating user stories priorities, etc. In addition, a well-defined change control process is required at any step of the scrum process, even within an ongoing sprint.

Requirements for a software system project are classified into three categories: Functional User Requirements (FUR), Non-Functional Requirements (NFR), and Project Requirements and Constraints (PRC) [5]. FUR express *"what the software shall do in terms of tasks and services"* [5]. NFR include *"any requirement for a hardware/software system or for a software product, including how it should be developed and maintained, and how it should perform in operation"* [5]. PRC describe *"how a software system project should be managed and resourced or constraints that affect its performance"* [5]. Depending on the changed requirements, change requests are classified as (i) functional changes, and (ii) technical changes [1]. In fact, a functional change affects the FUR. While, a technical change may affect the NFR or the PRC. In our research studies, we addressed the functional change requests.

In practice, change requests in scrum process are usually evaluated by "experts". Actually, the development team may have the required knowledge about the changed product and the required modifications that must be done with respect to the change request. However, change evaluations that is based only on the expert judgment is hardly criticized. Since there is no guarantee of their effectiveness [4]. Thus, it is necessary to use a well-defined measurement method to assess a change request.

In our previous work, we introduced an automated functional change evaluation approach applied in scrum process based on the COSMIC Functional Size Measurement (FSM) method [23]. Sizing a functional change in terms of COSMIC Function Point (CFP) units will provide a *real* evaluation of the change request [18]. An appropriate evaluation of a change request will help the decision-makers responding to the change. In this paper, we provide an empirical evaluation of the proposed automatic approach in [23].

The remaining of this paper is organized as follows: Sect. 2 presents firstly an overview of the scrum process, functional size measurement, and COSMIC ISO/IEC 19761 method. Secondly, it discusses some related works. Section 3 presents our proposed approach for change evaluation in scrum process. In Sect. 4, we present the recommendations to answer a functional change request. In Sect. 5, we evaluate our approach and discuss several threats to validity. Finally, Sect. 6 concludes the presented work and outlines some of its possible extensions.

2 Background

2.1 Overview of the Scrum Process

Scrum process allows a better communication between the development team and the product owner. For a successful scrum project, the development team must learn how to manage themselves efficiently. In addition, the product owner must be actively involved in every single phase of the software development. Scrum appears to work better with small projects that require five to nine persons in a development team including designers, developers and testers. Nevertheless, some companies adapt scrum for large-scale projects [13].

The scrum process, illustrated in Fig. 1, starts with a high-level definition of the project scope. Scrum uses the product backlog as a list of stories created by the product owner based on their initial requirements. These stories may increase or decrease in size based on decisions made throughout the software development. The list of stories is prioritized by the product owner to be used as an iterative input for different sprints (Iterations) [21]. Thus, the active involvement of the product owner is mandatory to explain, elucidate the next iteration that should be implemented and evaluate/test the work done.

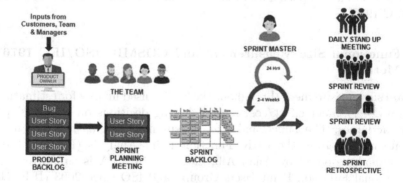

Fig. 1. Scrum software development process [2].

For a single sprint, four types of meetings should be held: sprint planning meeting, daily stand up meeting, sprint retrospective meeting, and sprint review meeting. The stories to be implemented in a sprint are captured during the planning meeting. They are selected from the product backlog according to their priorities and placed in a sprint backlog. In practice, usually, only the first two or three sprints are identified and planned. Daily stand up meetings are held during the sprint to discuss: what has been done, what are you going to do, and what are the issues [9]. Each sprint is ended by a sprint retrospective meeting, during which the team reviews the sprint and decides which change will be made, and how they can improve their work in the next sprint.

As we mentioned previously, scrum uses the user stories to represent the user requirements at different levels of details. A user story is a requirement written in a specific way illustrating the type of user, feature or functionality that the user want to do in order to realize some benefit [9]. Below the user story description adapted in practice.

This description identifies **Who** will do the user story or find it valuable <user type>, **What** it can be used for <feature or functionality>, and **Why** it is valuable or important <value or expected benefit>.

As a <user type>
I want to <feature or functionality>
so that <value or expected benefit>

Typically, development team members use the user story point to determine the effort required for the accomplishment of a user story compared to other user stories in the same product backlog. Although its popularity, user story point is not a good estimation technique. It has been widely criticized (cf., [8, 10, 12], etc.). In fact, user story point is only meaningful for a specific development team and project. Thus, it is necessary to use a standardized method that allows the measurement of the product functional size. In addition, the study in [10] proved that using COSMIC in agile projects gives a better results in estimating the effort needed to accomplish a user story. For these reasons, we selected COSMIC ISO/IEC 19761.

2.2 Functional Size Measurement and COSMIC ISO/IEC 19761 Method

Software size measurement throughout the SLC is used mainly for estimating the software development effort/cost and in driving decisions on the development project activities. The Functional Size Measurement (FSM) methods measure the software size from the FUR. Function Point Analysis (FPA) is the first FSM method proposed by Allan Albrecht in 1979. FPA is supported by the "International Function Point Users Group" and ISO since 2003 (IFPUG-ISO 20926:2009). Thereafter, researchers proposed several methods to improve the original FPA method such as NESMA, MK II, FiSMA, and finally COSMIC.

COSMIC considers that a FUR involves a number of functional processes. Each functional process is detailed by a set of sub-processes of two types: data movement and data manipulation. A data movement moves a data group from/to a functional user (respectively Entry and eXit data movement) or from/to a persistent storage (respectively Read and Write data movement). Software size is measured by counting one CFP (COSMIC Function Point) for each data movement. The size of each functional process is measured separately. The sizes of all functional processes are added to provide the software size.

COSMIC is the most straightforward method that measure the size of a change to software. It defines a functional change as *"any combination of additions of data movements or of modifications or deletions of existing data movements"* [11]. To measure the Functional Size of a Functional Change, referred to as FS(FC), COSMIC attribute one CFP for each changed data movement regardless of the change type (addition, deletion, or modification). The FS(FC) is given by the aggregation of the sizes of all the added, deleted and modified data movements. The functional size of the software after a functional change is given as the *sum* of all added data movements *minus* the functional size of all removed data movements [11] (Fig. 2).

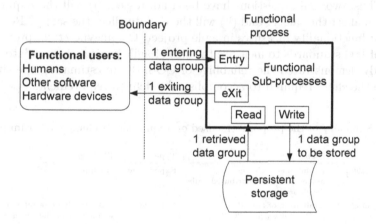

Fig. 2. COSMIC data movements [11].

2.3   Related Work

Decision-making process in agile project has received an increased interesting in recent years. For instance, Drury-Grogan & O'Dwyer explored the decision-making in scrum process and identified the factors that may influence the decisions made during the sprint planning and daily scrum meetings [14]. The authors conducted 34 semi-structured interviews and 18 observations with four agile teams. They showed that, in practice, agile teams follow sometimes a process for making-decisions during the sprint planning and daily scrum meetings. Decisions are made in a collaborative manner by the scrum team members. The main factors that may influence the decisions made according to this study are:

sprint duration, experience and resource availability. The decision-making process includes mainly the following steps: (i) problem identification, (ii) solution development, and (iii) selection of best alternative.

Decisions-making in agile, for example after a change request, are usually made based on the scrum team members' experiences. Although experts' judgment is much closer to reality, it is often considered as subjective [4]. For this reason, it is required to provide quantitative values to the decisions-makers in order to help them making appropriate decisions.

Researchers and practitioners agree that agile development provides a rapid response methodology to handle requirements change. Thus, many research studies have addressed the issues of managing changes in scrum process. For instance, Lloyd et al., addressed the problem of requirements changes during the software development in distributed agile development [20]. They proposed a supporting tool to help managing requirements changes in distributed agile development. On the other hand, Stålhane et al., proposed to analyze the impact of technical change requests [24]. In particular, this study focused on the safety requirements. Thus, two main questions have been addressed: (i) will the requirement and design affect the safety? and (ii) will the update affect the safety? Regarding the use of functionality measures in agile project, Commeyne et al., proved that the use of ISO standards to measure the size of agile projects is mandatory [10]. This study demonstrated the reliability of COSMIC in estimating the size and therefore the effort required to accomplish the defined requirements.

Table 1. Summary of the proposals focused on requirements change in scrum process.

Study	Focus	Type	Findings
Lloyd et al. [20]	Requirements change management in distributed agile development	Experimental	A supporting tool
Commeyne et al. [10]	Evaluation of teams' productivity using COSMIC	Experimental	COSMIC is more reliable in estimating models with much smaller variances
Stålhane et al. [24]	Impact of technical changes in safety requirements	Exploratory	A supporting tool that ensures the validity of safety

Table 1 summarizes the main proposals that focused on the requirements changes in scrum process. We noticed that some studies focused on functional changes (cf., [20]) while other studies focused on technical changes (cf., [24]). However, changes in these papers have been always considered as new requirements. In addition, none of the previous studies used a change control process. Thus, no changes evaluation is provided. However, it is important to evaluate requirements' changes and provide useful information for the right audience. This will certainly help during the software maintenance as well as for new software development. Moreover, change evaluation is usually based on experts' judgment. Whereas, experts' judgment evaluation is less transparent compared to any other techniques and depends mainly on the experts' skills.

In practice, usually, scrum teams do not allow changes in the middle of an iteration, since developers may already have preceded the implementation. In fact, practitioners consider that changes during an ongoing sprint may introduce defects. However, we consider that same changes must be authorized during an ongoing sprint. For example, a change request that proposes the deletion of a user story selected in the current sprint must be authorized. Since it is useless to implement a user story that will be deleted in the next sprint. Nevertheless, changes introduced during an ongoing sprint need prioritization.

3   Change Evaluation in Agile Context

This section illustrates our approach that proposes to evaluate a functional change in scrum process using COSMIC ISO/IEC 19761 [11]. Thus, we propose a detailed user story description that provides the required information to apply COSMIC. Thereafter, we provide our algorithm that can be used for user stories prioritization. Then, we present measurement formulas to measure the functional size of software products using user story format. Later, we describe our research method that suggests different phases to be used in evaluating a functional change and making-decision responding to a change request.

3.1   Detailed User Story Description

In scrum, there is no standard user story representation. Thus, different templates have been proposed mainly to describe what the users will need the software for. In addition, user stories are used at a high level of details [12]. This will impact not only the size measurement but also the quality of requirements statements. In order to guarantee the quality of measurement and requirements, we propose a detailed description of user story that represents all the information to apply COSMIC (see Fig. 3). Where:

- <**UserType**> is the user of the user story referred to as the functional user in COSMIC.
- <**Action**> and <**Object**> are used to replace the concept "feature or functionality" in the user story description provided in Sect. 2.1. In fact, the "feature or functionality" is a combination of an action and an object that the action will be applied on.
- <**value or expected benefit**>: It is used to characterize the successful ending of user story.
- <**NFR**> describes the non-functional requirements.
- <**Attachments**> any attachment that help defining the user story such as GUI.

The <value or expected benefit>, <NFR>, and <Attachments> are optional in the user story description.

In general, a user story could have finer or coarser granularity than functional processes. That is a user story could be a fraction of a functional process or a set of functional processes. In our study, we consider that each user story is associated to a functional process. Thus, two user stories could not have the same [<UserType>, <Action>, <Object>, and <value or expected benefit>]. The user story description in Fig. 3 provides more details in comparison with the old one. But, it does not represent the functional sub-process. Hence, moving to the scenario description is required to apply COSMIC. At this level, we distinguish the following concepts:

- **<User>**: External actor could be a human actor (*e.g.*, moderator, customer, etc.) or an external system in a direct relation with the software to be measured.
- **<ActionType>**: the action that will be applied on a data group is restricted to a number of verbs (*e.g.*, select, read, etc). These verbs are classified into four corpses: entry actions, read actions, write actions, and exit actions (see Appendix). These actions represent the sub-process in each user story. Thus, a sub-process can be a data movement or a data manipulation. This depends on whether or not it transfers data.
- **<DataTransfered>**: represents the data that have been transferred in each sub-process. <DataTransfered> in COSMIC corresponds to the "data group" concept.
- **<ActionDefinition>**: gives a summary of the user story purpose.

/*description*/
As a <UserType> **I want to** <Action> <Object> **so that** <value or expected benefit> <NFR> <Attachments>
/*Scenario description*/
<User> <ActionType: Entry, Read, Write, eXit, Expletive> <DataTransferred> <ActionDefinition>

Fig. 3. Detailed user story description format [23].

3.2   Prioritizing User Stories

Algorithm 1 is used to help prioritizing user stories in the product/sprint backlog. Hence, it can be used when selecting user stories from the product backlog and when re-organizing user stories in an on-going sprint after a change.

In scrum, user stories are prioritized as requested by the product owner [6]. However, the product owner may not have enough knowledge about the implementation details. Hence, ordering user stories based only on priority is not sufficient. In fact, the developer's view is also important in the user stories prioritization. Taking into account the developer's perspective is important to maximize the business value released at the end of every sprint. Therefore, we propose to balance the user story for product owner and development team perspectives according to mainly three parameters: importance, priority, and functional size. The priority of user stories is defined by the product owner (*i.e.,* P1 is more prior than P2, P2 is more prior than P3, etc.). The importance of a user story can be Essential or Desirable. User stories in the same cluster of classes (the same data base, service, etc.) have the same importance. The functional size is measured using COSMIC.

Algorithm 1. Prioritizing user stories.

    Aim   : Prioritizing user stories.
    Require: **P(US)** the priority of user story (US).
               Imp(US) the importance of user story (US).
               FS(US) the functional size of user story (US).
    Ensure : User stories organized by taking into account their priorities and
               importance first of all and then their functional sizes.

1 **begin**
2   **if** $Imp(USi) = Imp(USj)$ & $P(USi) != P(USj)$ **then**
3   Select the more prior user story ;
4   **else if** $Imp(USi) != Imp(USj)$ & $P(USi) != P(USj)$ || $P(USi) = P(USj)$
        then
5   Select the most important (Essential) user story ;
6   **else if** $Imp(USi) = Imp(USj)$ & $P(USi) = P(USj)$ **then**
7   Select the user story with minimum size ;
8   **else if** $Imp(USi) = Imp(USj)$ & $P(USi) = P(USj)$ & $FS(USi) = FS(USj)$
        then
9   Select the user story that requires less demand on resources (time or
          budget) ;

On the other hand, developers identify the status of a user story that can be used to control the development progress. Thus, the status of a user story[1], as shown in Fig. 4, can be:

- **New** is the status of a user story in the product backlog.
- **To do** is the status of a user story assigned to an on-going sprint.
- **In Progress** is the status of a user story currently being implemented.
- **To Verify** is the status of a user story ready for testing.
- **Done** is the status of a user story tested with success in the customer environment.

As it is described in [23], we kept only the **Done** and **In Progress** status.

---

[1] https://www.dreamstime.com/stock-illustration-scrum-task-kanban-board-
sticky-notes-whiteboard-post-agile-software-development-hanging-tasks-team-
image91765825.

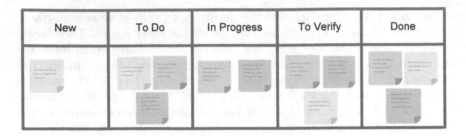

Fig. 4. User stories status in scrum process.

3.3 Sizing Software from User Stories Description

This section proposes measurement formulas that can be used to measure the software functional size based on the description of its user stories. Note that the functional size of the product backlog can be different from the functional size of the increment product. In fact, changes always happen in the scrum process. Hence, new functionality may appear, while others may be modified or deleted. The functional size of the product backlog is given by measuring the sizes of all sprints initially identified. While, the functional size of the increment product depends on the functional size of the implemented sprints.

The functional size of the product backlog or the increment product is equal to the sum of the functional sizes of *all* the sprints it includes (see Eq. 1).

$$FS(P) = \sum_{i=1}^{n} FS(S_i) \tag{1}$$

Where:

- FS(P) is the functional size of the product backlog or the increment product.
- FS(S_i) is the functional size of sprint i.
- n is the number of sprints initially identified in the case of product backlog size measurement or the number of implemented sprints in the case of increment product size measurement.

The functional size of a sprint is equal to the sum of the functional sizes of all the user stories it includes (see Eq. 2).

$$FS(S_i) = \sum_{j=1}^{m} FS(US_{ij}) \tag{2}$$

Where:

- FS(S_i) is the functional size of sprint i ($1 \leq i \leq n$).
- FS(US_{ij}) is the functional size of the user story j in S_i.
- m is the number of user stories in sprint S_i.

The functional size of a user story is equal to the sum of the functional sizes of its actions (see Eq. 3).

$$FS(US_{ij}) = \sum_{k=1}^{p} FS(Act_{ijk}) \tag{3}$$

Where:

- $FS(US_{ij})$ is the functional size of the user story j in S_i.
- $FS(Act_{ijk})$ is the functional size of action Act_{ijk} in US_{ij} ($1 \leq i \leq n$ and $1 \leq j \leq m$).
- p is the number of actions in user story j.

3.4   Research Method

Accepting or rejecting a functional change request depends on two main factors: the functional size of the changed user story and the user story status (done or undone). In fact, the functional size of a functional change gives a *real* evaluation of the change [18]. A change in an ongoing sprint, in an implemented sprint or in the product backlog may be handled with or without extra cost/time. Consequently, every functional change needs to be evaluated. In our previous study, we evaluate a functional change proposed in an ongoing or an implemented sprint [23]. This evaluation is used later to provide recommendations to the decision-makers to accept, defer or deny a functional change request.

In Fig. 5, we present the different phases of this study. In scrum, a change request is proposed by the product owner or the development team members. It should be expressed in terms of user story format to identify the changed user story (noted by USa). Then, we provide for its impact analysis. The status of the changed user story may be either done (*i.e.*, the change is in an implemented sprint or an ongoing sprint) or an undone user story (*i.e.*, the change is in an ongoing sprint). In the case of an ongoing sprint, we identify the attributes of the sprint where the change occurs (*e.g.*, size, start date, etc.) and measure respectively the FS(FC), the FS(USa) and the functional sizes of all the undone user stories in the same sprint. In the case of an implemented sprint, we measure the FS(FC) and the FS(USa). These measures are used to evaluate the functional change. This evaluation will be used to help in making decision (*i.e.*, accept, deny or defer a functional change request). More details about this step will be provided in Sect. 4. If a change is deferred or denied, the development team members must communicate the decision to the change requester. The communication is needed in order to resolve problems and ensure that expectations and values are understood. The development team members must explain to the product owner how long the change is going to take, and its impact on the project progress. After making the decision, it is required to update the documents to track all changes that are to be implemented. The change request is then implemented. It is send later for revision and testing.

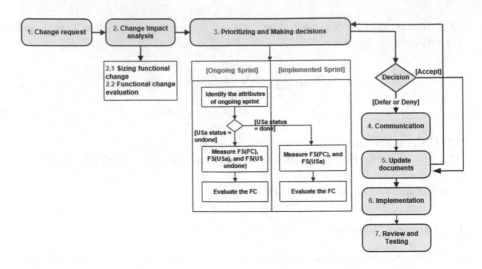

Fig. 5. Proposed method.

Functional Change Evaluation in an Ongoing Sprint. At the moment when a functional change appears, an ongoing sprint may contain both done and undone user stories. Thus, if the status of the changed user story (USa) is undone, our method proposes to compare the FS(FC) to the functional size of all the undone user stories in the same sprint. Hence, different baselines will be used to control the status of the functional change (see Table 2). Whereas, if the status of the USa is done, we compare the FS(FC) to the functional size of USa.

Table 2. Evaluating a functional change request where USa status = undone.

Low	Moderate	High
1 CFP	2 CFP ≤ FS(FC) ≤ FS(US undone)	FS(FC) > FS(US undone)

A "High" functional change is a change with a functional size bigger than the total functional sizes of undone user stories in the same sprint. It will have a potential impact on the software development progress. However, the functional size of a "Low" functional change is equal to 1 CFP. This change can be handled without any impact on the software development progress. Whereas, a "Moderate" functional change is a change with functional size lowest than the functional size of undone user stories in the same sprint. It will produce few changes in the software development progress.

Functional Change Evaluation in an Implemented Sprint. An implemented sprint in the increment product includes a number of done user stories.

Hence, a functional change affecting a done user story means that the work that has been already done must be changed. Thus, an additional time and effort may be required to handle the change (Table 3).

Table 3. Evaluating a functional change request where USa status = done.

Low	Moderate	High
1 CFP	2 CFP $\leq$ FS(FC) $\leq$ FS(USa)	FS(FC) > FS(USa)

A "High" functional change is a change with a functional size bigger than the functional size of the changed user story in the implemented sprint (USa). An important effort may be required to implement this change. However, the functional size of a "Low" functional change is equal to 1 CFP. This change can be handled without any required effort. However, a "Moderate" functional change is a change with functional size less than the functional size of the user story affected by the change in the implemented sprint. A little effort may be required to implement a "Moderate" change.

4   Deciding on a Functional Change Request

Software functional size can be used not only for effort/cost estimations but also for making decisions (*e.g.,* budget decision, portfolio decision, etc.) [3]. In this section, we provide some recommendations for the decision makers (*cf.,* product owner, development team, scrum master) that can be used to help in making decision regarding a functional change request. Recall that a functional change may affect either an ongoing sprint or an implemented sprint. These decisions are as follows:

- Accept the functional change request which means implement the change in the current sprint.
- Deny the functional change request which is made only if the change proposes a new software (re-start the development from the beginning).
- Defer the functional change request to the next sprint means accept the change and implement it in the next sprint not in the current one.

4.1   Functional Change in an Ongoing Sprint

Algorithm 2 provides recommendations that can be used in making decisions when the change type is a modification and affects a user story selected to be implemented in the ongoing sprint. These recommendations are based mainly on the comparison between the functional size of the functional change, the functional size of all undone user stories in the current sprint (noted by FS(US undone) in Algorithm 2), and the functional size of the changed user story (noted by FS(USa) in Algorithm 2). For instance, if the functional size of the functional change is greater than the total sizes of all the undone user stories in the current sprint, we suggest to defer the change request. Hence, the changed user story is deleted from the current sprint and added after modification, with respect to the change request, to the next sprint. In the case when the functional size of the functional change is less than the total sizes of all the undone user stories in the current sprint, it is required to compare the functional size of the functional change to the FS(USa) before the change (noted by FS(USa)i in Algorithm 2). Thus, if the FS(FC) is greater than the FS(USa)i, we suggest to defer the change request, and the USa after the change (noted by (USa)f in Algorithm 2) is added to the next sprint. Whereas, if the functional size of the functional change is less than the FS(USa)i, the decision will be made based on the impact of the change on the FS(USa)i. In the case when a functional change proposes the addition of a user story without changing any user story in the sprint, a comparison must be done between the functional size of the functional change and the functional sizes of all the undone user stories in the sprint. Hence, if the functional size of the functional change is less than the FS(US undone), the functional change is accepted. Otherwise, the functional change is deferred to the next sprint. The deletion of a change request do not have any affect on the development progress.

4.2 Functional Change in an Implemented Sprint

To carry out a functional change in an implemented sprint, it is required to discuss the change with the product owner. In fact, changing an implemented sprint means re-work (*i.e.,* re-doing a work that already has been done as requested by the product owner). In the case of an implemented sprint, we suggest to deny the change. However, in order to satisfy the product owner needs, we provide some analysis that allow the development team to determine the importance of the change such as a comparison between the time spent in implementing the changed user story and estimate the required time to re-develop the user story after the change. These analyses are provided in Algorithm 3. Hence, this algorithm do not provide recommendations to answer a functional change request but it provides some warnings to remember the product owner about the importance of the functional change, whether it is really needed or not.

5 Evaluation

This section evaluates our automatic approach for guiding the change evaluation process so that the decision makers will reach appropriate decisions responding to functional change requests. Firstly, in this evaluation, we used 15 end of studies projects implemented using scrum process. Then, we collected the feedback from two experts about our proposed approach. Finally, we discuss some threats to validity of our approach including internal, external, construct and conclusion validity.

Algorithm 2. Deciding on a functional change in an ongoing sprint [23].

   Aim   : Deciding on a FC in an ongoing sprint
   Require: FS(FC), FS(US undone), and FS(USa).
   Ensure : Recommendations

1 **begin**
2 | **if** *FS(FC) > FS (US undone)* **then**
3 | | defer the FC to the next sprint;
4 | | delete (USa)i from ongoing sprint /* (USa)i is US before the FC */
5 | | add (USa)f to next sprint /* (USa)f is US after the FC */
6 | **else if** *FS(FC) ≤ FS(US undone)* **then**
7 | | **if** *FS(FC) > FS(USa)i* **then**
8 | | | defer the FC to the next sprint;
9 | | | delete (USa)i from current sprint;
10 | | | add (USa)f to next sprint;
11 | | **else if** *FS(FC) ≤ FS(USa)* **then**
12 | | | **if** *FS(USa)f > FS(USa)i* **then**
13 | | | | /* the FS(USa) after the change is greater than the FS(USa)
   | | | | before the change */ **if** *remainingtime (USa)f ≤ requiredtime &*
   | | | | *teamprogress = early* **then**
14 | | | | | accept the FC;
15 | | | | | delete (USa)i from the current sprint;
16 | | | | | add (USa)f to the current sprint;
17 | | | | **else**
18 | | | | | defer the FC;
19 | | | | | delete (USa)i from the current sprint;
20 | | | | | add (USa)f to the next sprint;
21 | | | **else if** *FS(USa)f < FS(USa)i* **then**
22 | | | | /* the FS(USa) after the change is lower than the FS(USa)
   | | | | before the change */
23 | | | | accept the FC;
24 | | | | delete (USa)i from the current sprint;
25 | | | | add (USa)f to the current sprint;
26 | **else if** *FS(FC) = 1* **then**
27 | | accept the FC;
28 | | delete (USa)i from the current sprint;
29 | | add (USa)f to the current sprint;

5.1   Comparative Evaluation

To check how well the functional change status affects the decision making within the scrum process, we conduct an experiment with 15 end of studies projects between 2016 and 2018. The projects list is very diversified, it includes mobile apps, web applications, business applications, and real-time software. All these projects have been implemented during four months.

Algorithm 3. Deciding on a functional change in an implemented sprint.

Aim   : Deciding on a functional change in an implemented sprint
Require: FS(FC), FS(USa), USa priority, priorities P, FS(USs), devtime, USa
            real DevTime
Ensure : Warnings

1 **begin**
2   FC percentage = FS(FC) * 100 div FS(USa)
3   Avr DevTime = $\sum$ devtime div $\sum$ FS(USs)
4   **if** *USa importance = Essential* **then**
5   alert (you are going to change an Essential User Story with + FC
          percentage) ;

6   **else if** *USa priority < P(n div 2)* **then**
7   alert (This FC could highly impact other user stories as it was
          implemented in an early phase) ;

8   **else if** *Avr DevTime < USa real DevTime* **then**
9   alert (this US took more time in development then the average time
          needed to accomplish a US with the same functional size. It may
          contain extra data manipulation) ;

Case Studies and Results. The measurement results are given in Table 5. For each project we measure its functional size before and after the change noted in Table 5 respectively by **FSi(sw)** and **FSf(sw)**. Then we measure the functional size of the change request manually and automatically using our tool noted in Table 5 respectively by **FS(FC)m** and **FS(FC)aut**. Based mainly on the functional size of the functional change, we determine the functional change status manually and automatically as listed in Table 5 respectively by **FC status m** and **FC status aut**.

Evaluation Metrics. By analyzing all the results listed in Table 5, we noted that the tool gives exactly the same results (software functional size and status identification) for business applications, web applications and real time application. However, for the mobile apps (*e.g.*, Restaurant management system) our tool could not measure correctly the functional size of the functional change as well as the functional change status. In fact, this deviation can be related to the update or reading information from the data storage device. It depends on whether the data are stored in an internal or an external data storage devices [19].

We compared the manual results to the automatic results generated by our tool by using the precision (see Eq. 4) and the recall (see Eq. 5) metrics. Thus, our tool achieved a precision and a recall equal to 93%.

$$Precision = \frac{TP}{TP + FP} \qquad (4)$$

$$Recall = \frac{TP}{TP + FN} \tag{5}$$

Where:

- TP: number of functional changes' status correctly identified by our tool.
- FP: number of functional changes' status incorrectly identified by our tool.
- FN: False negatives are the number of functional changes' status incorrectly not identified.

5.2 Experts Evaluation

We verified our proposed automatic approach through an empirical evaluation based on a comparison between our results built by applying our algorithms and the results provided by two scrum experts.

The two experts are experienced and certified scrum practitioners. They have more than five years of experience in software industry, especially in leading scrum team analyzing and identifying customers needs, writing user stories, preparing maintaining, and prioritizing product backlog. However, they use user story point in their estimation and they do not have any idea about COSMIC.

Experts were asked to evaluate how important is a change request in the 15 selected end of studies projects. For this purpose, we provided the following information for each change request to the experts: software functional size before and after the change, the functional change description, and the functional size of the functional change. Experts were requested to classify each change request into low, moderate, and high. Each expert provided his own evaluation based on his experiences.

Experimentation results are given in Table 4. As shown in this Table, for 73% of the projects, the classification given by experts and our evaluation are exactly the same. All the high change requests have been correctly identified. In fact, the functional size of high change requests is usually considered as important in comparison to other change requests in different projects. However, for small change requests (with functional size equal to 3 CFP or 4 CFP), experts may provide an evaluation different to our evaluation. For example, for the change request proposed in the generic marketplace (with software functional size equal to 3 CFP) different evaluations have been provided. In fact, based on our proposed approach, this change request is classified as Moderate change while Expert 1 classified this change as Low. Hence, although the functional size of the functional change can be used as an indication of the change evaluation [18], experts usually compare the functional size of a change to other changes (in other projects) without taking into account the functional size of the changed software within the same project.

5.3 Threats to Validity

This work proposed an automatic approach to be used when software is being developed. This automatic approach generates the functional size of the software

Table 4. A comparison between our evaluation and experts' evaluations.

Software project	Our evaluation	Expert 1	Expert 2
Generic marketplace	Moderate	Low	Moderate
Worlds web travel guide	Moderate	Moderate	Low
Platform statistics	Moderate	Moderate	Moderate
Human resource management system	Moderate	Moderate	Low
E-commerce	High	High	High
Product lifecycle management	Moderate	Moderate	Moderate
Facial recognition system	Moderate	Moderate	Low
SWIFT messages management	Moderate	Moderate	Moderate
Stats forge detection	Moderate	Low	Moderate
Social network for FIFA 2022	Moderate	Low	Moderate
Socle drupal set up	High	High	High
Restaurant management system	Low	Low	Low
C-Reg system	High	High	High
Emergency monitoring system	Moderate	Low	Moderate
Salary ProVision	Moderate	Moderate	Low

before and after a change request, and the functional changes are measured and evaluated. Therefore, decision-makers will be guided to decide which functional change request should be accepted, deferred or denied.

The validity of the above results are subject to four types of threats (internal, external, construct, and conclusion) [25]:

- The internal validity threats are related to four issues. The first issue affecting the internal validity of our proposed approach is its dependence on a detailed description of the user story; such details may not always be available. Thus, for further work, we consider that approximate/rapid functional change evaluation is required for an urgent functional change request. The second issue is related to the productivity of the development team. In fact, two functional processes with exactly the same functional size do not require always the same development time. Moreover, the rapidity of the development team at the beginning of the sprint and the end of the sprint are not the same (this depends on the development team skills). Thus, for further work, we will use the structural size measurement method proposed by [22] for more precise change evaluation (*i.e.*, to take into account the data manipulations). The third issue is related to the evaluation of the functional change which is based only on its functional size without taking into account the functional change type (delete, addition or modification). However, we consider that this factor is important in the evaluation of a functional change request. Finally, in this study we did not take into account the relationship between the user stories. In fact, a functional change affecting a use story may lead to an impact

Table 5. Experimentation results.

Software project	FSi(sw)m	FSf(sw)	FC description	FS(FC)m	FS(FC)aut	FC status m	FC status aut
Generic marketplace	47 CFP	50 CFP	Add US "Contact administrator"	3 CFP	3 CFP	Moderate	Moderate
World's web travel guide	70 CFP	76 CFP	Add US "communicate with other client"	6 CFP	6 CFP	Moderate	Moderate
Platform statistics	80 CFP	88 CFP	Add US "Create user account"	8 CFP	8 CFP	Moderate	Moderate
Human resource management system	43 CFP	46 CFP	Add US "Create account"	3 CFP	3 CFP	Moderate	Moderate
E-commerce	40 CFP	56 CFP	Add three US	16 CFP	16 CFP	High	High
Product lifecycle management	50 CFP	57 CFP	Add user story "Create user account"	7 CFP	7 CFP	Moderate	Moderate
Facial recognition system	22 CFP	17 CFP	Delete US "add employee"	5 CFP	5 CFP	Moderate	Moderate
SWIFT messages management	27 CFP	31 CFP	Add US "add new category"	4 CFP	4 CFP	Moderate	Moderate
Stats forge detection	47 CFP	51 CFP	Add US "create a new account"	4 CFP	4 CFP	Moderate	Moderate
Social network for FIFA 2022	28 CFP	31 CFP	Add US "publish a welcome announcement"	3 CFP	3 CFP	Moderate	Moderate
Socle drupal set up	75 CFP	85 CFP	Add US "module management"	10 CFP	10 CFP	High	High
Restaurant management system	197 CFP	197 CFP	Modifying the US "Logon" users will logged on using an ID	3 CFP	1 CFP	Low	Moderate
C-Reg system	105 CFP	97 CFP	Changes between two versions V1.0 and V2.0	92 CFP	92 CFP	High	High
Emergency monitoring system	24 CFP	30 CFP	Add US "logon"	6 CFP	6 CFP	Moderate	Moderate
Salary ProVision	79 CFP	83 CFP	Add US "Registration"	4 CFP	4 CFP	Moderate	Moderate

on the functional size of other use stories. For further work, we will focus on the relationships between user stories and change propagation.

- The external validity threats deal with the possibility to generalize the results of this study to other case studies including the use of the proposed automatic approach or tool and the decision algorithms. In this paper, we used 15 end of projects studies to test the proposed tool. Although our experimentation showed that this tool provide exactly the measurement results for the majority of the software applications types, testing the proposed tool and algorithms in an industrial environment is required.
- The threats of construct validity is related to the relation between theory and observation. In fact, the experimental study showed that the proposed tool is able to correctly identify the functional change status for the web, business, and real time software applications. While the tool could not correctly identify the functional change status for mobile apps. To avoid this deviation,

it is required to distinguish between internal and external data storage. In addition, we believe that testing this tool with real data in industrial practice is important. On the other hand, the projects used in this paper include mobile apps, web applications, business applications, and real-time software. However, other projects types have not been considered in this paper such as embedded software. Future work in this topic should be performed.

– Conclusion Validity: in summary, we used 15 end of project studies, where two supported by the COSMIC-ISO 19761 Community (C-Reg system and restaurant management system). We tested the proposed automatic approach based on those case studies. The provided measurement results have been reviewed by two experts. Nonetheless, we believe that getting the feedback from the decision makers is important to guarantee the reliability of our results.

6   Conclusion

In practice, changes in software requirements are inevitable and present a main issue. Any deviation from those requirements may lead to project failure or induce an extra effort and much time through the software life cycle to satisfy the change request.

This paper proposed an automatic COSMIC-based approach that supports the functional changes control throughout the scrum process. It can be used by decision makers to meet user's expectations, identify problems in future projects, and estimating future software project effort. In fact, our tool is based on a detailed description of user stories and their sizing using COSMIC method. The evaluation of a change request and the decision made responding to the change are based mainly on its functional size and its impact on the development progress. This increase the users/product owner's satisfaction, and guarantee the project success.

For further work, we consider that approximate/rapid change evaluation is required especially for an urgent change request. In addition, it is important to estimate the change effort.

Appendix

Entry Corpus: These verbs express Entry data-movements: Assign, change, choose, click, create, edit, give, input, modify, provide, re-enter, select, submit, type, update.

Exit Corpus: These verbs express eXit data-movements: display, edit, list, output, post, present, print, return, send, Show update, view.

Read Corpus: These verbs express read data-movements: find, get, obtain, post, read, recognize retrieve, Validate, Verify.

Write Corpus: These verbs express write data-movements: add, archive, change, create, define, delete, edit, insert, record, register, remove, save, store, Update.

References

1. ISO/IEC 14143–1: Information Technology - Software Measurement - Functional Size Measurement. Part 1: Definition of Concepts (2007)
2. Scrum software development process (2018). https://www.maxxor.com/
3. Abran, A.: Software Metrics and Software Metrology. IEEE Computer Society (2010)
4. Abran, A.: Software Project Estimation: The Fundamentals for Providing High Quality Information to Decision Makers, 1st edn. Wiley/IEEE Computer Society Press (2015)
5. Abran, A., et al.: Guideline on non-functional & project requirements: how to consider non-functional and project requirements in software project performance measurement, benchmarking and estimating (2015)
6. Ambler, S.W.: User Stories: An Agile Introduction (2014)
7. Bano, M., Imtiaz, S., Ikram, N., Niazi, M., Usman, M.: Causes of requirement change - a systematic literature review. In: EASE 2012 (2012)
8. Berardi, E., Buglione, L., Santillo, L., Symons, C., Trudel, S.: Guideline for the use of COSMIC FSM to manage agile projects, v1.0 (2011)
9. Cohn, M.: User Stories Applied: For Agile Software Development. Addison-Wesley Professional (2004)
10. Commeyne, C., Abran, A., Djouab, R.: Effort estimation with story points and cosmic function points: an industry case study (2016)
11. COSMIC: The COSMIC Functional Size Measurement Method, Version 4.0.2, Measurement Manual, October 2017
12. Desharnais, J.M., Kocaturk, B., Abran, A.: Using the cosmic method to evaluate the quality of the documentation of agile user stories. In: 2011 Joint Conference of the 21st International Workshop on Software Measurement and the 6th International Conference on Software Process and Product Measurement, pp. 269–272, November 2011
13. Dikert, K., Paasivaara, M., Lassenius, C.: Challenges and success factors for large-scale agile transformations. J. Syst. Softw. **119**(C), 87–108 (2016)
14. Drury-Grogan, M., O'Dwyer, O.: An investigation of the decision-making process in agile teams. Int. J. Inf. Technol. Decis. Mak. **12**(6), 1097–1120 (2013)
15. Fairley, R.E.: Managing and Leading Software Projects. Wiley/IEEE Computer Society Press (2009)
16. Furtado, F., Zisman, A.: Trace++: a traceability approach to support transitioning to agile software engineering. In: The 24th International Requirements Engineering Conference (RE), pp. 66–75, September 2016
17. Gilb, T.: Why agile product development systematically fails, and what to do about it! (2018)
18. Haoues, M., Sellami, A., Ben-Abdallah, H.: Functional change impact analysis in use cases: an approach based on COSMIC functional size measurement. Sci. Comput. Program. Spec. Issue Adv. Softw. Meas. **135**, 88–104 (2017)
19. Haoues, M., Sellami, A., Ben-Abdallah, H.: A rapid measurement procedure for sizing web and mobile applications based on COSMIC FSM method. In: Proceedings of the 27th International Workshop on Software Measurement and 12th International Conference on Software Process and Product Measurement, IWSM-Mensura 2017, Gothenburg, Sweden, 25–27 October 2017, pp. 129–137 (2017)
20. Lloyd, D., Moawad, R., Kadry, M.: A supporting tool for requirements change management in distributed agile development. Future Comput. Inform. J. **2**(1), 1–9 (2017)

21. Schwaber, K.: Agile Project Management with Scrum (Developer Best Practices), 1st edn. Microsoft Press (2004)
22. Sellami, A., Hakim, H., Abran, A., Ben-Abdallah, H.: A measurement method for sizing the structure of UML sequence diagrams. Inf. Softw. Technol. **59**, 222–232 (2015)
23. Sellami, A., Haoues, M., Borchani, N., Bouassida, N.: Orchestrating functional change decisions in scrum process using COSMIC FSM method. In: Proceedings of the 13th International Conference on Software Technologies (ICSOFT), Porto, Portugal, 26–28 July, pp. 516–527 (2018)
24. Stålhane, T., Hanssen, G.K., Myklebust, T., Haugset, B.: Agile change impact analysis of safety critical software. In: Bondavalli, A., Ceccarelli, A., Ortmeier, F. (eds.) SAFECOMP 2014. LNCS, vol. 8696, pp. 444–454. Springer, Cham (2014). https://doi.org/10.1007/978-3-319-10557-4_48
25. Wohlin, C., Runeson, P., Höst, M., Ohlsson, M.C., Regnell, B., Wesslén, A.: Experimentation in Software Engineering: An Introduction. Kluwer Academic Publishers (2000)

Wise Objects for IoT (WIoT): Software Framework and Experimentation

Ilham Alloui$^{(\boxtimes)}$, Eric Benoit, Stéphane Perrin, and Flavien Vernier ⓘ

Université Savoie Mont Blanc - LISTIC, 5 chemin de Bellevue, Annecy-le-Vieux,
74940 Annecy, France
{ilham.alloui,eric.benoit,stephane.perrin,flavien.vernier}@univ-smb.fr

Abstract. Despite their expansion, Internet of Things (IoT) technologies remain young and require software technologies to ensure information management in order to deliver sophisticated services to their users. Users of IOT technologies particularly need systems that adapt to their use and not the reverse. To meet those requirements, we enriched our object oriented framework WOF (Wise Object Framework) with a communication structure to interconnect WOs (Wise Objects) and IoT. Things from IoT are then able to learn, monitor and analyze data in order to be able to adapt their behavior. In this paper, we recall the underlying concepts of our framework and then focus on the interconnection between WOs and IoT. This is enabled by a software bus-based architecture and IoT related communication protocols. We designed a dedicated communication protocol for IoT objects. We show how IoT objects can benefit from learning, monitoring and analysis mechanisms provided by WOF to identify usual behavior of a system and to detect unusual behavior. We illustrate our approach through two case studies in home automation. The first shows how a wise smart presence sensor learns on a classroom occupation. The second shows how a wise system helps us to see correlation among several WOs.

Keywords: Wise object · IoT · Software architecture · Communication · Knowledge analysis

1 Introduction

The Internet of Things (IoT) is known as the extension of current Internet to provide connection and communication between devices or physical objects referred to as "Things" [7]. Even growing substantially in number and use, the Internet of Things (IoT) technologies remain young and require software technologies to ensure data/information management among things in order to deliver sophisticated services to their users. Examples are home automation (HA) things which are getting more and more involved within our daily life: HA things are either within a ready-to-use systems (like boxes) or singles to be integrated to an existing system or platform. In both cases, when it is provided, support for data

© Springer Nature Switzerland AG 2019
M. van Sinderen and L. A. Maciaszek (Eds.): ICSOFT 2018, CCIS 1077, pp. 349–371, 2019.
https://doi.org/10.1007/978-3-030-29157-0_16

monitoring and analysis is very limited [11]. Users need to have a remote access to things, for instance to switch off lights they forgot or turn off the strove. Communication provided by existing IoT technologies should then involve basic data or information such as current state of things. Moreover, users of a HA need the technology adapts to their use and not the reverse: in our previous example, the system (instead of users) would for instance detect that unusually the lights are switched on at midnight. Then it would either adapt to this change (i.e. register this new behavior as usual) or take initiative to raise an alert or to switch the lights off depending on the knowledge it has (i.e. if no presence is detected).

This implies that the system is able to: (a) identify usual behavior; (b) detect the changes in the way it is being used and (c) either react by taking initiative or change its behavior to comply with those new usages. Our proposal is that intelligent software systems could enhance IoT with useful capabilities such as learning, monitoring and adaptation to meet users' requirements.

Starting from works on IoT and on intelligent software systems [6,12] we aim to add value to IoT through WOF (Wise Object Framework) [3], a software object framework that provides things (be them physical or software), built-in mechanisms for learning, monitoring, analyzing and managing data/information (see Fig. 1). Those software mechanisms allow IoT-based systems like in HA to: (a) identify common usage (i.e. usual behavior of their users); (b) detect changes in usage (unusual behavior); (c) adapt to the new usage (system in automatic mode) or simply give information to the users (manual mode).

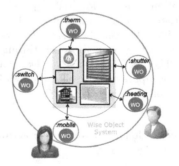

Fig. 1. Example of home automation wise object system [2].

Identifying a system common usage by software is not an easy work. At the best of our knowledge, common usage is usually studied from a psychological point of view for the human [1] or from the signal processing point of view with change detection methods [5] for data, but never from the software point of view. This research issue raises many questions such as: what is considered as common usage? Is common usage necessarily related to time? Is there an interval of acceptance of unusual behavior? Which one? What methods/techniques better identify common usage? In which context? etc.

As users' behavior identification and system adaptation rely on data collected from connected things that may be distributed as is the case in IoT, we realized a software bridge linking IoT objects to our WOF software objects. In this paper we focus mainly on this link between software "wise" objects (WOs) and IoT through the WOF. WOs can be seen as software avatars related to things. This paper extends [2] and introduces a new experiment which for the first time highlights the behavior of several WOs in the same environment and shows that correlated unusual behavior among several WOs may result from a same cause. The first case study presented in [2] illustrates the behavior of a single wise thing (a smart presence device) and mainly shows how such thing is able to manage and use presence events to result knowledge on a classroom occupation during a year. The new case study in this paper is based on a system of three wise things. Our aim is twofold: (a) show that our approach works also with several wise things and (b) highlight its ability to show correlated unusual behavior among several things. Such knowledge indicates that behavior change may result from a same triggering event which is very useful for diagnosing or explaining unusual behaviour of a system. In Sect. 2 we recall the concept of WO and WOF, the behavior of a WO, its interaction with other WOs as well as our first representation of common usage. Section 3 introduces the connection between a WO and an IoT, from the software interaction point of view in Sect. 3.1 and from the communication medium and protocol point of view in Sect. 3.2. In Sect. 4, we present two cases studies in home automation domain with the results we obtained using the framework. The first case study focus is on the behavior of a single wise thing while the second one focus is on a system of several wise things. Finally, we discuss our approach and conclude with ongoing work and some perspectives.

2 WO and WOF

2.1 WOF

WOF is founded on the concept of WO. Our design decisions behind the WOF are guided by the following requirements: software support should be the less intrusive possible, reusable and generic enough to be maintainable and used in different application domains with different strategies. Developers should be able to use the framework with the minimum of constraints and intrusion in the source code of the application. We consequently separated, in the WOF, the "wisdom" and intelligence logic (we name abilities) of the objects from application services (we name capabilities) they are intended to render. As shown by Fig. 2, we designed the WOF according to a layered architecture:

- the core layer, i.e. the framework building blocks, consists of a set of inter-related packages and classes that embed basic mechanisms for introspection, monitoring, analysis and communication among WO instances. WO is the main class from which a system developer may specialize application-level classes such as the Switch and Shutter classes within the home automation system in the example;

- the software system layer: contains the package and classes related to software systems developed for end-users. The home automation cited so far is
  a representative of such systems. Classes representing things can inherit the
  structure and behavior of the WO class in the Framework layer;
- the instantiated software system: gathers the instantiated application software
  systems from the previous layer. Instances of application-related classes are
  avatars for physical or logical objects (things).

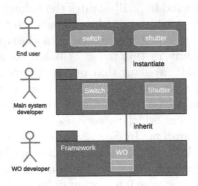

Fig. 2. WOF concrete architecture [2].

To build a WO system, the WOF provides a communication bus (Gava)
for the interaction between WOs. Interactions are managed through a manager
object that establishes the configured pairing between events and actions according to a publish-subscribe pattern. Figure 3 illustrates this interaction.

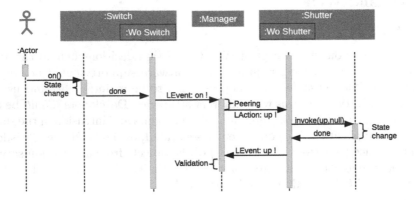

Fig. 3. UML sequence diagram of the interaction between a WO switch and a WO
shutter [2].

When a method is invoked on a WO instance: (a) the wise part of the instance
raises an event at the end of the invocation; (b) the manager catches the event

and sends orders to all WO instances interested in the initial event (paired WOs); (c) the paired WO instances execute the corresponding method; (d) the manager checks that the order has been correctly executed. The communication and pairing system are detailed in [4] and were initially limited to communication and pairing between WO instances.

2.2   Concept of WO

We define a Wise Object (WO) as a software object able to learn by itself on itself and on its environment (external knowledge), to deliver expected services according to the current state and using its own experience. Wisdom refers to the experience such object acquires by its own during its life. We intentionally use terms dedicated to humans as a metaphor. A Wise Object is intended to "connect" to either a physical entity/device (e.g. a vacuum cleaner) or a logical entity (e.g. a software component). As wise object could be a cleaner able to learn on how to clean a room depending on its shape and dimensions. In the course of time, the cleaner could in addition improve its performance (less time, less energy consumption, etc.). A WO is then characterized by:

- its autonomy: it is able to behave with no human intervention;
- its intelligence: it observes itself and its environment, analyzes them and uses its knowledge to decide how to behave (introspection, monitoring, analysis, planning);
- its adaptivity: it changes its behavior when its environment changes;
- its ability to communicate: with its environment that includes other WOs and end-users in different locations.

A WO built-in behavior involves two states: The dream state and the awake state, see Fig. 4.

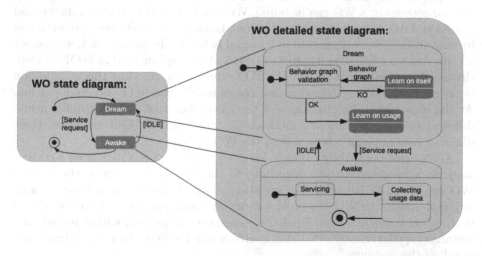

Fig. 4. UML state diagram of WO built-in behavior [4].

The dream state is dedicated to acquiring knowledge about its own capabilities and to analyzing usage-related knowledge. The awake state is the state where the WO executes its methods invoked by other objects (external service requests) or by itself (internal requests), and, monitors such execution while recording usage-related knowledge.

A WO's capability-related knowledge is itself stored as a state diagram. The WO executes the methods of its sub-class (i.e. an application class like Switch) to know the effect on the attributes of this sub-class instances. Each set of attribute values produces a state in the diagram and method invocation produces a transition (see Fig. 5). The main constraint in this step is that the method invocation must have no effect on the application when the WO is dreaming. This is solved thanks to a bus-based system architecture described in [3] with disconnection/re-connection mechanisms.

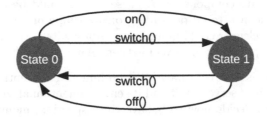

Fig. 5. UML state diagram of a switch built by its WO.

Regarding knowledge on an application object usage, two kinds of situations are studied: emotions and adaptation of behavior. We define an emotion of WO as a distance between its current usage and its common usage (i.e. unusual usage). WO can be stressed if one of its methods (services) is more frequently used or conversely, a WO can be bored. WO can be surprised if one of its method is used and this was never happened before. Emotions of a WO are a projection of its current behavior with regard to its usual behavior. In Subsect. 2.3, we present a Data Analyzer based on a statistical method we implemented in WOF to identify usual/unusual behavior. When a WO expresses an emotion, this information is caught by the WO system that may consequently lead to behavior adaptation. At the object level, two instances of the same class that are used differently – different frequencies, different methods... – may have different emotions, thus, different behavior and interaction in the WO system.

A WO uses its capability-related knowledge to compute a path from a current state to a known state [8]. According to the frequency of the paths used, a WO can adapt its behavior. For instance, if a path is often used between non-adjacent states, the WO can build a shortcut transition between the initial and destination states and then build the corresponding method within its subclass instance (application object). This consequently modifies the capability-related graph of this instance.

2.3 WOF and Data Analyzers

The WOF provides a connector to an evolving set of analyzers whose role is to identify a WO common behavior (usage) and to detect emotions when they occur. Each analyzer connected to a WO is waked-up during the WO's dream state to analyze the last events and to update its knowledge.

Let us recall our preliminary model of common usage introduced in [4]. It is based on a statistic approach and defines the common usage as weaker forms of stationarity (WSS) from the statistic point of view.

Let $x(i)$ be a continuous and stationary time random process. A process is a WSS process if and only if:

$$
\begin{aligned}
E\left[x(i)\right] &= \mu \quad \forall i, \\
Var\left[x(i)\right] &= \sigma^2 \neq \infty \quad \forall i, \\
Cov\left[x(i), x(i-k)\right] &= f(k) = \rho_k \quad \forall i \forall k.
\end{aligned}
$$

As the common usage can change along the time, we compute the stationarity – the common usage – on a sliding window of size w:

$$
\begin{aligned}
E\left[x(i)\right] &= \mu(t) \quad \forall i \in [t-w, t], \\
Var\left[x(i)\right] &= \sigma^2(t) \neq \infty \quad \forall i \in [t-w, t], \\
Cov\left[x(i), x(i-k)\right] &= f(k, t) = \rho_k(t) \forall i \in [t-w, t] \forall k,
\end{aligned}
$$

where the time series $x(i)$ are the occurrences $\left[e_\tau^{t-w} \ldots e_\tau^i \ldots e_\tau^t\right]$ of a given event – i.e. transition – τ between t−w and t.

As our system cannot be perfectly stationary, we relax the definition of WSS and consider that the system is in common use if and only if:

$$
\begin{aligned}
\mu(t+1) &\in [\mu(t-w), \mu(t)] \\
\sigma^2(t+1) &\in [\sigma^2(t-w), \sigma^2(t)] \\
\rho_k(t+1) &\in [\rho_k(t-w), \rho_k(t)].
\end{aligned}
$$

In other words, if the new mean, variance or autocovariance at time $t+1$ are in their corresponding ranges, the new event occurrence at time $t+1$ is considered as a common usage, otherwise it is unusual.

According to this definition, we define an emotion as the distance between the current usage at $t+1$ and the common usage between $t-w$ and t. This distance $d(x(i))$ is defined by the following centered normalized scale between -1 and 1, where:

$$
d(x(i)) = \begin{cases}
d(E\left[x(i)\right]), \\
d(Var\left[x(i)\right]), \\
d(Cov\left[x(i), x(i-k)\right]),
\end{cases}
$$

where

$$
d(E\left[x(i)\right]) = \frac{E[x(i)] - \overline{E[x(j)]}}{(\max(E[x(j)]) - \min(E[x(j)]))/2},
$$

$$
d(Var\left[x(i)\right]) = \frac{Var[x(i)] - \overline{Var[x(j)]}}{(\max(Var[x(j)]) - \min(Var[x(j)]))/2},
$$

$$d(Cov\,[x(i),x(i-k)]) =$$
$$\frac{Cov[x(i),x(i-k)]-\overline{Cov}[x(j),x(j-k)]}{(\max(Cov[x(j),x(j-k)])-\min(Cov[x(j),x(j-k)]))/2},$$

$j \in [t-w,t]$ and $\overline{E\,[x(j)]}$, $\overline{Var\,[x(j)]}$ and $\overline{Cov\,[x(j),x(j-k)]}$ are respectively the means of means, variances and autocovariances on the range $[t-w,t]$.

Thus, when a new event occurs at $t+1$, we compute the distance $d(x(i))$ with the common usage between $t-w$ and t. If all values of the distance – $d(E\,[x(i)])$, $d(Var\,[x(i)])$ and $d(Cov\,[x(i),x(i-k)])$ – are between -1 and 1, the behavior is considered as common, otherwise it is identified as unusual relatively to the knowledge on the common usage.

3   From WOF to IoT

To meet IoT related requirements cited in Sect. 1, we extended our framework WOF [4] with mechanisms to relate "things" to WOs. We thus define an object in WIoT as a peer composed of a physical object (thing) and a logical (software) object (WO). A WO can be viewed as an avatar of a thing. From now on, the term object will be used to refer to the thing-avatar peer (Fig. 6).

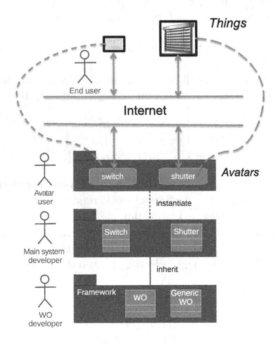

Fig. 6. WIoT architecture [2].

3.1 WO Model for IoT

When a thing (e.g. a physical switch) joins the application system (e.g. HA system), its corresponding avatar (a Switch class instance) is automatically instantiated and this pair forms then a new object. This means that the avatar's class of the thing exists. As it is not desirable and even not relevant to provide everything in the system with the ability of learning and analysis, we introduced a class named Generic WO without the introspection ability.

Like WO class instances, instances of Generic WO are able to construct their capability-related graph, but they cannot use introspection to analyze their behavior. A Generic WO instance learns its behavior from state change messages it receives from the thing it is related to. This way, a generic WO can be related to any "thing" able to communicate its state and state changes. This is not a strong constraint as recent physical connected objects are generally able to communicate changes in their state. In the case of home automation, devices using ZigBee [15], Z-Wave [14] or other modern systems, communicate their capabilities through profiles or other kinds of descriptions. Figure 7 presents the UML Class diagram of WOs including the Generic WOs. As shown in the figure, a generic WO is a WO where the "invoke" method is redefined. While through the "invoke" method, a WO can invoke methods of its sub-classes (i.e. application classes whose instances are avatars for things), the class Generic WO has no subclass. Then when the "invoke" method is called, it just updates its usage-related diagram (knowledge on the way the thing is being used).

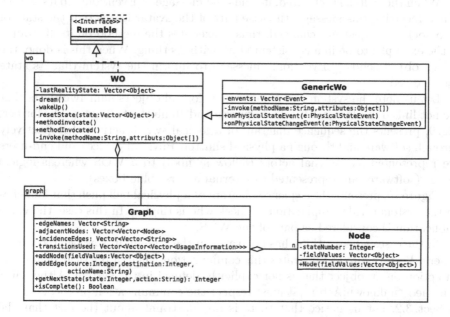

Fig. 7. UML class diagram of generic WO [2].

Figure 8 illustrates the communication flow between a physical switch and its associated physical shutter. The "PEvent/PAction" and "LEvent/LAction" are respectively sent through the physical (P) and logical (L) communication media.

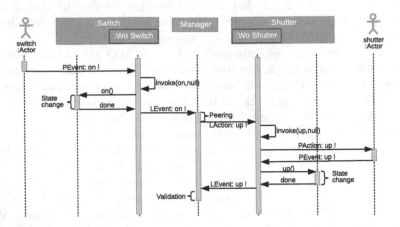

Fig. 8. UML sequence diagram of the interaction between a physical switch and a physical shutter [2].

When the switch is activated, it sends the message "PEvent:on!" to its avatar. When receiving this message, the wise part of the avatar learns that the state of its associated object has changed, thus it executes the method on itself, "on()" in the example, to be in a consistent state with its thing. When this is done, the switch object sends "LEvent:on!" message to inform the system that its state has changed.

Let us note the system can manage pure logical objects namely objects that are not linked to physical objects. Figures 9 and 10 illustrate 2 cases. The former, Fig. 9, presents the sequence diagram of a logical switch activated respectively through software and through a physical shutter. Physical devices and end-users are represented as external actors (fellow symbol) to a WOS whereas logical things (software) are represented as internal actors (blue boxes).

Figure 10, presents the sequence diagram of a physical bell push that launches on the system a video application to check who is ringing. In this case, the video application is considered as part of the WOS.

In the cases where a thing has no avatar in the system, it is associated with a generic WO. Figure 11 illustrates this configuration where a physical switch has an action on an object that is not explicitly defined in the system. Although it is named "unknown:Actor", it must respect the communication protocol defined in Sect. 3.2. Let us notice that there is no constraint about the fact that the "unknown:Actor" must be a logical or a physical object, it can be of both kinds.

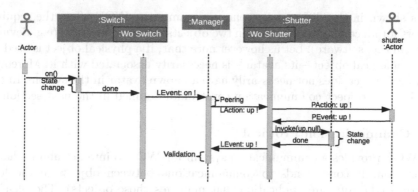

Fig. 9. UML sequence diagram of the interaction between a logical switch and a physical shutter [2]. (Color figure online)

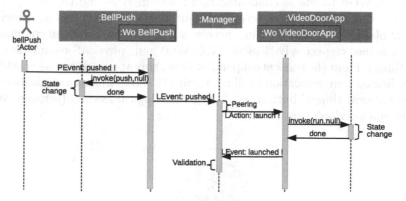

Fig. 10. UML sequence diagram of the interaction between a physical bell push and a logical video application [2].

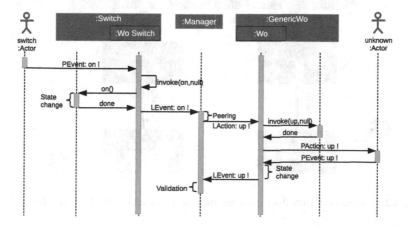

Fig. 11. UML sequence diagram of the interaction between a physical switch and a physical object not implemented as WO (no avatar) and managed as a generic WO [2].

As shown in the different sequence diagrams, the WOF offers the required support for all combinations between two objects, be them physical (e.g. devices) or logical (i.e. software). Let us however note that, if a physical object is used – a thing – a logical object – its avatar – is necessarily associated with it. Moreover, a physical object does not necessarily have a known avatar in the system. In this case, it must respect communication constraints detailed in the next section.

3.2   Communication Protocol

The WOF provides a communication system for WOs to interact and exchange information. It corresponds to communications between objects in the logical world (the software application that manages those objects). The physical objects/things are from IoT and communicate in our case through an MQTT communication system [13]. Thus we implemented a bridge between both those systems in WOF to enable communication between WOs and things.

As the communications between WOs and between a WO and its associated physical object are not of the same nature, we defined two kinds of communications we named respectively "logical" (WO-WO) and "physical" communications (WO-thing). From the conceptual point of view, this approach can be considered as a dedicated communication medium. Figure 12 shows this communication flow among physical things (button and light), their logical avatars (software WOs) and the manager software object.

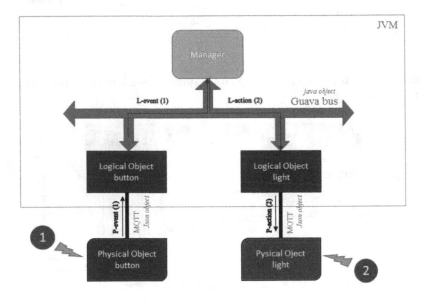

Fig. 12. Communication flow between manager, logical and physical objects [2].

From the implementation point of view, WOF uses the publish/subscribe-based Guava bus and IoT communication is based on MQTT with JSON format for messages. As both are publish/subscribe-based systems, a simple bridge is used to exchange messages from one to the other. To separate "logical" and "physical" communications, we use different types of messages that we defined as follows:

– Physical messages:
  • "PhysicNewDevice": message sent by a physical object when it connects to MQTT server.
  • "PhysicStateChange": message sent by a physical object when its state changes; it contains the event that generates the state change.
  • "PhysicAction": message sent to a physical object so that it performs an action.
  • "PhysicGetState": message sent to a physical object so that it sends its state; this message type is mainly dedicated to generic WOs so that they ask the things their state.
  • "PhysicState": message sent by a physical object to indicate its state; this message is the answer to "PhysicGetState" message.
– Logical messages:
  • "LogicNewDevice" message sent by a WO when it is created in the WOF.
  • "LogicalStateChange" message sent by a WO when its state changes.
  • "LogicalAction" message sent to a WO so that it performs an action.

The bridge only translates Java object messages to JSON objects and vice-versa according to the following rules:

– the MQTT topic is defined by [basetopic]/[Class] where:
  • basetopic is free, "Wo" in our example,
  • Class is the name of class message including the package name, for example a "PhysicAction" message of package "bus" is sent on topic "WO/bus.PhysicAction",
– any attribute of the Java object is an attribute of JSON.

Figures 13(a) and (b) illustrate respectively the "PhysicAction" class and an object that is translated as the following JSON message:

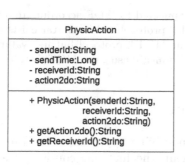

(a) PhysicAction class used to send "PhysicAction" message from a WO to its thing

(b) Example of PhysicAction object

Fig. 13. PhysicAction class used to receive "PhysicAction" message by a WO [2].

```
MqttConnector from MQTT: Wo/bus.PhysicAction->
{"senderId":"home_automation.Switch:1",
 "sendTime":1512984990902,
 "receiverId":"Switch:1",
 "action":"on"}
```

The WO identified by id "home_automation.Switch:1" sends, at time 1512984990902, the order "on" to its thing identified by "Switch:1".

Finally, the communication system we built between WOF and IoT allows us to connect:

- A thing defined in the WOF.
- A thing not defined in the WOF, but that can communicate using our protocol.
- A thing not defined in the WOF, that communicates with another medium (ZigBee, ZWave, WiFi...)

The constraint is that the thing must be able to give information on its state change. Figure 14 illustrates on a switch example the three communication cases.

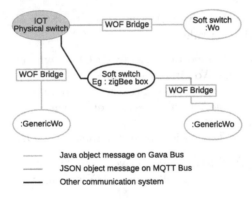

Fig. 14. An IoT object, like a switch can be connected to WOF according to 3 ways: (a) the thing can communicate using our MQTT protocol and its avatar exists in the WOF; (b) the thing can communicate using our MQTT protocol but its avatar does not exist in the WOF; (c) the thing cannot communicate using our MQTT protocol [2].

4   Experimental Implementation

We experimented our framework and its underlying approach on several examples. We present in this section two of them: the first one consists of a wise smart presence sensor in a real situation while the second one consists of a set of home automation related objects, namely a light, a shutter, a switch and a heating device. For each case we give a description of the objects, the goal of the experiment, data used/generated as well as the results and observations we did.

4.1   Use Case 1 Description and Experimental Results

To illustrate the use of WOF including the interconnection of WOs and IoT, we took the case of a presence smart sensor within a classroom with the objective to identify the usual usage of the room and detect habit change (unusual behavior). This allows us to experimentally validate our approach of habit change measurement.

One objective of the case study is to know if our system is able to detect habit change in relation to a common usage, especially regarding student vacation periods. The smart presence sensor provides the "presence" state when persons are in a room and the "no presence" state when not. It is worth noting that the smart capacity of the sensor offers the possibility to filter the output state: "no presence" state is delivered if no detection occurs for one minute.

Attempting to identify a common usage (habit) requires a significant volume of data that depends on the temporal observing window or the number of observations taken into account. To cover different volumes of data, it is obviously relevant to consider a long duration of observation. However to avoid a long experiment, one year in our case, we simulate the smart presence sensor outputs by using real data coming from the real-time scheduling system of our university. Thus, real data injected in the system corresponds to the outputs of the smart presence sensor placed into a classroom. At each "state change" event from the sensor, a physical timestamped message, including the sensor id, is sent using MQTT protocol. The next section presents some results of our experimentation.

Figures 15 and 16 illustrate the experiment results according to the definition of common usage given in Sect. 2.3, with only one k value for covariance. Our purpose is to highlight the strengths and weaknesses of our first modeling of common usage. As the focus of this paper is on interconnection between wise objects and IOT, we do not provide an in-depth analysis of common usage modeling. This issue will be studied in the future.

In this experiment, we observe for the sensor, the delay between events as well as the time spent by it in different states. The events are the detection of "new presence", when the sensor switches from "no presence" state to "presence" state and conversely, the detection of "no more presence", when the sensor switches from "presence" state to "no presence" state. Figures 15(a) and (b) give the common usage respectively computed from the "new presence" events and from the "no more presence" events. In other word, Fig. 15(a), gives the common variation of delay between two successive "new presence" events. Figures 16(a) and (b) give the common usage respectively computed from the duration of presence and the duration of no presence in the room. The results are computed with 15 days as window size w, any data older than 15 days are forgotten. Thus, in the range $[-1, 1]$, between green lines in the figures, the behavior is considered as common usage regarding the last 15 days. Outside the range $[-1, 1]$, behavior is considered as unusual, we qualify it as "emotion". The emotional force is represented by the distance of the behavior to the common usage.

These preliminary results are encouraging. They highlight, from different points of view – state changes and time spent in a state – the change in the

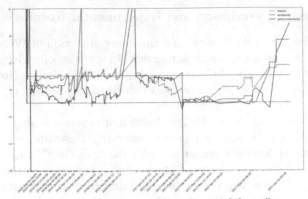

(a) Classroom usage representation computed from "new presence" events

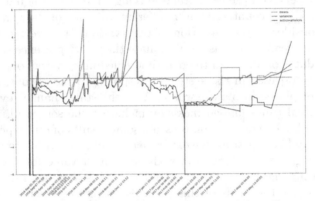

(b) Classroom usage representation computed from "no more presence" events

Fig. 15. Common usage and emotion representation based on events [2]. (Color figure online)

classroom usage. Each part with an important distance from the common usage corresponds to holidays (in France):

- 1 week for the Halloween holidays in October,
- 2 weeks for the Christmas holidays in December,
- 1 week for the winter holidays in February,
- 1 week for the Easter holidays in April and
- the end of the school year in June.

Each part with a small distance from the common usage corresponds to weekends. Let us note that each part detected as unusual depends on the usage done during the 15 days before. Thus weekends are strongly detected when the room is frequently used in the week for example between September and December.

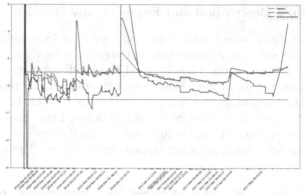

(a) Classroom usage representation computed from "presence" duration

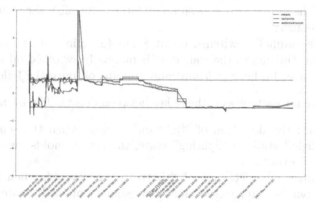

(b) Classroom usage representation computed from "no presence" duration

Fig. 16. Common usage and emotion representation based on time spent in state [2]. (Color figure online)

The holidays are strongly detected before January but, weakly detected after December. As the observed room is an amphitheater, it is more used at the beginning of the school year than at the end.

We consider those results as preliminary because there is a combinatorial problem in using the underlying analysis method. Sensor modeling with 2 states and 2 transitions leads to 12 graphics, with only one k value for the covariance, to identify common usage and emotions. For a given object, the maximum number of "common usage" related graphics is $n * a * (2 + n_k)$, where n is the number of states, a is the number of methods and n_k is the possible number of values of k. Thus, an information fusion step is required to reduce the combinatorial problem. Another point is that our system does not react if nothing happens during an unusual period; It detects changes only when an event occurs. The management of "no event" must also be performed by the system. Both those points will be addressed in future work.

4.2   Use Case 2 Description and Experimental Results

The second case study focus is on considering a set of objects instead of a single one as in the first case. The objective behind the experimentation is to be as close as possible to a real situation. Thus we used the WOF simulator to simulate a home automation system, within a classroom, composed of four physical objects: a switch, a light, a rolling shutter and a heating device. As in the previous case, we would like to know if our system is able to detect habit change in relation to a usual usage. As several objects are involved in the system, we also would like to study the behavior correlation among those objects. The usual behavior is the following:

- each day the heating system is automatically started at 6:00 am and it functions until 6:00 pm;
- each day at 8 am (±5 min), the shutter is manually opened by a teacher or a student of the first course. Eleven hours later (±30 min), the shutter is closed by the caretaker;
- the light is manually switched on at 8 am (±5 min), at the arrival of the teacher and students to the course. It is manually switched off at the end of the first course, 1 h later (±5 min) and remains off until the following day.

We observe for each object, the delay between events. The events are:

- for the light: the detection of "light on" events, when the sensor switches from "no light" state to "lighting" state; the reverse holds for the detection of "light off" events;
- for the shutter: the detection of "shutter open" events, when the actuator switches from "shutter closed" state to "shutter opened" state; the reverse holds for the detection of "shutter close" events;
- for the heating: the detection of "heating on" events, when the actuator switches from "no heating" state to "heating" state; the reverse holds for the detection of "heating off" events;

Figure 17 depicts the common usage computed respectively for the light, shutter and heating. Each sub-figure gives the common variation of delay between two successive events on an object (red) as well as the standard deviation (blue).

The results are computed within a memory window size w of 100 events corresponding to a duration of 3 months in our simulator. Data older than 3 months are forgotten (no longer considered in the computation). Thus, in the range $[-1, 1]$, between green lines in the figures, the behavior is considered as usual (common usage) during the last 3 months. Outside the range $[-1, 1]$, behavior is considered as unusual and the emotional force is represented by the distance of the behavior to the common usage.

As shown by Fig. 17:

- the heating system behaves as usual: no emotion detected; this is consistent with the fact that the heating is automatically started and stopped everyday exactly at the same instants (no random effect);

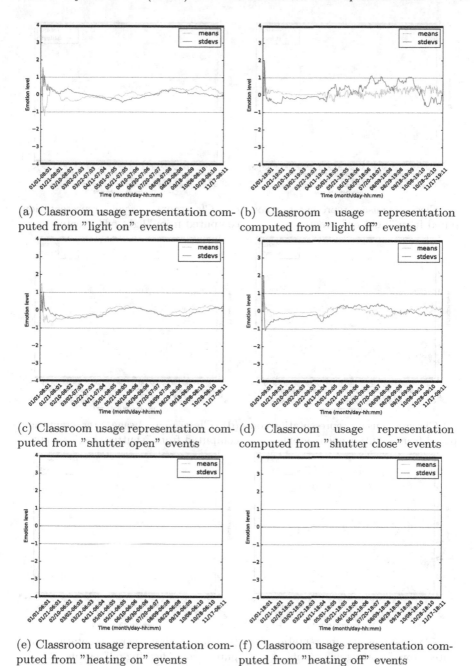

(a) Classroom usage representation computed from "light on" events

(b) Classroom usage representation computed from "light off" events

(c) Classroom usage representation computed from "shutter open" events

(d) Classroom usage representation computed from "shutter close" events

(e) Classroom usage representation computed from "heating on" events

(f) Classroom usage representation computed from "heating off" events

Fig. 17. Common usage and emotion representation based on events. (Color figure online)

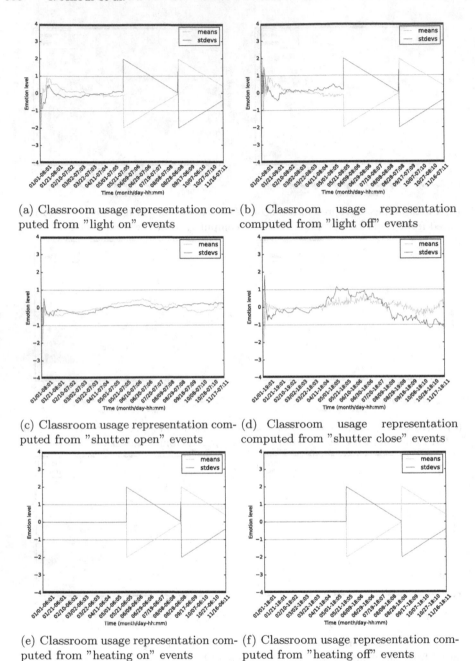

(a) Classroom usage representation computed from "light on" events

(b) Classroom usage representation computed from "light off" events

(c) Classroom usage representation computed from "shutter open" events

(d) Classroom usage representation computed from "shutter close" events

(e) Classroom usage representation computed from "heating on" events

(f) Classroom usage representation computed from "heating off" events

Fig. 18. Usage and emotion representation based on events, integrating an unusual event: a power cut at 10 am the 150th day of the experiment.

- we can notice that for both "light on" and "light off" events, at the beginning of the time window, there is a chaotic variation resulting an emotion (a surprise): as the events outside the time window are forgotten, events occurring in the new window are considered unusual by the object that progressively integrate them as a usual behavior;
- generally there is no significant change in the behavior of the shutter. We can however note sometimes a slight chaotic perturbation as in the sub-figure of "light off" events: this is due to the cumulative random effect.

While in the previous situation nothing special happened relatively to the common behavior, in Fig. 18, we can clearly see different shapes for the behavior of the light and the heating device. Something happened that disturbed the system without affecting the shutter: a power cut at 10 AM the 150th day of the experiment (May 21st). In this case we clearly see a variation value outside the normality boundaries. This translates an emotion that has an impact on the means computation. As the power cut lasted 2 h, the delay between successive events have been disturbed (around 2 h instead of 24). This highlights the ability of a wise system to show correlated unusual behavior among several things. Its knowledge monitoring and analysis capabilities are therefore useful for diagnosing or explaining unusual behaviour of IoT-based systems.

5 Concluding Remarks and Future Work

To meet the growing user requirements for IoT technology-based systems that adapt to their needs, we propose WOF (Wise Object Framework) [4], an object oriented framework to develop software-intensive systems ("wise systems") able to learn, monitor and analyze data/information among distributed things. We recalled in this paper the underlying concepts of WO (Wise Object) and WOF and focused in particular on how to interconnect IoT to WOF to benefit from its useful built-in mechanisms (namely learning, monitoring, adaptation) and meet users' requirements. The communication protocol we propose allows things to communicate themselves. It is designed as part of WOF. For each thing, we propose to use a software avatar, a WO in our case so that it become possible to manipulate and manage this representation of the thing. In this paper, we focus on the description of the communication structure and especially the corresponding software as well as the proposed protocol which makes possible interaction between a wise object and a physical thing.

We show that using the proposed structure, any thing from IoT is manageable. The only constraint is that the considered thing uses the proposed communication protocol. Thus, the system is able to communicate with any thing, whether known or unknown. If a thing is unknown – there is no WO implementation dedicated to this thing – a generic WO implementation can be used as an avatar for this thing.

We illustrated our approach on two case studies within home automation domain and showed how wise things (smart presence sensor, light, etc.) are able to identify common usage and unusual behavior. This is enabled by analyzers connectable to WOF: in this paper we presented one of them we built using a statistic method based on "stationarity" theory.

We show the interest for the system by performing a first experiment based on real data with a single thing then a second experiment based on simulated behavior of a classroom using home automation things (a smart presence sensor, shutter, etc.). One interesting finding comes from the fact that the results show the changes due to the usage context: vacation or weekends in the first case study or a power cut in the second case. In the broader context of home automation, we are convinced that our approach can be useful, for instance to assist old people in their home (individual or nursing). Authors in [9,10], adopt a user driven approach and present an interesting study on nursing home users' expectations from AAL (Ambient Assistant Living) technologies. One important outcome is that there is a need for systems able to detect users' activity level and to notify the care staff and/or family members about unusual behavior.

In future work, we plan to focus our research mainly on the modeling and the management of common usage and emotions. As highlighted in the experimental results, issues of information fusion and of management of situations like "nothing happens during an unusual time" must be addressed to obtain results that are more accurate, usable and up-to-date upon request. Another important issue is studying the correlation of behavior among a set of WOs composing a system, in particular measuring the impact of a WO emotion on the other WOs. The next step for us is to be able to express emotions with a higher semantic level than the present one (i.e. the statistical method) in order to communicate lighter amounts of information to the system. The system can then react according to an aggregated information rather than multiple pieces of information.

References

1. Aarts, H., Verplanken, B., Knippenberg, A.: Predicting behavior from actions in the past: repeated decision making or a matter of habit? J. Appl. Soc. Psychol. **28**(15), 1355–1374 (2006). https://doi.org/10.1111/j.1559-1816.1998.tb01681.x. https://onlinelibrary.wiley.com/doi/abs/10.1111/j.1559-1816.1998.tb01681.x
2. Alloui, I., Benoit, E., Perrin, S., Vernier, F.: Wiot: interconnection between wise objects and IOT. In: Proceedings of the 13th International Conference on Software Technologies, ICSOFT, vol. 1, pp. 494–505. INSTICC, SciTePress (2018). https://doi.org/10.5220/0006870205280539
3. Alloui, I., Esale, D., Vernier, F.: Wise objects for calm technology. In: 10th International Conference on Software Engineering and Applications (ICSOFT-EA 2015), Colmar, France, pp. 468–471. SciTePress, July 2015. https://doi.org/10.5220/0005560104680471, https://hal.archives-ouvertes.fr/hal-01226219
4. Alloui, I., Vernier, F.: WOF: towards behavior analysis and representation of emotions in adaptive systems. In: Cabello, E., Cardoso, J., Maciaszek, L.A., van Sinderen, M. (eds.) ICSOFT 2017. CCIS, vol. 868, pp. 244–267. Springer, Cham (2018). https://doi.org/10.1007/978-3-319-93641-3_12
5. Aminikhanghahi, S., Cook, D.J.: A survey of methods for time series change-point detection. Knowl. Inf. Syst. **51**(2), 339–367 (2017). https://doi.org/10.1007/s10115-016-0987-z

6. Brun, Y., et al.: A design space for self-adaptive systems. In: de Lemos, R., Giese, H., Müller, H.A., Shaw, M. (eds.) Software Engineering for Self-Adaptive Systems II. LNCS, vol. 7475, pp. 33–50. Springer, Heidelberg (2013). https://doi.org/10.1007/978-3-642-35813-5_2
7. IEC: IoT 2020: Smart and Secure IoT Platform: White Paper. International Electrotechnical Commission (2016). https://books.google.fr/books?id=aItwAQAACAAJ
8. Moreaux, P., Sartor, F., Vernier, F.: An effective approach for home services management. In: 20th Euromicro International Conference on Parallel, Distributed and Network-Based Processing (PDP), pp. 47–51. IEEE, Garching, February 2012. https://doi.org/10.1109/PDP.2012.45
9. Röcker, C., Ziefle, M., Holzinger, A.: Social inclusion in ambient assisted living environments: home automation and convenience services for elderly users. In: International Conference on Artificial Intelligence (ICAI 2011), pp. 55–59. CSERA Press, New York (2011). https://doi.org/10.1007/978-3-319-66808-6_17
10. Singh, D., Kropf, J., Hanke, S., Holzinger, A.: Ambient assisted living technologies from the perspectives of older people and professionals. In: Holzinger, A., Kieseberg, P., Tjoa, A.M., Weippl, E. (eds.) CD-MAKE 2017. LNCS, vol. 10410, pp. 255–266. Springer, Cham (2017). https://doi.org/10.1007/978-3-319-66808-6_17
11. Vishwajeet, H.B., Sanjeev, W.: i-learning IOT: an intelligent self learning system for home automation using IOT. In: International Conference on Communications and Signal Processing (ICCSP), April 2015. https://doi.org/10.1109/ICCSP.2015.7322825
12. Weyns, D., et al.: On patterns for decentralized control in self-adaptive systems. In: de Lemos, R., Giese, H., Müller, H.A., Shaw, M. (eds.) Software Engineering for Self-Adaptive Systems II. LNCS, vol. 7475, pp. 76–107. Springer, Heidelberg (2013). https://doi.org/10.1007/978-3-642-35813-5_4
13. Yassein, M.B., Shatnawi, M.Q., Aljwarneh, S., Al-Hatmi, R.: Internet of things: survey and open issues of MQTT protocol. In: 2017 International Conference on Engineering MIS ICEMIS, pp. 1–6, May 2017. https://doi.org/10.1109/ICEMIS.2017.8273112
14. Z-Vawe: Z-vawe aliance (2018). https://z-wavealliance.org/. Accessed 1 Apr 2018
15. Zigbee: Zigbee aliance (2018). http://www.zigbee.org/. Accessed 1 Apr 2018

A Software Product Line Approach to Design Secure Connectors in Component-Based Software Architectures

Michael Shin[1]($\boxtimes$), Hassan Gomaa[2], and Don Pathirage[1]

[1] Department of Computer Science, Texas Tech University, Lubbock, TX, USA
{michael.shin, don.pathirage}@ttu.edu
[2] Department of Computer Science, George Mason University,
Fairfax, VA, USA
hgomaa@gmu.edu

Abstract. This paper describes a software product line approach to design secure connectors in distributed component-based software architectures. The variability of secure connectors is modelled by means of a feature model, which consists of security pattern and communication pattern features. Applying separation of concerns, each secure connector is designed as a composite component that encapsulates both security pattern and communication pattern components. Integration of these components within a secure connector is enabled by a security coordinator, the high-level template of which is customized based on the selected security pattern features.

Keywords: Software product line · Feature model · Secure connector · Secure software architecture · Component-based software architecture · Message communication patterns · Security patterns · Model-based software design

1 Introduction

This paper describes the design of secure connectors in distributed component-based software architectures (CBSA) that are composed of components and connectors. Although connectors are typically used in software architecture [1] to encapsulate communication mechanisms between components, security concerns can also be encapsulated in software connectors separately from the application. In order to facilitate reuse of these connectors, which are referred to as secure connectors [2–6], it is necessary to design secure connectors that are both modular and reusable.

Each secure connector is designed as a composite component consisting of reusable security pattern components and communication pattern components. Each security pattern component encapsulates a security pattern, such as symmetric encryption or digital signature. Each communication pattern component encapsulates the communication protocol between application components, such as synchronous or asynchronous message communication. A secure connector is then constructed by composing security pattern components and communication pattern components. Integration of security

© Springer Nature Switzerland AG 2019
M. van Sinderen and L. A. Maciaszek (Eds.): ICSOFT 2018, CCIS 1077, pp. 372–396, 2019.
https://doi.org/10.1007/978-3-030-29157-0_17

patterns and communication patterns within a secure connector is provided by a security coordinator. Once a secure connector is constructed, it can then be reused in different applications.

This paper is an extension of our recent paper [7] that described modeling secure connectors by means of a software product line (SPL) approach. Our earlier work [2–6] focused on designing single reusable secure connectors in an ad hoc way. Our recent paper [7] investigated how applying SPL concepts can lead to a more systematic approach that addresses the inherent variability in the design of secure connectors that encapsulate the separate concerns of security and communication patterns. This paper extends our recent work in terms of the coordination templates needed to integrate security and communication patterns, explains the differences between SPL for secure connectors and traditional SPL approaches, provides an additional case study of a synchronous message communication connector, and validates our approach with android applications.

This paper is organized as follows. Section 2 describes existing approaches to modeling and designing security concerns in software applications. Section 3 describes a SPL approach for secure connectors, followed by the feature model for secure connectors in Sect. 4. Section 5 describes communication and security components. Section 6 describes security coordinator components and templates. Section 7 describes a secure asynchronous message communication connector derived from a SPL for secure connectors, followed by a secure synchronous message communication connector in Sect. 8. Section 9 describes the validation of reusable secure connectors. Section 10 discusses and compares the SPL approach for secure connectors with conventional SPL approaches. Section 11 describes the conclusions of this paper and future research.

2 Related Work

Related work focuses on approaches to designing software architectures for secure applications, patterns for distributed communication and component-based software product lines. The authors in [8] proposed SecureUML, which is a UML based modeling language for model-driven development of secure systems. An extension of UML for security called UMLsec [9] helps with the expression of security-relevant information within design diagrams. In model-driven security [10], a system is modeled with its security requirements and security infrastructures are generated.

A distributed CBSA in [1] consists of a set of components and connectors. Communication patterns in CBSA were investigated in [11, 12]. In [13], a connector centric approach is used to model, capture, and enforce security using software connectors. Methods in [14] propose SecArch to evaluate architectures with significant security concerns. Security patterns in [15, 16] address a range of security issues to be taken into account in the software development lifecycle. The authors describe the problem, context, solution, and implementation of security patterns, which are intended to help developers with little or no security expertise to construct secure systems.

A software product line (SPL) [17] is a family of software systems that have some common functionality and some variable functionality. The functionality of a SPL can be modeled by means of a feature model. In a component-based SPL, each component has ports with provided and required interfaces. The authors in [18–21] addressed multiple-view modeling and meta-modeling of SPLs and in [7] addressed a SPL approach for feature modeling and design of secure connectors. A co-author in [22–24] investigated respectively the design of SPL architecture for service-oriented systems, space flight systems, and smart spaces. Dynamic SPLs that dynamically adapt SPL members at run-time, were investigated in [25–27].

In recent work by the authors [3] described secure asynchronous and synchronous connectors for modeling the software architectures for distributed applications and the design of reusable secure connectors. The authors in [4–6] addressed the design of secure connectors in terms of maintainability and evolution. A co-author in [28–30] also investigated designing dynamically adaptable and recoverable connectors.

3   Software Product Line for Secure Connectors

A security service [31, 32] is software functionality for realizing a security goal, such as confidentiality, integrity and availability, which can be implemented by means of different security techniques. A security service is realized by means of different security patterns [15, 16], each of which addresses a specific security technique that realizes a security service. For instance, a confidentiality security service can be realized by means of a symmetric encryption or an asymmetric security pattern [16].

Typical message communication patterns between distributed components are synchronous message communication with reply and asynchronous message communication [12]. Communication patterns are frequently used protocols for inter-component communication. Each communication pattern is designed with a sender and receiver communication pattern component (CPC), which are encapsulated in a secure sender and secure receiver connector respectively. A secure connector is designed by considering the message communication and security patterns required by application components. A secure connector is a distributed connector, which consists of a secure sender and secure receiver connector. A secure sender or receiver connector consists of a security coordinator, one or more security objects, and a communication object.

In this paper, the reusability of secure connectors is enabled by applying SPL concepts to model the variability and design of secure connectors. The SPL approach models the variability of secure connectors in terms of security patterns and communication patterns. In the SPL, variability in these patterns are modeled as features in a feature model. The relationships between the features are modeled by means of feature dependencies. In addition, a feature/component table is used to determine which communication and security components are needed to realize each feature. To derive a given secure connector from the feature model, the appropriate features are selected and the components that realize those features are then selected and integrated.

4 Feature Model for Secure Connectors

The feature model (Fig. 1) for secure connectors describes the variability of secure connectors in terms of communication pattern (CP) and security pattern (SP) features and the dependency between the features. The feature model consists of one exactly-one-of-feature group, *Communication Patterns*, which means that one and only one feature can be selected from the group, and one at-least-one-of-feature group *Security Patterns*, which means that one or more features need to be selected from the group. The *Communication Patterns* feature group is composed of three further exactly-one-of feature groups: the *Unidirectional* feature group, which consists of three optional one-way message communication pattern features (CPFs), *SMC* (synchronous message communication) *without Reply, Broadcast* and *AMC* (asynchronous message communication) features; the *Bidirectional* feature group, which consists of two two-way optional message communication pattern features, *Bidirectional AMC* and *Subscription/Notification* features; and the *Message with Single Reply* feature group, which consists of two optional message communication features, *AMC with Callback* and *SMC with Reply* features. The optional communication pattern features are:

In *SMC with Reply* feature, a sender component sends a message to a receiver component and waits for a response from the receiver [12]. In *SMC without Reply* feature, a receiver component acknowledges a sender component when it receives a message from the sender [12]. In *AMC* feature, an asynchronous message is sent from a sender component to a receiver component and is stored in a queue if the receiver is busy [12]. *Bidirectional AMC* feature uses the asynchronous message communication pattern feature in both directions between the sender and receiver components [12]. In *AMC with Callback* feature, a sender component sends an asynchronous service request message to a server component, which includes the client operation (callback) handle [12]. *Subscription/Notification* feature uses the *SMC with Reply* for client components to subscribe to receive messages from a server component. The server component notifies client subscriber components through the AMC pattern [12]. In *Broadcast* feature, a server component sends unsolicited messages to all clients [12].

The security pattern features (SPFs) that constitute the *Security Patterns* at-least-one-of-feature group (Fig. 1) are the *Authenticator, Authorization, Symmetric Encryption,* and *Public Key Infrastructure* optional features in addition to the *Integrity* exactly-one-of-feature group, which consists of two optional mutually exclusive security pattern features: *Hashing* and *Digital Signature*. The *Hashing* security pattern feature provides message integrity, which is also provided by *Digital Signature* security pattern feature. In addition, *Digital Signature* feature provides non-repudiation security. The security pattern features are:

Symmetric Encryption feature prevents secret information from being disclosed to any unauthorized party. A message sent by a sender is encrypted using a secret key and is decrypted by the receiver [16]. *Hashing feature* protects against unauthorized changes to secret information. A hash value for a message is generated by a sender and the integrity of the message is verified by the receiver [16]. *Digital Signature* feature protects against one party to a transaction later falsely denying that the transaction occurred. A message is signed by a sender using the sender's private key and is verified by a receiver [16]. *Authenticator* feature allows an entity to identify itself positively to another entity using a password, personal-identification number or challenge response [16]. *Authorization* feature protects against unauthorized access to valuable resources using mandatory access control, discretionary access control, role-based access control or attribute-based access control [16]. *Public Key Infrastructure* feature provides security policies and procedures that create, revoke, manage, distribute, use, store public certificates and public keys [33].

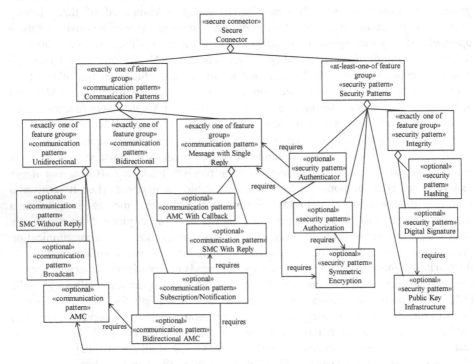

Fig. 1. Feature model for secure connectors.

The *Authenticator* and *Authorization* features each require the *Symmetric Encryption* feature because a sender's credentials for authentication and sender's parameter for requesting permission should be encrypted to prevent unauthorized access. Both *Authenticator* and *Authorization* features also require the *Message with Single Reply* feature due to their need for a response to the original request. In the *Authenticator* feature, a sender requests authentication from a server and the server needs to reply with the authentication result. Similarly, in the *Authorization* feature, a sender requests permission from a receiver and the receiver needs to send back the approval or denial to the sender. The *Digital Signature* feature requires the *Public Key Infrastructure* feature because a sender's message is signed using the sender's private key and a receiver verifies the signed message using the sender's public key.

5 Communication and Security Components

Each feature in the feature model for secure connectors is designed using components, which are then encapsulated into a secure connector. A security pattern feature is designed as one or more optional security pattern components, whereas a communication pattern feature is designed as sender and receiver optional communication pattern components, together with the appropriate variant optional security coordinator components, as described in Sect. 6.

Table 1 shows each feature in the feature model and their components. The *SMC with Reply* feature is designed as a *SMC with Reply Sender* component for sending messages to the receiver, a *SMC with Reply Receiver* component for receiving messages from the sender, and *SMC with Reply Security Sender Coordinator* and *Receiver Coordinator* components for sequencing the interactions with one or more security components and with the appropriate communication component. Similarly, the *Broadcast, AMC, Bidirectional AMC* and *SMC without Reply* features are designed as sender and receiver components respectively. Because the *Bidirectional AMC* feature depends on the *AMC* feature, it is designed to use components from the *AMC* feature. Also, the *Subscription/Notification* feature is designed to use components from both *AMC* and *SMC with Reply* features due to its dependency on these features. The *Authenticator* feature is designed as an *Authenticator* component whereas the *Authorization* feature is designed as an *Authorization* component. Each of the *Symmetric Encryption, Digital Signature*, and *Hashing* features is designed as two components, a sender and a receiver component. The *Public Key Infrastructure* feature is designed as a *Public Key Repository* component.

A security pattern feature (SPF) is designed using one or more security pattern components (SPCs), as depicted in Fig. 2. The *Symmetric Encryption* feature (Fig. 2a) is composed of the symmetric encryption encryptor and decryptor components [16]. The *Digital Signature* feature (Fig. 2b) is designed as the digital signature signer and digital signature verifier components (Fig. 2b) [16]. Each port of a component is defined in terms of provided and/or required interfaces [12]. Each security pattern component (Fig. 2) has a provided port through which the component provides security services to other components. Figure 3 depicts the interfaces provided by the ports of the SPCs in Fig. 2.

Each communication pattern is designed as a sender and a receiver communication pattern component (CPC), which are encapsulated in a secure sender connector and a secure receiver connector respectively. Figure 4a depicts the Asynchronous MC Sender CPC and Asynchronous MC Receiver CPC for the secure AMC connector. The Asynchronous MC Sender CPC (Fig. 4a) has the provided PAsyncMCSenderService port through which it receives from the Security Sender Coordinator component (Fig. 10a) a message to be sent to the Asynchronous MC Receiver CPC via the required RNetwork port. Similarly, the Asynchronous MC Receiver CPC (Fig. 4a) has the required RSecurityService port and provided PNetwork port. Figure 4b depicts the interfaces provided by each port of the AMC Sender and Receiver CPCs.

Table 1. Features and their components [7].

Feature	Components	Reuse Stereotype
SMC Without Reply Feature	SMC Without Reply Sender Component	Optional
	SMC Without Reply Receiver Component	Optional
	SMC Without Reply Security Sender Coordinator Component	Optional (Variant)
	SMC Without Reply Security Receiver Coordinator Component	Optional (Variant)
Broadcast Feature	Broadcast Sender Component	Optional
	Broadcast Receiver Component	Optional
	Broadcast Security Sender Coordinator Component	Optional (Variant)
	Broadcast Security Receiver Coordinator Component	Optional (Variant)
AMC Feature	AMC Sender Component	Optional
	AMC Receiver Component	Optional
	AMC Security Sender Coordinator Component	Optional (Variant)
	AMC Security Receiver Coordinator Component	Optional (Variant)
Bidirectional AMC Feature	Components from AMC Feature	
Subscription/ Notification Feature	Components from AMC Feature	
	Components from SMC Feature	
SMC With Reply Feature	SMC With Reply Sender Component	Optional
	SMC With Reply Receiver Component	Optional
	SMC With Reply Security Sender Coordinator Component	Optional (Variant)
	SMC With Reply Security Receiver Coordinator Component	Optional (Variant)
AMC With Callback Feature	AMC With Callback Sender Component	Optional
	AMC With Callback Receiver Component	Optional
	AMC With Callback Security Sender Coordinator Component	Optional (Variant)
	AMC With Callback Security Receiver Coordinator Component	Optional (Variant)
Authenticator Feature	Authenticator Component	Optional
Authorization Feature	Authorization Component	Optional
Symmetric Encryption Feature	Symmetric Encryption Encryptor Component	Optional
	Symmetric Encryption Decryptor Component	Optional
Digital Signature Feature	Digital Signature Signer Component	Optional
	Digital Signature Verifier Component	Optional
Hashing Feature	Hashing Generator Component	Optional
	Hashing Verifier Component	Optional
Public Key Infrastructure Feature	Public Key Repository Component	Optional

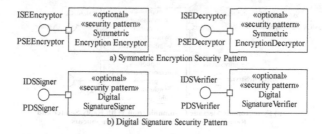

a) Symmetric Encryption Security Pattern

b) Digital Signature Security Pattern

Fig. 2. Security pattern components [7].

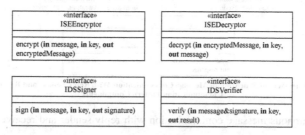

Fig. 3. Interfaces of security pattern components [7].

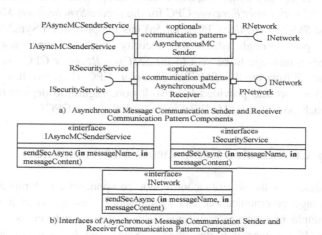

a) Asynchronous Message Communication Sender and Receiver Communication Pattern Components

b) Interfaces of Asynchronous Message Communication Sender and Receiver Communication Pattern Components

Fig. 4. Asynchronous message communication sender and receiver components [7].

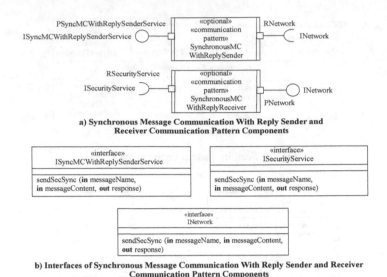

a) Synchronous Message Communication With Reply Sender and
Receiver Communication Pattern Components

b) Interfaces of Synchronous Message Communication With Reply Sender and Receiver
Communication Pattern Components

Fig. 5. Synchronous message communication with reply sender and receiver components

Figure 5a depicts the *SynchronousMC with Reply (SMCWR) Sender* CPC and *Synchronous MC with Reply Receiver* CPC for the secure *Synchronous MC with Reply* connector. The *SMCWR Sender* CPC (Fig. 5a) has the provided PSyncMCWithReply SenderService port through which the Security Sender Coordinator component (Fig. 14a) sends a message to be sent to the *SMCWR Receiver* CPC via the required RNetwork port. Similarly, the *SMCWR Receiver* CPC (Fig. 5a) has the required RSecurityService port and provided PNetwork port. Figure 5b depicts the interfaces provided by each port of the *SMCWR Sender* and *Receiver* CPCs.

6   Security Coordinator Components and Templates

This section describes the security coordinator components and templates for asynchronous message communication and synchronous message communication with reply. An example of a secure connector for a secure asynchronous message communication (AMC) connector is described in Sect. 7 while an example of a secure connector for a secure synchronous message communication with reply (SMCWR) connector is described in Sect. 8.

A security sender coordinator component receives messages from an application sender component, and a security receiver coordinator component delivers messages to an application receiver component. The security sender and receiver coordinator components are variant optional components (Table 1), optional because they are needed for each optional communication pattern, and variant because the design of each coordinator component needs to be customized for each secure connector based on one or more selected security features. Templates for the high-level security sender and receiver coordinator components are designed for each communication pattern.

A communication pattern needs one template for the high-level security sender coordinator component (Figs. 6 and 8) and another template for the receiver coordinator component (Figs. 7 and 9). These templates are customized for each secure connector based on the security features selected.

The pseudocode template for the security sender coordinator in a secure AMC sender connector is depicted in Fig. 6, in which the security related code (shown in italics) is replaced by the pseudocode for the security patterns selected for a secure AMC connector, as described in Sect. 7. A security pattern is applied to a message if the security feature condition is true, namely when a security feature is selected for a message. For instance, *SymmetricEncryption_feature = True* (Fig. 6) means that the Symmetric Encryption feature condition is true, so a message must be encrypted. The pseudocode template for the security sender coordinator is customized for a secure AMC connector that encapsulates Asymmetric Encryption and Digital Signature SCs, as described in Sect. 7 and depicted in Fig. 11.

```
loop

    -- Wait for message from sender component;
    receive (SenderComponentMessageQ, message);
    Extract MessageName, MessageContent and SenderSecurityPatternAttribute from message;

    -- Apply security patterns to message content;

        if (SymmetricEncryption_feature = True) then encrypt MessageContent; end if
        if (Hashing_feature = True) then generate hashValue of MessageContent; end if
        if (DigitalSignature_feature = True) then sign MessageContent; end if

    -- Send message to AMC Sender CPC;
    AMCSender.sendSecAsync (in MessageName, in MessageContent);

end loop;
```

Fig. 6. Pseudocode template for security sender coordinator in secure AMC connector.

Symmetric Encryption, Hashing and Digital Signature features can be applied to a message in a secure AMC. When both Symmetric Encryption and Hashing features are selected (Fig. 6), although Symmetric Encryption and Hashing security patterns could be applied to a message in an arbitrary order, the security coordinator applies the Symmetric Encryption feature to a message first and then applies the Digital Signature security pattern (Fig. 6) because an encrypted and then signed message is more secure and widely adopted. In contrast, a signed and then encrypted message could be exploited by a receiver to spoof the identity of the sender and send it to a third party.

Similarly, the pseudocode template for the Security Receiver Coordinator in a secure AMC receive connector is specified in Fig. 7. The security patterns in the pseudocode template (Fig. 7) are applied to a message in the reverse order of the security patterns (Fig. 6) applied by the security sender coordinator. As a security sender coordinator applies the security patterns in the order of Symmetric Encryption,

Hashing, and Digital Signature features (Fig. 6), a security receiver coordinator applies the security patterns in the order of Digital Signature, Hashing, and Symmetric Encryption features (Fig. 7). The pseudocode templates for security receiver coordinator component (Fig. 7) are customized for a secure AMC connector that encapsulates Symmetric Encryption and Digital Signature SCPs, as described in Sect. 7.

Loop

```
-- Wait for message from AMC Receiver CPC;
receive (AMCReceiverMessageQ, message);
Extract MessageName and MessageContent from message;

-- Apply security patterns to message content;
if (DigitalSignature_feature = True) then verify MessageContent; end if
if (Hashing_feature = True) then verify hashValue of MessageContent; end if
if (SymmetricEncryption_feature = True) then decrypt MessageContent; end if

-- Send message name and message content to receiver component;
if MessageContent is secure
then
         ReceiverComponent.sendSecAsync (in MessageName, in MessageContent);
end if;

end loop;
```

Fig. 7. Pseudocode template for security receiver coordinator in secure AMC connector.

```
loop
-- Wait for message from sender component;
receive (SenderComponentMessageBuffer&Response, message);
Extract MessageName, MessageContent and SenderSecurityPatternAttribute from message;

-- Apply security pattern to message content;
if (SymmetricEncryption_feature = True) then encrypt MessageContent; end if
if (Hashing_feature = True) then generate hashValue of MessageContent; end if
if (DigitalSignature_feature = True) then sign MessageContent; end if

-- Send message to SMCWR Sender CPC;
SMCWRSender.sendSecSync (in MessageName, in MessageContent, out Reply);

-- Apply security pattern to reply if reply is required;
if (DigitalSignature_feature = True) then verify reply; end if
if (Hashing_feature = True) then verify hashValue of reply; end if
if (SymmetricEncryption_feature = True) then decrypt reply; end if

-- Send reply to sender component;
if reply is secure
then
         reply(SenderComponentMessageBuffer&Response, Reply);
end if
end loop;
```

Fig. 8. Pseudocode template for security sender coordinator in secure SMCWR connector.

Figure 8 depicts the pseudocode template for the security sender coordinator in the secure SMCWR sender connector in which the security patterns are applied to a message sent to and a reply received from the secure SMCWR receiver connector. The pseudocode customized for the Symmetric Encryption security pattern in a secure SMCWR sender connector is described in Sect. 8 and depicted in Fig. 15.

Similarly, the pseudocode template for the Security Receiver Coordinator in the secure SMCWR receiver connector is specified in Fig. 9. When both Authenticator and Authorization features are selected for a message, Authenticator and then Authorization security patterns are applied to the message because the authenticity of message is checked and then the message is authorized if the message is authenticated successfully. Also, when the credentials for Authenticator or Authorization security patterns might be encrypted, hashed, and signed in the secure SMCWR receiver connector, the signature and hash value of the credentials are verified and then the credentials are decrypted in the secure SMCWR receiver connector. The pseudocode customized for the Symmetric Encryption security pattern for a secure SMCWR receiver connector is described in Sect. 8 and depicted in Fig. 16.

```
loop
-- Wait for message from SMCWR Receiver CPC;
receive (SMCWRReceiverMessageBuffer&Response, message);
Extract MessageName and MessageContent from message;

-- Apply security pattern to message content;
if (DigitalSignature_feature = True) then verify MessageContent; end if
if (Hashing_feature = True) then verify hashValue of MessageContent; end if
if (SymmetricEncryption_feature = True) then decrypt MessageContent; end if
if (Authenticator_feature = True) then authenticate MessageContent; end if
if (Authorization_feature = True) then authorize MessageContent; end if

-- Send message name and message content to receiver component;
if MessgeContent is secure
then
        ReceiverComponent.sendSecSync (in MessageName, in MessageContent,
out Reply&ReceiverSecurityPatternAttribute);
end if

-- Apply security pattern to reply;
if (SymmetricEncryption_feature = True) then encrypt reply; end if
if (Hashing_feature = True) then generate hashValue of reply; end if
if (DigitalSignature_feature = True) then sign reply; end if

-- Send reply to SMCWR Receiver CPC;
reply (SMCWRReceiverMessageBuffer&Response, Reply);
end loop;
```

Fig. 9. Pseudocode template for security receiver coordinator in secure SMCWR connector.

7 Secure Asynchronous Message Communication Connector

This section describes an example of a secure connector that can be derived from the SPL for secure connectors if an application requires the AMC feature together with the Symmetric Encryption and Digital Signature features. Deriving this secure connector needs the selection of one communication pattern (AMC) corresponding to the AMC feature, and two security patterns corresponding to the Symmetric Encryption and Digital Signature features (Fig. 1). The corresponding components (from Table 1) are the AMC Sender and Receiver components, Symmetric Encryption Encryptor (SEE) and Symmetric Encryption Decryptor (SED) components, and Digital Signature Signer (DSS) and Digital Signature Verifier (DSV) components. This secure AMC connector is composed of a secure AMC sender connector (Fig. 13) and secure AMC receiver connector (Fig. 13). The secure AMC sender connector (Fig. 13) is designed as a composite component in which the Security Sender Coordinator (SSC) component (Fig. 10a) integrates the SEE and DSS components (Fig. 2) with the AMC Sender component (Fig. 4). Similarly, the secure AMC receiver connector (Fig. 13) is designed as a composite component in which the Security Receiver Coordinator (SRC) component (Fig. 10b) integrates the SED and DSV components (Fig. 2) with the AMC Receiver component (Fig. 4).

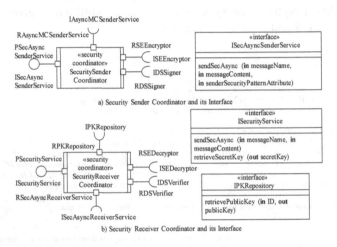

Fig. 10. Sender and receiver coordinators and their interfaces for secure AMC connector [7].

Figure 10a depicts the interface provided by the SSC for a secure AMC connector. The senderSecurityPatternAttribute parameter in sendSecAsync() specifies the private key and/or secret key that is needed by security pattern components to apply security services to a message. For integrating the components, the SSC component (Fig. 10a) has a required RSEEncryptor port to communicate with a provided PSEEncryptor port of the SEE component, which encrypts messages using the sender's secret key, and it also has a required RDSSigner port to communicate with a provided PDSSigner port of the DSS component, which signs a message using the sender's private key. The signed and encrypted messages are sent to the receiver component. The pseudocode for the SSC component is depicted in Fig. 11. Similarly, the AMC Receiver Connector (Fig. 13) is designed as a composite component that encapsulates the SRC component (Fig. 10b), SED component (Fig. 2), DSV component, and AMC Receiver component (Fig. 4). The pseudocode for the SRC component is depicted in Fig. 12.

```
loop
-- Wait for message from sender component;
receive (SenderComponentMessageQ, message);
Extract MessageName, MessageContent, PrivateKey, and SecretKey from message;

-- Apply security patterns to message content;
if MessageContent requires non-repudiation
then
        DigitalSignatureSigner.sign (in MessageContent,
                in PrivateKey, out SignedMessageContent);
        MessageContent = SignedMessageContent;
end if;
if MessageContent requires confidentiality
then
        SymmetricEncryptionEncryptor.encrypt (
                in MessageContent, in SecretKey,
                out EncryptedMessageContent);
        Message Content = EncryptedMessageContent;
end if;

-- Send message to AMC Sender CPC;
AsynchronousMCSender.sendSecAsync (in MessageName, in MessageContent);
end loop;
```

Fig. 11. Pseudocode of security sender coordinator for secure AMC connector with symmetric encryption and digital signature security pattern features [7].

```
loop
-- Wait for message from AMC Receiver CPC;
receive (AMCReceiverMessageQ, message);
Extract MessageName and MessageContent from message;

-- Apply security patterns to message content;
if MessageContent requires confidentiality
then
        ReceiverComponent.retrieveSecretKey (out SecretKey);
        SymmetricEncryptionDecryptor.decrypt (in
                EncryptedMessageContent&Signature,
        in SecretKey, out MessageContent&Signature);
end if;
if MessageContent requires non-repudiation
then
        PublicKeyRepository.retrievePublicKey (in SenderID,
                out SenderPublicKey);
        DigitalSignatureVerifier.verify (in MessageContent&Signature,
                in SenderPublicKey, out Result);
end if;

-- Send message name and message content to receiver component;
if Signature is verified
then
        ReceiverComponent.sendSecAsync (in MessageName, in MessageContent);
end if;
end loop;
```

Fig. 12. Pseudocode of security receiver coordinator for secure AMC connector with symmetric encryption and digital signature security pattern features [7].

Figure 13 depicts the structural view of the secure AMC connector with Symmetric Encryption and Digital Signature security patterns, which can be applied for confirming a shipment in a business to business (B2B) electronic commerce application. When a Supplier component sends a shipment confirmation to a Delivery Order Server, the shipment confirmation is signed by the DSS component in the secure AMC sender connector assuming the Digital Signature security pattern feature is selected for the Supplier component. The shipment confirmation and signature is then encrypted by the SEE component in the secure AMC sender connector assuming the Symmetric Encryption security pattern feature is also selected for the Supplier component. The encrypted shipment confirmation and signature are sent to the Delivery Order Server via the secure AMC receiver connector and then decrypted by the SED component using a secret key retrieved from the Delivery Order Server. The secure AMC receiver connector requests the sender component's public key from the Public Key Repository component (Table 1) that is designed for a certificate authority in the public key infrastructure feature (Table 1). The signature is verified by the DSV component in the secure AMC receiver connector using the sender's public key. The behavioral view of a secure AMC connector can be depicted using UML communication or sequence diagrams. An example is described in [4] for confidentiality and non-repudiation security services.

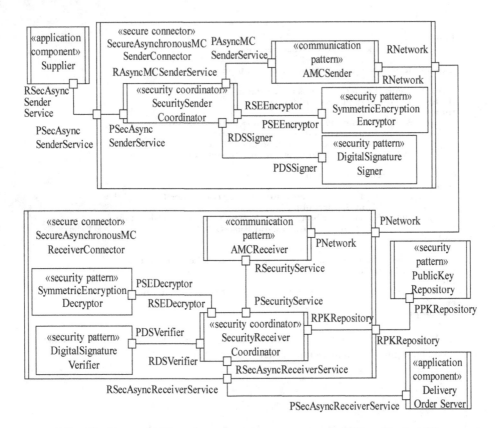

Fig. 13. Secure AMC sender and receiver connectors in B2B application [7].

8   Secure Synchronous Message Communication Connector

This section describes a secure SMCWR connector that is derived from the SPL for secure connectors if an application requires SMCWR feature with Symmetric Encryption. This needs selection of one communication pattern (SMCWR) and one security pattern (Symmetric Encryption) feature (Fig. 1). The corresponding components (from Table 1) are SMCWR Sender and Receiver components, SEE and SED components. This secure SMCWR connector is composed of a secure SMCWR sender connector (Fig. 17) and a secure SMCWR receiver connector (Fig. 17). The secure SMCWR sender connector (Fig. 17) is designed as a composite component in which the SSC component (Fig. 14a) integrates the SEE component (Fig. 2) with the SMCWR Sender component (Fig. 5). Similarly, the secure SMCWR receiver connector (Fig. 17) is designed as a composite component in which the SRC component (Fig. 14b) integrates the SED component with the SMCWR Receiver component.

Figure 14a depicts the interface provided by the SSC for a secure SMCWR connector. The SSC component (Fig. 14a) has a required RSEEncryptor port to communicate with a provided PSEEncryptor port of the SEE component, which encrypts messages using the sender's secret key. The encrypted messages are sent to the receiver component. The pseudocode for the Secure Sender Coordinator component is depicted in Fig. 15. Similarly, the SMCWR Receiver Connector (Fig. 17) is designed as a composite component that encapsulates the SRC component (Fig. 14b), SED component (Fig. 2) and SMCWR Receiver component (Fig. 4). The pseudocode for the Secure Receiver Coordinator component is depicted in Fig. 16.

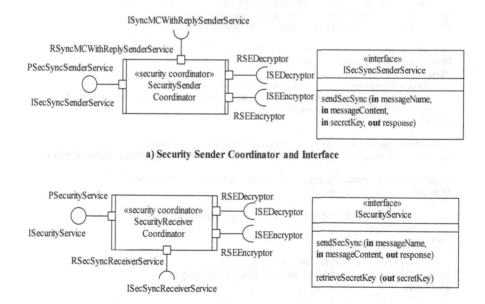

a) Security Sender Coordinator and Interface

b) Security Receiver Coordinator and Interface

Fig. 14. Sender and receiver coordinators and their interfaces for secure SMCWR connector.

```
loop
-- Wait for message from sender component;
receive (SenderComponentMessageBuffer, message);
Extract MessageName and MessageContent, and SecretKey from message;

-- Apply security pattern to message content;
if MessageContent requires confidentiality
Then
        SymmetricEncryptionEncryptor.encrypt (in MessageContent, in SecretKey,
        out EncryptedMessageContent);
end if;

-- Send message to SMCWR Sender CPC;
SynchronousMCWithReplySender.sendSecSync (in MessageName, in
EncryptedMessageContent, out EncryptedReply);

-- Apply security pattern to reply received from SMCWR Sender CPC;
If Reply requires confidentiality
then
        SymmetricEncryptionDecryptor.decrypt (in EncryptedReply, in SecretKey,
        out Reply);
end if;

-- Send reply to sender component;
reply(SenderComponent, Reply);
end loop;
```

Fig. 15. Pseudocode of security sender coordinator for secure SMCWR connector with symmetric encryption security pattern feature.

```
loop
-- Wait for message from SMCWR Receiver CPC;
receive (SMCWRReceiverMessageBuffer, message);
Extract MessageName and MessageContent from message;

-- Apply security pattern to message content;
if MessageContent requires confidentiality
then
        ReceiverComponent.retrieveSecretKey(out SecretKey);
        SymmetricEncryptionDecryptor.decrypt (in EncryptedMessageContent, in
            SecretKey, out MessageContent);
end if;

-- Send message name and message content to receiver component;
ReceiverComponent.sendSecSync (in MessageName, in MessageContent, out Reply);

-- Apply security pattern to reply received from receiver component;
If Reply requires confidentiality
then
        SymmetricEncryptionEncryptor.encrypt (in Reply, in SecretKey, out
EncryptedReply);
end if;

-- Send reply to SMCWR Receiver CPC;
reply (SMCWRReceiverMessageBuffer, EncryptedReply);
end loop;
```

Fig. 16. Pseudocode of security receiver coordinator for secure SMCWR connector with symmetric encryption security pattern feature.

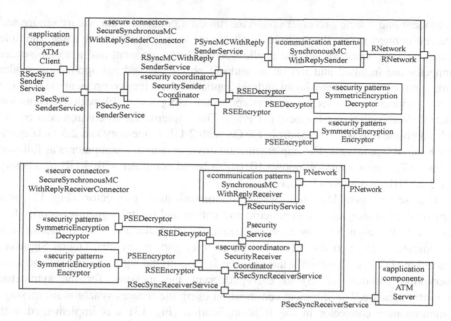

Fig. 17. Secure SMCWR sender and receiver connectors in ATM system.

Figure 17 depicts the structural view of the secure SMCWR connector with Symmetric Encryption security pattern for a service request and a reply, which can be applied for an ATM system. When an ATM Client component sends a service request to a ATM Server, the service request is encrypted by the SEE component in the secure SMCWR sender connector, assuming the Symmetric Encryption security pattern feature is selected for the ATM Client component. The encrypted service request is decrypted by the SED component, and then sent to the ATM Server component. Assuming the Symmetric Encryption security pattern feature is selected for the ATM Server component, a reply is encrypted by the SEE component in the secure SMCWR receiver connector. The encrypted reply is decrypted by the SED component in the secure SMCWR sender connector, and then sent to the ATM Client component.

9 Validation

The secure connectors derived from the SPL were validated from the perspectives of implementation and performance analysis of secure connectors for asynchronous message communication and synchronous message communication with reply.

9.1 Implementation of Secure Connectors

The secure connectors designed using the SPL approach were implemented in Java, Kotlin and XML for android applications, in which an application sender component and a secure sender connector run on an android phone, and an application receiver component and a secure receiver connector run on a computer. The secure sender and receiver connectors in the android applications were implemented using multiple threads in Java. Once an android application sender component and a secure sender connector are installed and run on an android phone, an android application sender component communicates with an android application receiver component via a secure sender connector and a secure receiver connector using a network with Transmission Control Protocol/Internet Protocol (TCP/IP). The implementation environment on the android phone is as follows: Android 6.0 OS with 2 GB of memory and 2.5 GHz quad-core Krait 400 processor. The implementation environment in a computer is as follows: Eclipse 4.7.1 version on a Windows 10, 64-bit-based computer with 4 GB of memory and 2.20 GHz quad-core i7 processor.

The secure asynchronous message communication connector (Fig. 13) was implemented to integrate the symmetric encryption and digital signature security features with the asynchronous message communication feature. The connector was implemented using two algorithms for the security pattern features, Digital Signature Algorithm (DSA) to sign/verify the message for the digital signature feature and Data Encryption Standard (DES) to encrypt/decrypt the message for the symmetric encryption feature. The shipment confirmation using the secure asynchronous message communication connector in the B2B application (Fig. 13) was implemented with seven threads, one for each of the following components: supplier, SSC, AMC sender, AMC receiver, SRC, public key repository, and delivery order server. In addition, a message queue was implemented and placed between threads (for example, a message queue between the supplier application thread and SSC thread, and a message queue between the SSC thread and the AMC sender thread).

Furthermore, a secure synchronous message communication with reply connector for the ATM application (Fig. 17) was implemented to integrate the symmetric encryption security feature with the secure synchronous message communication with reply communication feature. The Encryption and Decryption components for the symmetric encryption feature were implemented using the DES algorithm, which is a block cipher that operates on plain text blocks of a given size (64-bits) and returns cipher text blocks of the same size. The DES works by using the same 56-bit key to encrypt and decrypt a message. The encrypted service request is sent from the ATM Client component to the ATM Server component, the receiver connector of which decrypts the service request message using the DES algorithm with the same secret key. The service request using the secure SMC with reply connector was implemented with threads and separate message buffers.

9.2   Performance Analysis of Secure Connectors

This section describes the performance analysis of secure android application using the secure connectors derived from the SPL and compares them with secure android applications executing the same message communication patterns but using other approaches for providing or not providing security. The three approaches compared in this section are the (1) *with secure connector approach*, for secure android applications that use the approach described in this paper; (2) *without security service approach*, for android applications that do not provide any security services; (3) *without secure connector approach*, for secure android applications in which security services are mingled with the application logic. In the *with secure connector approach*, security services are encapsulated in secure connectors separately from application logic. The same application functionality is implemented in each approach. However, the underlying difference between *with secure connector approach* and *without secure connector approach* is that the security services in *without secure connector approach* are implemented within application components along with application business logic, whereas *with secure connector approach* separates the security services from application components and implements them as secure connectors. Also, the difference between *with secure connector approach* and *without security service approach* is that *with secure connector approach* provides security services encapsulated in secure connectors with application components, whereas *without security service approach* implements only business application logic without any security services.

For each communication pattern described in this paper, namely (a) asynchronous message communication with Symmetric Encryption and Digital Signature security patterns and (b) synchronous message communication with Symmetric Encryption security pattern, the performance of the *with secure connector approach* was evaluated by measuring the average time of message communication between sender and receiver components via a secure connector. Each message communication implemented in Sect. 9.1 was run 20 times to calculate the average communication time so that the performance evaluation would not be dependent on a few exceptional communication times. Message communication time (MCT) is measured by observing the overall run time from start to finish for each message communication pattern. For synchronous communication, MCT measures the time to send a message and receive a response. For asynchronous communication, MCT measures the time to send a message from sender to receiver.

Table 2 shows the average time of message communication and a comparison of the *with secure connector approach*, *without security service approach*, and *without secure connector approach* for the communication patterns. For the secure AMC connector with symmetric encryption and digital signature security patterns (Fig. 13 and top section in Table 2), the *with secure connector approach* (second column in Table 2) shows that the MCT is 46.3 milliseconds (ms) for the sender connector, 4.4 ms for the network connection, 50.2 ms for the receiver connector, giving a total of 100.9 ms. The *without security service approach* (third column in Table 2) shows that the MCT is 5.1 ms, 4.3 ms, and 4.0 ms for each portion, giving a total of 13.4 ms. The *without secure connector approach* (fourth column in Table 2) shows that the MCT is 46.0 ms, 4.4 ms and 49.1 ms for each portion, giving the overall MCT of 99.5 ms. The fifth column of Table 2 indicates that the time difference between the *with secure connector approach* and the *without security service approach* is 87.5 ms, which is highly significant. This is because *with secure connector approach* provides application components with security services such as confidentiality and non-repudiation. The security services in the *with secure connector approach* consume processing time for encrypting/decrypting messages and signing/verifying digital signature, whereas the *without security service approach* is much faster due to it providing no security services. The additional processing time taken by the *with secure connector approach* is to make android applications secure in comparison to insecure applications developed using the *without security service approach*. Comparing the performance *without secure connector approach* and *with secure connector approach* (sixth column in Table 2) shows that there is no significant difference in the runtime performance of the secure AMC connector with symmetric encryption and digital signature security patterns. The time difference between the approaches is 1.4 ms. These two approaches provide applications with security services; however, the *with secure connector approach* has the advantage of separating security services from application logic, which leads to secure software architectures that are more maintainable and evolvable than the *without secure connector approach*.

Table 2. Performance comparison of secure connector approaches.

Communication pattern	With secure connector approach	Without security service approach	Without secure connector approach	Time difference between with secure connector approach and without security service approach	Time difference between without secure connector approach and with secure connector approach
Secure AMC Connector with Symmetric Encryption and Digital Signature security patterns (Fig. 13)					
• Secure Asynchronous MC Sender Time	46.3 ms	5.1 ms	46.0 ms	41.2 ms	0.3 ms
• Network Time	4.4 ms	4.3 ms	4.4 ms	0.1 ms	0.0 ms
• Secure Asynchronous MC Receiver Time	50.2 ms	4.0 ms	49.1 ms	46.2 ms	1.1 ms
• Total Time for AMC with Symmetric Encryption & Digital Signature	100.9 ms	13.4 ms	99.5 ms	87.5 ms	1.4 ms
Secure SMC with Reply Connector with Symmetric Encryption security pattern (Fig. 17)					
• Secure Synchronous MC with reply Sender Time	39.3 ms	8.4 ms	38.4 ms	30.9 ms	0.9 ms
• Network Time	8.2 ms	7.9 ms	8.0 ms	0.3 ms	0.2 ms
• Secure Synchronous MC with reply Receiver Time	30.1 ms	3.1 ms	28.8 ms	27.0 ms	1.3 ms
• Total Time for SMCWR with Symmetric Encryption	77.6 ms	19.4 ms	75.2 ms	58.2 ms	2.4 ms

The performance analysis of the SMCWR with Symmetric Encryption security pattern (Fig. 17 and bottom section in Table 2) indicates a finding that is similar to the AMC with Symmetric Encryption and Digital Signature security patterns (Fig. 13 and top section in Table 2). For the SMCWR with Symmetric Encryption security pattern (Fig. 17 and bottom section in Table 2), the *with secure connector approach* shows that the MCT is 39.3 ms for the sender connector of SMCWR with Symmetric Encryption security pattern, 8.2 ms for the network connection, and 30.1 ms for the receiver connector. Thus the overall MCT for the SMCWR with Symmetric Encryption security pattern is 77.6 ms. The *without security service approach* (third column of Table 2) shows that the MCT is 8.4 ms, 7.9 ms and 3.1 ms for each portion, giving an overall average time of 19.4 ms. The *without secure connector approach* (fourth column of Table 2) shows that the MCT for SMCWR with Symmetric Encryption security pattern is 38.4 ms, 8.0 ms, 28.8 ms for each portion, giving an overall MCT of 75.2 ms. The fifth column of Table 2 indicates that the time difference between the *with secure connector approach* and the *without security service approach* is highly significant. This is because *with secure connector approach* provides application components with the confidentiality security service. Comparing the performance *without secure connector approach* and *with secure connector approach* (sixth column in Table 2) shows that there is no significant difference in the runtime performance of the SMCWR with Symmetric Encryption security pattern. The time difference between the approaches is 2.4 ms.

10 Discussion of SPL Approach for Secure Connectors

The SPL approach for secure connectors is different from typical SPL approaches. This section discusses the differences between SPL for secure connectors and traditional SPL approaches. A SPL consists of a family of software systems that have some common functionality and some variable functionality. Typical SPL approaches involve developing a feature model and SPL architecture for a family of software systems from which an application, which is a member of a SPL, is derived. The SPL for secure connectors focuses on a family of software artifacts rather than a family of software systems. Rather than features addressing variability in software requirements or configurations, the feature model focuses on variability in communication patterns and security patterns. The SPL architecture addresses the design of communication pattern components and security pattern components, and how these pattern components are selected and integrated within a secure connector. Thus, for the SPL for secure connectors, an appropriate communication pattern is selected from the feature model. The selected pattern is then customized based on the security features selected. Then the variant security coordinator template is customized based on the security pattern components it needs to interface to.

A secure AMC connector is created by customizing a selected AMC pattern based on the security patterns selected for an application. For a secure AMC connector with Symmetric Encryption and Digital Signature security patterns (Fig. 13), an AMC pattern is selected from the feature model (Fig. 1) and then components – AMC sender and receiver components, and AMC security sender and receiver coordinator components - supporting the selected AMC pattern is determined based on the feature/component table (Table 1). As Symmetric Encryption and Digital Signature security patterns are selected for an application from the feature model (Fig. 1), the templates (Figs. 6 and 7) for AMC SSC component and AMC SRC component are customized (Figs. 11 and 12) to interface to the selected security pattern components (Figs. 2 and 3).

11 Conclusions

This paper has described a SPL approach to modeling the variability of secure connectors in terms of security patterns and communication patterns, which makes it possible to design secure software architectures for concurrent and distributed software applications. The feature model for secure connectors captures various security pattern and communication pattern features, and describes the relationships between features. The security and communication pattern features are designed as security and communication pattern components that are encapsulated into secure connectors. Each secure connector is derived from the SPL for secure connectors, which is designed as a composite component that encapsulates both security and communication pattern components. A security coordinator enables security and communication pattern components to be integrated within a secure connector. A high-level pseudocode template for a security coordinator is customized to a pseudocode that interfaces to the security pattern components. This paper has also described a secure asynchronous message communication connector and a secure synchronous message communication with reply connector, which are designed and integrated based on the security pattern and communication pattern features selected for the applications.

This paragraph describes future research for secure connectors. The pseudocode templates described in this paper could be replaced with code, e.g., in Java or C++. The code of a security coordinator could be generated automatically from a code template of a high-level security coordinator. As security and communication pattern features are selected for an application, the template could be automatically filled with calls to the appropriate methods of the corresponding pattern components. A prototype tool could also be developed to automatically generate the code for security coordinators within secure connectors. In addition, we might need to investigate how multiple communication pattern components could be encapsulated within a secure connector when sender and receiver application components communicate with each other via different types of communication patterns.

Acknowledgements. This work was partially supported by the AFOSR grant FA9550-16-1-0030.

References

1. Taylor, R.N., Medvidovic, N., Dashofy, E.M.: Software Architecture: Foundations, Theory, and Practice. Wiley, West Sussex (2010)
2. Shin, M.E., Gomaa, H.: Software modeling of evolution to a secure application: from requirements model to software architecture. Sci. Comput. Program. **66**(1), 60–70 (2007)
3. Shin, M.E., Malhotra, B., Gomaa, H., Kang, T.: Connectors for secure software architectures. In: 24th International Conference on Software Engineering and Knowledge Engineering, pp. 394–399. Knowledge Systems Institute, San Francisco Bay (2012)
4. Shin, M.E., Gomaa, H., Pathirage, D., Baker, C., Malhotra, B.: Design of secure software architectures with secure connectors. Int. J. Software Eng. Knowl. Eng. **26**(05), 769–805 (2016)
5. Shin, M., Gomaa, H., Pathirage, D.: Reusable secure connectors for secure software architecture. In: Kapitsaki, G.M., Santana de Almeida, E. (eds.) ICSR 2016. LNCS, vol. 9679, pp. 181–196. Springer, Cham (2016). https://doi.org/10.1007/978-3-319-35122-3_13
6. Shin, M., Gomaa, H., Pathirage, D.: Model-based design of reusable secure connectors. In: 4th International Workshop on Interplay of Model-Driven and Component-Based Software Engineering (ModComp), Austin (2017)
7. Shin, M., Gomaa, H., Pathirage, D.: A software product line approach for feature modeling and design of secure connectors. In: The 13th International Conference on Software Technologies (ICSOFT). SciTePress, Porto (2018)
8. Lodderstedt, T., Basin, D., Doser, J.: SecureUML: a UML-based modeling language for model-driven security. In: Jézéquel, J.-M., Hussmann, H., Cook, S. (eds.) UML 2002. LNCS, vol. 2460, pp. 426–441. Springer, Heidelberg (2002). https://doi.org/10.1007/3-540-45800-X_33
9. Jürjens, J.: UMLsec: extending UML for secure systems development. In: Jézéquel, J.-M., Hussmann, H., Cook, S. (eds.) UML 2002. LNCS, vol. 2460, pp. 412–425. Springer, Heidelberg (2002). https://doi.org/10.1007/3-540-45800-X_32
10. Basin, D., Clavel, M., Egea, M.: A decade of model-driven security. In: Proceedings of the 16th ACM Symposium on Access Control Models and Technologies, pp. 1–10. ACM, Innsbruck (2011)
11. Gomaa, H., Menascé, D.A., Shin, M.E.: Reusable component interconnection patterns for distributed software architectures. In: Proceedings of the 2001 Symposium on Software Reusability Putting Software Reuse in Context, pp. 69–77. ACM, Toronto (2001)
12. Gomaa, H.: Software Modeling and Design: UML, Use Cases, Patterns, and software Architectures. Cambridge University Press, Cambridge (2011)
13. Ren, J., Taylor, R., Dourish, P., Redmiles, D.: Towards an architectural treatment of software security. ACM SIGSOFT SoftW. Eng. Notes **30**(4), 1–7 (2005)
14. Al-Azzani, S., Bahsoon, R.: SecArch: architecture-level evaluation and testing for security. In: Joint Working IEEE/IFIP Conference on Software Architecture and European Conference on Software Architecture, pp. 51–60. IEEE, Helsinki (2012)
15. Schumacher, M., Fernandez, E.B., Hybertson, D., Buschmann, F., Sommerlad, P.: Security Patterns: Integrating Security and Systems Engineering. Wiley, West Sussex (2006)
16. Fernandez-Buglioni, E.: Security Patterns in Practice: Designing Secure Architectures Using Software Patterns, 1st edn. Wiley, West Sussex (2013)
17. Gomaa, H.: Designing Software Product Lines with UML: From Use Cases to Pattern-Based Software Architectures. Addison-Wesley, Boston (2005)

18. Gomaa, H., Shin, M.E.: A multiple-view meta-modeling approach for variability management in software product lines. In: Bosch, J., Krueger, C. (eds.) ICSR 2004. LNCS, vol. 3107, pp. 274–285. Springer, Heidelberg (2004). https://doi.org/10.1007/978-3-540-27799-6_23

19. Gomaa, H., Shin, M.E.: Automated software product line engineering and product derivation. In: 40th Annual Hawaii International Conference on System Sciences, p. 285a. IEEE, Waikoloa (2007)

20. Gomaa, H., Shin, M.E.: Multiple-view modelling and meta-modelling of software product lines. IET Software 2(2), 94–122 (2008)

21. Gomaa, H., Shin, M.E.: Variability modeling in model-driven software product line engineering. In: Proceedings of the 2nd International Workshop on Model Driven Product Line Engineering (MDPLE 2010), Paris, p. 65 (2010)

22. Abu-Matar, M., Gomaa, H.: Variability modeling for service oriented product line architectures. In: 15th International Software Product Line Conference (SPLC), pp. 110–119. IEEE, Munich (2011)

23. Fant, J.S., Gomaa, H., Pettit, R.G.: Integrating and applying architectural design patterns in space flight software product lines. In: 10th International Joint Conference on Software Technologies (ICSOFT), vol. 1, pp. 1–11. IEEE, Colmar (2015)

24. Tzeremes, V., Gomaa, H.: Applying end user software product line engineering for smart spaces. In: Proceedings of the 51st Hawaii International Conference on System Sciences, Big Island, Hawaii (2018)

25. Gomaa, H., Hussein, M.: Software reconfiguration patterns for dynamic evolution of software architectures. In: Fourth Working IEEE/IFIP Conference on Software Architecture, Oslo (2004)

26. Gomaa, H., Hashimoto, K.: Dynamic software adaptation for service-oriented product lines. In: Fifth International Workshop on Dynamic Software Product Lines, Munich (2011)

27. Albassam, E., Gomaa, H., Menasce, D.: Variable recovery and adaptation connectors for dynamic software product lines. In: 10th International Workshop on Dynamic Software Product Lines, Sevilla, pp. 123–128 (2017)

28. Gomaa, H., Hashimoto, K., Kim, M., Malek, S., Menascé, D.A.: Software adaptation patterns for service-oriented architectures. In: Proceedings of the 2010 ACM Symposium on Applied Computing, pp. 462–469. ACM, Sierre (2010)

29. Albassam, E., Gomaa, H., Menascé, D.A.: Model-based recovery connectors for self-adaptation and self-healing. In: 11th International Joint Conference on Software Technologies, pp. 79–90. ICSOFT-EA, Lisbon (2016)

30. Albassam, E., Porter, J., Gomaa, H., Menascé, D.A.: DARE: a distributed adaptation and failure recovery framework for software architectures. In: 14th IEEE International Conference on Autonomic Computing and Communications (ICAC), Columbus (2017)

31. Farahmandian, S., Hoang, D.B.: SDS2: A novel software-defined security service for protecting cloud computing infrastructure. In: 16th International Symposium on Network Computing and Applications (NCA), pp. 1–8. IEEE, Boston (2017)

32. Taha, A., Trapero, R., Luna, J., Suri, N.: A framework for ranking cloud security services. In: International Conference on Services Computing (SCC), pp. 322–329. IEEE, Honolulu (2017)

33. Pfleeger, C.P., Pfleeger, S.L.: Security in Computing, 3rd edn. Prentice Hall, Upper Saddle River (2003)

Towards an Automatic Verification of BPMN Model Semantic Preservation During a Refinement Process

Yousra Bendaly Hlaoui[1], Salma Ayari[2(✉)], and Leila Jemni Ben Ayed[3]

[1] University of Tunis-Elmaner, Tunis, Tunisia
yousra.bendalyhlaoui@esstt.rnu.tn
[2] LATICE Laboratory, Paris, France
salma_ayari@yahoo.fr
[3] National School of Computer Science Manouba, Manouba, Tunisia
leila.jemni@fsegt.rnu.tn

Abstract. In this paper, we present a refinement approach for business processes specified with Business Process Modeling Notation (BPMN). The Business process or workflow refinement approach is a step-wise modeling approach which is composed of a set of abstraction levels. Each refinement step corresponds to an abstract level of a BPMN model. For each refined workflow model, we analyze, automatically, the workflow change impact using NuSMV model checker. The change impact concerns the semantic preservation of workflow models during the refinement process. We talk about workflow data and control flow dependencies. To realize this analysis, we have to transform at each level of modeling refinement, the BPMN model to a Kripke structure formalizing, hence, the semantics of the refined business process model.

Keywords: Workflow · BPMN modeling · Refinement ·
Change impact NuSMV · Kripke structure

1 Introduction

Workflow applications become increasingly popular in modern scientific computation and whose role is to automate processes. Typical examples of workflow applications are banking, customer services or travel agencies [1]. They could be complex and composed of a large number of heterogeneous linked entities. The step-wise specification is a solution to manage the complexity and allows a set of transformation from the highest level of the specification to the lowest one. We call this step-wise specification a *model refinement* [2]. A model refinement deals with adding more details to a given abstract model belonging to the previous level. At each refinement step, we have to prove that this refinement preserves the semantics of the abstract model as it is considered as a workflow change [3]. The verification of model semantic preservation allows the proof of

© Springer Nature Switzerland AG 2019
M. van Sinderen and L. A. Maciaszek (Eds.): ICSOFT 2018, CCIS 1077, pp. 397–420, 2019.
https://doi.org/10.1007/978-3-030-29157-0_18

the correctness [4] and the soundness [5] of the workflow model built by specification refinement. In fact, at each refinement level, we analyze the impact of the workflow or business process change. The impact of change deals with the data dependency change and the control flow change dependency. The dependency relationship determines the process semantics by simulating and modeling its execution using a dependency graph [6]. This graph includes the data and the control flow dependencies [6]. The dependency of data is defined by the exchanged data between the workflow activities as input and the output. The data dependency is determined by the data access mode affected to each workflow activity: an activity has the authorization to modify a data whereas an other uses this data to be performed. The control flow dependencies specify the causality order between workflow activities. Based on the dependency graph, the analysis of the impact of workflow change seems to be costly in terms of complexity. Therefore, we propose an automatic analysis of the workflow change impact using NusMV model checker [7] based on the Kripke structure [8] to specify the semantics of the refined model throughout the dependency relationships. Indeed, a kripke structure which is modeled by a property labeled transition system replaces the dependency graph used in the literature [6] to analyze the impact change. In this paper, we propose a refinement approach to specify business processes or workflow using BPMN language (Business Process Modeling and Notations) [9]. BPMN language is a standard notation used to express business processes [9]. To verify automatically the semantic preservation or the workflow change impact during the refinement process, we use NuSMV model checker. As mentioned above, we have to analyze the workflow data and control flow dependencies specified by a BPMN model belonging to a specific refinement level. As we propose an automatic approach, the refinement of a BPMN process is realized by introducing a refinement pattern. We have defined four refinement patterns [10] namely the *Sequence Refinement Pattern*, the *Parallel Refinement Pattern*, the *Exclusive Refinement Pattern*, and the *Loop Refinement Pattern*. Hence, we are brought about analyzing, automatically, the change impact caused by each refinement pattern when its introduced into the BPMN model at a specific level of refinement. The change impact analysis is performed by the verification, at each level of refinement, of the data and control flow dependencies using NuSMV. Therefore, we propose a translation process from BPMN models into Kripke structure to allow the NuSMV verification. So, to check the preservation of data and control flow dependencies, we have to specify them as linear temporal logic properties (LTL) [11]. In this paper, we detail how to define these properties, how to check them using NUSMV and How to proceed to transform a BPMN model to a Kripke structure.

This paper is organized as follows:

2   Related Works and Discussion

In the Literature, different works, dealing with the transformations based on refinement and using graphical notations, are proposed:

- UML AD (UML Activity diagram): Authors in [12] presents a refinement based modeling approach of workflow applications using UML AD. Limits of their work consists on the automatic verification of the refinement or the change. More, BPMN is becoming the leader in the modeling of business processes.
- Petri Net: Authors in [13] adopt an approach called property-preservation for verification of refinement. This verification technique is not automatic. PN tend to become large even for relatively small systems. The lack of hierarchical composition makes it difficult to specify and understand complex systems using the conventional model(PN) [10].
- BPMN: Author in [14] apply the refinement with a set of composition operators in a BPMN process and did not check the semantic preservation of this processes.

The change impact analysis has been studied in several works like [15,16]. The change and its impact are formalized in this works by a graph called dependency graph to represent dependencies existing inside the process. The impact is studied and does not allow a verification approach of such change.

In Our Contribution, differently to what was done and to overcome the limitations of the works mentioned above, we propose:

- BPMN is an ISO standard notation, provide a large collection of notation elements. Moreover, it supports the hierarchical approach to design; thus, the process can be modeled on several abstraction levels.
- Formal verification of the refinement BPMN processes with an automatic way by using the NuSMV model checking.
- The change and more particularly refinement requires an analysis of its impact since it allows to add details. Our analysis is done through a dependency graph depicted from [6] and for which it serves as a support for the impact studies.

3   Overview of Our Proposed Methodology

In this paper, and by extending our methodology approach from [10] we propose a transformation of BPMN refinement models to NuSMV. The first part is the modeling phase, when we develop with our team [20] a tool for BPMN abstract view in JAVA. XML files of the models are generated automatically from the views. The second phase, is the formalization phase where it includes the general idea of our work. The dependency graph is generated which is the Kripke structure. The Kripke structure is modeled with the framework **JUNG** which is used to visualize a graph. Kripke structure is the semantic notation of NuSMV. The last phase, is the verification phase who can check the validity of our model against a set of properties expressed in LTL. This is summarized in Fig. 1.

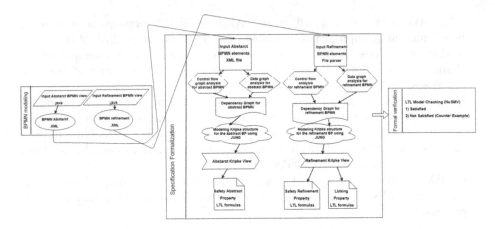

Fig. 1. Overview of our approach.

4 BPMN Specification

The Business Process Model & notation (BPMN) has been established as the standard notation to provide a graphical representations for business processes which is comprehensible to business users. We describe a core subset of BPMN elements in Fig. 2. These elements consist of:

- A set of objects connected by sequence flow transitions.
  Object could be:
  1. An activity which can be a simple task, a loop task or a sub-process,
  2. A gateway which is a routing construct that can only be connected by a sequence flow. There are many types of gateways such as parallel, exclusive, inclusive and complex types of gateways,
  3. Events can be triggered when something is happen during the running process. There are 3 types of events: Start, Intermediate and End events. Start event indicates when the process can starts, the Intermediate event which can occur in the middle of the execution of the process (between the Start and the End event) and the End event where there is no process to catch after this event,
- Artifacts namely annotations which that we use to present the pre and post conditions of an activity.

The BPMN specification definition is defined as follows:

Definition 1 *(Formal definition of BPMN)* [10]. *Let BP = (**O, Sf, Art, Sp**) be a Business process with:*

- $\boldsymbol{O} = O^{Event} \cup O^{Activity} \cup O^{Gateway}$ *is a set of objects with:*
  1. $O^{Event} = \varepsilon^S \cup \varepsilon^I \cup \varepsilon^E$, *i.e. the set of events partitioned into the disjoint subsets start, intermediate and end events.*
  2. $O^{Activity} = O^{simpletask} \cup O^{looptask} \cup O^{sub\text{-}process}$, *i.e. the set of activities partitioned into the disjoint subsets task atomic activity and sub-process.*

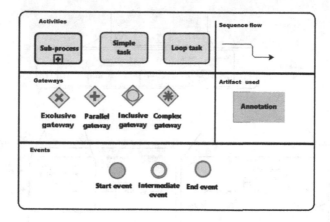

Fig. 2. BPMN constructs.

3. $O^{Gateway} = O^P \cup O^{Ex} \cup O^{In}$, *i.e. the set of gateways partitioned into the disjoint subsets parallel (AND), inclusive (XOR), exclusive (Or) and complex gateways. In this paper we use only parallel and exclusive gateways.*

- *Sf is a set of sequence flow or connecting of flow Objects.*
- *Art is the set of artifacts used to provide additional information.*
- *Sp is a function with Sp: O → Art where Art is a set of notations which Art = Art$_{pre}$ ∪ Art$_{post}$ representing the pre and post-conditions for an object.*

5   Business Process Refinement Approach

A refinement is a transformation that enriches system entities with specific detail or functionality. Hence, starting from the higher level of abstraction of the process specification which delivers as model a sub-process object annotated with its pre and post conditions and surrounded with the Start and End events. As Fig. 3 shows, the sub-process is refined with specific BPMN objects, sequence flows, start event, intermediate event, artifacts and gateways to bring more detail to the abstract sub-process. The obtained model belongs to the next abstract level of the initial sub-process. We continue the refinement process *model refinement* until no more detail could be added. The lower level of abstraction of the business process contains only simple tasks linked via sequence flows and gateways. The resulting model which belongs to the lower level of abstraction has to be semantically conformed to the highest specification. In fact, we are brought about developing a set of refinement patterns to ensure not only the conformity between the refined models but also to guarantee the automation of the refinement process. In order to verify the semantic conformity between models belonging to different abstraction levels, we have analyzed the impact of change when refining a model. Next, we bring more details concerning this analysis.

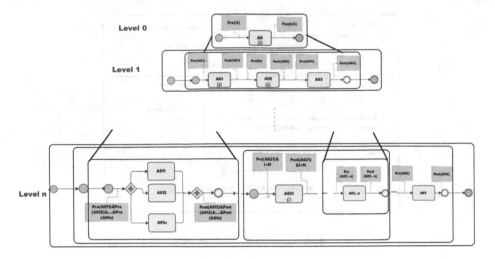

Fig. 3. The refinement approach steps.

5.1 Impact Analysis of Refinement

The purpose of the change impact analysis is to predict which parts of the BPMN model will be affected by a change. This analysis is essential to maintain the consistency of business processes and to estimate the development cost of this process. The consistency of a BPMN process can be used to prevent inconsistent or unsatisfactory operation from being occurred. It ensures the efficiency and quality of a process, at similar levels of abstraction, and provide the same behavior and look. The analysis of change in a preponed time will determine the consequences of changes before their introduction into the model. Especially, in our work we tackle the problem of change that can be defined by refinement. One of the most commonly identified relations as a common thread in the impact analysis process is the genetic relationship so-called dependency relationship [17]. A transformation can be applied in a business process if all the dependencies between the different parts of the process are respected. As a refinement is a special transformation, the dependency analysis which is performed over a transformation can be defined by a dependency graph.

5.2 Dependency Relationship

Dependency relationship is performed to analyze the effect of the change in software systems and which we can call the dependency analysis. The dependency analysis can identify the execution-order between elements in a business process models in order to maintain consistency. This can include Control flow dependency, in which it can represent the dependent relation between BPMN elements that define and use data. Another dependency relationship who is activity dependencies which defines the order of execution of the elements in a BPMN process. In refinement, the type of dependency which we can talk about occurs when the achievement of the refined (complex) activity is realized by the execution of different refinement activities. We will present the dependency graph for each dependency relationship *Control flow and data dependencies* applied to the refinement patterns [10] mentioned above. Each refined BP is presented as a graph in which every BPMN element is presented as a vertices connected by means of BPMN transitions called edges of the graph. Only one edge is allowed between two vertices.

Definition 2 *Dependency Graph (process graph)* [6]. *Let Γ_1 be a set of node types. Let Θ_1 a set of node labels. A process graph PG is represented by a tuple $PG = (V_1, E_1, \gamma_1, \theta_1)$ where:*

- V_1 *is a set of vertices,*
- E_1 *is a set of edges modeling the control flow of the business process,*
- $\gamma_1 : V_1 \rightarrow \Gamma_1$ *is a function that maps vertices to types and*
- $\theta_1 : V_1 \rightarrow \Theta_1$ *is a function mapping vertices to labels comprising $<$(vertex type,vertex name), unique number in the business process$>$.*

Consequently, a BP is transformed to a graph across the notation PG = (V, E). For example, if we have $v_1 \& v_2 \in V$ and $e \in E$ then the transition edge of the two nodes e = (v_1, v_2) represent the flow sequence between two activities $A^{T_1} \& A^{T_2}$ where $v_1.name = A^{T_1}, v_2.name = A^{T_2}$, e.type = sequence, *e.name* = $A^{T_1} \rightarrow A^{T_2}$, $v_1.type = A^T$, $v_2.type = A^T$. For the example in Table 1 we have the formal definition of the graph dependency for a simple BP.

Table 1. Graph dependency.

BPMN Object	PG
	Description
	$V_1 = \{A_1, A_2, \epsilon^S, \epsilon^E\}$
	$E_1 = \{e_1, e_2, e_3\}$
	$\gamma_1(A_1) = SimpleTask$
	$\gamma1(A_2) = Subprocess$
	$\theta_1(A_1) = (< simpletask >, A1), 1)$
	$\theta_1(A_2) = (< Subprocess >, A2), 2)$
	$\ldots =$

Control Flow Dependency. The Control flow dependency is a control dependency whose execution of an entity depends on the execution of a previous entity. In another way, X an activity that defines a variable "a" and Y another activity that uses this variable knowing that there is a direct path from X to Y and there is no intervening definition of a. Hence between two entities in execution, there is a control flow dependency between X and Y which Y's precondition depends on X post-condition. In other words, if D is modified by a new value then F will use and read this new value. The use of this value can be made with the precondition assertion. For that we consider that D transfers its current value with the assertion post-condition.

Definition 3 *Control flow dependency Graph (CFDG)* [6]. *Let Γ_2 be a set of edge types. Let Θ_2 a set of node labels and Ω_2 a set of edge labels. A CFDG is a labeled typed directed graph defined by a tuple $CFDG = (V_2, E_2, \gamma_2, \theta_2, \omega_2)$ where:*

- *$V_2 \subseteq V_1$, represent the nodes of the PG,*
- *$E_2 \subseteq V_2 X V_2$ is a set of edges, is a dominance relationship,*
- *$\gamma_2 : V_2 \rightarrow \Gamma_2$ is a function that maps edges to types (Sequence dependency, parallel dependency, exclusive dependency and loop dependency),*
- *$\theta_2 : E_1 \rightarrow \Theta_2$ and*
- *$\omega_2 : E_2 \rightarrow \Omega_2$ is a function that maps edges to labels (Pre & Post).*

Based on works of [3–6,15], we can represent our dependency graph for control flow dependency in refinement as follows:

- Control flow dependency for sequence Refinement pattern:
  The CFDG for sequence refinement pattern is shown in Table 2.

Table 2. Control flow dependency for sequence refinement pattern.

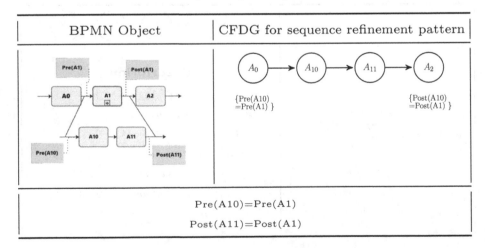

BPMN Object	CFDG for sequence refinement pattern
	Pre(A10)=Pre(A1)
	Post(A11)=Post(A1)

Table 3. Control flow dependency for parallel refinement pattern.

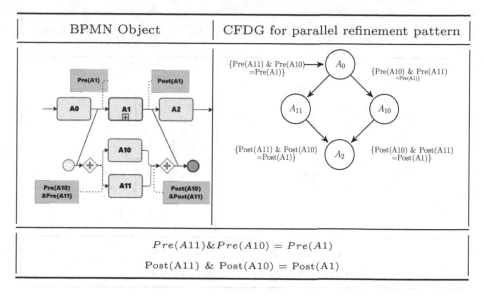

$$Pre(A11)\&Pre(A10) = Pre(A1)$$

$$Post(A11) \& Post(A10) = Post(A1)$$

- Control flow dependency for parallel refinement pattern:
  The CFDG for parallel refinement pattern is shown in Table 3.
- Control flow dependency for exclusive refinement pattern:
  The CFDG for exclusive refinement pattern is shown in Table 4.
- Control flow dependency for loop refinement pattern:
  The CFDG for loop refinement pattern is shown in Table 5.

Table 4. Control flow dependency for exclusive refinement pattern.

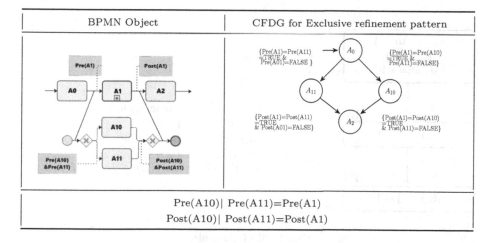

$$Pre(A10)|\ Pre(A11)=Pre(A1)$$

$$Post(A10)|\ Post(A11)=Post(A1)$$

Table 5. Control flow dependency for loop refinement pattern.

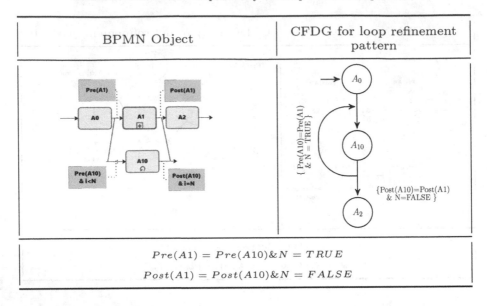

BPMN Object	CFDG for loop refinement pattern

$$Pre(A1) = Pre(A10)\&N = TRUE$$
$$Post(A1) = Post(A10)\&N = FALSE$$

Data Dependency. Data dependencies occur when a consumer of data is dependent on the provisioning of data from a producer [18]. The data dependency arises if one activity (A2) is the data consumer of (d1) then another activity (A1) needs to produce (d1) before (A2) tries the use of the data object. Data flow information can be collected by setting up and solving of equation systems that link information into a business process. An equation has the general form:

$$Data(A) = Out(A) \cup (In(A) - Del(A))$$

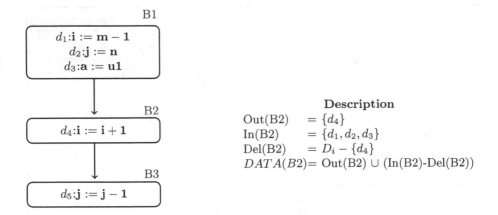

Fig. 4. DDG example.

This equation can be read as follows: Either the information at the end of an instruction is generated within that instruction, or it is entered at the beginning and is not deleted during the instruction. Such equations are called data flow equations. An example of data flow dependency graph (DFDG) is shown in Fig. 4.

By referring to works of [6] we conclude that:

Definition 4 *Data dependency Graph (DDG). Let Γ_3 be a set of edge types. Let Θ_3 a set of node labels and Ω_3 a set of edge labels. A DDG is a labeled typed directed graph defined by a tuple $DDG = (V_3, E_3, \gamma_3, \theta_3, \omega_3)$ where:*

- *$V_3 \subseteq V_1$, represent the nodes of the PG where
  $V_3 : Fo^{Activity} \rightarrow In(Fo)XOut(Fo)$,*
- *E_3 is a set of edges,*
- *$\gamma_3 : E_3 \rightarrow \Gamma_3$ is a function that maps edges to types (sequence data dependency, parallel data dependency, exclusive data dependency and loop data dependency),*
- *$\theta_3 : V_3 \rightarrow (\Theta_3, Out, del, In)$ is a function mapping vertices to labels corresponding BP activity name, data definition of the node, data to delete, data collected from the node before and*
- *$\omega_3 : E_3 \rightarrow \Omega_3$ is a function that maps edges to labels.*

We can represent our dependency graph for control flow dependency in refinement as follows:

- Sequence refinement data dependency:
  The DDG for sequence refinement pattern is shown in Table 6.

Table 6. Data dependency for sequence refinement pattern.

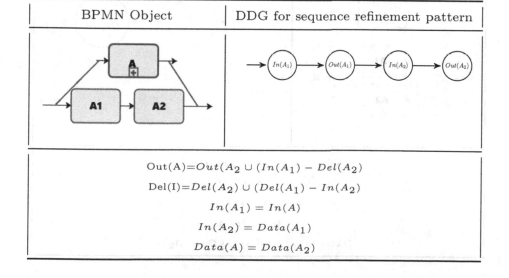

BPMN Object	DDG for sequence refinement pattern

$$Out(A)=Out(A_2 \cup (In(A_1) - Del(A_2))$$

$$Del(I)=Del(A_2) \cup (Del(A_1) - In(A_2))$$

$$In(A_1) = In(A)$$

$$In(A_2) = Data(A_1)$$

$$Data(A) = Data(A_2)$$

Table 7. Data dependency for parallel refinement pattern.

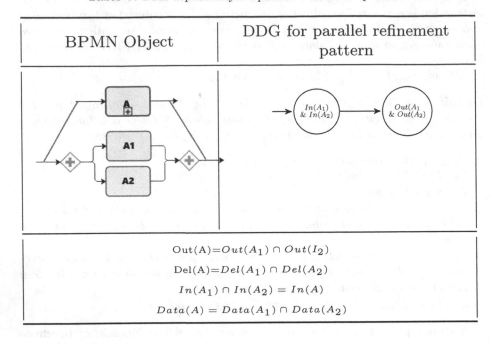

BPMN Object	DDG for parallel refinement pattern

$$Out(A)=Out(A_1) \cap Out(I_2)$$
$$Del(A)=Del(A_1) \cap Del(A_2)$$
$$In(A_1) \cap In(A_2) = In(A)$$
$$Data(A) = Data(A_1) \cap Data(A_2)$$

Table 8. Data dependency for exclusive refinement pattern.

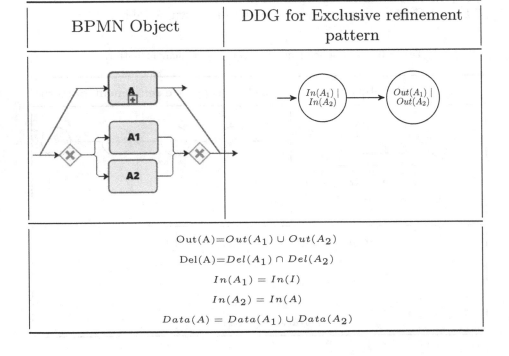

BPMN Object	DDG for Exclusive refinement pattern

$$Out(A)=Out(A_1) \cup Out(A_2)$$
$$Del(A)=Del(A_1) \cap Del(A_2)$$
$$In(A_1) = In(I)$$
$$In(A_2) = In(A)$$
$$Data(A) = Data(A_1) \cup Data(A_2)$$

Table 9. Data dependency for loop refinement pattern.

BPMN Object	DDG for Loop refinement pattern

$$\text{Out}(A)=Out(A_1)$$
$$\text{Del}(A)=Del(A_1)$$
$$In(I_1) = In(A) \cup Out(I_1)$$
$$Data(A) = Data(A_1)$$

- Parallel refinement dependency data:
  The DDG for parallel refinement pattern is shown in Table 7.
- Exclusive refinement data dependency:
  The DDG for the exclusive refinement pattern is shown in Table 8.
- Loop refinement data dependency:
  The DDG for the loop refinement pattern is shown in Table 9.

Graph Dependency Generation. The result of Control flow dependency and data dependency analysis can be presented in a directed graph called graph dependency generation. This graph analyses which structural and semantic changes are produced when applying refinement patterns to the BPMN model. The control flow dependency is represented through the labeled direct arcs of the graph. Thus, this graph is composed of a finite set of vertices, a finite set of edges and a typing of vertices. The graph dependency generation is a graph which verify the execution semantics of the desirable model. Here we study the semantics of BPMN processes using a set of refinement patterns. For example the data dependency graph of the sequence refinement pattern is shown in Fig. 5.

The execution semantics of a dependency graph generation simulates the behavior of the represented BPMN. In order to verify our execution semantics, we need to describe a tool supports verification of BPMN processes using refinement patterns for checking the refinement transformation in the graph dependency generation. Referring to our published work [10], we can see that the graph

in Fig. 5 is our defined kripke structure for checking the refinement of BPMN
processes that can be used for the model checking Nusmv.

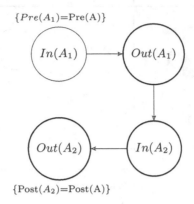

$$\{Pre(A_1)=\text{Pre}(A)\}$$

$$\{Post(A_2)=\text{Post}(A)\}$$

Fig. 5. Dependency Graph for a sequence refinement pattern.

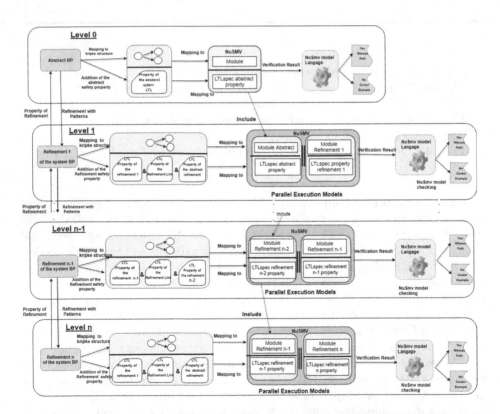

Fig. 6. Specification & verification of BPMN models with NuSMV.

6   Verification of BPMN Refinement Models Using NuSMV

The refinement of BPMN processes allows us to enrich a model at each $level_i$ of abstraction in a step-by-step approach. At each level we define a semantic execution behavior in which we define a formal definition for the transformation for BP_i to a Kripke structure. A set of properties is defined at each level. In our approach we deal with the abstract and refinement safety properties. Safety properties are added in each $level_i$. Therefore, we obtain the system behavior describing by the Kripke structure and the property of each level. Then the model checker NuSMV, takes models from Kripke structure and the safety properties from each level. And verifies if the formula is satisfied or not. Figure 6 summarizes the illustrated approach of this paper.

NuSMV is a widely used tool for the verification & validation of systems. It is open source, it has a widespread use in academia, and it accepts properties formalized not only in Computation Tree Logic (CTL) [19] but also in Linear Temporal Logic (LTL). Kripke structure provide a semantic for the NuSMV model checker in order to check the validity of refinement for BPMN models. For that we need to check this validity against a set of refinement properties.

6.1   Properties Generation

The graph dependency generation should specify under which requirements the transformation or the refinement is applicable for every vertices $v \in V_1$ that controls an activity with a pre and post-condition assertions. This assertions are the labels of the vertices for the graph and can be used as conditions for statements in order to verify the correctness of the transformation. To ensure that our system never exhibit a bad behavior, we need to check the safety property of the model. For that we have to verify that if a task try to run, it will use the precondition assertion depicted from the post-condition of the precedent BPMN object. After that, the task must terminate its execution and reach its post-condition.

Definition 5 *(Safety property)* [10]. *For functions Pre and Post over an object $A \in O^{Activity}$ in BPMN:*

$$P \triangleq (pre(A) \Rightarrow post(A)).$$

The symbol $\triangleq$ is read "is defined to be equal".

Likewise, in order to verify the refinement consistency we need to define a property for each refinement pattern. The refinement must guarantee the behavior preservation.

Definition 6 *(Safety refinement property)* [10]. *A BP_{i-1} at level $i-1$ with a specification property P_{i-1} implements a BP_i at level i with a specification property P_i and by preserving the linking property $P_{LinkRef_i}$, if a correspondence between them is given and called P_{ref_i}.*

$$P_{ref_i} \triangleq P_{LinkRef_i} \wedge P_{i-1} \wedge P_i, \forall i \in [1 \cdots n].$$

The implementation of a Kripke structure representing each semantic BPMN model must be equivalent to a set of specifications to avoid the structural errors which can be fixed by the safety and refinement properties of the system.

6.2   Kripke Structure

Definition 7 *(Kripke structure)* [10]. *A kripke structure is a quadruple $K = (S, I, T, \mathcal{L})$ where:*

- *S is a finite non-empty set of states,*
- *$I \subseteq S$ is a set of initial states,*
- *T is a transition relation between states such as $T \subseteq S \times S$ and*
- *$\mathcal{L} : S \to 2^{AP}$ assigns truth values to the set of atomic propositions (AP).*

A kripke structure is a graph dependency where all the vertices V of the graph corresponds to a set of states S. The initial vertices $v_0 \in V$ is the start vertex which is represented in the kripke structure with a set of Initial states I. E, the finite set of arcs, corresponds to the transition relation T. Let "x" be a variable and v a vertex. If v represent a statement referencing "x" then we can label the state $s \in S$. We define L the function labeling each state with a set of atomic propositions denoted AP where AP = {pre, end}. ϕ is the labeling function of the dependency generation graph then we have $\phi : N \to P(AP)$ where P(AP) is a subset of the set AP. The formal semantic using Kripke structure for BPMN processes is:

Definition 8 *(Formal semantics of BPMN using Kripke structure)* [10]. *A process BP = (Fo, Sf, Art, Sp) induces a Kripke structure $K = (S, I, T, \mathcal{L})$ with:*

1. *S being the set of all valid system states which present the behavior of objects in BP called Ins(O) where $O \in Fo^{Activity}$ such that:*

$$Ins : Fo^{Activity} \to In\_Fo \times Out\_Fo$$

   where:
   $In\_Fo = \{in\_O | O \in Fo^{Activity}\}$ and $Out\_Fo = \{out\_O | O \in Fo^{Activity}\}$
2. *I being the set of initial states;*
3. *T being the transition relation between the instantiate object Flow; Ins(O) $\times$ Ins(O);*
4. *$\mathcal{L} : S \to 2^P$. P is a set of elementary properties verified by each state of the entire system.*

To define the semantic description of BPMN using kripke structure, we need a formal description of each refinement pattern including the refinement properties [10].

1. The formal semantic using Kripke structure for a BPMN abstract Activity A $\in$ Fo is given as follows [10]:
   $\mathcal{L}(in(A)) = \{pre(A) | \nexists s \in S \wedge s \neq in(A), (s, in(A)) \in T\}$
   $\mathcal{L}(out(A)) = \{post(A) | \forall s \in S, (out(A), s) \notin T\}$

2. The formal semantic using Kripke structure for a BPMN sequence refinement activities $(>, \{A_1, \cdots, A_N\}) \in$ Fo and $A \in$ Fo the refined activity is given as follows: [10]

   $\mathcal{L}_>(in(A_1) = \{pre(A_1), P_{linkRef_i}| \nexists s \in S \wedge s \neq in(A_1); (s, in(A_1)) \in T \wedge P_{LinkRef_i} \hateq pre(A_1) = pre(A)\}$

   $\mathcal{L}_>(out(A_N)) = \{post(A_N), P_{linkRef_i}| \forall s \in S; (out(A_N), s) \notin T \wedge P_{LinkRef_i} \hateq post(A_N) = post(A)\}$

3. The formal semantic using Kripke structure for a BPMN parallel refinement activities $(\|, \{A_1, \cdots, A_N\})$ where $A \in$ Fo is the refined activity [10]:

   $\mathcal{L}_\|(\cap_{X \in (1, \cdots, N)} in(A_X) = \{\cap_{X \in (1, \cdots, N)} Pre(A_X), P_{linkRef_i}| \nexists s \in S \wedge s \neq in(A_1); (s, in(A_1)) \in T \wedge P_{LinkRef_i} \hateq \cap_{X \in (1, \cdots, N)} Pre(A_X) = pre(A)\}$

   $\mathcal{L}_\|(\cap_{X \in (1, \cdots, N)} out(A_X)) = \{\cap_{X \in (1, \cdots, N)} Post(A_X), P_{linkRef_i}| \forall s \in S; (out (A_N), s) \notin T \wedge P_{LinkRef_i} \hateq \cap_{X \in (1, \cdots, N)} Post(A_X) = post(A)\}$

4. The formal semantic using Kripke structure for a BPMN exclusive refinement activities $([], \{A_1, \cdots, A_N\})$ where $A \in$ Fo is the refined activity [10]:

   $\mathcal{L}_{[]}(\cup_{X \in (1 \cdots N)} in(A_X)) = \{\cup_{X \in (1 \cdots N)} Pre(A_X), P_{LinkRef_i}| \nexists s \in S \wedge s \neq in(A_1); (s, in(A_1)) \in T \wedge P_{LinkRef_i} \hateq \cup_{X \in (1, \cdots, N)} Pre(A_X) = pre(A)\}$

   $\mathcal{L}_{[]}(\cup_{X \in (1 \cdots N)} out(A_X)) = \{\cup_{X \in (1 \cdots N)} Post(A_X), P_{LinkRef_i}| \forall s \in S; (out (A_N), s) \notin T \wedge P_{LinkRef_i} \hateq \cup_{X \in (1, \cdots, N)} Post(A_X) = post(A)\}$

5. The formal semantic using Kripke structure for a BPMN loop refinement activities $(\curvearrowright N, B)$ where $A \in$ Fo is the refined activity [10]:

   $\mathcal{L}_\curvearrowright(in(A_1)) = \{Pre(A_1) \wedge N, P_{LinkRef_i}| \nexists s \in S \wedge s \neq in(A_1); (s, in(A_1)) \in T \wedge P_{LinkRef_i} \hateq Pre(A_1) \wedge N = Pre(A)\}$

   $\mathcal{L}_\curvearrowright(out(A_1)) = \{Post(A_1) \wedge \neg N, P_{LinkRef_i}| \forall s \in S; (out(A_1), s) \notin T \wedge P_{LinkRef_i} \hateq Post(A_1) \wedge \neg N = Post(A)\}$

6.3   NuSMV

NuSMV is a symbolic model checker. An SMV program consists of a tuple (V, init, next, AP) where:

- V i a set of Symbolic variables on a domain *ID* declared in the **VAR** section;
- A state transition variables *init* defined in section **ASSIGNMENTS** that define the valid initial state **init()** and the transition relation *next* that define the next state; **next()** defined as follows: "init(var):= initial_state; next(var):= next_state" and
- AP is a set of atomic propositions.

The BPMN process model can be transformed to kripke structure which is produced from the graph dependency then to implement a local model checking to check the refinement against properties expressed in LTL specification with the NuSMV language.

A Formal Transformation from BPMN to NuSMV. The formal transformation from BPMN to NuSMV for a sub-process is shown in Table 10:

Table 10. Code NuSMV generated for a BPMN sub-process.

BPMN Objects	Kripke structure.	NuSMV language.
| | | ```
ASSIGN
next(Pre(A)) := case
      state=In(A) : TRUE
      & Pre(A)=TRUE ;
      TRUE : FALSE;
      esac;
next(Post(A)) := case
      state=Out(A) : TRUE
      & Post(A)=TRUE;
      TRUE : FALSE;
      esac;
``` |

The formal transformation from BPMN to NuSMV for a sequence refinement pattern is shown in Table 11:

Table 11. Code NuSMV generated for a sequence refinement pattern.

BPMN Objects	Kripke structure.	NuSMV language.
| | | ```
ASSIGN
next(Pre(A1)) := case
      state=In(A1) : TRUE
      & Pre(A1)=TRUE ;
      TRUE : FALSE;
      esac;
...
next(Post(An)) := case
      state=Out(An) : TRUE
      & Post(An)=TRUE;
      TRUE : FALSE;
      esac;
``` |

The formal transformation from BPMN to NuSMV for a sequence refinement pattern is shown in Table 12:

Table 12. Code NuSMV generated for refinement with a parallel pattern.

BPMN Objects	Kripke structure.	NuSMV language.
	$\{\cap_{X \in (1,\cdots,N)} Pre(A_X), P_{LinkRef_i}\}$ In(A1) $\cap \cdots$ $\cap$In(An) Out(A)$\cap \cdots$ $\cap$Out(An) $\{\cap_{X \in (1,\cdots,N)} Post(A_X), P_{LinkRef_i}\}$	ASSIGN next(Pre(AND)) := case state=$\cap_{X \in (1,..,N)} In(A_X)$: $\cap_{X \in (1,..,N)} Pre(A_X)$= TRUE & Pre(AND)= TRUE ; TRUE : FALSE; esac; next(Post(AND)) := case state=$\cap_{X \in (1,..,N)} Out(A_X)$: $\cap_{X \in (1,..,N)} Post(A_X)$= TRUE & Post(AND) = TRUE ; TRUE : FALSE; esac;

The formal transformation from BPMN to NuSMV for a sequence refinement pattern is shown in Table 13:

Table 13. Code NuSMV generated for refinement with an exclusive pattern.

BPMN Objects	Kripke structure.	NuSMV language.
	$\{\cup_{X \in (1,\cdots,N)} Pre(A_X), P_{LinkRef_i}\}$ $In(A_1)|\cdots$ $|In(A_N)$ $Out(A_1)|\cdots$ $|Out(A_N)$ $\{\cup_{X \in (1,\cdots,N)} Post(A_X), P_{LinkRef_i}\}$	ASSIGN next(Pre(OR)) := case state=$\cup_{A \in (1,..,N)} In(A\_\{X\})$: $\cup_{X \in (1,..,N)} Pre(A\_\{X\})$= TRUE & Pre(OR)= TRUE ; TRUE : FALSE; esac; next(Post(OR)) := case state=$\cup_{A \in (A,..,N)} Out(A\_\{X\})$: $\cup_{X \in (1,..,N)} Post(A\_\{X\})$= TRUE & Post(OR) = TRUE ; TRUE : FALSE; esac;

The formal transformation from BPMN to NuSMV for a sequence refinement pattern is shown in Table 14:

Table 14. Code NuSMV generated for refinement with a loop pattern.

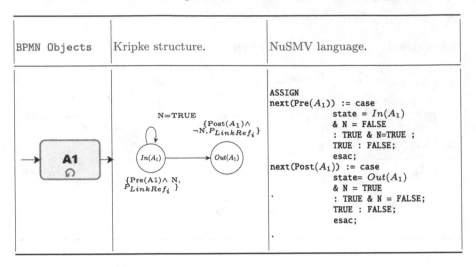

BPMN Objects	Kripke structure.	NuSMV language.

```
ASSIGN
next(Pre(A1)) := case
                state = In(A1)
                & N = FALSE
                : TRUE & N=TRUE ;
                TRUE : FALSE;
                esac;
next(Post(A1)) := case
                state= Out(A1)
                & N = TRUE
                : TRUE & N = FALSE;
                TRUE : FALSE;
                esac;
```

7 Case Study

We illustrate the verification of a BPMN process using NuSMV with the help of an example. The given case study consists of a simple booking site, as shown in Fig. 7. This site must allow an easy and quick search of travels. For this, the search will be possible with the sub-process Reservation. The user can register by completing a form that contains information and then make his reservation by specifying the number of people to travel for example. Finally the site determines if the number of places is available and returns a feedback determining yes or no the confirmation of its reservation.

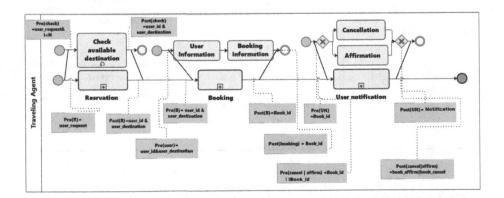

Fig. 7. Case study example.

The Screen-shots of the specification of the sub-process Reservation, the loop refinement check available destination and Kripke structure of both models is shown in Fig. 8. The verification results of the safety abstract and refined properties also are presented in Figs. 9 and 11.

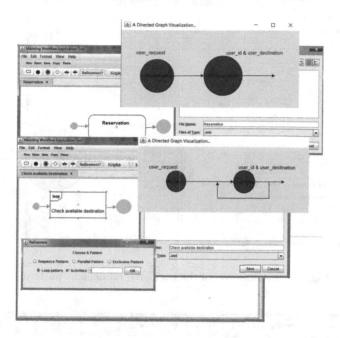

Fig. 8. Screen-shots of the specification of the loop refinement pattern.

```
93          " EF(phi)
94          */
95          else if (f.getValue().equals(CtplOperator.EF)) {
96
97              CtplTreeNode phi = f.getChild(0);
98              boolean changed = false;
99              System.out.print("Checking EF, Iterations:");
100
101             // If any state is labelled with the formula f
102             // within EF, then label this state with EF(f).
103             for (Iterator iter = k.getGraph().vertexSet().iterator(); iter.hasNext();) {
104                 KripkeNode s = (KripkeNode)iter.next();
105                 if (s.hasLabel(phi))
106                                                                        et(phi).clone());
107
108
109
110
111
112
113
114
115
116
117
118
119
120
121
122         /* Iterate parents */
```

```
C:\Windows\system32\cmd.exe - NuSMV -int loopreser.smv

*** See http://minisat.se/MiniSat.html
*** Copyright (c) 2003-2006, Niklas Een, Niklas Sorensson
*** Copyright (c) 2007-2010, Niklas Sorensson

NuSMV > go
WARNING *** Processes are still supported, but deprecated.    ***
WARNING *** In the future processes may be no longer supported. ***

WARNING *** The model contains PROCESSes or ISAs. ***
WARNING *** The MRC hierarchy will not be usable. ***
NuSMV > check_ltlspec
-- specification  G (user_request_r -> X user_id_destination_r)  is true
-- specification  G ((user_request_c = user_request_r & user_request_c) -> X (u
ser_id_destination_c & user_id_destination_r = user_id_destination_c))  is true
NuSMV >
```

Fig. 9. NuSMV verification response for the loop pattern.

The Screen-shots of the refinement with the exclusive process refinement and its verification result is shown in Figs. 10 and 11.

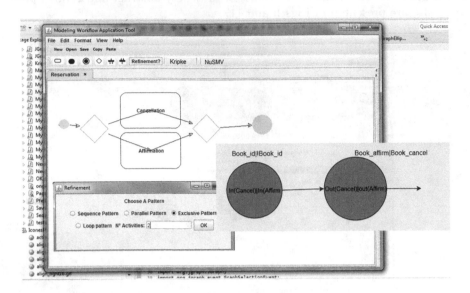

Fig. 10. Specification of the exclusive refinement pattern.

Fig. 11. NuSMV verification response for the exclusive pattern.

8   Conclusion

To get a manageable complexity of workflow modeling, we have introduced in this paper a BPMN modeling refinement approach. This approach allows developers to introduce gradually more details within BPMN models at each level of refinement.

In fact, we have proposed an automatic refinement approach based on a set BPMN refinement patterns. For each pattern, we have analyzed the change impact brought by the refinement pattern to the workflow model. The change impact concerns the workflow data and control flow dependencies. To prove the preservation of these dependencies throughout the refinement process, we have transformed, at each level of refinement, the BPMN model to a Kripke structure formalizing the model semantics. Once semantic requirements are specified, they are verified using NUSMV model checker. To validate our approach, we have illustrate the refinement process and the automatic verification of the semantic preservation via an example. As future work, we plan to finalize the tool supporting our approach and to define a syntaxe driven definition generated by the BPMN grammar allowing a systematic transformation of the workflow model to the corresponding Kripke structure.

References

1. Vaz, C., Ferreira, C.: Towards automated verification of web services. arXiv preprint arXiv:1111.2824 (2011)
2. Van Der Straeten, R., Jonckers, V., Mens, T.: A formal approach to model refactoring and model refinement. Softw. Syst. Model. **6**(2), 139–162 (2007)
3. Cao, J., Zhao, H., Wang, J., Zhang, S., Li, M.: Verifying dynamic workflow change based on executable path. Int. J. Intell. Control Syst. **12**(1), 37–44 (2007)
4. Rinderle, S., Reichert, M., Dadam, P.: Correctness criteria for dynamic changes in workflow systems–a survey. Data Knowl. Eng. **50**(1), 9–34 (2004)
5. Van Der Aalst, W.M., et al.: Soundness of workflow nets: classification, decidability, and analysis. Formal Aspects Comput. **23**(3), 333–363 (2011)
6. Bouchaala, O., Yangui, M., Tata, S., Jmaiel, M.: DAT: dependency analysis tool for service based business processes. In: IEEE 28th International Conference on Advanced Information Networking and Applications (AINA), pp. 621–628. IEEE, May 2014
7. Clarke Jr., E.M., Grumberg, O., Kroening, D., Peled, D., Veith, H.: Model Checking. MIT Press, Cambridge (2018)
8. Baier, C., Katoen, J.P.: Principles of Model Checking. MIT Press, Cambridge (2008)
9. White, S.A., Bock, C.: BPMN 2.0 Handbook Second Edition: Methods, Concepts, Case Studies and Standards in Business Process Management Notation. Future Strategies Inc. (2011)
10. Ayari, S., Bendali, H.Y., Jemni, B.L.: A refinement based verification approach of BPMN models using NuSMV. In: Proceedings of the 13th International Conference on Software Technologies, ICSOFT 2018, Porto, 26–28 July 2018

11. Lodaya, K., Sreejith, A.V.: LTL can be more succinct. In: Bouajjani, A., Chin, W.N. (eds.) ATVA 2010. LNCS, vol. 6252, pp. 245–258. Springer, Heidelberg (2010). https://doi.org/10.1007/978-3-642-15643-4_19
12. Younes, A.B., Hlaoui, Y.B., Ayed, L.J.B., Jlassi, R.: Refinement based modeling of workflow applications using UML activity diagrams. In: IEEE 37th Annual Computer Software and Applications Conference Workshops (COMPSACW), pp. 187–192. IEEE, July 2013
13. Huang, H., Cheung, T.Y., Mak, W.M.: Structure and behavior preservation by Petri-net-based refinements in system design. Theoret. Comput. Sci. **328**(3), 245–269 (2004)
14. Istoan, P.: Defining composition operators for BPMN. In: Gschwind, T., De Paoli, F., Gruhn, V., Book, M. (eds.) SC 2012. LNCS, vol. 7306, pp. 17–34. Springer, Heidelberg (2012). https://doi.org/10.1007/978-3-642-30564-1_2
15. Oliva, G., Milojicic, D., Gerosa, M.A., Smith, V.: A change impact analysis approach for workflow repository management. In: IEEE 20th International Conference on Web Services, ICWS 2013, June 2013
16. Strecker, M.: Modeling and verifying graph transformations in proof assistants. Electron. Notes Theor. Comput. Sci. **203**(1), 135–148 (2008)
17. Kherbouche, M.O.: Contribution à la gestion de l'évolution des processus métiers. (Contribution to the business process evolution management). University of the Littoral Opal Coast, Dunkerque, June 2013
18. Winkler, M.: Managing Service Dependencies in Service Compositions (2010)
19. Emerson, E.A., Halpern, J.Y.: Decision procedures and expressiveness in the temporal logic of branching time. J. Comput. Syst. Sci. **30**(1), 1–24 (1985)
20. Ben Fradj, I., Hlaoui, B.Y., Jemni, B.L.: Patterns for modeling and composing flexible workflows from cloud services. In: Proceedings of the 20th International Conference on Enterprise Information Systems, ICEIS 2018, Funchal, 21–24 March 2018, vol. 2 (2018)

Author Index

Alloui, Ilham 349
Ayad, Amani 3
Ayari, Salma 397
Ayed, Leila Jemni Ben 397

Ben Ahmed, Samir 282
Ben Noureddine, Dhouha 282
Benoit, Eric 349
Borchani, Nour 327
Bouassida, Nadia 327

Cavalli, Ana 194
Çergani, Ervina 79
Cerqueira, Italo 247
Chong, Chun Yong 266

da Silva, Fabio B. Q. 247
Dahab, Sarah 194
Dulz, Winfried 55

Florentin, Fabiana 247

Gharbi, Atef 282
Gol Mohammadi, Nazila 150
Gomaa, Hassan 372

Haidar, Hassan 124
Haoues, Mariem 327
Heisel, Maritta 150
Herber, Paula 28
Hlaoui, Yousra Bendaly 397

Kamei, Yasutaka 220
Kolp, Manuel 124

Lacerda, Rosberg 247
Laforcade, Pierre 104
Laghouaouta, Youness 104

Lee, Sai Peck 266
Loh, JiMeng 3

Maag, Stephane 194
Mallouli, Wissam 194
Marsit, Imen 3
Melemciuc, Marius-Constantin 307
Mezini, Mira 79
Mili, Ali 3
Moesus, Nikolai 28
Mohamed Omri, Nazih 3

Paduraru, Ciprian 307
Paduraru, Miruna 307
Pathirage, Don 372
Perrin, Stéphane 349
Pfahl, Dietmar 173

Quintino, Jonysberg P. 247

Santos, Andre L. M. 247
Sato, Ryosuke 220
Schlesinger, Sebastian 28
Scholze, Matthias 28
Sellami, Asma 327
Shah, Faiz Ali 173
Shin, Michael 372
Siebra, Clauirton 247
Sirts, Kairit 173

Ubayashi, Naoyasu 220
Ulfat-Bunyadi, Nelufar 150

Vernier, Flavien 349

Wautelet, Yves 124
Wirtz, Roman 150

Author Index

Printed in the United States
By Bookmasters